Lecture Notes in Computer Science 2634

Edited by G. Goos, J. Hartmanis, and J. van Leeuwen

T0189204

Springer
Berlin
Heidelberg
New York
Hong Kong
London
Milan
Paris
Tokyo

Feng Zhao   Leonidas Guibas (Eds.)

Information Processing
in Sensor Networks

Second International Workshop, IPSN 2003
Palo Alto, CA, USA, April 22-23, 2003
Proceedings

 Springer

Series Editors

Gerhard Goos, Karlsruhe University, Germany
Juris Hartmanis, Cornell University, NY, USA
Jan van Leeuwen, Utrecht University, The Netherlands

Volume Editors

Feng Zhao
Palo Alto Research Center (PARC)
3333 Coyote Hill Road, Palo Alto, CA 94304, USA
E-mail: fz@alum.mit.edu

Leonidas Guibas
Stanford University, Computer Science Department
Gates Building 374, Stanford, CA 94305, USA
E-mail: guibas@cs.stanford.edu

The illustration appearing on the cover of this book is the work of Mark Wong from
Palo Alto Research Center.

Cataloging-in-Publication Data applied for

A catalog record for this book is available from the Library of Congress.

Bibliographic information published by Die Deutsche Bibliothek.
Die Deutsche Bibliothek lists this publication in the Deutsche Nationalbibliografie;
detailed bibliographic data is available in the Internet at <http://dnb.ddb.de>.

CR Subject Classification (1998): C.2.4, C.2, F.2, D.1.3, D.2, E.1, H.5.3, C.3, H.4

ISSN 0302-9743
ISBN 3-540-02111-6 Springer-Verlag Berlin Heidelberg New York

Springer-Verlag Berlin Heidelberg New York
a member of BertelsmannSpringer Science+Business Media GmbH

http://www.springer.de

© Springer-Verlag Berlin Heidelberg 2003
Printed in Germany

Typesetting: Camera-ready by author, data conversion by PTP-Berlin GmbH
Printed on acid-free paper   SPIN: 10925966   06/3142   5 4 3 2 1 0

Preface

This volume contains the Proceedings of the 2nd International Workshop on Information Processing in Sensor Networks (IPSN 2003). The workshop was held at the Palo Alto Research Center (PARC), Palo Alto, California, on April 22–23, 2003.

Information processing in sensor networks is an interdisciplinary research area with deep connections to signal processing, networking and protocols, databases and information management, as well as distributed algorithms. Because of advances in MEMS microsensors, wireless networking, and embedded processing, ad hoc networks of sensors are becoming increasingly available for commercial and military applications such as environmental monitoring (e.g., traffic, habitat, security), industrial sensing and diagnostics (e.g., factories, appliances), infrastructure maintenance (e.g., power grids, water distribution, waste disposal), and battlefield awareness (e.g., multitarget tracking).

From the engineering and computing point of view, sensor networks have become a rich source of problems in communication protocols, sensor tasking and control, sensor fusion, distributed databases and algorithms, probabilistic reasoning, system/software architecture, design methodologies, and evaluation metrics. This workshop took a systematic approach to address crosslayer issues, from the physical sensor layer to the sensor signal processing and networking levels and then all the way to the applications.

Following the successful first Workshop on Collaborative Signal and Information Processing in Sensor Networks at PARC in 2001, this new workshop brought together researchers from academia, industry, and government to present and discuss recent work concerning various aspects of sensor networks such as information organization, querying, routing, and self-organization, with an emphasis on the high-level information processing tasks that these networks are designed to perform.

Seventy-three papers were submitted to the workshop, of which 23 were accepted for oral presentation and 21 for presentation by poster. Each paper was reviewed by approximately four reviewers. The reviewing process was handled electronically, using CyberChair software. The program chairs are indebted to the Technical Program Committee members for their efforts in putting together an outstanding technical program.

We wish to acknowledge the generous support from the US National Science Foundation (NSF) and the Defense Advanced Research Projects Agency (DARPA), through Dr. Mari Maeda and Dr. Sri Kumar. We also wish to thank many individuals who helped to make this workshop possible: Dr. Ying Zhang of PARC for putting together this proceedings volume, Jaewon Shin of Stanford for all his assistance with the paper-handling software and related matters, Jim Reich and Markus Fromherz of PARC for all the local arrangements, Jesse Durham of Strategic Analysis Inc. for conference management, Prof. Jennifer

Hou of UIUC for handling financial support for student and speaker travel, and PARC for providing organizational and logistical support for the entire workshop through its Communications and Facilities Departments.

April 2003   Leonidas J. Guibas
                                                                    Feng Zhao

Organization

IPSN 2003 was sponsored by the National Science Foundation (NSF) and the Defense Advanced Research Projects Agency (DARPA), technically cosponsored by the IEEE Signal Processing Society and the IEEE Circuits and Systems Society, in cooperation with the American Association for Artificial Intelligence (AAAI).

Program Chairs

Leonidas J. Guibas	Stanford University
Feng Zhao	Palo Alto Research Center (PARC)

Advisory Committee

Vincent Chan	Massachusetts Institute of Technology (MIT)
Deborah Estrin	University of California at Los Angeles (UCLA)
Johan de Kleer	PARC
Sri Kumar	DARPA
Mari Maeda	NSF
Shankar Sastry	University of California at Berkeley (UCB)
Larry Smarr	University of California at San Diego Cal-$(IT)^2$

Technical Program Committee

John Apostolopoulos	HP Labs
Victor Bahl	Microsoft Research
Chee-Yee Chong	Booz Allen Hamilton
Hugh Durrant-Whyte	University of Sydney
Johannes Gehrke	Cornell University
Rajesh Gupta	University of California at Irvine
Horst Haussecker	Intel Research
John Heidemann	University of Southern California, Information Sciences Institute
Alfred Hero	University of Michigan
Jennifer Hou	University of Illinois at Urbana-Champaign (UIUC)
Yuhen Hu	University of Wisconsin
S.S. Iyengar	Louisiana State University
Warren Jackson	HP Labs

Local Arrangements

Publication

Publicity

Table of Contents

Information Processing in Sensor Networks

On the Many-to-One Transport Capacity of a Dense Wireless Sensor Network and the Compressibility of Its Data*

Daniel Marco, Enrique J. Duarte-Melo, Mingyan Liu, and David L. Neuhoff

University of Michigan, Ann Arbor, MI 48109-2122, USA
{idaniel, ejd, mingyan, neuhoff}@eecs.umich.edu

Abstract. In this paper we investigate the capability of large-scale sensor networks to measure and transport a two-dimensional field. We consider a data-gathering wireless sensor network in which densely deployed sensors take periodic samples of the sensed field, and then scalar quantize, encode and transmit them to a single receiver/central controller where snapshot images of the sensed field are reconstructed. The quality of the reconstructed field is limited by the ability of the encoder to compress the data to a rate less than the single-receiver transport capacity of the network. Subject to a constraint on the quality of the reconstructed field, we are interested in how fast data can be collected (or equivalently how closely in time these snapshots can be taken) due to the limitation just mentioned. As the sensor density increases to infinity, more sensors send data to the central controller. However, the data is more correlated, and the encoder can do more compression. The question is: Can the encoder compress sufficiently to meet the limit imposed by the transport capacity? Alternatively, how long does it take to transport one snapshot? We show that as the density increases to infinity, the total number of bits required to attain a given quality also increases to infinity under *any* compression scheme. At the same time, the single-receiver transport capacity of the network remains constant as the density increases. We therefore conclude that for the given scenario, even though the correlation between sensor data increases as the density increases, any data compression scheme is *insufficient* to transport the required amount of data for the given quality. Equivalently, the amount of time it takes to transport one snapshot goes to infinity.

1 Introduction

In this paper we investigate the ability of a dense wireless sensor network to measure and transport independent *snapshots* of a two-dimensional field to a central location, i.e. a *collector*, where reconstructions of these field snapshots are formed.

More specifically, N sensors are uniformly spaced over some finite geographical region. At regular time intervals, each sensor measures the field value at its

---

* This work is supported by NSF ITR grant number ANI-0112801.

F. Zhao and L. Guibas (Eds.): IPSN 2003, LNCS 2634, pp. 1–16, 2003.

location; then quantizes its value and losslessly encodes it with bits. The wireless network, which has a transceiver at each sensor, operates in slotted time steps to transport the bits generated by the sensor encoders to the central collector. Multiple hops may be required. There is a number W such that each sensor can transmit or receive at most W bits in one slot. Note that because a sensor value is known only at its own location, the quantization and encoding must be done independently at each sensor location.

When the central collector has received from each sensor the encoded quantized value corresponding to a particular sampling time, i.e. corresponding to one complete snapshot, it forms a reconstruction of that snapshot. The sampling and data transport are pipelined in the sense that further snapshots may be taken by the sensors and their transport may begin before the network has finished transporting prior snapshots to the collector.

The principal question to be addressed is how frequently can a new snapshot be taken and transported successfully to the collector. If new snapshots can be received by the collector every u slots, then we say the network has *throughput* $1/u$ snapshots per slot. Clearly, large throughput is desired. Alternatively, one may ask how many network slots are needed (i.e. how many times the network must be used) to transport a snapshot. If new snapshots can be received by the collector every u slots, then we say the network has *usage rate* u slots per snapshot, which is the inverse of the throughput. Clearly, small usage rate is desired.

One might also ask how much time must transpire between the time the snapshot is taken by the sensors and the time the collector has the data needed for its reconstruction. This *delay* will not be discussed here, except to say that due to pipelining the usage rate is at most as large as the delay, and usually substantially smaller.

We are particularly interested in how the network throughput and usage rate vary as N, the number of sensors, increases. Of course, the sensor spacing decreases with N, and the sensor density increases with N. Must the usage rate (i.e. the number of slots/snapshot) increase with N? If so, does it saturate at some finite value? Or does it increase without bound?

To answer these questions, one must answer a *compressibility* question and a *capacity* question: How many bits must be generated by each sensor's quantizer/encoder per snapshot? And how many bits can be transported on the average by the network to the collector per sensor per slot? (Here, we only count new bits generated at the sensors – not bits relayed by the sensors.) Suppose the answer to the compressibility question is b_N, i.e. b_N is the minimum number of bits per sensor per snapshot that must be generated for a network of size N, and suppose the answer to the capacity question is c_N, i.e. c_N is the maximum average number of bits that can be transported to the collector per sensor per slot. (c_N is less than W – usually much less.) Then the smallest possible usage rate is $u_N = b_N/c_N$ slots/snapshot. Equivalently, the maximum possible throughput is $t_N = c_N/b_N$ snapshots/slot.

To answer the capacity question, we adopt a transmission and interference model similar to that of Gupta and Kumar [1], and we show in Section 3 that

$$c_N = \Theta\left(\frac{1}{N}\right) \text{ bits/sensor/slot },\tag{1}$$

where $\Theta(\frac{1}{N})$ means there exist constants a_1 and a_2 such that $\frac{a_1}{N} \leq c_N \leq \frac{a_2}{N}$ for sufficiently large N. That is, c_N, which may be considered to be the *many-to-one capacity* of the network, is bounded. This is essentially due to the fact that the number of bits per slot that the collector can receive is bounded by W. As a result, there is a bottleneck at the collector. In comparison, Gupta and Kumar [1] found the *peer-to-peer capacity* of a similar network to be $c_N = \Theta\left(\frac{1}{\sqrt{N \log N}}\right)$.

On the other hand, the compressibility question is not well posed until one specifies a model for the two-dimensional field being measured and the criteria with which the fidelity of the reconstructed snapshots are judged. These are described in the next two paragraphs.

The model for the field is a stationary two-dimensional, random field $X(u, v)$. That is, $X(u, v)$ is a real-valued random variable representing the field value at Euclidean coordinates (u, v), where u and v vary continuously. We make only benign assumptions about the random field. We make no assumption as to whether the random field is bandlimited or not (bandlimited refers to spatial frequency content). A principal characteristic of the random field is its autocorrelation function $R(\tau_1, \tau_2)$, which indicates the correlation between values of X separated horizontally and vertically by distances τ_1 and τ_2, respectively. For example, $R(\tau_1, \tau_2) = \exp\left\{-\sqrt{\tau_1^2 + \tau_2^2}\right\}$ is an example of an isotropic autocorrelation function that decays exponentially with Euclidean distance. We require that the autocorrelation function not be a constant, i.e. the field cannot be spatially constant, even if the constant is random. Finally, we assume that successive snapshots are independent. That is, each snapshot is modeled as a random field that is independent of the random fields modeling other snapshots.

In effect, the sensors take samples of the random field at locations denoted $(u_1, v_1), (u_2, v_2), ..., (u_N, v_N)$. It is these samples that are quantized, encoded and transported to the collector. The collector creates a reproduction $\widehat{X}(u, v)$, $(u, v) \in G$ as a reproduction of the original snapshot $X(u, v)$, $(u, v) \in G$, where G denotes the geographic region of interest over which the sensors are dispersed. This obviously involves interpolation. We quantify the fidelity of the $\widehat{X}$ reproduction with mean squared error:

$$\text{MSE} = \frac{1}{|G|} \int_G E\left(X(u, v) - \widehat{X}(u, v)\right)^2 du\, dv,\tag{2}$$

where E denotes expected value with respect to the random field, the integral is taken over the region G, and $|G|$ denotes its area. Note that due to interpolation and quantization errors, it is not possible to have MSE $= 0$. Therefore, the sensor network performs, in effect, lossy, rather than lossless coding of the random field. (Sampling, followed by scalar quantization and lossless binary encoding is a common method of lossy coding.) When N is large and, consequently, the sensors are closely spaced, the component of MSE due to interpolation error is negligible, and the MSE is well approximated simply by the average MSE between the N sensor samples and their reconstructions. That is,

$$\mathrm{MSE} \cong \frac{1}{N} \sum_{i=1}^{N} E \left(X(u_i, v_i) - \widehat{X}(u_i, v_i) \right)^2 . \tag{3}$$

From now on, we will fix a positive number D, and assume throughout the paper that the goal of the sensor network is to sample, quantize, encode and transport snapshots of the field with a mean squared error of D or less, as given by (2) or (3).

We will assume also that the quantizers used by the various sensors are identical. Every such quantizer maps a sensor value $X(u_i, v_i)$ to an integer that indexes the possible quantization cells/bins. This index is then encoded in some lossless fashion. Though only the X's at the sensor locations will be quantized, we nevertheless need to assume that the random field and quantizer are such that the probability that each $X(u, v)$ in the entire region of interest G would quantize to the same integer is less than one. (Equivalently, the probability that all $X(u, v)$'s are in the same quantization cell is less than one.) This is another benign assumption, because if it does not hold, i.e. if with probability one all X's lies in the same quantization cell, then clearly the quantizer is too coarse to be of use.

We can now pose the compressibility question. With the above models for the random field and the fidelity measure, and with a fixed MSE target D, then as discussed in Section 2, one may show that $b_N \longrightarrow 0$ as $N \longrightarrow \infty$, where b_N is the minimum number of encoded bits per sensor per snapshot that must be transported to the collector to attain MSE less than or equal to D. The idea is that as N increases, the sensors become increasingly close, the correlation between the values produced by nearby sensors increases, and it is possible to exploit this correlation using schemes such as conditional coding or Slepian-Wolf distributed lossless coding[1] on the quantizer outputs to make $b_N \longrightarrow 0$. On the other hand, although $b_N \longrightarrow 0$, we also show in Section 2 that no matter how the lossless coding is done, b_N does not decrease as rapidly as $1/N$. That is,

$$N b_N \longrightarrow \infty \text{ as } N \longrightarrow \infty . \tag{4}$$

---

[1] Slepian-Wolf coding is a remarkable method that permits lossless coders to independently encode the data from correlated sources (such as the data produced by neighboring sensors) as efficiently as if each encoder could see the values produced by the other data sources. Also, note that Slepian-Wolf coding entails the simultaneous encoding of a block of successive outputs from the quantizer of a given sensor.

Note that Nb_N is the total number of bits coming from the quantizer/encoders from all sensors. Note also that the above result is quite general and not limited to a particular lossless coding scheme.

Combining (4) with the many-to-one capacity result (1), we find that the smallest usage rate for which the mean squared error can be D or less is

$$U(N, D) = \frac{b_N}{c_N} = \frac{Nb_N}{Nc_N} \longrightarrow \infty \text{ as } N \longrightarrow \infty . \tag{5}$$

This indicates that to obtain a given MSE D, the number of slots per snapshot must grow without bound as N increases.

It must be said that this is somewhat disappointing, as it had been hoped that as N increases, the inter-sensor correlation would increase sufficiently rapidly to make Nb_N (and $U(N, D)$) saturate at a finite value, rather than approach infinity. Note, however, that this result does not say that sensor networks cannot do the desired job of measuring and transporting a two-dimensional field. Rather it says that the efficiency with which it does so, as expressed by the usage or throughput, degrades as the density of the sensors becomes very large.

It should be noted that the efficiency also degrades when N becomes too small. Specifically, there is some threshold value N_o such that for $N < N_o$, the interpolation error by itself exceeds D. Thus, there is no quantization-encoding-transport scheme that attains MSE D. Moreover, as N approach N_o from above, the quantizer must have increasingly fine resolution, which causes $b_N \longrightarrow \infty$. And since in this case $N > N_o$, we also have $Nb_N \longrightarrow \infty$. Thus as in (5), $U(N, D) \longrightarrow \infty$ as $N \searrow N_o$. We conclude that given a target MSE D and a random field model, there is an optimum value of N. This is the value for which Nb_N is smallest. This conclusion applies to bandlimited and non-bandlimited fields alike. For bandlimited fields the optimum value of N is not necessarily the value that leads to Nyquist sampling.

Based on the above analysis, an alternative strategy, to be pursued in future work, is to fix the number of sensors at the value of N that minimizes Nb_N, and then to permit there to be an additional set of transceivers at locations between the sensors. This is equivalent to having a network of $N' > N$ sensors, and putting all but N of them to sleep, while keeping all transceivers active.

We assert that the result in (4) is not at all obvious. Indeed, the limiting behavior of Nb_N has been a long standing question in the theory of sampling and quantization, which has only recently been resolved in [2]. The discussion we give in Section 2 is for one-dimensional random processes, but clearly extends to two-dimensional random fields as well. To see just how delicate the question is, in Section 2, we discuss how the rate-distortion theory branch of information theory shows that if *ideal* lossy coding were used instead of scalar quantization plus binary lossless coding, then Nb_N would not increase to infinity. However, the sensor network requires that coding be done independently at each sensor. This is why we use scalar quantization, rather than say vector or predictive quantization. On the other hand, it can be shown that even if one were allowed to use vector quantization, unless the dimension of the quantizer increases with N, Nb_N would still grow without bound.

Having shown that Nb_N grows to infinity, the question arises as to how fast it grows. In Section 2, we find the rate with which Nb_N increases for the special case of Gaussian random fields and a particular form of Slepian-Wolf coding. This also leads to a result on how fast $U(N, D)$ grows in this special case. Specifically, for a one-dimensional Gaussian field with exponential autocorrelation, it is shown that $U(N, D) \longrightarrow \infty$ at rate $\Theta(\sqrt{N} \log N)$.

In addition to the many-to-one capacity, we also consider the *many-to-many capacity*, which is the maximum average number of bits per sensor per slot that can be transported from each sensor to every other sensor. Section 3 shows that the many-to-many capacity is:

$$c_N = \Theta\left(\frac{1}{N}\right) \text{ bits/sensor/slot} . \tag{6}$$

This is the same as the many-to-one capacity. Thus the behavior of a network operating in many-to-many fashion, e.g. the asymptotic usage rate $U(N, D)$ is the same as the behavior of a network operating in many-to-one fashion.

We conclude this introduction with a comment on the results of a recent paper by Scaglione and Servetto [3]. The latter appears to claim that as N increases, the capability of the dense sensor network and the correlation structure of a typical random field are sufficient to permit any node to obtain the two-dimensional field quantized to within any prescribed distortion value. (It focuses on the many-to-many scenario.) If by such sufficiency the paper means to say that this can happen with bounded network usage (i.e., the number of slots per snapshot does not go to infinity), then our results show otherwise. That is, the number of slots needed between successive snapshots does indeed grows without bound. If such sufficiency does not involve any notion of time, then it is not clear to us what the claim means. The paper's intermediate results seem to indicate that a network can transport the field in $\Theta(\sqrt{N})$ slots, which is unbounded. Therefore its overall claim of sufficiency does not appear to match this result. Furthermore, the $\Theta(\sqrt{N})$ result (Equation (1) in [3]) is based on the assumption that the information theoretic rate-distortion function is attainable. However, in a sensor network, quantization must be done independently at each node, and our results show that in this case the ratio of the number of required encoded bits to the rate-distortion function approaches infinity. Therefore, the $\Theta(\sqrt{N})$ result is also in doubt.

The remainder of the paper is organized as follows. The next section presents the results on the number of bits b_N resulting from quantizing and encoding the sensor samples. Section 3 derives the many-to-one and many-to-many transport capacity of the sensor network when N is large. Section 4 summarizes and concludes.

2   The Compressibility of Sensor Data

We need to assess the minimum number of bits that an encoder could produce when encoding a quantized sensor value, when sensors are densely placed, and consequently, their values are highly correlated. We will summarize and use the recent results of [2].

As stated in the introduction, we view the sensors as taking uniformly spaced samples of a stationary two-dimensional random field over a finite geographical region. The collection of all samples taken at one time instance form a snapshot. Successive snapshots are assumed to be independent.

Though the field is two-dimensional, the basic ideas are more readily apparent and simpler to describe in one dimension. Therefore, we will focus on the case that N sensors are uniformly spaced on a straight line of length $L < \infty$. In this case, let $X(s)$, $0 \leq s \leq L$ denote the field value at location s. $X(s)$ is assumed to be a continuous parameter stationary random process. Let $(X_1, \dots, X_N)$ denote the N sensor values taken at a spacing of $d = L/N$. Let $(I_1, \dots, I_N)$ denote the integers resulting from quantizing $(X_1, \dots, X_N)$ with some fixed quantizer.

2.1 $b_N \longrightarrow 0$

From basic information theory we know that no lossless compression technique could compress the output of the quantizer with fewer than

$$H(I_1, \dots, I_N) \text{ bits.} \tag{7}$$

Equivalently, it requires on average at least

$$\frac{1}{N} H(I_1, \dots, I_N) \text{ bits per sample} \tag{8}$$

to losslessly encode each quantized sensor value.

The lower bound in (7) can in fact be attained using Slepian-Wolf distributed lossless coding. This requires every sensor to simultaneously encode a block of, say, M successive outputs from *its* quantizer. Observe that the block of outputs is a temporal block rather than a spatial one. Temporal blocks are needed in order for the encoder, at each sensor, to operate at rate close to some conditional entropy value (these conditional entropies will be stated shortly). Spatial blocks, however, are not used since every sensor knows only its own values and so the quantization and encoding must be done independently at each sensor.

The lower bound in (7) is attained in the following way. Let all sensors quantize their values independently. Let sensor 1 losslessly encode its block of M successive quantizer outputs into approximately $MH(I_1)$ bits using conventional block lossless coding[2], where $H(I_1)$ denotes the entropy of one of its quantizer

---

[2] This and subsequent similar approximations can be made arbitrarily tight by choosing M large. Moreover, this and subsequent block encodings are *nearly* rather than *perfectly* lossless, meaning that there is a nonzero probability that the decoder output does not match the encoder input. However, such decoding error probabilities can be made arbitrarily small by choosing M large, thereby having negligible effect on the overall MSE.

outputs, and where the independence of successive outputs has been used. Let sensor 2 encode its values using Slepian-Wolf style coding with respect to sensor 1. Then, it losslessly encodes its block of M successive quantizer outputs into approximately $MH(I_2|I_1)$ bits, where $H(I_2|I_1)$ denotes the conditional entropy of an output of sensor 2 given an output of sensor 1 in the same snapshot. (The decoder will already have decoded the I_1's, before decoding the I_2's.) Similarly, sensor 3 uses Slepian-Wolf coding with respect to sensors 1 and 2, thus mapping its M quantizer outputs into approximately $MH(I_3|I_2, I_1)$ bits. And so on. It follows that for the kth sensor, the number of bits per snapshot generated by its quantizer/encoder is approximately $b_N(k) = H(I_k|I_1, \ldots, I_{k-1})$. It is well known that $b_N(k)$ decreases monotonically with k. Thus, for large N, most of the $b_N(k)$'s are approximately the same. That is, there is a value b_N such that $b_N(k) \cong b_N$ for most k. It is this value to which Section 1 refers when prescribing the number of bits per sensor per slot produced by each sensor's quantizer/encoder.

It also follows that the total number of bits B_N produced by all the sensors is given by:

$$B_N = \sum_{k=1}^{N} b_N(k)$$
$$= H(I_1) + H(I_2|I_1) + \ldots + H(I_N|I_{N-1}, I_{N-2}, \ldots, I_1)$$
$$= H(I_1, \ldots, I_N) , \tag{9}$$

where the last equality is an elementary property of entropy. This shows that the Slepian-Wolf approach does indeed attain the lower bound in (7).

We now show $b_N \longrightarrow 0$ as $N \longrightarrow \infty$. Using elementary information theory relations,

$$b_N = \sum_{k=1}^{N} b_N(k)$$
$$= \frac{1}{N} \sum_{k=1}^{N} H(I_k|I_{k-1}, I_{k-2}, \ldots, I_1)$$
$$\leq \frac{1}{N} \sum_{k=1}^{N} H(I_k|I_{k-1})$$
$$= \frac{H(I_1)}{N} + \frac{(N-1)}{N} H(I_2|I_1)$$
$$\longrightarrow H(I_2|I_1) \text{ as } N \longrightarrow \infty . \tag{10}$$

As N increases the sensors become closer and closer. Consequently their correlation increases. Specifically, as $N \longrightarrow \infty$, the distance between sensors 1 and 2 goes to zero. Thus their sample values become essentially identical resulting in $H(I_2|I_1) \longrightarrow 0$, which in turn implies that $b_N \longrightarrow 0$.

2.2 $Nb_N \longrightarrow \infty$

It has recently been shown [2] that $H(I_1, \ldots, I_N) \longrightarrow \infty$ as $N \longrightarrow \infty$. The following briefly sketches the basic idea. Let T_o denote a quantization threshold that $X(s)$ crosses with probability one in the interval $[0, L]$. Let S_o denote the location of the first crossing of this threshold. The assumptions in Section 1 about the random field and quantizer insure the existence of T_o. Furthermore, they imply that S_o is a continuous random variable, thus having infinite entropy. When N is large and consequently the sample spacing d is small, from the quantizer outputs $(I_1, \ldots, I_N)$, one can immediately and easily determine in which time interval of length d the first threshold crossing occurs. Thus one obtains an estimate $\widehat{S}_o$ of S_o that is accurate to within d. Since $d \longrightarrow 0$ as $N \longrightarrow \infty$ and since S_o has infinite entropy, it follows from elementary information theory that the entropy $H(\widehat{S}_o)$ tends to infinity. Finally, since $\widehat{S}_o$ is a function of $(I_1, \ldots, I_N)$,

$$H(I_1, \ldots, I_N) \geq H(\widehat{S}_o) \longrightarrow \infty . \tag{11}$$

Since from (7) $B_N = Nb_N$ can be no smaller than $H(I_1, \ldots, I_N)$, we see that $Nb_N \longrightarrow \infty$.

This argument can be generalized to the case of a two-dimensional field. We note also that if the snapshots of the field were dependent, it can be shown that using an encoding scheme that encodes based on previous snapshots will do no better.

2.3   The Growth of Rate for a Gaussian Random Field

As mentioned, although the encoding of the sensor value X_i must be done without knowledge of the other sensor values with which it is correlated, one could nevertheless losslessly encode it with approximately $b_N = \frac{1}{N}H(I_1, \ldots, I_N)$ bits, provided Slepian-Wolf distributed coding is used [4]. A suboptimal but easier to analyze case is where Slepian-Wolf coding is used to encode each sensor value with approximately $b_N = H(I_2|I_1)$ bits. For this situation, it has been shown in [2] that when $X(s)$ is a stationary Gaussian random process and the scalar quantizer is uniform with step size Δ and an infinite number of levels, then

$$\lim_{\rho \to 1} \frac{H(I_2|I_1)}{-\sqrt{1 - \rho^2} \, \log \sqrt{1 - \rho^2} \, M_{\sigma, \Delta}} = 1 \tag{12}$$

where ρ is the correlation coefficient of X_1, X_2 and $M_{\sigma, \Delta}$ is a constant that depends on the variance σ^2 of $X(s)$ and the quantization step size Δ.

Let us consider now, as examples, two autocorrelation functions for the random process $X(s)$. To keep notation simple, let the process $X(s)$ have unit variance.

1. $R_X(s) = e^{-|s|}$: The correlation coefficient in this case is $\rho = e^{-d}$, recalling that $d = L/N$ is the spacing between adjacent sensors. It follows from

the usual expansion of the exponential that $\sqrt{1-\rho^2} \longrightarrow \sqrt{2d}$ as $d \longrightarrow 0$. Therefore, (12) can be rewritten as follows:

$$\lim_{d\to 0} \frac{H(I_2|I_1)}{-\sqrt{2d}\ \log \sqrt{2d}\, M_{1,\Delta}} = 1\ . \tag{13}$$

Consequently for large N,

$$B_N \approx -N\sqrt{2d}\, M_{1,\Delta}\ \log \sqrt{2d} = \sqrt{2L}\, M_{1,\Delta}\ \sqrt{N} \log \sqrt{\frac{N}{2L}} \longrightarrow \infty \text{ as } N \longrightarrow \infty\ . \tag{14}$$

In this case, B_N increases as $\sqrt{N} \log N$.

2. $R_X(s) = e^{-s^2}$: The correlation coefficient in this case is $\rho = e^{-d^2}$. It follows from the usual expansion of the exponential that $\sqrt{1-\rho^2} \longrightarrow \sqrt{2}d$ as $d \longrightarrow 0$. Therefore, (12) can be rewritten as follows:

$$\lim_{d\to 0} \frac{H(I_2|I_1)}{-\sqrt{2}d\ \log \sqrt{2}d\, M_{1,\Delta}} = 1\ . \tag{15}$$

Consequently for large N,

$$B_N \approx -N\sqrt{2}d\, M_{1,\Delta}\ \log(\sqrt{2}d) = \sqrt{2L}\, M_{1,\Delta}\ \left(\log \frac{N}{\sqrt{2L}}\right) \longrightarrow \infty \text{ as } N \longrightarrow \infty\ . \tag{16}$$

In this case B_N increases as $\log N$.

In light of the previous discussion that the total number of bits must increase to infinity as N increases, it should not be surprising that (14) and (16) increase without bound as $N \longrightarrow \infty$. Note that in these examples the number of bits per sensor $b_N = B_N/N$ goes to 0.

On the other hand, suppose that instead of independently scalar quantizing each sensor value, a hypothetical omniscient encoder could jointly quantize a block of, say, K_N adjacent sensor values from the same snapshot. Then if K_N is permitted to grow with N, information theoretic rate-distortion theory can be used to show that B_N, the number of bits per snapshot required to attain a target MSE D, will remain bounded rather than grow to infinity. However, if K_N is not permitted to grow with N, then an argument like that used above for scalar quantization shows that B_N must again go to infinity. This indicates the criticality of the independent quantization/encoding requirement. Moreover, it indicates that even if the latter were not required, it would still be very difficult to have B_N remain bounded.

3   Transport Capacity

In this section we analyze the transport capacity of a network where communication is of a many-to-one fashion (or more specifically all-to-one in this case).

This follows from the motivating application illustrated in Section 1 whereby all sensors send sampled data to a single collector/receiver. We will extend this analysis to discuss the capacity when the communication is of a many-to-many fashion as well. We present two types of results in this section. The first type of result is in the form of an upper bound, i.e., a level that the transport capacity cannot possibly exceed given our assumptions. The second type is in the form of a constructive lower bound, i.e., the transport capacity that is achievable via a particular construction of routing and scheduling mechanisms. These two results serve different purposes in this paper. The upper bound is used jointly with Sections 2.1 and 2.2 to show that the number of slots required per snapshot grows without bound. The lower bound is used jointly with Section 2.3 to characterize the usage rate in the special case of a Gaussian random field with known autocorrelation functions. Capacity of wireless networks has attracted much attention in recent studies with the assumption that source traffic is uncorrelated. The seminal work by Gupta and Kumar [1] first developed the transport capacity of a wireless network where sources and destinations are randomly chosen. The main results of [1] state that the total transport capacity of a network of N nodes is $\Theta(\frac{\sqrt{N}}{\sqrt{\log N}})$. Equivalently, the per source transport capacity is $\Theta(\frac{1}{\sqrt{N \log N}})$. Both are throughput capacities in amount of data transported end-to-end per unit of time. The main difference of the scenario studied in this section is that there is a single receiver.

Throughout this section the transport capacity is defined in two ways, the *total transport capacity*, which is the total rate at which the network transports data to the single receiver, and the *per-node transport capacity*, which is the rate at which each sensor transports to the single receiver. When each sensor has equal amount of data to send these two definitions become equivalent. We will use terms *collector*, *sink*, and *receiver* interchangeably, and use terms *sensor*, *node*, and *source* interchangeably.

We assume that the network used for our calculations is deployed following a uniform distribution over a field of area A. For simplicity we also assume that this field has a circular shape and that the collector is located at the center of the field. We assume that the collector cannot simultaneously receive from multiple sensors. The sensors are stationary once deployed and cannot transmit and receive simultaneously. As mentioned before, time is slotted, and all nodes share a channel with capacity of W bits per slot. We assume nodes use omnidirectional antennas, and use a fixed transmission power and achieve a fixed transmission range, denoted by r. We use transmission and interference models similar to those used in [1]. Let X_i and X_j be two sources with distance $d_{i,j}$ between them. Then the transmission from X_i to X_j will be successful if and only if

$$d_{i,j} \leq r \quad \text{and} \quad d_{k,j} > r + \delta, \quad \delta \geq 0 \tag{17}$$

for any other source X_k that is simultaneously transmitting. Here δ denotes the interference range. We assume that the transmission range r is sufficiently large to guarantee connectivity with high probability.

3.1 Capacity Upper Bound

We first consider an obvious upper bound on the total transport capacity in the case of a single receiver. From the collector's point of view, the maximum rate of transport is achieved when it is receiving 100% of the time. Since W is the transmission capacity of the shared channel, it follows that the collector cannot receive at rate faster than W. We thus have the following result:

Theorem 1. *The total transport capacity in a wireless network featuring many-to-one communications is upper bounded by W.*

Equivalently, if each sensor sends an equal amount then the per-node transport capacity is upper bounded by $\frac{W}{N}$.

Note that this result is independent of the assumption of the shape of the field, the location of the collector and the interference model. It also is not an asymptotic result so it can be applied to networks with finite N. It is simply a (direct) consequence of the assumption that the collector cannot receive simultaneously from multiple sensors. In [5] we show that this upper bound is in general not achievable with high probability as the number of sensors increases to infinity.

We now extend the above result to the many-to-many case. More specifically we consider the all-to-all broadcast scenario where data generated at each sensor is to be delivered to all other sensors in the network. Note in this case there is not a single collector, but rather that every sensor is a collector. Again we note that receiving at a rate of W for a given sensor can only be achieved when the sensor is continuously receiving. This is clearly infeasible since each sensor also needs to transmit its own data. Thus in this case the total transport capacity is also upper bounded by W bits per slot. Here the transport capacity refers to the number of distinct bits delivered per slot, thus a bit that reaches multiple destinations (since each bit has a destination of all other sensors in the network) is not counted multiple times.

3.2 Achievable Capacity

In this subsection we show constructively that a transport capacity on the order of W (but less than W) can be achieved. Here we will explicitly assume that all nodes need to transmit the same number of bits, or need to achieve a same rate. This assumption coincides with the suboptimal encoding scheme in subsection 2.3 where each sensor value is encoded using approximately $b_N = H(I_i|I_{i-1}) = H(I_2|I_1)$ bits. Consequently we will determine the achievable per-node capacity or per-node throughput, denoted by λ, and then multiply this result by N to obtain the total transport capacity instead of considering the total transport capacity directly. The result here is obtained with high probability in the asymptotic regime as N goes to infinity. We assume that the area A contains at least a circular area of radius $2r + \delta$. This is not an unreasonable assumption since the range r required to maintain connectivity decreases as $N \longrightarrow \infty$. We begin with the following lemma.

Denote by A_R the area of a circle of radius R, i.e., $A_R = \pi R^2$. Let random variable V_R denote the number of nodes within an area of size A_R. We then have the following lemma.

Lemma 1. *In a randomly deployed network with N nodes,*

$$Prob\left(\frac{NA_R}{A} - \sqrt{\alpha_N N} \le V_R \le \frac{NA_R}{A} + \sqrt{\alpha_N N}\right) \longrightarrow 1 \quad as \quad N \longrightarrow \infty, \text{(18)}$$

where the sequence $\{\alpha_N\}$ is such that $\lim_{N\to\infty} \frac{\alpha_N}{N} = \epsilon$, ϵ positive but arbitrarily small.

This result can be easily shown using Chebychev's inequality and noting that the mean of V_R is $\frac{NA_R}{A}$ and the variance σ^2 is $\frac{NA_R}{A}(1 - \frac{A_R}{A})$:

$$\text{Prob}\left(\frac{NA_R}{A} - \sqrt{\alpha_N N} \le V_R \le \frac{NA_R}{A} + \sqrt{\alpha_N N}\right) \ge 1 - \frac{\sigma^2}{\alpha_N N} = 1 - \frac{\frac{A_R}{A}(1 - \frac{A_R}{A})}{\alpha_N}. \tag{19}$$

The second term on the right hand side of (19) goes to zero since $\alpha_N \longrightarrow \infty$ as $N \longrightarrow \infty$.

This lemma shows that the number of nodes in a fixed area is bounded within $\sqrt{\alpha_N N}$ of the mean where α_N goes to infinity as $N \longrightarrow \infty$ but $\lim_{N\to\infty} \frac{\alpha_N}{N}$ is arbitrarily small.

Using this lemma, the following theorem constructs capacity that can be achieved with high probability as $N \longrightarrow \infty$ in the many-to-one case. Note that our result is as a function of the transmission range r and we have assumed that r is sufficiently large to guarantee connectivity. We construct this bound assuming that the routing and relaying scheme is such that each of the nodes one hop away from the sink carries an equal share of the total traffic. This is feasible given that the collector is at the center, the nodes are uniformly distributed and each sensor generates the same amount of bits.

Theorem 2. *A uniformly deployed network using multi-hop transmission for many-to-one communication can achieve per-node throughput $\lambda \ge \frac{W}{N}\frac{\pi r^2 - \sqrt{\epsilon}}{4\pi r^2 + 4\pi r\delta + \pi\delta^2 + \sqrt{\epsilon}}$ with high probability as $N \to \infty$, where ϵ is as given in Lemma 1.*

To see this, consider a source that is at least $2r + \delta$ away from the closest border of the network. The area of interference is thus a circle of radius $r' = 2r + \delta$ centered at this source. Using Lemma 1, with high probability the number of interfering neighbors including the source, k_1, is

$$\frac{NA_{r'}}{A} - \sqrt{\alpha_N N} \le k_1 \le \frac{NA_{r'}}{A} + \sqrt{\alpha_N N}. \tag{20}$$

Consider the entire network represented as a connected graph G(V,E), with edges connecting nodes that are within each other's interference range. Then the highest degree of this graph is $k_1 - 1$, since k_1 is the number of nodes within any interference area. Using the known result from graph theory, see for example [6,7], that the chromaticity of such a graph is upper bounded by the highest degree plus one, i.e., $k_1 - 1 + 1 = k_1$ in this case, there exists a schedule of length at most $l \leq k_1$ slots that would allow all nodes to transmit at least once during this schedule. The nodes one hop away from the sink carry the traffic of the entire network. Denote the number of these one hop nodes by k_2, there thus exists a schedule of length l such that $\frac{N}{k_2}\lambda = \frac{W}{l}$. Note that k_2 is bounded with high probability by Lemma 1: $\frac{NA_r}{A} - \sqrt{\alpha_N N} \leq k_2 \leq \frac{NA_r}{A} + \sqrt{\alpha_N N}$. Therefore we have

$$\frac{N}{\frac{NA_r}{A} - \sqrt{\alpha_N N}}\lambda \geq \frac{N}{k_2}\lambda = \frac{W}{l} \geq \frac{W}{k_1} \geq \frac{W}{\frac{NA_{r'}}{A} + \sqrt{\alpha_N N}}$$

$$\frac{1}{\frac{A_r}{A} - \sqrt{\alpha_N/N}}\lambda \geq \frac{W}{\frac{NA_{r'}}{A} + \sqrt{\alpha_N N}}$$

$$\text{as } N \longrightarrow \infty, \quad \lambda \geq \frac{W}{N}\cdot\frac{\frac{A_r}{A} - \sqrt{\epsilon}}{\frac{A_{r'}}{A} + \sqrt{\epsilon}}$$

$$= \frac{W}{N}\cdot\frac{\pi r^2 - \sqrt{\epsilon}}{4\pi r^2 + 4\pi r\delta + \pi\delta^2 + \sqrt{\epsilon}}$$

(since $\sqrt{\epsilon}$ arbitrarily close to 0) $\approx \dfrac{W}{4N\left(1 + \delta\left(\frac{1}{r} + \frac{\delta}{4r^2}\right)\right)}.$ (21)

Since there are N nodes transmitting with $\lambda \geq \frac{W}{N}\frac{\pi r^2 - \sqrt{\epsilon}}{4\pi r^2 + 4\pi r\delta + \pi\delta^2 + \sqrt{\epsilon}}$, and considering the result of Section 3.1 the achievable total transport capacity of the network is $\Theta(1)$.

We now briefly discuss the many-to-many case. Consider a node at any location in the network. When it first transmits its data, the data reaches every node within a distance r from the this node. Nodes on the edge of this area then retransmit the data to other nodes which were not reached in the first transmission. Because the size of the field is finite, it takes a finite number of transmissions k to cover the whole field. Once the whole field is covered, all intended destinations must have received the data. Consider a network where each node transmits its data this way, one starting as soon as the previous one has just finished. Under such a construction it would take at most Nk transmissions to transmit data from every node to every other nodes in the network. Therefore

$$\lambda \geq \frac{W}{kN}.$$ (22)

Since there are N nodes in the network, each with $\lambda \geq \frac{W}{kN}$, the total transport capacity of the network will again be $\Theta(1)$.

Note that the parameter k does not depend on N since an increase in N only means an increase in density when the size of the field is fixed. An increase in density means that every transmission reaches more nodes, but does not affect the number of transmissions needed to cover the field. An increase in the field size or a decrease in r will increase k, but as long as $r > 0$ and the field size is finite, k will be finite.

To summarize we have shown in this section that overall the total transport capacity of the network is $\Theta(1)$ in both the many-to-one and the many-to-many cases. Equivalently the per-node capacity is $\Theta(\frac{1}{N})$. The key is that the total capacity does not grow as the size of the network increases. This is a major difference from what was derived in [1] for the peer-to-peer case. At the same time, the per-node throughput decays as fast as $\frac{1}{N}$ as N increases.

4 Conclusion

In this paper we characterized the amount of data required to sample, quantize, and encode a field densely deployed with wireless sensors, and the amount of data that can be transported by the wireless sensor network, motivated by an imaging application where there is a single receiver/collector. We showed that as the number of sensors increases to infinity, the total amount of data generated for every snapshot also goes to infinity. At the same time, while the number of bits generated per sensor per snapshot may go zero, it can only do so at a rate strictly less than $\frac{1}{N}$. On the other hand, as the size grows, the total transport capacity of the network remains constant on the order of 1, and the transport capacity per node is on the order of $\frac{1}{N}$. Therefore the amount of data required for a fixed MSE cannot be transported within finite network usage. We would like to emphasize that this result holds for both a bandlimited and non-bandlimited random field, regardless of the encoding scheme used.

We showed that in the special case of a one-dimensional Gaussian random field with two example autocorrelation functions, there exists a coding scheme with which the number of bits per sensor per snapshot is on the order of $\frac{\log N}{\sqrt{N}}$ and $\frac{\log N}{N}$. We also constructively showed that the achievable per node capacity is on the order of $\frac{1}{N}$. Therefore in this special case the network usage is $\Theta(\sqrt{N}\log N)$ and $\Theta(\log N)$, respectively.

We also discussed that since the number of slots per snapshot increases with the number of sensors, there should exist an optimal number of sensors that minimizes the number of slots per snapshot. We do not know what this optimum is, but if we did, it would place a limit on how densely sensors should be deployed, beyond which one should *suppress* sensors, e.g. put sensors to sleep, to prevent over-sampling.

References

1. P. Gupta and P. R. Kumar, "The capacity of wireless networks," *IEEE Transactions on Information Theory*, vol. 46, no. 2, March 2000.
2. D. Marco and D. L. Neuhoff, "On the entropy of quantized data at high sampling rates," in preparation.
3. A. Scaglione and S. Servetto, "On the interdependence of routing and data compression in multi-hop sensor networks," in *Mobicom*, September 2002.

4. D. Slepian and J. Wolf, "Noiseless coding of correlated information sources," in *Trans. Information Theory*, July 1973, vol. IT-19, pp. 471–480.
5. E. J. Duarte-Melo and M. Liu, "Data-gathering wireless sensor networks: Organization and capacity," Tech. Rep., EECS Department, University of Michigan, 2002, CSPL-333.
6. G. Chartrand, *Introductory Graph Theory*, Dover Publications, INC, 1985.
7. J. A. Bondy and U. S. R. Murty, *Graph Theory with Applications*, American Elsevier Publishing INC, 1976.

Distributed Sampling for Dense Sensor Networks: A "Bit-Conservation Principle"*

Prakash Ishwar, Animesh Kumar, and Kannan Ramchandran

Department of Electrical Engineering and Computer Sciences,
University of California, Berkeley, CA 94720, USA.
{ishwar, animesh, kannanr }@eecs.berkeley.edu

Abstract. We address the problem of deterministic oversampling of bandlimited sensor fields in a distributed communication-constrained processing environment, where it is desired for a central intelligent unit to reconstruct the sensor field to maximum pointwise accuracy. We show, using a dither-based sampling scheme, that is is possible to accomplish this using minimal inter-sensor communication with the aid of a multitude of low-precision sensors. Furthermore, we show the feasibility of having a flexible tradeoff between the average oversampling rate and the Analog to Digital (A/D) quantization precision per sensor sample with respect to achieving exponential accuracy in the number of bits per Nyquist-period, thereby exposing a key underpinning *"conservation of bits" principle*. That is, we can distribute the bit budget per Nyquist-period along the amplitude-axis (precision of A/D converter) and space (or time or space-time) using oversampling in an almost arbitrary discrete-valued manner, while retaining the same reconstruction error decay profile. Interestingly this oversampling is possible in a highly localized communication setting, with only nearest-neighbor communication, making it very attractive for dense sensor networks operating under stringent inter-node communication constraints. Finally we show how our scheme incorporates security as a by-product due to the presence of an underlying dither signal which can be used as a natural encryption device for security. The choice of the dither function enhances the security of the network.

1 Introduction

Remote sensing of bandlimited physical phenomena of interest using a network of sensors is directly related to the classical sampling problem, a mature topic in signal processing [1]. The sensor network setting however has a unique set of attributes that impose challenging constraints on the sampling paradigm. First, individual sensors are low-power devices with limited processing capability. Second, inter-node communication costs are prohibitive leading to the constraint of only highly local inter-node communication (e.g., nearest-neighbor, see Figure 1).

---

* This research was supported by NSF under grant CCR-0219722 and DARPA under grant F30602-00-2-0538.

F. Zhao and L. Guibas (Eds.): IPSN 2003, LNCS 2634, pp. 17–31, 2003.

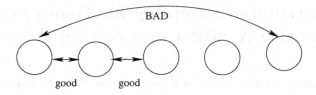

Fig. 1. Sensor networks typically have coarse resolution, high spatial density, and high inter-sensor communication costs.

This paper is accordingly motivated at addressing the question of deterministic sampling of bandlimited signals under these distributed or localized communication constraints. Consider the scenario where a large number of sensors are deployed over a region of interest in order to collect and return sensor measurements to a central processing unit (CPU). We use the term CPU to refer to any point of data collection and/or processing. The CPU need not be a remote entity that is associated with high communication costs. For instance, the nodes of the network can be dynamically organized into clusters and different nodes in each cluster can assume the role of the CPU at different times [2]. Many physical signals are approximately bandlimited and can be reconstructed in a stable manner from samples taken slightly above the Nyquist-rate on a uniform lattice. In practice, however, the samples of the signal are quantized due to the finite precision of A/D converters, leading to unavoidable signal reconstruction errors.

When signals are uniformly sampled at the critical Nyquist-rate, which we will refer to as the Pulse Code Modulation (PCM) style sampling setup, the worst case pointwise reconstruction error decays exponentially with the bit rate (measured in number of bits per Nyquist-interval) of the A/D converters [3]. However, high-precision A/D operations are expensive (this is true even outside the sensor network world). This leads to the following question: is it possible to trade-off A/D converter resolution in terms of bits per sample for (average) oversampling rate (attained through denser oversampling) while maintaining the same worst-case pointwise reconstruction error performance as a function of the number of bits per Nyquist-interval? In the sequel we answer this question in the affirmative, and show how it is possible to compensate for lack of precision in the A/D elements via spatial oversampling without compromising accuracy.

Our main result is the uncovering of an underpinning *"conservation of bits"* *principle* that can be useful in guiding the analysis and design of distributed sensor nodes including such questions as what tradeoffs in sampling density and A/D precision are needed to attain a desired worst-case pointwise reconstruction accuracy. A direct outcome of this framework is the ability to do spatially adaptive sampling: we can have critically sampled PCM-style sampling using higher resolution A/D converters when the sampling density is light (i.e. near the Nyquist-rate), and use proportionately lower resolution sensors when the sampling density is high. The bit-conservation principle also implies a certain degree of robustness to node failures. Node failures reduce the average sampling density and have the same effect as loss of amplitude resolution. This leads to a graceful degradation of reconstruction quality with node failures. This also has direct bearing on A/D precision versus inter-sensor communication cost trade-offs. Densely spaced low-resolution sensors would need to communicate fewer bits while sparsely spaced high-resolution sensors need to to communicate more bits. However, the total number of bits exchanged in a Nyquist-interval (bit-meters) would be about the same.

An interesting and useful by-product of the proposed sampling framework is its measure of security to eavesdropping that comes "for free" due to the use of dither functions underlying the approach, with the added flexibility of using different covert dither functions over different spatio-temporal Nyquist-regions. In this paper we address only deterministic aspects of distributed sampling, and the (worst-case) analysis is done in the context of sampling 1-D (spatially) bandlimited fields[1].

Extensions to more general spatio-temporal models are part of our ongoing and future studies, as also generalizations from the deterministic to the stochastic setting.

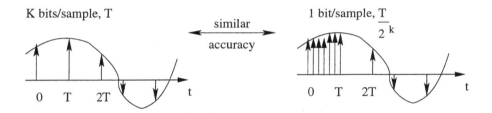

Fig. 2. Illustrating the "conservation of bits" principle. On the left, a bandlimited signal is sampled at near-Nyquist-rate T using k-bit A/D converters in a PCM-style sampling framework. On the right, the same signal is oversampled at 2^k times the Nyquist-rate using 1-bit A/D converters under a dither-based sampling framework (see Section 2.2). Both schemes use the same total number of bits in a Nyquist-interval. If the oversampling is done appropriately, using a suitable dither function, the two schemes achieve similar exponential decay in reconstruction error with bitrate.

2   Sampling Bandlimited Signals

2.1   PCM-Style Sampling at Near-Nyquist-Rates

For the rest of this paper, $f(t)$ is a bandlimited signal with bounded dynamic range. We assume, without loss of generality, that the spectral support and

---

[1] Actually, one could construe the scope of this paper to apply to spatio-temporal sampling of bandlimited signals, where the results of this paper apply to the 1-D spatial dimension corresponding to a "frozen" time instant, assuming the time-dimension has been sampled at the temporal Nyquist-rate.

dynamic range of $f(t)$ are respectively normalized to the intervals $[-\pi, \pi]$ and $[-1, 1]$. The Nyquist sampling period for $f(t)$ is $T_{NQ} = 1$ and classical sampling theory tells us that $f(t)$ can be perfectly reconstructed from the samples $\{f(n)\}_{n \in \mathbb{Z}}$ according to the well known interpolation formula [1]:

$$f(t) = \sum_{n=-\infty}^{\infty} f(n)\operatorname{sinc}(t - n), \quad \forall t \in \mathbb{R}, \tag{1}$$

where $\operatorname{sinc}(t) := \frac{\sin(\pi t)}{\pi t}$ for $t \neq 0$ and one otherwise. In practice, however, the reconstruction (1) is not stable to bounded perturbations in the sample values due to the poor decay properties of the sinc interpolation kernel, i.e., the series in (1) is not absolutely convergent. All practical A/D converters have finite precision and the sampling process is invariably accompanied by ambient noise. The instability in the reconstruction implies that the quantization noise can potentially build up and lead to unbounded reconstruction errors in parts of the signal. The instability can, however, be happily overcome by taking samples slightly above the Nyquist-rate:

Proposition 1. *[4] For each $\lambda > T_{NQ} = 1$, there exists a kernel $\phi_\lambda(t)$ bandlimited to $[-\pi, \pi]$ such that $C_\lambda := \sup_{t \in \mathbb{R}} \left(\sum_n |\phi_\lambda \left(t - \frac{n}{\lambda} \right)| \right) < \infty$ and*

$$f(t) = \frac{1}{\lambda} \sum_{n \in \mathbb{Z}} f\left(\frac{n}{\lambda} \right) \phi_\lambda \left(t - \frac{n}{\lambda} \right), \quad \forall t \in \mathbb{R}. \tag{2}$$

The finiteness of C_λ ensures that the reconstruction series (2) is absolutely convergent. The interpolation kernel $\phi_\lambda(t)$ in fact decays faster than $\frac{c_n}{t^n}$ for all positive integers n and some constant c_n. If $Q_k(\cdot)$ denotes a k-bit quantization operation, we have

$$\left| f\left(\frac{n}{\lambda} \right) - Q_k \left(f\left(\frac{n}{\lambda} \right) \right) \right| \leq 2^{-k}, \quad \forall n \in \mathbb{Z}$$

and the worst-case pointwise reconstruction error can be bounded as

$$\sup_{t \in \mathbb{R}} \left| f(t) - \frac{1}{\lambda} \sum_{n \in \mathbb{Z}} Q_k \left(f\left(\frac{n}{\lambda} \right) \right) \phi \left(t - \frac{n}{\lambda} \right) \right| \leq \frac{C_\lambda}{\lambda} \cdot 2^{-k}$$

$$= \frac{C_\lambda}{\lambda} \cdot 2^{-R/\lambda}, \tag{3}$$

where $R = \frac{k}{(1/\lambda)}$ is the bitrate in bits per sampling period used to quantize the signal. For a fixed oversampling rate λ, (3) reveals that the reconstruction error decays exponentially in rate R, however, since $R \propto k$ in the PCM-style sampling framework, the quality of reconstruction can be improved only by using higher resolution A/D converters.

The near-Nyquist stable sampling rate $\lambda > 1$ will be held fixed for the rest of this paper and the term oversampling will be used to refer to uniform sampling at rate strictly greater than the stable sampling rate λ. We shall also use the term 'Nyquist-interval' to refer to any stable sampling interval of the form $\left(\frac{n}{\lambda}, \frac{n+1}{\lambda} \right)$.

2.2 1-Bit A/D Dithered Oversampling

Recently, a dither-based, single-bit, oversampled A/D scheme was proposed in [5,6] with a worst-case reconstruction error that decays exponentially in the bitrate as in (3). However, unlike in PCM-style sampling where the bit budget for each Nyquist-interval is exhausted at a single high-resolution sampling point, the dither-based approach "spreads" the bit-budget over many single-bit A/D converters in a Nyquist-interval. The key component of dither-based sampling schemes is the dither function that has the following properties:

1. $|d\left(\frac{n}{\lambda}\right)| > 1, \forall n \in \mathbb{Z}$;
2. $\mathrm{sgn}\left[d\left(\frac{n}{\lambda}\right)\right] = -\mathrm{sgn}\left[d\left(\frac{n+1}{\lambda}\right)\right], \quad \forall n \in \mathbb{Z}$;
3. $d(t)$ is differentiable and $\Delta := \sup_{t \in \mathbb{R}} |d'(t)| < \infty$;

For example, $d(t) = \gamma \cos(\lambda \pi t)$ with $|\gamma| > 1$ is a valid dither function. The third property of dither functions implies that $d(t)$ is continuous. A bandlimited function is also continuous $\Rightarrow$ the dithered signal $f(t) + d(t)$ is continuous. This together with the first two properties of the dither function guarantees (by the intermediate value theorem for continuous functions [7]) that $f(t) + d(t)$ will have a zero-crossing in every Nyquist-interval $\left(\frac{n}{\lambda}, \frac{n+1}{\lambda}\right)$. Let 2^k 1-bit A/D converters be placed uniformly in every Nyquist-interval to record the sign of the dithered signal $f(t) + d(t)$, i.e., sensors are placed at the locations $\{m\tau_k\}_{m \in \mathbb{Z}}$ where $\tau_k := \frac{(1/\lambda)}{2^k}$ is the uniform oversampling period. To avoid clutter, we shall henceforth drop the subscript k in τ_k. Let $m_n \in \{0, \ldots, 2^k - 1\}$ be the smallest index for which $[f + d]\left(\frac{n}{\lambda} + m_n\tau\right)$ and $[f + d]\left(\frac{n}{\lambda} + (m_n + 1)\tau\right)$ have opposite signs in $\left[\frac{n}{\lambda}, \frac{n+1}{\lambda}\right]$. It follows from the intermediate value theorem that $f(z_n) + d(z_n) = 0$ at some point $z_n \in \left(\frac{n}{\lambda} + m_n\tau, \frac{n}{\lambda} + (m_n + 1)\tau\right)$. Bandlimited functions have bounded derivatives. Specifically, according to Bernstein's inequality for bandlimited signals [8],

$$|f'(t)| \leq \pi \sup_{t \in \mathbb{R}} |f(t)| \leq \pi. \tag{4}$$

The third condition on the dither function ensures that $f(t) + d(t)$ is differentiable and has a derivative bounded by $\pi + \Delta$. From Lagrange's mean value theorem [7] applied to the points $x_n = \left(m_n + \frac{1}{2}\right)$ and z_n it easily follows that

$$\left| [f + d](z_n) - [f + d]\left(\frac{n}{\lambda} + x_n\tau\right) \right| \leq (\pi + \Delta)\left| z_n - \frac{n}{\lambda} - x_n\tau \right|,$$

$$\text{i.e., } \left| f\left(\frac{n}{\lambda} + x_n\tau\right) - \left(-d\left(\frac{n}{\lambda} + x_n\tau\right)\right) \right| \leq \frac{(\pi + \Delta)\tau}{2} = \frac{(\pi + \Delta)}{2\lambda}2^{-k}.$$

Thus uniform oversampling of the dithered signal using 1-bit A/D converters give samples of f with linear precision in τ at the nonuniformly spaced points $\left\{\frac{n}{\lambda} + \left(m_n + \frac{1}{2}\right)\tau\right\}$. There are $2^k = \frac{1}{\tau\lambda}$ oversampling positions in a stable sampling period $\frac{1}{\lambda}$. Hence, it requires k bits to specify the identity of the the the 1-bit sensor just following the location of the first zero-crossing of the dithered signal in each Nyquist-interval, i.e., the bit rate required is $R = k\lambda$ bits/interval.

The worst case sample error is no more than $\frac{\pi+\Delta}{2\lambda}2^{-\frac{R}{\lambda}}$. The decay of the worst-case pointwise reconstruction error will have a similar behavior only if $\left\{\left(\frac{n}{\lambda}+\left(m_n+\frac{1}{2}\right)\tau\right)\right\}_{n\in\mathbb{Z}}$ constitutes a stable sampling set for the bandlimited function f. The following proposition proved in [5] shows that this is indeed the case if the sampling positions do not get too close to each other and at the same time they do not stray too far away from the stable Nyquist points.

Proposition 2. *[5] If* $\inf_{j,l\in\mathbb{Z},j\neq l}|t_j-t_l|>0$ *and* $\sup_{n\in\mathbb{Z}}|t_n-\frac{n}{\lambda}|<\infty$ *then there exist interpolating functions* $\psi_n(t)$ *with* $C':=\sup_{t\in\mathbb{R}}\left[\sum_{n\in\mathbb{Z}}|\psi_n(t-t_n)|\right]<\infty$ *such that for any function* $f(t)$ *with spectral support contained in* $[-\pi,\pi]$,

$$f(t)=\sum_n f(t_n)\psi_n(t-t_n).$$

Using the above proposition with $t_n=\frac{n}{\lambda}+\left(m_n+\frac{1}{2}\right)\tau$ it follows that the worst-case pointwise reconstruction error is bounded by

$$|f(t)-\widehat{f}_D(t)|\leq\frac{C'(\pi+\Delta)}{2\lambda}2^{-\frac{R}{\lambda}},\text{ where} \tag{5}$$

$$\widehat{f}_D(t):=\sum_{n\in\mathbb{Z}}\left(-d\left(\frac{n}{\lambda}+x_n\tau\right)\right)\psi_n\left(t-\frac{n}{\lambda}-x_n\tau\right)$$

is the dither-based reconstruction of $f(t)$ and the constant C' does not depend on $f(t)$. Observe that the reconstruction accuracy, in terms of bitrate, is similar to the PCM-style sampling scheme, i.e., it is exponentially decaying in rate with the same exponent. The reconstruction accuracy can be improved by reducing τ, i.e., by packing more sensors inside each Nyquist-interval. Unlike the PCM-style sampling scheme, there is no need to use higher precision A/D converters. However, determining the location of the first zero-crossing would require local communication among sensors in each Nyquist-interval. For example each sensor can send one bit to its right neighbor if it has not detected a crossing. The local communication cost is therefore limited to one bit per Nyquist-interval.

3 Tradeoffs in Amplitude and Spatial Resolution

In PCM-style sampling, signals are sampled at low, near-Nyquist-rates. The entire bit-budget of k bits per Nyquist-interval is spent in recording the signal amplitude at a single high precision (k-bit) sensor. The 1-bit dither-based sampling scheme on the other hand spends all available bits into specifying a spatial event in the form of zero-crossings by using many (2^k) poor-precision (1-bit) sensors in each Nyquist-interval. These sampling schemes represent two extreme scenarios. This section explains how k-bit PCM-style reconstruction accuracy can be achieved using b-bit A/D converters and an appropriate dither-based oversampling scheme for any $1<b<k$. This leads to a "bit-conservation principle"– a trade-off between the oversampling factor and A/D precision for "similar" reconstruction accuracy. To the best of our knowledge this tradeoff has not been discussed before in the deterministic sampling literature.

3.1   Oversampling Factor versus A/D Precision

PCM-style sampling uses only one k-bit A/D converter per Nyquist-interval of length $1/\lambda$. The 1-bit dithered sampling scheme uses 2^k, 1-bit A/D converters uniformly distributed over the same interval, i.e., the A/D converters are placed at intervals of length $\tau = 1/(\lambda 2^k)$. For definiteness, assume that the sensors are placed at the beginning of every τ-length interval, i.e., at locations $\{m\tau\}_{m\in\mathbb{Z}}$. Now consider the scenario where b-bit A/D converters ($1 \leq b \leq k$) are uniformly placed at intervals of length τ. Notice that, 1-bit A/D converters only detect one level crossing (the 0 level), 2-bit A/D converters can detect 3 distinct level crossings, and in general, b-bit A/D converters can detect $2^b - 1$ distinct level crossings given by $\left\{0, \pm\frac{1}{2^b-1}, \ldots, \pm\left(1 - \frac{1}{2^b-1}\right)\right\}$. Hence, it requires $\log_2(2^b-1) < b$ bits to index a level crossing. We shall presently show how to design a dither function $d_b(t)$ so that $f(t) + d_b(t)$ always crosses some level in every interval of the form $[A_n, B_n] := \left[\frac{n}{\lambda}, \frac{n}{\lambda} + \left(2^{k-b+1} - 1\right)\tau\right] \subset \left[\frac{n}{\lambda}, \frac{n+1}{\lambda}\right]$ which covers 2^{k-b+1} b-bit A/D converters. It would require only $\log_2(2^{k-b+1} - 1) < k - b + 1$ bits per Nyquist-interval to specify the location of the sensor *just* following the location of the first level crossing of $[f + d_b](t)$. Hence the total number of bits required with this sampling method would be not more than $(k - b + 1) + b = k + 1$ bits (or $R = \lambda(k+1)$ bits per interval) which, ignoring the additional 1 bit, is the same as that needed for the k-bit PCM-style sampling and the 1-bit dither based sampling schemes. (The source of this additional bit can be explained as follows: In 1-bit dithered sampling, the A/D converters do not need to explicitly specify which level was crossed since there is only one level; only zero-crossing locations need to be described. In the k-bit PCM-style sampling, the locations of the A/D converters need not be explicitly specified since they are known; however, the sensors need to specify the quantization interval in which the signal sample lies. Note: specifying the quantization interval needs k bits unlike $\log_2(2^k - 1)$ bits needed to specify a level crossing). We shall further show that the approximation accuracy achieved by this approach is (as in the 1-bit dithered sampling scheme) of the order of τ. Since τ and k are related through $\tau = \frac{1}{\lambda 2^k}$, it follows that the worst-case sample approximation error is of the order of $2^{-(\frac{R}{\lambda} - 1)}$ in the rate (bits per interval).

The proposed sampling and quantization scheme (illustrated in Figure 3) can be summarized as follows:

- For $1 < b < k$ let $d_b(t)$ be an appropriate dither function (see Section 3.2).
- b-bit A/D converters per Nyquist-interval are placed at locations $\{\frac{n}{\lambda} + m\tau\}$ for $m = 0, \ldots, 2^{k-b+1} - 1$, $n \in \mathbb{Z}$.
- Each b-bit A/D adds dither $d_b(t)$ to the signal $f(t)$ and determines the quantization interval in which the resulting sum lies.
- The number of bits required for specifying the location of the sensor *just* following the first level crossing is not more than $(k - b + 1)$.
- The number of bits required for specifying the level crossed is not more than b.
- The total number of bits needed per Nyquist-interval is not more than $(k+1)$.

- The worst-case pointwise reconstruction error is proportional to τ with the result that the error profile decays exponentially in $R = \lambda(k+1)$ bits per meter.

For the described sampling scheme, the reconstruction accuracy can be improved either by improving the precision of available sensors or equivalently by using more sensors of the same precision in every Nyquist-interval. This leads to the following principle.

"Conservation of bits" principle: *Let k be the number of bits available per Nyquist interval. For each $1 \leq b \leq k$ there exists a (dither-based) sampling scheme with not more than 2^{k-b+1}, b-bit A/D converters per Nyquist-interval achieving a worst-case pointwise reconstruction accuracy of the order of 2^{-k}.*

3.2 Dither Function Design

We now investigate conditions on $d_b(t)$ under which $f(t) + d_b(t)$ will cross a quantization level in $[A_n, B_n]$. Let $M := 2^b$ then $B_n - A_n = \frac{2}{M\lambda} > 0$. From Bernstein's inequality (4) and the mean value theorem, we have:

$$f(B_n) \leq f(A_n) + \pi(B_n - A_n) = f(A_n) + \frac{2\pi}{M\lambda}. \tag{6}$$

We assume that $d_b(t)$ is continuous in each $[A_n, B_n]$. This implies that $[f+d_b](t)$ is also continuous and the intermediate value theorem can be used, whenever applicable, to deduce the existence of a level crossings. For $i = 0, \ldots, \frac{M-2}{2}$ consider the following scenarios:

1. $f(A_n) \in \left[\frac{2i}{M}, \frac{2(i+1)}{M} \right)$; The upper level $\frac{2(i+1)}{M}$ in this quantization interval is just outside the dynamic range of the A/D converter when $i = \frac{M-2}{2}$. Hence we shall derive conditions under which $f(t) + d_b(t)$ crosses the lower level $\frac{2i}{M}$ in $[A_n, B_n]$. Without loss of generality we can assume that the level crossing is from above to below, i.e.,

$$\frac{2i}{M} < f(A_n) + d_b(A_n), \tag{7}$$

$$f(B_n) + d_b(B_n) < \frac{2i}{M}. \tag{8}$$

The first condition (7) is satisfied if

$$0 < d_b(A_n). \tag{9}$$

From (6) and the fact that $f(A_n) < \frac{2(i+1)}{M}$ it follows that $f(B_n) - \frac{2i}{M} \leq \frac{2\pi}{M\lambda} + \frac{2}{M}$. Hence, the second condition (8) will be satisfied if

$$0 < \frac{2}{M} + \frac{2\pi}{M\lambda} < -d_b(B_n). \tag{10}$$

Note that the sufficient condition (10) implies that $d_b(B_n)$ is negative.

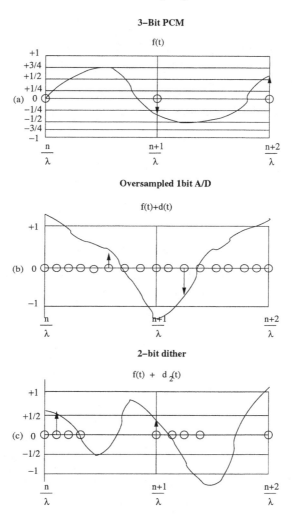

Fig. 3. Illustrating amplitude precision and oversampling rate tradeoffs in conventional and dither-based sampling frameworks. The top figure depicts conventional PCM-style sampling using 3-bit A/D converters placed at (near) Nyquist sampling locations $\{\frac{n}{\lambda}\}_{n\in\mathbb{Z}}$. The entire budget of 3 bits is exhausted at a single sample point in any Nyquist-interval. The middle figure shows a dither-based sampling scheme that uses eight, 1-bit A/D converters uniformly distributed over a Nyquist-interval to locate the zero crossing of the dithered signal. The bottom figure shows how to achieve a flexible tradeoff between these extremes. Four, 2-bit A/D converters uniformly distributed over half the Nyquist-period detect level crossings at 0 and $\pm\frac{1}{2}$. All three schemes have similar exponential error accuracy in bitrate.

2. $f(A_n) \in \left(-\frac{2(i+1)}{M}, -\frac{2i}{M}\right]$; the lower level $-\frac{2(i+1)}{M}$ in this quantization interval is just outside the dynamic range of the A/D converter when $i = \frac{M-2}{2}$. Hence we shall derive conditions under which $f(t) + d_b(t)$ crosses the upper level $-\frac{2i}{M}$ in $[A_n, B_n]$. Since $d_b(A_n) > 0$, we see that we no longer have a choice in the direction of the level crossing. To avoid conflicting requirements on $d_b(A_n)$, the level crossing must be from above to below, i.e.,

$$-\frac{2i}{M} < f(A_n) + d_b(A_n), \tag{11}$$

$$f(B_n) + d_b(B_n) < -\frac{2i}{M}. \tag{12}$$

Since, $-\frac{2i}{M} - f(A_n) < \frac{2}{M}$, condition (11) is satisfied if

$$\frac{2}{M} < d_b(A_n). \tag{13}$$

Again, from (6) and the fact that $f(A_n) \leq -\frac{2i}{M}$ it follows that $f(B_n) + \frac{2i}{M} \leq \frac{2\pi}{M\lambda}$. Hence, condition (12) will be satisfied if

$$0 < \frac{2\pi}{M\lambda} < -d_b(B_n). \tag{14}$$

Hence, the level crossing requirements on $d_b(t)$ are given by (9), (10), (13), and (14). These conditions can be summarized as

$$\frac{1}{2^{b-1}} < d_b(A_n),$$

$$0 < \frac{1}{2^{b-1}} + \frac{\pi}{\lambda 2^{b-1}} < -d_b(B_n).$$

Let $\alpha_b := \left(\frac{1}{2^{b-1}} + \frac{\pi}{\lambda 2^{b-1}}\right)$ and note that $\alpha_b > \frac{1}{2^{b-1}}$. If $d_b(t)$ is any function with the following properties:

1. $|d_b(A_n)| = |d_b(B_n)| > \alpha_b$ for all $n \in \mathbb{Z}$;
2. $\operatorname{sgn}[d_b(A_n)] = -\operatorname{sgn}[d_b(B_n)]$ for all $n \in \mathbb{Z}$;
3. $d_b(t)$ is differentiable in every $[A_n, B_n]$ and $\Delta_b := \sup_{t \in \cap_n (A_n, B_n)} |d_b'(t)| < \infty$;

then it is straightforward to verify that $d_b(t)$ meets all the level-crossing requirements. For instance, let $d(t)$ be any dither function used by the 1-bit dithered sampling scheme of Section 2.2 with derivative bounded by Δ. A valid b-bit dither function can be defined in terms of $d(t)$ as follows:

$$d_b(t) = \alpha_b \sum_{n \in \mathbb{Z}} d\left(\frac{2^{b-1}t}{1 - 2^{-(k-b+1)}} + \frac{n}{\lambda}\left(1 + \frac{1}{1 - 2^{-(b-1)}}\right)\right) 1_{[\frac{n}{\lambda}, \frac{n+1}{\lambda})}(t),$$

where $1_S(t)$ is the indicator function of set S. Note that the amplitude constraint on $d_b(t)$ is smaller (by a factor of around 2^{b-1}) than that on $d(t)$. However, $d_b(t)$ is also required to swing between positive and negative extremes over an interval that is shorter (by a factor of around 2^{b-1}) than that for $d(t)$. Hence, with respect to the derivative, these effects approximately cancel. If $d_b(t)$ is expressed in terms of $d(t)$ as above, $\Delta_b = \Delta(1 + \frac{\pi}{\lambda}) \frac{1}{1 - 2^{-(k-b+1)}}$.

Let $m_n \in \{0, \ldots, 2^{k-b+1} - 2\}$ be the smallest index[2] for which $[f + d_b](A_n + m_n \tau)$ and $[f + d_b](A_n + (m_n + 1)\tau)$ are on opposite sides of some level $l_n \in \{0, \pm\frac{1}{2^{b-1}}, \ldots, \pm(1 - \frac{1}{2^{b-1}})\}$ and let $z_n \in (A_n + m_n \tau, A_n + (m_n + 1)\tau)$ be the actual point of level crossing, i.e., $f(z_n) + d_b(z_n) = l_n$. From the mean value theorem applied to $[f + d_b](t)$ for the end-points $x_n = m_n + \frac{1}{2}$ and z_n we obtain

$$|[f + d_b](z_n) - [f + d_b](A_n + x_n \tau)| \leq \sup_{t \in (A_n, B_n)} |[f' + d_b'](t)| \, |z_n - A_n - x_n \tau|,$$

$$\Rightarrow \left| f\left(\frac{n}{\lambda} + x_n \tau\right) - \left(l_n - d_b\left(\frac{n}{\lambda} + x_n \tau\right)\right)\right| \leq \left(\frac{\pi + \Delta_b}{2}\right)\tau. \tag{15}$$

This shows that the accuracy of the nonuniform samples $\{f\left(\frac{n}{\lambda} + (m_n + \frac{1}{2})\tau\right)\}$ is still linear in τ, independent of the resolution of the A/D converters. As was pointed out earlier, only b bits are needed to specify the quantization level crossed and only $k - b + 1$ bits are needed to specify the first location of level crossing. The total number of bits needed is therefore $(k + 1)$ bits per $\frac{1}{\lambda}$ or $R = \lambda(k + 1)$ bits/interval. Hence, $\tau = \frac{2}{\lambda} 2^{-\frac{R}{\lambda}}$ and the worst-case sample error (15) is no more than

$$\frac{1}{\lambda}[\pi + \Delta_b] 2^{-\frac{R}{\lambda}}.$$

Using Proposition 2 with $t_n = \frac{n}{\lambda} + x_n \tau$ it is easy to confirm that $\{\left(\frac{n}{\lambda} + x_n \tau\right)\}_{n \in \mathbb{Z}}$ forms a set of stable sampling points for functions bandlimited to $[-\pi, \pi]$. Hence, the worst-case pointwise reconstruction error is bounded by

$$|f(t) - \widehat{f}_{D_b}(t)| \leq \frac{C'}{\lambda}[\pi + \Delta_b] 2^{-\frac{R}{\lambda}},$$

where

$$\widehat{f}_{D_b}(t) := \sum_{n \in \mathbb{Z}} \left(-d_b\left(\frac{n}{\lambda} + x_n \tau\right)\right) \psi_n\left(t - \frac{n}{\lambda} - x_n \tau\right)$$

is the b-bit dither-based reconstruction of $f(t)$ and the constant C' does not depend on $f(t)$. Observe that the reconstruction accuracy, in terms of bitrate, is similar to the PCM-style sampling scheme, i.e., it is exponentially decaying in rate R with the same exponent.

PCM as a special case: We would like to note that the PCM-style sampling scheme is also subsumed by the proposed generalized dithered sampling framework. Indeed, for $b = k$, the described framework suggests using two, k-bit A/D converters at locations $\frac{n}{\lambda}$ and $\frac{n}{\lambda} + \tau$. However, the dithered signal is guaranteed to have a level crossing in $[\frac{n}{\lambda}, \frac{n}{\lambda} + \tau]$. Hence, the second sensor is redundant and there is no need for the first sensor to add a dither value (except maybe for security reasons).

---

[2] The design of the dither function $d_b(t)$ ensures that a level crossing of $[f + d_b](t)$ will always occur in $[A_n, B_n]$ which covers 2^{k-b+1} sensors.

Number of sensors vs A/D precision: For the b-bit case, we need 2^{k-b+1} sensors per Nyquist interval, which means the number of sensors is less by a factor of 2^{b-1} compared to the 1-bit case. Thus, there is considerable flexibility in designing a sensor network. The number of sensors can be traded off with the precision of sensors. Note: throughout our analysis, the number of sensors has been a power two. However, this is only for the ease of illustration and is not a restrictive assumption.

4   Distributed Sampling in Sensor Networks

We have so far described, in an application-independent context, how it is possible to have a bit-conservation oversampling principle which allows for fairly flexible tradeoffs in A/D quantizer resolution versus the oversampling rate. In this section, we show how our proposed framework is particularly germane to the sensor network application as motivated in the introduction. Recall the key relevant features of (a) high spatial density (corresponding to oversampling), and (b) high inter-sensor communication costs (corresponding to local communication constraints – see Figure 1). In this context, it is better to have a dense set of low-precision sensors that have minimal-rate inter-node communication (nearest-neighbor only), as well as limited node-to-central-unit communication over the baseline case of coarse (Nyquist-rate) sensor density and potentially high node-to-central-unit communication cost. The dither-based oversampling method associated with the bit-conservation principle is particularly attractive in this application context, and offers a flexible array of tradeoffs between the precision of the sensors and the number of sensors.

Consider the following simple protocol that is friendly to the distributed sensor network application:

- Assume that sensors are placed uniformly at every $\tau = \frac{1}{\lambda 2^k}$ in $[\frac{n}{\lambda}, \frac{n}{\lambda} + (2^{k-b+1} - 1)\tau]$. The sensors at $\frac{n}{\lambda}$ are starting nodes.
- Each starting node passes a message to its neighbor (say its right neighbor), indicating the level-crossing index of $f(t) + d_b(t)$ at its location.
- Only the sensor(s) observing a level mismatch between what the neighbor reports and its own reading communicates with the base station, and indicates the level-crossing value (in the binary case, the level is always a zero-crossing and need not be sent).

A simple protocol like this provides accuracy through the A/D converter precision as well as the sampling separation τ. As we increase the A/D precision (b increases), we can get a reduction in the number of sensors according to the "conservation of bits" principle (the number of sensors needed is 2^{k-b+1}). How about the maximum pointwise reconstruction error? The sensors which broadcast their level-crossing to the central processor indicate their level-crossing index as well as their ID or address, requiring $(k + 1)$ bits. The reconstruction error is uniformly bounded by τ upto a proportionality constant. Hence, the overall accuracy is exponential in "bit rate to the central processor".

Local inter-sensor communication cost: For a reconstruction accuracy of the order of 2^{-k}, b-bit precision sensors, and the above local communication protocol, each sensor transmits b-bits to its right neighbor over a distance of τ. Since there are no more than 2^{k-b+1} sensors needed for the target reconstruction accuracy, b bits travel no more than $(2^{k-b+1} - 1)\tau$ meters in each sampling interval. Hence, the local communication cost is no more than $\frac{b}{\lambda 2^{b-1}} < \frac{1}{\lambda}$ bit-meters or 1 bit per Nyquist-interval. Thus, with limited local communication cost, the sampling task can be nicely distributed among the sensors.

Sensor distribution: Sensors need to be placed only in intervals of the form $\left[\frac{n}{\lambda}, \frac{n}{\lambda} + (2^{k-b+1} - 1)\tau\right]$. This leaves intervals over which there is no need to sample the signal at all. Hence for a given reconstruction quality (determined by the parameter k) the number of sensing units goes down exponentially with b: 1-bit dithered sampling needs 2^k sensors, b-bit dithered sampling needs 2^{k-b+1} sensors, and PCM-style sampling needs only one sensor per Nyquist-interval. Since the scheme naturally allows "inactive" regions in oversampling, we can have bunched irregular sampling using sensors. A direct advantage of this is that it allows for design flexibility in sensor deployment (e.g. in rugged terrain or in the presence of occluding obstacles, etc.).

In some cases the central unit can estimate the location of the sensor which is transmitting by the use of directional antennas and beamforming techniques. In this case, the sensors detecting the first level crossing need not identify themselves. This can provide significant savings in communication cost because the sensors need to send only the level crossing information. The dither-based oversampling method also offers robustness to node failures in terms of a graceful degradation of reconstruction error. For example, if every alternate node fails, the effective inter-node separation would increase to 2τ. This has the same effect as halving the resolution of the A/D converters by the bit-conservation principle. The same dither function will continue to work because it was designed for a higher spatial density. The worst-case local communication cost in bit-meters will also remain the same but the sensors would need to use more power to ensure that their message gets across a distance of 2τ as opposed to τ when all nodes were functioning. If we assume that temporal variation is uniform over a Nyquist interval (recall that we are considering an arbitrarily "frozen" time-instant in our analysis here), each sensor has an equal opportunity/load of communicating to the central unit, allowing for natural load-balancing.

Security: The design of the underlying dither function $d_b(t)$ can be chosen arbitrarily (within the constraints of the dither function properties). This allows for a secure sampling by selecting a covert dither function. The dither can be implementation-specific, and furthermore, can be different for each Nyquist-interval. However, the choice of the dither function also affects the reconstruction accuracy (through the slope of the dither function). Hence, a larger distortion for the eavesdropper's will also imply a larger reconstruction error in general. Quantifying the tradeoff between reconstruction error and security is part of our ongoing work.

5   Future Research Directions

We have addressed the problem of deterministic oversampling of bandlimited sensor fields. We have shown how, using a dither-based sampling scheme, it is possible to do this using only local inter-sensor communication and a multitude of low-precision sensors. More importantly, we have shown the feasibility of having a flexible tradeoff between the average oversampling rate and the Analog to Digital (A/D) quantization precision per sensor sample with respect to achieving exponential accuracy in the number of bits per Nyquist-interval, thereby exposing a key underpinning *"conservation of bits" principle*. This allows one to arbitrarily distribute the per-Nyquist-interval bit budget between the quantizer resolution and the spatial sampling resolution. Interestingly, this is possible using only neighbor-to-neighbor single-hop communication, making it attractive for sensor networks. Finally we pointed out how one can get security as a side-benefit due to the choice of the underlying dither function.

This paper is but the first step towards understanding the fundamentals of distributed sampling theory. The setup of a bandlimited 1-D deterministic signal model is somewhat simplistic but a necessary first step in probing further. The range of topics for future work is vast. There is a large body of literature on DPCM, delta-modulation, and sigma-delta modulation which needs to be revisited. The latter has been used in audio consumer electronic equipment for many years. Extensions to 2-D spatio-temporal sampling would be the next logical step for the work presented here. Other directions include incorporation of non-bandlimited signal models with "finite rate of innovation" that has recently been developed in [9] but with a distributed mindset. We would also like to explore connections to the seminal work on the throughput of ad-hoc networks in [10]. Finally, in contrast to the deterministic analysis of this work, extensions to sampling of bandlimited stochastic processes that incorporate the appropriate statistical signal and noise models is of great interest, and will be part of our future study.

References

1. R. J. Marks, II, *Introduction to Shannon Sampling and Interpolation Theory*. New York, USA: Springer-Verlag, 1990.
2. J. Chou, D. Petrovic, and K. Ramchandran, "Tracking and exploiting correlations in dense sensor networks," in *Asilomar Conference on Signals, Systems and Computers*, (Pacific Grove, CA), Nov 2002.
3. Z. Cvetković and M. Vetterli, "Error-rate Characteristics of Oversampled Analog-to-Digital Conversion," *IEEE Trans. on Information Theory*, vol. 44, pp. 1961–1964, Sep 1998.
4. I. Daubechies, *Ten Lectures on Wavelets*. Philadelphia: SIAM, 1992.
5. Z. Cvetković and I. Daubechies, "Single Bit oversampled A/D conversion with exponential accuracy in bit rate," *Proceeding DCC*, pp. 343–352, March 2000.
6. Z. Cvetković, I. Daubechies, and B. F. Logan, "Interpolation of Bandlimited functions from quantized Irregular Samples," *Proceeding DCC*, pp. 412–421, April 2002.

7. W. Rudin, *Principles of Mathematical Analysis.* USA: McGraw-Hill Companies, 1976.
8. G. H. Hardy, J. E. Littlewood, and G. Polya, *Inequalities.* London, UK: Cambridge University Press, 1959.
9. M. Vetterli, P. Marzilliano, and T. Blu, "Sampling Signals with Finite Rate of Innovation," *IEEE Trans. Signal Proc.*, pp. 1417–1428, June 2002.
10. P. Gupta and P. R. Kumar, "The Capacity of Wireless Networks," *IEEE Trans. on Information Theory*, vol. IT-46, pp. 388–404, Mar. 2000.

Energy-Quality Tradeoffs for Target Tracking in Wireless Sensor Networks

Sundeep Pattem[1], Sameera Poduri[2], and Bhaskar Krishnamachari[1]

[1] Department of Electrical Engineering,
[2] Department of Computer Science,
University of Southern California,
Los Angeles, CA 90036, USA
{pattem, spoduri, bkrishna}@usc.edu, http://ceng.usc.edu/~bkrishna/

Abstract. We study the tradeoffs involved in the energy-efficient localization and tracking of mobile targets by a wireless sensor network. Our work focuses on building a framework for evaluating the fundamental performance of tracking strategies in which only a small portion of the network is activated at any point in time. We first compare naive network operation with random activation and selective activation. In these strategies the gains in energy-savings come at the expense of increased uncertainty in the location of the target, resulting in reduced quality of tracking. We show that selective activation with a good prediction algorithm is a dominating strategy that can yield orders-of-magnitude energy savings with negligible difference in tracking quality. We then consider duty-cycled activation and show that it offers a flexible and dynamic tradeoff between energy expenditure and tracking error when used in conjunction with selective activation.

1   Introduction

There is an emerging trend towards the use of sophisticated wireless networks of unattended sensor devices for intelligence gathering and environmental monitoring [1] -[6]. One canonical application of sensor networks that has received considerable attention in the literature is the tracking of a mobile target (point source) by the network.

In a tracking scenario, information obtained from nodes far away from the region of activity is of little or no use. For a typical sensor network with a large number of nodes, a major portion of these falls in the above category. In addition, if the nodes are densely deployed, information obtained from some sensors close to the region of activity might be redundant. An obvious way to save energy is to switch on only a subset of the sensor nodes. We discuss in this paper various possible activation strategies: (1) naive activation, (2) randomized activation (3) selective activation based on trajectory prediction and (4) duty-cycled activation.

In these sensor activation strategies, energy savings come at the expense of a reduction in the quality of tracking. In other words, relying on the information provided by a small subset of the sensor nodes results in an increased uncertainty

F. Zhao and L. Guibas (Eds.): IPSN 2003, LNCS 2634, pp. 32–46, 2003.

in the sensed location of the mobile. In this paper we study the energy-quality tradeoffs involved by building a model to quantify both the energy expenditure and the quality of tracking. Also for a particular strategy, we study the impact of the following: a) deployed/activated density of sensors b) their sensing range c) capabilities of activated and un-activated nodes d) the target's mobility model.

Our efforts are not directed *per se* at proposing new techniques for mobile tracking. Rather the focus is on the evaluation and analysis of general strategies which may be incorporated into a real system. We start with a simple model for tracking and substantiate the intuition that it is possible to obtain orders of magnitude savings in energy while keeping the uncertainty within acceptable limits. We also discuss the extensions of the model to relate closely with real life scenarios. The results in this work are a first step in our attempt to understand the fundamental bounds on the the tracking quality that can be obtained under various energy constraints and sensor models.

The rest of the paper is organized as follows. In section 2, we discuss related work from the existing literature, presenting the context for our work. We describe our basic model, assumptions and evaluation metrics for target tracking in section 3. The general tracking strategies that we investigate are detailed in section 4. Section 5 contains the description of our experiments to evaluate the performance of these strategies, and an analysis of the results presented. Finally, we present concluding comments in section 6.

2   Related Work

Target tracking is considered a canonical application for wireless sensor networks, and work in this area has been motivated in large part by DARPA programs such as SensIT [18].

Zhao *et al.* present the information driven sensor querying (IDSQ) mechanism in [8], [7]. IDSQ is a sensor-to-sensor leader handoff based scheme in which at any given time there is a leader sensor node which makes the decisions about which sensors should be selectively turned on in order to obtain the best information about the target. A combined cost function which gives weight to both energy expenditure and information gain is considered. The generic selective activation strategy which we describe in this paper is closest in spirit to IDSQ. As our focus in this paper is to evaluate general strategies, our findings regarding selective activation are applicable to the performance of intelligent tracking strategies such as IDSQ. Liu *et al.* develop a dual-space approach to tracking targets which also enables selective activation of sensors based on which nodes the target is likely to approach next.

Along these lines, Ramanathan, Brooks, *et al.* advocate a location-centric approach to performing collaborative sensing and target tracking in [13], [14]. The idea is to develop programming abstractions that provide addressing and communication between localized geographic regions within the network rather than individual nodes. This makes localized selective-activation strategies simpler to implement.

Brooks *et al.* present self-organized distributed target tracking techniques with prediction based on Pheromones, Bayesian, and Extended Kalman Filter techniques [21], [22]. The implementation and testing of a real distributed sensor network collaborative tracking algorithm in a military context is described in [23].

A number of recent papers have focused on the question of deploying sensors to ensure adequate coverage of moving targets. Megerian, Meguerdichian, Potkonjak, et al. [20], [19], investigate the question of the minimum exposure path that a target can take in a given sensor field - which is a worst-case metric to evaluate the tracking quality that can be obtained for a given deployment. Clouquer *et al.* [16] use a related metric to evaluate sensor deployment strategies that enhance the worst-case probability of target detection, taking into account factors such as equipment and deployment costs. Chakrabarty, Iyengar *et al.* discuss the problem of tolerating faults while ensuring sensor coverage of an area to ensure that the target moving through the area can be tracked at all times [10]. Jung and Sukhatme examine target tracking by a mobile robotic sensor network in [12].

The problem of multiple targets has also attracted some attention. Bejar, Krishnamachari, *et al.* formulate a sensor tracking problem as that of distributed constraint satisfaction. They show that there is a critical combination of sensing and communication needed to ensure that multiple targets can be tracked satisfactorily by a sensor network. In [15], Li, Wong *et al.* tackle the problem of distinguishing between multiple targets, describing and developing several target classification mechanisms. Fang, Zhao and Guibas describe a distributed mechanism for counting the number of targets in a given field in [9].

In the context of these related works, we should emphasize that our attention is primarily focused on single-target tracking. Our interest is in analyzing and evaluating the fundamental energy-quality tradeoffs involved in tracking with different generic tracking strategies, rather than designing/advocating yet another tracking protocol.

3   Model and Metrics

We now describe the models, assumptions and metrics used in our work.

3.1   Basic Model

We consider a sensor network consisting of N nodes deployed in some operational area, operating for a total time duration T. There is a single target moving through the area. We assume that all sensors in the network are binary detectors with a fixed sensing range S. In other words, at each instant, each sensor returns a '1' if the target is present within a distance S of that sensor, and a '0' otherwise. Given this simple sensor model, we take the centroid of the *locations* of all detecting sensors as an estimate of the target's location at any given time t. Say there are k sensors at locations $X_i = (x_i, y_i)$, $i = 1 \ldots k$, detecting the target at time t. Then the estimated location of target $X_s(t) = (x_s(t), y_s(t))$, where

$$x_s(t) = \frac{\Sigma^k x_i}{k} \tag{1}$$

$$y_s(t) = \frac{\Sigma^k y_i}{k} \tag{2}$$

We assume two different modes of operation for each node:

1) A high power tracking mode : Nodes in this mode use a higher power H, which depends on their sensing capabilities. A node in this mode is capable of both sensing a target and also communicating with neighbor nodes.

2) A low power communication mode : Nodes in this mode use a lower power L, which is an indicator of the farthest distance they can communicate. A node in this mode can only communicate with neighbor nodes.

3.2   Quality Metric: Tracking Error

The two performance measures of interest to us in evaluating different tracking strategies are the average total energy expenditure P (averaged over a period of time T), and some measure of the tracking quality, which reflects the uncertainty in the target's location. We use the Euclidean distance between the estimated and actual locations of the target to measure the tracking error. If $X_a(t) = (x_a(t), y_a(t))$ is the actual position of the target at time t, we denote the *instantaneous* tracking error metric as $q(t)$:

$$q(t) = d(X_s(t), X_a(t)) = \sqrt{(x_s(t) - x_a(t))^2 + (y_s(t) - y_a(t))^2} \tag{3}$$

For the time T spent by a target in the area of interest, the time average error, which we denote as Q is given as

$$Q = \frac{1}{T} \int_0^T q(t)dt \tag{4}$$

We note that one drawback of the tracking error metric Q is that it is dependent on the target's specific trajectory[1] $X_a(t)$, $t = 0 : T$. An alternative trajectory-independent metric can be obtained by assuming that the target's movement is an *Ergodic* random process, and that its location probability distribution is independent of time. (A random process is ergodic if the time average of any instantiation of the process converges to the mathematical expectation.) Then we can use an alternative tracking error metric Q', the expected distance between the estimated and actual positions of the target:

$$Q' = E[q(t)] = E[\sqrt{(x_s(t) - x_a(t))^2 + (y_s(t) - y_a(t))^2}] \tag{5}$$

---

[1] Note that in our model, once the location of all N nodes in the network is fixed, and assuming the nodes that are sensing at each time is known, the estimated trajectory $X_s(t)$ can be determined from the actual trajectory $X_a(t)$.

Note that this tracking error metric Q' depends not on a time-dependent trajectory, but rather the probability distribution of the target's location in the operational area.

3.3 Energy Metric: Tracking Energy

For a given tracking strategy, let n_s denote the number of nodes that are in tracking/sensing mode and $n_c = N - n_s$ the number of nodes that are in communication mode. The average energy expenditure for a network of N nodes is then

$$P = (n_s H + n_c L) = P = (n_s H + (N - n_s)L) \qquad (6)$$

To simplify our analysis, we assume that the cost of communication is comparable across the different tracking strategies[2]. We therefore compare strategies primarily on the basis of their respective energy expenditure for tracking. To the first order, one can consider the sensing power expenditure as being a power law function of the sensing range S of the nodes: $H(S) = H_0 S^\alpha$, where α could be considered the decay exponent for the sensed signal and would depend upon the sensor modality and deployment factors such as terrain characteristics. Normalizing $H_0 = 1$, we get the following energy metric useful for evaluating a tracking strategy:

$$P_t = n_s H = n_s S^\alpha \qquad (7)$$

4 Tracking Strategies

We now describe some general tracking strategies:

– **Naive activation (NA):** In naive activation, all nodes in the network are in tracking mode all the time. While clearly this strategy offers the worst energy efficiency, it is a useful baseline for comparison because it provides the best possible quality of tracking. For this strategy, we have that

$$n_{s,NA} = N \qquad (8)$$
$$P_{t,NA} = NS^\alpha \qquad (9)$$

– **Randomized activation (RA):** In this strategy, each node is on with a probability p. On average a fraction p of all the nodes will be on and in tracking mode. In this case,

$$n_{s,RA} = pN \qquad (10)$$
$$P_{t,RA} = pNS^\alpha \qquad (11)$$

---

[2] This is a reasonably valid assumption particularly when one takes into account recent studies suggesting that reception power for wireless sensor nodes can be comparable to the transmission power.

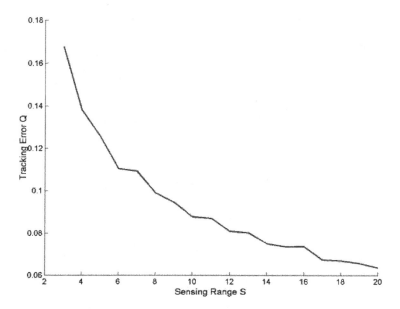

Fig. 1. Tracking Error versus Sensing Range for Naive Activation

- **Selective activation based on prediction (SA):** In this strategy, only a small subset of all the nodes are in tracking mode at any given point of time. They also predict the "next" position of the target and hand over tracking to nodes best placed to track the target in the "next" position. The rest of the nodes are in communication mode and can switch to tracking mode on being alerted by signals from tracking nodes.

  Let X_a be the actual position of the target, and $X_b = X_s$ the belief position of target as before; define X_p as the predicted target position. The idea of selective activation is to use prior history of X_b to determine X_p for the next step. (For example, if we discretize time, knowing sensors could use a simple linear predictor to predict the next location of the target $X_p(t+1)$, using the two latest previous belief positions to estimate the target velocity and assuming that it will continue to move in a straight line). All the sensors within a circle of radius S_p around $X_p(t+1)$ are then alerted to start sensing. Only the sensors within the sensing range S of the actual position $X_a(t+1)$ can possibly sense the target. Hence, the sensors lying in the overlap of the two circles sense the target and the new belief location $X_b(t+1)$ is obtained by finding the centroid of the positions of these sensors. This is illustrated in figure 3. With selective activation based on prediction, only the sensors within a radius S_p around X_p are in tracking mode at any point of time. If ρ is the density of deployment, we get

$$n_{s,SA} = \pi S_p^2 \rho \tag{12}$$

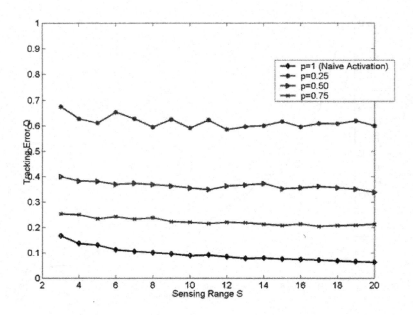

Fig. 2. Tracking Error versus Sensing Range for Random Activation

$$P_{t,SA} = \pi S_p{}^2 \rho S^\alpha \tag{13}$$

– **Duty-cycled Activation (DA):** In duty-cycled activation, the entire sensor network periodically turns off and on with a regular duty cycle. One key feature of duty-cycled activation is that it can actually be used in conjunction with any other activation strategy for target tracking (including NA, RA and SA). Let T_D be the period of the cycle, t_{ON} the on-time, and $n_{s,U}$ be the average number of tracking sensors in the underlying activation strategy U. Then

$$n_{s,DA} = \frac{n_{s,U}t_{ON}}{T_D} \tag{14}$$

$$P_{t,DA} = \frac{P_{t,U}t_{ON}}{T_D} = \frac{n_{s,U}S^\alpha t_{ON}}{T_D} \tag{15}$$

5   Experiments and Results

In the previous two sections we have developed useful common metrics for energy and tracking quality based on our sensor network model, described the tracking strategies we will consider, and their energy expenditure model. In order to compare these strategies, we now turn to simulation experiments.

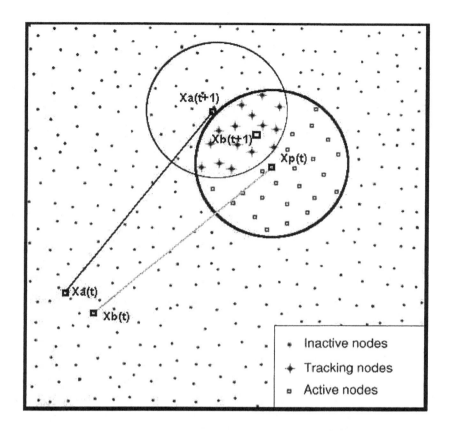

Fig. 3. Illustration of Selective Activation (note: $X_b = X_s$, the believed position)

We simulated a virtual large scale sensor network on a 200 unit x 200 unit area with random placement of sensors and density of deployment $\rho = 1$ sensor/unit area (i.e. a total of 40000 nodes). Linear, sinusoidal and other reasonable trajectories for the target motion were considered. To avoid edge effects in estimating uncertainty, our calculations are for trajectories in which the target stays away from the boundaries of the region. In the results presented, the target is assumed to follow a representative trajectory of the form $y(t) = Ax^B(t) + C \sin Dx(t) + E$.

5.1 Performance of Naive Activation, Random Activation, and Selective Activation

Since we are using the centroid of the sensors tracking at any point of time as the sensed position, this estimate can be improved by considering a larger number of sensors. One way of achieving this is to increase the sensing range S. Figure 1 shows how tracking error decreases with S for naive activation. Similarly, figure 2 shows the performance of randomized activation for different

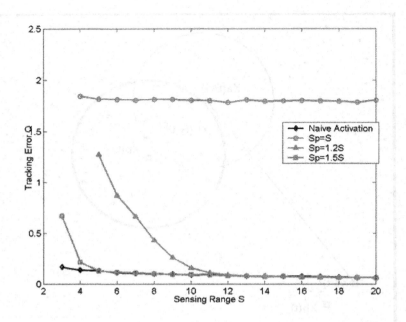

Fig. 4. Tracking Error versus Sensing Range for Selective Activation

values of p. It can be seen that the tracking quality of network-wide randomized activation deteriorates significantly as p is decreased. We also observe that while increasing S does result in a decrease in the tracking error, the decrease is not very substantial and diminishes with increasing S. This evidence of diminishing returns on quality leads us to conclude that it is best not to set the sensing range within the network too high.

Figure 4 compares the performance of selective activation with different settings of S_p. Naive activation is also plotted in the same figure as a baseline. It can be seen that the tracking error is quite high when $S_p = S$. In predictive selective-activation, as the intersection area of the two circles (the circle of radius S around the actual position and the circle of radius S_p around the belief position) becomes larger, sensors closer to the target's actual position are activated. This can be achieved by increasing S_p. For the particular trajectory considered, we find that selective activation with $S_p = 1.5S$ performs nearly as well as a naive network.

Figure 5 shows the energy-quality tradeoff between the NA, RA and SA strategies. It is a plot of the tracking error vs $log(P_t)$ for these strategies, with respect to the energy metric in log scale (as defined in section 3). In this figure, data points to the bottom left represent dominating, Pareto-optimal strategies, since they represent low tracking error (hence high tracking quality) as well as low energy expenditure. It is clear from the figure that selective activation with

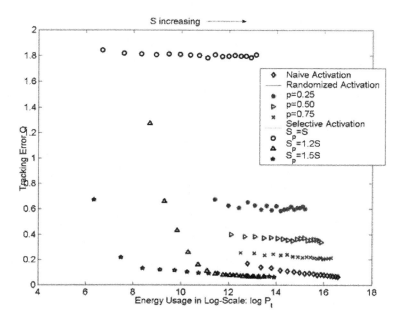

Fig. 5. Energy-Quality Tradeoff for Basic Activation Strategies: NA, RA, SA

reasonably high S_p is a dominating strategy. It provides overall significantly reduced traffic error for low energy expenditure.

Clearly, selective activation can provide a dominating design in terms of the energy-quality tradeoffs considered. Figure 5 shows that selective activation with optimal settings can offer 4 orders of magnitude savings in energy (corresponding to the size of the network) compared to NA or RA, for essentially the same tracking quality. Also, the sensing range should be chosen carefully and kept to a minimum based on the desired quality in order to effect the best tradeoff. For selective activation, the results suggest using the lowest feasible value of S and corresponding S_p. In general, the feasible values of S and S_p would depend on the mobility model of the target. The average speed of the target can provide a good indicator for determining these parameters. We found that the results do not vary much with trajectory for comparable values of target speed.

5.2 Performance of Duty-Cycled Activation

Let us now turn to the final strategy: duty-cycled activation. Let us understand the functioning of this scheme. If we consider a particular time period T_D, the instantaneous tracking error during time t_{ON} would be the same as for the network without duty-cycling (let's call this $q_U(t)$). However, once the network is shut down, the tracking error increase with time until the next time period starts - this is due to the drift between the estimated target location and the

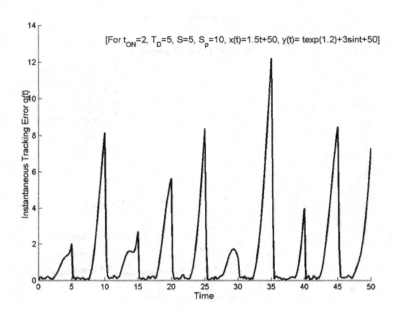

Fig. 6. Instantaneous Tracking Error versus Time for Selective Activation with Duty Cycling

actual target movement during the off-time. For the time period T_D, if v is the mean target speed, the tracking error at time t is

$$q(t) \simeq \begin{cases} q_U(t) & ,0 < t < t_O N \\ q_U(t) + v(t - t_{ON}) & ,t_{ON} < t < T_D \end{cases} \tag{16}$$

Hence the average tracking error for duty-cycled activation Q_{DA} can be approximated as

$$Q_{DA} \simeq Q_U + 0.5v(1 - \frac{t_{ON}}{T_D})^2 T_D \tag{17}$$

As we noted before, DA can be used in conjunction with other underlying strategies. Since our previous results have shown that selective activation is a dominating strategy, we focus on this combination: duty-cycled selective activation. Figure 6 shows a sample run illustrating how instantaneous tracking error varies with time for selective activation with duty-cycling. Figure 7 shows (as suggested by equation (17)) that for the same ratio t_{ON}/T_D, the average tracking error Q increases with the period T_D. Given an acceptable value for the tracking error and the mobility model of the target (v), the above approximation can help us arrive at the feasible values of T_D (t_{ON} should be kept to the minimum possible value, which might depend on the time-constants associated with device start-up and shut-down).

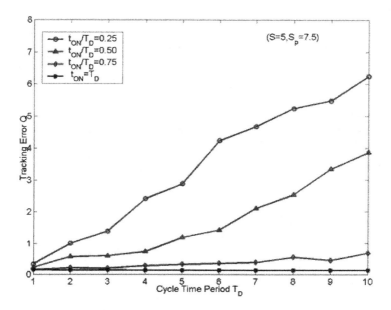

Fig. 7. Tracking Error versus Cycle Time for Selective Activation with Duty Cycling

Figure 8 shows the tracking error varies with energy usage when choosing different values of T_D and t_{ON}. The figure shows that duty-cycled activation is a flexible and efficient mechanism for tuning the energy-quality tradeoff of tracking.

6   Conclusions

The following is a summary of the main contributions of this paper:

- We identified four generic sensor activation strategies for target tracking that can be used to provide different energy-quality tradeoffs: naive activation, random activation, selective activation with prediction and duty-cycled activation.
- We developed simple metrics to evaluate the performance of these strategies with respect to energy usage and tracking quality.
- We examined how tracking performance for the basic strategies (NA, RA, SA) varies with sensor range, showing that there are diminishing returns in terms of tracking quality. This suggests that sensor range settings should be carefully chosen and kept to a minimum with these strategies.
- We showed that with the right parameters selective activation can provide orders of magnitude improvements in energy usage with near-optimal track-

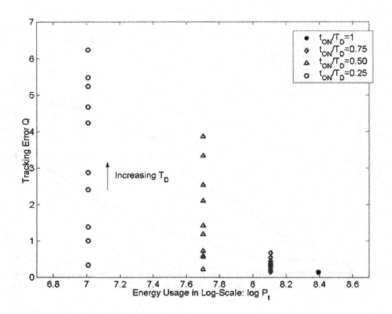

Fig. 8. Energy-Quality Tradeoff for Selective Activation with Duty Cycling

ing quality. With respect to random and naive activation, SA is a dominating strategy with Pareto-optimal points on an energy-quality plot.

– We then examined duty-cycled activation. Our analysis showed that for best energy performance the ratio t_{ON}/T_D should be kept as small as possible, while minimizing T_D improves the tracking quality. This allows us to use t_{ON} and T_D as tuning knobs to effect a flexible tradeoff between energy and tracking quality in conjunction with other base strategies such as selective activation.

Although we have taken a significant step in this direction, as future work, we would like to extend the mathematical treatment of the energy-quality tradeoffs involved in tracking. This will require the use of more tractable assumptions about the target mobility model. We would also like to consider richer sensor models and energy cost models to validate the generality of our findings.

References

1. A. Cerpa *et al.*, "Habitat monitoring: Application driver for wireless communications technology," *2001 ACM SIGCOMM Workshop on Data Communications in Latin America and the Caribbean*, Costa Rica, April 2001.
2. G.J. Pottie, W.J. Kaiser, "Wireless Integrated Network Sensors," *Communications of the ACM*, vol. 43, no. 5, pp. 551–8, May 2000.

3. J. Warrior, "Smart Sensor Networks of the Future," *Sensors Magazine*, March 1997.
4. D. Estrin, R. Govindan, J. Heidemann and S. Kumar, "Next Century Challenges: Scalable Coordination in Sensor Networks," *ACM/IEEE International Conference on Mobile Computing and Networks (MobiCom '99)*, Seattle, Washington, August 1999.
5. D. Estrin *et al. Embedded, Everywhere: A Research Agenda for Networked Systems of Embedded Computers*, National Research Council Report, 2001.
6. I. Akyildiz, , W. Su, Y. Sankarasubramaniam, and E. Cayirci, "A Survey on Sensor Networks," *IEEE Communications Magazine*, Vol. 40, No. 8, pp. 102–114, August 2002.
7. M. Chu, H. Haussecker, F. Zhao, "Scalable information-driven sensor querying and routing for ad hoc heterogeneous sensor networks." *International Journal on High Performance Computing Applications*, vol. 16, no. 3, Fall 2002.
8. F. Zhao, J. Shin, J. Reich, "Information-Driven Dynamic Sensor Collaboration for Tracking Applications." *IEEE Signal Processing Magazine*, March 2002.
9. Q. Fang, F. Zhao, L. Guibas, "Counting Targets: Building and Managing Aggregates in Wireless Sensor Networks." Palo Alto Research Center Technical Report pp. 2002–10298, June 2002.
10. K. Chakrabarty, S. S. Iyengar, H. Qi, E.C. Cho, "Grid Coverage of Surveillance and Target location in Distributed Sensor Networks" *To appear in IEEE Transaction on Computers*, May 2002.
11. R. Bejar, B. Krishnamachari, C. Gomes, and B. Selman, "Distributed constraint satisfaction in a wireless sensor tracking system," *Workshop on Distributed Constraint Reasoning, International Joint Conference on Artificial Intelligence*, Seattle, Washington, August 2001.
12. Jung, B. and Sukhatme, G.S. "Tracking Targets using Multiple Robots: The Effect of Environment Occlusion", *Autonomous Robots*, 2002.
13. P. Ramanathan, "Location-centric Approach for Collaborative Target Detection, Classification, and Tracking," *IEEE CAS Workshop*, 2002.
14. R. R. Brooks, P. Ramanathan, and A. Sayeed, "Distributed Target Tracking and Classification in Sensor Networks," *Proceedings of the IEEE*, Invited Paper, Submitted for review, September 2002.
15. D. Li, K. Wong, Y. Hu and A. Sayeed, "Detection, Classification, Tracking of Targets in Micro-sensor Networks," *IEEE Signal Processing Magazine*, pp. 17–29, March 2002
16. T. Clouqueur, V. Phipatanasuphorn, P. Ramanathan and K. K. Saluja, "Sensor Deployment Strategy for Target Detection," *The First ACM International Workshop on Wireless Sensor Networks and Applications (WSNA'02)*, Sep. 2002.
17. J. Liu, P. Cheung, L. Guibas, and F. Zhao, "A Dual-Space Approach to Tracking and Sensor Management in Wireless Sensor Networks," *The First ACM International Workshop on Wireless Sensor Networks and Applications (WSNA'02)*, Sep. 2002.
18. J. Reich, *SensIT Collaborative Signal Processing Scenario Discussions*, (http://www2.parc.com/spl/projects/cosense/pub/tracking_benchmarks.pdf).
19. S. Megerian, F. Koushanfar, G. Qu, G. Veltri, M. Potkonjak, "Exposure In Wireless Sensor Networks: Theory And Practical Solutions", *Journal of Wireless Networks, Vol. 8, No. 5, ACM Kluwer Academic Publishers*, pp. 443–454, September 2002.
20. S. Meguerdichian, F. Koushanfar, G. Qu, M. Potkonjak, "Exposure In Wireless Ad Hoc Sensor Networks", *International Conference on Mobile Computing and Networking (MobiCom '01)*, pp. 139–150, Rome, Italy, July 2001.

21. R. Brooks, and C. Griffin, "Traffic model evaluation of ad hoc target tracking algorithms," *Journal of High Performance Computer Applications*, Accepted, 2002.
22. R. Brooks, C. Griffin, and D. S. Friedlander, "Self-Organized distributed sensor network entity tracking," *International Journal of High Performance Computer Applications, special issue on Sensor Networks*, vol. 16, no. 3, Fall 2002
23. J. Moore, T. Keiser, R. R. Brooks, S. Phoha, D. Friedlander, J. Koch, A. Reggio, and N. Jacobson, "Tracking Targets with Self-Organizing Distributed Ground Sensors," *2003 IEEE Aerospace Conference*, Invited Paper, Accepted for publication, November 2002.

Adaptive and Decentralized Operator Placement for In-Network Query Processing

Boris Jan Bonfils and Philippe Bonnet

Department of Computer Science, University of Copenhagen, Universitetsparken 1,
2100 Copenhagen, Denmark
bbo@bording.dk, bonnet@diku.dk
http://www.distlab.dk/vaquita/

Abstract. In-network query processing is critical for reducing network traffic when accessing and manipulating sensor data. It requires placing a tree of query operators such as filters and aggregations but also correlations onto sensor nodes in order to minimize the amount of data transmitted in the network. In this paper, we show that this problem is a variant of the task assignment problem for which polynomial algorithms have been developed. These algorithms are however centralized and cannot be used in a sensor network. We describe an adaptive and decentralized algorithm that progressively refines the placement of operators by walking through neighbor nodes. Simulation results illustrate the potential benefits of our approach. They also show that our placement strategy can achieve near optimal placement onto various graph topologies despite the risks of local minima.

1 Introduction

Sensor networks are a promising platform for a new generation of monitoring applications [4]. In the recent years, research has shown that clusters of densely deployed sensor nodes arranged in a multi-hop network allow for improved sensing (via collaborative signal processing [17]) and improved energy efficiency [14]. Because data transmission is orders of magnitude more costly than processing on a sensor node [14], data processing should be pushed inside the sensor network whenever it reduces the amount of data to be transmitted [7]. The term *in-network processing* has been tossed to denote data processing that takes place inside the network [6].

It is now generally admitted that access to data in a sensor network should be declarative [5]: Users formulate queries to access the data they are interested in. The exact definition of these queries is an open issue. We take a database perspective and consider that a query is a tree of *operators* that aggregate, correlate or filter data streams [2,3,16]. In this paper we tackle the issue of operator placement for in-network query processing, i.e., on which sensor nodes should query operators be placed?

We give an example to illustrate the importance of operator placement. A user is correlating detections obtained from two distinct regions (in the context

F. Zhao and L. Guibas (Eds.): IPSN 2003, LNCS 2634, pp. 47–62, 2003.

of animal monitoring or vehicle observation): The user should be notified whenever similar targets are detected in the two distinct regions within a given time window. For the sake of simplicity we consider that one node generates detections in each region[1]. A correlation operator is pushed inside the network. This operator takes as input the detections from the two regions and generates an output whenever a similar target has been detected in the two regions within a given time window. A gateway node is the sink that consumes the data generated by the correlation operator.

Let us now discuss the ideal placement for the correlation operator, i.e. the operator placement that minimizes the amount of data transmitted in the network. Consider that initially both regions produce detections that are not correlated and that one region produces more detections than the other. The correlation operator is very reductive (it does not output data). Intuitively, its optimal placement is on the shortest path between the two nodes that generate detections, and closer to the node that produce more data (see Figure 1(a)). The exact position of the correlation operator depends (i) on the rate at which data is produced by the operator and both sources, as well as (ii) on the path length between the sources, the operators and the sink. In a second configuration, the detections are somewhat correlated. As a result, the correlation operator produces more data and its optimal placement is closer to the sink (see Figure 1(b)).

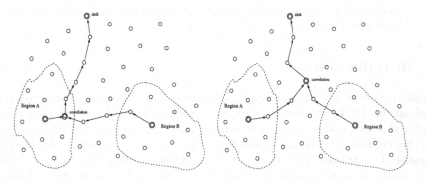

(a) Inequal number of detections in each region – Low correlation

(b) Equal number of detections in each region – Low correlation

Fig. 1. Examples of Operator Placements

The optimal placement of the correlation operator corresponds to the solution of a task assignment problem: The problem is to find the mapping of operators to sensor nodes that minimizes the amount of data transferred over the network.

---

[1] Possibly, a collaborative signal processing algorithm generates detections and elects a representative node in each region. At different points in time, different nodes might be elected to produce the detections.

We give a more formal problem definition in Section 2. Even though polynomial algorithms exists for some versions of the task assignment problem, they cannot be used for our purpose because:

1. We do not assume global knowledge about the sensor network. The algorithms that solve the task assignment problem are centralized and require complete topological information [1]. It would be expensive in terms of data transfer and quite inaccurate for a central site to maintain this information. In addition, the amount of information maintained on each node should be minimal because of memory limitation, In order to limit maintenance overhead, this information should be local - each node should only maintain information about close-by nodes. As a result, we need to devise a *decentralized* solution where each node maintains local information.

2. The placement of an operator needs to be recomputed as the conditions in the network change. In our example, the optimal placement of the correlation operator changes as the correlation between the detection evolves, but also as the number of detections produced in each region changes. It would be inefficient to place an operator on a sensor node once and for all. In our example, if the correlation operator is permanently placed at the sink node while the detections from both regions are not correlated, then data is transmitted all the way to the sink for no result. It would have been more efficient to compute the correlation as close to the sources as possible. Our solution must thus be *adaptive*.

In this paper, we propose a decentralized and adaptive solution to the operator placement problem. In our solution, sensor nodes continuously refine the placement of operators in order to minimize the amount of data transferred over the network. While one node is *active* executing an operator, a set of candidate nodes, that we denote *tentative* nodes, estimate the cost of running this operator (the cost is a function of the amount of data received and produced by a node). At regular intervals estimated costs are compared with the actual cost measured on the active node and execution is transferred to the node with the lowest cost.

We first give a formal problem definition and then we detail our contributions:

- We define *neighbor exploration*: a decentralized exploration strategy that continously refine the placement of operators towards the nodes with minimal costs.
- We describe a decentralized and adaptive algorithm that implements the neighbor exploration strategy based on the notions of active and tentative nodes.
- We present simultation results that illustrate the potential benefits of our approach.

Our simulation results show that our approach is viable. However, they do not allow us to lead a complete study. A key question that we do not tackle in this paper concerns the overhead generated by our decentralized algorithm - in terms of messages exchanged. Another interesting question concerns the reactivity of our approach (how fast it can adapt to changing conditions – e.g., data rate, data correlation). In order to study these issues, we have implemented our solution on top of directed diffusion [6]. We are currently running experiments using NS. Our initial results are very promising.

2 Problem Statement

Before we proceed to the formal problem definition, let us state our assumptions:

1. Queries are long-running: They are submitted to the system and run until the user decides to interrupt query execution. In our work, we assume that the (collaborative) signal processing algorithms that produce sensor data are implemented and deployed separately from the queries formulated by users to access these data.
2. We define a query as a tree of operators[2]. The leaves of the trees correspond to the *source* nodes, i.e., the nodes that return data on behalf of the (collaborative) signal processing algorithms that produce *data streams*. The internal nodes of the trees are correlation, filtering, aggregation, or duplicate elimination *operators* that take as input one or several data streams and output another data stream. The root of the query tree is an operator that takes one data stream as input and forwards it; typically this root operator is placed on a gateway node that we denote *sink* in the rest of the paper. Note that we assume that there is one fixed sink per query. Relaxing this assumption is an interesting topic for future work.

Let us now proceed to the formal problem definition. We aim at placing operators on sensor nodes in order to minimize data transfer in the network. We consider a sensor network to be a directed graph where vertices represent sensor nodes and where edges represent communication links, and a query as a tree of operators. We define:

1. An oriented sensor network graph (SNG) as
   a) ζ - a set of sensor nodes. In the rest, p and q are elements of ζ.
   b) π - a set of communication links connecting the nodes in ζ. We denote (p, q), the link between nodes p and q, an element of π.
   c) w_{pq} - a weight is a positive integer associated with the link (p, q) of π
2. An oriented query tree (QT) as
   a) η - a set of operators. In the rest, operators i and j are elements of η.
   b) λ - a set of communication dependencies connecting the operators. We denote (i, j), the link between operators i and j, an element of λ. We denote i as the child and j as the parent in this communication link. Because QT is an oriented query tree, each operator has zero, one or more children and at most one parent.
   c) d_{ij} - a weight associated with the link (i, j) of λ

---

[2] Possibly such a tree of operators is generated from a declarative query language [2, 16]

w_{pq} denotes the unit cost of communicating data through the link (p, q). This cost might for example vary with the battery power of the sensor node. We define the cost of a path $P = \{(p, x), \cdots, (y, q)\}$ between node p and q as $C_p(P) = \sum_{e \in P} w_e$ – note that x and y are nodes in ζ. We denote the cheapest path between p and q by $P_{min}(p, q)$.

d_{ij} denotes the rate at which data is transmitted between operator i and j. Because queries are long-running, the rate at which an operator produces data might vary in time (e.g., more detections are produced or a correlation operator produces more data as its input become more correlated).

The *transfer cost* of sending data between operator i on node p and operator q on node j may be denoted by a function $S_{pq}(d_{ij})$ defined by $S_{pq}(d_{ij}) = C_p(P_{min}(p, q)) \cdot d_{ij}$, i.e., the transfer cost is a function of the path cost and the amount of data sent through the path.

A placement of a query tree onto a sensor network graph may be expressed as a mapping, i.e., a set $M = \{(i, p), ...\}$ where every operator $i \in \eta$ is assigned to a node $p \in \zeta$.

The placement problem can now be stated as the assignment of operators onto nodes that minimizes the following global cost:

$$\sum_{(i,j) \in \lambda} x_{ip} x_{jq} S_{pq}(d_{ij}) \tag{1}$$

subject to

$$\sum_{p \in \zeta} x_{ip} = 1, \forall i \in \eta, \forall p \in \pi : x_{ip} \in \{0, 1\} \tag{2}$$

where $x_{ip} = 1$, if operator i is assigned to node p, and $x_{ip} = 0$, otherwise. Equation (2) ensures that each operator is assigned to exactly one node of the network.

This problem of operator placement is an instance of the *task assignment problem*. The task assignment problem considers the problem of assigning a set of tasks onto a network of processors. The general task assignment problem is known to be NP-complete. Bokhari [1] has devised an $O(mn^2)$ algorithm for the case where the set of tasks is tree-structured, which is the case of our query tree (m denotes the number of taks and n the number of processors in the network). This algorithm is centralized; as a consequence it cannot be used in a sensor network.

3   Placement Strategy

We aim at defining a decentralized and adaptive algorithm for the placement of a query tree onto a sensor network. More precisely, our objective could be stated as follows: *Given an initial arbitrary placement of operators, our goal is to define a decentralized algorithm that progressively refine the placement of operators towards an optimal placement.*

It can be shown that the optimal placement of a query tree is composed of local optimal placements for each operator in the query tree. By *local optimal placement* we mean an assignment of operator i on node p that minimizes the amount of data that i receives from its children and transmits to its parent[3]. We omit the proof of this result because of lack of space.

This notion of local optimal placement constitutes an objective for the placement of individual operators. Now the question is: How can a decentralized algorithm move individual operators to their local optimal placement? Before we detail our algorithm in the next section, we give here the intuition behind our placement strategy.

If we disregard the limitations imposed by the sensor network topology in terms of operator placement and shortest paths, we may imagine that operators could be placed anywhere in a euclidean space. Data could be transferred along straight lines between operators. Transfer cost would be proportional to the distance between operators (multiplied by the transfer rate).

We could then view the transfer cost between two operators as a force pulling the operator towards one another. From the laws of physics we know that the equilibrium is the center of gravity of n particles. The net force determining the direction of the movement is the sum of the individual force vectors acting on the body. As the body moves in the direction dictated by the net force it reaches the optimal position through the shortest path (a straight line). The net force (and cost) will decrease monotonically along this path. In the equilibrium the net force acting on the body is zero and the cost is minimal. This equilibrium constitutes the local optimal operator placement. This analogy with forces has previously been used by Heiss and Schmitz [8] to develop a decentralized algorithm that achieves dynamic load balancing in a multicomputer system.

To understand the usefulness of these observations we now restrict operator positioning and possible paths between operators to those of a Manhattan graph (Figure 4(a)). Such a graph is a simplified but useful idealization of a wireless ad-hoc sensor network and is often used in analytic models (e.g. [15]). Possible operator positions are confined to the vertices of the graph. Assuming equal weights on links and equal data rates, the cheapest paths between operators corresponds to the path with the minimal Manhattan distance.

If an operator is not in the optimal position, there will exist a cheapest path between the operator and its local optimal position along which operator placement becomes progressively cheaper. An operator can reach its local optimal placement by walking this cheapest path. In a Manhattan graph, an operator initially placed on an arbitrary node will thus progressively reach its local optimal placement by greedily moving to the neighbor with lowest estimated cost. We call this placement strategy *neighbor exploration*.

We use the neighbor exploration as the placement strategy for the decentralized algorithm that we present in the next section. Note that in a sensor network with an arbitrary graph topology, the neighbor exploration policy might reach

---

[3] Recall that we denote i as the child and j as the parent in any communication link between operators $(i, j) \in \lambda$

local minima different from a global optimum. We present simulation results in Section 5 that show that our algorithm performs well in sensor networks with various graph topologies despite the potential pitfall of local minima.

4   Adaptative and Decentralized Operator Placement

Let us assume that an operator assignment has been defined for a given operator. We denote the node on which the operator is placed and executed, the *active* node. The sink and the sources constitute special active nodes. They run operators that respectively consume and produce data, they are involved in the algorithm and their placement is fixed.

As we have seen in the introduction, any assignment may become suboptimal. In order to adapt to changing conditions (e.g., data rate, data correlation), our decentralized algorithm implements the neighbor exploration strategy: It (i) evaluates the cost incurred by the execution of the operator at the active node, (ii) estimates the cost for alternative assignments of the operator, (iii) compares the cost on the active node and on alternative nodes, and (iv) transfers the operator to the node with lowest cost that thus becomes the new active node.

4.1   Decentralized Cost Computation

We define the cost of an operator j assigned to node q as:

$$C_o(j,q) = \sum_{(i,j) \in \lambda} (C_o(i,p) + S_{pq}(d_{ij})) \tag{3}$$

where variables and functions are as defined in Section 2.

Since equation (3) is recursive, the cost of an operator includes the accumulated cost of all operators delivering data for the operator. The cost of the query tree – defined in equation (1) - is the cost of the root operator.

A node needs the cost of the child operators in order to evaluate the cost of an operator. As a consequence child operators send cost messages to their parent operator along the data path. The term $S_{pq}(d_{ij})$ represents the cost of sending data between the child and parent operator. This cost may be accumulated while the cost message travels the path between node p and q if we assume (i) that the cost w_{xy} of sending data to a neighbor y is available at every node x and (ii) that we include the data rate d_{ij} with each cost message. The following equation states that the cost may be calculated by summing the product of the data rate with the link cost of each hop in the path[4]:

$$S_{pq}(d_{ij}) = C_p(P_{min}(p,q)) \cdot d_{ij} = \left(\sum_{e \in P_{min}} w_e \right) \cdot d_{ij} = \sum_{e \in P_{min}} (w_e \cdot d_{ij}) \tag{4}$$

---

[4] Note that though equation (3) refers to node mappings for technical reasons, information about the actual mapping on the child operator is not necessary for the parent to perform the cost calculation.

As a matter of fact the accumulated cost may simply be added to the cost of the child operator as the cost message travels to the parent operator, since the parent operator is only interested in the total sum. Cost messages flowing from each child to parent operator contain the accumulated cost and the data rate, e.g., the message sent by node i on node p to operator j on node q is: $(C_o(i, p), d_{ij})$. Any operator in the query tree will have information about the cost attributed by each of its sub-trees and will be able to calculate and forward its own cost.

4.2   Exploration

Exact data rates are necessary to calculate cost. The data rate of a given operator does not depend on its placement (but on the rate of the input data streams and on their contents). As a consequence the data rate calculated by operators on active nodes may be used for calculating costs on alternative nodes[5]

The idea is simply to have the active operators communicate their data rates to alternative nodes so that cost can be computed. Since there is a set of alternative nodes associated to each active node that only serve to probe the solution space for better alternatives we shall term them *tentative nodes*. These tentative nodes execute *tentative operators* responsible for the cost calculation. Cost is computed in the same way as for the active node. Cost messages flow from children (both active and tentative) to parents (both active and tentative) operators, while data flows from active children to active parent operators.

To explore the space of tentative nodes, we need to define:

1. An *exploration policy* for choosing what nodes should be elected tentative nodes. The sheer complexity of the solution space prohibits considering more than a tiny fraction, so the policy must choose the tentative nodes based on heuristics that will increase the probability of including an optimal, or at least better assignment in the face of data rate variations. Following our neighbor exploration strategy, only immediate neighbors of an active node are considered as its associated tentative nodes.
2. We also need an *adaptation policy* for choosing a new active node among the tentative nodes explored. We only consider two possible actions: either to continue query execution using the active node or switching to a new active node. Following our neighbor exploration strategy, the adaptation policy simply greedily picks the cheaper tentative node as the new active position since this would be closer to the optimal position than more expensive neighbors.

The close proximity of tentative nodes means that the communication overhead incurred by the transmission of data rates between the active and tentative nodes will be minimal. No tentative node is more than one hop away so multi-hop path establishment will not be necessary. If the MAC layer supports message

---

[5] Alternative methods would consist in executing several instances of the same operator, which would be costly if complete data streams were duplicated, and inaccurate if cost was estimated using a non-representative fraction of a data stream.

multicasting all tentative nodes may receive information from the active node using only one transmission.

The cost of an operator relative to its neighbors depends on the incoming as well as outgoing transfer cost. Since the outgoing transfer cost is not available until the transfer has actually been made through a path between the operator and its parent, it is natural to have the parent operator make decisions on active child operator assignments, i.e. the adaptation policy is executed by the active parent nodes.

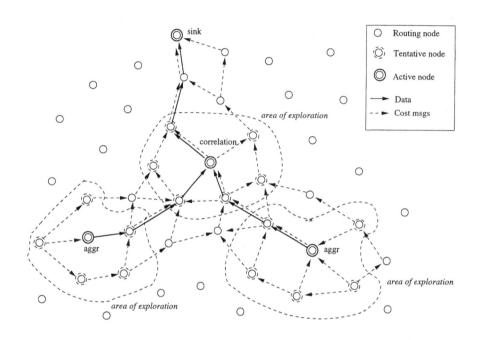

Fig. 2. Tentative and active Nodes

Figure 2 illustrates the flow of cost messages and data between active and tentative operators in the context of a complex query tree composed of an operator correlating the output of two aggregation operators.

4.3   Node Switching

At any point in time, there is only one active instance of each operator. The cost information received by the active parent operator allows it to implement the adaptation policy. When a tentative child operator instance has a lower estimated cost than the active child, the active operator may initiate a node switch. This switch consists of recursive signaling down two subtrees. Active operators in the active subtree must be informed that data flow is to cease. The cheaper tentative operator, on the other hand, must be informed that active dataflow is to start. The cheaper tentative operator will propagate this signal to its cheapest child instances. When the signal reaches the leaves, the leaf operators then begin to send data through the new active path. We shall term the two signal types *activation* and *deactivation* respectively.

There is one more issue to active plan switching: we need to support operator state transfer. Long-running operators on continuous data streams often need historic or accumulated information for their operation. Aggregation operators may keep a sliding window of values [13,16] and correlation operators usually store two sets of tuples that are probed and updated when new tuples arrive [2]. For the transition to be seamless such information must be transferred between the old and new active operators. Since we have already assumed that data rates can be communicated from the active operator to tentative operators, the same channel may be used for operator state transfer[6].

Operator state transfer could also be used to replicate the state of the active operator so that tentative nodes could take over in case the active node fails or runs out of energy. Designing an efficient fault tolerant placement of operators is a topic for future work.

4.4   Summary

Our algorithm, based on the exchange of cost messages and data between active and tentative operators, is adaptive and decentralized. It is adaptive because the placement of active operators is continuously refined depending on the estimated cost on their associated tentative nodes. It is decentralized because decisions are taken at the level of each operator. The information maintained on each node is local: active nodes merely maintain information about their children. Cost messages are transmitted in the network in addition to the data streams. The frequency at which cost messages are exchanged is a parameter of our algorithm (resulting in a trade-off between the responsivity of operator placement and the transmission overhead).

Note that our algorithm does not dictate how data should be routed between operators. We can thus use any routing protocol that relies on logical naming of nodes; we are currently implementing our algorithm on top of directed diffusion [6], using the filter mechanism to implement cost computation.

Figure 3 summarizes the exchanges between active and tentative operators (both parents and children) in our neighbor exploration policy:

- An active operator is defined as the instance of an operator which is actually executed; it receives input data streams, process them and generates an output data stream. An active operator is located on an active node.

---

[6] The design of efficient mobile operators is beyond the scope of this paper. Topics for future work include the design of operators requiring minimal internal states, and the design of efficient mechanisms supporting the marshalling/unmarshalling of the internal state and ensuring the continuity of execution while an operator is being moved from one node to another.

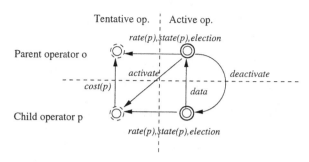

Fig. 3. Illustration of the communications between active and tentative operators

- A tentative operator is associated to an active operator in order to explore the cost of execution on alternative nodes (called tentative nodes). A tentative operator computes cost messages and transmits them to its parent. In order to compute cost, tentative operators receive data rate from their associated active node.
- Given the cost obtained from its children (both tentative and active), an active parent operator can decide to switch execution to a new active child operator. It then sends a deactivation message to the current active child operator and an activation message to the newly chosen active child operator. The current active child operator transfers its state to the new chosen active child operator.

5   Simulation Results

Our objective was to verify that the neighbor exploration strategy for operator placement is viable in sensor networks with various topologies. We focus on the placement of a single operator towards its local optimal placement, which is the basis of the neighbor exploration strategy.

The results we present in this section are essentially a proof-of-concept. We have now implemented our decentralized and adaptive algorithm on top of directed diffusion in order to measure the overhead incurred by our approach. This implementation allows us to experiment with the placement of complex query trees (with several operators) and with the adaption of the placement to changing conditions in the sensor network. Initial results confirm the good performances suggested by the simulations.

5.1   Simulation Framework

Topologies. Three types of basic network topologies were used in the simulations: (i) the maximal planar graph (MPG), (ii) the Manhattan graph (MG) and (iii) controlled random graphs (CRG)[7]. These graphs represent both abstract and realistic sensor network topologies.

The topologies were gradually degraded in terms of connectivity. This was done in one of two ways: (i) for the MPG and MG by removing a percentage of the nodes at random and (ii) for CRG by increasing the area in which a number of nodes were deployed thereby reducing the number of reachable neighbors gradually (fig.4). The CRG was produced by spreading a fixed number of nodes across a square area at random. When placing a node we try to ensure that the distance to any other node is at least half of the reach of the node. This is to avoid unrealistically close nodes. If we don't succeed in a few attempts we place the node anywhere. The x and y dimensions of the area is calculated as:

$$\sqrt{n} \cdot R \cdot f$$

where R is the reach of node radios and f is a factor varied between 0.55 and 0.90. A number of topologies where the area is gradually increased this way produce quite realistic random networks with decreasing density (10 to <3.8 neighbors) (fig.4). At higher values of f connected networks becomes harder to generate and less realistic.

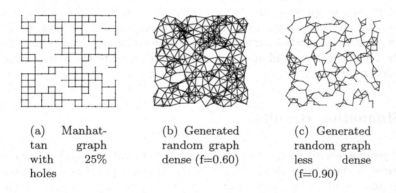

| (a) Manhattan graph with 25% holes | (b) Generated random graph dense (f=0.60) | (c) Generated random graph less dense (f=0.90) |

Fig. 4. Network Topologies

Query Plan. The query plan used for the simulations consists of two fixed sources, a correlation operator and a fixed sink at which the result is delivered. The two sources are equally productive and the correlation operator half as productive as the sources. We consider this to be slightly more challenging than having different rates of the source operators because the equal pull from the sources may get the operator stuck in a local optima, i.e., the operator could be stuck on one side of a hole in topologies with a source on either side of the hole.

---

[7] We term these graphs *controlled random* because we tried to avoid unrealistically close nodes during generation.

Simulator. For each type of topology and density, we generated 30 network instances with 225 nodes each. We ran 100 simulations on each network instance with random initial placements of the fixed sources and sink.

In order not to favor our scheme we have disregarded "easy" adaptation scenarios where the optimal assignment was less than 4 hops away from the initial operator assignment. In particular this does away with the trivial case where the operator is already in the optimal position.

For each run the cost of the optimal assignment, the assignment achieved through adaptation as well as the cost of data extraction was calculated. By data extraction we denote the case without in-network processing: each source sends the data it produces to the sink and data is processed outside the sensor network. These results were averaged for each topology type and density type and used for depicting the cost development of a topology as density decreases. This should provide a good statistical picture of the adaptation behaviour for a given topology and density.

The optimal assignment of the operator was found by performing an exhaustive search for cheapest position. Doing so was feasible because only one operator was at play. With complex query trees the mapping complexity would have required a more efficient method like that of Bokhari [1].

5.2 Results

Quality of Operator Placement. Figure 5(a) shows the cost of data extraction and the cost of optimal assignment together with the cost of the assignment achieved through neighbor exploration.

At high densities perfect or near-perfect adaptation is achieved. The dense random graphs are very likely to have Manhattan subgraphs explaining the initial coinciding graphs of optimal and adapted assignment costs.

The somewhat surprising findings are that our simple scheme does very well even in the least dense topologies. In no case is the average cost deviation greater than 10% of the optimal cost.

The slightly increasing tendency of the curves is caused by longer average inter-operator shortest paths as the networks get less connected. I.e. the direct way to a neighbor operator becomes less direct. These longer paths result in higher data transfer costs.

Since average measures says little about worst-cases, we also depict the constituents of the cost achieved through adaptation grouped by percentual deviation from the optimal cost on Figure 5(b)).

Even for the topologies of lowest density more than 70 % of the cost is attributed by adaptations deviating less than 10 % from the optimal assignment. We obtained equally good results with MG and MPG topologies but we omit the figures because of space constraints.

In our simulations the extraction cost was approximately twice the optimal cost due to the network size, the specific number of operators, their productivity and selectivity. We have been conservative with these parameters not to

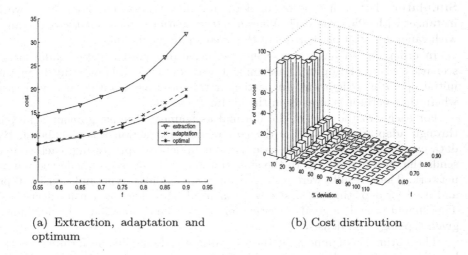

(a) Extraction, adaptation and optimum

(b) Cost distribution

Fig. 5. Cost random graphs

favor our approach unreasonably. Still our results indicate that in-network query processing is very promising.

6 Related Work

The notion of in-network processing in a sensor network was first introduced in order to opportunistically eliminate duplicates in the context of directed diffusion [6]. Intanagonwiwat et al. [11] extended this work by constructing a routing tree where paths are shared as much as possible to increase the possibilities of eliminating duplicates. The potential benefits of in-network duplicate elimination have also been studied from a theoretical perspective [12]. By comparison, we consider queries that embed richer application-level data processing (correlations, filters, aggregates). Those query trees are fixed a priori, which imposes a strong constraint on the routing tree. Also the cost function that we consider for operator placement includes the rate at which data is transmitted across operators in addition to the length of the path between those operators.

Madden et al. [13] were the first to study in-network query processing. They focused on simple aggregation queries, whose execution can be distributed over an arbitrarily large set of operators. They defined both (i) aggregate operators adapted to motes with limited ressources running tinyOS, and (ii) a routing strategy that imposes a spanning tree onto the network: data is aggregated at every internal node in the routing tree. Note that they assume that queries are submitted in a declarative, SQL-like form. The placement of the query tree is constrained by the characteristics of the routing tree. We have taken the alternative approach where the routing tree is constrained by the query tree and where data is processed only at a few nodes. Our approach is particularly relevant when the query contains *holistic aggregates* such as correlations or median [13] or materialization operators such as storage points [9].

Recently, Yao and Gehrke [16] have devised a general framework for in-network query processing. Each query is decomposed into *flow blocks* determining a set of sensor nodes that elect a leader on which a query fragment is executed. They applied this strategy to queries complex aggregates (with group by clauses) as well as joins (similar to our correlation operator). Our approaches are very much complementary in the sense that they defined a general framework for the optimization of declarative queries into query trees that could be a way to generate our query tree. Also, our algorithm could be seen as an election protocol, particularly well-suited for the adaptive placement of flow block leaders.

7   Conclusion

The problem of operator placement is crucial for in-network query processing. We showed that it was a variant of the task assignment problem and we described an adaptive and decentralized algorithm based on the *neighbor exploration* strategy: the placement of operators is progressively refined from neighbor node to neighbor node until a local optimal placement is reached. Simulation results stress the potential benefits of in-network query processing. They also show that neighbor exploration can achieve near optimal placement of a single operator with various graph topologies, despite the risks of local minima.

Future work includes a complete performance study of our algorithm. We have implemented it on top of directed diffusion and we have started to run experiments using NS. These experiments include a measure of the communication overhead introduced by our algorithm, as well as measures of the quality of adaptation with changing network conditions for single operators as well as complex query trees.

Other topics for future work are the design of query operators that can be moved from node to node with minimal overhead as well as the design of fault tolerant operator placement algorithms.

Acknowledgements. We would like to thank Mads Dydensborg, Stefan Røpke, Jacob Simonsen and Christian Stefansen for their help debugging this paper as well as Pawel Winter and Sam Madden for interesting discussions.

References

1. S.H. Bokhari: A shortest Tree Algorithm for optimal Assignments Across Space and Time in a Distributed Processor System. *IEEE Transactions on Software Engineering, Vol. se-7 no. 6*, November 1981.
2. Ph. Bonnet, J. Gehrke and P. Seshadri. Towards sensor database systems. *2nd International Conference on Mobile Data Management*, Hong Kong, Jan. 2001.

3. N.H. Cohen, A. Purakayastha, J. Turek, L. Wong, D. Yeh. Challenges in Flexible Aggregation of Pervasive Data. *IBM Research Division*, January 2001.
4. D. Estrin, R. Govindan, and J. Heidemann. Embedding the internet: Introduction. *Communications of the ACM*, 43(5), 2000.
5. D. Estrin, M. Srivastava, and A. Sayeed. Tutorial on Wireless Sensor Networks *ACM Mobicom*, Sep. 2002.
6. J. Heidemann, F. Silva, C. Intanagonwiwat, R. Govindan, Deborah Estrin, and Deepak Ganesan. Building efficient wireless sensor networks with low-level naming. In *SOSP*, 2001.
7. W. Heinzelman, A. Chandrakasan, and H. Balakrishnan. Energy-efficient Communication Protocol for Wireless Microsenset Network *Hawaii International Conference on System Sciences*, 2000.
8. H-U. Heiss, and M. Schmitz. Decentralized Dynamic Load Balancing: The Particles Approach. *Information Sciences 84(1&2*. 1995.
9. J. Hellerstein, W. Hong, S. Madden, and K. Stanek Beyond Average: Towards Sophisticated Sensing with Queries *IPSN*, 2003.
10. C. Intanagonwiwat, R. Govindan, D. Estrin: Directed Diffusion: A Scalable and Robust Communication Paradigm for Sensor Networks, Proceedings of the Sixth Annual International Conference on Mobile Computing and Networks (Mobicom 2000), August 2000, Boston, MA.
11. C. Intanagonwiwat, R. Govindan, D. Estrin, and J. Heiderman. Impact of Network Density on Data Aggregation in Wireless Sensor Networks. *DEBS'02*
12. B. Krishnamachari, D. Estrin, S. Wicker. The Impact of Data Aggregation in Wireless Sensor Networks *Distributed Event Based Systems*, 2002.
13. S. Madden, M.J. Franklin, and J. Hellerstein. TAG: a Tiny AGregation Service for Ad-Hoc Sensor Networks. *OSDI*, 2002.
14. G. J. Pottie and W. J. Kaiser. Wireless integrated network sensors. *Communications of the ACM*, 43(5):51–58, 2000.
15. S.D. Servetto, G. Barrenechea: Constrained Random Walks on Random Graphs: Routing Algorithms for Large Scale Wireless Sensor Networks, First ACM International Workshop on Wireless Sensor Networks & Applications, September 2002, Atlanta, Georgia.
16. Y. Yao and J. Gehrke. Query Processing in Sensor Networks *First Biennal Conference on Innovative Data Systems Research. CIDR 2003.*.
17. F. Zhao, J. Shin, and J. Reich. Information-driven dynamic sensor collaboration for tracking applications. *IEEE Signal Processing Magazine*, March 2002.

Beyond Average: Toward Sophisticated Sensing with Queries*

Joseph M. Hellerstein[1,2], Wei Hong[2], Samuel Madden[1], and Kyle Stanek[1]

[1] UC Berkeley
{jmh,madden}@cs.berkeley.edu, kyles@uclink.berkeley.edu
[2] Intel Research, Berkeley
whong@intel-research.net

Abstract. High-level query languages are an attractive interface for sensor networks, potentially relieving application programmers from the burdens of distributed, embedded programming. In research to date, however, the proposed applications of such interfaces have been limited to simple data collection and aggregation schemes. In this paper, we present initial results that extend the TinyDB sensornet query engine to support more sophisticated data analyses, focusing on three applications: topographic mapping, wavelet-based compression, and vehicle tracking. We use these examples to motivate the feasibility of implementing sophisticated sensing applications in a query-based system, and present some initial results and research questions raised by this agenda.

1 Introduction

Sensor networks present daunting challenges to potential application developers. Sensornet programming mixes the complexities of both distributed *and* embedded systems design, and these are often amplified by unreliable network connections and extremely limited physical resources. Moreover, many sensor network applications are expected to run unattended for months at a time. These challenges have motivated research into higher-level programming interfaces and execution environments, which try to relieve programmers from many of the burdens of distributed and embedded programming (e.g. [10,22]). In our own work, we have designed a framework called TAG [14] for sensornet data aggregation via an SQL-like language. More recently we have implemented the TAG framework in a system called TinyDB [15] that runs in networks of TinyOS-based Berkeley motes [8].

We have received initial feedback indicating that TinyDB's SQL-based interface is very attractive to a number of users interested in distributed sensing. However, we have also heard concerns about apparent limits to the functionality of simple SQL queries. This feedback resulted in part from our early work, which performed fairly traditional SQL queries for relatively simple tasks: periodically collecting raw readings, and computing simple summarizations like averages and counts.

In this paper, we present a status report on our efforts to do deploy more complex sensing tasks in TinyDB. Our intention is both to illustrate TinyDB's potential as a

---

* This work partially supported by NSF grants IIS-0086057 and SI0122599, by DARPA grant F33615-01-C-1895, and by funds from IBM, Intel, Microsoft, and the UC Micro program.

F. Zhao and L. Guibas (Eds.): IPSN 2003, LNCS 2634, pp. 63–79, 2003.

vehicle for complex sensing algorithms, and to highlight some of the unique features and constraints of embedding these sensing algorithms in an extensible, declarative query framework.

In the paper we review and extend the TAG framework [14], and show how it can be used to implement three sensing applications that are relatively distant from vanilla database queries:

1. *Distributed Mapping:* One commonly cited [4] application for sensor networks is to produce contour maps based on sensor readings. We present simple topographic extensions to the declarative query interface of TAG that allow it to efficiently build maps of sensor-value distributions in space. Our approach is based on finding *isobars*: contiguous regions with approximately the same sensor value. We show how such maps can be built using very small amounts of RAM and radio bandwidth, remaining useful in the face of significant amounts of missing information (e.g. dropped data or regions without sensor nodes.) Results from an initial simulation are included.

2. *Multiresolution Compression and Summarization:* Traditional SQL supports only simple aggregates for summarizing data distributions. We develop a more sophisticated wavelet-based aggregation scheme for compressing and summarizing a set of readings. Our technique also has the ability to produce results of increasing resolution over time. We describe a hierarchical wavelet encoding scheme that integrates naturally into the standard TAG framework, and is tuned to low-function devices like Berkeley motes. We also discuss a number of open research questions that arise in this context.

3. *Vehicle Tracking:* Several research papers have investigated distributed sensornet algorithms that track moving objects [2]. We show how a declarative, event-based query infrastructure can serve as a framework for such algorithms, and discuss how the TAG approach can be extended to allow sensor nodes to remain idle unless vehicles are near to them. This is work in progress: we have yet to instantiate this infrastructure with a sophisticated tracking algorithm, but hope that this framework will seed future efforts to combine intelligent tracking with the other ad-hoc query facilities afforded by a full-function sensornet query process like TinyDB.

The remainder of this paper is organized as follows: after a brief summary of TAG in Section 2, we present some new language features needed for these advanced applications in Section 3. The remaining sections then discuss each of these applications in turn as well a discussion of related work and future directions.

2   Background

In this section, we describe the declarative, SQL-like language we have developed for querying sensor networks, which is an extension of the simple language presented in TAG [14] and has been implemented in TinyDB [15]. We present a basic overview of the scheme here. In TinyDB, queries are posed at a powered *basestation*, typically a PC, where they are parsed into a simple binary representation, which is then flooded to sensors in the network. As the query is flooded through the network, sensors organize into a *routing tree* that allows the basestation to collect query results. The flooding works as follows: the basestation injects a query request at the *root* sensor, which broadcasts the query on its radio; all *child* nodes that hear the query process it and re-broadcast it on to their children, and so on, until the entire network has heard the query

Each request contains a hop-count (or *level*), indicating the distance from the broadcaster to the root. To determine their own level, nodes pick a *parent* node that is (by definition) one level closer to the root than they are. This parent will be responsible for forwarding the node's query results (and its children's results, recursively) to the basestation.

Queries in TinyDB have the following basic structure:

```
SELECT expr₁, expr₂, ...
  FROM sensors
  WHERE pred₁ [AND | OR] pred₂ ...
  GROUP BY groupExpr₁, groupExpr₂, ...
  SAMPLE PERIOD t
```

The SELECT clause lists the fields (or *attributes*) to retrieve from the sensors; $expr_n$ specifies a transform on a single field. Each transform may be a simple arithmetic expression, such as light + 10, or an aggregate function, which specifies a way in which readings should be combined across nodes or over time (aggregation is discussed in more detail in the following section.) As in standard SQL, aggregates and non-aggregates may not appear together in the SELECT clause unless the non-aggregate fields also appear in the GROUP BY clause.

The FROM clause specifies the table from which data will be retrieved; in the language presented in [14], there is only one table, sensors, which contains one attribute for each of the types of sensors available to the devices in the network (e.g. light, acceleration, or temperature). Each device has a small *catalog* which it uses to determine which attributes are locally available; the catalog also includes cost information and other metadata associated with accessing the attribute, and a pointer to a function that allows TinyDB to retrieve the value of the attribute.

The (optional) WHERE clause filters out readings that do not satisfy the boolean combination of predicates. Predicates in TinyDB are currently restricted to simple boolean and arithmetic operations over a single attribute, such as light / 10 > 25.

The (optional) GROUP BY clause is used in conjunction with aggregate expressions. It specifies a partitioning of the input records before aggregation, with aggregates in the SELECT clause being computed on each partition. In the absence of a GROUP BY aggregates are computed over the entire set of sensors; a GROUP BY partitions the sensors into groups whose group expressions each have the same value. For example, the query fragment:

```
SELECT roomNumber, AVG(light)
  GROUP BY roomNumber
      ...
```

partitions sensors into groups according to the value of the roomNumber attribute, and computes the average light reading within each group.

Finally, the SAMPLE PERIOD clause specifies the time between successive samples or *epochs*. Each node samples its sensors once per epoch and applies its query processing operators to that sensor.

2.1 Aggregation in Sensor Networks

Given this basic description of the query language, we now discuss how TinyDB processes queries, focusing on how aggregate queries are handled.

Structure of Aggregates. Recall that an aggregation expression may be specified in the SELECT clause of a query. In standard SQL, that expression contains one of a few basic aggregation functions: MIN, MAX, AVERAGE, COUNT, or SUM. As in TAG, TinyDB provides an *extensible* mechanism for registering new aggregates, derived from literature on extensible database languages. In TinyDB, aggregates are implemented via three functions: a merging function f, an initializer i, and an evaluator, e. In general, f has the following structure:

$$< z >= f(< x >, < y >)$$

where $< x >$ and $< y >$ are multi-valued *partial state records* (PSRs), computed over one or more sensor values, representing the intermediate state of the aggregation processing based on those values. $< z >$ is the partial-state record resulting from the application of function f to $< x >$ and $< y >$. For example, if f is the merging function for AVERAGE, each partial state record will consist of a pair of values: SUM and COUNT, and f is specified as follows, given two state records $< S_1, C_1 >$ and $< S_2, C_2 >$:

$$f(< S_1, C_1 >, < S_2, C_2 >) =< S_1 + S_2, C_1 + C_2 >$$

The initializer i is needed to specify how to instantiate a state record for a single sensor value; for an AVERAGE over a sensor value of x, the initializer $i(x)$ returns the tuple $< x, 1 >$. Finally, the evaluator e takes a partial state record and computes the actual value of the aggregate. For AVERAGE, the evaluator $e(< S, C >)$ simply returns S/C.

Processing Aggregate Queries. Aggregate queries produce one result per group per epoch. Once a query has been disseminated as described above, each leaf node in the routing tree produces a single tuple of sensor readings each epoch, applies the initialization function to the appropriate column, and forwards the initialized result to its parent. On the next epoch, the parent merges its own PSR from the previous epoch with PSRs from its children in the previous epoch, and forwards that result on to its parent. Results propagate up the tree, epoch-by-epoch, until a complete PSR from d epochs ago arrives at the root of the routing tree (where d is the depth of the tree). Once a result has arrived at the root, the basestation applies the evaluation function to it to produce a complete aggregate record and outputs the result to the user. Depending on the sample period, there may be enough time in each epoch to send aggregates up multiple levels of the routing tree, resulting in a delay of less than d epochs; see TAG and the complimentary workshop submission [14,16] for more information, and also for a discussion of other aspects of aggregate processing, such as handling GROUP BY queries.

Temporal Aggregates. All the aggregates that we described above aggregate sensor values sampled from multiple nodes at the same epoch. We have extended this framework to support *temporal aggregates* which aggregate sensors values across multiple consecutive epochs from the same or different nodes. Temporal aggregates typically take two extra arguments: *window size* and *sliding distance*. Window size specifies the number of consecutive epochs the temporal aggregate operates on, and the sliding distance specifies the number of epochs to skip over for the next window of samples. One frequently used temporal aggregates in TinyDB is the running average aggregate `winavg(window_size, sliding_dist, arg)`. It is typically used to reduce noise in sensor signals. For example, `winavg(10, 1, light)` computes the 10-sample running average of light sensor readings. It accumulates light readings from 10 consecutive epochs, averages them, then replaces the oldest value in the average window with the latest light sensor reading and keeps on computing averages over the window of samples. In addition to `winavg`, TinyDB also supports similar temporal aggregates such as `winmin`, `winmax`, `winsum`, etc. More sophisticated custom temporal aggregates such as one that computes the trajectory of a moving vehicle can be developed using the same extensible aggregate framework described above.

3   New Language Features

The query language described above provides a foundation for many kinds of simple monitoring queries. However, as sensor networks become more autonomous, the language needs to move beyond passive querying: rather than simply monitoring the environment and relaying results, the sensors will need to detect and initiate automatic responses to nearby events. Furthermore, sensor networks will need to collect and store information locally, since it is not always possible or advantageous to get data out of the network to a powered, storage-rich PC. We introduce two extensions to our query language to handle these situations.

3.1   Events

Events provide a mechanism for initiating data collection in response to some external stimulus. Events are generated explicitly, either by another query, by software in the operating system, or by specialized hardware on the node that triggers the operating system. Consider the following query for monitoring the occupancy of bird nests:

```
ON EVENT bird-detect(loc):
  SELECT AVG(light), AVG(temp)
  FROM sensors AS s
  WHERE dist(s.loc, event.loc) < 10m
  SAMPLE INTERVAL 2 s FOR 30 s
```

When a bird is detected in a nest (e.g. via a pressure switch in the nest), this query is executed to collect the average light and temperature level from sensors near the nest, and send these results to the root of a network. (Alternatively, the results could be stored locally at the detecting node, using the storage point mechanism described in the next section.) The semantics of this query are as follows: when a `bird-detect` event occurs, the query is issued from the detecting node and the average light and temperature are collected from nearby nodes (those nodes that are 10 or less meters from the collecting node) every 2 seconds for 30 seconds.

3.2 Storage Points

Storage points accumulate a small buffer of data that may be referenced in other queries. Consider, as an example:

```
CREATE
   STORAGE POINT recentlight SIZE 5s
   AS (SELECT nodeid, light
   FROM sensors
   SAMPLE INTERVAL 1s)
```

This STORAGE POINT command provides a shared global location to store a streaming view of recent data, similar to materialized views in conventional databases. Note that this data structure is accessible for read or write from any node in the network; its exact location within the network is not fixed – that is, it can be moved as an optimization. Typically, these storage points are partitioned by nodeid, so that each sensor stores its own values locally. The specific example here stores the previous five seconds worth of light readings (taken once per second) from all of the nodes in the network.

In this paper, we use storage points as a mechanism for storage and offline delivery of query results. Queries that select all of the results from a storage point, or that compute an aggregate of a storage point, are allowed; consider, for example:

```
SELECT MAX(light)
   FROM recentLight
```

This query selects the maximum light reading from the recentLight storage point defined above. The storage point is continually updated; this query returns the maximum of the values at the time the query is posed.

4 Isobar Mapping

In this section, we explore the problem of building a topographic (contour) map of a space populated by sensors. Such maps provide an important way to visualize sensor fields, and have applications in a variety of biological and environmental monitoring scenarios [4]. We show how TinyDB's aggregation framework can be leveraged to build such maps. Conceptually, the problem is similar to that of computing a GROUP BY over both space and quantized sensor readings – that is, our algorithms partition sensors into *isobars* that are contiguous in space and approximately equal in sensor value. Using in-network aggregation, the storage and communication costs for producing a topographic map are substantially less than the cost of collecting individual sensor readings and building the map centrally. We discuss three algorithms for map-building: a centralized, *naive* approach, an exact, *in-network* approach, and an approximate, *lossy* approach. The general process to build a topological map is as follows: each sensor builds a small representation of its local area, and sends that map to its parent, where it is combined with the maps from neighbors and ancestors and eventually becomes part of a complete map of the space at the root of the tree. To support topographic operations on sensors, we require a few (very) simple geometric operators and primitives. To determine adjacency in our maps, we impose a rectangular grid onto the sensors, and assign every sensor into a cell in that grid. Our goal is to construct isobars, which are orthogonal polygons with holes; we need basic operations to determine if two such polygons overlap and to find their union. Such operations can be performed on any polygon in $nlog(n)$ time (where n is the number of edges in the polygon) using the Leonov-Nitkin algorithm [13]. There are a number of free libraries which implement such functionality.

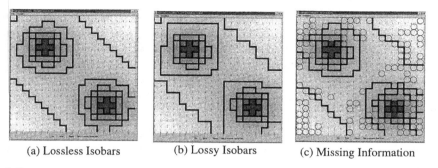

(a) Lossless Isobars	(b) Lossy Isobars	(c) Missing Information

Fig. 1. Screenshots of a visualization of isobars imposed on a grid of sensors. Each cell represents a sensor, the intensity of the background color indicates sensor value, and black lines frame isobars. See text for a description of the individual figures.

We begin with a discussion of the three algorithms, assuming that every cell in the grid is occupied. We return to mapping sparse grids in Section 4.4.

4.1 Naive Algorithm

In the naive algorithm, we run an aggregate-free query which returns the location and attribute value of all of the sensors in the network; these results are combined via code outside the network to produce a map. We implemented this approach in a simulation and visualization, as shown in figure Figure 1(a). In this first simulation, sensors were arranged in a grid, and could communicate losslessly with their immediate neighbors. The isobars were aggregated by the node at the center of the network. The network consisted of 400 nodes in a depth 10 routing tree. In the screenshot, the saturation of each grid cell indicates the sensor value, and the thick black lines show isobars.

4.2 In-Network Algorithm

In the in-network approach, we define an aggregate, called *contour-map* where each partial state record is a set of isobars, and each isobar is a container polygon (with holes, possibly) and an attribute value, which is the same for all sensors in the isobar. The structure of an isobar query is thus:

```
SELECT contour-map(xloc,yloc,floor(attr/k))
    FROM sensors
```

where k defines the width (in attribute-space) of each of the isobars. We can then define the three aggregation functions, i, f, and e, as follows:

- i: The initialization function takes an `xloc`, `yloc`, and `attr`, and generates as a partial state record the singleton set containing an isobar with the specified `attr` value and a container polygon corresponding to the grid cell of the sensor.
- f: The merging function combines two sets of isobars, I_1 and I_2 into a new isobar set, I_3, where each element of I_3 is a disjoint polygon that is the union of one or more polygons from I_1 and I_2. This new set may have several non-contiguous isobars with the same attribute value. Conversely, merging can cause such disjoint

isobars in I_1 to be joined when an isobar from I_2 connects them (and vice-versa.) Figure 2 shows an example of this happening as two isobar sets are merged together.

- e: The evaluation function generates a topographic map of contiguous isobars, each labeled with their attribute value.

4.3   Lossy Algorithm

The lossy algorithm works similarly to the in-network algorithm, except that the number of vertices v used to define the bounding polygon of each isobar is limited by a parameter of the aggregate. This reduces the communication cost of the approach, but makes it possible for isobars to overlap, as they will no longer perfectly trace out the edges of the contours.

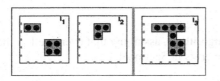

Fig. 2. Two isobar sets, I_1 (with two elements) and I_2 (with one element) being merged into a new isobar set, I_3 (also with one element).

In the lossy algorithm, i is the same as in the in-network case. For f, we compute I_3 as above, but we do not use it as the partial state record. Instead, for the containing polygon p in each set of I_3, we compute a bounding box, b, and then take from b a number of maximally sized rectangular "cuts" that do not overlap p. We continue taking cuts until either b contains v vertices, or the next cut produces a polygon with more than v vertices. We omit the details of how we compute maximal cuts; because our polygons are orthogonal, this can be done via a scan of the vertices of p. We use these cut-bounding-boxes as approximations of the containing polygons in the isobars of the PSRs resulting from our merge function. Figure 3 shows a containing polygon approximated by a bounding rectangle with a single cut.

In the lossy evaluation function e, one or more isobars in the final aggregate state record may overlap, and so some policy is needed to choose which isobar to assign to a particular cell. We use a simple "containment" principle: if one isobar completely contains another, we assume the true value of the cell is that specified by the innermost isobar. When the containment principle does not apply, we assign grid cells to the nearest isobar (in terms of number of grid cells), breaking ties randomly.

We simulated this lossy algorithm for the same sensor value distribution as was shown in Figure 1(a), using a maximum of 4 "cuts" per isobar. The results are shown in Figure 1(b); notice that the shape of the isobars is preserved.

We compared the total amount of data transmitted by our simulation of the lossy, in-network, and naive algorithms for the isobars shown in Figure 1(a) and 1(b), and found that the naive algorithms algorithm used a factor of four more communication than the lossy algorithm and about 40% more communication than the in-network algorithm.

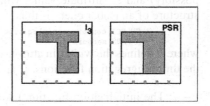

Fig. 3. A lossy approximation of a containing polygon (I_3) as a bounding box with a single cut (PSR).

4.4 Sparse Grids

Finally, we consider the case of sparse grids, where sensors do not exist at every cell in the grid. In sparse grids, the lossy algorithm described above can be used to infer an isobar for missing points. Since the merging function no longer tracks exact contours but uses bounding boxes, cells without sensors will often end up as a part of an isobar. Cells that aren't assigned an isobar as a part of merging can be assigned using the nearest-isobar method described in the lossy algorithm.

A similar situation arises in dense topologies with network loss, when some sensor values are not be reported during a particular epoch. We implemented this sparse grid approach and used it to visualize isobars with a high-loss radio model, where the probability that two sensors can communicate with each other falls off with the distance between the sensors. For adjacent sensors, loss rates are about 5%; for sensors that are three cells away (the maximum communication range), loss rates are about 20%. The result is shown in Figure 1(c), with black circles on the nodes whose values were lost during the epoch being visualized. Notice that, despite the large number of losses, the shape of the isobars is largely preserved.

5 Wavelet Histograms via Hierarchical Aggregation

SQL's built-in aggregates provide some basic statistical information about the distribution of a set of readings. But in many cases it is useful to get a richer synopsis of the distribution for further data analysis. Histograms are a form of synopsis that are familiar and intuitive. However, due to bandwidth constraints in sensor nets, we would like to have a *multiresolution* histogram, which can optionally provide additional resolution of "buckets" at the expense of additional communication. To that end, we explore using *wavelet histograms*. Wavelets are one of the best-known and most effective multiresolution coding techniques, and unlike traditional histograms are applicable for coding either sets or arrays (uni- or multi-dimensional). Wavelets have been widely applied for approximate querying and data mining settings ([12] provides a tutorial), and it is natural to revisit them in the sensor query context.

In this section, we sketch a TAG aggregate function for encoding a set of readings in a sensor network using Haar wavelets, the simplest and most widely-used wavelet encoding[1]. Our discussion here focuses on *wavelet histograms* [18], which capture information about the statistical distribution of sensor values, without placing significance on any ordering of the values. We drop coefficients with low absolute values ("thresholding") to keep the communication costs down, but always retain the value of coefficient 0; in Haar wavelets, the 0th coefficient represents the average of the values, and hence is often of interest to users.

Our wavelet compression setting here is somewhat unique. First, recall that aggregates in TinyDB must be computed by merging partial state records passed up the network communication tree. We present a new distributed wavelet encoding technique that works in this fashion, combining pairs of smaller wavelets without decoding and

---

[1] In the interest of brevity, we do not overview wavelets here; the interested reader is referred to [21] for a good practical overview of wavelets, or to [18] for a simple introduction to Haar wavelets.

recoding. Second, our processors do not have floating-point arithmetic and are generally rather slow, so we will use integer wavelets [1] , and do as much as possible in place to minimize copies. Finally, since we are constrained in both memory and bandwidth, we will be dropping low coefficients, and using a sparse array representation for the coefficients we keep.

The core of our logic is in the merging function f, which takes the PSRs from two subtrees (which are themselves wavelets) and combines them into a new PSR (another wavelet). Our wavelet PSR will be a sparse array represented by $2N + 2$ short integers. In order to maintain wavelet properties, N must be a power of 2 ($N = 8$ in our current implementation.) The first $2N$ values capture the non-zero elements of the sparse array: N array offsets, and N data values of the coefficients at those offsets. The next short integer is the count, which tracks the number of actual sensor readings rolled up into this wavelet. One additional short, called loglen, represents the $\log_2$ of the number of array entries in the (possibly zero-padded) wavelet.

The merging function considers 4 cases for merging two state records, r1 and r2:[2]

1. r1.count + r2.count $< N$: In this case, we do not compress, but simply store all the values. We concatenate the values from r2.data to the end of r1.data, and update the offsets and count of r1 accordingly. The loglen variable remains at the initialization value of $\log_2 N$.
2. r1.count $< N$ and r2.count $< N$, *but their sum is* $> N$: In this case we need to compress the output. Conceptually, we think of the two input arrays as one array of length $2^{\text{loglen}+1}$, and use the *lifting* scheme [20] to wavelet-compress the double-length array in place. We then keep only the top N coefficients by overwriting r1's data and offsets fields appropriately. We add r2.count to the value in r1.count, and increment the r1.loglen variable to reflect the effective doubling of the array.
3. *Both inputs have* count $> N$: In this case, we need to merge two wavelets.
   Our merge technique will assume that both inputs have the same loglen. If one input has a smaller loglen than the other, we need to zero-pad the smaller to match the larger. For example, if r1.loglen $<$ r2.loglen, we zero-pad r1 until it is of equal length. Pseudocode for efficiently doubling a Haar wavelet with 0's is given in Figure 4.
   Once both wavelets have the same loglen, we need to merge r2 into r1 to form a wavelet with twice as many coefficients. We then run the pseudocode given in Figure 5 to merge r2 into r1 without decoding and re-encoding. Finally we copy the top N coefficients of the result into r1.data, update r1's offsets appropriately, add r2.count to r1.count, and increment r1.loglen to reflect the doubling of the array.
4. *Exactly one input has* count *larger than* N: In this case, we zero-pad the smaller array to be size N, convert it to a wavelet of N coefficients, and invoke Case 3.

At the top of the aggregation tree, this technique produces a wavelet that lossily represents the concatenation of all the readings in the network, along with a large number of padded 0's. Given the count and loglen variables, a PC at the root of the network

---

[2] Note that the choice of ordering r1 before r2 is rather arbitrary: for now, we assume that the network topology and scheduling determines which input is first, and which is second.

```
// for all coefficients i except 0th, bump up offsets carefully
for i from 1 to N-1
    offsets[i] += 2^(floor(log_2(offsets[i])));
    // keep track of min coefficient, too
    if (abs(data[i]) < min) then { min = abs(data[i]);  minpos = i; }
// New 1st coefficient is 0 - (old 0th coefficient).
// If it's in the top N, make room for it in data and offsets arrays
if (abs(data[0]) > min)
    move offsets[1] through offsets[minpos-1] one position rightward;
    move data[1] through data[minpos-1] one position rightward;
    offsets[1] = 1; data[1] = 0 - data[0];
// overall average is halved, reflecting the 0-padding.
data[0] >>= 2; // i.e. data[0] = floor(data[0] / 2);
loglen++; // we doubled the size
```

Fig. 4. Double a Haar wavelet of N coefficients by zero-padding in place, without decoding/recoding. The result should have $N + 1$ coefficients; we drop the lowest of these other than the 0th coefficient, which we always keep in position 0 in the arrays.

```
// Double r1 and r2, but bump r2 rightward by an extra factor of 2.
for i from 1 to N-1
    r1.offsets[i] += 2^(floor(log_2(r1.offsets[i])));
    r2.offsets[i] += 2^(floor(log_2(r2.offsets[i])) + 1);
// merge r1's {offsets,data} pairs with r2's, sorted by offset
cursor1 = 1; cursor2 = 1;
for k from 2 to (N*2) - 1
    if (cursor1 < N && r1.offsets[cursor1] <= r2.offsets[cursor2])
        { smaller = r1; curs = cursor1; }
    else { smaller = r2; curs = cursor2; }
    wtmp.offsets[k] = smaller.offsets[curs];
    wtmp.data[k] = smaller.data[curs];
    curs++;
// 0th coefficient of wtmp is avg of old 0-coefs, 1st is diff
wtmp.offsets[0] = 0; wtmp.offsets[1] = 1;
wtmp.data[0] = floor((r1.data[0] + r2.data[0])/2);
wtmp.data[1] = r1.data[0] - r2.data[0];
// pack top N coefficients of wtmp into first N slots
// of wtmp.data, update wtmp.offsets appropriately,
topN_coeffs(wtmp);
copy N wtmp.{data,offsets} into r1.{data,offsets}
r1.count += r2.count;   r1.loglen++;
```

Fig. 5. Given two Haar wavelets r1 and r2 of N non-zero coefficients, merge them without decoding/recoding.

can discard the extraneous 0's, and perform the appropriate normalization to recreate both the overall average, and somewhat finer approximations of the densities of values.

Note that the coefficients produced by the recursive application of the merge procedure are not the top N coefficients of a Haar wavelet on the full array of readings. In particular, the $N + 1$'st coefficient of one network subtree will be discarded even though it may be much larger than the top N coefficients of another subtree. The effect of such an error may be spread across higher-order coefficients as further merges happen. We are investigating heuristics for improving this situation, including probabilistic updating schemes from [18] and coefficient confidence intervals based on [6].

5.1 MultiResolution Snapshots, Temporal Queries

In the spirit of image coding and *online aggregation* in databases [7], we might want the answer to a snapshot query to improve with additional rounds of communication.

In order to achieve this, we can augment the logic above so that at the lowest point in the tree where the merge function would have dropped coefficients, it sends the second highest set of N coefficients on round 2. At the top of the tree, the second round of coefficients needs to be merged into the previous coefficients from right to left in order to spread the updates correctly. This process can be repeated for additional rounds. In this scheme, the low valued coefficients can either be stored, or can be recommunicated and recomputed from the base snapshot readings. Given the relative costs of storage and communication in modern sensor networks, we expect to store the coefficients – in practice, storage limitations will bound the number of rounds we can support.

Multiresolution snapshot queries are complicated when we consider change in the time dimension. Online aggregation as described in [7] is targeted at traditional databases, where snapshot semantics are guaranteed via transactional mechanisms. Since online aggregation requires multiple rounds, it is quite possible that the sensor readings will change before much data can be propagated to the output.

Continuous queries with time-varying results are supported in TinyDB by buffering the state of aggregates from multiple epochs within the network, and delivering better estimations for prior epochs alongside new estimations [14]. However, this increases the storage overhead in the network by a factor of the depth of the network.

We are exploring ideas for intelligently managing the total storage across both time and space. The mix of multiresolution results and time-varying data raises a number of questions with respect to both the encoding (which may be analogous to work on video), and to human-computer issues and performance metrics. A driving question for performance metrics may be to consider different possible interfaces for users to specify their desires by fixing resources in one or both dimensions. Of course, in principle there is some pareto-optimal set of strategies across these dimensions, but naive users are unlikely to be able to reason in that fashion. One can imagine fairly natural temporal controls like "animation speed" sliders and spatial controls in terms of visual selection, zoom, or foveation. One can also imagine that the dependency across dimensions could be demonstrated by having adjustments in one dimension be reflected in the controls of the other dimension. We hope to explore these inter-disciplinary issues in future work.

6   Vehicle Tracking

In this section, we provide a rough illustration of TinyDB's support for a vehicle tracking application, where a fixed field of nodes detects the magnetic field, sound, or vibration of a vehicle moving through them. We choose the tracking application because it is a representative Collaborative Signal Processing (CSP) application for sensor networks and because it demonstrates the relative ease with which such applications can be expressed in TinyDB. As will become clear, our focus to date has not been on sophisticated algorithms for tracking, but rather on extending our platform to work reasonably naturally for collaborative signal processing applications. Target tracking via a wireless sensor network is a well-researched area [2]. There are different versions of the tracking problem with varying degrees of complexities. For ease of illustration, in our discussion we only deal with a very simple version of the tracking problem, based on the following assumptions and constraints:

– There is only a single target to track.

- The target is detected when the running average of the magnetometer sensor readings go over a pre-defined threshold.
- The target location at any point in time is reported as the node location with the largest running average of the sensor reading at that time.
- The application expects to receive a time series of target locations from the sensor network once a target is detected.

We believe that more sophisticated versions of tracking can also be supported in TinyDB, using more sophisticated signal processing logic for dynamic threshold adjustment, signal strength based localization, multiple targets, etc.

There are some clear advantages to implementing tracking applications on top of TinyDB. First, TinyDB's generic query language is available as a resource, allowing applications to mix and match existing spatial-temporal aggregates and filters in a query. Applications can also run multiple queries in the sensor network at the same time, for example one tracking query and one network health monitoring query. Second, TinyDB takes care of many of sensor-network systems programming issues such as multi-hop routing, coordination of node sleeping, query and event dissemination, etc. Third, by registering tracking subroutines as user-defined aggregates in TinyDB, they become reusable in other TinyDB queries in a natural way. Fourth, we are optimistic that TinyDB's query optimization techniques [14] can benefit tracking queries. For example, each node can "snoop" the messages from its neighboring nodes and suppress its output if any neighbor has detected a stronger sensor signal.

We will describe below how two versions of the tracking application could be implemented in TinyDB with increasing levels of query complexity for better energy efficiency. We describe these implementations in TinyDB's SQL-like query language, though some off the language features used in this section are not available in the current TinyDB release. In all the TinyDB SQL statements, mag is a TinyDB attribute for the magnetometer reading, $time$ is an attribute that returns the current timestamp as an integer. We assume the sensor nodes are time synchronized within 1 millisecond using protocols like [3]. $nodeid$ is a TinyDB attribute for the unique identifier of each node. We assume the target is detected when the magnetometer reading goes over a constant value, $threshold$. $winavg(10, 1, mag)$ is for the 10-sample running average for the magnetometer readings. $max2(arg1, arg2)$ is another TinyDB aggregate that returns the value of $arg2$ corresponding to the maximum value of $arg1$. $max2(avgmag, nodeid)$ is used in our implementations to find the $nodeid$ with the largest average magnetometer reading. As mentioned above, we use this to represent the location of our target and assume that the basestation is capable of mapping $nodeid$ to some spatial coordinate. $max2$ is really a place holder that can be replaced with much more sophisticated target localization aggregates. In both implementations, we need to apply $max2$ to group of values with the same timestamp. Values are grouped by $time/10$ to accommodate minor time variations between nodes.

6.1 The Naive Implementation

Figure 6 shows the TinyDB queries that implement our initial tracking application. In this implementation, each sensor node samples the magnetometer every 100 milliseconds and computes the 10-sample running average of the magnetometer readings. If the running average of magnetometer readings is over the detection threshold, the current time, nodeid and average value of the magnetometer are inserted into the storage point *running_avg_sp*.

Recall that storage points in TinyDB provide temporary in-network storage for query results and facilitate applications to issue nested queries. The second query in Figure 6 is a query that runs over the storage point *running_avg_sp* every second and computes the target locations using the *max2* aggregate.

6.2   The Query-Handoff Implementation

The problem with the naive implementation is that all sensor nodes must wake up and sample the magnetometer every 100 milliseconds. This is extremely power-inefficient because at any point in time, the target can only be detected by a small number of nodes assuming the sensor nodes are spread over a wide area. Thus, for a large percentage of nodes, the energy spent on waking up and sampling the magnetometer is wasted.

Ideally, we would like to only start the target tracking query on a node when the target is near it and stop the query when the target moves away. TinyDB will put a mote to sleep when there are no queries running. This means that we need a TinyDB event to trigger the tracking query. The query-handoff implementation that we are about to describe requires some special standalone hardware such as a motion detector that detects the possible presence of the target, interrupts the mote processor, and pulls it out of sleep mode. *target_detected* is the TinyDB event corresponding to this external interrupt. It is unrealistic to require this special hardware be installed with every node. However it might be feasible to only install them on a small number nodes near the possible entry points for the target to enter the sensor field (e.g. endpoints of a line of sensors along a road). These nodes will be woken up by the *target_detected* event and start sampling the magnetometer to determine the current target locations. At the same time, they also try to predict the possible locations the target may move to next via a custom aggregate *next_location* and signal a remote event *target_approaching* on nodes at these locations to alert them to start sampling their magnetometers and tracking the incoming target. Nodes that receive the *target_approaching* event will wake up and basically do the same. The *target_approaching* event relies on the functionality of remotely waking up a neighboring node via a special radio signal. Such functionality is available on the Berkeley Rene motes (TinyOS 0.6) or the PicoRadios described in [11]. The TinyDB queries for this implementation is shown in Figure 6.2. We call this the *query-handoff* implementation because the node hands the tracking queries off from one set of nodes to another set of nodes following the target movement.

Query handoff is probably the most unique query processing feature required by tracking applications, and one that at first we expected to provide via low-level network routing infrastructure. However, we were pleased to realize that event-based queries and storage points allow handoff to be expressed reasonably simply at the query language level. This bodes well for prototyping other application-specific communication patterns as simple queries. An ongoing question in such work will be to decide when these patterns are deserving of a more efficient, low-level implementation inside of TinyDB.

```
// Create storage point holding
// 1 second worth of running
// avg. of magnetometer readings
// with a sample period of 100 ms
// and filter the running
// average with the target
// detection threshold.
CREATE STORAGE POINT running_avg
SIZE 1s AS
    (SELECT time,
     nodeid,
     winavg(10,1,mag) AS avgm
     FROM sensors
     GROUP BY nodeid
     HAVING avgm > threshold
     SAMPLE PERIOD 100ms);

// Query the storage point every
// second to compute target
// location for each timestamp.
SELECT time, max2(avgm,nodeid)
FROM running_avg
GROUP BY time/10
SAMPLE PERIOD 1s;
```

Fig. 6. Naive Implementation

```
// Create an empty storage point
CREATE STORAGE POINT running_avg_sp
SIZE 1s (time, nodeid, avgm);

// When the target is detected,
// run query to compute running
// average.
ON EVENT target_detected DO
SELECT time, nodeid, winavg(10,1,mag) AS avgm
INTO running_avg_sp
FROM sensors GROUP BY nodeid
HAVING avgm > threshold
SAMPLE PERIOD 100ms
UNTIL avgm <= threshold;

// Query the storage point every
// sec. to compute target location;
// send result to base and signal
// target_approaching to the possible
// places the target may move next.
SELECT time, max2(avgm, nodeid)
FROM running_avg_sp GROUP BY time/10
SAMPLE PERIOD 1s
OUTPUT ACTION SIGNAL EVENT target_approaching
WHERE location IN
(SELECT next_location(time,nodeid,avgm)
 FROM running_avg_sp ONCE);

// When target_approaching event is
// signaled, start sampling &
// inserting into storage point
ON EVENT target_approaching DO
SELECT time, nodeid, winavg(8,1,mag) AS avgm
INTO running_avg_sp
FROM sensors GROUP BY nodeid
HAVING avgm > threshold UNTIL avgm <= threshold
SAMPLE PERIOD 100ms;
```

Fig. 7. Handoff Implementation

7 Related Work

Several groups have proposed high-level or declarative interfaces for sensor-networks [22,14,10]. There has also been some work on aggregation-like operations in sensor networks, such as [23,9]. Neither of these bodies of work specifically addresses any of the more sophisticated types of aggregates or queries we discuss in this paper. Building contour maps is a frequently mentioned target application for sensor networks; see, for example, [4], though, to our knowledge, no one has previously described a viable algorithm for constructing such maps using sensor networks. There is a large body of work on building contour maps in the image processing and segmentation literature – see [17] for an excellent overview of the state of the art in image processing. These computer vision algorithms are substantially more sophisticated than those presented here, but assume a global view where the entire image is at hand.

Wavelets have myriad applications in data compression and analysis; a practical introduction is given in [21]. Wavelet histograms have been proposed for summarizing database tables in a number of publications, e.g. [18,6]. In the sensor network environment, a recent short position paper proposed using wavelets for in-network storage and summarization [5]. This work is related to ours in spirit, but different in focus at both the system architecture and coding level. It sketches a routing-level approach for relatively power-rich devices, focused on encoding regularly-gridded, spatial wavelets over timeseries. By contrast, we focus on highly-constrained devices, and integrate with the multi-purpose TinyDB query execution framework. We also provide efficient algorithms for hierarchically encoding Haar wavelets, with a focus on wavelet histograms.

The query handoff implementation for the tracking application in Section 6 is based on the single-target tracking problem discussed in [2]. The tracking algorithms described in [2] is implemented on top of UW-API [19] which is a location-centric API for developing collaborative signal processing applications in sensor networks. UW-API is implemented on top of Directed Diffusion [10] focusing on routing of data and operations based on dynamically created geographical regions. While TinyDB can shield application developers from the complexities of using such a lower level API, it can potentially leverage this work to do location-based event and query dissemination.

8   Future Work and Conclusions

Many potential users of sensor networks are not computer scientists. In order for these users to develop new applications on sensor networks, high-level languages and corresponding execution environments are desirable. We are optimistic that a query-based approach can be a good general-purpose platform for application development. The work described here attempts to justify this optimism with some non-trivial applications outside the realm of traditional SQL queries. All three of these applications have been partially implemented in TinyDB, though preliminary evaluations have only been done of the isobar application. In addition to evaluating and pursuing the work here further, we also hope to continue this thrust by collaborating with domain experts in the development of new applications; this includes both application experts outside computing, and experts in other aspects of computing including collaborative signal processing and robotics. Our intent is for TinyDB to serve as an infrastructure that allows these experts to focus on issues within their expertise, leaving problems of data collection and movement in the hands of TinyDB's adaptive query engine. As with traditional database systems, we do not expect a TinyDB-based implementation to always be as efficient as a hand-coded implementation, but we hope the ease of use and additional functionality of TinyDB will justify any modest performance overheads.

Acknowledgments. We thank Kannan Ramchandran and Michael Franklin for helpful discussions.

References

[1] R. Calderbank, I. Daubechies, W. Sweldens, and B.-L. Yeo. Wavelet transforms that map integers to integers. 5(3):332–369, 1998.

[2] Y. H. H. Dan Li, Kerry Wong and A. Sayeed. Detection, classification and tracking of targets in distributed sensor networks. *IEEE Signal Processing Magazine*, 19(2), Mar 2002.

[3] J. Elson, L. Girod, and D. Estrin. Fine-grained network time synchronization using reference broadcasts. In *OSDI*, 2002.

[4] D. Estrin. Embedded networked sensing for enviromental monitoring. Keynote, circuits and systems workshop. Slides available at http://lecs.cs.ucla.edu/ estrin/talks/CAS-JPL-Sept02.ppt.

[5] D. Ganesan, D. Estrin, and J. Heidemann. Dimensions: Why do we need a new data handling architecture for sensor networks? In *Proceedings of the First Workshop on Hot Topics In Networks (HotNets-I)*, Princeton, New Jersey, Oct. 2002.

[6] M. Garofalakis and P. B. Gibbons. Wavelet synopses with error guarantees. In *Proc. ACM SIGMOD 2002*, pages 476–487, Madison, WI, June 2002.

[7] J. M. Hellerstein, P. J. Haas, and H. Wang. Online aggregation. In *Proceedings of the ACM SIGMOD*, pages 171–182, Tucson, AZ, May 1997.

[8] J. Hill, R. Szewczyk, A. Woo, S. Hollar, and D. C. K. Pister. System architecture directions for networked sensors. In *ASPLOS*, November 2000.

[9] C. Intanagonwiwat, D. Estrin, R. Govindan, and J. Heidemann. Impact of network density on data aggregation in wireless sensor networks. ICDCS-22, November 2001.

[10] C. Intanagonwiwat, R. Govindan, and D. Estrin. Directed diffusion: A scalable and robust communication paradigm for sensor networks. In *MobiCOM*, Boston, MA, August 2000.

[11] J. Rabaey, et al. Picoradios for wireless sensor networks: The next challenge in ultra-low-power design. In *Proceedings of the International Solid-State Circuits Conference*, San Francisco, CA, Feb. 2002.

[12] D. Keim and M. Heczko. Wavelets and their applications in databases. In *ICDE*, Heidelberg, Germany, Apr. 2001.

[13] M. V. Leonov and A. G. Nitikin. An efficient algorithm for a closed set of boolean operations on polygonal regions in the plane. Technical report, A.P. Ershov Institute of Informatics Systems, 1997. Preprint 46 (In Russian.) English translation available at http://home.attbi.com/ msleonov/pbpaper.html.

[14] S. Madden, M. J. Franklin, J. M. Hellerstein, and W. Hong. TAG: A Tiny AGgregation Service for Ad-Hoc Sensor Networks. In *OSDI*, 2002.

[15] S. Madden, W. Hong, J. M. Hellerstein, and M. Franklin. TinyDB web page. http://telegraph.cs.berkeley.edu/tinydb.

[16] S. Madden, R. Szewczyk, M. Franklin, and D. Culler. Supporting aggregate queries over ad-hoc wireless sensor networks. In *WMCSA*, 2002.

[17] J. Malik, S. Belognie, T. Leung, and J. Shi. Contour and texture analysis for image segmentation. *International Journal of Computer Vision*, 43(1):7–27, 2001.

[18] Y. Matias, J. S. Vitter, and M. Wang. Wavelet-based histograms for selectivity estimation. In *SIGMOD*, pages 448–459, Seattle, Washington, June 1998.

[19] P. Ramanathan, K. Saluja, K.-C. Wang, and T. Clouqueur. UW-API: A Network Routing Application Programmer's Interface. Draft version 1.0, January 2001.

[20] W. Sweldens. The lifting scheme: A construction of second generation wavelets. *SIAM J. Math. Anal.*, 29(2):511–546, 1997.

[21] W. Sweldens and P. Schröder. Building your own wavelets at home. In *Wavelets in Computer Graphics*, pages 15–87. ACM SIGGRAPH Course notes, 1996. http://cm.bell-labs.com/who/wim/papers/athome.pdf.

[22] Y. Yao and J. Gehrke. The cougar approach to in-network query processing in sensor networks. In *SIGMOD Record*, September 2002.

[23] J. Zhao, R. Govindan, and D. Estrin. Computing aggregates for monitoring wireless sensor networks. Technical Report 02-773, USC, September 2003.

Boundary Estimation in Sensor Networks: Theory and Methods

Robert Nowak[1]* and Urbashi Mitra[2]**

[1] Department of Electrical & Computer Engineering, Rice University
nowak@rice.edu
[2] Electrical Engineering Department, University of Southern California
ubli@usc.edu

Abstract. Sensor networks have emerged as a fundamentally new tool for monitoring spatially distributed phenomena. This paper investigates a strategy by which sensor nodes detect and estimate non-localized phenomena such as "boundaries" and "edges" (e.g., temperature gradients, variations in illumination or contamination levels). A general class of boundaries, with mild regularity assumptions, is considered, and theoretical bounds on the achievable performance of sensor network based boundary estimation are established. A hierarchical boundary estimation algorithm is proposed that achieves a near-optimal balance between mean-squared error and energy consumption.

1 Introduction

Sensor networks have emerged as a fundamentally new tool for monitoring inaccessible environments such as non-destructive evaluation of buildings and structures; contaminant tracking in the environment; habitat monitoring in the jungle; and surveillance in military zones. These *ad hoc* networks are envisioned to be a collection of embedded sensors, actuators and processors. We shall assume that communication between sensors is done in a wireless fashion. Sensor networks are distinguished from more classical networks due to strict limitations on energy consumption, the density of nodes, the simplicity of the processing power of nodes and possibly high environmental dynamics. An important problem in sensor networking applications is *boundary estimation*. Consider a network sensing a field composed of two or more regions of distinct behavior (e.g., differing mean values for the sensor measurements). An example of such a field is depicted in Figure 1(a). Boundary estimation is the process of determining the delineation between homogeneous regions.

There are two fundamental limitations in the boundary estimation problem. First, the accuracy of a boundary estimate is limited by the spatial density of

* Supported by the National Science Foundation, grant nos. MIP–9701692 and ANI–0099148, the Office of Naval Research, grant no. N00014-00-1-0390, and the Army Research Office, grant no. DAAD19-99-1-0290.
** Supported by the Texas Instruments Visiting Professorship.

F. Zhao and L. Guibas (Eds.): IPSN 2003, LNCS 2634, pp. 80–95, 2003.
© Springer-Verlag Berlin Heidelberg 2003

sensors in the network and by the amount of noise associated with the measurement process. Second, energy constraints may limit the complexity of the boundary estimate that is ultimately transmitted to a desired destination. The trade-off between accuracy and energy consumption can be characterized as follows. Assume that n sensor nodes are arranged on an $\sqrt{n} \times \sqrt{n}$ square lattice (assuming a planar, square sensor field). Suppose that the field being sensed consists of two homogeneous regions separated by a one-dimensional boundary (like the case depicted in Figure 1(a)). A broad class of boundaries is considered in this paper. Specifically, we only assume that the boundary is a Lipschitz function[6,3] or, more generally, has a box-counting dimension of one [9]. This class includes linear boundaries and other parametric curves, but also includes boundaries that cannot be described parametrically.

Each sensor node makes a (noisy) measurement of the field. Under these assumptions, there will be $O(\sqrt{n})$ nodes lying on the boundary. The boundary nodes provide a description of the boundary to within a resolution of $1/\sqrt{n}$. Noise present in the measurements limits the achievable accuracy of a boundary estimate. It is known that, under the assumptions on the class of boundaries above, the mean-square error (MSE) cannot, in general, decay faster than $O(1/\sqrt{n})$ [6, 3]. That is, no estimator (based on centralized or distributed processing) can exceed this convergence speed-limit. It is important to point out that if one restricts the class of boundaries, then faster decay rates are certainly possible. For example, if one assumes that the boundary is a line, then the problem is a parametric estimation problem and the rate of decay is $O(1/n)$. Assuming a line or parametric curve is, of course, very restrictive (and probably unreasonable for natural phenomena), and therefore this paper focuses on a much more general class of boundaries.

To quantify the total energy required to transmit a boundary estimate of this accuracy, note that each boundary node must send one message to the desired destination (indicating that it is on the boundary). Thus, the total energy required to transmit the boundary description is $O(\sqrt{n})$. Combining these results yields a fundamental trade-off between accuracy and energy of the form

$$\text{MSE} \sim \frac{1}{\text{Energy}}.$$

This tradeoff does not take into consideration the additional energy required to determine whether a sensor is in fact a boundary. It is important to note that this relation should not be interpreted to mean that a fixed number of sensor nodes using more energy can provide more accuracy. Rather, both the MSE and the energy consumption are functions of the number of sensor nodes, and the above relation indicates how the accuracy and energy consumption behave as the density of nodes increases. Also, note that if a boundary can be described parametrically, then the energy required to transmit the description is proportional to the number of parameters, and does not depend on n. However, as discussed above, the aim here is to avoid such restrictive parametric assumptions. The boundaries of interest may not admit exact parametric descriptions, and therefore the accuracy of the boundary description and transmission cost both grow as density of nodes increases.

This paper explores the basic trade-off between MSE and energy consumption, as functions of node density. We propose and develop a boundary estimation algorithm based on multiscale partitioning methods. The algorithm is quite practical and maps nicely onto a sensor network architecture. Moreover, we demonstrate theoretically that our method nearly achieves the optimal MSE/Energy trade-off discussed above. The theory hinges on an application of our extension [5] of the Li-Barron bound for complexity regularized model selection [8] to bound the MSE and on a recent concentration inequality for chi-squared distributions to bound the expected energy consumption [7]. Since our method (nearly) achieves the optimal trade-off above, no other scheme can be devised that will (asymptotically) perform significantly better. Simulation experiments verify the predicted theoretical performance of our method.

1.1 Related Work

Due to the nascence of sensor network research, there is a limited literature concerning boundary estimation for such networks. At first glance, boundary estimation (or boundary detection) has goals that are similar to that of edge detection in image processing. However, a major distinction exists. Due to energy constraints, processing the entire "image" simultaneously is impractical, and hence a single node does not have access to all of the sensor measurements. In [2], several techniques based on averaging and thresholds are developed and compared for boundary detection. All of the techniques rely on the collection of measurements from sensor neighbors within a *probing radius*, R. The authors note that the performance of their methods will improve as the probing radius increases at the expense of communication cost. To contrast with our approach, we systematically increase the probing radius, however our communication cost does not increase as $O(R^2)$ due to the fact that lower dimensional statistics (versus all measurements) are passed to nodes within the sensor network hierarchy; and, furthermore, messages are only passed to clusterheads rather than all nodes.

The data collection algorithm in [4] shares many features with our proposed boundary estimation method. A hierarchical compression scheme is considered where clusterheads aggregate measurements from children nodes and then pass signal estimates to the next layer in the hieararchy. Our objective, herein, is to analytically determine the estimation capability of a tree-based boundary estimation scheme which is penalized by communication costs. We note that the scheme of [4] does not explicitly optimze the description of the phenomena being encoded (in our case, a boundary) and thus suffers in terms of the error between the estimated boundary and the true boundary; however, the communication cost is lessened. With our scheme, we can systematically tradeoff between communication cost and reconstruction error by increasing the penalty associated with communication.

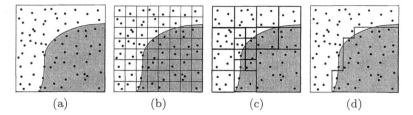

(a) (b) (c) (d)

Fig. 1. Sensing an inhomogeneous field. (a) Points are sensor locations. The environment has two conditions indicated by the gray and white regions of the square. (b) the sensor network domain is partitioned into square cells. (c) Sensors within the network operate collaboratively to determine a pruned partition that matches the boundary. (d) Final approximation to the boundary between the two regions which is transmitted to a remote point.

2 Problem Formulation and Approach

The basic problem is illustrated in Figure 1. Our objective is to consider measurements from a collection of sensors and determine the boundary between two fields of relatively homogeneous measurements.

We presume a hierarchical structure of "clusterheads" (see *e.g.* [4]) which manage measurements from nodes below them in the hierarchy. Thus, the nodes in each square of the partition communicate their measurements to a clusterhead in the square. Index the squares at the finest scale by row and column (i, j). The clusterhead in square (i, j) computes the average of these measurements to obtain a value $x_{i,j} \sim \mathcal{N}\left(\mu_{i,j}, \frac{\sigma^2}{m_{i,j}}\right)$, where $\mu_{i,j}$ is the mean value, σ^2 is the noise variance for each sensor measurement, and $m_{i,j}$ is the number of nodes in square (i, j). Thus we assume sensor measurements that have a Gaussian distribution. For simplicity, we assume $m_{i,j} = 1$. The random distribution is to account for noise in the system as well as for the small probability of node failure (outlier measurements).

Our approach to the boundary estimation problem is to devise a hierarchical processing strategy that enables the nodes to collaboratively determine a non-uniform rectangular partition of the sensor domain that is adapted to the boundaries. Specifically, the desired partition will have high, fine resolution along the boundary, and low, coarse resolution in homogeneous regions of the field, as depicted in Figure 1. The partition effectively provides a "staircase"-like approximation to the boundary. Similar strategies have been recently investigated to handle edges in images [3,10] and decision boundaries in classification problems [9]. The advantage of our approach is that, under mild conditions on the smoothness of the boundary curve, we can establish upper bounds on the MSE of the estimator using theoretical tools we have developed in previous work. These upper bounds can be used to tune the trade-off between data fitting and the complexity of the boundary estimate. The complexity of the boundary estimate relates directly to energy consumption in the network.

Our approach is as follows. Let us take the sensor domain to be the unit square $[0,1]^2$. Partition the domain into n sub-squares of sidelength $\frac{1}{\sqrt{n}}$, as shown in Figure 1(b). The sidelength $\frac{1}{\sqrt{n}}$ is the finest resolution of our analysis. In principle, this initial partition can be generated by a a *recursive dyadic partition* (RDP). First divide the domain into four sub-squares of equal size. Repeat this process again on each sub-square. Repeat this $1/2\log_2 n = J$ times. This gives rise to a *complete* RDP of resolution $\frac{1}{\sqrt{n}}$ (the rectangular partition of the sensing domain shown above in Figure 1(b)). The RDP process can represented with a quadtree structure. The quadtree can be pruned back to produce an RDP with non-uniform resolution as shown in Figure 1(c). The key issues are: (1) How to implement the pruning process in the sensor network; (2) How to determine the best pruned tree. Here, we discuss the first issue, and the second issue will be investigated in later sections of the paper.

Let $\mathcal{P}_n$ denote the set of all RDPs, including the initial complete RDP and all possible prunings. For each RDP $P \in \mathcal{P}_n$, there is an associated quadtree structure (generally of non-uniform depth corresponding to the non-uniform resolution of most RDPs). The leafs of each quadtree represent dyadic (sidelength equal to a negative power of 2) square regions of the associated partition. For a given RDP and quadtree, each sensor node belongs to a certain dyadic square. We consider these squares "clusters" and assume that one of the nodes in each square serves as a "clusterhead," which will assimilate information from the other nodes in the square. Notice that if one considers all RDPs in $\mathcal{P}_n$, then each sensor node actually belongs to a nested hierarchy of $1/2\log_2 n$ dyadic squares of sidelengths $\frac{1}{\sqrt{n}}, \frac{2}{\sqrt{n}}, \frac{4}{\sqrt{n}}, \ldots, 1$, respectively. Thus, we have a hierarchy of clusters and clusterheads.

Consider a certain RDP $P \in \mathcal{P}_n$. Define the estimator of the field as follows. On each square of the partition, average the measurements from the sensors in that square and set the estimate of the field to that average value. This results in a piecewise constant estimate, denoted by θ, of the field. This estimator will be compared with the data $x = \{x_{i,j}\}$. The data themselves are undesirable for two reasons. First, they are noisy and averaging over larger regions will reduce the noise. Second, the unprocessed data x will require the maximum amount of energy to transmit to the destination. Our empirical measure of performance is the sum-of-squared errors between $\theta = \theta(P)$ and the data $x = \{x_{i,j}\}$.

$$R(\theta, x) = \sum_{i,j=1}^{\sqrt{n}} \left(\theta(i,j) - x_{i,j}\right)^2, \qquad (1)$$

Define the complexity penalized estimator

$$\widehat{\theta}_n = \arg\min_{\theta(P):P\in\mathcal{P}_n} R(\theta(P), x) + 2\sigma^2 p(n)|\theta(P)|, \qquad (2)$$

where σ^2 is the noise variance, $|\theta(P)|$ denotes the total number of squares in the partition P, and $p(n)$ is a certain monotonically increasing function of n that discourages unnecessarily high resolution partitions (appropriate choices of $p(n)$

will be discussed in the sequel). It is well known that the optimization in (2) can be solved using a bottom-up tree pruning algorithm in $O(n)$ operations [1, 3,10]. This is possible because both the sum-of-squared errors and the penalty are additive functions, and therefore the squared error plus penalty cost can be separated into terms associated with each individual square of the partition θ. The hierarchy of clusterheads facilitates this process in the sensor network. At each level of the hierarchy, the clusterhead receives the best sub-partition/sub-tree estimates from the four clusterheads below it, and compares the total cost of these estimates with the cost of the estimate equal to the average of all sensors in that cluster.

3   Upper Bounds on Achievable Accuracy

We begin by recalling a fundamental upper bound on expected error of complexity penalized estimators, like that in (2). This particular bound was originally developed for mixture density modeling [8], and we later extended it to more general settings [5]. Here we state a specialized version of the bound, tailored to the estimator proposed in (2).

Let Θ_n denote the set of all possible models of the field. This set contains piecewise constant models (constant on the dyadic squares corresponding to one of the partitions in $\mathcal{P}_n$). The constant values are in a prescribed range $[-R, R]$, and are quantized to k bits. The range corresponds to the upper and lower limits of the amplitude range of the sensors. The set Θ_n consists of a finite number of models (a bound on the number of partitions is derived in the Appendix). Assume that $p(n)$ satisfies the summability condition (Kraft inequality)

$$\sum_{\theta \in \Theta_n} e^{-p(n)|\theta|} \leq 1 \ , \tag{3}$$

where again $|\theta|$ denotes the number of squares (alternatively we shall call this the number of leafs in the pruned tree description of the boundary) in the partition θ. It is shown in the Appendix that $p(n) \leq \gamma \log n$ satisfies (3). Let $\widehat{\theta}_n$ denote the solution to

$$\widehat{\theta}_n = \arg \min_{\theta \in \Theta_n} R(\theta, x) + 2\sigma^2 p(n)|\theta|, \tag{4}$$

where, as before, x denotes the array of measurements at the finest scale $\{x_{i,j}\}$, and $|\theta|$ denotes the number of squares in the partition associated with θ. This is essentially the same estimator as defined in (2) except that the values of the estimate are quantized in this case.

Let θ_n^* denote the true value of the field at resolution $1/\sqrt{n}$ (i.e., $\theta_n^*(i, j) = E[x_{i,j}]$). Then, applying Theorem 7 in [5], the MSE of the estimator $\widehat{\theta}_n$ is bounded above according to

$$\frac{1}{n} \sum_{i,j=1}^{\sqrt{n}} E\left[\left(\widehat{\theta}_n(i,j) - \theta_n^*(i,j)\right)^2\right] \leq$$

$$\min_{\theta \in \Theta_n} \frac{1}{n} \left\{ 2 \sum_{i,j=1}^{\sqrt{n}} (\theta(i,j) - \theta_n^*(i,j))^2 + 8\sigma^2 p(n)|\theta| \right\} \quad (5)$$

The upper bound involves two terms. The first term, $2 \sum_{i,j=1}^{\sqrt{n}} (\theta(i,j) - \theta_n^*(i,j))^2$, is a bound on the bias or approximation error. The second term, $8\sigma^2 p(n)|\theta|$, is a bound on the variance or estimation error. The bias term, which measures the squared error between the best possible model in our class and the true field, is generally unknown. However, if we make certain assumptions on the smoothness of the boundary, then the rate at which this term decays as function of the partition size $|\theta|$ can be determined.

Assume that the field being sensed is composed of homogeneous regions separated by a one-dimensional boundary. If the boundary is a Lipschitz function [3, 10] or more generally has a box-counting dimension (closely related to Hausdorf dimension) of 1, then by carefully calibrating quantization and penalization as discussed in the Appendix (taking $k \sim 1/4 \log n$ and setting $p(n) = 2/3 \log n$) it follows that

$$\frac{1}{n} \sum_{i,j=1}^{\sqrt{n}} E\left[\left(\widehat{\theta}_n(i,j) - \theta_n^*(i,j)\right)^2\right] \leq O\left(\sqrt{\frac{\log n}{n}}\right). \quad (6)$$

This result shows that the MSE decays to zero at a rate of $\sqrt{\log n / n}$. This rate cannot be significantly improved by any estimator. From [3,6] we know that for Lipschitz boundaries, the minimax rate is $O(1/\sqrt{n})$, which shows that our estimator is within a square-root of a logarithmic factor of the best possible convergence rate. The minimax rate is the fastest rate of convergence achievable with any estimator ("min") for the most challenging ("max") Lipschitz boundary. Faster rates of decay are theoretically possible if one assumes that the boundary is even smoother. As an extreme case, suppose the boundary can be exactly described parametrically (e.g., a line). Then the boundary problem is one of parameter estimation and the rate of convergence is $O(1/n)$. Extensions of our approach are possible which can take advantage of smoother boundaries, which may provide convergence rates approaching the parametric rate. These extensions are part of our ongoing work and will be discussed in Section 6.

4   Accuracy-Energy Trade-Off

A key characteristic of our proposed method is the explicit consideration of the cost of communication in the construction of the tree describing the boundary. Energy consumption is defined by two communication costs: the cost of communication due to the construction of the tree (*in-network* cost) and the cost of communicating the final boundary estimate (*out-of-network* cost). We will show that the expected number of leafs produced by our algorithm is $O(\sqrt{n})$, and that the in-network and out-of-network energy consumption is proportional to this number. Recall that the rate of decay for the MSE is MSE $\sim \sqrt{\log n/n}$. Therefore, ignoring the logarithmic factor, the accuracy-energy trade-off required to achieve this optimal MSE is roughly MSE $\sim 1/$Energy. Contrast this trade-off with that of a naive approach in which each of the n sensors transmits its data, directly or by multiple hops, to an external point. In this case, the in-network and out-of-network energy costs are $O(n)$, which lead to the trade-off MSE $\sim 1/\sqrt{\text{Energy}}$, since we know that no estimator exists that can result in an MSE decaying faster than $O(1/\sqrt{n})$. Thus, our proposed hierarchical boundary estimation method offers substantial savings over the naive approach while optimizing the tradeoff between accuracy and complexity of the estimate.

4.1   Out-of-Network Communication Cost

It is clear that the out-of-network communication cost is proportional to the final description of the boundary, thus it is of interest to compute the expected size of the tree, or $E[|\widehat{\theta}|]$. Each decision in the pruning process is based on comparing the complexity and fitness of an average value to the data in a certain dyadic square to that of the best subpartition model for that square (passed up from the bottom).

An upper bound on $E[|\widehat{\theta}|]$ is derived in the Appendix. The upper bound is based on the probability of pruning or not pruning at each node for our hierarchical algorithm. If no boundary is present, then the probability of pruning at each node can be bounded from above by the tail probability of a certain chi-square distribution. The chi-square distribution arises from the assumed Gaussian observation model and the sum-of-squared errors criterion used in pruning. Using another upper bound for the tail probability, we show in the Appendix that if no boundary is present in the square under consideration, and with a penalty $p(n) = 2/3 \log n$, the probability of not pruning tends to zero as n increases. This implies that $E[|\widehat{\theta}|] \to 1$ as $n \to \infty$. Thus, for large sensor networks, the expected number of leafs (partition pieces) in the case where there is no boundary (simply a homogeneous field) is one.

To consider the inhomogeneous case where a boundary does exist, if the boundary is a Lipschitz function or has a box counting dimension of 1, there exists a pruned RDP with at most $C'\sqrt{n}$ squares (leafs) that includes the $O(\sqrt{n})$ squares of sidelength $1/\sqrt{n}$ that the boundary passes through (see the Appendix for a fuller discussion of this property). Thus an upper bound on the number of leafs required to describe the boundary in the noiseless case is given by $C'\sqrt{n}$. In the presence of noise, we can use the results above for the homogeneous case to bound the number of spurious leafs due to noise (zero as n grows); as a result, for large sensor networks, we can expect at most $C'\sqrt{n}$ leafs in total. Thus, the expected energy required to transmit the final boundary description is Energy $= O(\sqrt{n})$.

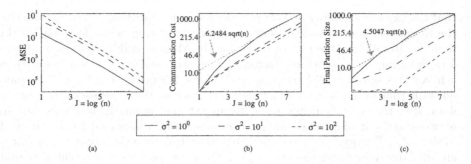

Fig. 2. (a)Estimation accuracy as a function of the total number of nodes. (b) In-network communication cost as a function of the total number of nodes. (c) Out-of-network communication cost, $E[|\hat{\theta}|]$, as a function of the total number of nodes.

4.2   In-Network Communication Cost

The in-network communication cost is intimately tied to the expected size of the final tree, as this value determines how much pruning will occur. We have seen above that the out-of-network cost is proportional to $\sqrt{n}$ and herein we shall show that the in-network communication cost is also $O(\sqrt{n})$. At each scale $2^j/\sqrt{n}$, $j = 0, \ldots, 1/2 \log_2 n - 1$, the hierarchical algorithm passes a certain number of data or averages, n_j, corresponding to the number of squares in the best partition (up to that scale), up the tree to the next scale. We assume that a constant number of bits k, is transmitted per measurement. These $k\, n_j$ bits must be transmitted approximately $2^j/\sqrt{n}$ meters (assuming the sensor domain is normalized to 1 square meter). Thus, the total in-network communication energy in bit-meters is:

$$\mathcal{E} = k \sum_{j=0}^{1/2 \log_2 n - 1} n_j 2^j / \sqrt{n}.$$

In the naive approach, $n_j = n$ for all j, and therefore $\mathcal{E} \approx kn$. In the hierarchical approach, first consider the case when there is no boundary. We have already seen that in such cases the tree will be pruned at each stage with high probability. Therefore, $n_j = n/4^j$ and $\mathcal{E} \approx 2k\sqrt{n}$. Now if a boundary of length $C\sqrt{n}$ is present, then $n_j \leq n/4^j + C\sqrt{n}$. This produces $\mathcal{E} \leq k(C + 2)\sqrt{n}$. Thus, we see that our hierarchical algorithm results in $\mathcal{E} = O(\sqrt{n})$.

5   Simulations

We next present representative simulation results on the efficacy of the proposed boundary estimation algorithm. We considered a host of sensor network densities observing the same phenomenon. Sensor networks of size 4^k for $k = 2, \cdots, 8$ distributed over a square meter were considered. The sensors operated in an

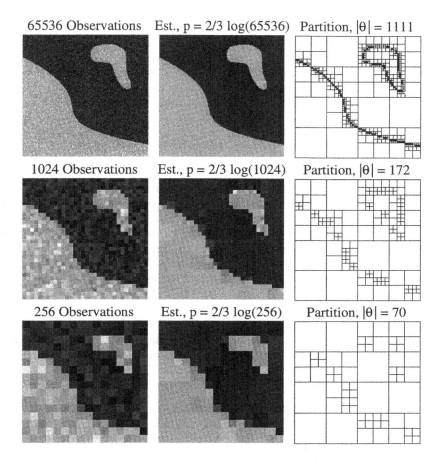

Fig. 3. Effect of sensor network density (resolution) on boundary estimation. Column 1 is the noisy set of measurements, Column 2 is the estimated boundary, and Column 3 is the associated partition.

environment with three different noise levels ($\sigma^2 = 1, 10, 100$). In Figure 2 (a), we see the mean-squared error (MSE) as a function of the network size (which relates directly to density). The MSE is averaged over 50 realizations of the noise. As predicted by the theoretical results, we see the expected decay in MSE. The in-network communication cost as scaled by the distance traveled is provided in Figure 2(b). As predicted, this cost is proportional to $\sqrt{n}$. Figure 2(c) shows the average size of the boundary estimate (number of leafs) as a function of the network size and a line fit to the data. This plot corresponds to the out-of-network communication costs. We see that the predicted bounds for both costs are in fact conservative, and in practice the constant in $O(\sqrt{n})$ is quite modest (here it is $4 - 6$). The final partition size (and hence the communication cost) decreases as the noise variance increases due to the fact that the overall penalty is a function of the noise variance. Thus as the noise variance increases, it is more likely that pruning will occur.

Figure 3 shows single realizations of the boundary estimation process for three resolutions/sensor network densities. The penalty function employed was that derived in the Appendix and we see that the resultant boundary estimates offer the desired tradeoff between accuracy and energy consumption.

6   Conclusions and Ongoing Work

In this work, we have proposed a method for boundary estimation in sensor networks. The boundary estimate is determined via complexity regularization of a hiearchical tree-based estimation method. We demonstrated theoretically that our method nearly achieves the optimal trade-off MSE $\sim$ 1/Energy, which shows that no other scheme can be devised that will (asymptotically) perform significantly better. Simulation experiments agreed very well with the theoretical predictions. In future work we plan to investigate more sophisticated boundary estimation techniques based on "wedgelets" [3] and "platelets" [10]. These methodologies are also based on hierarchical partitions and trees, but have additional flexibility which allows for a more parsimonious description of smooth boundaries and smooth variations in the mean of homogeneous regions. We are also currently incorporating the effects of imperfect wireless signaling into our theoretical framework and simulation studies. Finally, we are investigating the issue of tracking a slowly time-varying boundary.

Acknowledgments. The authors wish to thank Ms. Rebecca Willett for developing the simulation code for the proposed boundary estimator and for helpful comments on the manuscript, and thank Mr. Rui Castro for his careful reading of the proofs.

References

1. L. Breiman, J. Friedman, R. Olshen, and C. J. Stone. *Classification and Regression Trees*. Wadsworth, Belmont, CA, 1983.
2. K. Chintalapudi and R. Govindan.   Localized edge detection in sensor fields. *University of Southern California, Computer Science Department, Technical Report,02-773*, 2002. available at
    http://www.cs.usc.edu/tech-reports/technical-reports.html.
3. D. Donoho. Wedgelets: Nearly minimax estimation of edges. *Ann. Statist.*, 27:859–897, 1999.
4. D. Ganesan, D. Estrin, and J. Heideman. DIMENSIONS: Why do we need a new data handling architecture for sensor networks? In *Proceedings of IEEE/ACM HotNets-I*, Princeton, NJ, October 2002.
5. E. Kolaczyk and R. Nowak. Multiscale likelihood analysis and complexity penalized estimation. *Annals of Statistics* (tentatively accepted for publication). Also available at www.ece.rice.edu/~nowak/pubs.html, 2002.

6. A. P. Korostelev and A. B. Tsybakov. *Minimax theory of image reconstruction.* Springer-Verlag, New York, 1993.

7. B. Laurent and P. Massart. Adaptive estimation of a quadratic functional by model selection. *The Annals of Statistics*, (5), October 2000.

8. Q. Li and A. Barron. Mixture density estimation. In S.A. Solla, T.K. Leen, and K.-R. Müller, editors, *Advances in Neural Information Processing Systems 12*. MIT Press, 2000.

9. C. Scott and R. Nowak. Dyadic classification trees via structural risk minimization. In *Proc. Neural Information Processing Systems (NIPS)*, Vancouver, CA, Dec. 2002.

10. R. Willett and R. Nowak. Platelets: A multiscale approach to recovering edges and surfaces in photon-limited imaging. *IEEE Trans. Med. Imaging*, to appear in the Special Issue on Wavelets in Medical Imaging, 2003.

7 Appendix

7.1 Number of RDPs in $\mathcal{P}$

Recall the class $\mathcal{P}$ of RDPs under consideration (all RDPs resulting from pruning P_J, the uniform partition of the unit square into n squares of sidelength $\frac{1}{\sqrt{n}}$). In order to ensure that the Kraft inequality (3) is satisfied, we need to determine how many RDPs there are in $\mathcal{P}$. More specifically, we will need to know how many partitions there are with exactly ℓ squares/leafs. Notice that since the RDP is based on recursive splits into four, the number of leafs in every partition in $\mathcal{P}$ is of the form $\ell = 3m+1$, for some integer $0 \leq m \leq (n-1)/3$. The integer m corresponds to the number of recursive splits. For each RDP having $3m+1$ leafs there is a corresponding partially ordered sequence of m split points (at dyadic positions in the plane). In general, there are $\binom{n}{m} \equiv \frac{n!}{(n-m)!m!}$ possible selections of m points from n (n corresponding to the vertices of the finest resolution partition, P_J). This number is an upper bound on the number of partitions in $\mathcal{P}$ with $\ell = 3m + 1$ leafs (since RDPs can only have dyadic split points).

7.2 Kraft Inequality

Here we show that with k (recall that k is the number of bits employed per transmission) and $p(n)$ properly calibrated, we have

$$\sum_{\theta \in \Theta_n} e^{-p(n)|\theta|} \leq 1 \ . \tag{7}$$

Let $\Theta_n^{(m)}$ denote the subset of Θ_n consisting of models based on $\ell = 3m + 1$ leaf partitions. Begin by writing

$$\sum_{\theta \in \Theta_n} e^{-p(n)|\theta|} = \sum_{m=0}^{(n-1)/3} \sum_{\theta \in \Theta_n^{(m)}} e^{-(3m+1)p(n)}$$

$$\leq \sum_{m=0}^{(n-1)/3} \binom{n}{m} (2^k)^{3m+1} e^{-(3m+1)p(n)}$$

$$\leq \sum_{m=0}^{(n-1)/3} \frac{n^m}{m!} (2^k)^{3m+1} e^{-(3m+1)p(n)}$$

$$= \sum_{m=0}^{(n-1)/3} \frac{1}{m!} e^{[m \log n + (3m+1) \log(2^k) - (3m+1)p(n)]} .$$

If $A \equiv m \log n + (3m+1) \log(2^k) - (3m+1)p(n) < -1$ (then $e^A < e^{-1}$), then we have

$$\sum_{\theta \in \Theta_n} e^{-p(n)|\theta|} \leq 1/e \sum_{m=0}^{(n-1)/3} \frac{1}{m!} \leq 1 .$$

To guarantee $A < -1$, we must have $p(n)$ growing at least like $\log n$. Therefore, set $p(n) = \gamma \log n$, for some $\gamma > 0$. Also, as we will see later in the next section, to guarantee that the quantization of our models is sufficiently fine to contribute a negligible amount to the overall error we must select $2^k \sim n^{1/4}$. With these calibrations we have

$$A = [(7/4 - 3\gamma)m + (1/4 - \gamma)] \log n$$

In order to guarantee that the MSE converges to zero, we will see in the next section that m must be a monotonically increasing function of n. Therefore, for n sufficiently large, the term involving $(\frac{1}{4} - \gamma)$ is negligible, and the condition $A < -1$ is satisfied by $\gamma > 7/12$. We take $\gamma = 2/3$ in practice.

7.3   Rate of MSE Decay

Consider a complete RDP with m^2 squares of sidelength $1/m$. It is known that if the boundary is a Lipschitz function, or more generally has a box counting dimension of 1, then the boundary passes through $\ell \leq Cm$ of the squares, for some constant $C > 0$ [3,10,9]. Furthermore, there exists a pruned RDP with at most $C'm$ leafs, where $C' = 8(C + 2)$, that includes the above ℓ squares of sidelength $1/m$ that contain the boundary [3,9].

Now consider the upper bound (5), which as stated earlier follows as from an application of Theorem 7 in [5].

$$\frac{1}{n} \sum_{i,j=1}^{\sqrt{n}} E\left[\left(\widehat{\theta}_n(i,j) - \theta_n^*(i,j)\right)^2\right]$$

$$\leq \min_{\theta \in \Theta_n} \frac{1}{n} \left\{ 2 \sum_{i,j=1}^{\sqrt{n}} (\theta(i,j) - \theta_n^*(i,j))^2 + 8p(n)|\theta| \right\}$$

$$\leq 2 \int_{[0,1]^2} (\theta - \theta^*)^2 + 8 \frac{7}{12} \frac{\log n}{n} C'm ,$$

where the discretized squared error is bounded by the corresponding continuous counterpart. The squared error $\int_{[0,1]^2} (\theta - \theta^*)^2 \sim \frac{K_1}{m} + \frac{K_2}{\sqrt{n}}$, where the first term is due to the error between the $1/m$ resolution partition along the boundary, and the $1/\sqrt{n}$ term is due to the quantization error overall. Thus, the MSE behaves like

$$\text{MSE} \sim O(1/m) + O(1/\sqrt{n}) + O\left(m \frac{\log n}{n}\right).$$

Taking $m \sim \sqrt{\frac{n}{\log n}}$ produces the desired result: $\text{MSE} \sim O(\sqrt{\log n / n})$.

7.4   Expected Tree Size for Homogeneous Field

We construct an upperbound for $E[|\widehat{\theta}|]$ under the assumption of a homogeneous field with no boundary. Let P denote the tree-structured partition associated with $\widehat{\theta}$. Note that because P is an RDP it can have $d + 1$ leafs (pieces in the partition), where $d = 3m$, $m = 0, \ldots, (n-1)/3$. Therefore, the expected number of leafs is given by

$$E[|\widehat{\theta}|] = \sum_{m=0}^{(n-1)/3} (3m + 1) \Pr\left(|\widehat{\theta}| = 3m + 1\right).$$

The probability $\Pr\left(|\widehat{\theta}| = 3m + 1\right)$ can be bounded from above by the probability that one of the possible partitions with $3m + 1$ leafs, $m > 0$, is chosen in favor of the trivial partition with just a single leaf. That is, the event that one of the partitions with $3m + 1$ leafs is selected implies that partitions of all other sizes were not selected, including the trivial partition, from which the upper bound follows. This upper bound allows us to bound the expected number of leafs as follows.

$$E[|\widehat{\theta}|] \leq \sum_{m=0}^{(n-1)/3} (3m + 1) \#_m \, p_m,$$

where $\#_m$ denotes the number of different $(3m + 1)$-leaf partitions, and p_m denotes the probability that a particular $(3m+1)$-leaf partition is chosen in favor of the trivial partition (under the homogeneous assumption). The number $\#_m$ can be bounded above by $\binom{n}{m}$, just as in the verification of the Kraft inequality.

The probability p_m can be bounded as follows. Note this is the probability of a particular outcome of a comparison of two models. The comparison is made between their respective sum-of-squared errors plus complexity penalty, as given by (2). The single leaf model has a single degree of freedom (mean value of the entire region), and the alternate model, based on the $(3m+1)$-leaf has $3m+1$ degrees of freedom. Thus, under the assumption that the data are i.i.d. zero-mean Gaussian distributed with variance σ^2, it is easy to verify that the difference between the sum-of-squared errors of the models (single-leaf model sum-of-squares minus $(3m+1)$-leaf model sum-of-squares) is distributed as $\sigma^2 W_{3m}$, where W_{3m} is a chi-square distributed random variable with $3m$ degrees of freedom (precisely the difference between the degrees of freedom in the two models). This follows from the fact that the difference of the sum-of-squared errors is equal to the sum-of-squares of an orthogonal projection of the data onto a $3m$ dimensional subspace.

The single-leaf model is rejected if $\sigma^2 W_{3m}$ is greater than the difference between the complexity penalties associated with the two models; that is, if

$$\sigma^2 W_{3m} > (3m+1)2\sigma^2 p(n) - 2\sigma^2 p(n) = 6m\sigma^2 p(n),$$

where $2\sigma^2 p(n)$ is the penalty associated with each additional leaf in P. According to the MSE analysis in the previous section, we require $p(n) = \gamma \log n$, with $\gamma > 7/12$. To be concrete, take $\gamma = 2/3$, in which case the rejection of the single-leaf model is equivalent to $W_{3m} > 4m \log n$. The probability of this condition, $p_m = Pr(W_{3m} > 4m \log n)$, is bounded from above using Lemma 1 of Laurent and Massart [7]: If W_d is chi-square distributed with d degrees of freedom, then for $s > 0$

$$Pr(W_d \geq d + s\sqrt{2d} + s^2) \leq e^{-s^2/2}.$$

Making the identification $d + s\sqrt{2d} + s^2 = 4m \log n$ produces the bound

$$p_m = Pr(W_{3m} > 4m \log n) \leq e^{-2m \log n + m\sqrt{3/2(4 \log n - 3/2)}}.$$

Combining the upper bounds above, we have

$$E[|\widehat{\theta}|] \leq \sum_{m=0}^{(n-1)/3} (3m+1) \binom{n}{m} e^{-2m \log n + m\sqrt{3/2(4 \log n - 3/2)}},$$

$$= \sum_{m=0}^{(n-1)/3} (3m+1) \binom{n}{m} n^{-m} e^{-m \log n + m\sqrt{3/2(4 \log n - 3/2)}}.$$

For $n \geq 270$ the exponent $-\log n + \sqrt{3/2(4 \log n - 3/2)} < 0$ and therefore

$$E[|\widehat{\theta}|] \le \sum_{m=0}^{(n-1)/3} (3m+1) \binom{n}{m} n^{-m},$$

$$\le \sum_{m=0}^{(n-1)/3} (3m+1) \frac{n^m}{m!} n^{-m},$$

$$\le \sum_{m=0}^{(n-1)/3} (3m+1)/m! \; < \; 11.$$

Furthermore, note that as $n \to \infty$ the exponent $-\log n + \sqrt{3/2(4\log n - 3/2)} \to -\infty$. This fact implies that the factor $e^{-m\log n + m\sqrt{3/2(4\log n - 3/2)}}$ tends to zero when $m > 0$. Therefore, the expected number of leafs $E[|\widehat{\theta}|] \to 1$ as $n \to \infty$.

Scalable Control of Decentralised Sensor Platforms

Ben Grocholsky, Alexei Makarenko, Tobias Kaupp, and Hugh F. Durrant-Whyte

Australian Centre for Field Robotics, University of Sydney, Australia,
{ben,a.makarenko,t.kaupp,hugh}@acfr.usyd.edu.au,
http://www.acfr.usyd.edu.au

Abstract. This paper describes an information-theoretic approach to decentralised and coordinated control of multi-robot sensor systems. It builds on techniques long established for the related problem of Decentralised Data Fusion (DDF). The DDF architecture uses information measures to communicate state estimates in a network of sensors. For coordinated control of robot sensors, the control objective becomes maximisation of these information measures. A decentralised coordinated control architecture is presented. The approach taken seeks to achieve scalable solutions that maintain consistent probabalistic sensor fusion and payoff formulations. It inherits the many benefits of the DDF method including scalability, seamless handling of sub-system activation and deactivation, and interoperability among heterogeneous units. These features are demonstrated through application to practical multi-feature localisation problems on a team of indoor robots equipped with laser range finders.

1 Introduction

This paper addresses the problem of coordinating a group of mobile robots, equipped with sensors, engaged in a task of information acquisition. Several common mobile robot tasks may be formulated as problems of information acquisition, including target tracking, feature localisation, area search and exploration. The advantage of focusing on information acquisition problems is that the control objective is well defined and many tools exist for fusion of information in decentralised networks.

Figure 1 illustrates the operation of an active decentralised sensor network including: the representation, prediction and update of knowledge; placing value on the information gain achieved through sensing; choosing actions in order to maximise the expected value. In this light, approaches to active sensing can generally be categorised by three choices:

Sensor Fusion Algorithm – Combining multiple sensor observations to estimate the state of the world. Options include Bayesian estimators (e.g. Kalman or Particle filters) and non-probabilistic methods.

Payoff – Utility, cost or reward associated with the outcome of decisions. Most approaches are either heuristic or related to the information in the fusion process.

Control Solution – A decision rule or policy chosen to maximise the payoff. Methods differ in the use of discrete or parametric representations of the system states and actions.

F. Zhao and L. Guibas (Eds.): IPSN 2003, LNCS 2634, pp. 96–112, 2003.
© Springer-Verlag Berlin Heidelberg 2003

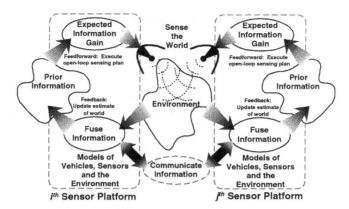

Fig. 1. Information flow in an active multi-sensor system. Models of vehicles, sensors and the environment provide means to capture and predict *a priori* the expected utility associated with a sequence of actions. Choosing appropriate actions requires solution to an optimal control problem. Fusing observed and communicated information updates the knowledge on which subsequent actions are selected.

The approach taken in this work seeks to achieve scalable solutions that maintain consistent probabilistic sensor fusion and payoff formulations. Sensor fusion is performed by the Decentralised Data Fusion (DDF) method [1] reviewed briefly in Appendix A. Only node-to-node communication and only local system knowledge are permitted in this method. This approach results in remarkably simple nodal algorithms with no central processing or communication facilities. The scalable coordinated control policies developed in this paper rely on this mechanism.

Existing approaches differ from that presented here in one or more aspects. Probabilistic approaches are distinguished by the choice of utility formulation and the estimation method. Zhao [2], Spletzer [3] and Burgard [4] apply probabilistic estimation techniques which are more flexible than the Kalman filter, but at the expense of computational effort, scalability and algorithm decentralisation.

Zhao [2] compares various information related utility formulations. Heuristic approaches such as Pirjanian [5] and Parker [6] are attractive because of their scalability and relatively low computational effort. Structure is imposed on the solution though geometric utility functions or low level controllers that relate to desirable steady state sensor configurations. But the system performance may suffer as they do not explicitly value prior knowledge, sensor characteristics and the evolution of uncertainty over time.

The rest of this paper is organised as follows. Section 2 describes the coordinated control architecture including formulation of the payoff and control solution along with a discussion of desirable characteristics. Section 3 outlines practical issues including hardware and software implementation. Simulation and experimental results are presented in Section 4.

2   Decentralised Multi-sensor Coordinated Control

In developing a decentralised control architecture, a distinction is made between coordinated and cooperative solutions. A *cooperative solution* is considered to be a predictive optimal negotiated group decision in the sense of a Nash equilibrium. In *coordinated solutions* there is no mechanism for this negotiated outcome. Decision makers act locally but exchange information that may influence each others subsequent decisions. A coordinated solution architecture is presented along with descriptions of the information-theoretic payoff used and control solution procedure. A negotiated cooperative solution in which decision makers are aware of and account for the cumulative expected observation information is detailed in [7].

2.1   Payoff for Information Gathering Tasks

Kalman filter algorithms generate an estimate of the state $\hat{\mathbf{x}}(t)$ together with an uncertainty measure, typically represented as a covariance matrix $\mathbf{P}(t)$. In DDF methods, these are replaced by the mathematically equivalent information filters which generate estimates of the information state $\hat{\mathbf{y}}(t)$ and the corresponding Fisher Information matrix $\mathbf{Y}(t)$ which are related to the state and covariance as:

$$\mathbf{Y}(t) = \mathbf{P}^{-1}(t), \quad \hat{\mathbf{y}}(t) = \mathbf{Y}(t)\hat{\mathbf{x}}(t) \tag{1}$$

The evolution of Fisher information in continuous linearised filtering is given by a Ricatti equation describing the information form of the Kalman filter

$$\underbrace{\dot{\mathbf{Y}}(t)}_{\substack{\text{Information} \\ \text{Rate}}} = \underbrace{- \mathbf{F}(t)\mathbf{Y}(t) - \mathbf{F}^T(t)\mathbf{Y}(t)}_{\substack{\text{Loss or Gain Through} \\ \text{Process Dynamics}}} - \underbrace{\mathbf{Y}(t)\mathbf{Q}(t)\mathbf{Y}(t)}_{\substack{\text{Loss Through} \\ \text{Process Noise}}} + \underbrace{\sum_{i=1}^{n} \mathbf{H}_i^T(t)\mathbf{R}_i^{-1}(t)\mathbf{H}_i(t)}_{\substack{\text{Gain Through} \\ \text{Observations}}}.$$

$$\tag{2}$$

Equation 2 describes how the system dynamics $\mathbf{F}$, process noise $\mathbf{Q}$ and observations $\mathbf{I}_i(t) = \mathbf{H}_i^T(t)\mathbf{R}^{-1}(t)\mathbf{H}_i(t)$ affect the probability distributions involved in the fusion process. The matrices $\mathbf{F}, \mathbf{Q}, \mathbf{R}$ and $\mathbf{H}_i$ are all potentially functions of the estimate $\hat{\mathbf{x}}$ of the environment, sensor platform and sensor states and the control inputs $\mathbf{u}$ to the vehicle and sensor systems. Entropy or Shannon information provides a natural quantitative measure of information in terms of the compactness of the probability distributions. For the n-dimensional Gaussian distributions considered, entropy provides a volumetric measure of information related to the determinant of the Fisher information matrix by

$$i(\mathbf{x}(k)) = \frac{1}{2} \log[(2\pi e)^n | \mathbf{Y}(k \mid k) |]. \tag{3}$$

Most importantly, the probabilistic modelling allows *a priori* prediction of the expected information outcome associated with a sequence of actions. For an action sequence $\mathbf{u}$ over N prediction and update stages, the change in entropy or mutual information gain provides a measure of the expected utility

$$\mathbf{J}(\mathbf{u}) = \frac{1}{2} \log \left[\frac{| \mathbf{Y}(k + N \mid \{\mathbf{u}, k - 1\}) |}{| \mathbf{Y}(k \mid k - 1) |} \right]. \tag{4}$$

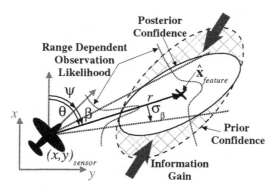

Fig. 2. Dependence of expected posterior information and information gain on prior information and relative location for a bearings-only sensor.

Example: Payoff for a Bearings-Only Sensor

Figure 2 shows a visual interpretation of the mutual information gain performance metric for the case of a sensor platform making bearings-only observations of a point feature.

Given the sensor platform heading angle $\psi(k)$ at time k, the observation model for a bearings measurement $\beta(k) = \mathbf{h}(\mathbf{x}(k))$ is

$$\mathbf{z}(k) = \beta(k) + \nu(k) = \hat{\theta}(k) - \psi(k) + \nu(k), \quad \hat{\theta}(k) = \arctan\left[\frac{\hat{y}_f(k) - y_s(k)}{\hat{x}_f(k) - x_s(k)}\right] \quad (5)$$

The Jacobian of the observation model with respect to the feature state estimate is

$$\mathbf{H}(k) = \nabla_{\hat{\mathbf{x}}}\mathbf{h}(\hat{\mathbf{x}}(k \mid k-1), \mathbf{x}_s)$$
$$= 1/\hat{r}(k)\left[-\sin\hat{\theta}(k), \cos\hat{\theta}(k)\right].$$

The expected observation Fisher information is

$$\mathbf{I}_\beta(k) = \mathbf{H}^T(k)\mathbf{R}^{-1}\mathbf{H}(k)$$
$$= \frac{1}{\sigma_\beta^2\hat{r}^2(k)}\begin{bmatrix} \sin^2\hat{\theta}(k) & -\sin\hat{\theta}(k)\cos\hat{\theta}(k) \\ -\sin\hat{\theta}(k)\cos\hat{\theta}(k) & \cos^2\hat{\theta}(k) \end{bmatrix} \quad (6)$$

The observation information depends on the relative range and bearing to the feature. The value of the sensing configuration and prior information is captured by the sensor model and the expected utility measure of Equation 4.

2.2   Coordinated Control

Local decision making builds upon the decentralised data fusion algorithm. This control algorithm predicts and maximises the expected information gain from local sensors without any knowledge of the choices made by other decision makers. The information on which the action selection is based is coupled through a static information structure. The DDF process propagates the current or delayed observation information throughout the network. This is fused with local information altering the prior on which subsequent local decisions are made. Consequently, by simply activating DDF network with independent

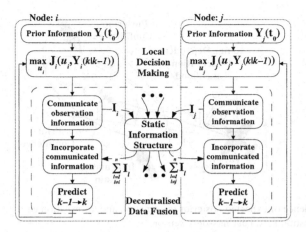

Fig. 3. Multi-platform coordinated decision making with a static information structure. The information structure is formed through a network interface at each decision maker. This allows the individual decision maker to incorporate the influence of other team members' observations over time, and inform the team of their own observations.

control rules at each node, leads to a coordinated control solution. The procedure is illustrated in Figure 3. It should be emphasised that this solution approach is fully decentralised. The static information structure consists of a communication network, a communication protocol and interface at each decision maker. The decision making and communication management mechanisms are internal to each system node. The only component external to the decision-making nodes is the medium and protocol through which they communicate.

2.3   Control Solution

The motion of platforms and sensors is subject to constrained dynamics. Modelling of platforms, sensors and environment as a set of continuous states, together with the use of information as payoff, allows the information acquisition problem to be formulated as a standard optimal control problem. For a system described by a set of ODEs, subject to constraints $\mathbf{c}(\boldsymbol{x}(t), \boldsymbol{u}(t)) = 0$, $\mathbf{g}(\boldsymbol{x}(t), \boldsymbol{u}(t)) \leq 0$, find the optimal control $\mathbf{u}^*(t)$ such that

$$\dot{\mathbf{x}}(t) = \boldsymbol{f}(\mathbf{x}(t), \mathbf{u}(t)) \ t \in [t_0 \ t_f] \tag{7}$$

$$\text{find } \mathbf{u}^*(t) = \arg\max_{\mathbf{u} \in \mathbf{U}} \mathbf{J}(\mathbf{x}(t), \mathbf{u}(t)) \tag{8}$$

The control vector parameterisation described by Goh [8] is used to determine a direct numerical solution on a receding time horizon.

2.4   Features of This Approach

Information-theoretic models offer a mathematically rigorous method of modelling large-scale sensor systems. Decentralised methods allow information gathering and decision making systems to be described in a modular and endogeneous manner. The global system can be considered as a system of interacting systems. Transparent handling of system heterogeneity, dynamic (re)configureability and scalability are particularly desirable characteristics of this approach.

Achieving Scalability

Inter-dependencies among the states of components of a network of sensors and actuators can lead to situations where the complexity of the estimation and control problem grows with the number of nodes. These dependencies arise when the sensor states, state estimates and observations are functionally dependent or statistically correlated. Fortunately, a broadly applicable class of practically useful situations exist where such dependencies either don"t exist, can be safely ignored or conservatively accounted for. In these cases the inter-nodal communication and nodal computational requirements are independent of the number of system nodes. A specific situation of interest where this occurs is when sensor platforms with known state observe an unknown environment. In this case the complexity of the estimation and control problem at each node is determined only by the dimension of the environment representation.

Handling Sensor and Sensor Platform Heterogeneity

This sensor fusion and control architecture requires explicit modelling of each component sensor and sensor platform. This modelling provides allows for specific sensor and platform details to be abstracted away at the information level. Observed and communicated information is propagated throughout the sensing and control network without knowledge of the nature of its source. The abstraction provided by the sensor observation model is illustrated by considering observation of a point feature by a heterogeneous sensor team composed of range-only and bearing-only sensors. For a range-only sensor the expected observation Fisher information is

$$\mathbf{I}_r(k) = \frac{1}{\sigma_{\mathbf{r}}^2} \begin{bmatrix} \cos^2 \hat{\theta}(k) & \sin \hat{\theta}(k) \cos \hat{\theta}(k) \\ \sin \hat{\theta}(k) \cos \hat{\theta}(k) & \sin^2 \hat{\theta}(k) \end{bmatrix} \tag{9}$$

The expected observation for a bearing only sensor is given by Equation 6. Data fusion amounts to communicating and summing the sensor information matrices $\mathbf{I}_{(\cdot)}(k)$ and vectors $\mathbf{i}_{(\cdot)}(k)$ (see Appendix A). The details only relevant to the individual sensors, in this case the sensor type, accuracy and relative distance to the feature are not communicated.

Heterogeneity of system components may be advantageous and is often required or unavoidable. It does not alter the algorithms and architecture fundamental to fusion, control and communication in distributed sensing.

Dynamic (Re)Configureability

Channel filters at each node manage inter-nodal connections and communication. These connections can be established dynamically allowing online addition of newly activated systems and recovery from system deactivation. An interface to the communications protocol in information form is all that is required to allow incorporation of an additional system into this architecture. Reconfiguration simply amounts to connecting or removing components having this decentralised interface. Particularly desirable from a systems engineering viewpoint is that implementing this on a new subsystem allows its use in the network without modification to existing systems. Enabling larger systems composed from decentralised sensing and control nodes to effortlessly acquire their complementary or redundant capabilities.

3   Implementation

This section focuses on practical aspects of the decentralised control architecture including hardware and software implementation. Section 3 focuses on the inter-node organisation while Section 3.1 provides details of the structure on the network level. Section 3.3 describes the details of applying the decentralised control architecture to a team of indoor robots.

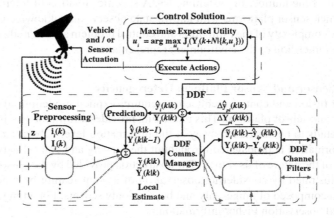

Fig. 4. Structure of a coordinated sensing node.

3.1   Node Architecture

A schematic of the inter-node architecture is shown in Figure 4. The DDF node is represented by the dashed frame in the centre. A bank of sensor preprocessing units connects the node to a set of sensors. Similarly, a bank of channel filters connects the node to a set of its neighbours in the DDF network. The control block calculates the control vector which maximises the expected payoff over the chosen time horizon. Notice that the shown configuration implements a controller which is *centralised* within the DDF node and is, therefore, a special case of a more general, fully decentralised, arrangement. The trade-offs inherent in this design decision are currently under investigation.

3.2   Network Architecture

A schematic of the DDF network is shown in Figure 5. Any number of nodes may be attached to a single platform. A static tree architecture was selected due to its simplicity

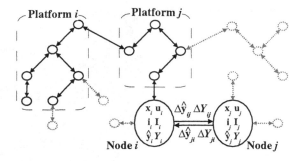

Fig. 5. Sensor and sensor platform network structure

and availability of theoretical results. Despite the pre-assigned connectivity structure, this network architecture is truly decentralised as no node needs to know the global topology in order to implement the DDF algorithm. According to the algorithm, the neighbouring nodes exchange new information in the form of $\Delta\hat{y}_{ij}$ and ΔY_{ij} as described in Appendix A.

3.3 Application to an Indoor Robot Team

The benefits of the decentralised control architecture are demonstrated on a team of indoor robots performing an information gathering task. A team of Pioneer robots equipped with laser range finders was used in the experiments. The bearing-only feature localisation was implemented by disregarding the range information available from the laser sensors. Experiments with other sensors, such as video cameras, are under way.

The property of DDF to abstract away the observation models of the individual sensors was complemented by a hardware abstraction layer provided by Player – an open-source robot server developed at USC [9].

The performance validation task for a large and complex system such as a sensor network is time consuming due to the statistical nature of performance metrics. In this situation, a realistic environment simulator is an invaluable tool. Stage [10] provides realistic 2-D simulation of indoor environment for the Pioneer family of robots and a set of common sensors. It also provides a maximum degree of code reuse in the transition from simulation to experiment.

Figure 6 illustrates the relationship between simulation, experiments, and the abstract notion of a DDF network. In this experiment, three Pioneer robots are performing the task of localising a set of stationary point features present in the environment. The features are marked with light-reflecting strips placed on the walls and free-standing poles. The robots in simulation and in the experiments are placed in the same positions relative to the features. Platform pose information is provided by the simulation engine in the former case and by a beacon localisation system in the latter.

The graphical user interface (GUI) developed for monitoring and interacting with the decentralised sensing and control network is shown in Figure 6(c). The topology of the DDF network is shown with dashed lines connecting the platforms into a star network with a centre at platform P1. One of the network branches connects platform

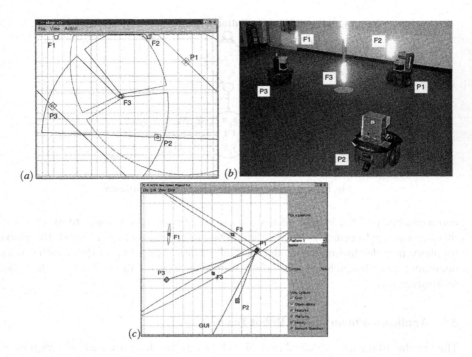

Fig. 6. Three Figures displaying a feature localisation problem (a) in Stage simulation environment, (b) the experimental setup using Pioneer robots, SICK laser scanning sensors and lasers beacons, and (c) on the GUI developed for monitoring and interacting with the decentralised sensing and control network.

P1 with the GUI node. Since the GUI node is an ordinary DDF node, it is exposed to the same information flow as the rest of the nodes and it can be attached at any point in the network. Furthermore, several GUI nodes with different purposes and capabilities may be present in the same network at the same time.

In one respect a GUI node is different from the rest of the network. It may be capable of accumulating non-local information about the network itself, such as the global topology shown in Figure 6(c). This information is used purely for visualisation purposes and, therefore, does not undermine the decentralised nature of the DDF approach.

The known features and their position uncertainty is shown with relatively small ellipses. Large ellipses represent the uncertainty of the latest observations made by platform P1. The difference in the size of the ellipses is due to the information accumulation inherent in the data fusion process.

Despite the intuitive representation of uncertainty currently present in the estimate of the feature locations, it is important to appreciate the abstract nature of the view provided by the GUI. Indeed, neither the individual nodes (including the GUI node), nor the DDF network in general, nor the controllers on the platforms are aware of the nature of the information source which led to the overall picture.

4   Results in Multi-platform Multi-feature Localisation

The use of information measures as a performance index in control problems is best illustrated through a motivational example. The bearings-only feature localisation problem is considered. Studies such as that by Oshman and Davidson [11] consider the single platform problem from an optimal control perspective. The vehicle control action and trajectory is sought that minimises the determinant of the feature error covariance at a fixed terminal time t_f. This is equivalent to maximising final information or information gain. This example is extended to multiple vehicles to demonstrate coordinated control architecture from Section 2.

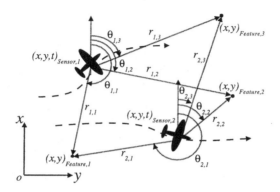

Fig. 7. 2D Multi-Vehicle Multi-Feature Localisation Problem

4.1   Problem Formulation

The problem consists of n sensor platforms $i = 1, \ldots, n$, localising m point features $j = 1, \ldots, m$. Each platform is moving in the xy plane with constant velocity V_i. The vehicle's location and heading at time t is captured in the state $\mathbf{x}_{s,i}(t)$. The single control variable $\mathbf{u}_i(t)$ for each platform is the heading rate.

$$\mathbf{x}_{s,i}(t) = \begin{bmatrix} x(t) \\ y_i(t) \\ \psi_i(t) \end{bmatrix}, \quad \dot{\mathbf{x}}_{s,i}(t) = \begin{bmatrix} V_i \cos \psi_i(t) \\ V_i \sin \psi_i(t) \\ \mathbf{u}_i(t) \end{bmatrix} \tag{10}$$

The features are modelled as stationary points on the xy plane modelled by two Gaussian random variables representing feature location $\mathbf{x}_{f,j} = [x_{f,j}, y_{f,j}]^T$. Each feature location is estimated by the conditional mean $\hat{\mathbf{x}}_{f,j}(k \mid k) = \mathrm{E}\{\mathbf{x}_{f,j}(k) \mid \mathbf{Z}^k\}$. The feature location uncertainty is captured by the covariance of the two dimensional Gaussian distribution $\mathbf{P}_{f,j}(k \mid k) = \mathrm{E}\{(\mathbf{x}_{f,j} - \hat{\mathbf{x}}_{f,j}(k \mid k))^T (\mathbf{x}_{f,j} - \hat{\mathbf{x}}_{f,j}(k \mid k)) \mid \mathbf{Z}^k\}$. In the information filter this is represented by the inverse covariance $\mathbf{Y}_{f,j}(k \mid k) = \mathbf{P}_{f,j}^{-1}(k \mid k)$. The feature state is not influenced by control input and has no process noise.

The global system equations are composed from these individual models. The global state consists of the current sensor platform locations and headings, feature location estimates and feature error covariance. Each vehicle maintains a local estimate of the feature states and a map of the feature information given by

$$\hat{\mathbf{x}}_f(k \mid k) = \begin{bmatrix} \hat{\mathbf{x}}_{f,1}(k \mid k) \\ \vdots \\ \hat{\mathbf{x}}_{f,m}(k \mid k) \end{bmatrix} = \mathbf{Y}_f^{-1}(k \mid k)\hat{\mathbf{y}}_f(k \mid k) \tag{11}$$

$$\mathbf{Y}_f(k \mid k) = \begin{bmatrix} \mathbf{Y}_{f,1}(k \mid k) & 0 & \cdots & 0 \\ 0 & \mathbf{Y}_{f,2}(k \mid k) & & \vdots \\ \vdots & & \ddots & 0 \\ 0 & \cdots & 0 & \mathbf{Y}_{f,m}(k \mid k) \end{bmatrix} \tag{12}$$

The local Fisher information prediction is simply

$$\mathbf{Y}_{f,j}(l+1 \mid \{\mathbf{u}, k-1\}) = \mathbf{Y}_{f,j}(l \mid \{\mathbf{u}, k-1\}) + \mathbf{I}_j(l \mid \mathbf{u}), \tag{13}$$

for $l = k, ..., k+N-1$. The state vector of interest to each sensor platform is the vehicle state combined with predicted feature Fisher information. The vehicle state is stacked with the 3 distinct elements of each 2x2 symmetric matrix.

$$\mathbf{x}_i(k) = \begin{bmatrix} \mathbf{x}_{s,i}(k) \\ \mathbf{x}_{f,1}(k) \\ \vdots \\ \mathbf{x}_{f,m}(k) \end{bmatrix}, \text{ where } \mathbf{x}_{f,j}(k) = \begin{bmatrix} Y_{x,j}(k) \\ Y_{xy,j}(k) \\ Y_{y,j}(k) \end{bmatrix}. \tag{14}$$

Maximising the mutual information gain is equivalent to maximising the log of the determinant of the predicted Fisher information. The expected utility used for this problem is

$$\mathbf{J}_i(\mathbf{u}) = \log \mid \mathbf{Y}_f(k+N \mid \{\mathbf{u}, k-1\}) \mid$$
$$= \sum_{j=1}^{m} \log \mid \mathbf{Y}_{f,j}(k+N \mid \{\mathbf{u}, k-1\}) \mid \tag{15}$$

4.2 A Special Control Case: Zero Look-Ahead

Planning with zero look ahead provides a special case in coordinated multi vehicle control. This can be used to form simple approximate solutions where the sensor platforms are directed by the dynamics of the mutual information rate gradient field.The Fisher information evolution in continuous linearised filtering is given by Equation 2. Using matrix calculus identities, the instantaneous rate of change of entropy, or mutual information rate is

$$\mathcal{I}(t) = \frac{1}{2}\frac{d}{dt}\log \mid \mathbf{Y}(t) \mid = \frac{1}{2}\text{trace}\left(\mathbf{Y}^{-1}(t)\dot{\mathbf{Y}}(t)\right). \tag{16}$$

Equation 16 represents a time varying vector field. It shows that the mutual information rate is determined by the current Fisher information and Equation 2. Equation 16 relates the sensor system state and control to the instantaneous rate of change of entropic information. Its gradient relates changes in the system state and control to changes in the rate of change of entropic information. Since $\mathbf{Y}(t)$ is not an explicit function of $\mathbf{x}$ or $\mathbf{u}$; the gradient field is given by

$$\nabla_{\mathbf{x}}\mathcal{I}(t) = \frac{1}{2}\text{trace}\left(\mathbf{Y}^{-1}(t)\nabla_{\mathbf{x}}\dot{\mathbf{Y}}(t)\right) \tag{17}$$

This allows evaluation of the gradient field in terms of the current Fisher information and the partial derivatives of Equation 2. Control actions can be scheduled according to the direction and magnitude of the local gradient field. In this example, the sensor platform motion is governed by the constant velocity vehicle model Equation 10. In order to maximise the information rate Equation 16, the platform should head in the direction of the gradient vector of information rate with respect to the vehicle state $\{x, y\}$

$$\psi^{\star}(t) = \arctan\left(\frac{\nabla_y\mathcal{I}(t)}{\nabla_x\mathcal{I}(t)}\right). \tag{18}$$

A simple approximate control solution is implemented by tracking $\psi^{\star}(t)$ with a constrained heading-rate controller, avoiding the multi-stage optimisation problem in Equation 8.

4.3 Results

Two solutions are presented to demonstrate the characteristics of this coordinated sensing and control framework. The first situation illustrates coordination resulting from the information shared though the DDF network. A second multi-feature, multi-vehicle example indicates transparent inter-operation among heterogeneous sensor systems.

Demonstrating Coordination: Point Feature Localisation by Two Sensor Platforms
A situation where two bearings-only sensor platforms localise a single point feature is considered in order to investigate the effect of the DDF process on the sensor platform trajectories. Two solutions are presented and discussed in Figure 8. Trajectories are shown for the same local controllers with and without the underlying DDF process activated. The comparative solutions demonstrate that coordinated control can be achieved simply by employing the DDF algorithm in the network of decision makers with local information seeking controllers.

Controlling Networks of Heterogeneous sensors
 The second example demonstrates the transparent handling of system heterogeneity by this architecture. It involves localisation of multiple point features by a team of robots equipped with different sensors; a fixed range-only sensor, a bearing-only sensor platform and a platform equipped with both range and bearing sensors. Details of an example solution are presented in Figure 9. The nodes influence the value of each others available actions through the propagation of their observation information. Selecting local actions that maximise information gain leads to platform motions that improve quality of the estimate of the environment derived from the system sensors.

4.4 Discussion

The platform trajectories in Figures 8 and 9 are a trade-off between range and bearing changes relative to the features that is affected by the existence and actions of other

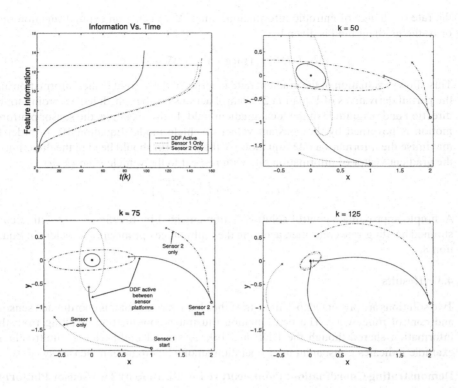

Fig. 8. Illustration of coordinated control arising through decentralised data fusion (DDF). Feature information over time is shown along with five snapshots of the locally optimal trajectories, with and without DDF active. Both vehicles implement local control laws which maximise their individual information gain from bearings-only observations given local prior knowledge. Coordination results from the DDF process updating local prior knowledge from which the optimal action is generated. There is no change in the control laws between cases.

sensors through the exchange of information over the DDF network. An isolated bearing-only vehicle tends to perform a pursuit curve to the nearest feature. Vehicles head more directly to features as prior information increases. Pairs of vehicles with bearings sensors tend to approach features at right-angles. These characteristics are not designed into low level controllers. They are artifacts of the "information seeking" control objective and the sensor, vehicle and feature modelling that agree with human intuition.

This framework provides three ingredients essential in constructing coordinated sensor networks:

Analytic: – Decentralised and information-theoretic methods provide an opportunity to analyse and reason about a system and its information gathering or decision making role. In particular, the process of local information formation, communication and assimilation, and decision making are well formulated.

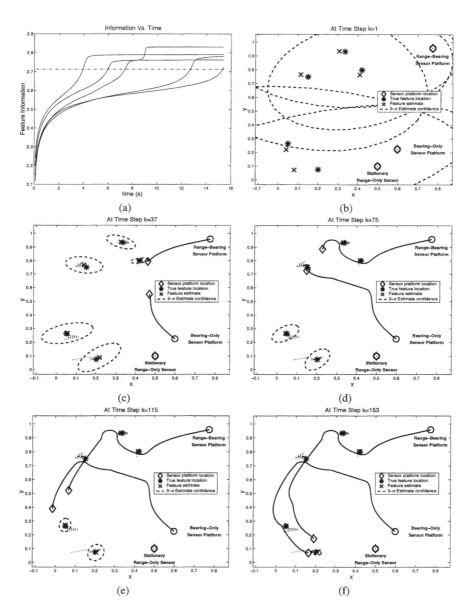

Fig. 9. Five snapshots of a coordinated feature localisation solution by decentralised heterogeneous sensor systems. The sensing system is composed from a fixed range-only sensor node, a bearing-only sensor platform node and a platform node equipped with both range and bearing sensors. Observations are transformed into information form and propagated throughout the sensing network. This anonymous information is assimilated influencing the future sensing and control actions. The system heterogeneity has implications for the capabilities and performance of the system as a whole but is not relevant to the nodal architecture and algorithms.

Composable and dynamically configurable: – Decentralised methods also provide an ability to compose mathematical descriptions of larger systems from descriptions of component sub-systems. The information filter formulation provides scalable and transparent sub-system inter-operation. Sensor, vehicle and task specific details irrelevant to the estimation task are abstracted away. Because of this, heterogeneity is handled transparently. Anonymous information is passed between system nodes which may be dynamically added or removed.

Predictive: – Information-theoretic methods provide a natural and powerful ability to predict expected "information" rewards associated with an action sequence. The system configuration is determined by coupling in the information seeking control objective rather than the interaction between characteristics embedded in low-level controllers or behaviours.

Only linearized Gaussian representations of uncertainty are considered in this analysis. This parameterization allows the formulation of a remarkably simple decentralized active sensing algorithm. A significant reduction in computation, storage and communication requirements is achieved at the expense of limiting the applicability of this framework to situations where this modeling is appropriate.

5   Conclusion

This paper presents a consistent decentralised and scalable system architecture for sensor planning. A control scheme was implemented that accomplishes coordinated execution of sensing tasks with efficient use of computational and communication resources. Decentralised coordinated control among heterogeneous sensor systems was demonstrated. Dynamic coordinated adjustment of the sensor platform spatial configuration to improve the estimate obtained from the system is the result of interaction among local information maximising controllers through the decentralised data fusion network.

References

1. Manyika, J., Durrant-Whyte, H.: Data Fusion and Sensor Management: An Information-Theoretic Approach. Prentice Hall (1994)
2. Zhao, F., Shin, J., Reich, J.: Information-driven dynamic sensor collaboration for tracking applications. IEEE Signal Processing Magazine **19** (2002) 61–72
3. Spletzer, J., Taylor, C.J.: Sensor planning and control in a dynamic environment. In: Proc. IEEE Int. Conf. Robotics and Automation. (2002) 676–681
4. Burgard, W., Fox, D., Moors, M., Simmons, R., Thrun, S.: Collaborative multi-robot exploration. In: Proc. of the IEEE Int. Conf. on Robotics and Automation (ICRA). Volume 1. (2000) 476–481
5. Pirjanian, P., Mataric, M.: Multi-robot target acquisition using multiple objective behavior coordination. In: Proc. IEEE Int. Conf. Robotics and Automation. (2000)
6. Parker, L.: Cooperative robotics for multi-target observation. Intelligent Automation and Soft Computing **5** (1999) 5–19
7. Grocholsky, B.: Information-Theoretic Control of Multiple Sensor Platforms. PhD thesis, The University of Sydney (2002) Available from http://www.acfr.usyd.edu.au.

8. Goh, C., Teo, K.: Control parameterization: A unified approach to optimal control problems with general constraints. Automatica **23** (1988) 3–18
9. Gerkey, B., Vaughan, R., Støy, K., Howard, A., Sukhatme, G., Mataric, M.: Most valuable player: A robot device server for distributed control. In: Proc. IEEE/RSJ Int. Conf. on Intelligent Robots and Systems (IROS). (2001) 1226–1231
10. Vaughan, R.T.: Stage: A multiple robot simulator. Technical Report IRIS-00-394, Institute for Robotics and Intelligent Systems, University of Southern California (2000)
11. Oshman, Y., Davidson, P.: Optimization of observer trajectories for bearings-only target localization. IEEE Trans. on Aerospace and Electronic Systems **35** (1999) 892–902
12. Grime, S., Durrant-Whyte, H.: Communication in decentralized systems. IFAC Control Eng. Practice **2** (1994) 849–863

A   The Decentralised Data Fusion Architecture

A key tool in decentralised sensor fusion systems is the information filter. A reformulation of the Kalman filter enabling scalable decentralised multi-sensor estimation. The information filter equations are stated briefly here. A full derivation can be found in [1]. Consider a system described in standard linear form

$$\mathbf{x}(k) = \mathbf{F}(k)\mathbf{x}(k-1) + \mathbf{G}(k)\mathbf{w}(k), \tag{19}$$

where $\mathbf{x}(j)$ is the n dimensional state vector of interest at time j, $\mathbf{F}(k)$ is the state transition matrix from time $k-1$ to k, and $\mathbf{G}(k)$ the noise input transition matrix, and where $\mathbf{w}(k)$ is the associated process noise input modelled as an uncorrelated white sequence with $E\{\mathbf{w}(i)\mathbf{w}^T(j)\} = \delta_{ij}\mathbf{Q}(i)$. The system is observed by a sensor according to the non-linear observation model

$$\mathbf{z}(k) = \mathbf{h}(k, \mathbf{x}(k)) + \mathbf{v}(k) \tag{20}$$

where $\mathbf{z}(k)$ is the vector of observations made at time k, and where $\mathbf{v}(k)$ is the associated observation noise modelled as an uncorrelated white sequence with $E\{\mathbf{v}(i)\mathbf{v}^T(j)\} = \delta_{ij}\mathbf{R}(i)$. The information form of the Kalman filter is obtained by replacing the representation of the state estimate $\hat{\mathbf{x}}$ and covariance $\mathbf{P}$ with the information state $\hat{\mathbf{y}}$ and Fisher information $\mathbf{Y}$. Notation $(i \mid j)$ is introduced to indicate a value at time i, conditional on observation information obtained up to time j. The information state and information matrix are defined as

$$\hat{\mathbf{y}}(i \mid j) \triangleq \mathbf{P}^{-1}(i \mid j)\hat{\mathbf{x}}(i \mid j),$$

$$\mathbf{Y}(i \mid j) \triangleq \mathbf{P}^{-1}(i \mid j), \tag{21}$$

and the information associated with an observation in the form

$$\mathbf{i}(k) \triangleq \mathbf{H}^T(k)\mathbf{R}^{-1}(k)(\mathbf{z}(k) - \mathbf{h}(\hat{\mathbf{x}}(k \mid k-1)) + \mathbf{H}(k)\hat{\mathbf{x}}(k \mid k-1),$$

$$\mathbf{I}(k) \triangleq \mathbf{H}^T(k)\mathbf{R}^{-1}(k)\mathbf{H}(k). \tag{22}$$

Where $\mathbf{H}^T(\cdot)$ is the Jacobian $\nabla_{\mathbf{x}}\mathbf{h}(\cdot)$. With these definitions, the information filter can be summarised in two stages as:

Prediction:

$$\mathbf{Y}(k \mid k-1) = \left[\mathbf{F}(k)\mathbf{Y}^{-1}(k-1 \mid k-1)\mathbf{F}^T(k) + \mathbf{Q}(k)\right]^{-1},$$

$$\hat{\mathbf{y}}(k \mid k-1) = \mathbf{Y}(k \mid k-1)\mathbf{F}(k)\mathbf{Y}^{-1}(k-1 \mid k-1)\hat{\mathbf{y}}(k-1 \mid k-1). \tag{23}$$

Estimation:

$$\mathbf{Y}(k \mid k) = \mathbf{Y}(k \mid k-1) + \sum_{i=1}^{N} \mathbf{I}_i(k),$$

$$\hat{\mathbf{y}}(k \mid k) = \hat{\mathbf{y}}(k \mid k-1) + \sum_{i=1}^{N} \mathbf{i}_i(k). \tag{24}$$

Where $\mathbf{I}_i(k)$ and $\mathbf{i}_i(k)$ are the information matrix and information state contributions of the sensors $i = 1, \ldots, N$. The posterior state estimate may be obtained from

$$\hat{\mathbf{x}}(k \mid k) = \mathbf{Y}^{-1}(k \mid k)\hat{\mathbf{y}}(k \mid k). \tag{25}$$

The information-filter form has the advantage that the update Equations 24 for the estimator are computationally simpler than the equations for the Kalman Filter, at the cost of increased complexity in prediction. The additive and associative property of information in the estimation stage is the key to scalable, decentralised data fusion. All system nodes can be made aware of global information through propagation of inter-node information differences through a communication network. This is studied in detail by Grime [12]. A channel filter at each fusion node manages the accumulation and communication of information. The inter-node communications requirement for this architecture is independent of the number of fusion nodes.

The algorithm is described graphically in Figure 4. Essentially, local estimates are first generated at each node by fusing (adding) locally available observation information $\mathbf{i}_i(k)$ with locally available prior information $\hat{\mathbf{y}}_i(k \mid k-1)$. This yields a local information estimate $\tilde{\mathbf{y}}_i(k \mid k)$. The difference between this local estimate and prediction (corresponding to new information gained) is then transmitted to other nodes in the network. In a fully connected or broadcast network, this results in every sensing node getting all new information. Communicated information is then assimilated simply by summing with the local information. An important point to note is that, after this step, the locally available estimates are *exactly* the same as if the data fusion problem had been solved on a single central processor using a monolithic formulation of the conventional Kalman filter.

Distributed Group Management for Track Initiation and Maintenance in Target Localization Applications

Juan Liu, Jie Liu, James Reich, Patrick Cheung, and Feng Zhao

Palo Alto Research Center
3333 Coyote Hill Road, Palo Alto, CA94304, USA
{juan.liu, jieliu, jreich, pcheung, zhao}@parc.com

Abstract. The tradeoff between performance and scalability is a fundamental issue in distributed sensor networks. In this paper, we propose a novel scheme to efficiently organize and utilize network resources for target localization. Motivated by the essential role of geographic proximity in sensing, sensors are organized into geographically local collaborative groups. In a target tracking context, we present a dynamic group management method to initiate and maintain multiple tracks in a distributed manner. Collaborative groups are formed, each responsible for tracking a single target. The sensor nodes within a group coordinate their behavior using geographically-limited message passing. Mechanisms such as these for managing local collaborations are essential building blocks for scalable sensor network applications.

1 Introduction

The study of distributed sensor networks is emerging as an exciting interdisciplinary research area, including aspects of signal processing, networking, distributed algorithms, and MEMS sensor technology. A wireless sensor network can be easily deployed in places where there is no a priori sensing infrastructure. This flexibility has led to an increasing interest in using these networks for large-scale applications such as environmental monitoring, security surveillance, and battlefield awareness. In contrast to traditional centralized sensor array processing where all processing occurs on a central processor, sensor networks distribute the computation among sensor units. Each sensor unit acquires local, partial, and relatively crude information from its surroundings. By exploiting the sensor network's spatial coverage and multiplicity of sensing modalities, the network can arrive at a good global estimate.

A key issue in distributed sensor networks is scalability, in both energy and spatial dimensions. Desirably, sensor networks must simultaneously track multiple phenomena, working within tight communication bandwidth, energy, and processing speed limits. Thus, it is critical to distribute the workload in an equitable way across only the "relevant" sensors, and leave other sensors available for other tasks. In this paper, we focus on target tracking applications, and present

F. Zhao and L. Guibas (Eds.): IPSN 2003, LNCS 2634, pp. 113–128, 2003.

a scalable track initiation and maintenance scheme based on collaboration between sensors in local groups. The scheme is built on the basis of our previous work [1,2] on single target tracking. To set up the proper context, we first briefly introduce the tracking problem.

1.1   Target Tracking Using Distributed Sensor Networks

Tracking is one of the major uses of sensor networks, essential in many commercial and military applications, such as traffic monitoring, facility security, and battlefield situational awareness. Assume a two-dimensional sensor field and a point target moving in it. The goal of a tracking system is to estimate the target location $x^{(t)}$ based on sensor measurements.

Each sensor node has a local measurement of the target over time. To be able to incorporate measurements from heterogeneous sensors, we use a statistical fusion method, where all sensor measurements are combined probabilistically in a common state space, based on the observational likelihood $p(z^{(t)}|x^{(t)})$. For sensor i, $\mathbf{z}_i^{(t)} = \{z_i^{(0)}, z_i^{(1)}, \cdots, z_i^{(t)}\}$ represents its local measurements, where the superscript indexes time. Let $\overline{z^{(t)}} = \{\mathbf{z}_1^{(t)}, \mathbf{z}_2^{(t)}, \cdots, \mathbf{z}_n^{(t)}\}$, where n is the number of nodes. The sensor network collectively computes the posterior belief $p(x^{(t)}|\overline{z^{(t)}})$ through Bayesian inference.

Noticing that the majority of the sensor measurements has little contribution to the global estimation of the target trajectory, we designed in [1] a leader-based tracking scheme to minimize resource usage. At any time instant t, there is only one leader k, which takes a new measurement $z_k^{(t)}$ and updates its estimate of the target location using sequential Bayesian filtering [3]. Based on this updated belief, the leader *selects* the most "informative" sensor (according to some criterion measuring information gain) from its neighborhood, and passes it the updated belief $p(x^{(t)}|\overline{z^{(t)}})$. This new sensor becomes the next leader at time $t+\delta$ (where δ is the communication delay), the previous leader returns to an idle state, and the process of sensing, estimation, and leader selection repeats. We call this approach *information-driven sensor query* (IDSQ).

1.2   Organization of This Paper

In theory, the IDSQ algorithm is scalable since all sensors except one (the leader) are in the idle state, freeing them to track other targets or perform other tasks. Thus, the number of active nodes is proportional only to the number of targets, and is independent of the size of the sensor network. However, without proper ways of initiating new target tracks and maintaining local collaboration groups, scalability cannot be achieved in practice. We need a mechanism to decide who is responsible for initialization and how to handle contention between multiple sensors detecting the same target. Furthermore, the co-existence of multiple tracks leads to the problem of track maintenance. Special care must be taken when two targets come into the vicinity of each other.

This paper establishes our solution to track initiation and maintenance problems in the following steps. Sec. 2 motivates the idea of organizing sensors into geographically-based local collaborative groups. Collectively, a group is responsible for the initiation and maintenance of one track (presumably corresponding to a single target). Sec. 3 describes in detail how a track is initiated, including detection and an efficient leader election scheme. Sec. 4 describes the algorithm for track maintenance, handling situations such as merging and splitting tracks. Overall, sensor nodes within the group coordinate their behavior by passing messages. Sec. 5 covers an implementation of the algorithms and an experiment on target tracking. Finally, we discuss in Sec. 6 the implications of distributed group management for more general sensor network applications.

2   Motivating Geographically-Based Group Management

A fundamental problem in sensor network design is the tradeoff between performance and scalability. Traditional centralized schemes move all sensor data to a central site and process it. While this is provably optimal in estimation performance, it exhibits poor scalability. The complexity of computation and communication grows rapidly with the total number of sensors, making these schemes impractical for sensor-rich systems. An interesting idea for balancing performance and scalability is to organize sensors into collaborative groups. Take tracking of some physical phenomena as an example. Sensors which jointly provide the best information about a phenomenon should form a group. Sensors which are less informative, or whose data are redundant, could be left out. By limiting the collaboration to a small number of sensors in a limited area, communication and computation are made independent of the size of network. Since the group contains the most informative sensors, impact on the tracking performance will be limited.

In practical sensor network applications, the effects of physical phenomena usually attenuate with distance, producing a decreasing signal-to-noise ratio (SNR) and lower-quality observations. This points toward the idea of geographically-based collaborative groups. In the target tracking problem, for example, we can organize the sensor network into geographical regions, as illustrated in Fig. 1. Sensors in the region around target A are responsible for tracking A, and the region around B handles B. Partitioning the network into local regions assigns network resources according to the potential contributions of individual sensors.

Furthermore, the physical phenomena being sensed change over time. This implies that the collaborative groups also need to be dynamic. As the target moves, the local region must move with it. Sensor nodes that were previously outside of the group may join the group, and current members may drop out. This requires some method for managing group membership dynamically.

Geographically-based group initiation and management have to be achieved by a light-weight protocol distributed on all sensor nodes. The protocol needs to be powerful enough to handle complex situations such as those where data from

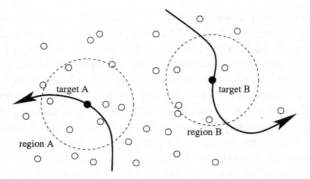

Fig. 1. Geographically-based collaborative groups. The small circles are sensor nodes. The nodes inside a specified geographical region (e.g., region A or B) form a collaborative group.

multiple leaders are contending for processing resources, and be robust enough to tolerate poor communication qualities such as out-of-order delivery and lost or delayed packets. In addition, the propagation region of group management messages should be restrained to only the relevant nodes without flooding the entire network. This is not trivial considering that the group membership is dynamic as the targets move, and that the network is formed in an *ad hoc* way such that no nodes have the knowledge of the global network topology. The difficulties are tackled in our approach by taking advantages of two facts: 1) a leader-based tracking algorithm where at any time each group has a unique leader who knows the geographical region of the collaboration; and 2) recent advances in geographical-based network routing [4,5] that do not require the leader to know the exact members of its group.

3   Distributed Detection and Track Initiation

Consider a distributed sensor network monitoring a large field. When there is no target in the field, the sensor nodes should be in an energy-saving mode. They should watch for possible targets using only low-cost computation and a minimal amount of communication. When a target enters the sensor field, the nodes need to select a leader and give it an initial belief state $p(x^{(0)}|z^{(0)})$. In this section, we describe an efficient geographically-based group formation scheme to accomplish this task. The algorithm is sketched out below, with more details in Secs. 3.1 — 3.4:

1. Each individual sensor performs a stand-alone detection by comparing the measurement with a precomputed threshold corresponding to the likelihood ratio test (LRT) described in Sec. 3.1.
2. Nodes with detections form a collaborative group and elect a single leader.
3. The leader suppresses all nodes in the collaborative group from further detection in order to prevent creation of multiple tracks for the same target.

4. The leader initializes the belief state $p(x^{(0)}|z^{(0)})$ and starts the tracking algorithm.

Throughout the algorithm's development, we assume that the nodes are globally time-synchronized up to some reasonable (e.g., sub-second) accuracy and communication between nodes are relatively reliable, though the group management scheme is designed with some robustness against occasional packet losses. We also assume nodes are aware of their one-hop neighborhood.

3.1 Target Detection on Individual Nodes

In many practical applications, activity within the network is sparse, and most of the sensor nodes spend the majority of their time in low-duty-cycle detection modes. Only when a target enters the region does the sensor field become actively involved in tracking. Since detection is the most frequent mode, the detection algorithm must be light-weight in terms of computation and communication. This helps maintain the longevity and stealth of the sensor network.

In distributed sensor networks, one can combine the measurements of multiple sensors to reach a detection decision, as done in [6], but such approaches require communication between multiple sensor nodes. The communication cost is significant because of the frequency of the detection operation. Here we take a simple standalone target detection approach, where each individual sensor detects independently of the others. The group collaboration scheme takes effects only after interesting phenomena have been detected. Much of the benefit of multi-node detections can also be realized by a two-stage detection process, with the first stage being single-node detections set conservatively to minimize missed targets, and the second stage verifying these detections using a multi-node process to minimize false alarms.

In single node detection, each node needs a decision rule to decide whether a target is present within some pre-specified detection range R_{detect} of itself. For this task, a common approach is LRT, which compares two hypotheses:

H_0: target not present, or outside of the detection range, i.e., $d(x, L_{sensor}) \geq R_{detect}$, where x is the target location, L_{sensor} is the sensor location, and $d(\cdot, \cdot)$ measures the Euclidean distance. The possibility of target not present is equivalent to $d(x, L_{sensor}) = \infty$, hence is included in this hypothesis.

H_1: target present in the detection range, i.e., $d(x, L_{sensor}) < R_{detect}$.

Assuming the two hypotheses are equally probable (i.e., no prior knowledge about whether the target is present or not), the decision rule takes the form:

$$p(z|H_0) \underset{H_1}{\overset{H_0}{\gtrless}} p(z|H_1), \qquad (1)$$

i.e., detection is declared if the presence hypothesis is more likely than the absence hypothesis. This decision rule guarantees the smallest probability of error.

Besides the standard LRT, other decision rules are also applicable and have similar forms. Depending on the application requirements, one might use the Neyman-Pearson rule [7], which maximizes the detection probability while keeping the false alarm probability below a specified value, or the minimax decision rule [7], which is more conservative and optimizes for worst case scenarios.

Let us illustrate a LRT using a sensing model similar to that in [1]. Assume a sensor network consists of microphone-based acoustic sensors. The sound wave received at the microphone takes the form:

$$f(t) = \frac{S(t - \tau)}{d(x, L_{sensor})} + n(t). \tag{2}$$

where t indexes time, $S(t)$ is the wave emitted by the target, τ is the wave propagation delay, and $n(t)$ is the measurement noise. The model is justifiable from the physics of wave propagation, assuming it is lossless and isotropic [8]. We further assume that signal and noise are statistically independent. The signal has energy denoted as E_s, and the noise sequence $n(t)$ is white with zero mean and some known variance σ_n^2.

Acoustic energy sensors compute the sound energy $z = \frac{1}{N} \sum_{t=1}^{N} |f(t)|^2$, where N is the buffer size. Based on z, the sensor decides whether a target is present. Under the sensing model described above, by the Central Limit Theorem [3], the observation $p(z|x)$ is approximately Gaussian with parameters:

- mean= $E_s/d^2 + \sigma_n^2$.
- variance = $2\sigma_n^4/N + 4 \cdot (E_s/d^2) \cdot \sigma_n^2/N$.

Under this observational model, the decision rule (1) boils down to a simple comparison of z to a decision threshold τ: if $z > \tau$, the sensor declares a target detection; otherwise no detection. The decision rule formalizes the intuition that when the perceived sound is loud enough, there is probably a target nearby.

The threshold τ is the dividing point which satisfies

$$p(\tau|H_0) = p(\tau|H_1). \tag{3}$$

It is computed numerically. From $p(z|x)$, one can compute the likelihoods $p(z|H_0)$ and $p(z|H_1)$ by numerical integration. Fig. 2 plots the likelihoods. It can be shown that $p(z|H_0)$ and $p(z|H_1)$ intersect at only one point, which is τ. Although the computation of τ is nontrivial, it only needs to be computed infrequently – at deployment time if the observation model is stationary, or during idle periods for background noise levels which change slowly. During detection, each sensor node periodically checks for detection simply by taking a measurement and comparing to the precomputed τ.

3.2   Group Formation and Leader Election

The single node detection scheme described above ignores the correlation between sensor measurements. It is very likely that multiple nodes simultaneously

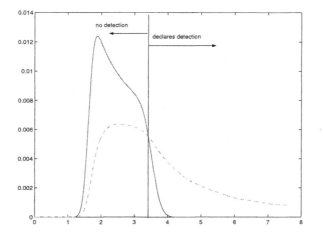

Fig. 2. Single node LRT. The horizontal axis is the energy measurement z, and the vertical axis is the value of the hypothesis likelihood functions $p(z|H_0)$ (the solid curve) and $p(z|H_1)$ (the dashed curve).

detect a single target. However, the leader-based tracking algorithm suggests that a single leader should be sufficient for the tracking of any individual target. Multiple sensor nodes with detections cause contention for leadership. In this section, we describe a geographically-based group management scheme which resolves contention and elects a single leader via message exchange.

First consider the ideal initialization condition: we have a sensor network covering a field in which the target has never appeared before. If sound propagates isotropically and attenuates monotonically with distance, the sensors physically closer to the target are more likely to detect than the sensors far away. One can compute an "alarm region", similar to a 3-σ region of a Gaussian distribution, such that most (e.g., 99%) of sensors with detections fall in the region. This is illustrated in Fig. 3. Sensor nodes are marked with small circles; the dark ones have detected a target. Assume the target is located at x (marked with a "+" in the figure), the alarm region is a disk centered at x with some radius R, where R is determined by the observation model. In practice, we use R_{detect} plus some moderate margin (to account for target motion during the sample period) as our choice of R.

Ideally, nodes in the alarm region should collaborate together to resolve their contention and elect a single leader from the region. However, the exact location of the alarm region is unknown since the target position x is unknown. Each node with a detection only knows that the target is within R distance of it, and a possible competitor could be another distance R from the target. Thus, in the absence of a "message center", a node notifies all nodes within a radius $2R$ of itself, which are potential "competitors" for leadership, of its detection.

Upon detection, each node broadcasts a DETECTION message to all nodes in this alarm region containing a time stamp recording when the detection is

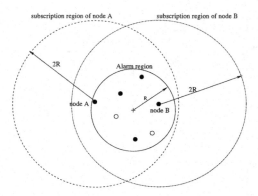

Fig. 3. Detection and collaborative regions

declared, and the likelihood ratio $p(z|H_1)/p(z|H_0)$. The higher this ratio, the more confident the detecting node is of its detection. We rely on the routing mechanisms to effectively limit the propagation of the detection messages to the specified region, a capability of critical importance for the algorithm to be scalable.

After sending out its own detection message, the node checks all detection packets received within an interval of t_{comm}. The value of t_{comm} should be long enough for all messages to reach their destination, yet not too long so that the target can be considered approximately stationary. These messages are then compared with the node's own detection. The node winning this election then becomes leader immediately, with no need for further confirmation. The election procedure is as follows:

- If none of the messages are timestamped earlier than the node's own detection, the node declares itself leader.
- If there are one or more messages with an earlier time stamp, the node knows that it is not the leader.
- If none of the messages contains earlier timestamps, but some message contains a time stamp identical to the node's detection time, the node compares the likelihood ratio. If the node's likelihood ratio is higher, the node becomes the leader.

Ideally, this algorithm will elect only one leader per target. In real networks, this algorithm is imperfect, and in some circumstances, multiple leaders may be elected. For example, if the DETECTION packet with the earliest detection time stamp fails to reach all the destination nodes, multiple nodes may find that they are the "earliest" detection and each may initiate a track. Since these tracks correspond to the same target, it is likely that they will collide with each other in the near future. This calls for methods to merge redundant tracks. Merging tracks is handled by the track maintenance scheme discussed in Sec. 4.

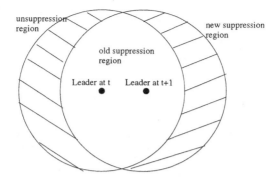

Fig. 4. Suppression and unsuppression regions.

3.3   Suppression within the Collaborative Group

Once the leader is elected, it initializes a belief state $p(x^{(0)}|z^{(0)})$ as a uniform disk of radius R centered at its own location. The disk contains the true target location with high probability. This belief provides a starting point for the tracking algorithm.

The leader plays a key role in maintaining the collaborative group. As the target moves, the sensors which did not previously detect may begin detecting. These sensors are potential sources of contention. The system uses SUPPRESSION messages to minimize this. Basically, a SUPPRESSION message is a claim of group membership. The leader sends out SUPPRESSION messages to notify the recipient nodes to abandon detection and join the group. The message goes out to a region known as the suppression region, which should contain potential sources of contention. Assuming the actual target position is contained in the belief state, the suppression region should cover all locations within R distance to the belief state. The actual implementation of this may depend on the belief representation used. In the case of the grid-based nonparametric representation used in [1], this region was found by starting with the bounding box containing all probability grids above a preset threshold level and adding margins of size R to all sides. Alternatively, one could identify a region containing the target with a specified probability and add margins of size R to that. The key factor is that the region must contain, with high probability, all nodes which might detect the target. In the special case of the original detection, as discussed in Sec. 3.2, the initial belief is a radius R disk centered at the leader, hence the suppression region is initially a concentric disk of radius $2R$.

As leadership moves in the network and the belief state is refined by successive measurements, the suppression region changes, and the group membership needs to be updated. Fig. 4 shows the two suppression regions at time t and $t+1$. The two regions are not identical, but overlap. We can further reduce network traffic by only notifying the delta regions, that is, the regions containing nodes which are added to or removed from the group. Three geographical regions need to be handled separately:

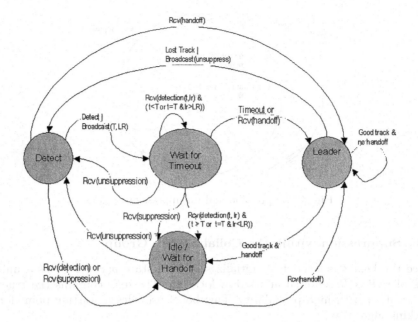

Fig. 5. Finite state machine on nodes

- The unsuppression region which contains nodes who are suppressed at t but not $t+1$. This is pictured in Fig. 4 as the crescent-shaped region on the left hand side. The leader sends to this region an UNSUPPRESSION message which basically reverses the effect of the SUPPRESSION message, equivalent to a dismissal from the collaborative group. Nodes receiving the UNSUPPRESSION message are freed, and go back to detection.
- The new suppression region which contains nodes who were not suppressed at t but suppressed at $t+1$. This is pictured in Fig. 4 as the crescent-shaped region on the right hand side. The leader sends SUPPRESSION message to claim membership.
- The region which sees no changes in group membership. No messages need to be sent to this region. The nodes in this region remain suppressed.

3.4 Group Management Process on Nodes

The protocol described in Secs. 3.2 and 3.3 can be implemented on each sensor node using a finite state machine. Fig. 5 shows the group management process on each node. The actual implementation was more complicated in order to be robust against packet loss and out-of-sequence message arrivals.

The node has four states:

- *Detecting*: the node is not in any collaborative group, and periodically monitors its measurement for detection of possible targets.

- *Leader*: the node takes measurements, updates the track and the collaborative group.
- *Idle*: the node belongs to a collaborative group, and is passively waiting for a handoff from the leader.
- *Waiting-for-time-out*: intermediate states waiting for potential detections to arrive from other nodes.

There are four types of messages in the process. In addition to DETECTION, SUPPRESSION, and UNSUPPRESSION messages described in previous sections, HANDOFF messages carry the belief state used in tracking. They contain a time stamp, a belief state, the sender and the receiver's IDs, and a flag indicating if the track is successful or lost. A track is considered successful if the uncertainty of the track is under some specified tolerance level, and lost if otherwise. All nodes in the collaborative group corresponding to a lost track dismiss their membership and restart detection immediately.

4 Distributed Track Maintenance

With collaborative group management, each group associated with tracking of a single target. The co-existence of multiple tracks in the network can be readily handled as long as the the tracks are far apart and the collaborative regions are non-overlapping.

In practice, however, collisions between tracks are possible. For example, as briefly discussed in Sec. 3.2, redundant tracks corresponding to the same target are very likely to collide as the tracking algorithm advances. In tracking of multiple targets, targets crossing each other's path will cause the collaborative regions to collide. In these cases, nodes in the overlapped collaborative regions need to resolve the ambiguity of which leader to follow, especially when the multiple leaders dictate conflicting actions. There are numerous ways collisions can be handled. Here we describe a simple method for maintenance and management of multiple tracks.

First, in order for the tracks to be distinguishable, each track is assigned a unique ID. A simple choice is the time stamp (in microseconds) when the track was initiated. This choice does not require global knowledge shared throughout the network beyond rough time synchronization. The chance of multiple tracks being assigned the same ID is very small. The ID is carried along with the track and shared among the nodes in the collaborative group. All messages originating from the group are tagged with it. When a node receives a message, by examining the ID, it knows which group (and hence which track) the message refers to.

Now consider a node which belongs to multiple collaborative groups. Each node keeps track of its multiple membership based on the received SUPPRESSION and UNSUPPRESSION messages. A non-leader node ("follower" in the group) can be suppressed by any leader, but freeing it requires UNSUPPRESSION messages from all the local leaders. In other words, a node is free only when no leader claims ownership over it.

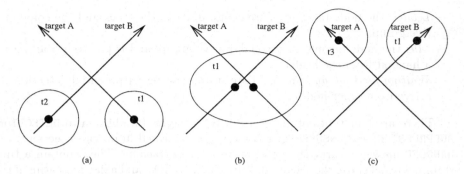

Fig. 6. Track merging and splitting when multiple targets cross over. The collaborative groups are plotted as circles or ellipsoids. The labels $t1$, $t2$, and $t3$ are track IDs.

For a leader node, a received SUPPRESSION message with a different ID than its own is a clear indication of multiple groups colliding. Without the help of a suitable target classification method, the nodes cannot tell whether the collision is due to multiple targets crossing over, or redundant tracks for the same target merging. Furthermore, the maintenance of overlapping tracks requires source separation and data association, which are in general notorious inverse problems and hard to implement in distributed networks. In view of the difficulties, we propose a simple track merging approach: One of the tracks survives; others are dropped. The collaborative groups merge together into a single group.

To decide which track to retain, each leader compares the ID of the incoming SUPPRESSION message, $t_{suppression}$, with its own, t_{leader}. We refer to the track corresponding to the incoming SUPPRESSION message as the incoming track. Between the incoming track and the track the leader currently has, the older one is retained. This is based on the intuition that an older track has already incorporated many measurements, hence is in general more accurate and reliable. The leader performs a comparison:

- If $t_{suppression} < t_{leader}$, i.e., the incoming track is older, the leader drops its own track, and relays the incoming SUPPRESSION message to its collaborative group, then gives up leadership. By this message, the two collaborative groups merge into one, obeying the leader of the incoming track.
- If $t_{suppression} \geq t_{leader}$, the leader's track survives. The leader sends a SUPPRESSION message to the leader of the incoming track.

This mechanism works well in merging multiple tracks corresponding to a single target. In the case where two (or more) targets approach each other closely, it basically tracks the superposition of the two targets as if the two targets could be regarded as a single "virtual" target. Without an accurate source separation scheme in place, the tracking algorithm is unable to tell the two targets apart. Once the targets separate, the second target will be re-detected as a new target. Fig. 6 illustrates this merging and splitting of tracks. As targets A and B approach each other, their groups merge, and then separate again. This example

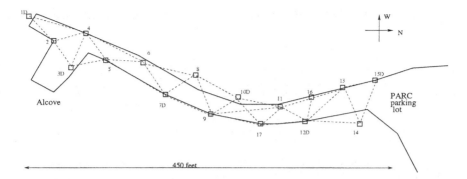

Fig. 7. Sensor network layout. The solid line plots the service road. The sensor nodes are marked with small squares. Labels with a "D" are DOA sensors. The dashed lines picture the connectivity between nodes.

shows that track merging and splitting enables the tracking of multiple targets, but cannot maintain the identities of either targets.

Alternatively, we can assign a new group ID when multiple groups merge into one. A time-contiguous series of location estimates with a consistent identity is considered as a "tracklet". For example, Fig. 6c contains four tracklets, two before the merging and two after. We can reacquire the target identity of each tracklet using classification schemes, and assemble tracklets into complete tracks.

The distributed track initiation and management scheme, combined with the leader-based tracking algorithm described in [1], forms a scalable system. The system works well in tracking multiple targets when the targets are not interfering (i.e., far apart), and can recover from inter-target interference once the targets move apart.

5 Experiment

We built a sensor network for multi-target tracking using the group management scheme. The sensor nodes in the experiment consists of 17 WINSNG 2.0 sensor nodes designed and manufactured by Sensoria Corp. Each node is essentially a Hitachi SH-4 based Linux PC with acoustic sensor inputs. Two type of sensors are used:

- Acoustic energy sensors. These output sound energy over a 256-sample window and estimate target distance based on the physics of sound attenuation.
- Direction-of-arrival (DOA) sensors. They are arrays of 4 microphones attached to a single node, and use beamforming techniques [9] to determine the bearing to the target.

The nodes in our experiment included 6 DOA sensors and 11 energy sensors. This diversity in sensing modality helps to balance the systematic biases of

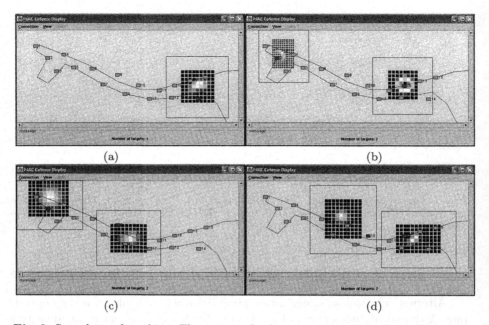

(a)   (b)

(c)   (d)

Fig. 8. Snapshots of tracking. The rectangular boxes correspond to the collaborative regions. Nodes in red are leaders.

individual sensors to obtain accurate target location. The nodes are placed along a service road outside the PARC building, as plotted in Fig. 7. Neighboring nodes talk to each other via 802.11b-based wireless links.

The geographically-based group management is built on top of the directed diffusion [10] network protocol. To avoid unnecessary flooding of network packets, we use the GEAR (Geographic and Energy Aware Routing) protocol, which is an implementation of geo-routing [4] in directed diffusion. The protocol allows data to be sent to a specified geographic region, and limits message propagation outside of the destination region by optimizing the routes to gradually approach the region. Only the destination region is flooded with data. To cope with the constraint in GEAR that the geographic regions has to be specified as rectangles, we use the rectangular bounding boxes. In our experiment, the leader-election time-out t_{comm} is set to 1 second, and the detect range $R = 45$ feet.

The tracking and group management algorithms run on the node in real time. Each node runs a process similar to that described in Sec. 3.4 to decide which sensing mode to use. Two non-interfering targets are tracked. One is a military truck, and the other is a speaker playing a recorded sound of an amphibious assault vehicle (AAV). The ground truth of target locations was measured using differential GPS, which reports an average accuracy of 6 — 10 feet. To measure the tracking performance, we have computed the displacement between the location estimates produced by the tracker and the GPS-measured ground truth. The standard deviation averaged over a complete run is about 19 feet. Given that GPS measurement error and tracking error are independent, the tracking accuracy of our system is actually better than the reported 19 feet.

Fig. 8 shows a few snapshots of the tracking result. The belief states are pictured using greyscales. A bright cell indicates that a target is very likely to be on the cell location, and a dark cell suggests otherwise. In Fig. 8a, the first target is detected as it enters the sensor field from the parking lot. The second target has not appeared yet. The rectangular box enclosing the belief state represents the suppression region. The nodes inside the region (nodes 12 — 16) form a collaborative group, led by node 14. The rest of the network is doing standalone detection.

Fig. 8b tracks the first target as it moves along the road (south bound) to the alcove end. Its collaborative region contains nodes 1 – 5. The second target has just been detected. Nodes 11 – 14, 16, and 17 form a collaborative group.

Fig. 8c and d tracks two targets simultaneously. The respective collaborative regions are plotted. The sensors are organized into independently coordinated groups, which enables the co-existence of multiple tracks and the simultaneous tracking of multiple targets.

Tracking of two targets which are occasionally interfering has also been tested in our experiment. The tracking system can successfully recover from mutual interference via track merging and splitting.

6 Discussion

The paper focuses on the group management method for track initiation and maintenance in target tracking applications. While we have experimentally validated the basic structure of the group management algorithm, through extensive simulations and field experiments on sensor nodes, a number of important theoretical and experimental characterizations remain as immediate future research tasks. For example, we have not characterized how the performance of the algorithm, measured as the frequency of spurious track initiation or track loss, varies as target speed increases or parameters such as t_{comm} changes. The current implementation is also limited in its capability to maintain information about multiple targets once they closely approach each other. It might, however, be viewed as a key stepping-stone towards future systems with these capabilities. Modules to perform data association, classification, and source separation may be added, and different sensor selection approaches may be chosen, but the concept of organizing sensors in local collaborative groups to control information propagation is essential to each of these modules, and hence fundamental to the scalability of the entire system.

Collaboration between sensors is especially important in cases where individual sensors are of limited capability, for example, on the Berkeley motes. Individually motes can only perform simple tasks, and only through collaboration can more sophisticated sensing tasks be accomplished.

A similar group management method is described in [11], where a group is defined as those nodes that satisfy a membership predicate conveyed by message passing among neighbors. Using a target counting problem as an example, sensors in a network attempts to determine the number of distinct targets (i.e., sources of signals) in an area using strictly local measurements. The collaborative groups correspond to local regions dominated by energy peaks induced by the target sources, and the groups are formed based on local communication and simple detection amplitude comparison. The interesting feature of this method is that the geographic groups are only implicitly defined, i.e., no geographic regions need to be specified, and a geographic group is self-organized as a result of the underlying signal field the network is sampling. An interesting future research direction is to generalize the geo-specified and physics-specified group management methods to the more generic attribute-based group management protocols.

Acknowledgment. This work is partially supported by the DARPA Sensor Information Technology program under Contract F30602-00-C-0139. We are indebted to Prof. John Heidemann and Dr. Fabio Silva of USC/ISI for their help on directed diffusion. We would also like to thank our colleagues Dave Duff, Jaewon Shin, and Rebecca Hinden for their assistance in carrying out the experiment.

References

1. J. Liu, J. E. Reich, and F. Zhao, "Collaborative in-network processing for target tracking," *EURASIP, Journal on Applied Signal Processing*, to appear in 2002.
2. M. Chu, H. Haussecker, and F. Zhao, "Scalable information-driven sensor querying and routing for ad hoc heterogeneous sensor networks," *International Journal of High-Performance Computing Applications*, vol. 16, no. 3, Fall 2002.
3. H. Stark and J. W. Woods, *Probability, Random Processes, and Estimation Theory for Engineers,* second edition. Upper Saddle River, NJ: Prentice Hall, 1994.
4. Y.-B. Ko and N. H. Vaidya, "Geocasting in mobile ad hoc networks: Location-based multicast algorithms," in *Proc. IEEE Workshop on Mobile Computer Systems and Applications*, (New Orleans), Feb 1999.
5. Y. Yu, R. Govindan, and D. Estrin, "Geographical and energy aware routing: a recursive data desemination protocol for wireless sensor networks," May 2001.
6. D. Li, K. Wong, Y. H. Hu, and A. Sayeed, "Detection, classification, and tracking of targets," *IEEE Signal Processing Magazine*, pp. 17–29, March 2002.
7. V. Poor, *An Introduction to Signal Detection and Estimation,* second edition. New York, NY: Springer-Verlag, 1994.
8. L. E. Kinsler, A. R. Frey, A. B. Coppens, and J. V. Sanders, *Fundamentals of Acoustics.* New York, NY: John Wiley and Sons, Inc., 1999.
9. J. Chen, R. Hudson, and K. Yao, "Joint maximum-likelihood source localization and unknown sensor location estimation for near-field wideband signals," *Proceedings of the SPIE*, vol. 4474, July 2001.
10. SCADDS Diffusion 3.1.2, developped by USC Information Science Institute, available on http://www.isi.edu/scadds/software, 2002.
11. Q. Fang, F. Zhao, and L. Guibas, "Couting targets: building and managing aggregates in wireless sensor networks." Palo Alto Research Center technical report P2002-10077, Mar. 2002.

Using Predictable Observer Mobility for Power Efficient Design of Sensor Networks

Arnab Chakrabarti, Ashutosh Sabharwal, and Behnaam Aazhang

Rice University, Houston TX 77005, USA

Abstract. In this paper, we explore a novel avenue of saving power in sensor networks based on predictable mobility of the observer (or data sink). Predictable mobility is a good model for public transportation vehicles (buses, shuttles and trains), which can act as mobile observers in wide area sensor networks. To understand the gains due to predictable mobility, we model the data collection process as a queuing system, where random arrivals model randomness in the spatial distribution of sensors. Using the queuing model, we analyze the success in data collection, and quantify the power consumption of the network. Even though the modeling is performed for a network which uses only single hop communication, we show that the power savings over a static sensor network are significant. Finally, we present a simple observer-driven communication protocol, which follows naturally from the problem formulation and can be used to achieve the predicted power savings.

1 Introduction

One of the major challenges in designing sensor networks is maximizing the useful network lifetime. Since many sensor networks deploy sensor nodes which are battery powered and which can possibly scavenge only a small amount of energy from their surroundings, limited battery is one of the major hurdles in achieving desired longevity of network operation. Reducing power consumption in sensing and subsequent data collection has been a topic of extensive study [1, 2, 3, 4, 5]. It has also been observed that communication power (which includes channel monitoring) is usually a significant component of the total power consumed in a sensor network [1,6]. In this paper, we explore the impact of predictable observer mobility in reducing communication power consumption in a sensor network.

Our contributions in this paper are two-fold. First, we propose a queuing formulation to accurately model data collection by the mobile observer over the region of interest. The queuing formulation captures the randomness due to random placement of sensors in the region. To achieve a pre-specified outage, defined as the fraction of nodes which fail to send their data, we show that predictability of the observer's motion can lead to large power savings over a network with no mobility. Second, we propose a simple observer-driven communication protocol which achieves a significant portion of the predicted gains. As the observer in our model is assumed to traverse the same path repeatedly, the data is *pulled* by the observer by waking up the nodes when it is close to them. Since the sensor

F. Zhao and L. Guibas (Eds.): IPSN 2003, LNCS 2634, pp. 129–145, 2003.

nodes only transmit when the observer is close to them, the power requirements are significantly reduced.

Many strategies for reducing power consumption in sensor networks have been explored. In [6], many of the important avenues were identified, such as, increasing the number of sensors to reduce transmission range, reducing the standby power through suitable protocol design, and energy-efficient hardware implementation. Power efficient topologies for situations where sensor locations can be precisely specified were explored in [3]. In [7, 8, 9] some communication issues such as modulation, coding and multiple-access were studied in the context of sensor networks and power-saving solutions were proposed. In a different direction, it was shown in [10] that mobility of nodes can increase the capacity of ad hoc networks for applications with loose delay constraints. None of the above work, however, looked at the special case of exploiting predictable observer mobility to save power in a sensor network.

Our work is particularly motivated by the fact that a prototype of this proposed model is currently being built at Rice University where university shuttle buses will carry mobile observers and sensors will be deployed on buildings. Since these carriers, such as buses, usually have a source of power that is more than sufficient for communicating, storing and processing data, the observer is not power constrained like the sensor nodes. Furthermore, the shuttle buses have fixed and predictable routes.

The rest of the paper is organized as follows. In Section 2, we describe the proposed model. Section 3 explains the process of data collection by the mobile observer. In Section 4, we provide a power comparison between the proposed sensor network model and two static sensor network models. A protocol suitable for our paradigm is proposed in Section 5. Finally, we conclude in Section 6.

2 Proposed Model

The sensor network consists of N sensor nodes distributed over an area A (see Fig. 1). Two node distribution models are studied in this paper. In the first model, nodes are assumed to be independently and uniformly scattered over the area A. Random scattering is a good model for cases where cheap sensor nodes are dropped with no particular plan, for rapid deployment. In the second model, we assume that the sensors are placed such that no two sensors are less than d meters apart, and the network is laid out to perform an efficient spatial sampling of the terrain.

The observer O moves repeatedly along a deterministic route inside A. When the observer has moved over the entire area A once and returned to the point from which it started, we say that it has completed a *cycle*. The speed of the observer is v. We assume that the path of the observer can be approximated by a straight line over distances of the order of the communication range of a sensor. We also assume that the observer is not power-constrained.

The sensors are all identical. Every sensor has the same kind of battery, uses the same communication range $R_{\max}$ and uses the same data rate to transmit information to the observer when it is within range. The rate at which sensors collect data about the phenomenon being monitored is also same for all nodes.

Each sensor needs time T to send all its data to the observer. The observer must be within range for the entire interval T, for if the observer moved out of range before T, communication would be unsuccessful resulting in a failure that we call *outage*. Communication takes place at constant rate and over a continuous time interval T. Communication between sensors and the observer is always single-user and over a single hop. There is no relaying, multiple-access or multicasting.

For single hop communication, the observer should come within communicable range of every sensor inside the given area A from some point on its fixed path. Let R be the distance for which every sensor node lies within a distance R from some point on the path of the observer. Note that R and the range R_{max} are different. Every sensor node comes within a distance R from the path of the observer. But for successful communication it is not simply enough that the observer should come within R_{max} of the sensor. It must remain within range for a period of T or more. The communication range R_{max} is chosen to satisfy

$$R_{max} \geq \sqrt{R^2 + (vT/2)^2} . \tag{1}$$

in order to ensure that every node remains within range for at least T seconds (this uses the straight-line path assumption). The relation between R and R_{max} is explained in Fig. 2.

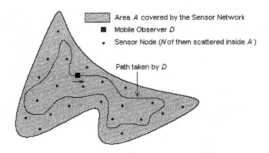

Fig. 1. Diagram of the Sensor Network

3 Process of Data Collection

As mentioned earlier, two node distribution models are studied in this paper. In the first model, nodes are assumed to be independently and uniformly scattered over the area A. In the second model, we assume that sensors are randomly

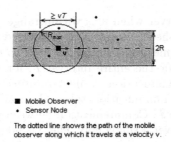

■ Mobile Observer
♦ Sensor Node

The dotted line shows the path of the mobile
observer along which it travels at a velocity v.

Fig. 2. Relation between R and $R_{\max}$

distributed subject to the constraint that no two sensors are less than d meters apart.

In the first model, we shall analyze the tradeoff between communication power and expected outage during data collection using a queuing formulation. In the second model, we shall show that it is possible to guarantee zero outage if the sensor separation is above a threshold.

3.1   Independently and Uniformly Distributed Nodes

Sensors are independently and uniformly scattered over the given area. Once they have been scattered, their locations are fixed. Thus, the distribution that we are referring to is the a priori distribution of sensors. The results we will obtain from the analysis below will indicate average performance over all possible sets of node positions.

Under this distribution, it may not be possible to collect data from all sensors. This is because random scattering introduces the possibility of several nodes being located close together, all trying to send data and the observer not being able to receive data from all of them. The presence of redundant nodes alleviates this problem to some extent. However, performance does get affected when the fraction of nodes unable to transmit is above a certain threshold. The fraction of nodes in outage may be reduced below this threshold by either increasing the transmission range $R_{\max}$ or by increasing the data rate. Note that increasing the transmission range and the data rate both involve increasing transmission power. The important questions to answer in this context are:

1. What is the minimum power with which we can collect data from the specified fraction of nodes?
2. What combination of $R_{\max}$ and T achieves this?

As the observer moves, new sensors come within range and ones that were within range go out of range. We now provide a suitable mathematical formulation for this process.

In a time interval of length t, the observer moves a distance vt. Nodes in an area $2Rvt$, which were previously out of range, come within range. The observer may be busy when a new node comes within range, in which case, the node has to wait in order to send its data. If the observer is not busy, the sensor can start sending its data immediately. Once the observer has started communicating with this node, it will not listen to any other node that may come within range. This is analogous to a queue where sensors arrive according to a certain random process and the observer listens to them one by one.

An important point is that it is futile to start communicating with a sensor node that will not stay within range long enough. For each sensor there is a maximum waiting time, which is a function of its distance from the path of the observer. If the observer does not start communicating with the node before this time, it will be impossible for the sensor to send all its data, resulting in outage. This is depicted in Fig. 3.

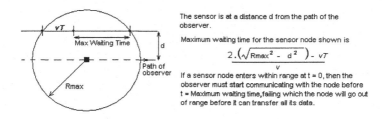

Fig. 3. Relation between Waiting Time and Outage

If N nodes are independently and uniformly distributed over area A, then the interarrival times may be modeled using the following *pdf* (see Appendix A)

$$p_{arrival}(t) = \frac{2RvN(A - 2Rvt)^{N-1}}{A^N}; \qquad 0 \le t \le \frac{A}{2Rv} \qquad (2)$$

Also, the distance d shown in Fig. 3 is uniformly distributed from 0 to R in magnitude as a consequence of the independent and uniform distribution of nodes. Based on this, the *pdf* of waiting times (see Appendix B) is

$$p_w(W) = \frac{v^2(W + T)}{4R\sqrt{R_{max}^2 - v^2(W + T)^2/4}}; \quad \frac{2\sqrt{R_{max}^2 - R^2}}{v} - T \le W \le \frac{2R_{max}}{v} - T \qquad (3)$$

A cycle, during which the observer moves through the entire area A once, can be simulated like a queue using these two distributions. For purposes of the simulation, it has been assumed that the observer has exact knowledge of the waiting time of each sensor that comes within range (as if aided by an oracle), which allows it to perform optimal scheduling. In practice, a protocol may be designed to ascertain the waiting times through exchange of information between the sensor and the observer (see Sect. 5).

Numerical Results. Increasing the value of $R_{\max}$ reduces outage and keeps the observer busy more often. When we increase the range, we increase the waiting times. As a consequence, sensors can wait longer for their turn before they finally go out of range resulting in outage. It is as if we have increased the size of the input buffer of a queue to smooth out burstiness in the input.

This improvement in performance comes at a price. Increasing the communication range while keeping the data rate same involves spending more power. For doubling $R_{\max}$, while keeping the worst case SNR same, one needs to increase transmission power at least four times (actually 2^γ times where γ is the path attenuation constant).

Performance is also seen to improve when T is reduced while keeping $R_{\max}$ fixed. As in the case of increasing $R_{\max}$, decreasing T also involves more power.

Fig. 4 and Fig. 5 show the pattern of changes in outage and the percent of time the observer is receiving information with changes in T and $R_{\max}$ respectively. These observations suggest that there may be multiple combinations of the parameters $R_{\max}$ and T that can be used to achieve outage below a specified limit. The designer must pick the one that consumes minimum energy in order to maximize network life.

We chalk out the procedure for power-optimization with the aid of an example. Table 1 contains a list of the system parameters used for simulations.

Table 1. List of System Parameters

Parameter	Value
Maximum allowable outage	20%
γ = Path attenuation of wireless channel	2
R	80 m
A = Area covered by the sensor network	100 sq km
v = Observer velocity	15 m/sec
N = Number of nodes	3000
R_{sens} = Rate at which a sensor collects data	160 bps
B = Bandwidth of the system	100 kHz
N_0 = Noise power spectral density	10^{-19} Watt/Hz
T_{cycle} = Time needed to complete one cycle	$\sim A/(2Rv)$
D_{cycle} = Data collected by a node in one cycle	$R_{sens} * T_{cycle}$

For different values of T, the minimum value of $R_{\max}$ is found (through simulation) for which the expected outage is not in excess of the specified 20%. The power P is calculated using Shannon's expression for channel capacity and equating it to the data rate D_{cycle}/T, i.e.,

$$P = BN_0R^\gamma(2^{D_{cycle}/TB} - 1) , \tag{4}$$

and the energy consumed by a node per cycle for the purpose of transmission is calculated by multiplying this power by the time T. The power and energy

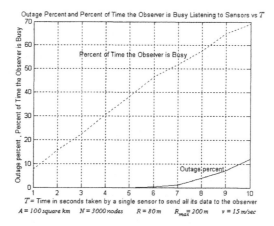

Fig. 4. Effect of T on performance

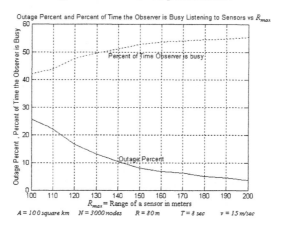

Fig. 5. Effect of $R_{\max}$ on performance

obtained for different T are plotted in Fig. 6 from which it can be seen that there exists a certain point where the energy consumed is minimized. Fig. 7 shows the different values of $R_{\max}$ that were found to ensure less than 20% outage. It is important to note that the energy spent varies significantly depending on the choices of T and $R_{\max}$, thus reiterating the fact that a suitable choice of the system parameters is crucial for power efficiency.

Comment on the Choice of Velocity. We have carried out all our analysis assuming that the observer moves at a fixed speed v. In practice, the velocity of the observer has a certain probability distribution and the outage that we measure depends on this distribution. Moreover, this distribution may not be

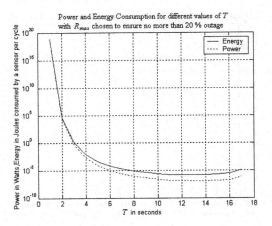

Fig. 6. Power and Energy Optimization

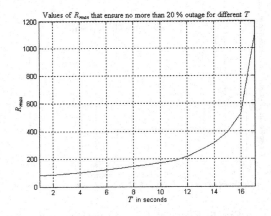

Fig. 7. Values of $R_{\max}$ to ensure outage $< 20\%$

stationary. The question is: which velocity should we consider as v for designing the system so that the specified maximum outage is not exceeded?

In most scenarios, we would recommend either the maximum speed, or a speed that is very rarely exceeded, as the choice for v. Note here that the worst outage results when the observer is moving fast, not when it is static or moving slowly. Choosing the average speed as v could be potentially harmful due to the non-stationary nature of the distribution of velocities. For example, the average speed of a bus could be 30 mph, but the bus might consistently travel at 40 mph on some roads, so that if v were chosen to be 30 mph, it would result in high outage near those roads thereby impairing the ability of the sensor network to gather data from there.

3.2   Randomly Distributed Nodes with Minimum Separation Constraint

In sensor networks where nodes are randomly distributed subject to the constraint that no two nodes can be closer than d (minimum separation), zero outage can be guaranteed by an appropriate choice of parameters. This is significant because outage is not acceptable in many applications and yet unavoidable if we allow the nodes to be randomly scattered without additional constraints.

It can be shown that the condition

$$d \geq \sqrt{(2R)^2 + (vT)^2} \ . \tag{5}$$

is sufficient for guaranteeing zero outage (see Appendix C). This condition ensures that the time gap between one sensor entering within the range of the observer and the next sensor is at least T. This condition can be met by reducing T if the sensors are positioned to satisfy

$$d > 2R \ . \tag{6}$$

4   Power Comparison with Sensor Networks Having Static Observers

To quantify the power savings afforded by observer mobility, we compare our sensor network model with static sensor network models covering an area A that is circular in shape with one observer at the center of the circle. The sensor network has N sensors in all cases. These sensors are uniformly distributed over the entire area. The three cases that we compare are shown in Fig. 8. Case 1 corresponds to our proposed model. In case 2, the observer is static and each sensor node transmits its data directly to the observer over a single hop. In case 3, each sensor node sends its data to the observer over multiple hops.

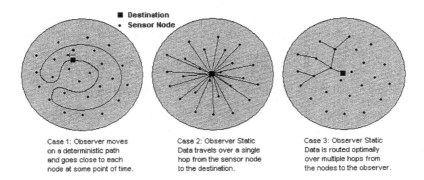

Case 1: Observer moves on a deterministic path and goes close to each node at some point of time.

Case 2: Observer Static Data travels over a single hop from the sensor node to the destination.

Case 3: Observer Static Data is routed optimally over multiple hops from the nodes to the observer.

Fig. 8. Sensor Network Models

For purposes of comparison, we consider an area of 100 sq km. Each sensor measures data at a rate of 1kbps. The remaining parameters have values provided in Table 1 unless mentioned otherwise.

4.1   Case 1: Mobile Observer

We choose $R = 500$m (this seems to be a reasonable distance for citywide public transport systems). The communication bandwidth available is 1MHz. In the proposed model, the energy consumed by a single sensor per cycle was found to be around 0.3 microjoule using the technique outlined in section 3.1. In general (see Table 1),

$$\text{Energy consumed per sensor} = TBN_0R^\gamma(2^{D_{cycle}/TB} - 1) \; Joule/cycle \; . \quad (7)$$

4.2   Case 2: Static Observer – Single Hop Communication

In this case, different sensors need to have different communication ranges in order to send their data to the observer. We assume that each sensor transmits at the same power. As a result, the sensors that are farther away from the observer will be able to transmit at a slower data rate and their communication will take more time. We would like to find how much power P each sensor needs to have so that the rate at which the network collects data can be matched by the rate at which data is communicated to the observer. For fair comparison, we assume that 20% nodes do not send anything as in case 1. Since a node at a distance r from the observer transmits at a data rate of

$$D(r) = B \log_2(1 + \frac{P}{BN_0r^\gamma}) \; bps \quad (8)$$

over a cycle period of T_{cycle} , the node collects D_{cycle} bits of data (see Table 1). The time taken to communicate this to the observer is $D_{cycle}/D(r)$. This quantity, summed over all nodes should equal T_{cycle}. The value of P, for which this equality occurs, is the transmission power required by every node. This value of P was calculated to be about 6.44 microwatts (for uniformly distributed sensors) from which the average energy spent per node per cycle was calculated to be 111.8 microjoules. This is over 300 times the average energy consumption per node per cycle in case 1.

4.3   Case 3: Static Observer – Multi Hop Communication

The power consumption in this case is difficult to calculate. It depends on the actual routes chosen for communication between different nodes and the sensor, which in turn depend on the locations of nodes. To simplify the situation, we consider an optimistic scenario where sensors are located in a uniform triangular lattice as shown in Fig. 9. As earlier, here also, for the sake of fair comparison, we assume that 20% of the nodes do not send data to the observer.

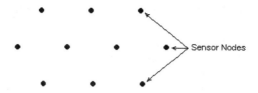

Fig. 9. Arrangement where sensors lie on the vertices of equilateral triangles

If N nodes were placed in this fashion over an area A, then the separation between neighboring nodes would be approximately

$$d = \sqrt{2A/\sqrt{3}N} \ . \tag{9}$$

In such a situation, a node, which is at a distance r from the observer, would have to send its data over at least $\lceil r/d \rceil$ hops, each of length d. The value of d is calculated to be 196.2 m in our case.

Over a cycle period of T_{cycle}, a node at a distance r from the observer collects D_{cycle} bits of data (see Table 1). This data has to travel over $\lceil r/d \rceil$ hops, each of length d. Here again, we assume that the nodes are identical, they use the same transmission power and have a transmission range of d (they need no more). Since, we have also assumed that the observer can receive only from one sensor at a time, it follows that a single link should be able to transmit at the rate at which the network collects information. From this it follows that the transmission power over a single hop will be

$$P' = BN_0 d^\gamma (2^{0.8NR_{sens}/B} - 1) \ . \tag{10}$$

Over a cycle period of T_{cycle} , a single node collects D_{cycle} bits of data (see Table 1). If this information is transmitted at a rate of $0.8NR_{sens}$, the time taken will be $D_{cycle}/(0.8NR_{sens}) = T_{cycle}/(0.8N)$ secs. The energy consumed to send a single sensor's information over a single hop per cycle is then $T_{cycle}P'/(0.8N)$ Joule. Multiplying this by the average number of hops over which data travels gives us the average energy consumed per sensor. The average number of hops is almost equal to $(2\sqrt{A})/(3\sqrt{\pi}d)$. Thus, on average, $(2\sqrt{A}T_{cycle}P')/(2.4\sqrt{\pi}Nd)$ Joule will be expended per sensor per cycle. For our system, this is 0.88 microjoule, which is about thrice the energy expended by a sensor per cycle in case 1.

5   Communication Protocol

The protocol for communication between nodes and the observer needs to be designed in such a way that individual sensors have very little responsibility apart from that of collecting data and communicating when requested. Medium access control, resolving contention, dealing with collisions and various kinds of failures will be handled by the observer since, by our assumption, it is not power constrained.

The life of a sensor network may be loosely divided into three phases- *startup*, *steady state* and *failure* [11]. We will describe briefly, the tasks to be performed by the protocol at each stage.

5.1   Startup Phase

Sensor nodes boot up individually. Each sensor has a unique address. At this time, the observer knows nothing about the positions of individual sensors. Neither do sensors know anything about the path of the observer. During the startup phase, the observer and the sensors exchange information that helps them to acquire such knowledge about each other. The startup phase consists of two different *cycles*.

Cycle 1. Sensors listen to the channel periodically at quick intervals to check if there is an observer within range. The observer, in this phase, goes on its regular path while continuously broadcasting a beacon signal. The strength of this beacon is same as the strength at which sensor nodes will typically transmit in the steady phase. Each sensor is able to measure:

1. How often the observer comes within range?
2. How long it stays within range?

Wireless channels are time varying and to obtain reliable estimates of these parameters, this cycle should be repeated a stipulated number of times.

Cycle 2. Here, the observer travels on its regular path broadcasting a beacon. When a sensor hears the observer, it responds with an RTS (Request To Send) packet containing its address. A collision-resolution strategy, based on random backoff (similar to 802.11), is used to resolve collisions among RTS packets sent by different sensors. When the observer hears an RTS from a particular sensor, it stops broadcasting the beacon, sends a CTS (Clear To Send) addressed to the sensor, and then the sensor node sends a small packet, which contains information about the parameters measured in cycle 1. This information will help the observer to decide priority when there are multiple sensor nodes in range waiting to transfer data (during the steady phase). The observer sends an ACK (ACKnowledgement) to the sensor node after it has received this packet.

Since there is the possibility of packet loss, this cycle should also be repeated several times. When cycle 2 is repeated, the only sensors that respond to the observer's beacon are those that have not received an ACK. The information exchanged in this cycle is crucial for efficient steady phase operation and all sensors should be able to send their packets to the observer.

5.2   Steady Phase

The observer has accurate knowledge about the positions of different sensor nodes. Using this information, and using the knowledge of its own position, the observer initiates communication, using a *wake* signal, with sensors that it knows to be within range. When there are several sensors within range, the observer initiates communication with that node which will go out of range first. In a sense, the observer assigns higher priority to sensors that can wait less.

In the steady phase, sensor nodes predict when the observer is likely to come close based on the information gathered during startup. They monitor the channel only when the observer is expected to be nearby. In [6], it has been indicated that the power consumed in channel monitoring can be a major chunk of the total power consumption of a sensor node. By reducing channel monitoring time, the life of a sensor node is increased significantly.

This protocol should perform well for sensor networks with static nodes. If the nodes are mobile and move by distances of the order of the separation between sensors or more in a relatively short time period, then it is difficult to do efficient scheduling. In certain cases, it may help to keep updating the information collected during the startup phase every cycle or once in every few cycles.

5.3   Failure Detection

The observer can detect node failures through their consistent inability to respond to wake calls and suitably reschedule the remaining nodes. When a significant number of nodes have failed, the network will no longer be able to gather sufficient data.

6   Conclusions

We showed that predictable mobility can be used to significantly reduce communication power in sensor networks. There are several advantages that predictability has over random mobility. One of them is boundedness of the transmission delay. Determinism of the path also makes it possible to predict the point where the observer and the mobile should communicate to save maximum power.

Much work on exploiting mobility remains to be done. Our future work will focus on, among other issues, combining relaying with predictable mobility to yield even higher power savings over multi-hop static sensor networks. For applications with loose performance requirements, random mobility can also be exploited.

References

1. R. Min and A. Chandrakasan, Energy-efficient communication for ad-hoc wireless sensor networks. In: Conference Record of the Thirty-Fifth Asilomar Conference on Signals, Systems and Computers. Volume 1. (2001) 139–143

2. G. J. Pottie, Wireless sensor networks. In: Information Theory Workshop (1998) 139–140

3. A. Salhieh, J. Weinmann, M. Kochha, and L. Schwiebert, Power efficient topologies for wireless sensor networks. In: International Conference on Parallel Processing. (2001) 156–163

4. R. Min, M. Bhardwaj, S.-H. Cho, A. Sinha, E. Shih, A. Wang, and A. Chandrakasan, An architecture for a power-aware distributed microsensor node. In: IEEE Workshop on Signal Processing Systems. (2000) 581–590

5. D. Estrin, Wireless sensor networks: Application driver for low power distributed systems. In: International Symposium on Low Power Electronics and Design. (2001) 194

6. J. M. Rabaey, J. Ammer, T. Karalar, S. Li, B. Otis, M. Sheets, and T. Tuan, Picoradios for wireless sensor networks: the next challenge in ultra-low power design. In: Digest of Technical Papers. ISSCC. IEEE International. Volume 2. (2001) 156–445

7. C.-H. Liu and H. Asada, A source coding and modulation method for power saving and interference reduction in ds-cdma sensor network systems. In Proceedings of the American Control Conference. Volume 4 (2002) 3003–3008

8. G. Pei and C. Chien, Low power tdma in large wireless sensor networks. In Military Communications Conference. Volume 1 (2001) 347–351

9. C. Chien, I. Elgorriaga, and C. McConaghy, Low-power direct-sequence spread-spectrum modem architecture for distributed wireless sensor networks. In: International Symposium on Low Power Electronics and Design. (2001) 251–254

10. M. Grossglauser and D. Tse, Mobility increases the capacity of ad hoc wireless networks. In: INFOCOM. Proceedings. IEEE. Volume 3 (2001) 1360–1369

11. K. Sohrabi, J. Gao, V. Ailawadhi, and G. J. Pottie, Protocols for self-organization of a wireless sensor network. IEEE Personal Communications **7** (2000) 16–27

A   Distribution of Interarrival Times

The *pdf* of interarrival times may be derived as follows.

In a time period t, the observer travels a distance vt. Nodes within an area $2Rvt$ that were previously out of range now come within range. If $p(t)$ were the interarrival pdf then[1]:

$\int_0^t p(x)dx$

= Probability that at least one node enters within range in time t

= 1 - (Probability that no node enters within range in time t)

= 1 - $(\frac{A-2Rvt}{A})^N$

Taking the derivative on both sides with respect to t yields Eqn. 2, which is the *pdf* of interarrival times.

---

[1] This follows from the fact that nodes are independently and uniformly distributed and the probability for any single node to be outside the area $2Rvt$ equals $(A - 2Rvt)/A$. Note that the time t cannot exceed $(A/2Rv)$ because in this time the observer's range covers an area A i.e. the entire area.

B   Distribution of Waiting Times

The *pdf* of maximum waiting times may be derived as follows. The concept of maximum waiting time is explained in Fig. 3. The maximum waiting time for a sensor node that is at a distance r from the path of the observer is

$$W(r) = (2\sqrt{R_{\max}^2 - r^2} - vT)/v \; . \tag{11}$$

Note that r is uniformly distributed from 0 to R. Hence the *pdf* of waiting times may be obtained by transforming this uniform *pdf*

$$p_w(W) = \frac{p_r(r)}{\left|\frac{dW(r)}{dr}\right|} \tag{12}$$

which yields the *pdf* given in Eqn. 3.

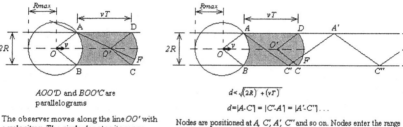

$AOO'D$ and $BOO'C$ are parallelograms

The observer moves along the line OO' with a velocity v. The circle denotes its range.

(a)

$d < \sqrt{(2R) + (vT)}$

$d = |A\text{-}C'| = |C'\text{-}A'| = |A'\text{-}C''| \dots$

Nodes are positioned at A, C', A', C'' and so on. Nodes enter the range of the observer at a rate such that the time in between arrivals is less than T and outage is inevitable after some time.

(b)

Fig. 10.

C   Condition for Guaranteeing Zero Outage

The sufficient condition for ensuring zero outage with minimum separation of nodes d is derived as follows(see Fig. 10(a)). Data transfer from a node to the observer takes time T. If we can ensure that the entry of two nodes into the range of the observer is spaced in time by T, then outage will not occur. Thus, if a sensor node is placed anywhere on the arc AB (see Fig. 10(a)), then no other node can lie within the shaded region $ABCD$. This implies that the minimum separation d must be greater than or equal to the distance from any point on arc AB to any other point on the boundary of $ABCD$ i.e.

$$d \ge \max(|x - y|); \quad x \in AB, y \in ABCD \; . \tag{13}$$

Let $x = U$ and $y = V$ be the pair for which $|x - y|$ is maximized.
Proposition: $U = A$ and $V = C$ (or $U = B$ and $V = D$) are the pair that maximizes $|x - y|$. This is proved as follows:

Claim 1: Choose and fix an arbitrary point $x = P \in AB$. Then, the point $y = Q \in ABCD$, for which $|P - y|$ is maximized does not lie on the line segments BC or AD except possibly that Q is one of the end points A,B,C or D.

Proof: Assume, for a contradiction that $Q \in BC \ Q \neq B,C$ (similar proof if $Q \in AD$). Then $\max(\angle PQB, \angle PQC) \geq 90°$. Thus, $\max(|P - B|, |P - C|) > |P - Q|$. Hence, we have a contradiction to the fact that $y = Q$ maximizes $|P - y|$.

Corollary 1: Since this claim holds for arbitrary x, it must hold for $x = U$, the point which achieves the overall maximum. Therefore, $V \in \{AB, CD\}$.

Claim 2: Choose and fix an arbitrary point $x = P \in AB$. Suppose that the point $y = Q \in ABCD$ is the point for which $|P - y|$ is maximized. Then, unless P is one of the end points of AB, $|P - Q| < |U - V|$. In other words, $U \in \{A, B\}$.

Proof: This is similar to the previous proof. Since $\max(\angle QPB, \angle QPA) > 90°$, therefore $\max(|A - Q|, |B - Q|) > |P - Q|$ which means $|P - Q| < |U - V|$.

Corollary 2: V lies on CD for if V were to lie on AB, by moving horizontally to the corresponding point on CD, one could show that this point is farther from U than V is.

The problem has therefore reduced to that of finding V from the set of points on CD. U has been ascertained to be either A or B (which one we choose makes no difference). Consider the line passing through A and O'. This line cuts the arc CD if and only if

$$(2R)^2 + (vT)^2 > (2R_{\max}^2) \tag{14}$$

which is in direct contradiction to Eqn. 1. The case of interest is when the line passing through A and O' does not cut CD. This happens when A is a point that lies within the circle centered at O' and having radius $R_{\max}$. We propose the following theorem for this situation.

Theorem: When the line passing through A and O' does not cut CD,

$$|A - C| = \max(|x - y|); \quad x \in AB, y \in ABCD . \tag{15}$$

Proof: If A were to lie on the circumference of the circle centered at O' having radius $R_{\max}$, and F were an arbitrary point on arc CD, then $\angle AFC$ would have been 90°. Now as A is moved along a straight line towards D, so that it enters within the circle, $\angle AFC$ increases monotonically. The important point is that $\angle AFC > 90°$. As a consequence, $|A - C| > |A - F|$ for all choices of F.

This is the result using which we obtain a meaningful relationship between the minimum separation d and our system parameters. Since

$$|A - C| = |B - D| = \sqrt{(2R)^2 + (vT)^2} , \tag{16}$$

we conclude that

$$d \geq \sqrt{(2R)^2 + (vT)^2} \qquad (17)$$

is a sufficient condition to guarantee zero outage.

An interesting point to note is that the above condition is also necessary to *guarantee* zero outage, meaning that if this condition is not satisfied, then it is possible to arrange sensors in a bad way, so that outage occurs. Fig. 10(b) shows one such arrangement of sensors where outage is unavoidable with

$$d < \sqrt{(2R)^2 + (vT)^2} \; . \qquad (18)$$

Bounds on Achievable Rates for General Multi-terminal Networks with Practical Constraints

Mohammad Ali Khojastepour, Ashutosh Sabharwal, and Behnaam Aazhang

Department of Electrical and Computer Engineering
Rice University
6100 Main St., MS-366
Houston, TX 77005
{amir, ashu, aaz}@rice.edu

Abstract. We consider the problem of communication in a general multi-terminal network where each node of the network is a potential sender or receiver (or both) but it cannot do both functions together. The motivation for this assumption comes from the fact that current radios in sensor nodes operate in TDD mode when the transmitting and receiving frequencies are the same. We label such a radio as a *cheap* radio and the corresponding node of the network as a *cheap* node.
We derive bounds on the achievable rates in a general multi-terminal network with finite number of states. The derived bounds coincide with the known cut-set bound [11] of network information theory if the network has just one state. Also, the bounds trivially hold in the network with cheap nodes because such a network operates in a finite number of states when the number of nodes is finite. As an example, application of these bounds in the multi-hop network and the relay channel with cheap nodes is presented. In both of these cases, the bounds are tight enough to provide converses for the coding theorems [16], and thus their respective capacities are derived.

1   Introduction

Network information theory in general deals with the problem of communication and information transfer between intended subsets of the nodes in a multi-terminal network of senders and receivers. Current results in network information theory are mainly a collection of results for special network topologies or channel models, like: two-way channel, interference channel, multiple access channel, and broadcast channel, and relay channel. The development of multiple user information theory started with the definition of various types of multiple user channels and attempt to find the corresponding capacity regions. Among the investigated channels there are a few channels for which the exact capacity has been derived, and usually the capacity is not known in general.

In this introduction we first give a brief history of the known results in network information theory, which starts with the introduction of various spacial

F. Zhao and L. Guibas (Eds.): IPSN 2003, LNCS 2634, pp. 146–161, 2003.

multiple user channels. Then, we will consider more general results on the multi-terminal network information theory. After that, a short overview of the recent works on characterizing the capacity of wireless network is given, and finally, we summarize the results of this paper.

1.1 Known Results in Network Information Theory

The definition of the two-way channel by Shannon in one of his pioneering papers in 1961 [22] might be considered as the first work on multiple user information theory. It is quite interesting that in different parts of his paper, Shannon also considered two other types of multiple user channels that almost a decade later developed into the multiple access channel and interference channel.

Shannon did not find the capacity result for the general two-way channel (and it is still not known), but in his paper [22], Shannon informally defined a channel (which has later been called as multiple access channel) and mentioned that "a complete and simple solution of the capacity region" for this channel has been found. He never published this result on the multiple access channel, and almost a decade later, in 1971, Ahlswede presented a simple characterization of the multiple access channel [1].

Shannon also considered a 'restricted' two-way channel where sender and receiver points at each end are in different places with no direct cross communication. This channel later defined in terms of two pairs of sender-receiver where the transmission of information from each sender to its corresponding receiver interferes with the communications between other sender-receiver pairs [7,6].

The broadcast channel was also introduced in the same decade. In 1972, Cover first introduced the broadcast channel which involves sending different pieces of information from a single source to several destination [9].

The relay channel was first defined and studied by Van der Mullen [19] for the case of three terminals (or nodes) and later considered by Cover [10]. Cover's results on the relay channel are still the most comprehensive in terms of achievability and capacity bounds (converse). Although in the relay problem there is just one sender and receiver, it is considered in the domain of network information theory due to the presence of relay node (or nodes).

The aforementioned works were first steps in finding better achievable rates or capacities. Although not many capacity results have been derived, these efforts usually have resulted in derivation of better achievable rates, consideration of special cases and special constraint, investigation of the corresponding channel with continuous alphabet (usually as AWGN channel), and exploration of the effect of feedback.

1.2 Multi-terminal Network Information Theory

In the aforementioned multiple user channels and in general in network information theory new elements such as interference, cooperation, and feedback make the problem of reliable communications more challenging. Due to the difficulty of the problem, capacity results are only known for very limited cases with special constraints. In most of the cases where the capacity results are known, they coincide with the cut-set bound on the achievable rates in a network [11]. The bounds have nice and simple max-flow min-cut representation: The rate of flow of information across any boundary is less than or at most equal to the mutual information between the inputs on one side of the boundary (senders' side) and the output on the other side (receivers' side) conditioned on the inputs on receiver's side.

The cut-set theorem is one of the most general results in network information theory. Although the converse (if it exists) to the coding theorem for different channels has been proved independently, in most of the cases it corresponds to a simple representation of the cut-set bounds. For example, the capacity region of multiple access channel is known due to the fact that the discovered achievable region for this channel is large enough to coincide with the cut-set bound. Another example is the relay channel for which an achievable rate was derived by Cover [10]. This achievable rate simply coincides with the cut-set bound for the degraded relay channel, and so the capacity of degraded relay channel is known, while the bound of non-degraded relay channel is higher and is still not shown to be achievable.

On the other hand, there are some cases where an upper bound on the capacity has been derived which is tighter than direct application of the cut-set theorem. For example, the capacity region of general broadcast channel is still not known because either the outer bounds are not tight enough or the achievable rate region is not large enough. But recently, the sum capacity of Gaussian vector broadcast channel (GVBC) has been considered and derived [5,23,27,24], which is lower than the corresponding suggested cut-set bound on the sum rate. The outer bound on this sum rate capacity is derived based on the work of Sato [21] and the achievablility part is based on Costa's precoding [8] or Marton's achievable region for the general broadcast channel [18].

Some recent works on network information theory have considered the problem of multi-casting in the networks which can be regarded as the network information flow. Ahlswede et al. [2,3] introduced a new class of multiuser source coding problems inspired by network communications, and proposed the use of coding in the network for the purpose of multi-casting. This work can be regarded as the max-flow min-cut theorem for the network information flow. Meanwhile, this work reveals that in general coding at the nodes (*network coding*) is required to achieve the best rates and the information should not be treated as a 'fluid' which can simply be routed and replicated at the nodes. Li and Yeung [17] presented a linear code for multi-casting from a single-source which is an example of such a network code. Borade applied the cut-set theorem [11] to the problem of the network information flow and derived an information theoretic upper bound on the information flow in discrete memoryless networks [4].

1.3   Information Theory of the Wireless Networks

Since information theoretic analysis of capacity and achievable rates in the network is complicated, it might not give much intuition on construction and limits of practical communication systems. Gupta and Kumar presented another look at the capacity of large networks and characterized the achievable throughput of the nodes [14]. The assumption of point-to-point coding in their work precludes any kind of cooperation and network coding which is possible for example in broadcast or multiple access channels.

New interest in sensor networks and network information theory has sparkled new research into the relay channel. Subsequent work by Gupta and Kumar [15] on an extension of the relay channel shows that using more sophisticated multiuser coding schemes can provide sizable gains in terms of *transport capacity*. Also a follow-up paper by Xie and Kumar [26] established an explicit achievable rate expression for the degraded Gaussian channel with multiple relays and characterized the bounds on transport capacity. Reznik et al. [20] considered Gaussian physically degraded relay channels and extended the results for multiple relay stages with a total average power constraint.

Gasper and Vetterli [12] derived a lower bound on the capacity of the relay channel by allowing arbitrarily complex network coding. Also, they considered upper bounds from the cut-set theorem [11] and showed that these upper and lower bounds meet asymptotically as the number of relay nodes goes to infinity. This result again shows that network coding is essential.

1.4   In This Paper

As we discussed, there are many new elements in network information theory and especially sensor networks that should be considered in the communication problem, such as: interference, feedback, and cooperation. Feedback and cooperation have received most of the attention so far, in order to derive better achievable rates or increase the network capacity in different scenarios, while the effect of interference even in the relay case can be quite capacity limiting and it has not received enough attention. On the other hand another limiting property is the fact that most of the current radios in sensor nodes operate in TDD mode when the transmitting and receiving frequencies are the same. Thus, sensor nodes cannot transmit and receive at the same time, and as a result the achievable rate in the network is lower.

This practical constraint will force us to use the nodes of the network as either a sender or receiver at any given time, which can be interpreted as having more than one mode of operation in the network. Each mode of operation in the network corresponds to the valid partitioning of the nodes into two disjoint subsets of sender and receiver nodes such that there is no node in the sender nodes set which is going to communicate with another node in that subset.

The motivation for the current work comes from the aforementioned practical constraint. We consider a more general case of the problem where the network has a finite number of states and derive some upper bounds on the achievable information rate in such a network. The derived bounds coincide with the known cut-set bound in network information theory [11] when the network has just one state. On the other hand, the bounds trivially hold for the network with the mentioned practical constraint if modes are considered as states, and the number of nodes in the network is finite. Later, we will give two applications of the derived bound which provides a tight upper bound where the cut-set bound [11] is unable to provide such bounds. In these two specific examples, we show that the derived bounds are tight enough to characterize the capacity.

Channels with finite number of states have been considered first in the context of compound channels [25], and the capacity expression for discrete memoryless channels with different cases of channel state information at the receiver and the transmitter have been derived. Extension of the results for the AWGN channel with infinite number of states (fading) can also be found in [13]. In the compound channel, besides the fact that knowledge of the channel state information may or may not be available at the sender or receiver, the state is considered to be varying stochastically. Throughout this paper, we assume that the network state information is known to all sender and receiver nodes, and in Corollaries 1, 2 we even let the nodes choose the state of the channel in order to optimize the intended achievable communication rates. As another direct application of the derived bound, Theorem 1 also provides a tight bound for the capacity of the compound channel with the known channel state information both at the transmitter and receiver [Theorem 4.6.1 in [25]].

2   Problem Formulation

We consider a general multi-terminal network of senders and receivers. The network can be considered as a directed graph where each node of the network represents a potential sender or receiver (or both), and each link represents existence of a (one-way) channel between two nodes. Most radios operate in TDD mode when the transmitting and receiving frequencies are the same. Thus, they can either send or receive at a given time or use of the network. We label such a radio as a *cheap* radio and the corresponding node of the network as a *cheap* node.

In accordance with the term of *channel use* in a single discrete memoryless channel we define *network use* which corresponds to the simultaneous one time use of each existing nodes of the network either as a sender or receiver. Also in each network use, set of *active links* is defined as all links which are departing from the set of sender nodes. With this definition, the mentioned practical constraint translates to the fact that in each network use there is no active link that arrives at a sender node.

We define operating mode of the network (or state of the network) as a valid partitioning of the nodes of the network into two sets of 'sender nodes' and 'receiver nodes' such that there is no active link that arrives at a sender node. It is obvious that if the number of nodes in the network is finite then the number of operating modes of the network of cheap nodes are finite.

In the following discussion we consider the network with finite states in general, where the network state is known to all nodes at each time and it is predefined. In other words sequence of the network states is a deterministic function or we can choose it in advance in order to maximize the throughput or optimize other network characteristics.

Results of this section are easily applicable to the network with cheap nodes where operating mode of the network is considered as the state of the network. Thus, although most of the discussion in the rest of paper applies to the network with cheap nodes, it is not limited to such a network. In other words state of the network in this section is not necessarily derived from the mentioned practical constraint.

Assume that there are N nodes and for every node i, $X^{(i)}$ is the transmitted variable, $Y^{(i)}$ is the received variable , and $R^{(ij)}$ represents the rate in which node i transmits information to node j. We assume that all intended messages $W^{(ij)}$ from node i to the node j are independent and uniformly distributed over their respective ranges $\{1, 2, 3, ..., 2^{nR^{(ij)}}\}$

Considering the network of discrete memoryless channels (DMC) with finite number of states and following the notation of [25] , the channel transition function or channel probability function (c.p.f.) is defined as: $P(y^{(1)}, y^{(2)}, \ldots, y^{(N)} | x^{(1)}, x^{(2)}, \ldots, x^{(N)} | m)$ where m is the state of the network. Each network use corresponds to the use of all present channels one time in a specific state. For example in the mentioned network with cheap nodes existing channels in each state is the set of active links or active channels. For every transmitter-receiver node pair (i, j) there is an intended message $W^{(ij)} \epsilon \{1, 2, 3, ..., 2^{nR^{(ij)}}\}$ to be transmitted from node i to node j in n network uses. The input symbol $X_k^{(i)}$ which is the transmitted signal from node i in time k (or k'th channel use) depends on $W^{(ij)} \forall j \epsilon \{1, 2, \ldots, N\}$, and also the past values of the received signal $Y^{(i)}$, i.e. $Y_1^{(i)}, Y_2^{(i)}, \ldots, Y_{k-1}^{(i)}$. Thus, the encoding and decoding functions of block length n code for node i have the following structure and properties:

Encoder: $X_k^{(i)}(W^{(i1)}, W^{(i2)}, \ldots, W^{(iN)}, Y_1^{(i)}, Y_2^{(i)}, \ldots, Y_{k-1}^{(i)})$ for any network use $k \epsilon \{1, 2, \ldots, N\}$

Decoder: $\widehat{W}^{(ij)}(Y_1^{(j)}, Y_2^{(j)}, \ldots, Y_N^{(j)}, W^{(j1)}, W^{(j2)}, \ldots, W^{(jN)}$ for all values of $j, i \epsilon \{1, 2, \ldots, N\}$ which is estimate of the receiver of node i at node j based on the received signal of node j for the whole block of transmission (from 1, to n) and its own transmitted information for the other nodes.

The probability of error for each decoder is defined as: $P_e^{(n)(ij)} = Pr(\widehat{W}^{(ij)} \neq W^{(ij)})$ which is defined based on the assumption that the messages are independent and uniformly distributed over their respective ranges.

A set of rates $\{R^{(ij)}\}$ is said to be achievable if there exist an encoding and decoding function with block length n such that $P_e^{(n)(ij)} \longrightarrow 0$ when $n \longrightarrow \infty$ for all $j, i \epsilon \{1, 2, \ldots, N\}$

Now suppose that state of the network is a deterministic function for every network use k as m_k, $m_k \epsilon \{1, 2, \ldots, M\}$, where M is the number of possible states assuming finite number of states. For any state m define $n_m(k)$ as the number of states which is equal to m in the first k network uses. Let $t_m = \lim_{k \to 0} n_m(k)/k$ define the portion of the time that network have been used in state m as the total number of network use goes to infinity.

For any cut-set which partitions set of all the nodes into two disjoint set S, S^c we will drive a bound on the information flow from one side to the other side, i.e from sender nodes in the set S to the receiver nodes in the set S^c As Theorem 1 states the bound is not function of the choices of deterministic function m_k directly rather it depends only on the asymptotic values $t_1, t_2, \ldots t_M$. In fact this theorem bounds the achievable rate of the transmission across a cut-set with the best choice of the deterministic function m_k with the fixed asymptotical properties, i.e. fixed $t_i, i\epsilon\{1, 2, \ldots, M\}$

Theorem 1. *Consider a general network with finite number of states, M, for which the sequence m_k of the states of the network is fixed and is known to all nodes. If the information rates $\{R^{(ij)}\}$ are achievable then there exist some joint probability distribution $p(x^{(1)}, x^{(2)}, \ldots, x^{(N)}|m)$ such that*

$$\sum_{i\epsilon S, j\epsilon S^{(c)}} R^{(ij)} \leq \sum_{m=1}^{M} t_m I(X_{(m)}^S, Y_{(m)}^{S^c}|X_{(m)}^{S^c}) \tag{1}$$

for all $S \subset \{1, 2, \ldots, N\}$

Proof See appendix I.

Theorem 1 provides a bound on the information flow across any cut-set of the network when the sequence of channel states is a known deterministic function. Thus, considering all possible sequence of Network states the bound across each cut-set would be the supremum of the achievable bounds in Theorem 1 for all choices of deterministic function m_k. Specifically we have the following corollary.

Corollary 1. *Consider a general network with finite states, M, for which the sequence m_k of the states of the network is known to all nodes. Maximum achievable information rates $\{R^{(ij)}\}$ across the cut-set $S \subset \{1, 2, \ldots, N\}$ for the proper choice of network state sequence m_k is bounded by:*

$$\sum_{i\epsilon S, j\epsilon S^{(c)}} R^{(ij)} \leq \sup_{t_m} \sum_{m=1}^{M} t_m I(X_{(m)}^S, Y_{(m)}^{S^c}|X_{(m)}^{S^c}) = \sup_{m} I(X_{(m)}^S, Y_{(m)}^{S^c}|X_{(m)}^{S^c}) \tag{2}$$

for some joint probability distribution $p(x^{(1)}, x^{(2)}, \ldots, x^{(N)}|m)$ where $\sum_{i=1}^{M} t_m = 1$.

Thus, in order to maximize the sum rate of the information transfer across a cut-set the above result suggests using the network in a fixed state m which allows for the maximum mutual information $I(X_{(m)}^S, Y_{(m)}^{S^c} | X_{(m)}^{S^c})$.

We can also consider an upper bound for the achievable rate of the information flow between two disjoint subsets of the nodes $\{S_1, S_2\}$. This upper bound proves useful when we just try to maximize the rate of information transfer from a given subset of the nodes to the other disjoint subset of the nodes without any interest in other communications in the network. For example this situation happens in the relay problem when a sender node (or set of sender nodes) transmits information to a destination node (or set of destination nodes) by the help of some intermediate relay node (or relay nodes). In this case, the aim is to maximize the rate from sender to destination.

A simple observation suggest that the sum of information rates from the set S_1 to the set S_2 is bounded by the sum of the rates across all the cut-set S such that $S \subset \{1, 2, \ldots, N\}$, $S \cap S_1 = S_1$, $S \cap S_2 = \phi$ which is given by corollary 1. Thus, we have:

$$\sum_{i \in S_1, j \in S_2} R^{(ij)} \leq \min_S \sup_m I(X_{(m)}^S, Y_{(m)}^{S^c} | X_{(m)}^{S^c}) \tag{3}$$

for some joint probability distribution $p(x^{(1)}, x^{(2)}, \ldots, x^{(N)} | m)$.

We can further elaborate result of theorem 1 directly to find better upper bound for the achievable rate of the information flow between to disjoint subsets of the nodes $\{S_1, S_2\}$.

Theorem 2. *Consider a general network with finite states, M, for which the sequence m_k of the states of the network is fixed and known to all nodes. If the information rates $\{R^{(ij)}\}$ are achievable then there exist some joint probability distribution $p(x^{(1)}, x^{(2)}, \ldots, x^{(N)} | m)$ such that sum rate of information transfer from a node set S_1 to a disjoint node set S_2, $S_1, S_2 \subset \{1, 2, \ldots, N\}$, is bounded by:*

$$\sum_{i \in S_1, j \in S_2} R^{(ij)} \leq \min_S \sum_{m=1}^M t_m I(X_{(m)}^S, Y_{(m)}^{S^c} | X_{(m)}^{S^c}) \tag{4}$$

when the minimization is taken over all set $S \subset \{1, 2, \ldots, N\}$ subject to $S \cap S_1 = S_1$, $S \cap S_2 = \phi$.

Proof Direct application of the Theorem 1 and considering the fact that the sequence of channel state is fixed results in the mentioned bound.∎

Again, considering all possible sequence of channel states, the bound of the achievable rate of information transfer from a node set S_1 to a disjoint node set S_2, $S_1, S_2 \subset \{1, 2, \ldots, N\}$, is bounded by the supremum of the achievable bounds in theorem 2 for all choices of deterministic function m_k.

Corollary 2. *Consider a general network with finite states, M, for which the sequence m_k of the states of the network is known to all nodes. Maximum achievable information rates $\{R^{(ij)}\}$ from a node set S_1 to a disjoint node set S_2, $S_1, S_2 \subset \{1, 2, \ldots, N\}$ for the proper choice of network state sequence m_k is bounded by:*

$$\sum_{i \epsilon S_1, j \epsilon S_2} R^{(ij)} \leq \sup_{t_m} \min_{S} \sum_{m=1}^{M} t_m I(X_{(m)}^S, Y_{(m)}^{S^c} | X_{(m)}^{S^c}) \tag{5}$$

for some joint probability distribution $p(x^{(1)}, x^{(2)}, \ldots, x^{(N)} | m)$ when the minimization is taken over all set $S \subset \{1, 2, \ldots, N\}$ subject to $S \cap S_1 = S_1$, $S \cap S_2 = \phi$ and the supremum is over all the non-negative t_m subject to $\sum_{i=1}^{M} t_m = 1$.

In the next section we will consider some specific examples of the networks and application of this bound on the achievable rates of communication in such networks.

3   Application of the New Bounds

Theorem 1 provides general bounds on the achievable information rates across any cut-set in the network and these bounds are not necessarily tight. For example, for the networks with just one state of operation, it coincides with the known cut-set bounds [11] which provide tight enough bounds to find the capacity region or capacity rate in some cases like discrete memoryless multiple access channel, degraded discrete memoryless relay channel, or arbitrary discrete memoryless relay channel with feedback [10]. On the other hand, the cut-set bounds [11] for even some other simple examples, such as general (non-degraded) broadcast channel do not provide a tight bound and thus the capacity region is not yet known.

Although having more than one state of operation in the network seems to increase degrees of freedom and thus the achievable rates in the network, but it is not always true. For example in the problem of communication in a network with cheap nodes, having more than one state is a result of imposing the condition that each node cannot transmit and receive at the same time. It is somehow trivial that posing this condition will not increase any sets of achievable rates in the network in comparison to the same network without this constraint (which has obviously just one state of operation but all of the links or channels between the nodes can be used at the same time).

In this section, we will give applications of derived bounds in the previous section in cascaded channels (multi-hop network) and relay channel with cheap nodes. In both of the examples, achievable rate of information transmission is considerably lower than the rate of the same network topology without the mentioned practical constraint. Thus, the known cut-set theorem of network information theory is unable to provide tight enough bounds. On the other hand, the derived bounds in this paper prove to be most effective in these cases and they

capture the effect of the introduced practical constraint on the network nodes
to the extent that we can actually drive the capacity in both of the examples.

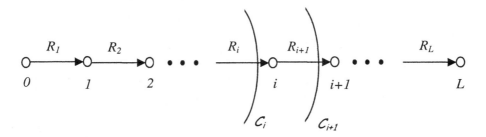

Fig. 1. Cascaded Discrete Memoryless Channels

3.1 Cascaded Channels (Multi-hop Network)

Consider L discrete memoryless channel in cascade, Figure 1, and index each
channel from left to right as $i = 1, 2, \ldots, L$, and each node from left to right as
$0, 1, 2, \ldots, L$ in which we are interested in transmitting information from node
0 to node L. Thus node i receives Y_i which is the output of the channel i and
transmit its information, X_{i+1} via channel $i+1$ which is the input to this channel. Since we have assumed that channels are cascaded and there are no other
connection between the nodes other than stated, the channel output Y_i just depends on the input X_i but no other transmitted signals. For each channel i,
$i\epsilon\{1, 2, \ldots, L\}$ define capacity of each individual link as $R_i := \max I(X_i, Y_i)$
where maximization is taken over all possible distributions of X_i.

It has been known that the capacity of such cascaded system without the
mentioned practical limitation on transmission and reception at the same time is
the minimum of the individual rates of the channels $C_1 = \min\{R_1, R_2, \ldots, R_L\}$.
Since each channel can transmit information at least with the rate of C_1 without
any restriction on receiving data from previous node, achievablity of this minimum rate is immediate. Also, the known cut-set bound of network information
theory states that no higher rate is achievable.

On the other hand, imposing the mentioned practical limitation will decrease
the achievable rate in this cascaded channel and the mentioned known cut-set
bound is no longer tight. In this case, by using the results of Corollary 2 we have:

$$R \triangleq R^{(0L)} \leq \sup_{t_m} \min_i \{(\sum_{m=1}^{M} t_m * \delta_{im}) R_i\} \tag{6}$$

when the minimization is taken over i, $i\epsilon\{1, 2, \ldots, L\}$ and the supremum is over
all the non-negative t_m subject to $\sum_{i=1}^{M} t_m = 1$. In the above expression $\delta_{im} = 1$
iff link i is used in state m of the network, otherwise $\delta_{im} = 0$.

It is also possible to prove that the above bound is actually achievable. The proof is based on the fact that for any given sets of $\{t_1, t_2, \ldots, t_M\}$ associated with the states $1, 2, \ldots, M$ satisfying $\sum_{i=1}^{M} t_m = 1$, the rate of $\min_i\{(\sum_{m=1}^{M} t_m * \delta_{im}) R_i\}$ is achievable with arbitrarily small probability of error [16]. Thus, the above rate $\sup_{t_m} \min_i\{(\sum_{m=1}^{M} t_m * \delta_{im}) R_i\}$ is the capacity of the network of the cascaded channels with cheap nodes.

Furthermore, we have proved that the above expression can be simplified to the following form:

$$R = R^* := \min\{\frac{R_1 R_2}{R_1 + R_2}, \frac{R_2 R_3}{R_2 + R_3}, \ldots, \frac{R_{L-1} R_L}{R_{L-1} + R_L}\} \tag{7}$$

For each $i \epsilon \{1, 2, \ldots, L-1\}$, consider two cut-set C_i, C_{i+1}. since for each i, m we have $\delta_{im} * \delta_{(i+1)m} = 0$ it can easily be verified that $R \leq \frac{R_i R_{i+1}}{R_i + R_{i+1}}$ and thus $R \leq R^*$. On the other hand it is possible to show that states $1, 2, \ldots, M$ and their associated set of $\{t_1, t_2, \ldots, t_M\}$ exist such that the rate R^* is achievable, and thus $R = R^*$ [16].

3.2 Relay Channel

Consider discrete memoryless relay channel of Figure 2, in which source node S is willing to transmit information to the destination node D by using direct link between the node pair (S, D) as well as help of another relay node R (if it improves the achievable rate of transmission) by using link pairs (S, R) and (R, D). Furthermore assume that relay node R is a cheap node and thus it cannot transmit and receive at the same time.

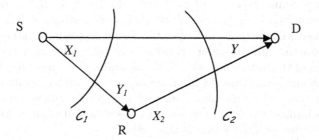

Fig. 2. Discrete Memoryless Relay Channel

With this assumption there are two possible states of operation in the network. In the state m_1 relay node R acts as a receiver and thus channel probability function is given by: $p(y, y_1|x_1|m_1)$, while in the state m_2 relay node functions as a transmitter and the channel probability function is given by: $p(y|x_1, x_2|m_2)$.

From Corollary 2, an upper bound for the information transfer rate R from source node S to the destination node D would be:

$$R \leq \sup_{t,\, 0 \leq t \leq 1} \min\{t\, I(X_1; Y, Y_1 | m_1) + (1-t)\, I(X_1; Y | X_2, m_2),$$
$$t\, I(X_1; Y | m_1) + (1-t)\, I(X_1, X_2; Y | m_2)\} \qquad (8)$$

For every t, $0 \leq t \leq 1$, it is possible to show that the rate R^* is achievable where R^* is given by:

$$R^* \triangleq \min\{t\, I(X_1; Y_1 | m_1) + (1-t)\, I(X_1; Y | X_2, m_2),$$
$$t\, I(X_1; Y | m_1) + (1-t)\, I(X_1, X_2; Y | m_2)\} \qquad (9)$$

Thus, if in the state m_1 the received signal y at the destination node D is degraded form of the received signal y_1 at the relay node then the the bound of (8) would coincide with this achievable rate for some value of t. Hence, the bound derived in Corollary 2 provides the converse for the capacity theorem of degraded cheap relay channel, and the capacity is given by $C = R^*$ defined in (9).

4 Concluding Remarks

Theorems 1, 2, (and Corollary 1, 2) establish general bounds on the achievable information rates in the network with finite number of states. While these bounds are not necessarily tight in general, they provide tight enough bounds for the network of cascaded channels with cheap nodes and also cheap relay network which results in derivation of the capacity in these cases. The derived Bounds coincide with the known cut-set Bounds [11] of network information theory if the network has just one state. In addition, Theorem 1 provides a tight bound for the capacity of the compound channel (which is a multiple state channel) with the known channel state information both at the transmitter and receiver [Theorem 4.6.1 in [25]].

References

1. R. Ahlswede: Multi-way communication channels. in Proc. 2nd Int. Symp. information Theory, Tsahkadsor, Armenian S.S.R., pp. 23-52,, (1971)
2. R. Ahlswede, N. Cai, R.W. Yeung: Network Information Flow Theory, In: Proc. IEEE ISIT 1998, pp. 186, (1998)
3. R. Ahlswede, N. Cai, S.-Y. R. Li, R.W. Yeung: Network Information Flow, IEEE Trans. on Information Theory, Vol.46, No.4, pp. 1204–1216, (2000)
4. S.P. Borade: Network Information Flow: Limits and Acheivability, In: Proc. IEEE ISIT 2002, pp. 139, (2002)
5. G. Caire, S. Shamai: On the Achievable Throughput in Multiple Antenna Gaussian Broadcast Channel, submitted to IEEE Transactions on Information Theory, July (2001)
6. A. B. Carleial: A case where interference does not reduce capacity, IEEE Trans. Inform. Theory, vol. IT-21, pp. 569–570, Sept. (1975)

7. A.B. Carleial: Interference Channels, IEEE Trans. on Information Theory, Vol. IT-24, No. 1, January, pp. 60–70 (1978)
8. M. H. M. Costa: Writing on dirty paper, IEEE Transactions on Information Theory, pp. 439–441, May (1983)
9. T. M. Cover: Broadcast channels, IEEE Trans. Inform. Theory, vol. IT-18, pp. 2–14, Jan. (1972)
10. Thomas M Cover, Abbas S. El Gammal: Capacity Thorems for the Relay Channel. IEEE Transactions on Information Theory, Vol-25, No.5, pp. 572–584, September. (1979)
11. Thomas M Cover, Joy A Thomas: Elements of Information Theory. John Wiley and Sons, Inc., New York (1991)
12. Michael Gastpar, Martin Vetterli: On the Capacity of Wireless Networks: The Relay Case. (2002)
13. A. J. Goldsmith, P. Varaiya: Capacity of fading channels with channel side information, IEEE Transactions on Information Theory. November (1997)
14. Piyush Gupta and P. R. Kumar: The Capacity of Wireless Networks, IEEE Transactions on Information Theory, pp. 388–404, vol. IT-46, no. 2, March (2000)
15. P.Gupta, P.R. Kumar: Towards an Information Theory of Large Networks: An Achievable Rate Region, Submitted to the IEEE Trans. on Information Theory, September (2001), Revised November (2002)
16. Mohammad A. Khojastepour, Ashutosh Sabharwal, Behnaam Aazhang: On the Capacity of 'Cheap' Relay Networks. to be submitted to the 37th Annual Conference on Information Sciences and Systems, Baltimore, Maryland, March 12–14 (2003)
17. S.-Y. R. Li, R.W. Yeung: Linear Codes for Network Information Flow, In: Proc. IEEE ISIT 1999, pp. 25, (1999)
18. K. Marton: A coding theorem for the discrete memoryless broadcast channel, IEEE Transactions on Information Theory, pp. 306–311, May (1979)
19. E. C. van der Meulen: Three-terminal communication channels, In: Adv. Appl. Prob., vol. 3, pp. 120–154, (1971)
20. A. Reznik, S.R. Kulkarni, S. Verdu: Capacity and Optimal Resource Allocation in the Degraded Gaussian Relay Channel with Multiple Relays, In: 40th Allerton Conference on Communication, Control, and Computing, September (2002)
21. H. Sato: An outer bound to the capacity region of broadcast channels, IEEE Trans. on Information Theory, Vol. 24, No. 3, pp. 374–377, May (1978)
22. C. E. Shannon: Two-way communication channels, In: Proc. 4th Berkelev Svm . Math. Statist. and Prob. vol. 1. VD. 611–644. (1961). Reprinted in: Key Papers in the Development-of Information Theory, (D. Slepian, Ed.) New York: IEEE Press, pp. 339–372, (1974)
23. S. Vishwanath, N. Jindal, and A. Goldsmith: On the Capacity of Multiple Input Multiple Output Broadcast Channels, International Conference on Communications, (2002)
24. Pramod Viswanath, David Tse: Sum Capacity of the Multiple Antenna Gaussian Broadcast Channel and Uplink-Downlink Duality , submitted to IEEE Transactions on Information Theory, July (2002)
25. Jacob Wolfowitz : Coding Theorems of Information Theory. 3rd edn. Springer-Verlog, Berlin Heidelberg New York (1978)
26. L. Xie, P.R. Kumar: A network information Theory for Wireless Communication: Scaling Laws and Optimal Operation, Submitted to the IEEE Trans. on Information Theory, April (2002)

27. W. Yu, and J. Cioffi: Sum Capacity of Gaussian Vector Broadcast Channels, submitted to IEEE Transactions on Information Theory, Nov., (2001)

Appendix I: *Proof of Theorem 1*

Let $T = \{(i,j) : i\epsilon S, j\epsilon S^c\}$ be the set of all links that cross from node set S to the node set S^c and T^c be all the other links in the network. Based on the definition of $W^{(ij)}$ such that they are independent and uniformly distributed over their range and also following the definitions and conditions of Section 2, we have:

$$\sum_{i\epsilon S, j\epsilon S^{(c)}} R^{(ij)}$$

$$= \sum_{i\epsilon S, j\epsilon S^{(c)}} H(W^{(ij)}) \tag{10}$$

$$= H(W^T) \tag{11}$$

$$= H(W^T|W^{T^c}) \tag{12}$$

$$= I(W^T, Y_1^{(S^c)}, Y_2^{(S^c)}, \ldots, Y_N^{(S^c)}|W^{(T^c)})$$
$$+ H(W^T|Y_1^{(S^c)}, Y_2^{(S^c)}, \ldots, Y_N^{(S^c)}, W^{(T^c)}) \tag{13}$$

$$\leq I(W^T, Y_1^{(S^c)}, Y_2^{(S^c)}, \ldots, Y_N^{(S^c)}|W^{(T^c)}) + n\epsilon_n \tag{14}$$

$$= \sum_{k=1}^{N} I(W^T, Y_k^{(S^c)}|Y_1^{(S^c)}, Y_2^{(S^c)}, \ldots, Y_{k-1}^{(S^c)}, W^{(T^c)}) + n\epsilon_n \tag{15}$$

$$= \sum_{k=1}^{N} \{H(Y_k^{(S^c)}|Y_1^{(S^c)}, Y_2^{(S^c)}, \ldots, Y_{k-1}^{(S^c)}, W^{(T^c)})$$
$$- H(Y_k^{(S^c)}|Y_1^{(S^c)}, Y_2^{(S^c)}, \ldots, Y_{k-1}^{(S^c)}, W^{(T^c)}, W^T)\} + n\epsilon_n \tag{16}$$

$$\leq \sum_{k=1}^{N} \{H(Y_k^{(S^c)}|Y_1^{(S^c)}, Y_2^{(S^c)}, \ldots, Y_{k-1}^{(S^c)}, W^{(T^c)}, X_k^{(S^c)})$$
$$- H(Y_k^{(S^c)}|Y_1^{(S^c)}, Y_2^{(S^c)}, \ldots, Y_{k-1}^{(S^c)}, W^{(T^c)}, W^T, X_k^{(S^c)}, X_k^{(S)})\} + n\epsilon_n \tag{17}$$

$$\leq \sum_{k=1}^{N} \{H(Y_k^{(S^c)}|X_k^{(S^c)}) - H(Y_k^{(S^c)}|X_k^{(S^c)}, X_k^{(S)})\} + n\epsilon_n \tag{18}$$

$$= \sum_{k=1}^{N} I(X_k^{(S)}, Y_k^{(S^c)}|X_k^{(S^c)}) + n\epsilon_n \tag{19}$$

$$= \sum_{k=1}^{N} I(X_{Q_{m(k)}}^{(S)}, Y_{Q_{m(k)}}^{(S^c)}|X_{Q_{m(k)}}^{(S^c)}, Q_{m(k)} = k) + n\epsilon_n \tag{20}$$

$$= \sum_{m=1}^{M} n_m(n) I(X_{Q_m}^{(S)}, Y_{Q_m}^{(S^c)}|X_{Q_m}^{(S^c)}, Q_m) + n\epsilon_n \tag{21}$$

$$= \sum_{m=1}^{M} n_m(n)\{H(Y_{Q_m}^{(S^c)}|X_{Q_m}^{(S^c)}, Q_m) - H(Y_{Q_m}^{(S^c)}|X_{Q_m}^{(S^c)}, X_{Q_m}^{(S)}, Q_m)\} + n\epsilon_n(22)$$

$$\leq \sum_{m=1}^{M} n_m(n)\{H(Y_{Q_m}^{(S^c)}|X_{Q_m}^{(S^c)}) - H(Y_{Q_m}^{(S^c)}|X_{Q_m}^{(S^c)}, X_{Q_m}^{(S)})\} + n\epsilon_n \qquad (23)$$

$$= \sum_{m=1}^{M} n_m(n)I(X_{Q_m}^{(S)}, Y_{Q_m}^{(S^c)}|X_{Q_m}^{(S^c)}) + n\epsilon_n \qquad (24)$$

where

(10) follows from the assumption that $W^{(ij)}$'s are distributed uniformly over their respective ranges $\{1, 2, 3, ..., 2^{nR^{(ij)}}\}$,

(11) follows from the assumption that $W^{(ij)}$'s are independent and also definition $W^{(T)} = \{W^{(ij)} : i\epsilon S, j\epsilon S^c\}$,

(12) follows from the independence of $W^{(T)}$, $W^{(T^c)}$,

(13) follows from the definition of the mutual information,

(14) follows from the Fano's inequality, because message $W^{(T)}$ can be decoded from $Y^{(S)}$ and $W^{(T^c)}$. (Since we have assumed that the set of rates $\{R^{(ij)}\}$ are achievable; and also note that $\epsilon_n \longrightarrow 0$ as $n \longrightarrow \infty$),

(15) follows from the chain rule,

(16) follows from the definition of the mutual information,

(17) follows from the fact that first term has been changed due to the definition of $X_k^{(S^c)}$ which is function of the past received symbols $Y(S^c)$ and the message $W^{(T^c)}$. Also the second term has not been increased since conditioning can only reduce the entropy,

(18) follows from the fact that $Y_k^{(S^c)}$ only depends on the current input symbols $X_k^{(S^c)}$, $X_k^{(S)}$. (Note that although $Y_k^{(S^c)}$ depends on the state m_k but it is deterministic and predefined before transmission for all the nodes),

(19) follows from the definition of the mutual information,

(20) follows from introducing time sharing random variables $Q_1, Q_2, ..., Q_M$ for each state of the network, where each state m, Q_m is uniformly distributed over all values of the time index k, $k\epsilon\{1, 2, 3, ..., N\}$, for which $m_k = m$,

(21) follows from rearranging the summation and using definition of the average mutual information,

(22) follows from the definition of the mutual information,

(23) follows from the fact that conditioning cannot increase the entropy for the first term and the fact that second term has not been changed since $Y_{Q_m}^{(S^c)}$ only depends on the current input symbols $X_{Q_m}^{(S^c)}$, $X_{Q_m}^{(S)}$ and conditionally is independent of Q_m,

(24) follows from the definition of the mutual information.

Thus, by dividing both sides of inequality (24) by n and finding the limit as $n \longrightarrow \infty$ we have:

$$\sum_{i \epsilon S, j \epsilon S^{(c)}} R^{(ij)} \leq \sum_{m=1}^{M} \frac{n_m(n)}{n} I(X_{Q_m}^{(S)}, Y_{Q_m}^{(S^c)} | X_{Q_m}^{(S^c)}) + \epsilon_n \qquad (25)$$

and as $n \longrightarrow \infty$ we have:

$$\sum_{i \epsilon S, j \epsilon S^{(c)}} R^{(ij)} \leq \sum_{m=1}^{M} t_m I(X_{Q_m}^{(S)}, Y_{Q_m}^{(S^c)} | X_{Q_m}^{(S^c)}) \qquad (26)$$

and it completes the proof.∎

Source-Channel Communication in Sensor Networks

Michael Gastpar[1] and Martin Vetterli[12]

[1] University of California, Berkeley CA 94720, USA,
gastpar@eecs.berkeley.edu,
http://www.eecs.berkeley.edu/~gastpar
[2] Ecole Polytechnique Fédérale (EPFL), Lausanne, Switzerland.

Abstract. Sensors acquire data, and communicate this to an interested party. The arising coding problem is often split into two parts: First, the sensors compress their respective acquired signals, potentially applying the concepts of distributed source coding. Then, they communicate the compressed version to the interested party, the goal being not to make any errors. This coding paradigm is inspired by Shannon's separation theorem for point-to-point communication, but it leads to suboptimal performance in general network topologies. The optimal performance for the general case is not known.

In this paper, we propose an alternative coding paradigm based on joint source-channel coding. This coding paradigm permits to determine the optimal performance for a class of sensor networks, and shows how to achieve it. For sensor networks outside this class, we argue that the goal of the coding system could be to approach our condition for optimal performance as closely as possible. This is supported by examples for which our coding paradigm significantly outperforms the traditional separation-based coding paradigm. In particular, for a Gaussian example considered in this paper, the distortion of the best coding scheme according to the separation paradigm decreases like $1/\log M$, while for our coding paradigm, it decreases like $1/M$, where M is the total number of sensors.

1 Introduction

In a sensor network, the goal is typically to reconstruct the measured physical phenomenon to within some prescribed distortion level, and this at the smallest possible cost on the communication link. What coding strategy should the sensors use? For the case of a single sensor, i.e., for the ergodic point-to-point communication scenario, Shannon proved that separate source and channel code design is an optimal strategy (asymptotically as the delay and the complexity become unconstrained [12]). This fact, known as the separation principle, is both conceptually and practically appealing. Therefore, it is also a tempting coding paradigm in a network context: each sensor compresses its measurements using the best possible distributed coding techniques, see e.g. [1,13,15];

F. Zhao and L. Guibas (Eds.): IPSN 2003, LNCS 2634, pp. 162–177, 2003.
© Springer-Verlag Berlin Heidelberg 2003

the resulting source codewords are then transmitted across the channel using capacity-achieving codes, see e.g. [4, Ch. 14]. It is well known that in spite of its elegance, this coding paradigm does *not* lead to optimal performance in networks, see e.g. [4, p. 449], [7]. In other words, the concepts of capacity and rate-distortion do not characterize the best achievable performance. Rather, joint source-channel coding techniques can significantly outperform the separation-based coding paradigm in these cases.

In this paper, we propose an alternative coding paradigm based on recent results on the source-channel communication problem in the point-to-point case [5, 6,7]. We investigate a particular sensor network topology, which is defined in detail in Section 2. M separate sensors observe each a different noisy version of a physical phenomenon S. The sensors communicate over a multi-access channel to a central observer who wishes to produce an estimate $\hat{S}$ of the physical phenomenon in such a way as to minimize the distortion. The precise shape of the distortion measure $d(s, \hat{s})$ depends on the problem at hand.

In Section 3, we evaluate the performance achievable by the separation-based coding paradigm in our sensor network topology. Results are given in particular for a Gaussian example, for which we prove that the achievable distortion decays like $1/\log M$, where M is the number of sensors.

In Section 4, we develop a simple joint source-channel coding strategy for the same Gaussian example. We establish two key facts for our strategy: First, we determine that the distortion decays like $1/M$, where M is the number of sensors, thus considerably outperforming the separation-based coding paradigm. Second, we prove that as M tends to infinity, our strategy achieves the smallest possible distortion.

Thereafter, we extend our results beyond the Gaussian example, establishing a general joint source-channel coding paradigm for the considered sensor network topology, using the arguments of [5,6,7]. We show that it sometimes leads to provably optimum performance, but even when it does not, we illustrate that it can considerably outperform the separation-based coding paradigm.

In Section 5, we outline the extension of our basic sensor network topology to include communication *between* the sensors. In particular, we find for a class of sensor networks that this additional degree of freedom does not enhance the asymptotic performance (as the number of sensors M tends to infinity).

2   The Considered Sensor Network

Consider the sensor network shown in Figure 1: The physical phenomenon is characterized by the sequence of random vectors

$$\{S[n]\}_{n \in Z} = \{(S_1[n], S_2[n], \dots, S_L[n])\}_{n \in Z}. \tag{1}$$

To simplify the notation in the rest of the paper, we denote sequences as

$$S^n \overset{def}{=} \{S[n]\}_{n \in Z}. \tag{2}$$

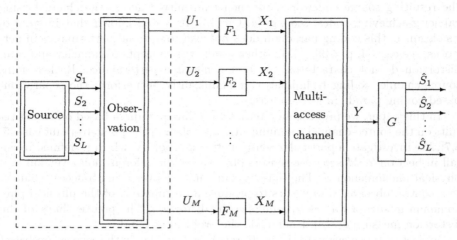

Fig. 1. The sensor network topology considered in this paper.

We use the upper case S to denote the random variable, and the lower case s to denote its realization. The distribution of S is denoted by $P_S(s)$. To simplify notation, we will also use the shorthand $P(s)$ when the subscript is just the capitalized version of the argument in the parentheses. The random vector $S[n]$ is not directly observed by the sensors. Rather, sensor k observes a sequence $U_k^n = \{U_k[n]\}_{n \in Z}$ which depends on the physical phenomenon according to a conditional probability distribution, which we denote by

$$P(u_k | s_1, \ldots, s_L). \tag{3}$$

Based on the observations $U_k[n]$, sensor k transmits a signal

$$X_k^n = F_k(U_k^n) \tag{4}$$

on the multi-access channel. The transmitted signals satisfy a power, or more generally, a cost constraint of the form

$$E\rho(X_1^n, X_2^n, \ldots, X_M^n) \leq \Gamma. \tag{5}$$

This is a generalization of the sum power constraint for all the sensors together. In some variations of our problem, it is also interesting to consider a family of simultaneous constraints, with cost functions $\rho_i(\cdot)$ and maximum expected cost Γ_i. This is a generalization of the individual power constraints for each sensor.

The final destination uses the output of the multi-access channel to construct estimates

$$\hat{S}^n = (\hat{S}_1^n, \hat{S}_2^n, \ldots, \hat{S}_L^n). \tag{6}$$

For a fixed code, composed of the encoders $F_1, F_2, \ldots, F_M$ at the sensors and the decoder G, the achieved distortion Δ is computed as follows:

$$\Delta = Ed\left(S^n, \hat{S}^n\right). \tag{7}$$

For a particular coding scheme $(F_1, F_2, \ldots, F_M, G)$, the performance is determined by the required cost Γ and the incurred distortion Δ. The goal of the analysis is to determine the set of optimal trade-offs (Γ, Δ), where optimal is to be understood in an information-theoretic sense, i.e., irrespective of delay and complexity.

Example 1 (Gaussian case). An important special case of the sensor network topology of Figure 1 is illustrated in Figure 2: In this case, $L = 1$, and

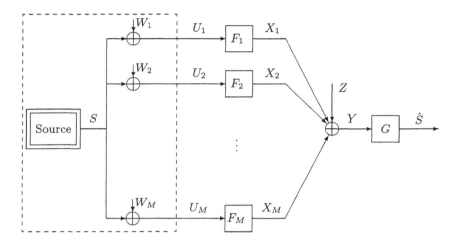

Fig. 2. The Gaussian example.

$$U_k[n] = S[n] + W_k[n], \tag{8}$$

where $\{S[n]\}_n$ is a sequence of independent and identically distributed (iid) Gaussian random variables of variance σ_S^2, and $\{W_k[n]\}_n$ is a sequence (in n, for $n = 1, 2, 3, \ldots$) of iid Gaussian random variables of mean zero and variance σ_W^2. Moreover, for the sake of the example, we also assume that W_k and W_l are independent for all $k \neq l$. The constraint on the signals transmitted by the sensors is a sum power constraint, i.e.,

$$\sum_{k=1}^{M} E|X_k|^2 \leq MP. \tag{9}$$

The final destination receives

$$Y[n] = \sum_{k=1}^{M} X_k[n] + Z[n], \tag{10}$$

where $Z[n]$ is iid Gaussian noise of variance σ_Z^2. The distortion measure in this example is the mean-squared error, i.e.,

$$D = \sum_{j=1}^{n} E|S[n] - \hat{S}[n]|^2. \tag{11}$$

The goal of the analysis is to determine the best power-distortion trade-off. More precisely, we want to determine the minimum distortion for a fixed power MP. The performance of a communication scheme employing source-channel separation is analyzed in two steps: the rate-distortion and the capacity-cost problem.

3   Separate Source and Channel Coding

In extension of the point-to-point case (summarized in Appendix A), a general coding paradigm for sensor networks can again be formulated as the combination of source coding and channel coding. In this section, we outline the performance that can be achieved using a separation-based coding strategy. Then, we provide an explicit answer for a simple Gaussian sensor network with a topology according to Figure 1. Note that it is well-known that this coding paradigm does not lead to optimal network designs in general, see e.g. [4, p. 449].

3.1   Distributed Source Coding

The particular source coding problem corresponding to Figure 1 is known as the CEO problem, proposed and partially solved in [2]. More precisely, the problem for sensor k is to encode its observations into a bit stream of R_k bits per sample. The determination of the set of the smallest $(R_1, R_2, \ldots, R_M)$ that permit the source decoder to reconstruct $S_1, \ldots, S_L$ at a specified fidelity Δ (as in Equation (7)) is an open problem in general. We call this the rate-distortion region, denoted by $\mathcal{R}(\Delta)$.

Example 2 (Gaussian case). For the Gaussian sensor network of Example 1, the particular problem of encoding U_k as in Figure 2 into bits and reconstructing S from these bits, has been studied in the shape of the so-called quadratic Gaussian CEO problem in the literature [11,14]. The distortion D_{CEO} depends on the total rate used by the sensors, $R_{tot} = R_1 + R_2 + \ldots + R_M$ as

$$D_{CEO} = \frac{\sigma_W^2}{2R_{tot}}, \tag{12}$$

when the total rate R_{tot} is large. More precise results for small R_{tot} can be found in [11].

3.2   Multi-access with Dependent Messages

For the multi-access problem in Figure 1, the goal is to determine the set of all achievable rate pairs (R_1, R_2) when the channel inputs satisfy the cost constraint Γ (as in Equation (5)), i.e., the capacity region $\mathcal{C}(\Gamma)$. When the messages of the different users are independent from each other, the capacity region is known, see e.g. [4]. However, in a sensor network situation, the messages of the sensors may typically be correlated since the underlying signals are. The capacity region for the case where the messages are potentially correlated is only partially known [3].

Example 3 (Gaussian case). For the Gaussian sensor network of Example 1, the goal is to determine the capacity region for the additive white Gaussian multiple-access channel with inputs $X_1, X_2, \ldots, X_M$ and output Y. When the messages may be dependent, the maximum sum rate R_{tot} can be upper bounded by

$$R_{tot} \leq \frac{1}{2} \log_2 \left(1 + \frac{M^2 P}{\sigma_Z^2} \right). \tag{13}$$

This bound follows by allowing *arbitrary* dependence between the inputs of the multi-access channel. However, in the Gaussian sensor network of Example 1, since the encoders are separate, the messages cannot be arbitrarily dependent; rather, their dependence follows from the source structure. For this reason, the bound should not be expected to be tight, but rather too optimistic.

3.3   Achievable Cost-Distortion Trade-Offs

For separate source and channel coding, a cost-distortion trade-off (Γ, Δ) is achievable only if

$$\mathcal{R}(\Delta) \cap \mathcal{C}(\Gamma) \neq \emptyset. \tag{14}$$

This follows immediately from the definition of the rate-distortion and the capacity-cost regions. In other words, if the two regions do not intersect, it is not possible to achieve the trade-off (Γ, Δ) by a strategy composed of optimal source compression followed by capacity-approaching channel coding.

Remark 1. Condition (14) is only achievable if each sensor is allowed to observe the entire sequence U_k^n before deciding what X_k^n to transmit.

Example 4 (Gaussian case). For the Gaussian sensor network of Example 1, the optimum power-distortion trade-offs that can be achieved by separate source and channel coding can be determined by combining the results of Examples 2 and 3. For a fixed total sensor power MP, the smallest achievable distortion is bounded by inserting the upper bound to the total rate R_{tot} on the multi-access channel (from Equation (13)) in the minimum distortion for the CEO problem

(Equation (12)). Hence, the distortion achieved by the separation-based scheme behaves at best like

$$D_{sep}(MP) \geq \frac{\sigma_W^2}{\log_2\left(1 + \frac{M^2 P}{\sigma_Z^2}\right)}, \tag{15}$$

when the number of sensors M is large. Here, σ_W^2 is the variance of the observation noise and also the variance of the noise in the multi-access channel, and MP is the total sensor transmit power.

4   Joint Source-Channel Coding

Since it is well-known that the separation-based coding paradigm does not lead to optimal system designs in general, we now develop an alternative coding paradigm for our sensor network topology, illustrated in Figure 1. This is motivated by a particular feature of the Gaussian example discussed above. Therefore, we first study an alternative coding scheme for the Gaussian case that outperforms separation-based strategies considerably. Thereafter, we extend this insight into a general coding paradigm, using an approach reminiscent of [5,6,7].

4.1   The Gaussian Case

An Achievable Distortion. For the point-to-point transmission of an iid Gaussian source across an additive white Gaussian channel, it is well-known that uncoded transmission is optimal [10], see also [5,6,7]. For the Gaussian example illustrated in Figure 2 and defined in Example 1, it is therefore intuitive to study the strategy of uncoded forwarding by the sensors. The following power-distortion trade-off is achieved by this strategy.

Theorem 1. *For the Gaussian sensor network defined in Example 1, with source variance σ_S^2, observation noise variance σ_W^2, and total transmit power at the sensors of MP, the following distortion is achievable:*

$$D_1(MP) = \frac{\sigma_S^2 \sigma_W^2}{\frac{M^2}{M+(\sigma_Z^2/\sigma_W^2)(\sigma_S^2+\sigma_W^2)/P}\sigma_S^2 + \sigma_W^2}. \tag{16}$$

Proof. Suppose the sensors apply uncoded transmission. More precisely, sensor k scales $U_k[n]$ to meet its power constraint P,

$$X_k[n] = \sqrt{\frac{P}{\sigma_S^2 + \sigma_W^2}} U_k[n]. \tag{17}$$

Recalling that $U_k[n] = S[n] + W_k[n]$, the received signal for the uncoded strategy is

$$Y[n] = \sqrt{\frac{P}{\sigma_S^2 + \sigma_W^2}}\left(MS[n] + \sum_{k=1}^{M} W_k[n]\right) + Z[n]. \tag{18}$$

It remains to specify the decoder. Since the encoding operation is memoryless, the optimum decoder (or estimator) G is also memoryless: there is no benefit from considering multiple symbols jointly. The optimum decoder G is then simply the minimum mean-squared error estimator of $S[n]$, given by the standard formula:

$$\hat{S}[n] = \frac{E\left[SY\right]}{E\left[Y^2\right]} Y[n] = \frac{\sqrt{\frac{P}{\sigma_S^2 + \sigma_W^2}} M \sigma_S^2}{\frac{P}{\sigma_S^2 + \sigma_W^2}(M^2 \sigma_S^2 + M \sigma_W^2) + \sigma_Z^2} Y[n]. \tag{19}$$

The resulting distortion is evaluates to

$$D_1(MP) = \sigma_S^2 - \frac{\frac{P}{\sigma_S^2 + \sigma_W^2} M^2 \sigma_S^4}{\frac{P}{\sigma_S^2 + \sigma_W^2}(M^2 \sigma_S^2 + M \sigma_W^2) + \sigma_Z^2}$$

$$= \frac{\sigma_S^2 \sigma_W^2}{\frac{M^2}{M + (\sigma_Z^2/\sigma_W^2)(\sigma_S^2 + \sigma_W^2)/P} \sigma_S^2 + \sigma_W^2}. \tag{20}$$

□

The main result of Theorem 1 follows from the comparison of (16) with (15): The separation-based scheme is clearly suboptimal in our example. More precisely, the decreasing behavior of the distortion as a function of the number of sensors M is fundamentally different for the two schemes: The separation-based scheme achieves at best a decreasing behavior of $1/\log M$, while Theorem 1 establishes an achievable decreasing behavior of $1/M$.

Asymptotic Optimality. In this paragraph, we first derive a lower bound to the minimum achievable distortion $D_{min}(MP)$ at total sensor power MP. We then establish that this lower bound coincides with $D_1(MP)$ in the limit as the number of sensors becomes large. This proves that asymptotically in M, the strategy of Theorem 1 performs optimally.

The lower bound is found by analyzing the system in which the sensors are ideally linked to the destination. This system can be interpreted as a point-to-point multi-antenna system, where the sender has one antenna with output S and the receiver has M antennas with inputs $U_1, U_2, \ldots, U_M$. The minimum distortion achievable in this system cannot be larger than the minimum distortion achievable in our sensor network. The lower bound can stated as follows:

Theorem 2. *For the Gaussian sensor network defined in Example 1, with source variance σ_S^2, observation noise variance σ_W^2, and total transmit power at the sensors of MP, the minimum achievable distortion satisfies $D_{min}(MP) \geq D_{lower}(MP)$, where*

$$D_{lower}(MP) = \frac{\sigma_S^2 \sigma_W^2}{M \sigma_S^2 + \sigma_W^2}. \tag{21}$$

Proof. The lower bound is found by idealization: The receiver is ideally linked to the sensors, and we suppose that the physical phenomenon $S[n]$ itself uses optimal coding.

The smallest distortion achievable in this idealized system obviously cannot be larger than the smallest distortion achievable in the original system.

The idealized system is an ergodic point-to-point source-channel communication system; the separation theorem applies. The capacity of the idealized channel is simply the capacity of the multi-antenna channel with one transmit antenna (the source itself) and M receive antennae (the M sensors, now ideally linked to the destination). The capacity of such a system is well-known:

$$C = \frac{1}{2} \log_2 \left(1 + \frac{M\sigma_S^2}{\sigma_W^2} \right). \tag{22}$$

By the separation theorem, the minimum (mean-squared error) distortion that can be achieved for a Gaussian source across this channel is

$$D_{\mathcal{N}}(C) = \frac{\sigma_S^2 \sigma_W^2}{M\sigma_S^2 + \sigma_W^2}, \tag{23}$$

where $D_{\mathcal{N}}(\cdot)$ denotes the distortion-rate function of the iid Gaussian source of variance σ_S^2. This concludes the proof.   □

In the limit as $M \to \infty$, the upper and lower bounds of this paper coincide, establishing the following result on the optimal power-distortion trade-off in the Gaussian sensor network of Example 1.

Theorem 3. *For the Gaussian sensor network defined in Example 1, with source variance σ_S^2, observation noise variance σ_W^2, and a total transmit power at the sensors of MP,*

$$\lim_{M \to \infty} \frac{D_{lower}(MP)}{D_1(MP)} = 1, \tag{24}$$

hence,

$$D_{min}(MP) = \frac{\sigma_S^2 \sigma_W^2}{M\sigma_S^2 + \sigma_W^2}, \tag{25}$$

and the minimum is achieved when the sensors use a simple scaling, $X_k[n] = \gamma_k U_k[n]$, and the final destination uses $\hat{X}[n] = \gamma Y[n]$.

Proof. The theorem follows directly by combining Theorems 1 and 2.   □

Remark 2. In the limiting case as $M \to \infty$, the minimum distortion $D(MP)$ does not depend on P and σ_Z^2. Note however that the result *does* depend on the fact that the total available power at the sensor increases linearly with the number of sensors M. This can be extended to cases where the total sensor power behaves according to a different law along the lines of the analysis in [8, 9].

Remark 3 (real-time processing). There is no causality or real-time constraint on the encoding and decoding functions in the setup of Example 1; in fact, the scheme discussed in Section 3 does not satisfy any such constraint. In contrast to this, Theorem 3 shows that the globally optimum trade-off (in the limit $M \to \infty$) *can be achieved* by a causal and real-time system in the sense that $X_k[n]$ can be generated without waiting for future source outputs $U_k[n+j]$, $j = 1, 2, \ldots$.

The Gaussian example can be extended using concepts similar to [5,6,7]. This is the issue of the next section.

4.2   Generalization of the Gaussian Case

The Gaussian case discussed above can be summarized by two key insights:

1. Uncoded transmission (at the sensors) considerably outperforms any approach based on the separation paradigm (even for a relatively small number of sensors M).
2. In the limit as $M \to \infty$, uncoded transmission performs optimally.

In this section, both of these features are extended beyond the Gaussian case. We first establish a general sufficient condition for a given sensor coding system $(F_1, F_2, \ldots, F_M, G)$ to perform optimally, thus extending the second feature of the Gaussian case. Thereafter, we extend the first feature of the Gaussian case by suggesting a general coding paradigm as an alternative to the separation-based coding paradigm. We show that for a class of sensor networks that includes the Gaussian case, our coding paradigm, while not necessarily optimal, considerably outperforms the separation-based paradigm.

Optimal Performance. We now establish a general sufficient condition for the optimality of a sensor network with a topology according to Figure 1. It can be stated as follows.

Theorem 4. *If in the sensor network of Figure 1, the code $(F_1, F_2, \ldots, F_M, G)$ satisfies the cost constraint $E\rho(X_1, X_2, \ldots, X_M) \leq \Gamma$, and*

$$d(s, \hat{s}) = -c_2 \log_2 P(s|\hat{s}) + d_0(s) \tag{26}$$
$$I(S; U_1, U_2, \ldots, U_M) = I(S; \hat{S}), \tag{27}$$

then it performs optimally.

Proof. The proof works by idealizing the sensor network of Figure 1 by a point-to-point communication system. In particular, we consider the communication system where the final destination has direct access to the observations $U_1, \ldots, U_M$. If the code $(F_1, F_2, \ldots, F_M, G)$ achieves optimal performance in this point-to-point communication system, then it *must* achieve optimal performance in the original sensor network of Figure 1.

The conditions for optimality for the idealized point-to-point source-channel communication system can be stated as follows (see Appendix A and [5,6,7]): The point-to-point communication system is optimal if

$$\rho(s) = c_1 D(p_{U_1,U_2,\ldots,U_M|s} \| p_{U_1,U_2,\ldots,U_M}) + \rho_0 \tag{28}$$

$$d(s,\hat{s}) = -c_2 \log_2 P(s|\hat{s}) + d_0(s) \tag{29}$$

$$I(S;\hat{S}) = I(S;U_1,U_2,\ldots,U_M), \tag{30}$$

where $D(\cdot\|\cdot)$ denotes the Kullback-Leibler distance, see e.g. [4]. If the sensor network satisfies these conditions, it must perform optimally. However, in our problem, there is no cost constraint on the source signal S. In other words, $\rho(s)$ can always be chosen appropriately. Hence, the condition on $\rho(s)$ can be removed, which completes the proof. $\square$

The conditions of Theorem 4 are sufficient for optimality, but they are only achievable for a particular class of sensor networks; in the general case of Figure 1, they cannot be met. The goal of the following discussion is to illustrate the special class for which the conditions of Theorem 4 can be satisfied. We first illustrate these two issues for the Gaussian example studied above.

Example 5 (Gaussian case). Let us study conditions (26) and (27) for the Gaussian example. Consider first condition (26). Since $S[n]$ and $\hat{S}[n]$ are jointly Gaussian, we can write $S[n]$ in terms of $\hat{S}[n]$ as follows:

$$S[n] = \frac{E\left[S\hat{S}\right]}{E\left[\hat{S}^2\right]} \hat{S}[n] + W'[n], \tag{31}$$

where $W'[n]$ is additive white Gaussian noise. Since $\hat{S}$ is the minimum mean-squared error estimate of S, we find that $E[S\hat{S}]/E[\hat{S}^2] = 1$, and hence $S[n] = \hat{S}[n] + W'[n]$. This immediately reveals that $P(s|\hat{s})$ is given by the distribution of $W'[n]$. Since it is Gaussian, we find

$$- \log_2 P(s|\hat{s}) = d_1(s - \hat{s})^2 + d_0(s), \tag{32}$$

i.e., mean-squared error distortion. The variance of the noise $W'[n]$ is irrelevant for this argument; it only influences the constant d_1. This means that even for finite M, condition (26) is satisfied by the Gaussian example.

For condition (27) in our Gaussian example, equality is only achieved asymptotically as the number of sensors tends to infinity. We now analyze this in detail. From (19), $\hat{S}$ can be rewritten as

$$\hat{S}[n] = \frac{\frac{P}{\sigma_S^2+\sigma_W^2} M\sigma_S^2}{\frac{P}{\sigma_S^2+\sigma_W^2}(M^2\sigma_S^2 + M\sigma_W^2) + \sigma_Z^2} \left(MS[n] + \sum_{i=1}^{M} W_k[n] + \sqrt{\frac{\sigma_S^2 + \sigma_W^2}{P}} Z[n] \right).$$

It follows immediately that

$$I(S;U_1,U_2,\ldots,U_M) = I(S;\hat{S},U_1,U_2,\ldots,U_M)$$

$$= I(S;\hat{S}) + \sum_{k=1}^{M} I(S;U_k|\hat{S},U_1,\ldots,U_{k-1}). \tag{33}$$

The next goal is to determine the first term in the sum, i.e., $I(S; U_1|\hat{S})$. This term is easily calculated by first replacing $\hat{S}$ by a scaled version $\hat{S}' = MS[n] + \sum_{k=1}^{M} W_k[n] + \sqrt{(\sigma_S^2 + \sigma_W^2)/P}Z[n]$. Using the shorthand

$$\beta = \frac{\sigma_S^2 + \sigma_W^2}{P}\frac{\sigma_Z^2}{\sigma_W^2}, \tag{34}$$

we can evaluate

$$
\begin{aligned}
I(S; U_1|\hat{S}) &= I(S; U_1|\hat{S}') \\
&= \frac{1}{2}\log\frac{(M+\beta)\sigma_S^2\sigma_W^2\left((\sigma_S^2+\sigma_W^2)(M^2\sigma_S^2+(M+\beta)\sigma_W^2)-(M\sigma_S^2+\sigma_W^2)^2\right)}{(M+\beta-1)\sigma_S^2\sigma_W^4(M^2\sigma_S^2+(M+\beta)\sigma_W^2)} \\
&= \frac{1}{2}\log\frac{(M+\beta)\sigma_S^2\sigma_W^2((M^2-M+\beta)\sigma_S^2\sigma_W^2+M\sigma_W^4)}{(M+\beta-1)\sigma_S^2\sigma_W^4(M^2\sigma_S^2+(M+\beta)\sigma_W^2)} \\
&= \frac{1}{2}\log\frac{M^3\sigma_S^2+M^2((\beta-1)\sigma_S^2+\sigma_W^2)+M((\beta-1)\sigma_S^2+\beta\sigma_W^2)+\beta^2\sigma_S^2}{M^3\sigma_S^2+M^2((\beta-1)\sigma_S^2+\sigma_W^2)+M(2\beta-1)\sigma_W^2+\beta(\beta-1)\sigma_W^2}, \tag{35}
\end{aligned}
$$

and hence, as $M \to \infty$,

$$I(S; U_1|\hat{S}) \to 0. \tag{36}$$

Note that this convergence is very rapid: the coefficients of both M^3 and M^2 are the same in the numerator and the denominator. A similar argument establishes that

$$I(S; U_k|\hat{S}, U_1, U_2, \ldots, U_{k-1}) \to 0, \tag{37}$$

as $M \to \infty$, hence

$$I(S; U_1, U_2, \ldots, U_M) \to I(S; \hat{S}), \tag{38}$$

hence condition (27) is satisfied in the limit as $M \to \infty$.

This short argument immediately reveals a class of extensions of the Gaussian example for which the conditions of Theorem 4 are also achievable, as follows:

Example 6 (Simple extension of Gaussian case). Suppose that the source S in Figure 2 is still Gaussian, that the observation noises W_k satisfy

$$\sum_{k=1}^{M} W_k \sim \mathcal{N}(0, M\sigma_W^2), \tag{39}$$

i.e., the sum of the observation noises is Gaussian and its variance grows linearly in the number of sensors M, and finally that the variance of W (see Figure 2) vanishes in comparison to the signal. Then, the same asymptotic behavior is observed.

Remark 4. This example is particularly interesting because only the sum of the observation noises has to be Gaussian: by the central limit theorem, this condition is satisfied in many practical cases as the number of sensors becomes large.

General Coding Paradigm. In the Gaussian case, the performance of the scheme of Theorem 1 cannot be argued to be optimal. Nevertheless, it is considerably superior to the performance of separate source and channel coding: In the latter, the distortion (as a function of the number of sensors) only decays like $1/\log M$, while in the former, it decays like $1/M$. Hence, even at relatively small M, the joint source-channel coding approach of Theorem 1 outperforms the separate source and channel coding.

This behavior can also be observed in terms of the conditions of Theorem 4: For the Gaussian case, condition (26), i.e.,

$$-\log_2 P(s|\hat{s}) = d_1(s - \hat{s})^2 + d_0(s), \tag{40}$$

was shown to be satisfied (for any M), while condition (27) was evaluated in (35) to be

$$
\begin{aligned}
&I(S; U_1, U_2, \ldots, U_M) \\
&= I(S; \hat{S}) + \frac{1}{2} \log \frac{M^3 \sigma_S^2 + M^2 \ldots}{M^3 \sigma_S^2 + M^2 \ldots} + \ldots.
\end{aligned} \tag{41}
$$

This converges rapidly as M tends to infinity, and condition (27) is asymptotically satisfied.

These observations propose an alternative coding paradigm for sensor networks with a topology according to Figure 1, namely to code in such a way as to approach the conditions of Theorem 4 as closely as possible:

Coding Paradigm. *The goal of the coding scheme for sensor networks with a topology according to Figure 1 is to approach*

$$d(s, \hat{s}) = -c_2 \log_2 P(s|\hat{s}) + d_0(s) \tag{42}$$

$$I(S; U_1, U_2, \ldots, U_M) = I(S; \hat{S}), \tag{43}$$

as closely as possible.

Remark 5. Note that *neither* the above coding paradigm *nor* the separation-based coding paradigm can be shown to lead to optimal performance in general sensor networks with a topology according to Figure 1. Recall that the optimal performance for the general case of Figure 1 is *not known* to date.

In our coding paradigm, the precise meaning of approaching the formulae of Theorem 4 "as closely as possible" is currently under investigation. For the Gaussian case studied in this paper, one such approaching behavior is achieved by the strategy of Theorem 1, as shown in Equation (41).

5   Communication between the Sensors

In the sensor network topology of Figure 1, the sensors can only communicate to the destination; they cannot communicate with each other. An interesting variation on the consideration of this paper is to allow the sensors to communicate with each other. Our arguments can be used to obtain directly the following statement:

Theorem 5 (communication between the sensors). *Consider the sensor network of Figure 1, but allow now for communication between the sensors. If in this revised sensor network, the code $(F_1, F_2, \ldots, F_M, G)$ satisfies the cost constraint $E\rho(X_1, X_2, \ldots, X_M) \leq \Gamma$, and*

$$d(s, \hat{s}) = -c_2 \log_2 P(s|\hat{s}) + d_0(s) \tag{44}$$

$$I(S; U_1, U_2, \ldots, U_M) = I(S; \hat{S}), \tag{45}$$

then it performs optimally.

Proof. This follows again by the idealization used to prove Theorem 4: This idealization does include communication between the sensors.   □

Remark 6. For the general case involving communication between the sensors, we cannot compare to the separation-based code design: Its performance it unknown to date. However, it must be expected to perform suboptimally, in line with the arguments discussed above.

Remark 7. While in general, the possibility of the sensors to communicate with each other may be expected to enhance the performance, Theorem 5 establishes that for all sensor networks that satisfy Theorem 4, communication between the sensors *does not* improve the performance. This includes in particular our Gaussian example (Example 1). To emphasize the point, suppose that in the Gaussian example, each sensor is linked to every other sensor by an ideal cable. Then, not only can the sensors apply a much more efficient compression, but they can also act like a multiple-antenna transmitter, thus harvesting gains in capacity. Do we get a better performance than without the ideal cables between the sensors? Theorem 5 establishes that the answer is negative (asymptotically as the number of sensors $M \to \infty$): The uncoded transmission scheme of Theorem 1 achieves just the same performance. In other words, in this case, there is *no penalty* for the fact that the sensors are distributed, rather than joint.

6   Conclusions

In this paper, we analyzed a particular sensor network topology. We first derived the performance of a coding scheme designed according to the source-channel separation principle. For the considered Gaussian example, for instance, it was shown that the distortion decays like $1/\log M$, where M is the total number of sensors. Thereafter, we considered *joint* source-channel coding. The optimal performance and coding scheme is not known in general. We proposed an alternative coding paradigm and derived a class of sensor networks for which codes designed according to our paradigm achieve optimal performance. For the considered Gaussian example, it was shown that the distortion for a code according to our paradigm decays like $1/M$, i.e., considerably better than the separation-based scheme.

References

1. T. Berger. Multiterminal source coding. *Lectures presented at CISM Summer School on the Information Theory Approach to Communications*, July 1977.
2. T. Berger, Z. Zhang, and H. Viswanathan. The CEO problem. *IEEE Transactions on Information Theory*, IT–42:887–902, May 1996.
3. T. M. Cover, A. A. El Gamal, and M. Salehi. Multiple access channels with arbitrarily correlated sources. *IEEE Transactions on Information Theory*, 26(6):648–657, November 1980.
4. T. M. Cover and J. A. Thomas. *Elements of Information Theory*. Wiley, New York, 1991.
5. M. Gastpar. *To Code Or Not To Code*. PhD thesis, Ecole Polytechnique Fédérale (EPFL), Lausanne, Switzerland, 2002.
6. M. Gastpar, B. Rimoldi, and M. Vetterli. To code or not to code. In *Proc IEEE Int Symp Info Theory*, page 236, Sorrento, Italy, June 2000.
7. M. Gastpar, B. Rimoldi, and M. Vetterli. To code, or not to code: Lossy source-channel communication revisited. *submitted to IEEE Transactions on Information Theory*, May 2001. Revised July 2002.
8. M. Gastpar and M. Vetterli. On the capacity of large Gaussian relay networks. *submitted to IEEE Transactions on Information Theory*, September 2002.
9. M. Gastpar and M. Vetterli. On the capacity of wireless networks: The relay case. In *Proc IEEE Infocom 2002*, New York, NY, June 2002.
10. T. J. Goblick. Theoretical limitations on the transmission of data from analog sources. *IEEE Transactions on Information Theory*, IT–11(4):558–567, October 1965.
11. Y. Oohama. The rate-distortion function for the quadratic Gaussian CEO problem. *IEEE Transactions on Information Theory*, IT–44(3):1057–1070, May 1998.
12. C. E. Shannon. A mathematical theory of communication. *Bell Sys. Tech. Journal*, 27:379–423, 623–656, 1948.
13. D. Slepian and J. K. Wolf. Noiseless coding of correlated information sources. *IEEE Transactions on Information Theory*, IT–19:471–480, 1973.
14. H. Viswanathan and T. Berger. The quadratic Gaussian CEO problem. *IEEE Transactions on Information Theory*, IT–43(5):1549–1559, September 1997.
15. A. D. Wyner and J. Ziv. The rate-distortion function for source coding with side information at the receiver. *IEEE Transactions on Information Theory*, IT–22:1–11, January 1976.

A   Review: Point-to-Point Source-Channel Communication

In this section, we provide a brief review of the information-theoretic results for the point-to-point source-channel communication system, illustrated in Figure 3. The source is defined by a source distribution $P_S(s)$ and a distortion measure $d(s, \hat{s})$. The channel is defined by a conditional distribution $P_{Y|X}(y|x)$ and an input cost function $\rho(x)$. For the purpose of this brief review, we suppose that the encoder F maps a sequence of n source symbols onto a sequence of n channel input symbols. We also suppose that the decoder is synchronized with the encoder, and maps a sequence of n channel output symbols onto a sequence of

Fig. 3. The general point-to-point source-channel communication problem.

n source reconstruction symbols. The goal of the code (F, G) is to produce a minimum distortion,

$$\Delta = Ed\left(S^n, \hat{S}^n\right), \tag{46}$$

using, simultaneously, a minimum power (or more generally, cost) on the channel,

$$\Gamma = E\rho(X^n). \tag{47}$$

The key problem of source-channel communication is to determine the optimal cost-distortion pairs (Γ, Δ). We consider this problem in the information-theoretic sense, i.e., we are interested in the optimum *irrespective of the coding complexity and delay*.

Shannon's separation theorem determines the optimal trade-off between cost and distortion by the condition

$$R(\Delta) = C(\Gamma). \tag{48}$$

For a more detailed treatment, see e.g. [5, Ch. 1]. By the operational meaning of the rate-distortion and capacity-cost function, this simultaneously furnishes a coding paradigm, i.e., a way to implement the optimal coding (F, G). Hence, the communication system is optimal if it satisfies a *rate-matching* condition: the minimum rate for the source compression (the rate-distortion function) must be equal to the maximum rate for the channel code (the capacity-cost function).

Recently, an alternative perspective has been presented [5,6,7]. The optimal trade-off satisfies

$$\rho(x^n) = c_1 D(P_{Y^n|x^n}\|P_{Y^n}) + \rho_0 \tag{49}$$

$$d(s^n, \hat{s}^n) = -c_2 \log_2 P_{S^n|\hat{S}^n} + d_0(s^n) \tag{50}$$

$$I(S^n; \hat{S}^n) = I(X^n; Y^n), \tag{51}$$

where $c_1 \geq 0, c_2 \geq 0$ and ρ_0 are constants, $d_0(s)$ is an arbitrary function of s, and $D(\cdot\|\cdot)$ denotes the Kullback-Leibler distance, see e.g. [4]. Hence, the communication system is optimal if it satisfies a *measure-matching* condition: the probability measures of the source and the channel and the cost and distortion measure must be matched in the right way by the coding system.

In this paper, we extend both these perspectives to the case of the considered sensor network. Previously, we have also applied our measure-matching perspective to obtain capacity results for relay networks [9,8].

On Rate-Constrained Estimation in Unreliable Sensor Networks[*]

Prakash Ishwar[1], Rohit Puri[1], S. Sandeep Pradhan[2], and
Kannan Ramchandran[1]

[1] Department of Electrical Engineering and Computer Sciences,
University of California, Berkeley, CA 94720, USA.
{ishwar, rpuri, kannanr}@eecs.berkeley.edu
[2] Department of Electrical Engineering and Computer Science,
University of Michigan, Ann Arbor, MI 48103, USA.
pradhanv@eecs.umich.edu

Abstract. We study a network of non-collaborating sensors that make
noisy measurements of some physical process X and communicate their
readings to a central processing unit. Limited power resources of the
sensors severely restrict communication rates. Sensors and their communication links are both subject to failure; however, the central unit
is guaranteed to receive data from a minimum fraction of the sensors,
say k out of n sensors. The goal of the central unit is to optimally estimate X from the received transmissions under a specified distortion
metric. In this work, we derive an information-theoretically achievable
rate-distortion region for this network under symmetric sensor measurement statistics.
When all processes are jointly Gaussian and independent, and we have a
squared-error distortion metric, the proposed distributed encoding and
estimation framework has the following interesting optimality property:
*when any k out of n rate-R bits/sec sensor transmissions are received,
the central unit's estimation quality matches the best estimation quality
that can be achieved from a completely reliable network of k sensors, each
transmitting at rate R. Furthermore, when more than k out of the n sensor transmissions are received, the estimation quality strictly improves.*
When the network has clusters of collaborating sensors should clusters
compress their raw measurements or should they first try to estimate
the source from their measurements and compress the estimates instead.
For some interesting cases, we show that there is no loss of performance
in the distributed compression of local estimates over the distributed
compression of raw data in a rate-distortion sense, i.e., encoding the
local sufficient statistics is good enough.

1 Introduction

With the recent proliferation of distributed sensor networks designed to capture
physical phenomena of interest to the scientific and military communities, there

---

[*] This research was supported by NSF under grant CCR-0219722 and DARPA under
grant F30602-00-2-0538.

F. Zhao and L. Guibas (Eds.): IPSN 2003, LNCS 2634, pp. 178–192, 2003.

has arisen the need to develop a fundamental understanding of the performance bounds for different signal processing tasks (such as estimation, detection, and classification) under a distributed regime for sensing, communicating, and processing. More specifically, while the classical signal processing literature has a mature knowledge-base on the problems of estimation and detection [1], the distributed dense sensor network setting imposes additional constraints. These include (i) bandwidth (due to low power requirements), (ii) distributed processing (due to prohibitive inter-sensor communication costs), and (iii) robustness requirements (due to the wireless transmission channel).

This paper addresses the estimation problem under these relevant constraints with the goal of providing fundamental information-theoretic performance bounds for an important class of estimation problems. In our problem formulation, we translate the three sensor network requirements listed above into the specific constraints of (i) bit-rate, (ii) fully distributed processing of the sensors, and (iii) a packet-erasure communication model respectively.

Figure 1 depicts a mathematical abstraction of a sensor network consisting of individual sensors that make synchronous, correlated, noisy measurements of some physical process X (e.g., temperature). Individual sensors are typically lightweight devices that have very limited battery power. Inter-sensor communication has heavy power and protocol overhead that strongly discourages information exchange between sensors. The goal is to communicate sensor measurements to a central query in a manner that allows the central unit to form the best possible estimate of the physical process with respect to a specified (distortion) metric of estimation quality. Note that the central unit is only a logical entity and can also be one of the other sensors which acts as a "cluster-head" with different sensors taking turns.

The wireless communication links from the sensors to the central processing unit are often through multiple hops that are time-varying and characterized by deep fades. Furthermore, the availability of only limited transmission power severely constrains sensor communication rates. Motivated by this, in this work, the effective communication links from individual sensors to the central unit are modeled as independent, discrete, rate-constrained channels that are subject to erasures. The erasure pattern is assumed to remain fixed over some large block length of sensor measurements. We invoke a rate-constrained communication model in keeping with the existing base of digital communication architectures[1].

Prior work on information-theoretic aspects of this sensor network has focused exclusively on the case when all sensors and their effective communication links to the central decoding unit are functional [3]. In [3], Oohama provides a complete characterization of the rate-distortion region when all sensors and their communication links are reliable, and when the source and measurement

---

[1] Note that in some scenarios where multihop communication is not needed, and when the physical process, the communication channel, and the distortion measure are statistically "matched" to one another [2] then an uncoded "analog" transmission might be desirable if distributed synchronization of these sensor signals can be orchestrated at the physical layer.

processes are independent across sensors and time and are Gaussian distributed. However, in most practical scenarios, the sensor nodes and their communication links are subject to failure.

In Section 2, we present an achievable rate-distortion region for the sensor network when, out of a total of n rate-R sensor transmissions, at least some k are guaranteed to successfully arrive at the decoding unit while the remaining transmissions are "erased". Our analysis assumes symmetric sensor measurement noise statistics, i.e., the measurements of all sensors are statistically indistinguishable. This assumption is motivated by the consideration that in practice, due to lack of information exchange between sensors, it will be difficult to estimate the relative measurement noise power of individual sensors. With this assumption, the reconstruction quality depends only on the number of sensor transmissions received, and not on *which* specific subset of sensors measurements is received. We would like to note, however, that the presented results and methods of analysis can be extended to handle asymmetric sensor noise as well. As discussed above, transmission power and bandwidth limitations impose severe communication rate restrictions on the sensors: it is assumed that each sensor cannot use more than R bits per noisy sample of the physical process being measured. We present an information-theoretic code construction that enables reconstruction of X with a quality that is commensurate with a total network rate of kR bits per source sample when *some* k out of n encoded sensor transmissions are received. The estimation quality strictly improves when more transmissions are received.

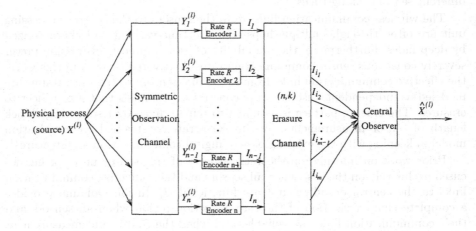

Fig. 1. An unreliable sensor network. A noisy version of source X is observed at each of the n sensors. The noisy observations $Y_1, ..., Y_n$, which are statistically indistinguishable, are encoded and the encoded indices $I_1, ..., I_n$ transmitted. The network delivers *some* $m \geq k$ indices. The decoder obtains the best possible reconstruction of X from the received indices.

There are two important aspects associated with the sensor network of Figure 1. First, the sensor measurements are correlated, and the power and protocol overhead of inter-sensor communication precludes any collaboration between sensors. Since both the transmission power and bandwidth are at a premium, efficient compression is a necessity. This motivates the development of algorithms that provide efficient distributed compression. The problem of distributed compression was first studied within an information-theoretic framework by Slepian and Wolf for lossless distributed compression [4]. The second important aspect associated with the sensor network is that only some k out of the n sensor readings are guaranteed to be received by the central unit. This implies an inherent uncertainty at the sensor encoders as to which measurements will be received by the central unit. The decoder, however, knows which sensor transmissions were successfully received and which got "erased". This can be interpreted as *side information* known only to the decoder but not to the encoders. The encoders, however, do know the network reliability in terms of the number of transmissions that are guaranteed to reach the decoder. Thus the encoders have access to the "statistics" of the side information process but not its particular realization. This observation provides a link to the theory of source coding with side information at the decoder studied by Wyner and Ziv in [5] where the statistics of the side information is available to the source encoder but the actual realization is not. In some interesting cases (e.g., for jointly Gaussian statistics), there is no loss of performance if the side-information is available at only one end (the receiver). Constructive algorithms using error control codes, inspired by information-theoretic random binning (hashing) ideas in [4,5], have been developed recently in [6,7].

Central to the problems of distributed compression of correlated sources and source coding with side information at the decoder is the notion of random binning [4,5]. The concept of random binning involves each encoder sending an index for a *list of messages* (a bin) rather than a unique index for each message. This reduces the rate of transmission. If the bin size is small enough, it is possible to construct message lists for each encoder in a manner that allows the decoder to disambiguate the transmitted messages from the list using the side information available to it. The construction of these bins relies only on the joint statistics of the correlated messages that the encoders need to communicate to the central decoding unit. To further develop intuition for the problem at hand, suppose that the encoder alphabet sizes are all finite, the sensor measurements are symmetrically correlated, and the total rate available to the network as a whole equals the joint entropy [8] of *any* k noisy observations. In this case, a straightforward application of the Slepian-Wolf coding theorem for multiple sources [8] shows that if the total rate is split equally amongst all n sensors, then with the reception of *any* k transmissions, the decoder can reconstruct the corresponding noisy observations perfectly (also see [9]). This shows that it is possible to achieve the same performance in the unreliable case as when the encoders know in advance *which* specific k sensor transmissions will reach the decoder.

In Section 3 we specialize the achievability results of Section 2 to the Gaussian setting. This reveals an interesting optimality property of the proposed robust, distributed encoding and estimation framework: When *any* k out of n *unreliable* sensor transmissions are received, the central observer's estimation quality can be as good as the best reconstruction quality that can be achieved by deploying only k *reliable* sensors and the central decoding unit is able to receive the encoded noisy observations from all k sensors. Furthermore, when more than k out of the n sensor transmissions are received, the estimation quality strictly improves.

Section 4 discusses an important question associated with distributed, rate-constrained estimation: if sensors could collaborate in small local clusters, should they compress their raw measurements or should they first try to estimate the source from their measurements and compress the estimates instead. We show, under suitable conditions, that distributed compression of local estimates is optimal.

2   Problem Set-Up and Main Result

Random quantities are denoted by capital letters while their specific realizations are denoted by small letters. Let $\{X(t)\}_{t=1}^{\infty}$ be an i.i.d. sequence of source symbols and $Y_1(t), ..., Y_n(t)$ the noisy measurements of the n sensors at time t. The noisy sensor measurements take values in a common finite alphabet $\mathcal{Y}$ and are assumed to be symmetrically correlated conditioned on the source values[2]. Let $\{\mathbf{Y}(t)\}_{t=1}^{\infty}$ be an i.i.d. sequence of noisy sensor measurements where $\mathbf{Y}(t) := (Y_1(t), ..., Y_n(t))$. Let

$$F_i^{(l)} : \mathcal{Y}^l \longrightarrow \mathcal{I}_{2^{lR}},$$

be the rate-R encoding function for the ith sensor ($i = 1, \ldots, n$) for block-length l, where $\mathcal{I}_m := \{1, ..., m\}$ and $\mathcal{Y}^l$ is the l-fold Cartesian product of the observation alphabet $\mathcal{Y}$. In other words, sensor observations are encoded in blocks of length l at a time by each sensor. Every block of observations is mapped to an index in the set $\{1, \ldots, 2^{lR}\}$. The encoding rate is therefore R bits per sample. Let $\widehat{\mathcal{X}}$ be the reconstruction alphabet and let

$$G_m^{(l)} : \mathcal{I}_{2^{lR}}^m \longrightarrow \widehat{\mathcal{X}}^l$$

be the decoding function when measurements from $m \geq k$ sensors are received by the central observer. Here, $\widehat{X}^{(l)} := \widehat{X}(1), ..., \widehat{X}(l)$. In other words, the decoder at the central unit maps a set of $m \geq k$ indices it receives to a reconstruction vector of length l. Let $d : \mathcal{X} \times \widehat{\mathcal{X}} \longrightarrow \mathbb{R}^+$ be a bounded distortion metric (i.e., $d(x, \widehat{x}) \leq d_{\max} < \infty$ for all $(x, \widehat{x}) \in \mathcal{X} \times \widehat{\mathcal{X}}$). The distortion metric on $\mathcal{X}^l \times \widehat{\mathcal{X}}^l$ is defined as $d^{(l)}(x^{(l)}, \widehat{x}^{(l)}) := \frac{1}{l} \sum_{t=1}^{l} d(x(t), \widehat{x}(t))$.

---

[2] All subsets of random variables of the same cardinality have the same joint conditional mass function.

Definition 1. *A rate-distortion tuple* $(R, D_k, ..., D_n)$ *is said to be achievable if for every* $\epsilon > 0$ *there exists a sufficiently long block length* $l(\epsilon)$ *and rate-R encoders* $\{F_i^{(l)}\}_{i=1}^n$ *and decoders* $\{G_m^{(l)}\}_{m=k}^n$ *such that*

$$E\left[d^{(l)}\left(X^{(l)}, G_m^{(l)}\left(F_{i_1}^{(l)}(Y_{i_1}^{(l)}), ..., F_{i_m}^{(l)}(Y_{i_m}^{(l)})\right)\right)\right] \leq D_m + \epsilon,$$

for all $k \leq m \leq n$.

Here, E denotes the expectation operator. The expected distortion depends only on m, and not on the specific values of $i_1, ..., i_m$ due to symmetric observation statistics. In plain words, a rate-distortion tuple is achievable if for arbitrarily stringent tolerance specifications ϵ there exist rate-R encoders and decoders for which the expected estimation quality at the reception of m sensor readings is within ϵ of D_m, for all $m = k, ..., n$.

Conditioned on $\mathbf{Y}$, let $U_1, ..., U_n$ be independent random variables taking values in a common finite alphabet $\mathcal{U}$ with

$$p_{\mathbf{U}|\mathbf{Y}}(u_1, ..., u_n|y_1, ..., y_n) := \prod_{i=1}^n p_{U|Y}(u_i|y_i), \qquad (1)$$

where $\mathbf{U} := (U_1, ..., U_n)$. The random variables U_i may be thought of as arising from a rate-distortion quantization of Y_i. Define

$$R_k^*(p_{\mathbf{U}|\mathbf{Y}}) := \frac{1}{k}\left[H(U_1, ..., U_k) - \sum_{i=1}^k H(U_i|Y_i)\right], \qquad (2)$$

$g_m : \mathcal{U}^m \longrightarrow \widehat{\mathcal{X}}$, $k \leq m \leq n$, and

$$D_m^*(p_{\mathbf{U}|\mathbf{Y}}, g_m) := E\left[d(X, g_m(U_{i_1}, ..., U_{i_m}))\right]. \qquad (3)$$

Due to the symmetry of the underlying probability distributions, $H(U_i|Y_i)$ is the same for all i and the expected distortion in (3) only depends on m, g_m, and $p_{\mathbf{U}|\mathbf{Y}}$ and not on the specific values of $i_1, ..., i_m$. The main result of this paper is contained in the following theorem whose proof is outlined in Section 4.

Theorem 1. *If* $R > R_k^*(p_{\mathbf{U}|\mathbf{Y}})$ *and* $D_m \geq D_m^*(p_{\mathbf{U}|\mathbf{Y}}, g_m)$ *for all* $m \geq k$ *then the rate distortion tuple* $(R, D_k, ..., D_n)$ *is achievable.*

The above theorem describes the estimation quality that can be achieved at the central processing unit for a given bit budget. In the above description, the dependence of estimation quality on the bit-budget is expressed in terms of the quantization strategy (governed by $p_{\mathbf{U}|\mathbf{Y}}$) and the estimation algorithm governed by $\{g_m\}_{m=k}^n$. By varying the quantization and estimation strategies, one can trade off the required rate R and estimation quality $\{D_m\}_{m=k}^n$.

Figure 2 shows the detailed structure of sensor encoders and the central decoder that can asymptotically achieve the rate-distortion region of Theorem 1 for long block lengths. The encoders have two parts. The first stage is a rate R', block-length l, rate-distortion quantizer matched to the statistics of the sensor measurements. The second stage involves a random binning that exploits the correlation between the quantized observations across different sensors to get a rebate of $R' - R$ bits per sample. The decoder first reconstructs the quantized sensor observations from the bin indices of different sensors and then forms the best estimate of the physical process of interest.

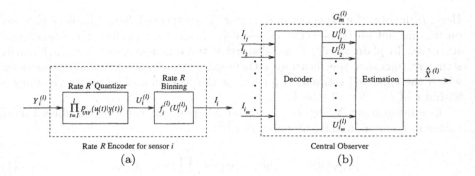

Fig. 2. Structure of sensor encoders: (a) and the central observer decoder: (b) that can achieve the rate-distortion performance of Theorem 1. The encoder of each sensor consists of a rate R' quantizer, for block length l, followed by a rate R random binning function. The central observer first decodes the received indices to intermediate representations, of length l, and then forms the best estimate of the source. Here, $m \geq k$.

3   The Gaussian Sensor Network

The result of the previous section can be extended to continuous alphabet sources – with differential entropy [8] replacing discrete entropy in all expressions – using techniques similar to those used in [10]. In this section, we specialize our results to the setting described in [3]: $\{X(t)\}_{t=1}^{\infty} \sim \mathcal{N}(0, \sigma_X^2)$ is an i.i.d. Gaussian source and $Y_i(t) = X(t) + N_i(t), \forall i \in \mathcal{I}_n$. The observation noise processes $N_i(t)$ are independent of each other and the source process. Across time, the noise processes are i.i.d., zero-mean, and Gaussian distributed with variance σ_N^2. With this setup note that the noisy sensor observations are conditionally independent and symmetrically correlated given the source samples. Estimation quality is measured by mean squared error, i.e., $d(x, \hat{x}) = (x - \hat{x})^2$. Our problem differs from the one considered by Oohama in [3] in the following important aspect: In [3], the transmissions from *all* sensors are assumed to be available to the central observer; in our problem only *some* k out of n transmissions are guaranteed to be available.

Let $U_i(t) := Y_i(t) + q_i(t)$ for each sensor i and time t where $\{q_i(t)\}_{t=1}^{\infty}$ is a zero-mean, i.i.d. Gaussian quantization noise process for sensor i with common variance σ_q^2. Hence (we refer the reader to [8] for expressions of joint and conditional differential entropies of Gaussian random variables),

$$\sum_{i=1}^{k} h(U_i|Y_i) = \frac{k}{2} \log_2(2\pi e \, \sigma_N^2 \, \text{DNR}), \qquad (4)$$

where DNR is the Distortion to Noise Ratio given by σ_q^2/σ_N^2. The eigenvalues of the correlation matrix of $U_1, \ldots, U_k$ can be shown to be $\sigma_N^2(1 + \text{DNR} + k \cdot \text{SNR})$ with multiplicity 1 and $\sigma_N^2(1 + \text{DNR})$ with multiplicity $(k-1)$, where σ_X^2/σ_N^2 is the Signal to Noise Ratio (SNR). Hence,

$$h(U_1, \ldots, U_k) = \frac{k}{2} \log_2 \left[2\pi e \, \sigma_N^2 \left(1 + \frac{k \cdot \text{SNR}}{1 + \text{DNR}} \right)^{\frac{1}{k}} \left(1 + \frac{1}{\text{DNR}} \right) \right].$$

Using these expressions in (2), yields

$$R_k^* = \frac{1}{2} \log_2 \left[\left(1 + \frac{k \cdot \text{SNR}}{1 + \text{DNR}} \right)^{\frac{1}{k}} \left(1 + \frac{1}{\text{DNR}} \right) \right]. \qquad (5)$$

On the reception of any $m \geq k$ transmissions, the central observer first decodes the appropriate set of quantized sensor observations $u_{i_1}^{(l)} \ldots u_{i_m}^{(l)}$ and then computes the minimum mean squared error (MMSE) estimate of $X^{(l)}$. The MMSE estimate is the conditional mean of the posterior distribution of $X^{(l)}$ given the quantized observations [1]. Since the source, observation noise, and quantization noise processes are independent and Gaussian, the MMSE estimate is a linear function of the quantized observations [1]:

$$\widehat{x}_m^{(l)} = \frac{\text{SNR}}{1 + \text{DNR} + m \cdot \text{SNR}} \sum_{j=1}^{m} u_{i_j}^{(l)}.$$

The optimal mean square error for this estimate is given by

$$D_m^* = \frac{\sigma_X^2(1 + \text{DNR})}{1 + \text{DNR} + m \cdot \text{SNR}}. \qquad (6)$$

Suppose that $k = n\alpha$ and $m = n\beta$ where $0 < \alpha \leq \beta \leq 1$. Here, α and β respectively represent the fraction of guaranteed and the fraction of received sensor measurements. For fixed α and β as $n \longrightarrow \infty$, the asymptotic rate reduces to $\frac{1}{2} \log_2 \left(1 + \frac{1}{\text{DNR}} \right)$. The distortion with the reception of a fraction β of the sensor observations decays as $\frac{\sigma_X^2(1+\text{DNR})}{n\beta}$ which is similar, up to proportionality constants, to the decay of distortion when the central decoder has direct access to *all* the uncoded sensor measurements.

In [3] Oohama proves the following result: if there are there exactly k sensors, all their transmissions reach the central unit, and the total rate available to the k-sensor network is kR_k^* (given by (5)), then the best estimation quality that can be achieved is D_k^* (given by (6)) under the Gaussian statistics assumptions of this section. However, R_k^* and D_k^* are respectively the rate and distortion achievable when $n \geq k$ sensors are used and it is not a priori known exactly which of the k sensor readings will be available to the central unit. Hence, regardless of which k sensor observations reach the decoding unit, the performance is as good as that of k completely reliable transmissions. Thus we get robustness to erasures without any loss in performance. Furthermore, the estimation quality strictly improves with the reception of more sensor observations: D_m^* is a strictly decreasing function of m; see (6). The source of this optimality property can be traced to the structure of the encoders in [3]. The encoder and decoder structures are further elaborated in Section 6.1.

4   Compressing Raw Data versus Local Estimates

In some scenarios, small clusters of sensors have the communication resources to locally collaborate. In other situations, a sensor node may consist of a sensor-array or sensors with multiple modalities (acoustic, seismic, infra red, etc.). Both these scenarios can be captured by allowing vector-valued sensor data $\{\mathbf{Y}_i\}_{i=1}^n$ in the model of Figure 1 (also see Figure 3) . Individual components of the vector-valued observations would then represent the scalar measurements of collaborating sensors in each cluster or the component measurements in sensor-arrays or the measurements corresponding to different modalities in multi-modal sensors. A natural question that arises in this context is: how should these vector measurements be processed and encoded by the sensor-clusters/multi-modal sensors to be rate-distortion optimal. The approach in the scalar case would suggest doing a rate-distortion quantization of the vector measurements followed by random binning that exploits the correlation between measurements across sensor-clusters. When all associated processes are jointly Gaussian, rate-distortion quantization amounts to doing a reverse water-filling on the locally decorrelated components of the measurements, i.e., a Karhunen-Loève transform followed by reverse water-pouring [8].

A different approach would be to first form local estimates $T_i(\mathbf{Y}_i)$ of X at each cluster and then compress the estimates in a distributed manner. Under what conditions will there be no loss in (rate-distortion) performance? There are two possible sources of loss. First, compression of $\{T_i\}_{i=1}^n$ might be sub-optimal even when infinite rate is available, i.e., the best estimate of X based on $\{T_i(\mathbf{Y}_i)\}_{i=1}^n$ is not the same as the best estimate based on $\{\mathbf{Y}_i\}_{i=1}^n$. The availability of finite rate is another potential source of loss. However,

Proposition 1. *For MSE as the distortion metric, if there is no performance loss in encoding local statistics at high (infinite) rates, i.e., if*

$$Z := E\left[X | \mathbf{Y}_1, \ldots, \mathbf{Y}_n\right] = h\left(T_1(\mathbf{Y}_1), \ldots, T_n(\mathbf{Y}_n)\right), \tag{7}$$

for some function $h()$ of local statistics, then there will be no performance loss for any finite rate R.

Proposition 1, proved in the Appendix, is a generalization of a result due to Sakrison in [11], where it was shown that for a point-to-point communication scenario, i.e., when there is only one sensor, estimation (forming $T_1(\mathbf{Y}_1) := E[X|\mathbf{Y}_1]$) followed by quantization is optimal in a rate-distortion sense. This is a consequence of the orthogonality principle[3] and the structure of optimal, fixed-rate, vector quantizers. Note that (7) and the orthogonality principle together imply that $h(T_1, \ldots, T_n) = E[X|T_1(\mathbf{Y}_1), \ldots, T_n(\mathbf{Y}_n)]$ (cf. Appendix for details).

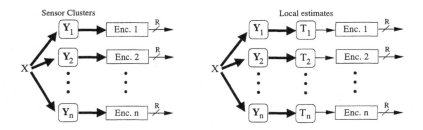

Fig. 3. Distributed compression of raw data (left) versus distributed compression of local estimates (right).

Thus, under the assumption of no performance loss at high rates given by (7) the problem of compressing correlated, vector-valued observations reduces to a problem of compressing local, scalar-valued statistics T_i. These ideas can be illustrated by considering a simple vector-version of the Gaussian CEO problem studied by Oohama in [3]. Here, the source X is a discrete, zero-mean, Gaussian random process. The noise processes are assumed to be i.i.d., zero-mean, and Gaussian across all sensor-clusters and across all components in each cluster. The local and global observation statistics in this example have the same structure. Hence, intuitively, it is clear that the form of the local and global MMSE estimators will also be the same. In fact, all (local as well as global) MMSE estimators in this example will compute the simple average of the constituent observations followed by scaling. From this it follows that the global MMSE estimate can be expressed as a function of local MMSE estimates so that condition (7) holds. Hence, there will be no loss in rate-distortion performance in first forming local averages at each sensor-cluster. The vector-version of the CEO problem is thereby reduced to the regular scalar Gaussian CEO problem for which the optimal distributed compression encoder structure is known (see Section 6.1 and [3]). In general, we have the following result which is proved in the Appendix.

Proposition 2. *If $(X, \mathbf{Y}_1, \ldots, \mathbf{Y}_n)$ are jointly Gaussian and $\mathbf{Y}_1, \ldots, \mathbf{Y}_n$ are conditionally independent given X then (7) holds with $T_i(\mathbf{Y}_i) := E[X|\mathbf{Y}_i]$, $\forall i$.*

---

[3] The MMSE estimation error $(X - E[X|\text{data}])$ is orthogonal to any measurable statistic of the data [1].

Thus, there will be no loss in compressing local estimates even when clusters have arbitrary local noise correlation structure as long as the noise processes are independent across clusters and everything is jointly Gaussian.

How do things change if condition (7) does not hold? In other words, what if the clusters went ahead and formed local estimates even when doing so is not optimal? Clearly, there would be additional distortion due to the fact that the best MMSE estimate of X based on all data is not the same as the best estimate based on local statistics. The process of forming local estimates looses some information that is useful for estimating X. However, will there be additional rate-dependent performance loss due to (finite-rate) compression? Intuitively, although the process of compression looses information with respect to the estimation of source X, the local estimates should be easier to encode for the same rate provided that the statistics are "well-behaved". The local estimates are in some sense "less random" than the raw data and should be easier to compress. Hence, we strongly believe that finite-rate compression would not introduce any more performance loss than that at high (infinite) rates, for well-behaved local estimates, i.e., there will be no rate-dependent excess loss. *For jointly Gaussian statistics, and linear local estimators, this result can be shown to be true.* The proof is similar to that of Proposition 1 with the additional observation that both the global MMSE estimate based on raw data and the global MMSE estimate based on local linear estimates are Gaussian and the latter is easier to compress because it has smaller variance. Whenever there is no rate-dependent excess loss, the task of designing distributed estimation algorithms for sensor networks with finite rate constraints can be decoupled into two tasks: (i) designing good distributed estimation algorithms assuming infinite rates and (ii) designing good distributed compression algorithms. The decoupling is in the sense that the second task will not introduce any rate-dependent excess distortion.

5   Concluding Remarks

This work represents a step towards developing a fundamental understanding of the performance limits for estimation in a distributed, rate-constrained, unreliable environment. We have provided an information-theoretically achievable rate-distortion region for the sensor network setup of Figure 1. For a Gaussian sensor network, we have shown how robustness can be incorporated without sacrificing rate-distortion performance. Our ongoing work includes evaluating fundamental estimation performance limits for increasingly complex source and sensor statistics and channel models. More realistic models for sensor networks should incorporate correlation between sensor noise processes and also have the ability to deal with a vector-valued source process having general spatio-temporal dependencies. We are also looking at practical code constructions to be used in sensor networks for robust, distributed estimation. This involves constructing quantizers for capturing independent signal components to mimic the performance of independent random codes. This can be done using quantizers that are shifted versions of one another (see [7] for details). A structured way of realizing independent binning of multiple codebooks presented in this paper is by using algebraic trellis and lattice codes along the lines of [7,12]. The key idea is to construct "linearly independent" partitions of different codebooks under consideration. The algebraic structure of trellis and lattice codes is amenable to such partitions. Ongoing work involves finding computationally efficient constructions for such partitions, and fast algorithms for doing index assignment.

References

1. H. V. Poor, *An Introduction to Signal Detection and Estimation.* New York, NY: Springer–Verlag, 1994.
2. M. Gastpar, B. Rimoldi, and M. Vetterli, "To code, or not to code: Lossy source-channel communication revisited," *IEEE Transactions on Information Theory.* To appear.
3. Y. Oohama, "The Rate-Distortion Function for the Quadratic Gaussian CEO Problem," *IEEE Transactions on Information Theory*, vol. 44, pp. 55–67, May 1998.
4. D. Slepian and J. K. Wolf, "Noiseless Coding of Correlated Information Sources," *IEEE Transactions on Information Theory*, vol. 19, pp. 471–480, July 1973.
5. A. Wyner and J. Ziv, "The Rate-Distortion Function for Source Coding with Side Information at the Decoder," *IEEE Transactions on Information Theory*, vol. 22, pp. 1–10, January 1976.
6. S. S. Pradhan and K. Ramchandran, "Distributed Source Coding Using Syndromes (DISCUS): Design and Construction," *Proceedings of the Data Compression Conference (DCC)*, March, Snowbird, UT, 1999.
7. S. S. Pradhan and K. Ramchandran, "Distributed Source Coding: Symmetric Rates and Applications to Sensor Networks," *Proceedings of the Data Compression Conference (DCC)*, March, Snowbird, UT, 2000.
8. T. M. Cover and J. A. Thomas, *Elements of Information Theory.* New York: John Wiley and Sons, 1991.
9. S. S. Pradhan, R. Puri, and K. Ramchandran, "n-Channel Symmetric Multiple Descriptions - Part I: (n,k) Source-Channel Erasure Codes," *IEEE Transactions on Information Theory.* To appear.
10. R. G. Gallager, *Information Theory and Reliable Communication.* New York: John Wiley and Sons, 1968.
11. D. J. Sakrison, "Source Encoding in the Presence of Random Disturbance," *IEEE Trans. on Information Theory*, vol. IT-14, Jan. 1968.
12. S. S. Pradhan and K. Ramchandran, "Generalized Coset Codes for Symmetric Distributed Coding," *IEEE Transactions on Information Theory,* 2003. Submitted.
13. T. Berger, "Multiterminal Source Coding," *Information Theory Approach to Communication, (CISM Courses and Lecture Notes No. 229)*, G. Longo, Ed., Wien and New York: Springer-Verlag, 1977.

6   Appendix

6.1   Proof of Theorem 1

We now present the key ideas in the proof of the theorem. For clarity, we shall only present a sketch of the proof and omit technical details. Consider a symmetric distribution $p_{\mathbf{U}|\mathbf{Y}}$ of the form given by (1) and decoders $\{g_m\}_{m=k}^n$. Let $R' \geq R$.

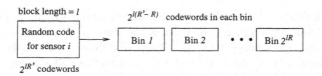

Fig. 4. Random code construction: n independent random codebooks of block length l are constructed each containing $2^{lR'}$ codewords. Each codebook is randomly partitioned into 2^{lR} bins each with approximately $2^{l(R'-R)}$ codewords.

Random Coding: For each sensor $i \in \mathcal{I}_n$, generate a codebook $\mathcal{C}_i$ containing $2^{lR'}$ codewords of blocklength l. The codewords of $\mathcal{C}_i$ are generated by drawing i.i.d. symbols from the marginal distribution p_{U_i}. The rate R' has to be large enough to ensure that there exists at least one codeword in $\mathcal{C}_i$ that is jointly (strongly) typical [8,13] with the sensor observation $y_i^{(l)}$. Using properties of strongly typical sequences, the probability that there exists a codeword which is jointly typical with $y_i^{(l)}$, to the first order with respect to l in the exponent, is $2^{-lI(Y_i;U_i)} = \frac{2^{lH(Y_i,U_i)}}{2^{lH(Y_i)}2^{lH(U_i)}}$. Intuitively, the desired probability will be close to one if the expected number of jointly typical codewords: $2^{lR'}2^{-lI(Y_i;U_i)}$ is exponentially large. This can be ensured if

$$R' > I(Y_i; U_i). \tag{8}$$

Note: since distributions are symmetric,

$$R' > I(Y_i; U_i) = \frac{1}{k}\sum_{j=1}^{k} I(Y_j; U_j) = \frac{1}{k}\sum_{j=1}^{k}\left[H(U_j) - H(U_j|Y_j)\right], \tag{9}$$

for all $i = 1, \ldots, n$.

Random Binning: For each sensor, construct 2^{lR} bins, each having approximately $2^{l(R'-R)}$ codewords (see Figure 4). The codewords are drawn independently, uniformly and with replacement from the corresponding codebook. Random binning is a technique that enables each encoder to transmit data at the *reduced* rate R by leveraging the fact that the quantized noisy observations of all sensors are correlated and the decoder will have access to $k-1$ additional correlated sensor observations.

Encoding: Given a noisy sensor observation $y_i^{(l)}$ find a codeword $u_i^{(l)}$ from $\mathcal{C}_i$ that is jointly typical with it. If (8) is satisfied, there exists at least one such codeword. The index I_i of the bin containing the codeword $u_i^{(l)}$ is transmitted.

Decoding: Let the decoder receive some k bin indices $I_{i_1}, ..., I_{i_k}$. The decoder searches through the corresponding bins to identify a k tuple of codewords that is jointly typical. If (8) holds, there is at least one such k tuple, namely the one that was transmitted. The size of each bin should be small enough so that the probability of finding another jointly typical k tuple is very small. There are $2^{kl(R'-R)}$ combinations of k-tuples of codewords from k bins. The probability that a random k tuple of codewords is jointly typical is, to the first order in the exponent w.r.t. l, given by $p \approx \frac{2^{lH(U_1,\ldots,U_k)}}{2^{lH(U_1)}2^{lH(U_2)}\ldots 2^{lH(U_k)}}$. Intuitively, the desired probability goes to zero if the expected number of jointly typical k-tuples: $p \cdot 2^{kl(R'-R)}$ is exponentially small. This can be ensured if the exponent satisfies

$$k(R' - R) < \sum_{i=1}^{k} H(U_i) - H(U_1, \ldots, U_k). \tag{10}$$

Combining (9) and (10) we get the desired result: $R > R_k^*$ (cf. (2)). With these conditions, the decoder successfully recovers the quantized noisy observations $u_{i_1}^{(l)} \ldots u_{i_k}^{(l)}$ with high probability and can optimally estimate the source from them.

If $m > k$ indices are received, the above decoding procedure can be repeatedly used on subsets of k indices at a time to recover all m quantized noisy observations with high probability.

6.2   Proof of Proposition 1

First note that the both $X - Z$ and $Z - E[Z|T_1, \ldots, T_n]$ are orthogonal to $\{T_i\}_{i=1}^{n}$. Hence, $X - E[Z|T_1, \ldots, T_n]$ is also orthogonal to the local statistics and $E[X|T_1, \ldots, T_n] = E[Z|T_1, \ldots, T_n] = h(T_1, \ldots, T_n)$, where the last equality follows from (7).

Let X take values in $\mathbb{R}$, $\mathbf{Y}_i$ take values in $\mathcal{Y}_i$ and consider l i.i.d. realizations of the tuple $(X, \mathbf{Y}_1, \ldots, \mathbf{Y}_n)$ denoted by $X^{(l)}$, and $\mathbf{Y}_i^{(l)}$ for $i = 1, \ldots, n$. Let $T_i : \mathcal{Y}_i :\to \mathbb{R}, i = 1, \ldots, n$ be some measurable maps for which (7) holds. Let $T_i^{(l)}(\mathbf{Y}_i^{(l)})$ denote $(T_i(\mathbf{Y}_i(1)), \ldots, T_i(\mathbf{Y}_i(l)))^T$. Since the realizations are independent and (7) holds, we have

$$Z^{(l)} := E\left[X^{(l)}|\mathbf{Y}_1^{(l)}, \ldots, \mathbf{Y}_n^{(l)}\right] = h^{(l)}\left(X^{(l)}|T_1^{(l)}, \ldots, T_n^{(l)}\right),$$

where in fact,

$$Z^{(l)}(j) = E[X(j)|\mathbf{Y}_1(j), \ldots, \mathbf{Y}_n(j)] = h(T_1(\mathbf{Y}_1(j)), \ldots, T_n(\mathbf{Y}_n(j))),$$

for all $j = 1, \ldots, l$. Now consider a set of n rate-R encoders and decoders (distributed vector-quantizers) of block-length l:

$$f_i : \mathcal{Y}_i^l \longrightarrow \mathcal{I}_{2^{lR}}, \ i = 1, \ldots, n,$$
$$g : (\mathcal{I}_{2^{lR}})^n \longrightarrow \mathbb{R}^l.$$

Let the set of reconstruction vectors in $\mathbb{R}^l$ be denoted by $\{\mathbf{v}_1, \ldots, \mathbf{v}_{2^{nlR}}\}$. We shall show that if the $\{f_i\}$'s and g are optimized for yielding the smallest MSE, then it is necessary that for each sensor i, observations $\mathbf{Y}_i^{(l)}$ which map to the same value of the statistic $T_i^{(l)}$, should have the same encoding index. By the orthogonality principle,

$$E\left\|X^{(l)} - g(F_1, \ldots, F_n)\right\|^2 = E\left\|X^{(l)} - Z^{(l)}\right\|^2 + E\left\|Z^{(l)} - g(F_1, \ldots, F_n)\right\|^2.$$

The first term on the right-hand side of the last equation does not depend on the encoders and decoder used. The second term is of the form

$$E\left\|h^{(l)}\left(T_1^{(l)},\ldots,T_n^{(l)}\right)-g\left(F_1,\ldots,F_n\right)\right\|^2.$$

If g is optimal, the reconstruction vectors in $\{\mathbf{v}_j\}_{j=1}^{2^{nlR}}$ must be all distinct otherwise one could use additional reconstruction vectors to reduce the MSE without increasing the rate. Now,

$$E\left\|h^{(l)}\left(T_1^{(l)},\ldots,T_n^{(l)}\right)-g\left(F_1,\ldots,F_n\right)\right\|^2 =$$
$$E\left[E\left[\left\|h^{(l)}\left(T_1^{(l)},\ldots,T_n^{(l)}\right)-g\left(F_1,\ldots,F_n\right)\right\|^2\middle| T_1^{(l)}=\mathbf{t}_1,\ldots,T_n^{(l)}=\mathbf{t}_n\right]\right].$$

Let

$$\mathbf{v}(\mathbf{t}_1,\ldots,\mathbf{t}_n):=\arg\min_{\mathbf{v}\in\{\mathbf{v}_1,\ldots,\mathbf{v}_{2^{nlR}}\}}\left\|h^{(l)}(\mathbf{t}_1,\ldots,\mathbf{t}_n)-\mathbf{v}\right\|.$$

Then it is clear that over the region of space $\bigotimes_{i=1}^n \mathcal{Y}_i^{(l)}$ where $T_i^{(l)}=\mathbf{t}_i, i=1\ldots,n$, we must have $g(F_1,\ldots,F_n)=\mathbf{v}(\mathbf{t}_1\ldots,\mathbf{t}_n)$ otherwise the MSE will be larger. Since different indices map to different reconstruction vectors, it follows that all points of $\bigotimes_{i=1}^n \mathcal{Y}_i^{(l)}$ for which $T_i^{(l)}(\mathbf{Y}_i^{(l)})=\mathbf{t}_i, i=1\ldots,n$, have the same the n-tuple of encoding indices as was claimed.

6.3   Proof of Proposition 2

First note that $E[\mathbf{Y}_i|X]=\frac{E[X\mathbf{Y}_i]}{E[X^2]}$. From the conditional independence assumption we have

$$E[\mathbf{Y}_i\mathbf{Y}_j^T]=E[E[\mathbf{Y}_i\mathbf{Y}_j^T]|X]=E[E[\mathbf{Y}_i|X]E[\mathbf{Y}_j^T|X]]=\frac{E[X\mathbf{Y}_i]E[X\mathbf{Y}_j^T]}{E[X^2]}.$$

The MMSE estimator of X based on all observations has the form $\sum_{i=1}^n \mathbf{a}_i^T\mathbf{Y}_i$. The local MMSE estimator of X based on $\mathbf{Y}_i$ is given by $E[X|\mathbf{Y}_i]=E[X\mathbf{Y}_i^T]K_i^{-1}\mathbf{Y}_i$, where $K_i:=E[\mathbf{Y}_i\mathbf{Y}_i^T]$. From the orthogonality principle and the conditional independence assumption we obtain for $j=1,\ldots,n$,

$$E[X\mathbf{Y}_j^T]=\mathbf{a}_j^T K_j+\sum_{i\neq j}\mathbf{a}_i^T E[\mathbf{Y}_i\mathbf{Y}_j^T],$$
$$=\mathbf{a}_j^T K_j+\beta_j E[X\mathbf{Y}_j^T],$$

where $\beta_j:=\sum_{i\neq j}\mathbf{a}_i^T E[X\mathbf{Y}_i]/E[X^2]$. This shows that

$$\mathbf{a}_j^T\mathbf{Y}_j=(1-\beta_j)E[X\mathbf{Y}_j^T]K_j^{-1}\mathbf{Y}_j=(1-\beta_j)E[X|\mathbf{Y}_j]$$

for all j. Hence, the global MMSE estimate has the form $\sum_i(1-\beta_i)E[X|\mathbf{Y}_i]$ which conforms to (7) as claimed.

Collaborative Signal Processing for Distributed Classification in Sensor Networks

Ashwin D'Costa and Akbar M. Sayeed*

Electrical and Computer Engineering
University of Wisconsin-Madison
dcosta@cae.wisc.edu, akbar@engr.wisc.edu

Abstract. Sensor networks provide virtual snapshots of the physical world via distributed wireless nodes that can sense in different modalities, such as acoustic and seismic. Classification of objects moving through the sensor field is an important application that requires collaborative signal processing (CSP) between nodes. Given the limited resources of nodes, a key constraint is to exchange the least amount of information between them to achieve desired performance. Two main forms of CSP are possible. Data fusion – exchange of low dimensional feature vectors – is needed between correlated nodes, in general, for optimal performance. Decision fusion – exchange of likelihood values – is sufficient between independent nodes. Decision fusion is generally preferable due to its lower communication and computational burden. We study CSP of multiple node measurements for classification, each measurement modeled as a Gaussian (target) signal vector corrupted by additive white Gaussian noise. The measurements are partitioned into groups. The signal components within each group are perfectly correlated whereas they vary independently between groups. Three classifiers are compared: the optimal maximum-likelihood classifier, a data-averaging classifier that treats all measurements as correlated, and a decision-fusion classifier that treats them all as independent. Analytical and numerical results based on real data are provided to compare the performance of the three CSP classifiers. Our results indicate that the sub-optimal decision fusion classifier, that is most attractive in the context of sensor networks, is also a robust choice from a decision-theoretic viewpoint.

1 Introduction

Wireless sensor networks are an emerging technology for monitoring the physical world with a densely distributed network of wireless nodes [1]. Each node has limited communication and computation ability and can sense the environment in a variety of modalities, such as acoustic, seismic, and infra red [1,2, 3]. A wide variety of applications are being envisioned for sensor networks, including disaster relief, border monitoring, condition-based machine monitoring,

---

* This work was supported by DARPA SensIT program under Grant F30602-00-2-0555.

F. Zhao and L. Guibas (Eds.): IPSN 2003, LNCS 2634, pp. 193–208, 2003.
© Springer-Verlag Berlin Heidelberg 2003

and surveillance in battlefield scenarios. Detection and classification of objects moving through the sensor field is an important task in many envisioned applications. Exchange of sensor information between different nodes in the vicinity of the object is necessary for reliable execution of such tasks due to a variety of reasons, including limited (local) information gathered by each node, variability in operating conditions, and node failure. Consequently, development of theory and methods for collaborative signal processing (CSP) of the data collected by different nodes is a key research area for realizing the vision of sensor networks.

The CSP algorithms have to be developed under the constraints imposed by the limited communication and computational abilities of the nodes as well as their finite battery life. A key goal of CSP algorithms in sensor networks is to exchange the least amount of data between nodes to attain a desired level of performance. In this paper, with the above goal in mind, we investigate CSP algorithms for single-target classification based on multiple acoustic measurements at different nodes. The numerical results presented here are based on real data collected in the DARPA SensIT program.

Some form of region-based processing is attractive in sensor networks in order to facilitate CSP between nodes and also for efficient routing of information in applications involving tracking of moving targets [3]. Typically, the nodes in the network are partitioned into a number of regions and a manager node is designated within each region to facilitate CSP between the nodes in the region and for communication of information from one region to another. Single target classification and tracking generally involves the following steps [3]:

1. **Target detection and data collection.** A target is detected in a particular region which becomes the active region. The nodes that detect the target also collect time series data that may be communicated to the manager node for classification purposes.
2. **Target localization.** Target detection information (for example, the time of closest point of approach and energy detector outputs) from different nodes is used by the manager node to estimate the location of the target.
3. **Target location prediction.** Location estimates over a period of time are used by the manager node to predict target location at future time instants.
4. **Creation of new potential active regions.** When the target gets close to exiting the current region, the estimates of predicted target location are used to put new regions on alert.
5. **Determination of new active region.** Once the target is detected in a new region it becomes the new active region. The above four steps are repeated for target tracking through the sensor field.

In this paper, we are primarily concerned with CSP techniques for combining the data collected by different nodes for single-target classification within a particular active region. However, the basic principles apply to distributed decision making in sensor networks in general.

There are two main forms of information exchange between nodes dictated by the statistics of measured signals. If two nodes yield correlated measurements, *data fusion* is needed, in general, for optimal performance – exchange of (low-dimensional) feature vectors that yield sufficient information for desired classification performance. On the other hand, if two nodes yield independent measurements, *decision fusion* is sufficient – exchange of likelihood values (scalars) computed from individual measurements. In general, the measurements would exhibit a mixture of correlated and independent components and would require a combination of data and decision fusion between nodes. In the context of sensor networks, decision fusion is clearly the more attractive choice. First, it imposes a significantly lower communication burden on the network, compared to data fusion, since only scalars are transmitted to the manager node [3]. Second, it also imposes a lower computational burden compared to data fusion since lower dimensional data has to be jointly processed at the manager node.

In this paper, we investigate the design of CSP classifiers and assess their performance in an idealized abstraction of measurements from multiple nodes. We consider $K = Gn_G$ measurements corresponding to a particular event. The K measurements are split into G groups with n_G measurements in each group. The signal component in the n_G measurements in a particular group is identical (perfectly correlated), but it varies independently from group to group. We compare the performance of three classifiers: 1) the optimal maximum-likelihood (ML) classifier, 2) a sub-optimal (decision-fusion) classifier that treats all the measurements as independent, and 3) a sub-optimal (data-averaging) classifier that treats all the measurements as perfectly correlated. Our results indicate that the decision-fusion classifier is remarkably robust to the true statistical correlation between measurements. Thus, the decision-fusion classifier, that is the most attractive choice in view of the computational and communication constraints, is also a robust choice from a decision-theoretic viewpoint.

2 CSP Classifiers for Multiple Measurements

We consider Gaussian classifiers which assume that the underlying data has complex circular Gaussian statistics. The notation $x \sim \mathcal{CN}(\mu, \Sigma)$ means that $\mathrm{E}[x] = \mu$ and $\mathrm{E}[xx^H] = \Sigma$ and $\mathrm{E}[xx^T] = 0$ (circular assumption). We first discuss the classifier structure for a single measurement and then generalize it to multiple measurements.

2.1 Single Measurement Classifier

Consider M target classes. Let x denote a complex-valued N-dimensional feature vector corresponding to a detected event. Under hypothesis $j = 1, \cdots, M$ (corresponding to j-th target class), x is modeled as

$$H_j \ : \ x = s + n \ , \ j = 1, \cdots, M, \tag{1}$$

where $s \sim \mathcal{CN}(\mu_j, \Sigma_j)$ denotes the Gaussian signal component corresponding to the j-th class, and $n \sim \mathcal{CN}(0, I)$ denotes additive white Gaussian noise. A classifier C maps the event feature vector $\boldsymbol{x}$ to one of the target classes. We assume that all classes are equally likely. Thus, the optimal classifier is the maximum-likelihood (ML) classifier which takes the form [4]

$$C(\boldsymbol{x}) = \arg \max_{j \in \{1, \cdots, M\}} p_j(\boldsymbol{x}) \tag{2}$$

where $p_j(\boldsymbol{x})$ denotes the likelihood function for j-th class which takes the following form under the complex Gaussian assumption

$$p_j(\boldsymbol{x}) = \frac{1}{\pi^N |\boldsymbol{\Sigma}_j + \boldsymbol{I}|} e^{-(\boldsymbol{x} - \boldsymbol{\mu}_j)^H (\boldsymbol{\Sigma}_j + \boldsymbol{I})^{-1} (\boldsymbol{x} - \boldsymbol{\mu}_j)}. \tag{3}$$

In this paper, we assume zero-mean signals so that $\boldsymbol{\mu}_j = \boldsymbol{0}$ for all j and, thus, all information about the targets is contained in the covariance matrices $\boldsymbol{\Sigma}_j$. In practice, $\boldsymbol{\Sigma}_j$ has to be estimated from available training data. We assume that $\mathrm{tr}(\boldsymbol{\Sigma}_j)$ (signal energy) is the same for all j.

2.2 Multiple Measurement Classifier

Suppose that we have K measurements (in a given modality), $\{\boldsymbol{x}_1, \cdots, \boldsymbol{x}_K\}$, from different nodes available to us. We are interested in combining these measurements to achieve improved classification performance. Consider the concatenated NK-dimensional feature vector

$$\boldsymbol{x}^{cT} = [\boldsymbol{x}_1^T, \boldsymbol{x}_2^T, \cdots, \boldsymbol{x}_K^T] \tag{4}$$

which has the same form as (1) under different hypotheses except for the larger number of dimensions. The noise is still white but the signal correlation matrix under H_j can be partitioned as

$$\boldsymbol{\Sigma}_j^c = \begin{bmatrix} \boldsymbol{\Sigma}_{j,11} & \boldsymbol{\Sigma}_{j,12} & \cdots & \boldsymbol{\Sigma}_{j,1K} \\ \boldsymbol{\Sigma}_{j,21} & \boldsymbol{\Sigma}_{j,22} & \cdots & \boldsymbol{\Sigma}_{j,2K} \\ \vdots & \ddots & \vdots & \vdots \\ \boldsymbol{\Sigma}_{j,K1} & \boldsymbol{\Sigma}_{j,K2} & \cdots & \boldsymbol{\Sigma}_{j,KK} \end{bmatrix} \tag{5}$$

where $\boldsymbol{\Sigma}_{j,kk'} = \mathrm{E}[\boldsymbol{x}_k \boldsymbol{x}_{k'}^H]$ denotes the cross-covariance between the k-th and k'-th measurements. The optimal classifier operates on $\boldsymbol{x}^c$ and takes the form (2) with $p_j(\boldsymbol{x}^c)$ given by (3) by replacing $\boldsymbol{x}$ with $\boldsymbol{x}^c$ and $\boldsymbol{\Sigma}_j$ with $\boldsymbol{\Sigma}_j^c$.

2.3 A Simple Measurement Model

We now present a model for measurements that is used throughout the paper. Let $K = G n_G$. Suppose that the signal component of $\boldsymbol{x}^c$ can be partitioned into G groups of n_G measurements each as

$$\boldsymbol{s}^{cT} = [\boldsymbol{s}_1^T, \cdots, \boldsymbol{s}_1^T, \boldsymbol{s}_2^T, \cdots, \boldsymbol{s}_2^T, \cdots, \boldsymbol{s}_G^T, \cdots, \boldsymbol{s}_G^T] \tag{6}$$

where the signal component of the n_G measurements in each group is identical and it varies independently from group to group. That is, $\{s_1, \cdots, s_G\}$ are i.i.d. according to $\mathcal{CN}(0, \Sigma_j)$ under H_j. The noise measurements, on the other hand, are independent across all measurements. The above signal model can capture a range of correlation between measurements. For $K = G$ ($n_G = 1$), all the measurements have independent signal components (no correlation), whereas for $K = n_G$ ($G = 1$), all the measurements have identical signal components (maximum correlation). We consider three classifiers based on the above model.

Optimum Classifier. There are two sources of classification error: background noise and the inherent statistical variability in the signals captured by Σ_j's. The optimal classifier performs signal averaging within each group to reduce the noise variance and statistical averaging over the groups to reduce the inherent signal variations. The optimum classifier operates on the NG dimensional vector

$$y = \begin{bmatrix} y_1 \\ \vdots \\ y_G \end{bmatrix} = \begin{bmatrix} s_1 \\ \vdots \\ s_G \end{bmatrix} + \begin{bmatrix} w_1 \\ \vdots \\ w_G \end{bmatrix} = s + w \tag{7}$$

where y_i are obtained by averaging the measurements in each group

$$y_i = \frac{1}{n_G} \sum_{j=1}^{n_G} x_{(i-1)G+j} = s_i + w_i \,, i = 1, \cdots, G. \tag{8}$$

Note that w_i are i.i.d. $\mathcal{CN}(0, I/n_G)$ due to signal averaging and s_i are i.i.d. $\mathcal{CN}(0, \Sigma_j)$ under H_j. It can be shown that the optimal classifier takes the form

$$C_{opt}(y_1, \cdots, y_G) = \arg \min_{j=1,\cdots,M} l_{opt,j}(y_1, \cdots, y_G) \tag{9}$$

where the (negative) log-likelihood function $l_{opt,j}(y)$ is given by

$$l_{opt,j}(y) = \log|\Sigma_j + I/n_G| + \frac{1}{G} \sum_{i=1}^{G} y_i^H (\Sigma_j + I/n_G)^{-1} y_i$$

$$= \log|\Sigma_j + I/n_G| + \mathrm{tr}((\Sigma_j + I/n_G)^{-1} \hat{\Sigma}_y) \tag{10}$$

and $\hat{\Sigma}_y = \frac{1}{G} \sum_{i=1}^{G} y_i y_i^H$ is the estimated data correlation matrix of $\{y_i\}$.

It is insightful to consider two limiting cases. First, suppose that $K = n_G$ ($G = 1$ – perfectly correlated measurements). In the limit of large K

$$\lim_{K \to \infty} l_{opt,j}(y) = \log|\Sigma_j| + y_1^H \Sigma_j^{-1} y_1 \tag{11}$$

which shows that noise is completely eliminated and the only remaining source of error is the inherent statistical variation in the signal. Now, suppose that $K = G$ ($n_G = 1$ – independent measurements). In the limit of large K

$$\lim_{K \to \infty} l_{opt,j}(y) = \log|\Sigma_j + I| + \mathrm{tr}((\Sigma_j + I)^{-1} \Sigma_y) \tag{12}$$

where $\boldsymbol{\Sigma}_y = \boldsymbol{\Sigma}_m + \boldsymbol{I}$ under H_m. In this case, all statistical variation in the signal is removed due to ensemble averaging. However, there is a bias in the estimated data correlation (relative to $\boldsymbol{\Sigma}_j$) due to noise. Both data averaging (correlated measurements) and ensemble averaging (uncorrelated measurements) contribute to improved classifier performance. However, as we will see, ensemble averaging is more critical in the case of stochastic signals.

Decision-Fusion Classifier. The sub-optimal decision-fusion classifier treats all measurements as independent:

$$C_{df}(\boldsymbol{x}_1, \cdots, \boldsymbol{x}_K) = \arg \min_{j=1,\cdots,M} l_{df,j}(\boldsymbol{x}_1, \cdots, \boldsymbol{x}_K)$$

$$l_{df,j}(\boldsymbol{x}) = \log|\boldsymbol{\Sigma}_j + \boldsymbol{I}| + \frac{1}{K} \sum_{i=1}^{K} \boldsymbol{x}_i^H (\boldsymbol{\Sigma}_j + \boldsymbol{I})^{-1} \boldsymbol{x}_i$$

$$= \log|\boldsymbol{\Sigma}_j + \boldsymbol{I}| + \mathrm{tr}((\boldsymbol{\Sigma}_j + \boldsymbol{I})^{-1} \hat{\boldsymbol{\Sigma}}_x) \qquad (13)$$

where $\hat{\boldsymbol{\Sigma}}_x = \frac{1}{K} \sum_{i=1}^{K} \boldsymbol{x}_i \boldsymbol{x}_i^H$ is the estimated data correlation matrix of $\{\boldsymbol{x}_i\}$. Note that C_{opt} and C_{df} are identical for $K = G$ in the measurement model. Note also from (13) that the M scalars $\{\boldsymbol{x}_i^H(\boldsymbol{\Sigma}_j + \boldsymbol{I})^{-1}\boldsymbol{x}_i\}$ for $j = 1, \cdots, M$ need to be transmitted from the K nodes to the manager node. Thus, C_{df} imposes a much smaller communication (and computational) burden on the network since $M \ll N$ in general. We consider only soft decision fusion in this paper. Several other forms, including hard decision fusion, are also possible [5].

Data-Averaging Classifier. The data-averaging classifier treats all measurements as correlated. It operates on the average of all measurements

$$\boldsymbol{y}_{da} = \frac{1}{K} \sum_{i=1}^{K} \boldsymbol{x}_i = \frac{1}{G} \sum_{i=1}^{G} \boldsymbol{y}_i = \boldsymbol{s}_{da} + \boldsymbol{w}_{da} \qquad (14)$$

where $\boldsymbol{s}_{da} \sim \mathcal{CN}(\boldsymbol{0}, \boldsymbol{\Sigma}_j/G)$ under H_j and $\boldsymbol{w}_{da} \sim \mathcal{CN}(\boldsymbol{0}, \boldsymbol{I}/K)$ in the measurement model. The data-averaging classifier takes the form

$$C_{da}(\boldsymbol{y}_{da}) = \arg \min_{j=1,\cdots,M} l_{da,j}(\boldsymbol{y}_{da})$$

$$l_{da,j}(\boldsymbol{y}_{da}) = \log|\boldsymbol{\Sigma}_j + \boldsymbol{I}/K| + \boldsymbol{y}_{da}^H (\boldsymbol{\Sigma}_j + \boldsymbol{I}/K)^{-1} \boldsymbol{y}_{da}. \qquad (15)$$

Note that C_{opt} and C_{da} are identical for $K = n_G$. All K measurements $\{\boldsymbol{x}_i\}$ have to be communicated to the manager node for the computation of C_{opt} and C_{da}. However, the computational burden of C_{da} is lower than that of C_{opt}.

3   Performance Analysis of the Three Classifiers

We analyze the performance of the three classifiers for $M = 2$ classes. The analysis for $M > 2$ is more involved and is the beyond the scope of this paper. Simple union bounds can be obtained for $M > 2$ via the $M = 2$ analysis presented here. We also analyze the asymptotic performance in the limit of large number of independent measurements and also provide an entropy comparison between data and decision fusion.

We assess the performance in terms of the average probability of (correct) detection (PD)

$$PD_j = P(l_j < l_m \ , \ \forall m \neq j | H_j) \ , \ PD = \frac{1}{M} \sum_{j=1}^{M} PD_j \qquad (16)$$

and the average probability of false alarm (PFA)

$$PFA_j = \frac{1}{M-1} \sum_{k=1, k \neq j}^{M} P(l_j < l_m, \forall m \neq j | H_k) \ , \ PFA = \frac{1}{M} \sum_{j=1}^{M} PFA_j. \qquad (17)$$

For $M = 2$ the above expressions simplify to

$$PD_1 = P(l_1 < l_2 | H_1) = 1 - PFA_2 \ , \ PD_2 = P(l_2 < l_1 | H_2) = 1 - PFA_1 \qquad (18)$$
$$PD = 1 - PFA. \qquad (19)$$

Our analysis is based on a signal model in which the covariance matrices of different targets are simultaneously diagonalizable. This model is motivated in the next section and it also simplifies the exposition to gain insight into the performance of the classifiers.

3.1   Simultaneously Diagonalizable Classes

We assume that all the covariance matrices share the same eigenfunctions

$$\Sigma_j = U \Lambda_j U^H \ , \ j = 1, \cdots, M \qquad (20)$$

where U represents the matrix of common (orthonormal) eigenvectors for all the classes – the different classes are characterized by the diagonal matrix of eigenvalues $\Lambda_j = \mathrm{diag}(\lambda_j[1], \cdots, \lambda_j[N])$. One scenario in which this assumption is approximately valid is when the source signals for different targets can be modeled as stationary processes over the duration of the detected event. In such a case, choosing U as a discrete Fourier transform (DFT) matrix would serve as an approximate set of eigenfunctions [6]. The eigenvalues will then correspond to samples of the associated power spectral densities (PSD's). The numerical results in Section 4 are based on this assumption and rely on experimental data collected in the SensIT program. Note that given the knowledge of Λ_j in the measurement model of Section 2.3, a realization for the signal in the i-th group, from the j-th class, can be generated as

$$s_i = U \Lambda_j^{1/2} z_i \ , \ z_i \sim \mathcal{CN}(0, I) \ , \ i = 1, \cdots, G. \qquad (21)$$

The same z_i realization is used in the i-th group and it changes independently from group to group. We assume the above signal model and analyze the classifiers in the eigen (Fourier) domain so that $\{\Sigma_j\}$ are replaced with $\{\Lambda_j\}$.

3.2 Optimal Classifier

The test statistic for the optimal classifier takes the form

$$l_{opt,j}(\boldsymbol{y}_1, \cdots, \boldsymbol{y}_G) = \log |\widetilde{\boldsymbol{\Lambda}}_j| + \frac{1}{G} \sum_{i=1}^{G} \boldsymbol{y}_i^H \widetilde{\boldsymbol{\Lambda}}_j^{-1} \boldsymbol{y}_i \ , \quad \widetilde{\boldsymbol{\Lambda}}_j = \boldsymbol{\Lambda}_j + \boldsymbol{I}/n_G \qquad (22)$$

where $\boldsymbol{y}_i$ are i.i.d. according to $\mathcal{CN}(\boldsymbol{0}, \widetilde{\boldsymbol{\Lambda}}_j)$. Thus, $\boldsymbol{y}_i$ can be representated as $\boldsymbol{y}_i = \widetilde{\boldsymbol{\Lambda}}_j^{1/2} \boldsymbol{z}_i$ where $\{\boldsymbol{z}_i\}$ are i.i.d. $\mathcal{CN}(\boldsymbol{0}, \boldsymbol{I})$. Consider the computation of PD_1 first. It can be readily shown that under H_1

$$l_{opt,1} = \log |\widetilde{\boldsymbol{\Lambda}}_1| + \frac{1}{G} \sum_{i=1}^{G} \|\boldsymbol{z}_i\|^2 \ , \quad l_{opt,2} = \log |\widetilde{\boldsymbol{\Lambda}}_2| + \frac{1}{G} \sum_{i=1}^{G} \boldsymbol{z}_i^H \widetilde{\boldsymbol{\Lambda}}_1 \widetilde{\boldsymbol{\Lambda}}_2^{-1} \boldsymbol{z}_i. \qquad (23)$$

Thus,

$$PD_1 = P\left(\frac{1}{G} \sum_{i=1}^{G} \boldsymbol{z}_i^H \left[\boldsymbol{I} - \widetilde{\boldsymbol{\Lambda}}_1 \widetilde{\boldsymbol{\Lambda}}_2^{-1} \right] \boldsymbol{z}_i < \log |\widetilde{\boldsymbol{\Lambda}}_2| - \log |\widetilde{\boldsymbol{\Lambda}}_1| \right) \qquad (24)$$

where the quadratic form

$$\frac{1}{G} \sum_{i=1}^{G} \boldsymbol{z}_i^H \left[\boldsymbol{I} - \widetilde{\boldsymbol{\Lambda}}_1 \widetilde{\boldsymbol{\Lambda}}_2^{-1} \right] \boldsymbol{z}_i = \frac{1}{G} \sum_{i=1}^{G} \sum_{n=1}^{N} |z_i[n]|^2 \left(\frac{\lambda_2[n] - \lambda_1[n]}{\lambda_2[n] + 1/n_G} \right) \qquad (25)$$

is a weighted sum of NG χ_2^2 random variables ($\{|z_i[n]|^2\}$) whose density and distribution functions can be analytically computed but are tedious [7]. Similarly, under H_2

$$PD_2 = P\left(\frac{1}{G} \sum_{i=1}^{G} \boldsymbol{z}_i^H \left[\boldsymbol{I} - \widetilde{\boldsymbol{\Lambda}}_2 \widetilde{\boldsymbol{\Lambda}}_1^{-1} \right] \boldsymbol{z}_i < \log |\widetilde{\boldsymbol{\Lambda}}_1| - \log |\widetilde{\boldsymbol{\Lambda}}_2| \right). \qquad (26)$$

We note that the PD can be computed in closed form for $M = 2$, as indicated above, but we do not provide the explicit expression since it is rather tedious.

3.3 Decision-Fusion Classifier

The test statistic for the decision-fusion classifier takes the form

$$l_{df,j}(\boldsymbol{x}_1, \cdots, \boldsymbol{x}_K) = \log |\widehat{\boldsymbol{\Lambda}}_j| + \frac{1}{K} \sum_{i=1}^{K} \boldsymbol{x}_i^H \widehat{\boldsymbol{\Lambda}}_j^{-1} \boldsymbol{x}_i \ , \quad \widehat{\boldsymbol{\Lambda}}_j = \boldsymbol{\Lambda}_j + \boldsymbol{I}. \qquad (27)$$

The quadratic form in the test statistic can be expanded as

$$\frac{1}{K} \sum_{i=1}^{K} \boldsymbol{x}_i^H \widehat{\boldsymbol{\Lambda}}_j^{-1} \boldsymbol{x}_i = \frac{1}{Gn_G} \sum_{i=1}^{G} \sum_{k=1}^{n_G} (\boldsymbol{s}_i + \boldsymbol{n}_{(i-1)G+k})^H \widehat{\boldsymbol{\Lambda}}_j^{-1} (\boldsymbol{s}_i + \boldsymbol{n}_{(i-1)G+k})$$

$$= \frac{1}{G} \sum_{i=1}^{G} \left[\boldsymbol{s}_i^H \widehat{\boldsymbol{\Lambda}}_j^{-1} \boldsymbol{s}_i + 2\mathrm{Re} \left[\boldsymbol{s}_i^H \widehat{\boldsymbol{\Lambda}}_j^{-1} \boldsymbol{w}_i \right] \right.$$

$$\left. + \frac{1}{n_G} \sum_{k=1}^{n_G} \boldsymbol{n}_{(i-1)G+k}^H \widehat{\boldsymbol{\Lambda}}_j^{-1} \boldsymbol{n}_{(i-1)G+k} \right] \tag{28}$$

where $\boldsymbol{s}_i$ and $\boldsymbol{w}_i$ are defined in (8) and (21). The density for the above quadratic form can be computed exactly but here we provide a simple approximation that yields fairly accurate (but conservative) PD estimates and relates $l_{df,j}$ to $l_{opt,j}$. We make two approximations. First, we replace the $\boldsymbol{w}_i \sim \mathcal{CN}(\boldsymbol{0}, \boldsymbol{I}/n_G)$ in (28) with $\boldsymbol{w}_i \sim \mathcal{CN}(\boldsymbol{0}, \boldsymbol{I})$. Second, we replace $\frac{1}{n_G} \sum_{k=1}^{n_G} \boldsymbol{n}_{(i-1)G+k}^H \widehat{\boldsymbol{\Lambda}}_j^{-1} \boldsymbol{n}_{(i-1)G+k}$ with $\boldsymbol{w}_i \widehat{\boldsymbol{\Lambda}}_j^{-1} \boldsymbol{w}_i$, $\boldsymbol{w}_i \sim \mathcal{CN}(\boldsymbol{0}, \boldsymbol{I})$. With the above approximations we have

$$\frac{1}{K} \sum_{i=1}^{K} \boldsymbol{x}_i^H \widehat{\boldsymbol{\Lambda}}_j^{-1} \boldsymbol{x}_i \approx \frac{1}{G} \sum_{i=1}^{G} \widehat{\boldsymbol{y}}_i^H \widehat{\boldsymbol{\Lambda}}_j^{-1} \widehat{\boldsymbol{y}}_i \tag{29}$$

where $\widehat{\boldsymbol{y}}_i$ are i.i.d. $\mathcal{CN}(\boldsymbol{0}, \widehat{\boldsymbol{\Lambda}}_j)$ under H_j. Thus, the PD_1 and PD_2 for the decision fusion classifier can be approximated by those of the optimal classifier given in (24) and (26) by replacing $\widetilde{\boldsymbol{\Lambda}}_j$ with $\widehat{\boldsymbol{\Lambda}}_j$. In particular, the quadratic form for PD_1 is given by

$$\frac{1}{G} \sum_{i=1}^{G} \boldsymbol{z}_i^H \left[\boldsymbol{I} - \widehat{\boldsymbol{\Lambda}}_1 \widehat{\boldsymbol{\Lambda}}_2^{-1} \right] \boldsymbol{z}_i = \frac{1}{G} \sum_{i=1}^{G} \sum_{n=1}^{N} |z_i[n]|^2 \left(\frac{\lambda_2[n] - \lambda_1[n]}{\lambda_2[n] + 1} \right) \tag{30}$$

which is a weighted sum of NG χ_2^2 random variables ($\{|z_i[n]|^2\}$), as for C_{opt}. However, the weights are different and essentially amount to a loss in SNR by a factor of n_G compared to C_{opt} since C_{df} does not do signal averaging within each group. The above conservative analysis shows that C_{df} fully exploits the independent observations across different groups, as C_{opt}, but incurs an effective loss in SNR compared to C_{opt}.

3.4 Data-Averaging Classifier

The test statistic for the data-averaging classifier takes the form

$$l_{da,j}(\boldsymbol{y}_{da}) = \log|\check{\boldsymbol{\Lambda}}_j| + \boldsymbol{y}_{da}^H \check{\boldsymbol{\Lambda}}_j^{-1} \boldsymbol{y}_{da} \;,\quad \check{\boldsymbol{\Lambda}}_j = \boldsymbol{\Lambda}_j + \boldsymbol{I}/K \tag{31}$$

where $\boldsymbol{y}_{da} \sim \mathcal{CN}(\boldsymbol{0}, \check{\boldsymbol{\Lambda}}_j)$, $\check{\boldsymbol{\Lambda}}_j = \boldsymbol{\Lambda}_j/G + \boldsymbol{I}/K$ under H_j. Thus, $\boldsymbol{y}_{da}$ can be represented as $\boldsymbol{y}_{da} = \check{\boldsymbol{\Lambda}}_j^{1/2} \boldsymbol{z}$ where $\boldsymbol{z} \sim \mathcal{CN}(\boldsymbol{0}, \boldsymbol{I})$. Proceeding similarly as above, it can be shown that

$$PD_1 = P \left(\boldsymbol{z}^H \check{\boldsymbol{\Lambda}}_1 \left[\check{\boldsymbol{\Lambda}}_1^{-1} - \check{\boldsymbol{\Lambda}}_2^{-1} \right] \boldsymbol{z} < \log|\check{\boldsymbol{\Lambda}}_2| - \log|\check{\boldsymbol{\Lambda}}_1| \right) \tag{32}$$

where the quadratic form can be expressed as

$$z^H \breve{\boldsymbol{\Lambda}}_1 \left[\breve{\boldsymbol{\Lambda}}_1^{-1} - \breve{\boldsymbol{\Lambda}}_2^{-1} \right] z = \sum_{n=1}^{N} |z[n]|^2 \left(\frac{\lambda_1[n]}{G} + \frac{1}{K} \right)$$
$$\left(\frac{\lambda_2[n] - \lambda_1[n]}{(\lambda_1[n] + 1/K)(\lambda_2[n] + 1/K)} \right) \tag{33}$$

which is a weighted sum of N χ_2^2 random variables ($\{|z[n]|^2\}$). Similarly,

$$PD_1 = P \left(z^H \breve{\boldsymbol{\Lambda}}_2 \left[\breve{\boldsymbol{\Lambda}}_2^{-1} - \breve{\boldsymbol{\Lambda}}_1^{-1} \right] z < \log |\breve{\boldsymbol{\Lambda}}_1| - \log |\breve{\boldsymbol{\Lambda}}_2| \right). \tag{34}$$

The density and distribution function of the quadratic form in (33) can be computed in closed form [7] and thus the PD of the data-averaging classifier can also be computed in closed form.

The data-averaging classifier provides maximum immunity against noise by averaging over all measurements. However, it does not exploit the independent signal components in different groups to reduce the inherent variations in the signal. Thus, in the limit of large number of uncorrelated measurements, we expect both C_{opt} and C_{df} to exhibit improved performance (perfect classification under certain conditions), but the performance of C_{da} will always be limited.

3.5   Asymptotic Performance

We now analyze classifier performance in the limit of large G (and K) for fixed n_G. In this analysis, we consider arbitrary $M > 2$. According to the analysis above, the only effect of n_G is to alter the effective SNR in the case of C_{opt} and C_{df}. First, consider the optimal classifier. Note that

$$l_{opt,j}(\boldsymbol{y}_1, \cdots, \boldsymbol{y}_G) = -\log p_j(\boldsymbol{y}_1, \cdots, \boldsymbol{y}_G)/G = -\frac{1}{G} \sum_{i=1}^{G} \log p_j(\boldsymbol{y}_i) \tag{35}$$

since $\boldsymbol{y}_i$ are i.i.d. $\mathcal{CN}(\boldsymbol{0}, \widetilde{\boldsymbol{\Lambda}}_m)$ under H_m. Thus, under H_m, it is well-known that by the law of large numbers [8]

$$\lim_{G \to \infty} l_{opt,j}(\boldsymbol{y}_1, \cdots, \boldsymbol{y}_G) = -\mathrm{E}_m[\log p_j(\boldsymbol{Y})] = D(p_m \| p_j) + h_m(\boldsymbol{Y}) \tag{36}$$

where $\mathrm{E}_m[\cdot]$ denotes expectation under H_m, $D(p_m \| p_j)$ is the Kullback-Leibler distance between p_j and p_m [8]

$$D(p_m \| p_j) = \mathrm{E}_m \left[\log(p_m(\boldsymbol{Y})/p_j(\boldsymbol{Y})) \right]$$
$$= \log \left(|\widetilde{\boldsymbol{\Lambda}}_j| / |\widetilde{\boldsymbol{\Lambda}}_m| \right) + \mathrm{tr} \left(\widetilde{\boldsymbol{\Lambda}}_j^{-1} \widetilde{\boldsymbol{\Lambda}}_m - \boldsymbol{I} \right) \tag{37}$$

and $h_m(\boldsymbol{Y})$ is the differential entropy (in bits) of $\boldsymbol{y}_i$ under H_m [8]

$$h_m(\boldsymbol{Y}) = -\mathrm{E}_m[\log p_m(\boldsymbol{Y})] = \log \left((\pi e)^N |\widetilde{\boldsymbol{\Lambda}}_m| \right). \tag{38}$$

From (36), we note that under H_m the different test statistics (for $j = 1, \cdots, M$) differ only in the term $D(p_m \| p_j) \geq 0$ which is identically zero for $j = m$. Thus, perfect classification ($PD = 1$, $PFA = 0$) is attained in the limit of large G if

$$D(p_m \| p_j) > 0 \ \forall j, m, j \neq m \tag{39}$$

which would be true in general for any given SNR (and any fixed n_G).

Now consider the decision-fusion classifier. Recall from (27) and (29) that the test statistics can be conservatively approximated as

$$l_{df,j}(\widehat{\boldsymbol{y}}_1, \cdots, \widehat{\boldsymbol{y}}_G) \approx -\log \widehat{p}_j(\widehat{\boldsymbol{y}}_1, \cdots, \widehat{\boldsymbol{y}}_G)/G = \frac{1}{G} \sum_{i=1}^{G} -\log \widehat{p}_j(\widehat{\boldsymbol{y}}_i) \tag{40}$$

since $\widehat{\boldsymbol{y}}_i$ are i.i.d. $\mathcal{CN}(\boldsymbol{0}, \widehat{\boldsymbol{\Lambda}}_m)$ under H_m and $\widehat{p}_j$ denotes the density of $\mathcal{CN}(\boldsymbol{0}, \widehat{\boldsymbol{\Lambda}}_j)$. Thus, in the limit of large G (under H_m)

$$\lim_{G \to \infty} l_{df,j}(\widehat{\boldsymbol{y}}_1, \cdots, \widehat{\boldsymbol{y}}_G) = -\mathrm{E}_m[\log \widehat{p}_j(\widehat{\boldsymbol{Y}})] = D(\widehat{p}_m \| \widehat{p}_j) + h_m(\widehat{\boldsymbol{Y}}) \tag{41}$$

where $D(\widehat{p}_m \| \widehat{p}_j)$ and $h_m(\widehat{\boldsymbol{Y}})$ are defined similar to (37) and (38). Consequently, in the limit of large G we expect perfect classification if

$$D(\widehat{p}_m \| \widehat{p}_j) > 0 \ \forall j, m, j \neq m \tag{42}$$

which would also be true in general for any given SNR (and any fixed n_G).

Finally, consider the data-averaging classifier whose test statistics are given in (31) where $\boldsymbol{y}_{da} \sim \mathcal{CN}(\boldsymbol{0}, \breve{\boldsymbol{\Lambda}}_m)$ under H_m. Recall that $\breve{\boldsymbol{\Lambda}}_j = \boldsymbol{\Lambda}_j + \boldsymbol{I}/K$ and $\grave{\boldsymbol{\Lambda}}_j = \boldsymbol{\Lambda}_j/G + \boldsymbol{I}/K$. As $G(K) \to \infty$, $\breve{\boldsymbol{\Lambda}}_j \to \boldsymbol{\Lambda}_j$ and $\grave{\boldsymbol{\Lambda}}_j \to \boldsymbol{0}$. Consequently,

$$\lim_{G \to \infty} l_{da,j}(\boldsymbol{y}_{da}) = \log |\boldsymbol{\Lambda}_j| \tag{43}$$

independent of the true underlying hypothesis. Thus, in the limit of large G (K), the data-averaging classifier assigns every event to the class with the smallest value of $\log |\boldsymbol{\Lambda}_j|$ and results in worst performance ($PD = PFA = 1/M$).

3.6   Entropy Comparison between Data and Decision Fusion

The above analysis indicates that C_{df} approximates the performance of C_{opt} except for an SNR loss depending on the fraction of correlated measurements n_G. The numerical results in the next section confirm the analysis. However, the attractiveness of C_{df} is also implicitly based on the assumption that communicating the likelihoods from the K nodes to the manager node puts a smaller communication burden on the network compared to communicating the N-dimensional feature vectors in the case of C_{opt}.

Recall from (13) that in C_{df} the M quadratic forms $\{\boldsymbol{x}_i^H(\boldsymbol{\Sigma}_j + \boldsymbol{I})^{-1}\boldsymbol{x}_i \, , \ j = 1, \cdots, M\}$ are communicated from the i-th node to the manager node for

$i = 1, \cdots, K$. In C_{opt}, on the other hand, the N-dimensional vectors x_i are communicated from the K nodes to the manager node. Thus, we need to compare the cost of communicating M quadratic forms (scalars) to that of communicating an N-dimensional Gaussian vector from each node to the manager node. We compare the communication cost in terms of differential entropy [8].[1]

The differential entropy of $x \sim \mathcal{CN}(0, \Sigma_m + I)$ is

$$h_m(X) = -\mathrm{E}[\log p_m(X)] = \log\left((\pi e)^N |\Sigma_m + I|\right) = \log\left((\pi e)^N |\Lambda_m + I|\right) \quad (44)$$

and quantifies the information content of any x_i from m-th class.

Now consider the differential entropy of the quadratic forms used by C_{df}. Let q_{jm} denote the quadratic form associated with $l_{df,j}$ under H_m

$$q_{jm} = x^H(\Sigma_j + I)^{-1}x = z^H \Lambda_{jm} z \quad (45)$$

where $x \sim \mathcal{CN}(0, \Sigma_m + I)$ and the second equality is based on the eigen-decomposition

$$(\Sigma_m + I)^{1/2}(\Sigma_j + I)^{-1}(\Sigma_m + I)^{1/2} = U \Lambda_{jm} U^H \quad (46)$$

which uses the representation $x = (\Sigma_m + I)^{1/2} z$, $z \sim \mathcal{CN}(0, I)$. Note that under the simultaneously diagonalizable signal model we have

$$\Lambda_{jm} = \widehat{\Lambda}_m \widehat{\Lambda}_j^{-1}, \quad \widehat{\Lambda}_j = \Lambda_j + I. \quad (47)$$

We want to compute the entropy of the quadratic form random variable Q_{jm} for all j, m. We first compute the worst case (highest) entropy by assuming that Q_{jm} is Gaussian. Using the fact that x is Gaussian, it can be readily shown that

$$\mathrm{E}[Q_{jm}] = \mathrm{E}_m[x^H(\Sigma_j + I)^{-1}x] = \mathrm{tr}\,(\Lambda_{jm}) \ , \ \mathrm{var}(Q_{jm}) = \mathrm{tr}\,(\Lambda_{jm}^2). \quad (48)$$

Thus, the worst-case entropy of Q_{jm} is given by [8]

$$h(Q_{jm}) = \frac{1}{2} \log\left(2\pi e \ \mathrm{tr}\,(\Lambda_{jm}^2)\right). \quad (49)$$

Note from (47) that $\Lambda_{jm} = I$ for $j = m$. Thus, $h(Q_{jj})$ is the same for all j. For $j = m$, the true entropy can also be easily computed since $q_{jj} = \|z\|^2$ from (45). Now, $q = \|z\|^2 \sim \chi_{2N}^2$ with density given by [7]

$$p_Q(q) = \frac{1}{(N-1)!} q^{N-1} e^{-q} \ , q \geq 0 \quad (50)$$

and thus

---

[1] We note differential entropy can be a bit misleading since it can be negative. However, a comparison of the difference in differential entropies is still valid – a quantity with higher entropy would require more bits to encode. A more intuitive interpretation of differential entropy is based on the fact that the entropy of an n-bit quantization of continuous random variable X is approximately $h(X) + n$ [8].

$$h(Q) = -\mathbb{E}[\log p_Q(Q)] = \log(N-1)! - N - (N-1)\int_0^\infty p_Q(q)\log(q)dq \ . \quad (51)$$

We note that the true entropy of q_{jm}, for $j \neq m$, can also be computed in closed-form but it is a bit more involved. Furthermore, as our numerical results indicate, $h(Q)$ is a good estimate for the entropy of q_{jm} for all j, m.

4   Simulation Results Based on Real Data

We now present numerical results based on real data collected in the SensIT program. We consider the problem of classifying a single vehicle. We consider $M = 2$ classes: Amphibious Assault Vehicle (AAV; tracked vehicle) and Dragon Wagon (DW; wheeled vehicle). We simulated $N = 25$ dimensional acoustic measurements from $K = Gn_G = 10$ nodes according to the model in Section 2.3. The eigenvalues (PSD samples) for the two vehicles were estimated from experimental data. The measurements at different nodes were generated using (21). The PD and PFA were estimated using Monte Carlo simulation over 5000 independent events. For $x \sim \mathcal{CN}(0, \Lambda + I)$, SNR $= \mathrm{tr}(\Lambda)/\mathrm{tr}(I)$.

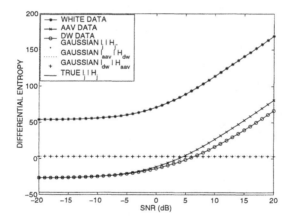

Fig. 1. Comparison between differential entropies of $N = 25$ dimensional Gaussian vectors used by l_{opt} and those of the quadratic forms used by l_{df}. The entropies for a white vector and two correlated vectors (AAV and DW) are plotted. The worst-case entropies for quadratic forms, assuming Gaussian statistics, are plotted. The true entropy of the quadratic forms, under the correct hypothesis, is also plotted. The entropy gains of decision fusion over data fusion are evident.

Figure 1 compares the differential entropy of Gaussian data in (44) with that of the quadratic forms in (49) and (51). The entropies for three data vectors are plotted: white data (maximum entropy), AAV data, and DW data. The worst-case entropy in (49) of the quadratic forms used by C_{df} are also plotted for all j, m (they are nearly identical). It can be seen that for SNR above 5dB, the worst-case entropy of Q_{jm} is lower than that of data. The true entropy of Q_{jj}, given in (51), is also plotted for comparison. The true entropy of Q_{jj} is seen to be substantially lower compared to that of data for the entire SNR range considered. This indicates the significant potential gains of C_{df} over C_{opt} in terms of the communication burden.

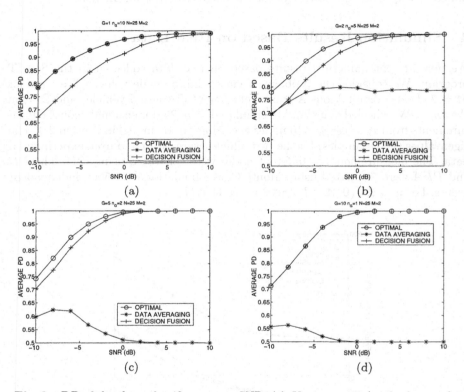

Fig. 2. PD of the three classifiers versus SNR. (a) $K = n_G = 10$ (perfectly correlated measurements). (b) $G = 2$ and $n_G = 5$. (c) $G = 5$ and $n_G = 2$. (d) $K = G = 10$ (independent measurements).

Figure 2 plots the PD as a function of SNR for the three classifiers for $K = 10$ and different combinations of G and n_G. The PFA is simply given by $1 - PD$ for $M = 2$. As expected, C_{opt} and C_{da} perform identically for $K = n_G$ (perfectly correlated case; Figure 2(a)), whereas C_{opt} and C_{df} perform identically for $K = G$ (independent case; Figure 2(d)). Note that C_{df} incurs a small loss in performance in the perfectly correlated (worst) case which diminishes at high SNRs. The performance loss in C_{da} in the independent (worst) case is very significant and does not improve with SNR. This is consistent with our analysis. At high SNR, all events are classified as DW by C_{da} since $\log |\Lambda_{DW}| < \log |\Lambda_{AAV}|$ due to the peakier eigenvalue distribution for DW, as evident from Figure 3(a). Figure 3(b) compares the PD of the three classifiers for an intermediate case

$(G = n_G = 2)$ with $K = 4$, $N = 15$-dimensional measurements. Analytically computed PD for C_{opt} and C_{da} and the conservative approximation for PD of C_{df} are also plotted and agree well with the simulation results.

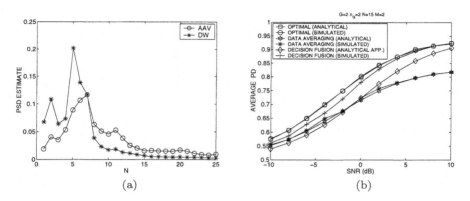

(a)   (b)

Fig. 3. (a) Covariance matrix eigenvalues (PSD estimates) for AAV and DW. (b) Comparison of simulated and analytical PD for $K = 4$, $G = 2$, $n_G = 2$ and $N = 15$.

Figure 4 plots the PD for the three classifiers as function of G ($K = 10$) for two different SNRs. It is evident that C_{df} closely approximates C_{opt} whereas C_{da} incurs a large loss when $K \neq n_G$. It is worth noting that for SNR=-5dB, the performance of C_{opt} and C_{df} first improves slightly with G and then gets worse again. This is consistent with the observation, in non-coherent communication over fading channels, that there is an optimal level of diversity (G) for a given SNR – increasing G beyond that level results in a loss in performance [7].

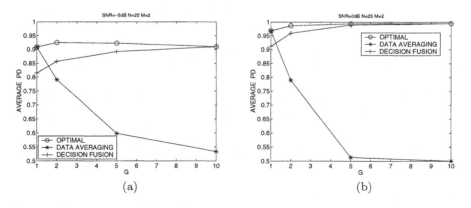

(a)   (b)

Fig. 4. Comparison of PD of the three classifiers for varying values of G ($K = 10$). (a) SNR = -5 dB. (b) SNR = 0 dB.

5   Conclusions

We have taken a first step in addressing the problem of how much information should be exchanged between nodes for distributed decision making in sensor networks. Our analysis is based on modeling the source signal as a stationary Gaussian process. In general, measurements from multiple nodes will provide a mixture of correlated and uncorrelated information about the source signal. The optimal classifier exploits the correlated measurements to improve the SNR and the independent measurements to stablize the inherent statistical variability in the signal. Both effects are important for improving classifier performance. However, for stochastic signals, the fusion of independent measurements is most significant. In this context, our results demonstrate that the simple sub-optimal decision-fusion classifier, that treats all measurements as independent, is not only an attractive choice given the computational and communication constraints in a sensor network, but is also a robust choice from a decision theoretic viewpoint. The decision-fusion classifier fully exploits the independent measurements and only incurs an effective SNR loss compared to the optimal classifier depending on the fraction of correlated measurements. However, if the source signal exhibits a non-zero mean or fewer degrees of freedom (lower-rank covariance matrix), data averaging to improve SNR might become more important. We note that exploiting a non-zero mean is difficult in practice due to various sources of measurement error. Directions for future research include hard decision fusion, quantized measurements, and multiple-target classification.

References

[1] Estrin, D., Girod, L., Pottie, G., Srivastava, M.: Instrumenting the world with wireless sensor network. In: Proc. IEEE Int. Conf. on Acoust., Speech and Signal Proc. – ICASSP'01. (2001) 2675–2678
[2] Special issue on collaborative signal and information processing in microsensor networks. In: IEEE Signal Processing Magazine, (S. Kumar and F. Zhao and D. Shepherd (eds.) (2002)
[3] Li, D., Wong, K., Hu, Y., Sayeed, A.: Detection, classification, tracking of targets in micro-sensor networks. In: IEEE Signal Processing Magazine. (2002) 17–29
[4] Duda, R., Hart, P., Stork, D.: Pattern Classification. 2nd edn. Wiley (2001)
[5] Kittler, J., Hatef, M., Duin, R., Matas, J.: On combining classifiers. IEEE Trans. Pattern Anal. Machine Intelligence 20 (1998) 226–238
[6] Gray, R.M.: On the asymptotic eigenvalue distribution of toeplitz matrices. IEEE Trans. Inform. Th. 18 (1972) 725–730
[7] Proakis, J.G.: Digitial Communications. 3rd edn. McGraw Hill, New York (1995)
[8] Cover, T.M., Thomas, J.A.: Elements of Information Theory. Wiley (1991)

Multi-target Sensor Management Using Alpha-Divergence Measures[*]

Chris Kreucher[1], Keith Kastella[1], and Alfred O. Hero[2]

[1] Veridian's Ann Arbor Research and Development Center, Ann Arbor, MI
{Christopher.Kreucher, Keith.Kastella}@Veridian.com
[2] The University of Michigan
Department of Electrical Engineering and Computer Science, Ann Arbor, MI
hero@eecs.umich.edu

Abstract. This paper presents a sensor management scheme based on maximizing the expected Rényi Information Divergence at each sample, applied to the problem of tracking multiple targets. The underlying tracking methodology is a multiple target tracking scheme based on recursive estimation of a Joint Multitarget Probability Density (JMPD), which is implemented using particle filtering methods. This Bayesian method for tracking multiple targets allows nonlinear, non-Gaussian target motion and measurement-to-state coupling. Our implementation of JMPD eliminates the need for a regular grid as required for finite element-based schemes, yielding several computational advantages. The sensor management scheme is predicated on maximizing the *expected* Rényi Information Divergence between the current JMPD and the JMPD after a measurement has been made. The Rényi Information Divergence, a generalization of the Kullback-Leibler Distance, provides a way to measure the dissimilarity between two densities. We evaluate the expected information gain for each of the possible measurement decisions, and select the measurement that maximizes the expected information gain for each sample.

1 Introduction

The problem of sensor management is to determine the best way to task a sensor where the sensor may have many modes and may be pointed in many directions. This problem has recently enjoyed a great deal of interest [9]. A typical application, and one that we focus on in our model problem, is to direct an electronically scanned aperture (ESA) radar [2]. An ESA provides great flexibility in pointing and mode selection. For example, the beam can be redirected in a few microseconds, enabling targets to be illuminated at will.

[*] This material is based upon work supported by the United States Air Force under Contract No. F33615-02-C-1199. Any opinions, findings and conclusions or recommendations expressed in this material are those of the author(s) and do not necessarily reflect the views of the United States Air Force.

F. Zhao and L. Guibas (Eds.): IPSN 2003, LNCS 2634, pp. 209–222, 2003.

One way of designing a sensor management system is by optimizing information flow. This is analogous to designing a communications system to maximize the channel capacity. Past work in this area has been based on maximizing Kullback-Leibler (KL) divergence. In this work, we use a more general information measure called the Rényi Information Divergence (also known as the α-divergence) [8], which reduces to the KL divergence under a certain limit. The Rényi divergence has additional flexibility in that in allows for emphasis to be placed on specific portions of the information.

We propose here an algorithm for sensor tasking that is motivated by information theory. First, we utilize a target tracking algorithm that recursively estimates the joint multitarget probability density for the set of targets under surveillance. We then strive to task the sensor in such a way that the sensing action it makes results in the maximum amount of information gain. To that end, we employ the Rényi information divergence as a measure of distance between two densities. The decision as to how to use a sensor then becomes one of determining which sensing action will maximize the expected information gain between the current joint multitarget probability density and the joint multitarget probability density after a measurement has been made. This methodology is similar in spirit to that of [10], although our application is quite different. In addition, [11] considers the sensor management as one of maximizing expected information and examines a variety of information driven criteria, including the Kullback-Leibler distance.

The paper is organized as follows. In Section 2, we present the target tracking algorithm that is central to our sensor management scheme. Specifically, we give the details of the JMPD and examine the numerical difficulties involved in directly implementing JMPD on a grid. In Section 3, we present a particle filter (PF) based implementation of JMPD. We see that this implementation provides for computationally tractable implementation, allowing realistic simulations to be made. A sensor management scheme, based on calculating the expected Rényi Information Divergence is given in Section 4. A comparison of the performance of the tracker using sensor management to the tracker using a non-managed scheme on a model problem is given in Section 5. We furthermore include some comments and results as the α parameter in the Rényi Divergence is varied. We conclude with some thoughts on future direction in Section 6.

2   The Joint Multitarget Probability Density (JMPD)

In this section, we provide the details of using the Joint Multitarget Probability Density (JMPD) for target tracking. The concept of JMPD was first discussed by Kastella in [1], where an association free method of tracking multiple targets that moved between discrete cells on a line based on a set of sensor measurements was presented. We generalize that discussion here to deal with targets that have N-dimensional continuous valued state vectors. In the model problem considered herein, we are interested in tracking the position (x, y) and velocity $(\dot{x}, \dot{y})$ of multiple targets and so we describe targets by the four dimensional state vector $[x, \dot{x}, y, \dot{y}]'$.

JMPD provides a means for tracking an unknown number of targets in a Bayesian setting. The statistics model uses the joint multitarget conditional probability density $p(\mathbf{x}_1^k, \mathbf{x}_2^k, ... \mathbf{x}_{T-1}^k, \mathbf{x}_T^k | \mathbf{Z}^k)$ as the probability density for exactly T targets with states $\mathbf{x}_1^k, \mathbf{x}_2^k, ... \mathbf{x}_{T-1}^k, \mathbf{x}_T^k$ at time k based on a set of observations $\mathbf{Z}^k$. The number of targets T is a variable to be estimated simultaneously with the states of the T targets. The observation set $\mathbf{Z}^k$ refers to the collection of measurements up to and including time k, i.e. $\mathbf{Z}^k = \{\mathbf{z}^1, \mathbf{z}^2, ... \mathbf{z}^k\}$, where each of the $\mathbf{z}^i$ may be a single measurement or a vector of measurements made at time i.

Each of the state vectors $\mathbf{x}_i$ in the density $p(\mathbf{x}_1^k, \mathbf{x}_2^k, ... \mathbf{x}_{T-1}^k, \mathbf{x}_T^k | \mathbf{Z}^k)$ is a vector quantity and may (for example) be of the form $[x, \dot{x}, y, \dot{y}]'$. We refer to each of the T target state vectors $\mathbf{x}_1^k, \mathbf{x}_2^k, ... \mathbf{x}_{T-1}^k, \mathbf{x}_T^k$ as a partition of the state $\mathbf{X}$. For convenience, the density will be written more compactly in the traditional manner as

$$p(\mathbf{X}^k | \mathbf{Z}^k) \tag{1}$$

With the understanding that the state-vector $\mathbf{X}$ represents a variable number of targets each possessing their own state vector. As an illustration, some examples illustrating the sample space of p are

$p(\emptyset | \mathbf{Z})$, the posterior likelihood for no targets in the surveillance volume
$p(\mathbf{x}_1 | \mathbf{Z})$, the posterior likelihood for one target in state $\mathbf{x}_1$
$p(\mathbf{x}_1, \mathbf{x}_2 | \mathbf{Z})$, the posterior likelihood for two targets in states $\mathbf{x}_1$ and $\mathbf{x}_2$
$p(\mathbf{x}_1, \mathbf{x}_2, \mathbf{x}_3 | \mathbf{Z})$, the posterior likelihood for three targets in states $\mathbf{x}_1, \mathbf{x}_2$ and $\mathbf{x}_3$

The temporal update of the posterior likelihood on this density proceeds according to the usual rules of Bayesian filtering. Given a model of target kinematics $p(\mathbf{X}^k | \mathbf{X}^{k-1})$, we may compute the time-updated or prediction density via

$$p(\mathbf{X}^k | \mathbf{Z}^{k-1}) = \int d\mathbf{X}^{k-1} p(\mathbf{X}^k | \mathbf{X}^{k-1}) p(\mathbf{X}^{k-1} | \mathbf{Z}^{k-1}) \tag{2}$$

Bayes rule enables us to update the posterior density as new measurements $\mathbf{z}^k$ arrive as

$$p(\mathbf{X}^k | \mathbf{Z}^k) = \frac{p(\mathbf{z}^k | \mathbf{X}^k) p(\mathbf{X}^k | \mathbf{Z}^{k-1})}{p(\mathbf{z}^k | \mathbf{Z}^{k-1})} \tag{3}$$

In practice, the sample space of $\mathbf{X}^k$ is very large. It contains all possible configurations of state vectors $\mathbf{x}_i$ for all possible values of T. The original formulation of JMPD given in [1] approximated the density by discretizing on a grid. It was immediately found that the computational burden in this scenario makes evaluating realistic problems intractable, even when using the simple model of targets moving between discrete locations in one-dimension. In fact, the number grid cells needed grows as $Locations^{Targets}$, where $Locations$ is the number of discrete locations the targets may occupy and $Targets$ is the number of targets.

Thus, we need a method for approximating the JMPD that leads to more tractable computational burden. In the next section, we show that the Monte Carlo methods collectively known as particle filtering break this logjam.

3   Particle Filter Implementation of JMPD

We expect that a particle filter based implementation of JMPD will break the computational logjam and allow us to investigate more realistic problems. To implement JMPD via a particle filter (PF), we first approximate the joint multitarget probability density $p(\mathbf{X}|\mathbf{Z})$ by a set of N_{part} weighted samples, $\mathbf{X}_p, (p = 1...N_{part})$:

$$p(\mathbf{X}|\mathbf{Z}) \approx \sum_{p=1}^{N_{part}} w_p \delta(\mathbf{X} - \mathbf{X}_p) \tag{4}$$

Here we have suppressed the time superscript k everywhere for notational simplicity. We will do this whenever time is not relevant to the discussion at hand.

Recall from Section 2 that our multitarget state vector $\mathbf{X}$ has T partitions, each corresponding to a target:

$$\mathbf{X} = [\mathbf{x}_1, \ \mathbf{x}_2, \ ..., \ \mathbf{x}_{T-1}, \ \mathbf{x}_T] \tag{5}$$

Furthermore, the joint multitarget probability density $p(\mathbf{X}|\mathbf{Z})$ is defined for $T = 0...\infty$. Each of the particles $\mathbf{X}_p$, $p = 1...N_{part}$ is a sample drawn from $p(\mathbf{X}|\mathbf{Z})$. Therefore, a particle $\mathbf{X}_p$ may have $0, 1, ...\infty$ partitions, each partition corresponding to a different target. We will denote the number of partitions in particle $\mathbf{X}_p$ by n_p, where n_p may be different for different $\mathbf{X}_p$. Since a partition corresponds to a target, the number of partitions that a particle has is that particle's estimate of the number of targets in the surveillance area.

To make our notation more concrete, assume that each target is modeled using the state vector $\mathbf{x} = [x, \dot{x}, y, \dot{y}]'$. Then a particular $\mathbf{X}_p$, which is tracking n_p targets, will be given as

$$\mathbf{X}_p = [\mathbf{x}_{p,1}, \ \mathbf{x}_{p,2}, \ ... \ \mathbf{x}_{p,n_p}] = \begin{pmatrix} x_{p,1} & x_{p,2} & \cdots & x_{p,n_p} \\ \dot{x}_{p,1} & \dot{x}_{p,2} & \cdots & \dot{x}_{p,n_p} \\ y_{p,1} & y_{p,2} & \cdots & y_{p,n_p} \\ \dot{y}_{p,1} & \dot{y}_{p,2} & \cdots & \dot{y}_{p,n_p} \end{pmatrix} \tag{6}$$

Where here we expand the notation a bit and use $x_{p,1}$ to denote the x position estimate that particle p has of target 1.

Notice that this method differs from traditional particle filter tracking algorithms where a single particle corresponds to a single target. We find that when each particle is attached to a single target, some targets become particle starved over time. All of the particles tend to attach to the target receiving the best measurements. Our method explicitly enforces the multitarget nature of the problem by encoding in each particle the estimate of the number of targets and the states of those targets. This helps top alleviate the particle starvation issue.

Note there is a permutation symmetry inherent in JMPD, i.e. $p(\mathbf{x}_1, \mathbf{x}_2 | \mathbf{Z}) = p(\mathbf{x}_2, \mathbf{x}_1 | \mathbf{Z})$. This is particularly relevant when targets are near each other and particle partitions begin to swap allegiances. We will have more to say about this issue in Section 3.5.

In the following subsections, we detail the particle filter implementation of JMPD.

3.1 Initialization

As this is primarily a target tracking application, we typically assume that an estimate of the actual ground truth is available at time 0. To this end, we typically initialize a small set of particles (e.g. 10%) to contain the true target states at time 0 and randomly assign values (both target states and number of targets) to the rest of the particles.

Alternatively, we have successfully employed the following detection scheme. All particles are initialized to believing there are 0 targets. For the first t time steps the algorithm is in detection mode and the sensor is scheduled to periodically scan the surveillance area. As targets are detected, particles are mutated to be consistent with the detection.

3.2 Particle Proposal

Several methods of particle proposal have been investigated. The standard method used, which will be referred to as sampling from the kinematic prior, proposes new particles at time k, $\mathbf{X}_p^k$, according to the traditional Sampling-Importance Resampling (SIR) method. For each particle at time $k-1$, $\mathbf{X}_p^{k-1}$, a new particle $\mathbf{X}_p^k$ is generated using the kinematic prior $p(\mathbf{X}^k | \mathbf{X}^{k-1})$. In the case where the targets are indistinguishable and move independently, each target in $\mathbf{X}_p^{k-1}$ behaves according to the same motion model and is proposed independently of the other targets.

In addition, we have investigated three alternate particle proposal techniques, all of which are developed as a means of biasing the proposal process towards the measurements.

First, the multi-particle proposal method proposes a set of M distinct particles, $\mathbf{X}_p^k(m)$, $m = 1...M$, for each particle at time $k-1$. The proposed particles $\mathbf{X}_p^k(m)$ are then given weights according to the likelihood and a single representative is selected as $\mathbf{X}_p^k$ based on the weights.

Second, the multi-partition proposal method proposes M possible realizations for each partition of a particle $\mathbf{X}_{p,j}^k(m)$. In this notation $\mathbf{X}_{p,j}^k(m)$ refers to the mth proposal for the jth partition of the pth particle at time k. See (6) for a concrete example of a particle and its partitions. The proposed partitions are then given weights according to the likelihood and a new particle $\mathbf{X}_p^k$ is chosen by selecting a representative from each of the proposed partition sets.

Third, the independent-partition method proposed by [7] proposes new partitions and weights each partition independently. Particles at time k, $\mathbf{X}_p^k$, are formed by selecting partitions from the set of weighted proposed partitions from the particles at time $k - 1$. This method assumes that the targets states are independent, which is not the case when targets cross.

Finally, in any of these methods, target birth and death may be accounted for by modifying the proposal density to incorporate a probability that the proposed particle $\mathbf{X}_p^k$ has either fewer or more targets then $\mathbf{X}_p^{k-1}$. For example, with some birth rate probability α we propose a particle with $n_p + 1$ targets at time $k + 1$ starting from a particle with only n_p targets at time k. Similarly, we may propose a particle with fewer targets according to some target death rate. In practice, targets enter and leave only along the boundaries of the surveillance area and so this must be taken into account as well.

3.3   Measurement Update

Each proposed particle is given a weight according to its agreement with the measurements, the kinematic model, and the importance density [4]. Since we are proposing particles based on $p(\mathbf{X}^k|\mathbf{X}^{k-1})$, it can be shown that the proper weighting is given by

$$w_p \propto p(\mathbf{z}|\mathbf{X}_p^k) \tag{7}$$

where the density p comes from the sensor model and incorporates both target detection and false alarm rates.

Recall that each particle $\mathbf{X}_p^k$ simultaneously postulates that a specific number of targets exist in the surveillance region (n_p) and that the target states are given by $[\mathbf{x}_1, \mathbf{x}_2, ..., \mathbf{x}_{n_p-1}, \mathbf{x}_{n_p}]$. In the case where the measurement set is made up of a scan i cells (e.g. measurements taken on a XY grid) where the measurement in each cell is independent of the measurements in the other cells, we compute the weight as

$$w_p \propto \prod_i p(z_i|\mathbf{X}_p) \tag{8}$$

where in this notation z_i refers to the measurement made in cell i. A particular particle $\mathbf{X}_p$ will postulate that there are targets in some cells i_x (not necessarily distinct):

$$i_x = i_1, i_2, ...i_{n_p} \tag{9}$$

We denote the measurement density when there are 0 targets present as p_0, and simplify the weight equation as

$$w_p \propto \prod_{i \notin i_x} p_0(z_i) \prod_{i \in i_x} p(z_i|\mathbf{X}_p) \tag{10}$$

$$w_p \propto \prod_i p_0(z_i) \prod_{i \in i_x} \frac{p(z_i|\mathbf{X}_p)}{p_0(z_i)} \tag{11}$$

$$w_p \propto \prod_{i \in i_x} \frac{p(z_i | \mathbf{X}_p)}{p_0(z_i)} \tag{12}$$

If we let $O_{i,p}$ (the occupation number) denote the number of targets that a particle p postulates exist in cell i, then we write the weight as

$$w_p \propto \prod_{i \in i_x} \frac{p(z_i | O_{i,p})}{p_0(z_i)} \tag{13}$$

Notice that there is no association of measurement to tracks as is done in conventional multi-target trackers. Each particle $\mathbf{X}_p$ is an estimate of the system state (both number of targets and their states) and has its weight w_p computed based on agreement with the measurements.

3.4   Resampling

As noted by [4], over time the variance of the weights w_p can only increase. If left unchecked, eventually all of the particles except one have near zero weight. To remedy this situation a resampling step is added. When the variance of the weights becomes too high, a new set of N_{part} particles is selected from the existing set with replacement based on the weights w_p. We then have a collection of N_{part} particles with uniform weight that approximate the density $p(\mathbf{X}|\mathbf{Z})$. At this step, particles that do not correspond to measurements are not retained – in particular, particles that have an n_p that is unsupported by measurements are not retained.

The particular resampling that we have implemented is called systematic resampling [4]. We like this scheme because it is easy to implement, runs in $O(N)$, is unbiased, and minimizes Monte Carlo variance. In addition, we favor resampling only when necessary as advocated by [6]. This saves time as well as reduces the variance of the estimate. Many other resampling schemes and modifications are presented in the literature [5]. Of these methods, we have found that adaptive resampling [6] and Markov Chain Monte Carlo (MCMC) moves using a Metropolis-Hasting scheme [5] lead to improved performance over straightforward resampling in our application.

3.5   Estimation

Estimates of various interesting quantities may be easily made using the particles. Estimation is best performed before resampling, as resampling has been shown to only increase the variance of the estimate.

To compute the probability that there are exactly n targets in the surveillance volume, first define the indicator variable

$$I_p = \begin{cases} 1 \text{ if } n_p = n \\ 0 \text{ otherwise} \end{cases} \tag{14}$$

Then the probability of n targets in the surveillance volume, $p(n|\mathbf{Z})$, is given by

$$p(n|\mathbf{Z}) = \sum_{p=1}^{N_{part}} I_p w_p \tag{15}$$

So to estimate the probability of n targets in the surveillance volume, we sum up the weights of the particles that have n partitions.

To compute the estimated state and covariance of target i, we first define a second indicator variable $\tilde{I}_p$ that indicates if particle p has a partition corresponding to target i:

$$\tilde{I}_p = \begin{cases} 1 \text{ if } n_p \geq n \\ 0 \text{ otherwise} \end{cases} \tag{16}$$

Furthermore, we define the normalized weights to be

$$\hat{w}_p = \frac{w_p \tilde{I}_p}{\sum_{l=1}^{N_{part}} \tilde{I}_l w_l} \tag{17}$$

So $\hat{w}_p$ is the relative weight of particle p, with respect to all particles tracking target i. Then the estimate of the state of target i is given by

$$\hat{\mathbf{X}}(i) = E[\mathbf{X}(i)] = \sum_{p=1}^{N_{part}} \tilde{I}_p \hat{w}_p \mathbf{X}_{p,i} \tag{18}$$

Which is simply the weighted summation of the position estimates from those particles that are tracking target i. The covariance is given by

$$\hat{\mathbf{\Lambda}}(i) = \sum_{p=1}^{N_{part}} \tilde{I}_p \hat{w}_p (\mathbf{X}_{p,i} - \hat{\mathbf{X}(i)})(\mathbf{X}_{p,i} - \hat{\mathbf{X}(i)})' \tag{19}$$

The indicator function $\tilde{I}_p$ causes the summations in (18) and (19) to be taken over only those particles that are tracking target i. The permutation symmetry issue mentioned in Section 3 comes to the forefront here. Notice that it is not necessarily true that partition i of particle j is tracking the same target that partition i of particle $j + 1$ is tracking. Therefore, before evaluation of (18) or (19) can be made, we must ensure that partition i, $(i = 1...T)$, corresponds to the same target in each particle. In our work, this is accomplished by taking care to retain the ordering during the particle proposal process.

4   Rényi Information Divergence for Sensor Management

Our paradigm for tasking the sensor is to choose the sensing action (i.e. sensing modality or sensor pointing direction) that maximizes the expected information gain. To that end, we introduce the Rényi information divergence (20), also known as the α-divergence, between two densities f_1 and f_0:

$$D_\alpha(f_1||f_0) = \frac{1}{\alpha - 1} ln \int f_1^\alpha(x) f_0^{1-\alpha}(x) dx \tag{20}$$

The function D_α gives a measure of the distance between the two densities f_0 and f_1. In our application, we are interested in computing the divergence between the predicted density $p(\mathbf{X}|\mathbf{Z}^{k-1})$ and the updated density after a measurement is made, $p(\mathbf{X}|\mathbf{Z}^k)$.

$$D_\alpha(p(\mathbf{X}|\mathbf{Z}^k)||p(\mathbf{X}|\mathbf{Z}^{k-1})) = \frac{1}{\alpha-1} ln \sum_{\mathbf{X}} p(\mathbf{X}|\mathbf{Z}^k)^\alpha p(\mathbf{X}|\mathbf{Z}^{k-1})^{1-\alpha} \qquad (21)$$

The integral in (20) reduces to a summation since any discrete approximation of $p(\mathbf{X}|\mathbf{Z}^{k-1})$ only has nonzero probability at a finite number of target states. After some algebra and the incorporation of Bayes rule (3), one finds that this quantity can be simplified to

$$D_\alpha(p(\mathbf{X}|\mathbf{Z}^k)||p(\mathbf{X}|\mathbf{Z}^{k-1})) = \frac{1}{\alpha-1} ln \frac{1}{p(\mathbf{z}|\mathbf{Z}^{k-1})^\alpha} \sum_{\mathbf{X}} p(\mathbf{X}|\mathbf{Z}^{k-1})p(\mathbf{z}|\mathbf{X})^\alpha \qquad (22)$$

Our particle filter approximation of the density reduces (22) to

$$D_\alpha(p(\mathbf{X}|\mathbf{Z}^k)||p(\mathbf{X}|\mathbf{Z}^{k-1})) = \frac{1}{\alpha-1} ln \frac{1}{p(\mathbf{z})^\alpha} \sum_{p=1}^{N_{part}} w_p p(\mathbf{z}|\mathbf{X_p})^\alpha \qquad (23)$$

where

$$p(\mathbf{z}) = \sum_{p=1}^{N_{part}} w_p p(\mathbf{z}|\mathbf{X}_p) \qquad (24)$$

We would like to make the divergence between the current density and the density after a new measurement has been made as large as possible. This indicates that the sensing action has maximally increased the information content of the measurement updated density, $p(\mathbf{X}|\mathbf{Z}^k)$, with respect to the density before a measurement was made, $p(\mathbf{X}|\mathbf{Z}^{k-1})$.

Of course, we cannot calculate (23) exactly until after the measurement at time k has been made. However, we can calculate the expected value of this quantity for different sensing actions. We propose as a method of sensor management, then, calculating the expected value of (23) for each of the $m, (m = 1...M)$ possible sensing actions and choosing the action that maximizes the expectation. In this notation m refers to any possible sensing action under consideration, including but not limited to sensor mode and sensor beam positioning. In this manner, we say that we are making the measurement that maximizes expected information gain. Notice that this is a greedy scheme, which chooses to make the measurement that optimizes information gain for the next time step.

The expected value of (23) may be written as an integral over all possible outcomes z_m when performing sensing action m:

$$< D_\alpha >_m = \int dz_m p(z_m|\mathbf{Z}^{k-1}) D_\alpha(p(\mathbf{X}|\mathbf{Z}^k)||p(\mathbf{X}|\mathbf{Z}^{k-1})) \qquad (25)$$

In the special case where measurements are thresholded and are therefore either detections or no-detections, this integral reduces to

$$< D_\alpha >_m = p(z = 0|\mathbf{Z}^{k-1})D_\alpha|_{m,z=0} + p(z = 1|\mathbf{Z}^{k-1})D_\alpha|_{m,z=1} \quad (26)$$

Which, using (23) results in

$$< D_\alpha >_m = \frac{1}{\alpha - 1} \sum_{z=0}^{1} p(z)ln\frac{1}{p(z)^\alpha} \sum_{p=1}^{N_{part}} w_p p(z|\mathbf{X}_p)^\alpha \quad (27)$$

Implementationally, the value of equation (27) can be calculated for a host of possible actions using only a single loop through the particles.

In summary, our sensor management algorithm is a recursive algorithm that proceeds as follows. At each occasion where a sensing action is to be made, we evaluate the expected information gain as given by (27) for each possible sensing action m. We then select and make the sensing action that gives maximal expected information gain.

We note here that the α parameter may be used to adjust how heavily one emphasizes the tails of the two distributions. In the limiting case of $\alpha \to 1$ the Rényi divergence becomes the more commonly known Kullback-Leibler (KL) discrimination (28).

$$\lim_{\alpha \to 1} D_\alpha(f_1||f_0) = \int f_0(x)ln\frac{f_0(x)}{f_1(x)}dx \quad (28)$$

5   Simulation Results

We test the performance of the sensor management scheme by considering the following model problem. We have three targets moving on a $12x12$ sensor grid. Each target is modeled using the four-dimensional state vector $[x, \dot{x}, y, \dot{y}]'$. Target motion is simulated using a constant-velocity (CV) model with a (relatively) large diffusive component. The trajectories have been shifted and time delayed so that there are two times during the simulation where targets cross paths.

The target kinematics assumed by the filter (2) are CV as in the simulation. At each time step, a set of L (not necessarily distinct) cells are measured. The sensor is at a fixed location above the targets and all cells are always visible to the sensor. When measuring a cell, the imager returns either a 0 (no detection) or a 1 (detection) governed by P_d, P_f, and SNR. This model is known by the filter and used to evaluate (3). In this illustration, we take $P_d = 0.5$, and $P_f = P_d^{(1+SNR)}$, which is a standard model for thresholded detection of Rayleigh returns.

We contrast in this section the performance of the tracker when the sensor uses a non-managed (periodic) scheme versus the performance when the sensor uses the management scheme presented in Section 4. The periodic scheme measures each cell in sequence. At time 1, cells 1...L are measured. At time 2, cells

$L + 1...2L$ are measured. This sequence continues until all cells have been measured, at which time the scheme resets. The managed scheme uses the expected information divergence to calculate the best L cells to measure at each time.

For the simulations that follow, we have taken α in (27) near 1. However, we still use the Rényi formulation of (20) rather than the KL formulation of (28) because the Rényi formulation provides some computational advantages.

In Fig. 1, we give a single-time snapshot, which graphically illustrates the difference between the two schemes. On the left, we show the managed scheme and on the right the periodic scheme. In both panes, the three targets are marked with an asterisk, the covariance ellipses of the estimated target position are shown, and we use grayscale to indicate the number of times each cell has been measured at this time step.

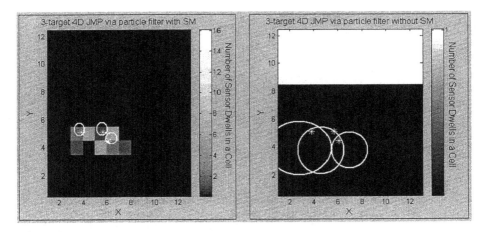

Fig. 1. A Comparison of Non-Managed and Managed Tracking. (L) Using Sensor Management, and (R) Using a Periodic Scheme. With Sensor Management, Dwells are Only Used in Areas that Contain Targets and the Covariance Ellipses are Much Tighter.

Qualitatively, in the managed scenario the measurements are focused in or near the cells that the targets are in. Furthermore, the covariance ellipses, which reflect the current state of knowledge of the tracker conditioned on all previous measurements, are much tighter. In fact, the non-managed scenario has confusion about which tracks correspond to which target as the covariance ellipses overlap.

A more detailed is provided in the Monte Carlo simulation results of Figure 2. The sensor management algorithm was run with $L = 24$ (i.e. was able to scan 24 cells at each time step) and is compared to the non-managed scheme with 24 to 312 looks. The unmanaged scenario needs approximately 312 looks to equal the performance of the managed algorithm in terms of RMSE error. We say that the sensor manager is approximately 13 times as efficient as allocating the sensors without management.

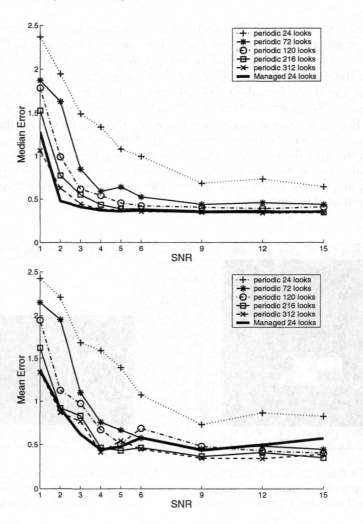

Fig. 2. Median and Mean Error vs. Signal To Noise Ratio (SNR). Managed Performance With 24 Looks is Similar to Unmanaged Performance With 312 Looks.

In addition, we have investigated the performance of the sensor management algorithm with different values of α in (27) under the same set of simulation parameters. As shown in 3, it appears that in the case under consideration that the technique is rather insensitive to the choice of α. We anticipate that values of α that deviate from unity may be useful in the case of model mismatch.

6   Conclusion

In this paper, we have proposed an algorithm for multiple target tracking and sensor management. The central element of interest in both the target track-

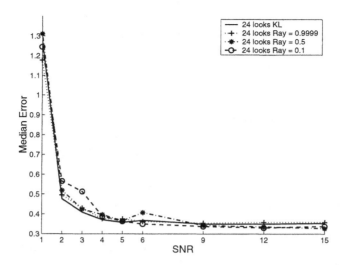

Fig. 3. Performance of the Sensor Management Technique for Different α.

ing and sensor management schemes is the posterior density $p(\mathbf{X}|\mathbf{Z})$, which is approximated using particle filtering methods.

The particle filter implementation we have proposed has three main benefits. First, by nature of being a particle filter implementation, it allows for non-linear measurement to state coupling, non-linear state evolution (target motion), and non-Gaussian densities. Second, the formulation explicitly enforces the multi-target nature of the problem. Each particle simultaneously postulates both the number of targets and their states, both of which are unknown. Finally, the particle filter implementation breaks the computational logjam that grid-based techniques have presented in the past. This makes this technique applicable to larger scale problems.

The information-based sensor management scheme presented in this paper is based on computing the expected information gain for each sensor tasking under consideration. The sensor management algorithm is integrated with the target tracking algorithm in that it too uses the posterior density $p(\mathbf{X}|\mathbf{Z})$. In this case, the posterior is used in conjunction with target kinematic models and sensor models to predict which measurements will provide the most information gain. In simulated scenarios, we find that the tracker with sensor management gives similar performance to the tracker without sensor management while using a factor of 13 fewer sensor dwells.

There are two interesting directions in which we see this work evolving. First, this method is amenable to incorporating auxiliary information such as ground elevation maps and sensor trajectories. For example, if the appropriate auxiliary information were incorporated, this method would clearly never choose to make a measurement in a region that was not visible to the sensor due to hill regions between the sensor and the desired look location. Second, the current algorithm is a greedy algorithm, choosing to make the measurement that is best at the current time step. It would be beneficial to extend the methodology to plan several time instances in the future.

References

1. K. Kastella, "Joint multitarget probabilities for detection and tracking", SPIE Proceedings, Acquisition, Tracking and Pointing XI, 21-25 April, 1997, Orlando, FL.
2. S.S. Blackman, Mulitple-Target Tracking with Radar Applications. Norwood, MA. Artech House, 1986.
3. Alfred O. Hero III, Bing Ma, Olivier J.J. Michel, and John Gorman, "Applications of Entropic Spanning Graphs", IEEE Signal Processing Magazine, September 2002, pp. 85-95.
4. Arulampalam, M., Maskell, S., Gordon, N. and Clapp, T. "A Tutorial on Particle Filters for Online Nonlinear/Non-Gaussian Bayesian Tracking", IEEE Transactions on Signal Processing, February 2002.
5. Doucet, A. de Freitas, N., and Gordon, N. "Sequential Monte Carlo Methods in Practice", Springer Publishing, New York, 2001.
6. Liu, J. and Chen, R. "Sequential Monte Carlo Methods for Dynamic Systems", Journal of the American Statistical Association, September 1998.
7. Matthew Orton and William Fitzgerald, "A Bayesian Approach to Tracking Multiple Targets Using Sensor Arrays and Particle Filters", IEEE Transactions on Signal Processing, vol. 50, no.2, February 2002, pp. 216-223.
8. A. Rényi, "On measures of entropy and information", Proc. 4th Berkeley Symp. Math. Stat. and Prob., volume 1, pp. 547-561, 1961.
9. D. Sinno and D. Kreithen, "A Constrained Joint Optimization Approach to Dynamic Sensor Configuration", Thirty Six Asilomar Conference on Signals, Systems, and Computers, November 2002.
10. D. Geman and B. Jedynak, "An active testing model for tracking roads from satellite images", IEEE Transactions on Pattern Analysis and Machine Intelligence, vol. 18, no. 1, January 1996, pp. 1-14.
11. F. Zhao, J. Shin, and J. Reich, "Information-Driven Dynamic Sensor Collaboration", IEEE Signal Processing Magazine, March 2002, pp. 61-72.

A Distributed Algorithm for Managing Multi-target Identities in Wireless Ad-hoc Sensor Networks

Jaewon Shin[1], Leonidas J. Guibas[1], and Feng Zhao[2]

[1] Computer Science Department
Stanford University
Stanford CA 94305, U.S.A
{jwshin, guibas}@cs.stanford.edu
[2] Palo Alto Research Center(PARC)
3333 Coyote Hill Road
Palo Alto, CA 94304, U.S.A
zhao@parc.com

Abstract. This paper presents a scalable distributed algorithm for computing and maintaining multi-target identity information. The algorithm builds on a novel representational framework, Identity-Mass Flow, to overcome the problem of exponential computational complexity in managing multi-target identity explicitly. The algorithm uses local information to efficiently update the global multi-target identity information represented as a doubly stochastic matrix, and can be efficiently mapped to nodes in a wireless ad hoc sensor network. The paper describes a distributed implementation of the algorithm in sensor networks. Simulation results have validated the Identity-Mass Flow framework and demonstrated the feasibility of the algorithm.

1 Introduction

A wireless ad-hoc sensor network (WASN) is a network of sensor nodes with limited on-node sensing, processing, and communication capabilities. At the heart of many WASN applications such as object tracking and environmental monitoring is the problem of estimating non-local parameters or states of the physical phenomenon being observed using only local information available to each node. This problem poses unique challenges that are not addressed in a centralized setting or fixed network:

- Scalable distributed information fusion: The global parameters or states of interest must be estimated, updated, and maintained using only local information.
- Sensor tasking: A sensor node may be tasked to compute or store state information based on its relevance and utility to the current task, as well as cost constraints.

F. Zhao and L. Guibas (Eds.): IPSN 2003, LNCS 2634, pp. 223–238, 2003.

In this paper, we study the problem of distributed multi-target identity management in WASN. The goal is to maintain information about *who is who* over time given targets' position estimates. In addition to its central importance in many of the monitoring and surveillance applications, the problem highlights the need for distributed information fusion and sensor tasking. The study of this problem is an important step towards establishing a general methodology for the design of scalable WASN algorithms.

Multi-target identity management is closely related to the multi-target tracking problem. The main difficulty in both problems is the exponential complexity in associating target position estimates with target identities. In the past three decades, a number of approaches have been developed for the multi-target tracking problem, mostly for centralized computational platforms. MHT ([2]) explicitly maintains associations, or hypotheses, over time and prunes the associations using a rank function. JPDA ([4]) computes an association matrix at each time and updates it with a combination of all new measurements weighted by their marginal probabilities. While widely used in practice, both MHT and JPDA algorithms still suffer from their computational complexity, in the worst case exponential in the number of targets or time steps. Moreover, for WASN applications, a significant challenge lies in distributing the information and computation to each node.

This paper develops an efficient distributed approach to computing and updating multi-target identity information. The **main contribution** of this work is twofold. First, it introduces a new distributed representation called identity belief matrix, a doubly stochastic matrix, that describes how identity information of each target is distributedly represented (a row in the matrix). The key advantage of this representation is that when the matrix is mapped to a set of nodes in a WASN, a node could efficiently maintain possible identifies of a target it is tracking (a column in the matrix), using its local evidence only. Second, the paper develops a distributed algorithm for computing and updating the cross-node identity belief matrix in a WASN. The algorithm exploits doubly-stochasticity of the matrix to renormalize identity probability masses stored on different WASN nodes. As soon as a piece of local/marginal evidence is available to a node, the local belief of target identity is updated, and the information is propagated through the network to other nodes. The computational complexity of our algorithm is $O(N^2)$, where N is the number of targets, a significant advantage over the exponential complexity of MHT and JPDA.

The rest of the paper is organized as follows. Section 2 introduces identity-mass flow (IMF) framework to represent multi-target identity information. To ease the introduction of mathematical materials and focus on key representational issues, the identify representation is first developed in a centralized setting. Sections 3 and 4 develop algorithms to distribute the computation and map the algorithm to WASN nodes. Section 3 describes an algorithm for updating global identity information using local identity information. Section 4 maps the identity representation and algorithm to a set of WASN nodes. Finally, Section 5 describes an implementation of the algorithm, and presents simulation results that validate the correctness of the representational framework and the basic structure of the algorithm.

2 Multiple Identity Management: A Mathematical Framework

Consider the following problem. There are N targets moving in the region of interest and their position-estimates are reported periodically. Assuming the initial identities are known, the goal of the multiple identity management is to maintain and update the identity information of all the targets as they are moving.

Apparently, the dynamics of the target - how they are moving - seems to be the only information available to do the job. Unlike the radar system, however, the subset of the nodes in the sensor network are very close to the targets and are able to sense more than position-estimate - the target signature information. This signature information is clear and dependable in the sparse target configuration, but is not informative when the targets are close to one another. Figure 1 illustrates the two target configurations, which are named as configuration of high uncertainty(COHU) and configuration of low uncertainty(COLU), respectively. The actions/decisions based on the information in COHU could be false and it would be nice to have a representational framework that could fix the poor actions/decisions in COHU using the better information in COLU. This is the main motivation behind our mathematical formulation in the upcoming subsections.

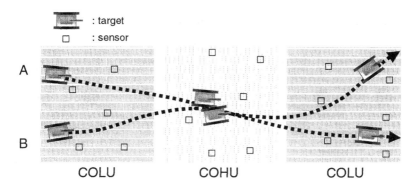

Fig. 1. Sparse(COLU) and crowded(COHU) target configurations

2.1 Formulation

In this section, we formulate the problem of multiple identity management as identity-mass distribution problem. The identity set $I = \{1, \cdots, N\}$ is a set of identities of all the targets and the position-estimates of N targets at time k is $X(k) = \{x_i(k) \in \mathbf{R}^2 | i = 1, \cdots, N\}$.[1] The identity management algorithm is supposed to compute the correct permutation of I given $X(k)$. The natural approach to this is to maintain all the possible permutations[2] at each time, although the number of possible permutations increases exponentially. Even with good rank functions and pruning heuristics, the number of possible permutations can easily go unmanageably large in a very short period of time.

To overcome the above combinatorial complexity and maintain the computational complexity as constant over time, we propose the idea of Identity-Mass Flow(IMF) to approximately represent all the possible permutations. Figure 2 (a) shows the basic idea behind our approach; Initially, a unit mass is assigned to each identity. Whenever the new position-estimate $X(k)$ is available, the whole or partial masses from $X(k-1)$ flow into $X(k)$ and the identities are mixed in this way. There, however, need to be constraints regarding how masses flow to make the resulting mixed identities physically meaningful. Figure 2 (b) and (c) explain the two constraints. (b) says no mass can be created or destroyed during the Identity-Mass Flow and (c) says the sum of all the masses arriving at $x_i(k)$ is one.

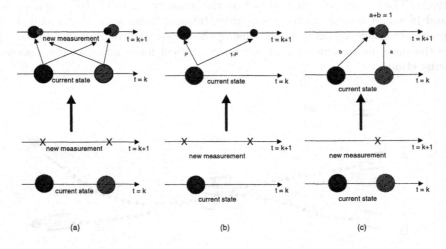

Fig. 2. Identity Mass Flow

To formulate the above idea, we define the identity belief matrix $B(k)$ and the mixing matrix $M(k)$.

---

[1] $x_i(k)$ and $x_i(k+1)$ are not related. i's are just random labels that come with the position estimate.

[2] In multi-target tracking community, this is also called an *association*.

Definition 1. *The identity belief matrix $B(k)$ is a $N \times N$ doubly-stochastic matrix[3], whose entry $b_{ij}(k)$ represents the amount of identity mass from $i \in I$ that arrives at $x_j(k)$. The j_{th} column $\mathbf{b_j}(k)$ of $B(k)$ is called the identity belief vector of $x_j(k)$.*

$$B(k) = \begin{bmatrix} \mathbf{b_1}(k) \; \mathbf{b_2}(k) \cdots \mathbf{b_N}(k) \end{bmatrix} \in [0,1]^{N \times N}$$

where

$$\mathbf{b_i}(k) = \begin{bmatrix} p(x_i(k)\text{'s ID is } 1) \\ p(x_i(k)\text{'s ID is } 2) \\ \vdots \\ p(x_i(k)\text{'s ID is } N) \end{bmatrix} \in [0,1]^{N \times 1}$$

Definition 2. *The mixing matrix $M(k)$ is a $N \times N$ doubly-stochastic matrices, whose entry $m_{ij}(k)$ represents the probability of $x_j(k)$ being originated from $x_i(k-1)$, and is statistically independent with $M(l)$ for all $l \neq k$.*

Given the definition of $M(k)$ and $B(k)$, the following theorem presents the basic equation relating the two quantities.

Theorem 1. *Let $B(k)$ and $M(k)$ be the identity belief matrix and the mixing matrix at time k as defined above, then the following is true.*

$$B(k+1) = B(k)M(k+1)$$

Proof. From the above definitions, the identity belief of $x_j(k+1)$ is computed as follows

$$\mathbf{b_j}(k+1) = \sum_{l=1}^{N} m_{lj}(k+1)\mathbf{b_l}(k) = B(k)\mathbf{m_j}(k+1)$$

where $\mathbf{m_j}(k+1)$ is the j_{th} column of $M(k+1)$. Therefore,

$$B(k+1) = B(k)M(k+1)$$

and this concludes the proof.

The above theorem shows that we can recursively compute the identity information $B(k)$ by computing $M(k)$ from $X(k)$ and $X(k-1)$ and is illustrated in Figure 3. The details on how to compute $M(k)$ is investigated in the next section.

The following lemma explains how the uncertainty in the system changes over time in this formulation.

Lemma 1. *Let $\pi_{B(k)} \in [0\ 1]^{N! \times 1}$ be the probability mass function over all the possible identity association in $B(k)$, then*

$$H(\pi_{B(k)}) \geq H(\pi_{B(k-1)})$$

where $H(\cdot)$ is the statistical entropy of a probability mass function.

---

[3] The doubly-stochastic matrix is a $N \times N$ non-negative matrix, whose rows and columns sum to one.

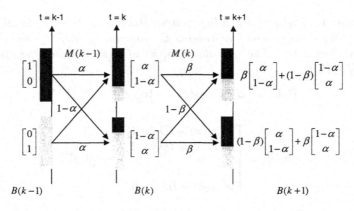

Fig. 3. Updating $B(k)$ using $M(k)$

Proof. The mixing matrix $M(k)$ can represented as a convex sum of permutation matrices as follows

$$M(k) = \sum_{i=1}^{N!} \alpha_i \Phi_i$$

where $\sum_i \alpha_i = 1$ and Φ_i is the i_{th} $N \times N$ permutation matrix. Then,

$$H(\pi_{B(k)}) = H(\pi_{B(k-1)} M(k))$$
$$= H(\sum_{i=1}^{N!} \alpha_i \pi_{B(k-1)} \Phi_i)$$
$$\geq \sum_{i=1}^{N!} \alpha_i H(\pi_{B(k-1)} \Phi_i)$$
$$= \sum_{i=1}^{N!} \alpha_i H(\pi_{B(k-1)})$$
$$= H(\pi_{B(k-1)})$$

where the inequality comes from the strict concavity of the entropy function. This concludes the proof.

The statistical entropy is a quantitative measure of uncertainty in the probability distribution and the above lemma shows the uncertainty on the possible identity associations does not decrease over time. Therefore, the uncertainty will grow until every identity association becomes equally like without any additional information available. As we have mentioned in section 2, the target identity information is more likely to be available in COLU and the proper use of this local information could make the uncertainty decrease in IMF formulation. The details on how to exploit the local identity information is investigated in section 3.

2.2 Computing Mixing Matrix $M(k)$

The mixing matrix $M(k)$ is a collection of marginal association probabilities and can be computed from the joint association probability[4] in theory. Computing the joint association probabilities is very expensive and should be avoided in practice. In this paper, we propose a simple heuristic with $O(N^2)$ empirical complexity that only requires the information on how fast the targets are moving. Let's assume that the speed information is given as a probability density function $p(s(k))$, where $s(k)$ is $|x(k) - x(k-1)|/\Delta T$.[5] Then, we compute a non-negative matrix $L(k) \in \mathbf{R}^{N \times N}$, whose (i,j) entry is $l_{ij}(k) = p(s(k) = |x_j(k) - x_i(k-1)|/\Delta T)$. In general, $L(k)$ is not doubly-stochastic and an optimization need to be done to transform this into a doubly-stochastic matrix. We use the Iterative Scaling algorithm to transform $L(k)$ into a doubly-stochastic matrix. The details on the Iterative Scaling algorithm are explained in section 3.2.

3 Multi-target Identity Update Using Local Information

In WASN, the ability to use local information efficiently is critical for distributed algorithms since non-local information only comes at the cost of communication. The IMF approach in multi-target identity management does provide a natural setting for exploiting local evidences. Figure 4 illustrate this in a simple two targets crossover scenario. Two targets are moving cross each other and their identity masses are mixed at the intersection of the two tracks. After the mixing, the identity belief matrix $B(k)$ becomes un-informative - each association is almost equally likely. When the two targets are well-separated, i.e., in COLU, one of the nodes near the bottom target observes a local evidence[6] that the bottom target is more likely to be yellow[7] . This observation increases the yellow-mass of the bottom target $b_{yellow,bottom}(k)$ and the rest of the elements in $B(k)$ can be updated from the doubly-stochasticity of $B(k)$. Therefore, the local information about the bottom target directly leads to the information about the top target in a unique way.

From the above example, only a local evidence seems to be enough to update the whole identity belief $B(k)$ uniquely. For the general N target case, however, the doubly-stochasticity of $B(k)$ is not enough to guarantee a unique solution since there are more unknowns (N^2) than the number of constraints (N). Therefore, we need more constraints or optimizations to compute a unique $B(k)$ given a local evidence. The upcoming sub-sections deal with this problem of computing $B(k)$ given a local evidence in a centralized setting. Section 4 discusses the distributed implementation of the algorithm for WASN.

---

[4] Probabilities of permutations/associations, i.e., how likely each permutation is.

[5] $p(s(k))$ is usually stationary, i.e., does not depend on k.

[6] A local evidence is the information enough to determine the whole or partial entries in $b_i(k)$. The simple example is "$x_i(k)$ is of ID j".

[7] Lighter color in a black and white printout

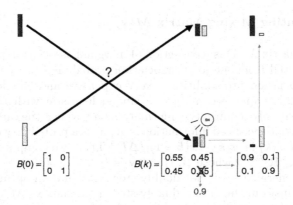

$$B(0) = \begin{bmatrix} 1 & 0 \\ 0 & 1 \end{bmatrix} \qquad B(k) = \begin{bmatrix} 0.55 & 0.45 \\ 0.45 & 0.55 \end{bmatrix} \qquad \begin{bmatrix} 0.9 & 0.1 \\ 0.1 & 0.9 \end{bmatrix}$$

0.9

Fig. 4. Example of using local evidence: The top left ID is colored as blue and the bottom left ID is yellow. The blue and yellow look dark and lighter grey, respectively, in a black and white printout.

3.1   Bayesian Normalization

Before we introduce a practical solution to compute unique $B(k)$ given a local evidence, we study the desirable properties of the *perfect solution* by computing $B(k)$ as a Bayesian posterior belief distribution given a local evidence, assuming the whole history of the mixing events are known. In this case, we assume that the joint probability distribution $\pi(k) \in \{Z \in \mathbf{R}^{N! \times 1} | \sum_i z_i = 1, z_i \geq 0\}$ over all the possible $N!$ associations at time k, from which $M(k)$ can be derived, is available for all k. Note that, for some k's, $\pi(k)$'s are deterministic and their associated $M(k)$ are permutation matrices. These $\pi(k)$ do not contribute in computing the $B(k)$ and its posterior. To consider only those random mixing events, we define $K \subset \{0, 1, \cdots, N\}$ be the set of time indices associated with $|\pi(k_i)| > 2$, where k_i is the i_{th} element in K and $|\cdot|$ represents the cardinality of a set. We also introduce a sequence of random variables R_i associated with $\pi(k_i)$, which takes values $j \in \{1, \cdots, |\pi(k_i)|\}$ with probability of $\pi_j(k_i)$, i.e., j_{th} value in $\pi(k_i)$.

Figure 5 illustrates the above formulation, where each box can be considered as a probabilistic switch governed by R_i, i.e., a specific permutation is chosen according to the value of R_i with some probability. Then, a single identity association at time k is a point ε in the joint event space $S = \{(R_1, R_2, \cdots, R_{|K|}) | R_i \in [1 \; |\pi(u_i)|]\}$ with $|S| = \prod_i |\pi(u_i)|$ and the probability of this event can be easily computed due to the statistical independence assumption in section 2.1.

$$p((R_1, \cdots, R_{|K|}) = \varepsilon)) = p(R_1 = \varepsilon_1) \cdots p(R_{|K|} = \varepsilon_{|K|}))$$
$$= \pi_{\varepsilon_1}(u_1) \cdots \pi_{\varepsilon_{|K|}}(u_{|K|})$$

Using the above equation, we can compute the posterior $B(k)$ given a local evidence L, which is a set of events in S satisfying the local observation, say, $ID(x_i(k)) = j$, using the following theorem.

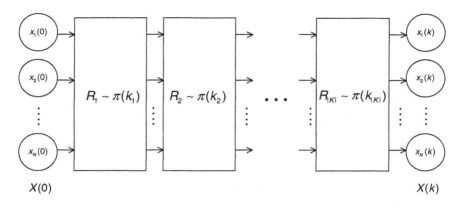

Fig. 5. Bayesian Normalization

Theorem 2. *Let $E_{ij}(k)$ be the subset of S satisfying $ID(x_j(k)) = i$ and L be the subset of S satisfying the local observation, then*

$$p(b_{ij}(k)|L) = p(E_{ij}|L) = \frac{\sum_{\varepsilon_l \in E_{ij} \cup L} p(\varepsilon_l)}{\sum_{\varepsilon_l \in L} p(\varepsilon_l)}$$

Proof. The proof is trivial using the Bayes' rule.

Now that we know how to update $B(k)$ given a local evidence L, but the effect of the evidence to the other columns is not obvious from the equation. The following lemma describes how the local evidence effect the uncertainty of the other columns.

Lemma 2. *The local observation L does not increase the entropies of the columns, i.e.*

$$H(\mathbf{b_i}(k)|L) \leq H(\mathbf{b_i}(k))$$

Proof. See [6] for the proof.

The lemma says that the local evidence does not increase the entropy of the other columns on the average.

The ideal solution obtained in the above theorem exhibits one very interesting characteristic, in which there are some elements in $B(k)$ - in addition to the zero elements in $B(k)$ - that are not affected by the local evidence. This can potentially save huge amount of communication energy in practice. The following theorem formally presents the property of the Bayesian solution.

Theorem 3. *Let $b_{pq}(k)$ be the entry that becomes 1 from the local evidence L, then the columns with zero at p_{th} entry and the rows with zero at q_{th} entry do not change.*

Proof. Let's first prove that the columns with zero at p_{th} entry do not change. If $\mathbf{b_i}(k)$ is such a column, then there does not exist any event in S that guarantees a path from $x_p(0)$ to $x_i(k)$, i.e., no path originated from $x_p(0)$ reaches $x_i(k)$. The local evidence L defines a subset of S, which guarantees the existence of at least one path between $x_p(0)$ and $x_q(k)$. None of these paths between $x_p(0)$ and $x_q(k)$, however, affect the paths arriving at $x_i(k)$. Due to the statistical independence assumption on the mixing events, $\mathbf{b_i}(k)$ does not change given the local evidence L. The row case can be proved in the same way. This concludes the proof.

The above theorem reduces the number of variables to be updated in $B(k)$ given a local evidence. In addition to that, this can help the number of communications required to update $B(k)$ given a local evidence assuming that each column $\mathbf{b_i}(k)$ is maintained by a node in the sensor network. The details on the distributed computation is discussed in section 4.

In addition to these rows and columns, the zero elements in $B(k)$ do not change given a local evidence L.

3.2   Iterative Scaling

In practice, the Bayesian formulation in the previous section is infeasible due to its exponential complexity. This section presents the practical alternative called the Iterative scaling. First, we present a version of the Iterative Scaling algorithm to achieve a doubly-stochastic matrix A given a $N \times N$ non-negative matrix B.

```
B := A;
B_old := A;
for k = 1 to maximum_number_of_iteration
    for i = 1 to number_of_row
        row_sum := 0;
        for k = 1 to number_of_column
            row_sum := row_sum + B(i,k);
        end
        for j = 1 to number_of_column
            B(i,j) := B(i,j)/row_sum;
        end
    end
    for i = 1 to number_of_column
        column_sum := 0;
        for k = 1 to number_of_row
            column_sum := column_sum + B(i,k);
        end
        for j = 1 to number_of_row
            B(j,i) := B(j,i)/column_sum;
        end
    end
    if |B - B_old| < error
```

```
        terminate;
    end
    B_old := B;
end
```

Basically, the algorithm divides each element in i_{th} row(column) by the sum of the i_{th} row(column) and repeats the normalization until the error margin is small. The following observations are made from the numerical simulations and we list them here without proofs.

- The algorithm converges to a unique doubly-stochastic matrix given an initial matrix.
- The ordering of row/column normalization does not affect the convergence.
- The total number of iteration is not affected by the size of the matrix.

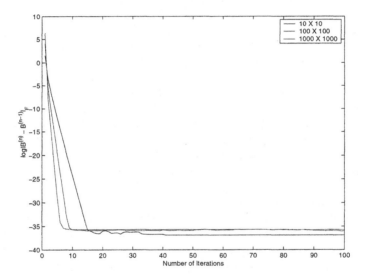

Fig. 6. Typical convergence of iterative scaling: The flat part of the plots are due to the Matlab precision limit.

From these observations, the Iterative Scaling algorithm scales as $O(N^2)$. The proof of the complexity result remains as an immediate task for future research. Figure 6 shows an example of the convergence behavior of the algorithm. Three different sizes of matrices (10×10, 100×100, 1000×1000) are generated randomly using Matlab $rand(\cdot)$ function, in which each entry is generated according to the uniform probability density over [0 1]. The plot shows that the Iterative Scaling method has fast convergence and the size of a matrix does not affect the convergence ratio. What seems to affect the convergence rate is how different the (scaled) initial matrix from being the doubly-stochastic matrix, although we do not have a proper quantitative measure for this at this point. This is why the larger matrices in the above figure converges a little faster than the smaller ones, since all the row/column sums of the larger matrices are close to $0.5N$ due to the Law of Large Numbers and effectively *close* to a doubly-stochastic matrix after scaling.

To benefit from the theorem 3, the Iterative scaling algorithm should be able to deal with the non-square matrix with the fixed row/column sums. Let $\mathbf{r}$ and $\mathbf{c}$ be $N \times 1$ vector of row and column sum satisfying $\sum_i c_i = \sum_j r_j$, then we can modify the above pseudo code as follows.

```
B(i,j) = B(i,j)/row_sum*r(i);
......
B(j,i) = B(j,i)/column_sum*c(i);
```

4 Distributed Implementation in WASN

The basic quantity to be distributed is $B(k)$, the belief matrix. One way of distributing $B(k)$ is to let each node in the sensor network maintain its own version of $B(k)$. This method is very robust and fault-tolerant due to the information redundancy in the system. However, this idealistic distribution is infeasible and non-scalable for the following the reason. To update the information, each node need to compute its version of $M(k)$, which requires information from at least one of the other nodes. This is exactly the scenario in the landmark paper [14], where per-node throughput goes to zero as the number of nodes goes to infinity even under optimal routing and power control scheme. Therefore, the idealistic distribution of each node maintaining $B(k)$ is impossible and this argument is true for all the algorithms of sensor networks that estimates the global quantity.

To overcome this problem, we adopt and extend the approach in [16] and [17], where a leader-based single target tracking in WASN is introduced. The basic idea is that, only a small number of nodes called *leaders* are active and responsible for maintaining/updating the information of interest. When the leaders are no longer the good subset of nodes for the information, they handoff the information to the other nodes based on a utility function and the nodes receiving the information become the new leaders. In this approach, whereabout of the information is easily maintained at the risk of the reduced robustness and fault-tolerance.

Applying the leader-based approach to our algorithm, each column $\mathbf{b}_i(k)$ of $B(k)$ and its position estimate $x_i(k)$ is maintained by each leader. When the mixing happens, the local version of $M(k)$[8] can be easily computed by the leader. When a leader node observes a local evidence about the ID of its target, say $ID(x_i(k)) = j$, then the leader needs to talk to some of the other leaders, who also think what they are tracking can be of the same ID. This type of multi-cast communication in network is usually dealt by a group management protocol,

---

[8] In the two target mixing, only non-zero entries in the i_{th} and j_{th} columns of $M(k)$ are required to update b_i and b_j and they are locally computable.

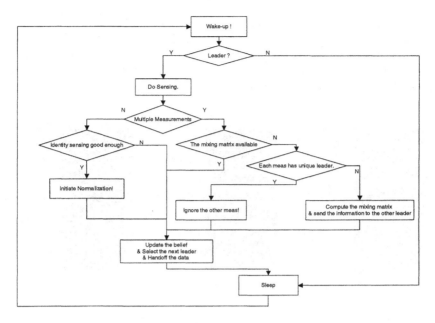

Fig. 7. Flowchart of the distributed algorithm for the multi-target identity management

which maintains and updates the different groups in the network according to a predefined membership. In our case, the i_{th} group is the set of the leader that have non-zero probability at i_{th} entry of their $\mathbf{b}(k)$ and we assume there exists a good (or optimal) group management protocol for our purpose. Figure 7 shows the main procedures and their relations of the distributed algorithm that each node is running.

5   Experimental Results

We make the following assumptions for the simulation.

- Each node can sense the positions of the targets within its sensing range.
- Each node can talk to all the nodes within its communication range.
- Initially, the number of the targets are known to the initial leaders.
- Each node has a signal processing module for the signal classification and the module performs better in COLU.
- Each node knows the relative positions of all the nodes in the communication range.

The initial leaders are manually selected for the simulation, although it's possible to detect them as long as their initial positions are well separated. Each leader updates its belief vector $\mathbf{b}_i(\mathbf{k})$ using the local version of $M(k)$ and handoffs the information to the next leader, which is selected based on its geographical location. The signal classification module of the leaders will keep collecting the information and initiates the identity normalization process by talking to the other leaders that are in the same group when the identity information from the signal classification is better than $\mathbf{b}_i(k)$ and some threshold.

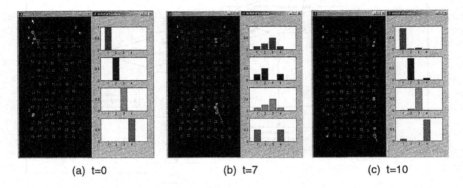

(a) t=0   (b) t=7   (c) t=10

Fig. 8. Simulation Example

Figure 8 shows the three screen shots from the simulation of the algorithm. Four targets - one tank and three dots - are moving along the straight lines for 10 seconds. The tank signature is much different from those of the other three, so it can be identified with high probability in COLU. This local identity information about the tank is the only available information and used to normalize the belief $\mathbf{b}_i(k)$ of the other leaders. The four leaders are colored differently and their corresponding beliefs are displayed with the same color. Figure 8 (a) is the initial configuration of the targets and their associated leaders. (b) shows that the belief $\mathbf{b}_i(k)$ of each leader gets uncertain after some number of mixing events at $t = 7$ and the leaders are no longer sure of the identities of the targets. (c), however, shows the beliefs get much better after the normalization using Iterative Scaling algorithm given local identity information.

In figure 9, how the identity uncertainty of each target evolves during the simulation is depicted using the entropy of each identity belief $\mathbf{b}_i$. The increases in the uncertainty are due to the mixing events and the decreases are by the local evidences. The two pieces of the local evidence on target 1 have reduced the uncertainties of all the other targets in this example, since the identity mass from the target 1 is mixed with all the other identities during the mixing events.

6   Summary and Future Work

We have developed a scalable distributed algorithm for the multi-target identity management problem, first presented as a mathematical framework for a centralized setting, and then mapped to a distributed WASN. Simulation results

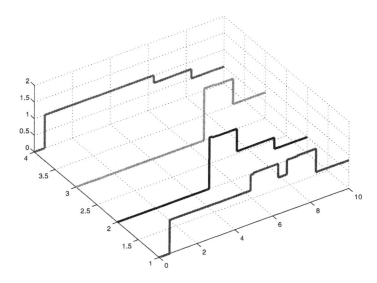

Fig. 9. An example of how uncertainty of each belief changes. The target numbers correspond to the track numbers in the previous figure.

have demonstrated the effectiveness of the framework and the efficiency of the algorithm.

Since the target identity computation is at the heart of many WASN tracking and classification applications, the work presented here is an important step towards building a comprehensive system for distributed inference in sensor networks. As our future work, we plan to relax some of the assumptions and models used in our framework. For example, we may exploit a signal processing model for target source separation, localization, and signature classification to obtain additional target identity information when targets are in close proximity of each other, and incorporate the ability to handle dynamic addition and deletion of targets. A more theoretical task is the convergence proof for the normalization step given multiple local evidences regardless of their chronological order.

References

1. I. Csiszar, "A geometric interpretation of Darroch and Ratcliff's generalized iterative scaling", *Annals of Probability*, 3, 146–158, 1975.
2. Reid, D.B., "An Algorithm for Tracking Multiple Targets", *IEEE Trans. on Automatic Control*, No. 6, December 1979, pp. 843–854
3. R.R. Tenny and N. R. Sandell Jr., "Detection with Distributed Sensors", *IEEE Transactions on Aerospace and Electronic Systems*, Vol. AES-17, No. 4, July 1981
4. Y. Bar-Shalom and T. E. Fortmann, *Tracking and Data Association,* Academic Press, New York, 1988
5. H. R. Hashemi and I. B. Rhodes, "Decentralized Sequential Detection", *IEEE Transactions on Information Theory*, Vol. 35, No. 3, May 1989

6. T. M. Cover and J. A. Thomas, "Elements of Information Theory", *Wiley*, 1991
7. I. J. Cox and S. L. Hingorani, "An Efficient Implementation of Reid's Multiple Hy-pohtesis Tracking Algorithm and its Evaluation for the Purpose of Visual Track-ing," *IEEE Trans. on PAMI*, Vol 18., No. 2, pp. 138–150, Feb. 1996
8. P. L. Combettes, "Hilbertian Convex Feasibility Problem: Convergence of Projec-tion Methods" *Appl. Math. Optim.* 35:311–330, 1997
9. M. Isard and A. Blake, "CONDENSATION – Conditional Density Propagation for Visual Tracking", *Int. J. Computer Vision* , 1998
10. L. J. Guibas, "Kinetic data structures – a state of the art report," *Proc. Workshop Algorithmic Found. Robot.,* pages 191–209, A. K. Peters, Wellesley, MA, 1998
11. H. Tao, H.S. Sawhney and R. Kumar, "A Sampling Algorithm for Tracking Mul-tiple Objects," *Proc. of the IEEE Wkshp. on Vision Algorithms, Corfu, Greece,* Sep. 1999
12. H. Pasula, S. Russel, M. Ostland and Y. Ritov, "Tracking Many Objects with many sensors," *Int. Joint Conf. on Artificial Intelligence (IJCAI), Stockholm,* pages 1160–1171, 1999.
13. D. Estrin, R. Govindan, J. Heidemann, and S. Kumar, "Next century challenges: Scalable coordination in sensor networks", *Proceedings of the Fifth Annual In-ternational Conference on Mobile Computing and Networks,* Seattle, Washington, August 1999
14. P. Gupta and P.R. Kumar, "The Capacity of Wireless Networks", *IEEE Trans. Inform. Theory,* 46(2):388–404, 2000.
15. J. MacCormick and A. Blake, "Probabilistic exclusion and partitioned sampling for multiple object tracking.", *Intl J. Computer Vision,* 39(1):57–71, 2000.
16. M. Chu, H. Haussecker, and F. Zhao, "Scalable Information-Driven Sensor Query and Routing for ad hoc Heterogeneous Sensor Network", *International Journal of High Performance Computing Applications,* 2002
17. F. Zhao, J. Shin, and J. Reich, "Information Driven Dynamic Sensor Collaboration for Tracking Application", *IEEE Signal Processing Magazine* 2002 March
18. Wei Ye, John Heidemann and Deborah Estrin, "An Energy-Efficient MAC Protocol for Wireless Sensor Networks", *IEEE INFOCOM 2002,* June, 2002.

Hypothesis Testing over Factorizations for Data Association

Alexander T. Ihler, John W. Fisher, and Alan S. Willsky

Massachusetts Institute of Technology
Cambridge, MA 02139
{ihler,willsky}@mit.edu, fisher@ai.mit.edu

Abstract. The issue of data association arises frequently in sensor networks; whenever multiple sensors and sources are present, it may be necessary to determine which observations from different sensors correspond to the same target. In highly uncertain environments, one may need to determine this correspondence without the benefit of an *a priori* known joint signal/sensor model. This paper examines the data association problem as the more general hypothesis test between factorizations of a single, learned distribution. The optimal test between known distributions may be decomposed into model-dependent and statistical dependence terms, quantifying the cost incurred by model estimation from measurements compared to a test between known models. We demonstrate how one might evaluate a two-signal association test efficiently using kernel density estimation methods to model a wide class of possible distributions, and show the resulting algorithm's ability to determine correspondence in uncertain conditions through a series of synthetic examples. We then describe an extension of this technique to multi-signal association which can be used to determine correspondence while avoiding the computationally prohibitive task of evaluating all hypotheses. Empirical results of the approximate approach are presented.

1 Introduction

Data association describes the problem of partitioning observations into like sets. This is a common problem in networks of sensors – multiple signals are received by several sensors, and one must determine which signals at different sensors correspond to the same source.

In many collaborative sensing scenarios, the signal models are assumed to be known and fully specified *a priori*. With such models, it is possible to formulate and use optimal hypothesis tests for data association. However, real-world uncertainty often precludes strong modelling assumptions. For example, it is difficult to analytically quantify dependence between data of different modalities. Additionally, nonlinear effects and inhomogenous media create complex interactions and uncertainty. When applicable, a learning/estimation based approach is appealing, but in the online case requires that one learn the signal distributions while simultaneously performing the test. For example, this is possible for data

F. Zhao and L. Guibas (Eds.): IPSN 2003, LNCS 2634, pp. 239–253, 2003.
© Springer-Verlag Berlin Heidelberg 2003

association because it is a test described in terms of the distribution *form*, in particular as a test over factorization and independence.

We show that the optimal likelihood test between two factorizations of a density learned from the data can be expressed in terms of mutual information. Furthermore, the analysis results in a clear decomposition of terms related to statistical dependence (i.e. factorization) and those related to modelling assumptions. We propose the use of kernel density methods to estimate the distributions and mutual information from data. In the case of high-dimensional data, where learning a distribution is impractical, this can be done efficiently by finding *statistics* which capture its interaction. Furthermore, the criterion for learning these statistics is also expressed in terms of mutual information. The estimated mutual information of these statistics can be used as an approximation to the optimal likelihood ratio test, by training the statistics to minimize a bound on the approximation error.

We will begin by describing a data association example between a pair of sensors, each observing two targets. We show first how the optimal hypothesis test changes in the absence of a known signal model and express the resulting test in terms of information. We then discuss how one may use summarizing features to estimate the mutual information efficiently and robustly using kernel methods. This can yield a tractable estimate of the hypothesis test when direct estimation of the observations' distribution is infeasible. Finally, we present an algorithmic extension of these ideas to the multiple target case.

2   An Information-Theoretic Interpretation of Data Association

Data association can be cast as a hypothesis test between density factorizations over measurements. As we will show, there is a natural information-theoretic interpretation of this hypothesis test, which decomposes the test into terms related to statistical dependency and terms related to modelling assumptions. Consequently, one can quantify the contribution of prior knowledge as it relates to a known model; but more importantly, in the absence of a prior model one can still achieve a degree of separability between hypotheses by estimating statistical dependency only. Furthermore, as we show, one can do so in a low-dimensional feature space so long as one is careful about preserving information related to the underlying hypothesis.

Consider the following example problem, which illustrates an application of data association within tracking problems. Suppose we have a pair of widely spaced acoustic sensors, where each sensor is a small array of many elements. Each sensor produces an observation of the source and an estimate of bearing, which in itself is insufficient to localize the source. However, triangulation of bearing measurements from multiple sensors can be used to estimate the target location. For a single target, a pair of sensors is sufficient to perform this triangulation.

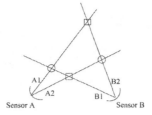

Fig. 1. The data association problem: two pairs of measurements results in estimated targets at either the circles or the squares; but which remains ambiguous.

However, complications arise when there are multiple targets within a pair of sensors' fields of view. Each sensor determines two bearings; but this yields four possible locations for only two targets, as depicted in Figure 1. With only bearing information, there is no way to know which one of these target pairs is real, and which is the artifact. We will show that it is possible to address this ambiguity under the assumption that the sources are statistically independent, without requiring a prior model of the relationship between observations across sensors.

2.1   Mutual Information

Mutual information is a quantity characterizing the statistical dependence between two random variables. Although most widely known for its application to communications (see e.g. [1]), here it arises in the context of discrimination and hypothesis testing [2].

Correlation is equivalent to mutual information only for jointly Gaussian random variables. The common assumption of Gaussian distributions and its computational efficiency have given it wide applicability to association problems. However, there are many forms of dependency which are not captured by correlation.

For example, Figure 2(a-c) shows three non-Gaussian joint distributions characterized by a single parameter θ, indicating an angle of rotation with respect to the random variables x, y. Although the correlation between x and y is zero for all θ, the plot of mutual information as a function of θ (Figure 2(d)) demonstrates that for many θ, x and y are far from independent. This illustrates how mutual information as a measure of dependence differs from correlation.

2.2   Data Association as a Hypothesis Test

Let us assume that we receive N *i.i.d.* observations of each source at each of the two sensors. When a full distribution is specified for the observed signals, we have a hypothesis test over *known*, factorized models

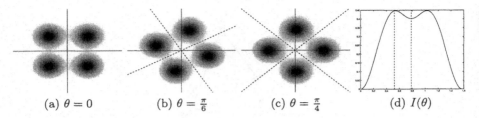

(a) $\theta = 0$ (b) $\theta = \frac{\pi}{6}$ (c) $\theta = \frac{\pi}{4}$ (d) $I(\theta)$

Fig. 2. Two variables x, y with joint distributions (a-c) are uncorrelated but not necessarily independent – (d) shows mutual information as a function of the angle of rotation θ.

$$H_1 : [A_1, B_1, A_2, B_2]_k \sim p_{H_1}(A_1, B_1)p_{H_1}(A_2, B_2)$$
$$H_2 : [A_1, B_1, A_2, B_2]_k \sim p_{H_2}(A_1, B_2)p_{H_2}(A_2, B_1) \tag{1}$$
$$\text{for } k \in [1 : N]$$

with corresponding (normalized) log-likelihood ratio

$$\frac{1}{N} \log L = \frac{1}{N} \sum_{k=1}^{N} \left[\log \frac{p_{H_1}([A_1, B_1]_k)p_{H_1}([A_2, B_2]_k)}{p_{H_2}([A_1, B_2]_k)p_{H_2}([A_2, B_1]_k)} \right] \tag{2}$$

As N grows large, the (normalized) log-likelihood approaches its expected value, which can be expressed in terms of mutual information (MI) and Kullback-Leibler (KL) divergence. Under H_1 this value is

$$E_{H_1}[\log L] = I_{H_1}(A_1; B_1) + I_{H_1}(A_2; B_2) + \\ D(p_{H_1}(A_1, \ldots, B_2) \| p_{H_2}(A_1, \ldots, B_2)) \tag{3}$$

and similarly when H_2 is true:

$$E_{H_2}[\log L] = - I_{H_2}(A_1; B_2) - I_{H_2}(A_1; B_2) - \\ D(p_{H_2}(A_1, \ldots, B_2) \| p_{H_1}(A_1, \ldots, B_2)) \tag{4}$$

The expected value of Equation (3) can be grouped in two parts – an information part (the two MI terms) measuring statistical dependency across sensors, and a model mismatch term (the KL-divergence) measuring difference between the two models. We begin by examining the large-sample limits of the likelihood ratio test, expressed in terms of its expected value; when this likelihood ratio is not available we see that another estimator for the same quantity may be substituted.

Often the true distributions p_{H_i} are unknown, e.g. due to uncertainty in the source densities or the medium of signal propagation. Consider what might be done with estimates of the densities based on the empirical data to be tested. Note that this allows us to learn densities *without* requiring multiple trials under similar conditions. We can construct estimates assuming the factorization under either hypothesis, but because observations are only available for the true hypothesis our estimates of the other will necessarily be incorrect. Specifically, let $\hat{p}_{H_i}(\cdot)$ be a consistent estimate of the joint distribution assuming the factorization under H_i and let $\tilde{p}_{H_i}(\cdot)$ denote its limit; then we have

if H_1 is true,

$$\hat{p}_{H_1} \to \tilde{p}_{H_1} = p_{H_1}(A_1, B_1)p_{H_1}(A_2, B_2)$$
$$\hat{p}_{H_2} \to \tilde{p}_{H_2} = p_{H_1}(A_1)p_{H_1}(B_1)p_{H_1}(A_2)p_{H_1}(B_2)$$

(5)

if H_2 is true,

$$\hat{p}_{H_1} \to \tilde{p}_{H_1} = p_{H_2}(A_1)p_{H_2}(B_1)p_{H_2}(A_2)p_{H_2}(B_2)$$
$$\hat{p}_{H_2} \to \tilde{p}_{H_2} = p_{H_2}(A_1, B_2)p_{H_2}(A_2, B_1)$$

Thus when $\hat{p}_{H_i}$ assumes the correct hypothesis we converge to the correct distribution, while assuming the incorrect hypothesis leads to a fully factored distribution. This is similar to issues arising in generalized likelihood ratio (GLR) tests [3].

We proceed assuming that our estimates have negligible error, and analyze the behavior of their limit $\tilde{p}(\cdot)$; we will examine the effect of error inherent in finite estimates $\hat{p}(\cdot)$ later. Now the expectation of the log-likelihood ratio can be expressed solely in terms of the mutual information between the observations. Under H_1 this is

$$E_{H_1}[\log \tilde{L}] = E_{H_1}\left[\log \frac{\tilde{p}_{H_1}(A_1, B_1)\tilde{p}_{H_1}(A_2, B_2)}{\tilde{p}_{H_2}(A_1, B_2)\tilde{p}_{H_2}(A_2, B_1)}\right]$$
$$= I(A_1; B_1) + I(A_2; B_2)$$

and similarly under H_2,

$$E_{H_2}[\log \tilde{L}] = -I(A_1; B_2) - I(A_2; B_1)$$

Notice in particular that the KL-divergence terms stemming from model mismatch in Equation (3) have vanished. This is due to the fact that both models are estimated from the same data, and quantifies the increased difficulty of discrimination when the models are unknown. We can write the expectation *independent* of which hypothesis is true as

$$E[\log \tilde{L}] = I(A_1; B_1) + I(A_2; B_2) - I(A_1; B_2) - I(A_2; B_1)$$

(6)

since for either hypothesis, the other two terms above will be zero; this casts the average log-likelihood ratio as an estimator of mutual information.

We have not assumed that the true distributions $p(\cdot)$ have any particular form, and therefore might consider using nonparametric methods to ensure that our estimates converge under a wide variety of true distributions. However, if the observations are high-dimensional such methods require an impractical number of samples in order to obtain accurate estimates. In particular, this means that the true likelihood ratio cannot be easily calculated, since it involves estimation and evaluation of high-dimensional densities. However, the log-likelihood ratio is acting as an estimator of the mutual information, and we may instead substitute another, more tractable estimate of mutual information if available.

Direct estimation of the MI terms above using kernel methods also involves estimating high-dimensional distributions, but one can express it succinctly using features which summarize the data interaction. We explore ways of learning such features, and shall see that the quality criterion for summarization is expressed as the mutual information between features estimated in a low-dimensional space.

Let us suppose initially that we possess low-dimensional sufficient statistics for the data. Although finding them may be difficult, we know that for the data association problem sufficient statistics should exist, since the true variable of interest, correspondence, is summarized by a single scalar likelihood. More precisely, let $f_i^{A_j}$ be a low-dimensional feature of A_j and $\bar{f}_i^{A_j}$ its complement, such that there is a bijective transformation between A_j and $[f_i^{A_j}, \bar{f}_i^{A_j}]$ (and similarly for B_k). If the following relation holds,

$$\begin{aligned} p_{H_i}(A_j, B_k) &= p_{H_i}(f_i^{A_j}, \bar{f}_i^{A_j}, f_i^{B_k}, \bar{f}_i^{B_k}) \\ &= p_{H_i}(f_i^{A_j}, f_i^{B_k}) p_{H_i}(\bar{f}_i^{A_j} | f_i^{A_j}) p_{H_i}(\bar{f}_i^{B_k} | f_i^{B_k}) \end{aligned} \tag{7}$$

then the log-likelihood ratio of Equation (6) can be written exactly as

$$E[\log \tilde{L}] = I(f_1^{A_1}; f_1^{B_1}) + I(f_1^{A_2}; f_1^{B_2}) - I(f_2^{A_1}; f_2^{B_2}) - I(f_2^{A_2}; f_2^{B_1}) \tag{8}$$

Although sufficient statistics are likely to exist, it may be difficult or impossible to find them exactly. If the features $f_i^{A_j}$ and $f_i^{B_k}$ are *not* sufficient, several divergence terms must be added to Equation (8). For *any* set of features satisfying $p_{H_i}(A_j, B_k) = p_{H_i}(f_i^{A_j}, \bar{f}_i^{A_j}, f_i^{B_k}, \bar{f}_i^{B_k})$, we can write

$$E[\log \tilde{L}] = I_1^{1;1} + I_1^{2;2} - I_2^{1;2} - I_2^{2;1} + D_1^{1;1} + D_1^{2;2} - D_2^{1;2} - D_2^{2;1} \tag{9}$$

where for brevity we have used the notation

$$I_i^{j;k} = I(f_i^{A_j}; f_i^{B_k})$$
$$D_i^{j,k} = D(\tilde{p}(A_j, B_k) \| \tilde{p}(f_i^{A_j}, f_i^{B_k}) \tilde{p}(\bar{f}_i^{A_j} | f_i^{A_j}) \tilde{p}(\bar{f}_i^{B_k} | f_i^{B_k}))$$

The data likelihood of Equation (9) contains a difference of the divergence terms from each hypothesis. Notice, however, that only the divergence terms involve high-dimensional data; the mutual information is calculated between low-dimensional features. Thus if we discard the divergence terms we can avoid all calculations on the high-dimensional compliment features $\bar{f}$. We would like to minimize the effect on our estimate of the likelihood ratio, but cannot estimate the terms directly without evaluating high-dimensional densities. However, by nonnegativity of the KL-divergence we can bound the difference by the sum of the divergences:

$$\left| D_1^{1;1} + D_1^{2;2} - D_2^{1;2} - D_2^{2;1} \right| \leq D_1^{1;1} + D_1^{2;2} + D_2^{1;2} + D_2^{2;1} \tag{10}$$

We then minimize this bound by minimizing the individual terms, or equivalently maximizing each mutual information term (which can be done in the low-dimensional feature space). Note that these four optimizations are decoupled from each other.

Finally, it is unlikely that with finite data our estimates $\hat{p}(\cdot)$ will have converged to the limit $\tilde{p}(\cdot)$. Thus we will also have divergence terms from errors in the density estimates:

$$
\begin{aligned}
E[\log \tilde{L}] =& \hat{I}_1^{1;1} + \hat{I}_1^{2;2} - \hat{I}_2^{1;2} - \hat{I}_2^{2;1} \\
&+ D(\tilde{p}_{H_1} \| \hat{p}_{H_1}) - D(\tilde{p}_{H_2} \| \hat{p}_{H_2})
\end{aligned}
\tag{11}
$$

where the $\hat{I}$ indicate the mutual information of the density estimates. Once again we see a difference in divergence terms; in this case minimization of the bound means choosing density estimates which converge to the true underlying distributions as quickly as possible. Note that if $\hat{p}_{H_1}(\cdot)$ is not a consistent estimator for the distribution $\tilde{p}_{H_i}(\cdot)$, the individual divergence terms above will never be exactly zero.

Thus we have an estimate of the true log-likelihood ratio between factorizations of a learned distribution, computed over a low-dimensional space:

$$
\begin{aligned}
E[\log \tilde{L}] =& \hat{I}(f_1^{A_1}; f_1^{B_1}) + \hat{I}(f_1^{A_2}; f_1^{B_2}) - \hat{I}(f_2^{A_1}; f_2^{B_2}) \\
&- \hat{I}(f_2^{A_2}; f_2^{B_1}) + divergence\ terms
\end{aligned}
\tag{12}
$$

where maximizing the $\hat{I}$ with regard to the features $f_i^{X_j}$ minimizes a bound on the ignored divergence terms. We can therefore use estimates of the mutual information over learned features as an estimate of the true log-likelihood ratio for hypothesis testing.

3 Algorithmic Details

The derivations above give general principles by which one may design an algorithm for data association using low-dimensional sufficient statistics. Two primary elements are necessary:

1. a means of estimating entropy, and by extension mutual information, over samples, and
2. a means of optimizing that estimate over the parameters of the sufficient statistic.

We shall address each of these issues in turn.

3.1 Estimating Mutual Information

In estimating mutual information, we wish to avoid strong prior modelling assumptions, i.e. jointly Gaussian measurements. There has been considerable research into useful nonparametric methods for estimating information-theoretic quantities; for an overview, see e.g. [4].

Kernel density estimation methods are often used as an appealing alternative when no prior knowledge of the distribution is available. Similarly, these kernel-based methods can be used to estimate mutual information effectively. Using estimates with smooth, differentiable kernel shapes will also yield simple calculations of a gradient for mutual information, which will prove to be useful in learning. An issue one must consider is that the quality of the estimate degrades as the dimensionality grows; thus we perform the estimate in a low-dimensional space.

To use kernel methods for density estimation requires two basic choices, a kernel *shape* and a *bandwidth* or smoothing parameter. For the former, we use Gaussian kernel functions $K_\sigma(x) = (2\pi\sigma^2)^{-\frac{1}{2}} \exp\{-x^2/2\sigma^2\}$, where σ controls the bandwidth. This ensures that our estimate is smooth and differentiable everywhere. There are a number of ways to choose kernel bandwidth automatically (see e.g. [5]). Because we intend to use these density estimates for likelihood evaluation and maximization, it is sensible to make this the criterion for bandwidth as well; we therefore make use of a leave-one-out maximum likelihood bandwidth, given by

$$\arg\max_\sigma \left[-\frac{1}{N} \sum_j \log \left(\frac{1}{N-1} \sum_{i\neq j} K_\sigma(x_j - x_i) \right) \right] \tag{13}$$

Because our variables of interest are continuous, it is convenient to write the mutual information in terms of joint and marginal entropy, as:

$$I(f_i^{A_j}; f_i^{B_k}) = H(f_i^{A_j}) + H(f_i^{B_k}) - H(f_i^{A_j}, f_i^{B_k}) \tag{14}$$

There are a number of possible kernel-based estimates of entropy available [4]. In practice we use either a leave-one-out resubstitution estimate:

$$\hat{H}_{RS}(x) = -\frac{1}{N} \sum_j \log \left(\frac{1}{N-1} \sum_{i\neq j} K_\sigma(x_j - x_i) \right) \tag{15}$$

or an integrated squared error estimate from [6]:

$$\hat{H}_{ISE} = H(\mathbf{1}) - \frac{1}{2} \int (1 - \hat{p}(x))^2 \, dx \tag{16}$$

where $\mathbf{1}$ is the uniform density on a fixed range, and

$$\hat{p}(x) = \frac{1}{N} \sum_j K_\sigma(x - x_j)$$

These methods have different interpretations – the former is a stochastic estimate of the true entropy, while the latter can be considered an exact calculation of an entropy approximation. In practice both of these estimates produce similar results. Both estimates may also be differentiated with respect to their arguments, yielding tractable gradient estimates useful in learning.

3.2   Learning Sufficient Statistics

In order to learn sufficient or relatively sufficient statistics, we must define a function from our high-dimensional observation space to the low-dimensional space over which we are able to calculate mutual information. By choosing a function which admits a simple gradient-based update of the parameter values, we can use gradient ascent to train our function towards a local information maximum [7,8].

Often, quite simple statistic forms will suffice. For example, all of the examples below were performed using a simple linear combination of the input variables, passed through a hyperbolic tangent function to threshold the output range:

$$f(x = [x^1 \ldots x^d]) = \tanh(\sum_i w_i x^i) \tag{17}$$

That is, using the method of [7,8] we apply gradient ascent of mutual information between the associated features with respect to the weight parameters w_i.

However, the methods are applicable to any function which can be trained with gradient estimates, allowing extension to much more complex functional forms. In particular, *multiple layer perceptrons* are a generalization of the above form which, allowed sufficient complexity, can act as a universal function approximator [9].

We may also wish to impose a capacity control or complexity penalty on the model (e.g. regularization). In practice, we put a penalty on the absolute sum of the linear weights (adding to the gradient a constant bias towards zero) to encourage sparse values.

4   Data Association of Two Sources

We illustrate the technique above with two examples on synthetic data. The first is a simulation of dispersive media – an all-pass filter with nonlinear phase characteristics controlled by an adjustable parameter α. The phase response for three example values of α are given in Figure 3(a). Sensor A observes two independent signals of bandpassed *i.i.d.* Gaussian noise, while sensor B observes the allpass-filtered versions of A.

If the filter characteristics are known, the optimal correspondence test is given by applying the inverse filter to B followed by finding its correlation with A. However when the filter is not known, estimating the inverse filter becomes a source reconstruction problem. Simple correlation of A and B begins to fail as the phase becomes increasingly nonlinear over the bandwidth of the sources. The upper curve of Figure 3(b) shows the maximum correlation coefficient between correct pairings of A and B over all time shifts, averaged over 100 trials. Dotted lines indicate the coefficient's standard deviation over the trials. To determine significance, we compare this to a baseline of the maximum correlation coefficient between incorrect pairings. The region of overlap indicates nonlinear phases for which correlation cannot reliably determine correspondence.

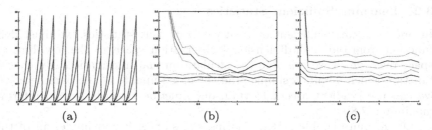

Fig. 3. Data association across a nonlinear phase all-pass filter: tunable filter (a) yields correlations (b) and mutual information (c).

Figure 3(c) shows an estimate of mutual information between the Fourier spectra of A and B, constructed in the manner outlined above. As α increases, the mutual information estimate assumes a steady-state value which remains separated from the baseline estimate and can accurately determine association.

The second example relates observations of non-overlapping Fourier spectra. Suppose that we observe a time series and would like to determine whether some higher-frequency observations are unrelated, or are a result of observing some nonlinear function (and thus harmonics) of the original measurements. We simulate this situation by creating two independent signals, passing them through a nonlinearity, and relating high-passed and low-passed observations. Sensor A observes the signals' lower half spectrum, and sensor B their upper half.

Synthetic data illustrating this can be seen in Figures 4-5. For Figure 4 we create a narrowband signal whose center frequency is modulated at one of two different rates, and pass it through a cubic nonlinearity. In the resulting filtered spectra (shown in Figure 4(a-d)), the correct pairing is clear by inspection. Scatterplots of the trained features (see Figure 4(e-h)) show that indeed, features of the correct pairings have high mutual information while incorrect pairings have nearly independent features.

Figure 5 shows the same test repeated with wideband data – Gaussian noise is passed through a cubic nonlinearity, and the resulting signal is separated into high- and low-frequency observations, shown in Figure 5(a-d). The resulting structure is less obvious, both visually and to our estimates of mutual information (Figure 5(e-h)), but the correct pairing is still found.

5   Extension to Many Sources

For the problem described above, the presence of only two targets means the data association problem can be expressed as a test between two hypotheses. However, as the number of targets is increased, the combinatorial nature of the hypothesis test makes evaluation of each hypothesis infeasible. Approximate methods which determine a correspondence without this computational burden

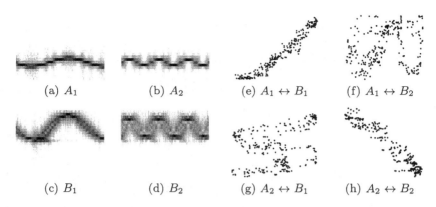

(a) A_1 (b) A_2 (e) $A_1 \leftrightarrow B_1$ (f) $A_1 \leftrightarrow B_2$

(c) B_1 (d) B_2 (g) $A_2 \leftrightarrow B_1$ (h) $A_2 \leftrightarrow B_2$

Fig. 4. Associating non-overlapping harmonic spectra: the correct pairing of data sets (a-d) is easy to spot; the learned features yield MI estimates which are high for correct pairings (e,h) and low for incorrect pairings (f,g).

offer an alternative which may be particularly attractive in the context of sensor networks. We describe an extension of the above method to perform data association between many targets without requiring evaluation of all hypotheses.

Let us re-examine the problem of Section 2, but allow both sensors to receive separate observations from M independent targets, denoted $A_1, \ldots, A_M$ and $B_1, \ldots, B_M$. One may still apply estimates of MI to approximate the hypothesis test as described in Section 2.2, but direct application will require that mutual information be estimated for each of the M^2 data pairs – a potentially costly operation.

However, we suggest an approximate means of evaluating the same test which does not compute each MI estimate. We can solve the data association problem by finding features which summarize *all* the signals received at a particular sensor. A test can then be performed on the learned feature coefficients directly, rather than computing all individual pairwise likelihoods.

Let us denote the concatenation of all signals from sensor A by $[A_1, \ldots, A_M]$. One can learn features which maximize mutual information between this concatenated vector and a particular signal B_j; we denote the feature of B_j by $f_A^{B_j}$, and the feature of $[A_1, \ldots, A_M]$ by $f_j^{[A_1, \ldots, A_M]}$.

Again, let us consider the linear statistics of Section 3.2:

$$f_A^{B_j} = \tanh(\sum_i w_i B_j^i) \tag{18}$$

$$f_j^{[A_1, \ldots, A_M]} = \tanh(\sum_{i,k} w_{i,A_k} A_k^i) \tag{19}$$

where A_k^i (B_j^i) indicates the ith dimension of the signal A_k (B_j).

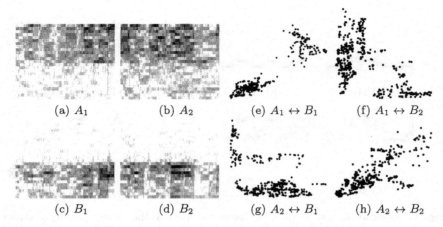

(a) A_1 (b) A_2 (e) $A_1 \leftrightarrow B_1$ (f) $A_1 \leftrightarrow B_2$

(c) B_1 (d) B_2 (g) $A_2 \leftrightarrow B_1$ (h) $A_2 \leftrightarrow B_2$

Fig. 5. Associating non-overlapping wideband harmonic spectra: though the correct pairing is harder to see than Figure 4, the estimated MI is still higher for the correct hypothesis (e,h).

We now consider tests based on the absolute deviation of the feature coefficients for each signal A_k:

$$\sum_i |w_{i,A_k}|$$

Under the assumption of independent sources, mutual information exists only between the correctly associated signals; i.e. if A_s and B_t represent a correct association, we have

$$I(A_s; B_t) = I([A_1, \dots, A_M]; B_t)$$
$$= I(A_s; [B_1, \dots, B_M])$$

We may then analyze the mutual information of a particular feature

$$I(f_t^{[A_1, \dots, A_M]}; f_A^{B_t}) = I(\tanh(\sum_{i,k} w_{i,A_k} A_k^i); f_A^{B_t})$$

$$= I(\sum_{i,k} w_{i,A_k} A_k^i; f_A^{B_t})$$

$$= \sum_k I(\sum_i w_{i,A_k} A_k^i; f_A^{B_t})$$

$$= I(\sum_i w_{i,A_s} A_s^i; f_A^{B_t})$$

Thus, for $k \neq s$ the weights w_{i,A_k} have no contribution to the mutual information. This tells us that among all features with maximal MI, the one with minimum absolute deviation $\sum_{i,k} |w_{i,A_k}|$ has support *only* on A_s. Whether distributions exist such that no linear feature captures dependence (i.e. $I(f_t^A; f_A^{B_t}) = 0$ for all linear f) is an open question.

As a means of exploiting this property, we impose a regularization penalty on the feature coefficients during learning. In particular, we augment the information gradient on the concatenated vector feature with a sparsity term, giving

$$\frac{\partial I(f_j^{[A_1,\ldots,A_M]}; f_A^{B_j})}{\partial w_{i_0,A_{k_0}}} - \alpha \max_{i,k} |w_{i,A_{k \neq k_0}}| \tag{20}$$

where the parameter α controls the strength of the regularization. This imposes a penalty on the absolute deviation of the weights which is proportional to the maximum weight from a *different* signal, giving sparse selection of signals – if only one of the M signals has nonzero coefficients, it has no regularization penalty imposed.

A decision can be reached more efficiently using the coefficient deviations, since only a few ($\mathcal{O}(M)$) statistics must be learned; a simple method such as greedy selection or the auction algorithm may be applied to determine the final association.

In the following example, we show the application of this technique to associating harmonics of wideband data passed through a nonlinearity; each of four signals is created in the same manner as those of the final example in Section 4. The signals' Fourier coefficients are shown in Figure 6; sensor A observes the lower half-spectrum and sensor B the upper. For demonstration purposes, we calculate statistics both for each B_k with $[A_1, \ldots, A_M]$, and each A_k with $[B_1, \ldots, B_M]$. Again, we use the ISE approximation of Equation (16) to calculate the information gradient.

Statistics trained in this way are shown in the upper half of Figure 7. To see how one would use these statistics to determine association, we can write the total absolute deviation of the statistic coefficients grouped by observation, and normalize by its maximum. This gives us the pairwise values shown in the lower part of Figure 7. In this example, a greedy method on either set of statistics is sufficient to determine the correct associations. More sophisticated methods might compute and incorporate both sets into a decision.

6   Discussion

We have seen that the data association problem may be characterized as a hypothesis test between *factorizations* of a distribution. An information-theoretic analysis led to a natural decomposition of the hypothesis test into terms related to prior modelling assumptions and terms related to statistical dependence. Furthermore, this analysis yielded insight into how one might perform data association in a principled way in the absence of a prior model. The approach described is similar to a nonparametric generalized likelihood ratio test.

In addition, we have presented an algorithm which utilizes these principles for the purposes of performing data association. This allows us to perform correspondence tests even when the source densities are unknown or there is uncertainty in the signals' propagation by learning statistics which summarize the

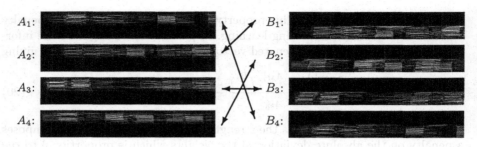

Fig. 6. Associating many signal pairs: a naive approach to finding the association above would require 4^2 estimates of mutual information.

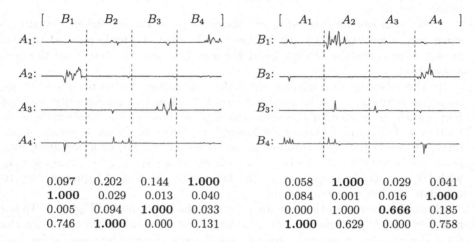

Fig. 7. Statistics learned on concatenated signals (above); each feature's region of support indicates probable associations. The row-normalized absolute sum (L^1 norm) of the statistics subdivided by signal index (below) may be used to determine correspondence; bold type indicates the correct association

mutual information between observed data vectors in a compact form. This was equivalent to approximating the likelihood ratio test with mutual information estimates in a low-dimensional space.

We have also suggested an approximate method of determining correspondence between larger signal sets based on the same techniques. Although this does not correspond directly to the optimal hypothesis test, it has the advantage that it does not require that mutual information be estimated for all M^2 signal pairs. Finally, we demonstrated the efficacy of this method with experiments on synthetic data.

References

1. T. Cover and J. Thomas. *Elements of Information Theory.* John Wiley & Sons, New York, 1991.
2. S. Kullback and R. A. Leibler. On information and sufficiency. *Annals of Mathematical Statistics,* 22:79–86, 1951.
3. E. J. Kelly. An adaptive detection algorithm. *IEEE Transactions on Aerospace and Electrical Systems,* 22(1):115–127, 1986.
4. J. Beirlant, E. J. Dudewicz, L. Györfi, and E. C. van der Meulen. Nonparametric entropy estimation: An overview. *International Journal of Math. Stat. Sci.,* 6(1):17–39, June 1997.
5. B.W. Silverman. *Density Estimation for Statistics and Data Analysis.* Chapman and Hall, New York, 1986.
6. J.W. Fisher III and J.C. Principe. A methodology for information theoretic feature extraction. In A. Stuberud, editor, *International Joint Conference on Neural Networks,* 1998.
7. J. W. Fisher III, A. T. Ihler, and P. Viola. Learning informative statistics: A nonparametric approach. In S. A. Solla, T. K. Leen, and K-R. Müller, editors, *Neural Information Processing Systems 12,* 1999.
8. A. Ihler, J. Fisher, and A. S. Willsky. Nonparametric estimators for online signature authentication. In *International Conference on Acoustics, Speech, and Signal Processing,* May 2001.
9. C. Bishop. *Neural Networks for Pattern Recognition.* Clarendon Press, 1995.

Energy-Constrained Collaborative Processing for Target Detection, Tracking, and Geolocation

Peter W. Boettcher and Gary A. Shaw*

MIT Lincoln Laboratory, 244 Wood St, Lexington, MA 02420
boettcher@ll.mit.edu

Abstract. While unattended ground sensors have traditionally relied upon acoustic, seismic, magnetic and non-imaging IR sensing modalities to perform detection, tracking, and recognition, imagery has the potential to greatly improve performance by introducing a rich feature set in the form of length, color, and shape metrics. This paper summarizes recent work in collaborative processing exploiting two extremes of sensor complexity: single-element acoustic sensors and panoramic image sensors. For the case of acoustic sensing, acoustic features from multiple nodes are combined to establish bearing to target bearing via time-difference of arrival algorithms. Multiple bearing estimates from different node clusters are combined to geolocate targets. We also present recent work in multi-node target tracking using panoramic imagers, where bearing estimates are derived by detecting and tracking moving objects within the panoramic image. Performance of both acoustic and image sensing modalities is illustrated using field data. We show that adoption of imagers is feasible in terms of size, weight, energy consumption, and bandwidth usage, and discuss the advantages and disadvantages relative to traditional unattended sensors.

1 Introduction

Until recently, research in unattended ground sensors for target detection and tracking was evolving toward ever more capable sensors in the form of imagers, range finders, and arrays of high-sensitivity microphones for coherent beamforming [1,2,3]. However, these large, high performance sensors are power-hungry, and have not proven affordable for remote surveillance over wide areas. Recently, researchers have been exploring low-cost distributed sensors as a means to lower deployed system cost and energy usage, while improving coverage, data quality and timeliness through proliferation of short-range, collaborative sensors [4].

Acoustic sensors spring quickly to mind as inexpensive, low power nodes. Indeed, acoustic sensors have been the focus of a number of recent collaborative sensing research efforts. Acoustics can certainly provide approximate locations of targets, as well as a reasonably accurate classification of each target, and

* This work is sponsored by DARPA under A/F Contract #F19628-00-C-0002. Opinions, interpretations, recommendations and conclusions are those of the authors and are not necessarily endorsed by the Department of Defense.

F. Zhao and L. Guibas (Eds.): IPSN 2003, LNCS 2634, pp. 254–268, 2003.

can do so with low power usage. However, the performance of acoustic sensors degrades significantly when tracking or classifying multiple targets, or targets not in the pre-defined classification library. Acoustic sensor performance also degrades severely in the presence of wind or multipath environments.

Furthermore, while acoustic sensors may correctly determine the class of vehicular target, other important features such as markings, occupants, and armament cannot be ascertained from acoustic data. In order to support comprehensive surveillance and situational awareness, it is clear that imagers must be involved in some form. However, since imagers consume much more power than acoustic sensors, it is inefficient if not impractical for them to operate continuously. Therefore, acoustic or another low-power sensing modality must be used for cueing the image sensors.

This paper describes a distributed acoustic bearing estimation system as well as a panoramic imager system. The acoustic bearing estimation system can serve as the low-power cueing system for the imager, which can perform more sophisticated and accurate tracking and classification of targets.

2   Acoustic Time-Difference of Arrival

Historically, applications involving acoustic unattended ground sensors are characterized by isolated sensor nodes, possibly with a small coherent array, that report results to human operators over ranges of a few kilometers or more [3]. In contrast, the distributed sensing community is exploring the utility of sensor platforms consisting of many small, low-cost sensors employing low-power, omnidirectional sensors (e.g., acoustic and seismic). Such sensors are effective in classifying targets according to signature, but, due to the lack of directionality, the sensors do not individually provide target geolocation or bearing information. Furthermore, the energy constraints imposed by the small sensor size require hardware and algorithm design that minimize energy utilization in processing and communication, and also minimize required inter-sensor communication.

In terms of collaborative bearing estimation, researchers have investigated the possibility of algorithms such as "blind" beamforming, which adapt traditional coherent direction-finding algorithms to cross-platform operation [5]. Such algorithms exemplify what we call *collaborative signal processing* (CSP). That is, since each sensor node has limited capability, information from multiple sensor nodes is combined to enhance overall performance. However, beamforming algorithms require a great deal of communication bandwidth, which increases energy consumption and is counter to the goal of small, low-cost, close-range sensing.

Acoustic time-difference of arrival (TDOA) is a technique for target localization that can be adapted to resource-constrained, omnidirectional acoustic nodes, with sufficiently low communication bandwidth requirements to be feasible in long-term deployments. This section provides a brief summary of one such algorithm. For a more detailed discussion, see [6] and [7].

2.1   Power Considerations

Since the cost, logistics, support, and covertness of a deployable sensor is proportional to its size and weight, power conservation is of the utmost importance. With current technology, rules of thumb for energy consumption vary between picojoules to nanojoules per instruction for processing, while communication consumes microjoules to millijoules per bit, depending on desired range and link geometry. This creates a strong argument for the use of local processing of sensor data to extract only essential information and thus minimize communication. Minimizing communication among nodes is particularly important when communicating at low elevation angles near the ground, where R^{-4} spreading losses occur [8]. This increases the energy cost of communication and reduces the achievable distance of radio transmission.

These observations lead us to limit collaborative processing to local clusters of sensors, and to avoid transmitting raw data between nodes in order to minimize bits communicated and commensurate energy expended.

2.2   TDOA Motivation

Single-element acoustic sensors are among the smallest and lowest power sensors available. However, to obtain useful directional information, a single sensor is insufficient. Instead, a network of individual sensor nodes is used, and the data is combined using some type of CSP algorithm. Coherent processing [1,2] is theoretically possible, but performance is limited by sensor location uncertainties, problems related to the long baselines, and errors in time synchronization. *Closest point of approach* (CPA) [9,10] has also been proposed, but is complicated by multi-target scenarios and by complex target motion. Furthermore, CPA is of no value in geolocating targets which lie outside the convex hull of a collaborative sensor cluster.

The TDOA method described in this paper shares some of the advantages of these two techniques. Instead of using phase difference information, as coherent beamforming does, TDOA techniques compare the travel time of sound through the air over much larger baselines. In order to avoid transmitting time-series data from one node to another, the relative time-difference of arrival of a signal is estimated using the dominant frequency of the acoustic spectrum as a feature. From this measurement, bearing or geolocation estimates can be calculated. The range is much greater than that allowed by CPA, while TDOA is much more tolerant to the uncertainties in location and time which plague coherent approaches.

2.3   Algorithm Summary

The block diagram shown in Fig. 1 illustrates the basic structure of the TDOA algorithm. Each node extracts the dominant frequency from its local acoustic data using an adaptive filter. This dominant frequency is used as a feature for

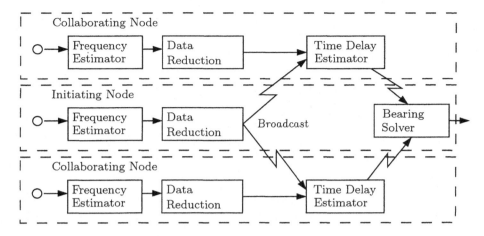

Fig. 1. Block diagram of TDOA bearing estimation algorithm. The dashed boxes indicate the physical node on which each block is run

matching acoustic signals between multiple sensors. Because the dominant frequency changes relatively slowly, the data rate is significantly less than the raw time series.

A single node initiates the bearing estimation procedure by sharing this frequency estimate with surrounding nodes. Each of these surrounding nodes then estimates the time delay between the local and remote frequency estimates using an approach similar to correlation over small blocks of data. This time delay estimate is returned to the initiating node. Finally, the initiating node can compute a bearing estimate from the estimated time delays.

2.4   TDOA Experimental Results

The DARPA SensIT program developed wireless sensor nodes and associated networking and collaborative processing algorithms for *ad hoc* networks of energy-constrained sensors [11]. In August 2000, a data collection experiment called SITEX00 was run at Twentynine Palms, CA, with the cooperation of the USMC. A total of 37 nodes were placed in three clusters along the roads at the test site. Each node was configured with acoustic, seismic, and non-imaging IR sensors, and the location of each node was determined using GPS. Over a period of two weeks, numerous collection runs were made on various military vehicles, with GPS receivers providing vehicle ground truth.

To validate performance of the distributed TDOA algorithms, six nodes near the intersection of the roads were chosen to form a cluster. Only the acoustic data from these nodes was used for this experiment. The acoustic data was low-pass filtered and sampled at 256 Hz by the sensor. The frequency estimates were shared from central node out to the other five nodes, and each of those five nodes

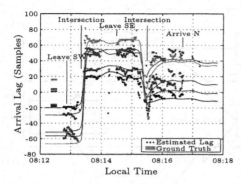

Fig. 2. Time delay estimates. The dots show the estimates of the time delay from the data. The solid lines are predicted from the ground-truth

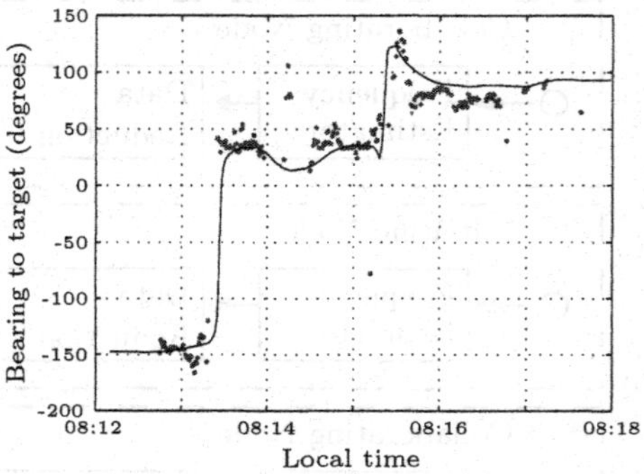

Fig. 3. Bearing results, using the approximate center of the 6-node cluster as reference. Ground truth bearing is the solid line, and the dots represent the estimated bearing

compared the received estimate with its own local frequency estimate, producing the TDOA estimates which are shown in Fig. 2.

The delay estimates were collected back at the central node, and bearing estimates were formed. These bearing estimates are shown in Fig. 3, superimposed on the GPS ground truth bearing-to-target.

2.5   CPU Complexity and Bandwidth Analysis

The frequency estimation stage requires very few CPU cycles, since it uses an extremely efficient adaptive filter structure. The most demanding computation is the delay estimation, but even this stage has modest requirements. For example, at the 256 Hz acoustic sampling rate, 10× decimation of the frequency estimate, and 5 second frames, the correlation is performed using approximately 12.8 Kop (kilo-operations) per frame. At a rate of 2 estimates per second, 24 Kop per second are required.

The most stressing communication requirements occur when transmitting the frequency estimate from the initiating node to the collaborating nodes. Depending on exact system parameters, as few as 400 bits/second could be required, with no compression beyond performed simple decimation. This requirement is low enough to admit the possibility of non-RF communication, such as non-line-of-sight UV communication [12].

Compare these numbers to an estimate of those required for distributed coherent beamforming. Using the Remote Sentry system [1] as a reference, beamforming would require approximately 500 Kop/s of processing, and 32 kbps of bandwidth [6].

Finally, given inter-node spacings of 100m, the algorithm can tolerate node position uncertainties of 5-10m, and time synchronization errors of up to a few

Fig. 4. Example of a panoramic image, taken using a zenith-looking fisheye lens

milliseconds. Accuracies in these ranges are achievable without specialized hardware or surveying of node locations.

3   Panoramic Imagers

In order to airdrop or otherwise remotely deploy an imaging sensor, a means for pointing the imager must be provided. Either a motorized pan/tilt system must be used to point the imager at the scene of interest, or some type of panoramic imager must be used. Combined with a one-shot mechanical deployment device, the camera can right itself. Since a panoramic camera has a 360° azimuthal field of view, no panning is necessary. This 360° field of view can be produced from a fisheye lens, a mirror assembly, or an array of imagers. Fig. 4 shows an example of a panoramic image obtained, in this case, with a fisheye lens.

3.1   Prototype Panoramic Vision Node

In order to demonstrate the utility of panoramic imagery in a distributed sensor network, and to provide a source of data for algorithm development and performance evaluation, several prototype image nodes were built from commercial off-the-shelf (COTS) hardware (See Fig. 5). The emphasis in the implementation of these prototype nodes was to provide a flexible platform for algorithm implementation and assessment, and to avoid the need for any custom hardware development. Size and power were not a concern in this COTS implementation.

Fig. 5. Prototype panoramic imager node

Each node is based on a PC-104 form factor, used for industrial embedded computing [13]. PC-104 modules are approximately 10cm × 10cm, and are stackable. Each node contains a main CPU board with Pentium-III class CPU, a 2.5" laptop hard drive, a digital frame grabber, and a power supply. This embedded computer runs Linux and is fully controllable via remote network.

The imager component is a 1 Megapixel, 12 bit color CCD with digital output, and a full hemisphere panoramic lens. The field of view extends from −5° to 90° in elevation and 0° to 360° in azimuth.

3.2   Video Motion Tracking

The lowest level of processing is performed on the raw panoramic images, and is presently limited to the detection and tracking of moving objects within the image. Motion detection is performed using adaptive background subtraction. However, motion tracking algorithms need also take into account distracters (blowing leaves, clouds), noisy pixels, uneven lighting, and long-term motion (objects becoming background and reverse). This section details the algorithms used in detecting and tracking motion. A block diagram of the algorithms is shown in Fig. 6.

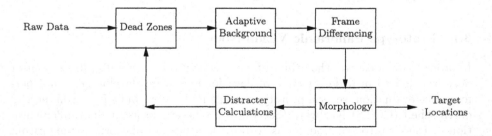

Fig. 6. Video processing block diagram

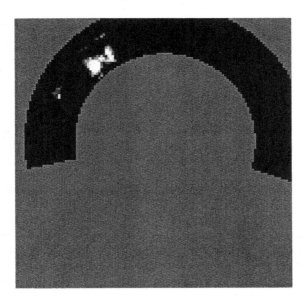

Fig. 7. *Dead zones* and pixel activity metric. The solid gray areas are a priori declared uninteresting. The bright white region is high pixel activity

This set of algorithms is by no means intended to be the final version for all future use. It does, however, provide a starting point for future development of motion tracking algorithms.

Dead Zones. In many cases scenes contain dead zones, or "regions of disinterest", known a priori. For example, when the panoramic imager is pointing skyward and attempting to track targets on the ground, the entire center of the image is unnecessary, and may distract the algorithms. At the least, processing time can be saved by setting up these dead zones. The four corners of the square focal plane are truly dead, as the panoramic lens produces a round image.

In addition, when the imagers are hand-emplaced, it is possible to specify a region of interest in azimuth, depending on deployment.

Dead zones are implemented simply as a pixel map. See Fig. 7 for an illustration of dead zones.

Adaptive Background Calculation. The background of a scene is by no means static. Lighting changes frequently (especially outdoors), and non-fixed stationary objects in the scene may be moved, for example. One way to deal with the constant background variation is to use a decaying average scheme. Each pixel p_{ij} is combined with its weighted average b_{ij} using $b_{ij_t} = \alpha p_{ij} + (1 - \alpha)b_{ij_{t-1}}$. In this equation, α determines the decay rate of the background, or how quickly old features fade from importance. To aid in the tracking stage, two different backgrounds are maintained: a long-term background and a short-term background.

Future work in this area will include incorporation of more sophisticated adaptive background techniques, such as Bayesian approaches [14] and Gaussian mixture models [15].

Frame differencing. Each pixel in a newly captured image is compared with the two background planes. Those pixels which have an absolute difference greater than some threshold are *motion pixels*. Morphological processing is then used to de-noise the motion pixels. That is, blocks of 8 × 8 pixels are declared *motion blocks* if they contain a certain number of motion pixels.

Objects entering background. Objects may enter the scene, then become part of the background. For instance, a car may enter, then park. After a short time, the parked car should no longer be detected as motion, but should become part of the background. A higher-level tracker can maintain state information about this potential target.

In this case, the short-term background fairly quickly adapts to include the parked car. Therefore, the pixels on the car will not register a difference with the short-term background, so it is not detected as motion.

Objects leaving background. Continuing with the previous example, the parked car may then continue on its way. Not only will the car be detected as motion, but the place formerly occupied by the car (the *hole*) will be detected as well. To avoid this, the pixels in the image are compared with the long-term background as well. Since the long-term background adapts very slowly, the pixels in the hole may not yet have adapted, and the hole will immediately be recognized as such and ignored. If an object has been in the scene too long, it will have been fully adapted into both backgrounds, and the hole will be detected as motion for a few seconds. At this point, the short-term background will quickly adapt, and the hole will be ignored.

Distracter pixels. Especially in an outdoor environment, some parts of the scene are constantly in motion, and thus would always register as motion pixels. Blowing leaves, artificial noise from saturated pixels, and clouds are all examples of phenomena that would create distracter pixels. To avoid confusing the tracking algorithms, these pixels are ignored using a *motion map*. As each pixel is classified as either moving or non-moving (using thresholded absolute difference), the corresponding entry in the motion map is respectively incremented or decremented. The end result is that the motion map adapts to ignore regions of continuous motion. Fig. 7 shows a region with a high level of pixel activity, which is ignored during tracking. The entire gray-shaded region, as well as the small, light region, is ignored during processing.

Fig. 8. Perspective-corrected image chip, extracted from a zenith-looking fisheye lens

Target reports. Two different versions of the prototype software use different methods to produce target location estimates. One system simply finds the centroid of the motion blocks remaining after this processing, assuming single-target scenes. When the scene truly is single-target, this simple approach produces reliable results that assists in development of other parts of the system. A developmental version of the software uses connected components to isolate disjoint objects. This version is easily confused by gaps in detected objects, but more sophisticated target tracking could do a much better job in tracking multiple targets. Approaches such as Kalman filtering and K-means clustering have been used with success [15,16].

The tracking stage outputs bearing and elevation to the target (or to multiple targets, in the multitarget case). These outputs are used as inputs to the fusion stage and to the perspective-corrected image extraction stage.

3.3   Perspective Corrected Image Extraction

One of the most useful features of panoramic imagery is the ability to use virtual pan, tilt, and zoom to extract arbitrary views (See Fig. 8). One can imagine a transparent viewplane placed somewhere inside the panoramic hemisphere view. This viewplane can be placed at any angle or distance from the origin, and the value of each pixel on the viewplane can be calculated by projecting through the plane and onto the panoramic image. The end result is a perspective view at any angle and zoom. Of course, since there are no moving parts, any number of perspective views can be calculated from the same panoramic source.

These perspective views can be highly compressed and communicated via network or communication link. Even video-rate extraction is possible, if the link can support that bandwidth.

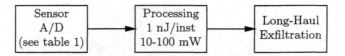

Fig. 9. Generic unattended remote sensor block diagram

3.4 Fusion

Once several imagers have independently estimated bearing-to-target, only the bearings need be sent to a fusion node for an estimate of position. This requires almost no bandwidth, and allows target location reports to be efficiently sent via long-haul communication link.

In the multitarget case, a more sophisticated tracker must be used at this stage, in order to disambiguate bearing and elevation information from multiple imager nodes, Kalman filters are one possibility [15,16]; another is Bayesian object matching [17,18].

4 Power Utilization Analysis

The prototype vision nodes described in Sec. 3.1 consume 10-25 W of power. They are intended for research purposes only, and are not feasible for a field-able unit. However, with current technology one could envision a deployable panoramic vision node with a lifetime of a month or more.

4.1 System Energy Balance

In terms of energy consumption, long-haul communication is usually the dominant subsystem for an unattended ground sensor, or network of sensors. If one can balance the energy consumption of the various subsystems of a sensor (see Fig. 9), overall performance and longevity will be improved.

Table 1. Typical sensor energy costs

Node Types	Power (mW)	Rate (kHz)	nJ/sample
Acoustic	.06	4	0.15
Seismic	.02	1	0.2
Visible Imager (APS)	30	12550	2.5
IR Imager (Microbolometer[19])	1200	7300	164

Table 1 shows the state-of-the-art energy usage of low-power sensors, in terms of energy per sample. Note that visible image acquisition requires approximately 10× more energy per sample than acoustic or seismic sensors. Uncooled infrared imagers require almost 1000× more energy per sample.

Table 2. Typical radio energy costs

Radio Type	Approx. Range	Power (W)	Energy (nJ/bit)
WaveLAN (S)	150m	1.4	125
SINCGARS (VHF)	8km	4	>350K
Freewave (L)	80km	6	50K
Iridium (L)	>780km	0.85	355K
Orbcom (VHF)	>800km	6	2,500K

Table 2 is a similar illustration of the energy usage of various commercial and military radios. Note that all the long-range radios require 4–5 orders of magnitude more energy per bit than the data acquisition.

Local processing is essential to extract information from the raw signal, effectively providing data compression at the sensor. Without reference to any particular processor, we note that the state-of-the-art in commercially available processing is about 1 mW/MIP, or effectively 1 nJ per instruction. This energy number for a single instruction is consistent with the cost of acquiring the signal, but the number of instructions per sample for typical signal processing operations can vary from hundreds to thousands of operations per sample. If communication required no energy, it would not be cost effective, from an energy perspective, to perform local processing. However, because the energy cost of both local and long-haul communication is high, processing to identify significant events and compress the data is essential.

4.2   Concept Low-Power Panoramic Imager

The fisheye lens of the prototype node is the heaviest, bulkiest, most fragile, and most expensive piece of entire system. Obviously a different solution is needed if a low-cost deployable imager node is desired. Instead of using a monolithic panoramic image, one could use an array of narrow field-of-view cameras, digitally calibrated and stitched. One such commercially available camera [20] measures less than $\frac{1}{3}$cm^3 in volume, and has built in lens, active pixel focal plane, and digital read-out, all at a cost of around 40 USD.

Each of these cameras has a field of view of 55°, so an octagonal array would cover the full 360° scene, with 10° of overlap between each view. The entire array assembly would be less than 2.5cm in diameter. Each of these cameras would feed into the processor, which could either sample all 8 simultaneously, or in sequence, or only 2 cameras based on a priori knowledge.

The cameras and processor would be kept in sleep mode until cued by an extremely low-power acoustic sensor.

4.3   Energy Utilization Example

In order to arrive at an estimate for long-term energy consumption of an unattended ground sensor, one must consider a specific scenario for use of the sensor.

Fig. 10. Sample image, dimensions 270 × 120

Fig. 11. Same image, compressed to 10 kilobits using JPEG2000

In this case, the hypothetical scenario under consideration involves surveillance in a rural environment. Specifically, the mission of the sensor field is to search vehicular traffic in an intersection, in order to ID tanks and heavy trucks. Spot reports of any positive IDs are exfiltrated via long-haul RF link.

It is assumed that a vigilant acoustic sensor cues the imager for further processing. The imager responds by powering up, taking approximately 20 frames of video, processing the video, and exfiltrating if necessary.

The traffic model assumed for the intersection is:

- Day: 200 vehicles/hour; 20 heavy trucks/hour
- Night: 30 vehicles/hour; 5 heavy trucks/hour

If the acoustic sensor has a 50% false alarm rate, then the imager will be turned on 30 times per hour, during the day. This duty cycle assumption is equivalent to 150s of active processing per hour, and assuming 250 operations per pixel and 1 nJ per operation, the image processing would likely require 5mW average power during the day.

Assuming 200 bits for a report of a confirmed detection, average power can be computed. In addition, a highly compressed still image of the target might require 10 kbits (See Figs. 10 and 11 for an example of high compression). These image chips would be exfiltrated only on request from a remote user. An Iridium-class link is assumed for the long-haul communication. Table 3 shows the estimated energy consumption of each of these subsystems of the hypothetical system.

Table 3. Energy consumption of hypothetical panoramic node

	Avg. Daytime Pwr.	Energy/day
Data Acquisition	350 μW	20 J
Image Processing	5 mW	300 J
Comms (Target Reports)	360 μW	23 J
Comms (Image Chips)	3 J/target	

Finally, by assuming state-of-the-art battery density of 1J/mm^3 and a 9V form factor battery, an estimate of deployed longevity is 65 days continuous operation, if no image chips are exfiltrated. If 100 images per day are requested and transmitted, lifetime drops to 34 days. These energy use estimates do not account for link acquisition or other types of processing tasks, and are therefore best case.

5   Conclusions

The TDOA algorithm presented here represents an example of a collaborative processing algorithm for distributed sensors. The algorithm architecture and implementation is driven by consideration of bandwidth and energy constraints, and uncertainties in node location and calibration. The algorithm provides bearing-to-target and geolocation estimates in a distributed sensor network where coherent processing is impractical. The bearing estimates provide useful tracking information at ranges far beyond those possible with closest point of approach based algorithms, but the algorithm still has quite modest processing and bandwidth requirements. Algorithm performance was illustrated using distributed sensor data collected at the recent SensIT SITEX00 experiment.

The prototype panoramic imager system provides a platform for more accurate tracking and classification of targets. Although an imager system consumes more power than an acoustic system, images carry much higher value in terms of providing comprehensive surveillance and actionable information. Furthermore, by intelligent cueing, the incremental energy cost of the imager can be minimized. The energy analysis of off-the-shelf hardware demonstrates the feasibility of building a deployable panoramic imager system. When coupled with an acoustic cueing system, several months of continuous operation is a reasonable goal for such a system.

References

1. Brooks, Jr., J.A., Gallo, M.A.: Remote sentry advanced technology demonstration. In: Proc. of the SPIE. Volume 2764. (1996) 154–164
2. Malone, K.T., Riblett, L., Essenmacher, T.: Acoustic/seismic identifications, imaging, and communications in *Steel Rattler*. In: Proc. of the SPIE. Volume 3081. (1997) 158–165
3. Stotts, L.B.: Unattended ground sensor related technologies; an army perspective. In: Proc. SPIE. Volume 4040. (2000) 2–10
4. Kumar, S., Shepherd, D.: SensIT: Sensor information technology for the warfighter. In: Proc. 2001 International Conf. on Information Fusion. Volume 1., Montreal (2001) TuC1–3
5. Yao, K., Hudson, R.E., Reed, C.W., Chen, D., Lorenzelli, F.: Blind beamforming on a randomly distributed sensor array. IEEE J. Select. Areas Commun. **16** (1998) 1555–1567
6. Boettcher, P.W., Sherman, J.A., Shaw, G.A.: Target localization using acoustic time-difference of arrival in distributed sensor networks. In: Proc. of the SPIE. Volume 4741. (2002)

7. Boettcher, P.W., Shaw, G.A.: A distributed time-difference of arrival algorithm for acoustic bearing estimation. In: Proc. 2001 International Conf. on Information Fusion. Volume 1., Montreal (2001)
8. Blaunstein, N.: Radio Propagation in Cellular Networks. Artech House Publishers, Boston (2000)
9. Dommermuth, F.M.: The estimation of target motion parameters from CPA time measurements in a field of acoustic sensors. J. Acoust. Soc. Am. **83** (1988) 1476–1480
10. Milios, E.E., Nawab, S.H.: Acoustic tracking from closest point of approach time, amplitude, and frequency at spatially distributed sensors. J. Acoust. Soc. Am. **87** (1990) 1026–1034
11. Coffin, D., Hook, D.V., Kolek, S., McGarry, S.P.: Declarative ad hoc sensor networking. In: Proc. of the SPIE. Volume 4126., San Diego, CA (2000)
12. Shaw, G.A., Nischan, M., Iyengar, M., Kaushik, S., Griffin, M.K.: NLOS UV communication for distributed sensor systems. In: Proc. of the SPIE. Volume 4126, San Diego, CA (2000)
13. PC/104 Consortium: http://www.pc104.org (2003)
14. Matthews, K., Namazi, N.: A bayesian approach to uncovered background and moving pixel detection. In: Intl. Conf. on Acoustics, Speech and Signal Proc. Volume 4. (1995) 2245–2248
15. Stauffer, C., Grimson, W.: Adaptive background mixture models for real-time tracking. In: Computer Vision and Pattern Recognition. Volume 2., IEEE Computer Society (1999) 246–253
16. KaewTraKulPong, P., Bowden, R.: An adaptive visual system for tracking low resolution color targets. In: British Machine Vision Conf. (2001) 243–252
17. Ellis, T., Xu, M.: Object detection and tracking in an open and dynamic world. In: Proc. of the 2nd IEEE International Workshop on PETS. (2001)
18. Kahn, S., Javed, O., Shah, M.: Tracking in uncalibrated cameras with overlapping field of view. In: Proc. of the 2nd IEEE International Workshop on PETS. (2001)
19. Kostrzewa, J., Meyer, W., Kraemer, D., Poe, G., Nguyen, V., Brown, M., Terre, W.: Overview of the UL3 Omega^{TM} uncooled camera and its applications. In: Proc. of the SPIE. Volume 4719. (2002) 189–195
20. Fujitsu Corporation: http://www.fma.fujitsu.com/pdf/cmos_fs.pdf (2002)

Array Processing for Target DOA, Localization, and Classification Based on AML and SVM Algorithms in Sensor Networks

L. Yip, K. Comanor, J.C. Chen, R.E. Hudson, K. Yao, and L.Vandenberghe

Electrical Engineering Department, University of California at Los Angeles,
Los Angeles, CA 90095-1594

Abstract. We propose to use the Approximate Maximum-Likelihood (AML) method to estimate the direction-of-arrival (DOA) of multiple targets from various spatially distributed sub-arrays, with each sub-array having multiple acoustical/seismic sensors. Localization of the targets can with possibly some ambiguity be obtained from the cross bearings of the sub-arrays. Spectra from the AML-DOA estimation of the target can be used for classification as well as possibly to resolve the ambiguity in the localization process. We use the Support Vector Machine (SVM) supervised learning method to perform the target classification based on the estimated target spectra. The SVM method extends in a robust manner to the nonseparable data case. In the learning phase, classifier hyperplanes are generated off-line via a primal-dual interior point method using the training data of each target spectra obtained from a single acoustical/seismic sensor. In the application phase, the classification process can be performed in real-time involving only a simple inner product of the classifier hyperplane with the AML-DOA estimated target spectra vector. Analysis based on Cramér-Rao bound (CRB) and simulated and measured data is used to illustrate the effectiveness of AML and SVM algorithms for wideband acoustical/seismic target DOA, localization, and classification.

1   Introduction

Recent developments in integrated circuits have allowed the construction of low-cost small sensor nodes with signal processing and wireless communication capabilities that can form distributed wireless sensor network systems. These systems can be used in diverse military, industrial, scientific, office, and home applications [1], [2]. One of the central tasks of these systems is to localize the target of interest by collaborative processing of the received sensing data. In this paper, we consider source localization by cross bearing from different subarrays. In this approach, processing of the data is performed locally within each subarray and no data communication is needed among the subarrays.

Source localization and DOA estimation using sensor arrays have received much attention in the array signal processing field for decades. Many high resolution algorithms such as Multiple Signal Classification(MUSIC)[3] and Maximum

F. Zhao and L. Guibas (Eds.): IPSN 2003, LNCS 2634, pp. 269–284, 2003.

Likelihood(ML)[4], [5] have been proposed for narrow band DOA estimation. Recently there has been an interest in locating wideband sources, for example, the tracking of multiple acoustic sources using a microphone array. The algorithm development in wideband source localization can be categorized into two classes. The first class of algorithms involves two steps: estimation of the time difference of arrivals(TDOAs) among the sensors followed by a least square(LS) fit to obtain the source location [6]. However, this class of methods is usually for a single source only. The second class of algorithms uses a ML parameter estimation method [7] to perform DOA estimation of the sources for far-field scenarios, which is capable of estimating multiple source DOAs. The Approximated ML(AML) algorithm discussed in this paper processes the data in the frequency domain as this may be more attractive for acoustic signals due to their wideband nature. Moreover, the estimated source spectrum can be obtained as a byproduct of the source angle estimation algorithm , and this spectrum can then be used for source identification and source classification.

We propose the use of the support vector machine (SVM) to perform the source classification from the estimated source spectra. The SVM is a supervised learning algorithm which attempts to linearly separate labeled training data by a hyperplane. Since its introduction by Vapnik in 1992 [14], it has received considerable attention and is widely used in a variety of applications [12]. The SVM method not only includes the simple linearly separable training data case, but extends in a robust manner to the nonseparable data case. In the learning phase, classifier hyperplanes are generated off-line via a primal-dual interior point method using the training data of each target spectra obtained from a single acoustical/seismic sensor. In the application phase, the classification process can be performed in real-time involving only a simple inner product of the classifier hyperplane with the AML beamforming estimated target spectra vector obtained from a sub-array.

Besides the development of different estimation and classification algorithms using a sensor array, we also derive the theoretical Cramer-Rao bound(CRB) for both performance comparison and basic understanding purposes. The CRB provides a common tool for all unbiased estimators. It has been shown that the CRB can be asymptotically approached by an ML estimator when SNR and sampling data length are sufficiently large [8]. The first explicit formula for the CRB on the covariance matix appeared in [8]. However, it was only restricted to the narrowband DOA estimation case. In [9], a CRB for a single source case was given for both wideband source localization and DOA estimation. In this paper, we extend the result in [9] to a multiple sources case. The resulting formula shows that the CRB for a particular source DOA is increased due to interference from the other sources. Most of the CRB derivations were focused on the received noise at each sensor. However, the time synchronization among each sensor is crucial for coherent type array signal processing and this error should be minimized to obtain good performance. However, analysis of this kind of error is rare in the array signal processing literature. In this paper, we derive a CRB equation for theoretical analysis of the time-synchronization error.

In section 2, we derive the theoretical Cramer-Rao bound for multiple source DOA estimation. The AML method for DOA estimation is described in section 3. In section 4, we review the formulation of the SVM as a quadratic programming (QP) problem and describe a primal-dual interior-point method for solving it. We present experimental results in section 5, and finally, we draw some conclusions in section 6.

2   CRB Analysis for Multiple Source DOA Estimation

2.1   Array Data Model for DOA Estimation

When the source is in the far-field of the array, wavefront arriving at the array is assumed to be planer and only the angle of arrival can be estimated. For simplicity, we assume both the source and sensor array lie in the same plane(a 2-D scenario). Let there be M wideband sources, each at an angle θ_m from the array. The sensor array consists of P randomly distributed sensors, each at position $\mathbf{r}_p = [x_p, y_p]^T$. The sensors are assumed to be omni-directional and have identical response. The array centroid position is given by $\mathbf{r}_c = \frac{1}{P} \sum_{p=1}^{P} \mathbf{r}_p = [x_c, y_c]^T$. We use the array centroid as the reference point and define a signal model based on the relative time-delays from this position. The relative time-delay of the mth source is given by $t_{cp}^{(m)} = t_c^{(m)} - t_p^{(m)} = [(x_c - x_p)\sin\theta_m + (y_c - y_p)\cos\theta_m]/v$, in where $t_c^{(m)}$ and $t_p^{(m)}$ are the absolute time-delays from the mth source to the centroid and to the pth sensor, respectively, and v is the speed of propagation. In a polar coordinate system, the above relative time delay can also be expressed as: $t_{cp}^{(m)} = r_p \cos(\theta_m - \phi_p)/v$, where r_p and ϕ_p are the range and angle of the p sensor with respect to the array centroid. The data received by the pth sensor at time n is then $x_p(n) = \Sigma_{m=1}^{M} S_c^{(m)}(n - t_{cp}^{(m)}) + w_p(n)$, for $n = 0, ..., N-1$, $p = 1, ..., P$, and $m = 1, ..., M$, where $S_c^{(m)}$ is the mth source signal arriving at the array centroid position, $t_{cp}^{(m)}$ is allowed to be any real-valued number, and w_p is the zero mean white Gaussian noise with variance σ^2.

For the ease of derivation and analysis, the received wideband signal can be transformed into the frequency domain via the DFT, where a narrowband model can be given for each frequency bin. However, the circular shift property of the DFT has an edge effect problem for the actual linear time shift. These finite effects become negligible for sufficiently long data. Here, we assume the data length N is large enough to ignore the artifact caused by the finite data length. For N-point DFT transformation, the array data model in the frequency domain is given by

$$\mathbf{X}(k) = \mathbf{D}(k)\mathbf{S}_c(k) + \eta(k), \tag{1}$$

for $k = 0, ..., N-1$, where the array data spectrum is $\mathbf{X}(k) = [X_1(k), ..., X_P(k)]^T$, the steering matrix $\mathbf{D}(k) = [\mathbf{d}^{(1)}(k), ..., \mathbf{d}^{(M)}(k)]$, the steering vector is given by $\mathbf{d}^{(m)}(k) = [d_1^{(m)}(k), ..., d_P^{(m)}(k)]^T$, $d_p^{(m)} = e^{-j2\pi k t_{cp}^{(m)}/N}$, and the source spectrum is given by $\mathbf{S}_c(k) = [S_c^{(1)}(k), ..., S_c^{(m)}(k)]^T$. The noise spectrum vector

$\eta(k)$ is zero mean complex white Gaussian distributed with variance $N\sigma^2$. Note, due to the transformation to the frequency domain, $\eta(k)$ asymptotically approaches a Gaussian distribution by the central limit theorem even if the actual time-domain noise has an arbitrary i.i.d. distribution (with bounded variance). This asymptotic property in the frequency-domain provides a more reliable noise model than the time-domain model in some practical cases. A more compact expression of (2) can be formed by stacking up the $N/2$ positive frequency bins of $X(k)$ into a single column, that is $\mathbf{X} = \mathbf{G}(\Theta) + \xi$, where $\mathbf{X} = [\mathbf{X}(1)^T, ..., \mathbf{X}(N/2)^T]^T$, $\mathbf{G}(\Theta) = [\mathbf{S}(1)^T, ..., \mathbf{S}(N/2)^T]^T$, $\mathbf{S}(k) = \mathbf{D}(k)\mathbf{S}_c(k)$, and $\mathbf{R}_\xi = E[\xi\xi^H] = N\sigma^2\mathbf{I}_{NP/2}$. Throughout this paper, we denote superscript ^{T} as the transpose, and ^{H} as the complex conjugate transpose.

2.2   CRB Derivation for Multiple Source DOA Estimation

The CRB for any unbiased estimator of parameters Θ with an arbitrary distribution is in general given by the inverse of the Fisher Information matrix[10], that is $\mathbf{CRB}(\theta_i) = \mathbf{F}^{-1}[\Theta]_{ii}$. In the white Gaussian noise case, the Fisher information matrix is given by

$$\mathbf{F} = 2\mathrm{Re}[\mathbf{H}^H\mathbf{R}_\xi^{-1}\mathbf{H}] = (2/N\sigma^2)\mathrm{Re}[\mathbf{H}^H\mathbf{H}], \tag{2}$$

where $\mathbf{H} = \frac{\partial\mathbf{G}}{\partial(\Theta)^T}$. We first assume the source signals are known and the unknown parameter is $\Theta = [\theta_1, ..., \theta_M]$. Applying (2), the element of Fisher Information matrix can be shown to be

$$\mathbf{F}_{ii} = \frac{2}{N\sigma^2}\sum_p\sum_k a_{ip}^2(\frac{2\pi kr_p}{v})^2\sin^2(\theta_i - \phi_p)|S_c^{(i)}(k)|^2 \tag{3}$$

$$\mathbf{F}_{ij} = \frac{2}{N\sigma^2}\sum_p\sum_k a_{ip}a_{jp}(\frac{2\pi kr_p}{v})^2\exp(-j\frac{2\pi kr_p[\cos(\theta_i - \phi_p) - \cos(\theta_j - \phi_p]}{v})$$

$$\sin(\theta_i - \phi_p)\sin(\theta_j - \phi_p)S_c^{(i)*}(k)S_c^{(j)}(k) \tag{4}$$

The Fisher Information matrix is a $M \times M$ Hermitian with real diagonal elements. The CRB can be obtained by the inverse of $\mathbf{F}$. In order to make comparison of the single source formula, assume the matrix $\mathbf{F}$ has the format of

$$\mathbf{F} = \begin{bmatrix} \mathbf{F}_{11} & \mathbf{F}_{1x} \\ \mathbf{F}_{x1} & \mathbf{F}_{xx} \end{bmatrix}, \tag{5}$$

where $\mathbf{F}_{11}$ is the scaler which is the same as the single source case, and $x \neq 1$. By applying the block matrix inverse lemma, the CRB of the source 1 angle is given by$[\mathbf{F}^{-1}]_{11} = (\mathbf{F}_{11} - \mathbf{F}_{1x}\mathbf{F}_{xx}^{-1}\mathbf{F}_{x1})^{-1}$. The penalty term $\mathbf{F}_{1x}\mathbf{F}_{xx}^{-1}\mathbf{F}_{x1}$ is due to the interference from the other sources. It can be shown that this term is always nonnegative, therefore, the CRB of DOA of source 1 in a single source case is always less than the multiple source case.

In practice, the source signals are usually unknown. In this case, the unknown parameter for estimation is $[\Theta, \mathbf{S}_c^T]$. The $\mathbf{H}$ matrix is given by $\mathbf{H} = [\frac{\partial \mathbf{G}}{\partial \Theta^T}, \frac{\partial \mathbf{G}}{\partial \mathbf{S}_c^T}]$. The Fisher information matrix can be shown as

$$\mathbf{F} = \begin{bmatrix} \mathbf{F}_\Theta & \mathbf{B} \\ \mathbf{B}^T & \mathbf{C} \end{bmatrix}, \tag{6}$$

where $\mathbf{B} = \frac{2}{N\sigma^2}(\frac{\partial \mathbf{G}}{\partial \Theta^T})^H \frac{\partial \mathbf{G}}{\partial \mathbf{S}_c^T}$, $\mathbf{C} = \frac{2}{N\sigma^2}(\frac{\partial \mathbf{G}}{\partial \mathbf{S}_c^T})^H \frac{\partial \mathbf{G}}{\partial \mathbf{S}_c^T}$. By the block matrix inversion lemma, the inverse of the upper left $M \times M$ submatrix is given by $[\mathbf{F}_{\Theta, \mathbf{S}_c}^{-1}]_{M \times M} = (\mathbf{F}_\Theta^{-1} - \mathbf{Z}_{\mathbf{S}_c})^{-1}$, where $\mathbf{Z}_{\mathbf{S}_c} = \mathbf{B}^T \mathbf{C}^{-1} \mathbf{B}$. It can be shown that the penalty matrix $\mathbf{Z}_{\mathbf{S}_c}$ due to unknown source signal is non-negative definite. Therefore, the DOA estimation error of the unknown signal case is always larger than that of the known case.

2.3   CRB Derivation for the Time Synchronization Error

In this subsection, we evaluate the theoretical performance of DOA estimation for the far-field case by CRB analysis. For clear illustration of the effect of the time synchronization error, we only consider the case of a single source here. From the data model of the far-field DOA case, when only the time synchronization error is considered, the received waveform of the pth sensor at the k frequency bin is given by

$$X_p(k) = S_c(k) \exp\left[\frac{-j2\pi k(t_p - \tau_p)}{N}\right], \tag{7}$$

where $S_c(k)$ is the received signal spectrum at the reference sensor, t_p is the relative time delay from the pth sensor to the reference sensor. For the far-field case, $t_p = \frac{r_p \cos(\theta_s - \phi_p)}{v}$. τ_p is the time synchronization error and assumed to be IID white Gaussian with zero mean and variance σ_τ^2. Taking natural logarithm of both sides of (7), and rearranging terms, we obtain

$$Z_p(k) = f_k - \frac{r_p \cos(\theta_s - \phi_p)}{v} + \tau_p, \tag{8}$$

for $k = 1, \ldots, K$ and $p = 1, \ldots, P$, where $Z_p(k) = \frac{N}{2\pi k}\Im\{\ln(X_p(k))\}$, $f_k = \frac{N}{2\pi k}\Im\{\ln(S_c(k))\}$, and $\Im\{\}$ represents the imaginary part of a complex value. At the frequency bin k, the P equations are stacked up to form a complete matrix. We have the following real-valued white Gaussian data model $\mathbf{X} = \mathbf{G}(\Theta) + \tau$, where Θ is the unknown parameter that we need to estimate, $\Theta = [\theta_s, f_k]$ in our case, i.e., the source angle and the source spectrum, $\tau = [\tau_1 \ldots \tau_P]^T$ and $\mathbf{G}(\Theta) = f_k[1 \ldots 1]^T - \left[\frac{r_1 \cos(\theta_s - \phi_1)}{v} \ldots \frac{r_P \cos(\theta_s - \phi_P)}{v}\right]^T$. From (2), the Fisher information matrix of this white Gaussian model is given by

$$\mathbf{F} = \frac{1}{\sigma_\tau^2} \begin{bmatrix} \sum_{p=1}^P \frac{r_p^2 \sin^2(\theta_s - \phi_p)}{v^2} & \sum_{p=1}^P \frac{r_p \sin(\theta_s - \phi_p)}{v} \\ \sum_{p=1}^P \frac{r_p \sin(\theta_s - \phi_p)}{v} & P \end{bmatrix}. \tag{9}$$

The CRB for the source angle can then be given by the first diagonal element of the inverse of the Fisher information matrix, which is given by

$$\text{CRB} = \frac{\sigma_\tau^2}{\sum_{p=1}^{P} \frac{r_p^2 \sin^2(\theta_s - \phi_p)}{v^2} - \frac{1}{P}\left(\sum_{p=1}^{P} \frac{r_p \sin(\theta_s - \phi_p)}{v}\right)^2}. \tag{10}$$

Some observation can be made from the CRB formula 10. First, the numerator of the CRB only depends on the variance of the time-synchronization error; while the denominator of the CRB depends on the array geometry and source angle. Therefore, the CRB is proportional to the time synchronization error. Furthermore, the array geometry also has effect on the CRB. Poor array geometry may lead to a smaller denominator, which results in a larger estimation variance. It is interesting to note that the geometric factor is the same as the CRB formula for additive Gaussian noise at [9], which means the array geometry produces the same effects on both kinds of errors. Second, although the derivation is limited to one frequency bin, the resulting CRB formula is independent of that particular frequency bin. Therefore, unlike the CRB of AWGN, the CRB can not be reduced by increasing the number of frequency bins. In other words, the time synchronization error can not be reduced by increasing the data length of the received signal.

2.4   Variance Lower Bound for Time Synchronization Error and AWGN

By considering time synchronization error and AWGN together, the received signal spectrum at the k frequency bin and the pth sensor, will be

$$X_p(k) = S_c(k) \exp\left[\frac{-j2\pi k(t_p - \tau_p)}{N}\right] + \eta_p(k), \tag{11}$$

where the first term is the same as (7), η_{pk} is the complex white Gaussian with zero mean and $N\sigma_n^2$ is the variance. Exact CRB requires the derivation of the probability density function (pdf) of the above data model, which may be a formidable task.

Here, we provide a variance bound based on the independence assumption of τ_p and η_{pk}. With this condition, the variance of the estimator will be the sum of the variance induced by these errors independently. By using $\text{var}(\theta; \tau, \eta) = \text{var}(\theta; \tau) + \text{var}(\theta; \eta)$, $\text{CRB}(\theta; \tau) \leq \text{var}(\theta; \tau)$ and $\text{CRB}(\theta; \eta) \leq \text{var}(\theta; \eta)$, we obtain

$$\text{var}(\theta; \tau, \eta) \geq \text{CRB}(\theta; \tau) + \text{CRB}(\theta; \eta). \tag{12}$$

The CRB induced by AWGN is given by

$$\text{CRB} = \frac{1}{\varsigma\left[\sum_{p=1}^{P} \frac{r_p^2 \sin^2(\theta_s - \phi_p)}{v^2} - \frac{1}{P}\left(\sum_{p=1}^{P} \frac{r_p \sin(\theta_s - \phi_p)}{v}\right)^2\right]}, \tag{13}$$

where $\varsigma = \frac{2}{N\sigma^2 V^2} \sum_{k=1}^{N/2} \left(\frac{2\pi k S_c(k)}{N}\right)^2$ and the geometric factor is the same as the time synchronization error. Although the variance bound may not be as tight as the CRB, it can be shown to match well with the root-mean-square (RMS) error of the simulation of AML algorithm. Furthermore, it offers a much simpler and more efficient way to evaluate the variance lower bound.

3   AML Method for DOA Estimation

3.1   Derivation of the AML Algorithm

In contrast to the TDOA-CLS method where the data is processed in the time domain, the AML estimator does the data processing in the frequency domain. The ML metric results in a coherent combination of each subband. Therefore, the AML approach can gain advantage where the signal is wideband, for example, the acoustic signal. By assuming both the source angles and spectrums are unknown, the array signal model defined in section 2.1 is given by $\mathbf{X} = \mathbf{G}(\mathbf{\Theta}, \mathbf{S}_c) + \xi$, and $\mathbf{R}_\xi = E[\xi\xi^H] = N\sigma^2 \mathbf{I}_{NR/2}$. The log-likelihood of this complex Gaussian noise vector ξ, after ignoring irrelevant constant terms, is given by $L(\mathbf{\Theta}, \mathbf{S}) = -||\mathbf{X} - \mathbf{G}(\mathbf{\Theta}, \mathbf{S})||^2$. The maximum-likelihood estimation of the source DOA and source signals is given by the following optimization criterion

$$\max_{\mathbf{\Theta}, \mathbf{S}} L(\mathbf{\Theta}, \mathbf{S}) = \min_{\mathbf{\Theta}, \mathbf{S}} \sum_{k=1}^{N/2} ||\mathbf{X}(k) - \mathbf{D}(k)\mathbf{S}(k)||^2, \tag{14}$$

which is equivalent to a nonlinear least square problem. Using the technique of separating variable[5], the AML DOA estimate can be obtained by solving the following likelihood function

$$\max_{\mathbf{\Theta}} J(\mathbf{\Theta}) = \max_{\mathbf{\Theta}} \sum_{k=1}^{N/2} ||\mathbf{P}(k, \mathbf{\Theta})\mathbf{X}(k)||^2 = \max_{\mathbf{\Theta}} \sum_{k=1}^{N/2} \text{tr}(\mathbf{P}(k, \mathbf{\Theta})\mathbf{R}(k)), \tag{15}$$

where $\mathbf{P}(k, \mathbf{\Theta}) = \mathbf{D}(k)\mathbf{D}^\dagger(k)$, $\mathbf{D}^\dagger = (\mathbf{D}(k)^H \mathbf{D}(k))^{-1}\mathbf{D}(k)^H$ is the pseudo-inverse of the steering matrix $\mathbf{D}(k)$ and $\mathbf{R}(k) = \mathbf{X}(k)\mathbf{X}(k)^H$ is the one snapshot co-variance matrix. Once the AML estimate of $\mathbf{\Theta}$ is found, the estimated source spectrum can be given by $\hat{\mathbf{S}}_c^{ML}(k) = \mathbf{D}^\dagger(k, \hat{\mathbf{\Theta}}^{ML})\mathbf{X}(k)$. The AML algorithm in effect performs signal separation by utilizing the physical separation of the sources, and for each source signal, the SINR is maximized in the ML sense.

3.2   Multiple Snapshot Implementation of AML

In the previous formulation, we derive the AML algorithm using only a single block data. A variant of the AML solution using multiple snapshots can also be formed. In this approach, a block of N data samples are divided into N_s snapshots, each snapshot contains N_t samples, i.e. $N = N_s \times N_t$. The sample covariance matrix $\mathbf{R}$ can then be obtained by averaging the N_s time snapshots $\mathbf{R} = \frac{1}{N_s} \sum_{t=1}^{N_s} \mathbf{X}(k)\mathbf{X}(k)^H$. Since the multiple snapshots approach uses less sample data to perform FFT, the edge effect becomes more severe that the single snapshot approach. Appropriate zero padding is necessary to reduce this artifact.

3.3   Alternating Projection of Multiple Source DOA Estimation

In the multiple source case, the computational complexity of the AML algorithm requires multi-dimensional search, which is much higher than the MUSIC type algorithm that requires only 1-D search. The alternating projection technique breaks the multi-dimensional search into a sequence of 1-D search, and reduced the computational burden greatly. The following describes the alternating projection algorithm for the case of M sources.

Step 1: Solve the problem for a single source, $\hat{\theta}_1^{(0)} = \arg\max_{\theta_1} J(\theta_1)$.

Step 2: Solve the second source $\hat{\theta}_2^{(0)} = \arg\max_{\theta_2} J(\hat{\theta}_1^{(0)}, \theta_2)$. by assuming the first source is at θ_1. Continuing in this fashion until all the initial values $\hat{\theta}_1^{(0)}, ..., \hat{\theta}_M^{(0)}$ are computed.

For k=1,..., repeat Step 3 until it converges.

Step 3: At every iteration a maximization is performed with respect to a single parameter while all the other parameter are held fixed. Therefore, at $(k+1)$ iteration, $\hat{\theta}_i^{(k+1)} = \arg\max_{\theta_i} J(\hat{\mathbf{\Theta}}_{(i)}^{(k)}, \theta_i)$, where $\hat{\mathbf{\Theta}}_{(i)}^{(k)}$ denotes the $(M-1) \times 1$ vector of the computed parameters at (k) iteration, i.e. $\hat{\mathbf{\Theta}}_{(i)}^{(k)} = [\hat{\theta}_1^{(k)}, ..., \hat{\theta}_{i-1}^{(k)}, \hat{\theta}_{i+1}^{(k)}, ..., \hat{\theta}_M^{(k)}]$.

3.4   Source Localization by Cross Bearing

When two or more subarrays simultaneously detect the same source, the crossing of the bearing lines can be used to estimate the source location. Without loss of generality, let the centroid of the first subarray be the origin of the coordinate system. Denote $\mathbf{r}_{ck} = [x_{ck}, y_{ck}]^T$ as the centroid position of the kth subarray, for $k = 1, ..., K$. Denote θ_k as the DOA estimate (with respect to north) of the kth subarray. From simple geometric relationship, we have $\mathbf{Ay} = \mathbf{b}$, where

$$\mathbf{A} = \begin{bmatrix} \cos(\theta_1) & -\sin(\theta_1) \\ \vdots & \vdots \\ \cos(\theta_K) & -\sin(\theta_K) \end{bmatrix}, \mathbf{y} = \begin{bmatrix} x_s \\ y_s \end{bmatrix}, \text{ and } \mathbf{b} = \begin{bmatrix} x_{c1}\cos(\theta_1) - y_{c1}\sin(\theta_1) \\ \vdots \\ x_{cK}\cos(\theta_K) - ycK\sin(\theta_K) \end{bmatrix}.$$

The source location estimate can be given by the least square (LS) solution of the above equation using normal equation pseudo-inverse $\hat{\mathbf{y}} = (\mathbf{A}^T\mathbf{A})^{-1}\mathbf{A}^T\mathbf{b}$, or Moore-Penrose pseudo-inverse. The residual of the LS solution can also be given by res $= \|\mathbf{A}\hat{\mathbf{y}} - \mathbf{b}\|$. In the multiple sources case, two or more DOA can be estimated from each subarray. For example, there are eight permutations in the case where three subarrays uield six DOA estimates (assuming each subarray yield two DOA estimates). The two source location estimates can be chosen by the two lowest residuals of the LS solutions.

4 Support Vector Machine

4.1 Standard QP Formulation

Suppose we are given training data in the form of N vectors $x_i \in \mathbf{R}^n$ and N binary labels $y_i \in \{-1, 1\}$. A support vector classifier is based on an affine decision function $a^T x - b$, where $a \in \mathbf{R}^n$ and $b \in \mathbf{R}$ are the solution of the following quadratic program

$$\begin{aligned} & \text{minimize} \quad (1/2)\|a\|_2^2 + \gamma \mathbf{1}^T u, \\ & \text{subject to } Y(Xa - \mathbf{1}b) \geq \mathbf{1} - u, \\ & \qquad\qquad u \geq 0. \end{aligned} \tag{16}$$

The variables are $a \in \mathbf{R}^n$, $b \in \mathbf{R}$, and $u \in \mathbf{R}^N$. The matrix $X \in \mathbf{R}^{N \times n}$ has rows x_i^T, $Y = \mathbf{diag}(y_1, \ldots, y_N)$, and $\mathbf{1}$ denotes a vector in $\mathbf{R}^N$ with all its components equal to one. The coefficient $\gamma > 0$ is a parameter set by the user.

The constraints in (16) have the following interpretation. The training vector x_i is considered correctly classified by the decision function $f(x) = a^T x - b$, if $a^T x_i - b \geq 1$, if $y_i = 1$, or $a^T x_i - b \leq -1$, if $y_i = -1$. The variable u is the *slack vector* in these inequalities, *i.e.*, measures the amount of constraint violation: $u_i = 0$ if the point is correctly classified and $u_i > 0$, otherwise.

The cost function is a weighted sum of two objectives. The second term $\mathbf{1}^T u$ is the total slack, *i.e.*, total constraint violation. The first term penalizes large a, and has a very intuitive geometrical meaning. It can be shown that $2/\|a\|_2$ is the distance between the hyperplanes $a^T x - b = 1$ and $a^T x - b = -1$. This distance is a good measure of the robustness of the classifier. By minimizing $\|a\|_2$ we maximize the margin between the two hyperplanes. In the QP (16), we control the trade-off between classification error (as measured by the total slack violation) and robustness (inversely proportional to the $\|a\|_2$) by the parameter γ.

We can also use the QP formulation (16) to solve nonlinear classification problems. We define a nonlinear decision function $f : \mathbf{R}^p \to \mathbf{R}$ of the form $f(v) = a^T F(v) - b$, where $F : \mathbf{R}^p \to \mathbf{R}^n$ consists of a set of specified basis functions (*e.g.*, all monomials of a certain maximum degree). Given a set of N training points $v_i \in \mathbf{R}^p$, $y_i \in \{-1, 1\}$, we can then define $x_i = F(v_i)$, and compute a and b by solving (16).

4.2 Solution via Primal-Dual Interior Point Method

Most SVM training methods solve the QP (16) via the dual problem

$$\begin{aligned} & \text{maximize} \quad -(1/2)z^T Q z + \mathbf{1}^T z, \\ & \text{subject to } 0 \leq z \leq \gamma \mathbf{1}, \\ & \qquad\qquad y^T z = 0, \end{aligned} \tag{17}$$

where the variable is $z \in \mathbf{R}^N$, and the matrix Q is defined as $Q = YXX^TY$, *i.e.*, $Q_{ij} = y_i y_j x_i^T x_j$, $i, j = 1, \ldots, N$. The dual problem has fewer variables (*i.e.*, N)

than the primal problem (which has $n+1+N$ variables). In nonlinear separation problems we usually have $n \gg N$, and the large dimension n affects the dual problem only through the length of the inner products $Q_{ij} = y_i y_j F(v_i)^T F(v_j)$. While a naive implementation would require $O(n)$ operations per inner product, for many common basis functions F the inner products can be computed much more efficiently, in $O(p)$ operations. This is referred to as the *kernel trick* in the SVM literature. Most SVM implementations therefore solve the dual problem using general-purpose interior-point solvers (such as LOQO [13] or MOSEK [11]).

However, similar savings can be achieved in any primal or primal-dual interior-point method directly applied to (16). We will explain this for Mehrotra's primal-dual predictor-corrector method, one of the most popular and efficient interior-point algorithms.

Skipping details, each iteration of the primal-dual method requires the solution of a set of linear equations

$$
\begin{bmatrix}
\mathbf{diag}(z) & \mathbf{diag}(s) & 0 & 0 & 0 & 0 \\
0 & 0 & \mathbf{diag}(u) & 0 & 0 & \mathbf{diag}(\lambda) \\
-I & 0 & 0 & YX & -y & I \\
0 & I & I & 0 & 0 & 0 \\
0 & y^T & 0 & 0 & 0 & 0 \\
0 & X^TY & 0 & -I & 0 & 0
\end{bmatrix}
\begin{bmatrix}
\Delta s \\
\Delta z \\
\Delta \lambda \\
\Delta a \\
\Delta b \\
\Delta u
\end{bmatrix}
=
\begin{bmatrix}
r_1 \\
r_2 \\
r_3 \\
r_4 \\
r_5 \\
r_6
\end{bmatrix}. \tag{18}
$$

where $s = Y(Xa - 1b) + u - 1$, $\lambda = \gamma 1 - z$, and a, b, u, z are the current primal and dual iterates. These equations are obtained by linearizing the optimality conditions (KKT conditions)

$$
\begin{aligned}
z_i s_i = 0, \quad u_i \lambda_i = 0 \quad i = 1, \dots, N, \\
Y(Xa - 1b) - 1 + u - s = 0, \quad u \geq 0, \quad s \geq 0, \\
\gamma 1 - z = \lambda, \quad y^T z = 0, \quad z \geq 0, \quad \lambda \geq 0, \\
a = X^T Y z,
\end{aligned} \tag{19}
$$

and provide search directions Δa, Δb, Δu, Δz for the primal and dual updates.

An efficient implementation of the primal-dual method requires solving the equation (18) fast. A first key observation is that if the starting values of a and z satisfy $a = X^T Y z$, then $r_6 = 0$ in the righthand side of (18). Therefore, the steps Δa and Δz satisfy $\Delta a = X^T Y \Delta z$, and the inequality $a = X^T Y z$ holds throughout the algorithm. As a result, the large-dimensional variable a or its update Δa is never needed. Instead, they are defined implicitly by the smaller dimensional variables z and Δz.

A second important observation is that by straightforward elimination of Δa, Δs, Δu, and $\Delta \lambda$, we obtain an equivalent system

$$
\begin{bmatrix}
Q + D & -y \\
y^T & 0
\end{bmatrix}
\begin{bmatrix}
\Delta z \\
\Delta b
\end{bmatrix}
=
\begin{bmatrix}
r_7 \\
r_5
\end{bmatrix}, \tag{20}
$$

where D is a positive diagonal matrix and r_7 is computed from the righthand sides of (18). The coefficient matrix of (20) can be constructed by adding a diagonal matrix to Q (evaluated efficiently via the kernel trick). The solution is obtained from the Cholesky factorization of $Q + D$. Given Δz and Δb, the remaining search directions readily follow from (18). Additional savings are possible by using approximate search directions obtained by replacing Q with an approximation (*e.g.*, diagonal plus low rank), or solving (20) iteratively.

5   Simulation and Experiment Results

5.1   Simulation Examples of CRB Analysis

In this subsection, we compare the derived CRB of DOA estimation with the RMS error of AML in several simulations. In the first simulation, multiple CRB of is calculated in a two-source scenario. The two far-field sources are located at 45° and 60° from the sensor array. The sensor array configuration is a uniform square with four acoustic sensors, each spacing 0.305 meter apart. The two sources are a prerecorded motorcycle and a car signal respectively. The sampling frequency is set to be 5KHz and the speed of propagation is 345m/sec. The RMS error of AML is computed via 100 Monte Carlo runs. Figure 1 shows the resulting RMS error of the first source as a function of the SNR. It can be seen that both the AML estimation error and CRB decrease as the SNR increases. The saturation behavior of the AML RMS error may be due to the quantization error of the angle sampling.

In the second simulation, we consider the time synchronization effect on the AML DOA estimation. The derived variance bound of (12) is compared with the RMS error of AML. Only a single source arrive to the sensor array from 45° in this case. The RMS error of AML and the derived variance bound are plotted as a function of SNR for various σ_t^2. It can be seen that the performance of AML matches well with the variance bound. Furthermore, the performance of AML is limited even in the high SNR region for fixed σ_t^2 as shown in figure 2. This is due to the time synchronization error becoming dominant at that region, which results in a error floor effect. The above theoretical as well as simulation analysis of the time synchronization error shows that it is crucial to obtain accurate time synchronization among sensors in order to yield good performance of the coherent array signal processing.

5.2   Experiment Results of Source Localization by Cross Bearing

Several acoustic experiments were conducted in PARC, Palo Alto, CA. In the first outdoor experiment (outside of the Xerox PARC building), three widely separated linear subarrays, each with four microphones, were used. A white Gaussian signal was played through the loud speaker placed at the two locations shown in figure 3. In this case, each subarray estimated the DOA of the source independently using the AML method, and the bearing crossing from the three subarrays provided an estimate of the source location. An RMS error of 32cm was reported for the first location, and an RMS error of 97cm was reported for

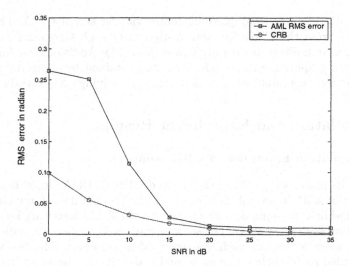

Fig. 1. RMS error comparison of CRB and AML as a function of SNR.

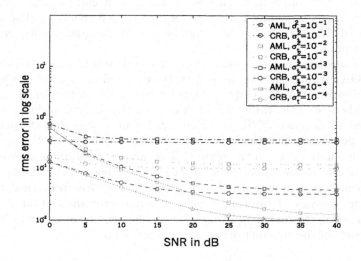

Fig. 2. RMS error comparison of variance bound and AML.

the second location. This shows the AML crossing bearing method can locate the wideband source effectively.

In a different outdoor configuration, two linear subarrays of four microphones were placed at the opposite sides of the road and two omni-directional loud speakers were placed between them, as depicted in figure 4. The two loud speakers play two independent pre-recorded sounds of light wheeled vehicles of different kinds. By using the alternating projection steps on the AML metric, the DOA's of the two sources were jointly estimated for each subarray under 11dB SNR (with respect to the bottom array). Then, the crossing yielded the location estimates of the two sources. An RMS error of 37cm was observed for the source 1 and an RMS error of 45cm was observed for source 2. We note, the AML DOA subarray angular resolution for multiple targets is significantly better than the classical Fourier limited resolution of the same subarray. This advantage is similar to the so-called "superresolution" effect of various parametric spectral estimators (e.g., MUSIC; subspaced-based method) as compared to classical DFT Fourier limited spectral estimator.

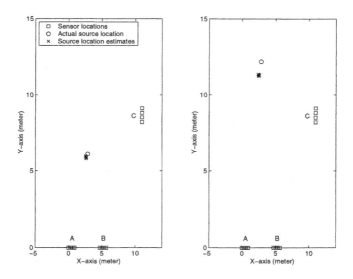

Fig. 3. Source localization of white Gaussian signal using AML DOA cross bearing in an outdoor environment.

5.3   Simulation Results of SVM Classification

We attempt to discriminate between two sources (a Harley motorcycle and a car from microphone data collected by BAE, Austin, TX, in Oct. 2002) based on the magnitude spectrum of their acoustic signals. A total of 382 training vectors were acquired. For each time signal, sampled at 5 kHz, we used a window of 1000 samples and moved the window by 100 samples until the end of the signal was reached. For each time window, we took the magnitude of the FFT, saving only the first 200 frequency bins to make up each training vector.

Shown in figure (5) is the solution of (16) for various γs. We see that for sufficiently large γ, the margin becomes small enough such that $1^T u$ is reduced to 0, $i.e.$, the training vectors are separable.

Figure (6) shows the result of testing our SVM classifier on source spectra estimated via the AML algorithm. The plot shows the fraction of misclassified

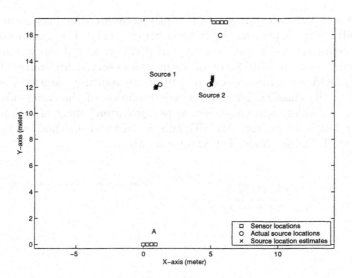

Fig. 4. Two-source localization using AML DOA cross bearing with alternating projection in an outdoor environment.

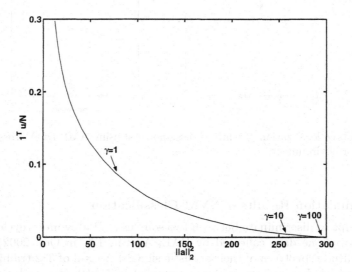

Fig. 5. Tradeoff curve between $\|a\|_2$ and $\mathbf{1}^T u$.

testing vectors as a function of the source SNR for γ set to 1,10, and 100. As expected, we see that for the larger values of γ, which corresponds to larger $\|a\|$ and hence smaller margin width, the classifier performs slightly worse at low SNRs and slightly better at high SNRs. This phenomenon illustrates the tradeoff between robustness and misclassification.

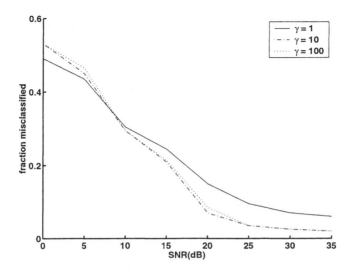

Fig. 6. Fraction of misclassified testing vectors from estimated source spectra as a function of SNR.

6   Conclusions

In this paper, an AML algorithm is derived for multiple sources DOA and spectra estimation. The source location can then be obtained via cross bearing from several widely separated arrays. Furthermore, the proposed SVM algorithm can be applied to the target classification based on the estimated source spectra. Theoretical analysis based on the CRB formula is also derived. Simulation and experimental results demonstrated the effectiveness of the AML and SVM algorithms.

Acknowledgments. We wish to thank J. Reich, F. Zhao, and P. Cheung of PARC, Palo Alto, CA, for supplying the data used in section 5.2 and S. Beck and J. Reynolds of BAE, Austin, TX, for supplying the data used in section 5.3. This work is partially supported by DARPA SensIT program under contract AFRL/IFG 315 330-1865 and AROD-MURI PSU contract S0126.

References

1. J. Agre and L. Clare, "An integraed arcitecture for cooperative sensing and networks," Computer, vol. 33, pp. 106–108, May 2000.
2. G.J. Pottie and W.J. Kaiser, "Wireless integrated network sensors," Comm. of the ACM, vol. 43, pp. 51–58, May 2000.
3. R.O. Schmidt, "Multiple emitter location and signal parameter estimation," IEEE Trans. on Antenna and Propagation, vol. AP-34, no. 3, pp. 276–80, Mar. 1986.

4. F.C. Schweppe, "Sensor array data processing for multiple signal sources," IEEE Trans. Information Theory, vol. IT-14, pp. 294–305, 1968.
5. I. Ziskine ad M. Wax, "Maximum likelihood localization of multiple sources by alternating projection," IEEE Trans. Acoust., Speech, and Signal Processing, vol. ASSP-36, no. 10, pp. 1553–60, Oct. 1988.
6. T.L. Tung, K. Yao, C.W. Reed, R.E. Hudson, D. Chen, and J.C. Chen, "Source localization and time delay estimation using constrained least squares and best path smoothing", Proc.SPIE, vol. 3807, Jul 1999, pp. 220–23.
7. J.C. Chen, R.E. Hudson, and K. Yao, "Maximum-likelihood source localization and unknown sensor location estimation for wideband signals in the near-field," IEEE Trans. on Signal Processing, vol. 50, no. 8, pp. 1843–54, Aug. 2002.
8. P. Stocia and A. Nehorai, "MUSIC, Maximum Likelihood, and Cramer-Rao Bound," IEEE Trans. Acoust. Speech, and Signal Processing, vol. 37. no. 5, pp. 720–41, May 1989.
9. L. Yip, J.C. Chen, R.E. Hudson, and K. Yao, "Cramer-Rao bound analysis of wideband source localization and DOA estimation," in Proc. SPIE, vol. 4971, Jul. 7–11, 2002
10. S.M. Kay, Fundamentals of Statistical signal Processing:Estimation Theory, Prentice-Hall, New Jersey, 1993.
11. MOSEK v2.0 User's manual, 2002. Available from http://www.mosek.com.
12. B. Scholkopf and A. Smola. Learning with Kernels. MIT Press, Cambridge, MA, 2002.
13. R.J. Vanderbei. LOQO: An interior point code for quadratic programming. Optimization Methods and Software, 11:451–484, 1999.
14. V. N. Vapnik. The Nature of Statistical Learning Theory. Springer, New York, NY, 1995.

Energy Based Acoustic Source Localization

Xiaohong Sheng and Yu-Hen Hu*

University of Wisconsin – Madison,
Department of Electrical and Computer Engineering
Madison WI 53706, USA,
sheng@ece.wisc.edu, hu@engr.wisc.edu,
http://www.ece.wisc.edu/~sensit

Abstract. A novel source localization approach using acoustic energy measurements from the individual sensors in the sensor field is presented. This new approach is based on the acoustic energy decay model that acoustic energy decays inverse of distance square under the conditions that the sound propagates in the free and homogenous space and the targets are pre-detected to be in a certain region of the sensor field. This new approach is power efficient and needs low communication bandwidth and therefore, is suitable for the source localization in the distributed sensor network system. Maximum Likelihood (*ML*) estimation with Expectation Maximization (*EM*) solution and *projection* solution are proposed to solve this energy based source location (*EBL*) problem. Cramer-Rao Bound (*CRB*) is derived and used for the sensor deployment analysis. Experiments and simulations are conducted to evaluate *ML* algorithm with different solutions and to compare it with the Nonlinear Least Square (*NLS*) algorithm using energy ratio function that we proposed previously. Results show that energy based acoustic source localization algorithms are accurate and robust.

1 Introduction

Efficient collaborative signal processing algorithms that consume less energy for computation and communication are important in wireless distributed sensor network communication system [1]. An important collaborative signal processing task is source localization. The objective is to estimate the positions of the moving targets within a sensor field that is monitored by a sensor network. In this paper, our focus will be on collaborative source localization based on acoustic signatures.

Most localization methods depend on three types of physical variables measured by or derived from sensor readings for localization: time delay of arrival (*TDOA*), direction of arrival (*DOA*) and received sensor signal strength or power. *DOA* can be estimated by exploiting the phase difference measured at receiving sensors [2], [3], [4], [5],[6] and is applicable in the case of a coherent, narrow band source. *TDOA* is suitable for broadband source and has been extensively

---

* This project is supported by DARPA under grant no. F 30602-00-2-0555

F. Zhao and L. Guibas (Eds.): IPSN 2003, LNCS 2634, pp. 285–300, 2003.

investigated [7], [8] [9], [10], [11], [12]. In practice, *DOA* measurements typically require costly antenna array on each node. The *TDOA* techniques require a high demand on the accurate measurement or estimation of time delay. In contrast, received sensor signal strength is comparatively much easier and less costly to obtain from the time series recordings from each sensor.

In [13], we show that, for single target at noiseless situation, each energy ratio dictates that the potential target location must be on a hyper-sphere within the sensor field. With noise taken into account, the target location is solved as the position that is closest to all the hyper-spheres formed by all energy ratios in the least square sense. Using this energy ratio function, the source energy is eliminated, the task of source localization estimation can be simplified by solving a Nonlinear Least Square (*NLS*) problem. Yet, this method can only be used for single target localization.

In this paper, we presented a novel approach to estimate the source location based on acoustic energy measured at individual sensors in the sensor field. We set up an acoustic energy decay model in the free and homogenous (no gusty wind) space under the conditions that the acoustic sources are not far away from the sensors and also not too close to the sensors so that they can be treated as omni-directional points.

Based on this acoustic energy decay model, we presented a new approach using acoustic energy measurements from the individual sensors in the sensor field to locate the targets in the region. Maximum Likelihood (*ML*) estimation with Expectation Maximization (*EM*) solution and project solution using *Exhaustive Search (ES)* and *Multi-Resolution (MR) search* are proposed to solve this *EBL* problem. *Cramer-Rao Bound (CRB)* is derived and used to analyze the sensor deployment to improve the performance of *EBL* algorithms.

Experiments and simulations were conducted to verify the energy decay model and to evaluate different algorithms and solutions of this *EBL* problem. Results show that energy based localization with *ML* estimation using *projection* solution outperforms other method by the cost of heavy computation burden. *Projection* solution with *MR* search reduces the computation burden a lot with the cost of reducing the performance a little bit.

Performance variation of *ML* estimation when targets have different energy intensity is also analyzed. It shows that, when the two targets have significant difference of energy source, the target with smaller energy becomes more ambiguous, and therefore, we get less accurate localization estimation for that target.

This paper is organized as follows: In section2, we formulate the acoustic energy decay model in the sensor network system when certain conditions are satisfied. Based on this energy decay model, we derive *ML* estimation and its *EM* solution and *projection* solution with *MR* and *exhaustive* search to solve this *EBL* problem. In section 3, we derive the *CRB* for this *EBL* problem. The effect of sensor deployment to the *CRB* is also analyzed in this section. Experiments and simulations are provided in section 4 to evaluate and compare different algorithms and solutions for solving the *EBL* problems. Conclusion and future work are given in section 5.

2   Energy-Based Source Localization

Energy-based source localization is motivated by a simple observation that the sound level decreases when the distance between sound source and the listener becomes large. By modelling the relation between sound level (energy) and distance from the sound source, one may estimate the source location using multiple energy reading at different, known sensor locations.

2.1   An Acoustic Energy Decay Model

The way sound propagates with the distance from the source is dependent on the size and shape of the source, the surrounding environment, prevailing air currents and the frequencies of the propagating sound. Other factors that may affect sound propagation may include wind direction, strength of wind, vegetation such as forest and other obstructions.

To simplify the problem, we make some assumptions in developing the energy decay model for energy based source localization in the wireless sensor network system. These assumptions are normally satisfied in certain sensor network systems. The assumptions we made are:

1. Sound propagates in the free air,

2. Target is pre-detected to be in a particular region of a sensor field. The region size is not very big so that targets are not far from the sensors. (For example, in our experiment, the region size is about $100 * 100M^2$)

3. Sound source can still be treated as an omni-directional point. (We can assume the dimension of the engine of the vehicle is relative small compared with the distance between the sensor and the vehicle).

4. The propagation medium (air) is roughly homogenous (i.e. no gusty wind) and there is no sound reverberation.

In such environment, the acoustic intensity attenuated at a rate that is inversely proportional to the distance between source and the sensor [14]. Since sound waveform is additive, the acoustic wave intensity signature received by each sensor is:

$$x_i(n) = s_i(n) + \nu_i(n) \tag{1}$$

Where: $s_i(n) = \gamma_i \sum_{k=1}^{K} \frac{a_k(n - t_{ki})}{\|\boldsymbol{\rho}_k(n - t_{ki}) - \mathbf{r}_i\|}$ and $i = 1, 2, ...N$

In the above equation, $x_i(n)$ is the nth acoustic signature sampled on the ith sensor over a time interval $[1/f_s]$ by a matched filter, f_s is the sampling frequency; $\nu_i(n)$ is the zero-mean additive white Gaussian noise (AWGN) on the nth time interval; K is the number of targets; N is the number of the sensors of the particular region in the sensor field; $a_k(n - t_{ki})$ is a scalar denoting the acoustic source intensity emitted by the kth target; t_{ki} is the propagation delay from the kth source to the ith sensor; $\boldsymbol{\rho}_k$ is the $p \times 1$ vector denoting the coordinates of the kth target; $\mathbf{r}_i$ is a $p \times 1$ vector denoting the Cartesian coordinates of the ith stationary sensor; p is the dimension of location; γ_i is a scaling factor corresponding to the sensor gain of the ith acoustic sensor.

Assume $s_i(n)$ and $v_i(n)$ are uncorrelated, a_{k_1} and a_{k_2} are uncorrelated for $k_1 \neq k_2$, $E[v_i(n)] = 0$, and $E[a_k(n)] = 0$, we get:

$$E\left[x_i^2(n)\right] = E\left[s_i^2(n)\right] + E\left[v_i^2(n)\right] \tag{2}$$

where $E\left[s_i^2(n)\right] = g_i \sum_{k=1}^{K} \frac{S_k(n - t_{ki})}{|\boldsymbol{\rho}_k(n - t_{ki}) - \mathbf{r}_i|^2}$

In above, $g_i = \gamma_i^2$ and $S_k(n - t_{ki}) = E\left[a_k^2(n - t_{ki})\right]$.

Since we assume that the targets are pre-detected to be in a particular region of a sensor field and the region size is not big, we can assume that the targets are not far from the sensors in the region. Therefore, the propagation delay t_{ki} is small enough that we can assume: $a(n - t_{ki}) \approx a(n)$ and $\boldsymbol{\rho}(n - t_{ki}) \approx \boldsymbol{\rho}(n)$.

The expectation of energy is calculated by averaging over a time window $T = M/f_s$, where M is the number of sample points we used for averaging the energy, f_s is the sampling frequency. Denote $E\left[x_i^2(n)\right]$ as $y_i(t)$, $E\left[a_k^2(n)\right]$ as $y_s(t)$ and $E\left[v_i^2(n)\right]$ as $\varepsilon_i(t)$, we get the energy decay model as:

$$y_i(t) = y_s(t) + \varepsilon_i(t) = g_i \sum_{j=1}^{K} \frac{S_j(t)}{\| \boldsymbol{\rho}_j(t) - \mathbf{r}_i \|^2} + \varepsilon_i(t) \tag{3}$$

Where $t = \frac{T}{2}, \frac{3T}{2}, \frac{5T}{2}, \dots$

Background noise $v_i(n)$ is independent zero mean AWGN with variance σ_n^2, $v_i^2(n)$ is independent χ^2 distributed with mean σ_n^2 and variance $\frac{2\sigma_n^4}{M}$. If M is sufficiently large (practically $M > 30$), by central limit theorem, ε_i is approximately normal: $\varepsilon \sim N(\sigma_n^2, \frac{2\sigma_n^4}{M})$.

2.2   Maximum Likelihood Estimation for *EBL* Problem

To simplify our notation, in the following parts, we will not denote time t explicitly in our equation. All parameters refer to the same time window automatically, i.e., we denote y_i for $y_i(t)$.

Following we will introduce the *ML* estimation with different solutions to estimate the source location. Note that the estimation is based on single frame of energy readings from different individual sensors. Estimation based on sequential energy readings are under developing.

Define

$$\mathbf{Z} = \left[\frac{y_1 - \mu_1}{\sigma_1} \; \frac{y_2 - \mu_2}{\sigma_2} \; \cdots \; \frac{y_N - \mu_N}{\sigma_N} \right]^{\Gamma} \tag{4}$$

Equation (3) can be simplified as:

$$\mathbf{Z} = \mathbf{GDS} + \boldsymbol{\xi} = \mathbf{HS} + \boldsymbol{\xi} \tag{5}$$

Where:

$$\mathbf{S} = \left[S_1 \; S_2 \cdots S_K \right]^{\Gamma} \tag{6}$$

$$\mathbf{H} = \mathbf{GD} \tag{7}$$

$$\mathbf{G} = diag \left[\frac{g_1}{\sigma_1} \; \frac{g_2}{\sigma_2} \; \cdots \; \frac{g_n}{\sigma_N} \right] \tag{8}$$

$$\mathbf{D} = \begin{bmatrix} \frac{1}{d_{11}^2} & \frac{1}{d_{12}^2} & \cdots & \frac{1}{d_{1K}^2} \\ \frac{1}{d_{21}^2} & \frac{1}{d_{22}^2} & \cdots & \frac{1}{d_{2K}^2} \\ \vdots & \vdots & \ddots & \vdots \\ \frac{1}{d_{n1}^2} & \frac{1}{d_{n2}^2} & \cdots & \frac{1}{d_{NK}^2} \end{bmatrix} \tag{9}$$

$d_{ij} = |\boldsymbol{\rho}_j - \mathbf{r}_i|$ is the Euclidean distance between the ith sensor and the jth source.

Then, $\xi_i = \frac{(\varepsilon_i - \mu_i)}{\sigma_i} \sim N(0, 1)$, $z_i = \frac{y_i - \mu_i}{\sigma_i} \sim N\left(\frac{g_i}{\sigma_i} \sum_{j=1}^{K} \frac{S_j}{d_{ij}^2}, 1 \right)$

The unknown parameters θ in the above function is:

$$\boldsymbol{\theta} = \left[\boldsymbol{\rho}_1^T \; \boldsymbol{\rho}_2^T \; \cdots \; \boldsymbol{\rho}_K^T \; S_1 \; S_2 \; \cdots \; S_K \right]^T$$

The log-likelihood function of equation (5) is:

$$\ell(\boldsymbol{\theta}) \sim \frac{-1}{2} \sum_{i=1}^{N} \| z_i - \frac{g_i}{\sigma_i} \sum_{j=1}^{K} \frac{S_j}{d_{ij}^2} \|^2 = \frac{-1}{2} \| \mathbf{Z} - \mathbf{GDS} \|^2 \tag{10}$$

ML estimate of the parameters $\boldsymbol{\theta}$ is the values that maximize $\ell(\boldsymbol{\theta})$, or equivalently, minimize

$$L(\boldsymbol{\theta}) = \| \mathbf{Z} - \mathbf{GDS} \|^2 \tag{11}$$

Equation (11) has $K(p+1)$ unknown parameters, there must be at least $K(p+1)$ or more sensors reporting acoustic energy readings to yield an unique solution to this nonlinear least square problem.

Expectation Maximization Solution. Define pseudoinverse of $\mathbf{H}$ as $\mathbf{H}^\dagger$, perform reduced SVD of $\mathbf{H}$, and setting $\frac{\partial L}{\partial \mathbf{S}}$ to be zero, we get:

$$\mathbf{S} = \mathbf{H}^\dagger \mathbf{Z} \tag{12}$$

Where:

$$\mathbf{H} = \mathbf{GD} = \mathbf{U}_H \boldsymbol{\Sigma}_H \mathbf{V}_H^T \tag{13}$$

$$\mathbf{H}^\dagger = \left(\mathbf{H}^T \mathbf{H} \right)^{-1} \mathbf{H}^T \tag{14}$$

Now, set the gradient of L with respect to $\boldsymbol{\rho}_j$ to zero, we get:

$$\nabla_{\boldsymbol{\rho}_j} L = 2 s_j \sum_{i=1}^{N} \frac{g_i}{\sigma_i} \left(\frac{\boldsymbol{\rho}_j - \mathbf{r}_i}{d_{ij}^4} \right) \left(z_i - \frac{g_i}{\sigma_i} \sum_{m=1}^{K} \frac{s_m}{d_{im}^2} \right) = 0 \tag{15}$$

Where the relation

$$\nabla_{\rho_j} \left(\frac{1}{d_{im}^2} \right) = \begin{cases} \frac{\rho_m - r_i}{-d_{im}^4}, & j = m \\ 0, & j \neq m \end{cases}$$

is used. Solving equation (15) for j, we have

$$\rho_j = \frac{\sum_{i=1}^{N} \frac{g_i}{\sigma_i} \left(\frac{1}{d_{ij}^4} \right) \left(z_i - \frac{g_i}{\sigma_i} \sum_{m=1}^{K} \frac{s_m}{d_{im}^2} \right) r_i}{\sum_{i=1}^{N} \frac{g_i}{\sigma_i} \left(\frac{1}{d_{ij}^4} \right) \left(z_i - \frac{g_i}{\sigma_i} \sum_{m=1}^{K} \frac{s_m}{d_{im}^2} \right)} \tag{16}$$

Equation (16) represents Kp nonlinear constraints on the target location coordinates $\{\rho_j, 1 \leq j \leq K\}$. Note that ρ_j appears on both sides of equation (16) because d_{ij} contains ρ_j implicitly. ρ_j can't be solved explicitly. Yet, we can solve it by iterative procedure, a special case of Expectation Maximization (EM) algorithm [15]. In [16], it is proved that such special case of EM algorithm is guaranteed to be convergence (in fact, all EM algorithms are guaranteed to be convergence). Besides, it avoids the complexities of non-linear optimization algorithms. The procedure of this algorithm is as follows:

EM Algorithm

Initialization: Initial estimates of $\{\rho_j, 1 \leq j \leq K\}$

Repeat until convergence

Expectation Step. Estimate **S** using equation (12), update **S**.

Maximization Step. Substitute **S** into equation (16), update ρ_j

Projection Solution with (MR) Search. Insert (12) into the cost function (11), we get modified cost function as follows:

$$\arg_{\{\rho_1, \rho_2, \dots \rho_k\}} \min L = \arg_{\{\rho_1, \rho_2, \dots \rho_k\}} \min \left(\mathbf{Z}^T (\mathbf{I} - \mathbf{P}_H)^T (\mathbf{I} - \mathbf{P}_H) \mathbf{Z} \right)$$

$$= \arg_{\{\rho_1, \rho_2, \dots \rho_k\}} \max \left(\mathbf{Z}^T \mathbf{P}_H^T \mathbf{Z} \right) = \arg_{\{\rho_1, \rho_2, \dots \rho_k\}} \max \mathbf{Z}^T \mathbf{U}_H \mathbf{U}_H^T \mathbf{Z} \tag{17}$$

Where

$$\mathbf{P}_H = \mathbf{H}(\mathbf{H}^T \mathbf{H})^{-1} \mathbf{H}^T = \mathbf{U}_H \mathbf{U}_H^T \tag{18}$$

is the projection matrix of **H**.

For single source, $j = 1$,

$$\mathbf{H} = \left[\frac{g_1}{\sigma_1 d_1^2}, \frac{g_2}{\sigma_2 d_2^2}, \cdots, \frac{g_n}{\sigma_n d_n^2} \right]^T, \qquad \mathbf{U_H} = \frac{\mathbf{H}}{\| \mathbf{H} \|}$$

Exhaustive search can be used to get the source location to maximize function (17). However, the computation complexity is very high. For example, suppose our detected search region is 128×128, if we use *exhaustive* search using the grid size of 8×8, we need 256^K times of search for every estimation point, where K is the number of the targets. Rather, we can use MR search to reduce the number of search times. For example, we can use the initial search grid size 16×16 followed by the fine search grid size 8×8, then, the number of search times is reduced to $64^K + 4^K$. For two targets, it needs 4112 search times using MR search with this search strategy and 256^2 search times using *exhaustive* search to get one estimation. We can further reduce the number of search times by reducing our search region based on the previous location estimation, the time interval between two localization operation, possible vehicle speed and estimation error. In our simulation, all these conditions are used. The search area we used for the *projection* solution is $(x_i - 32, x_i + 32) \times (y_i - 32, y_i + 32)$, where (x_i, y_i) is the previous estimation location of the ith target. Therefore, for single target, we need only 20 search; for two targets, we need 272 search for every localization estimation, which is feasible for our distributed wireless networking system.

3   Cramer-Rao Bounds and Sensor Deployment Analysis

Cramer-Rao Bound (CRB) is a theoretical lower bound of the variance that we can reach for the unbiased estimation. It is useful to indicate the performance bounds of a particular algorithm. CRB also facilitates analysis of factors that impact most on the performance of an algorithm. CRB is defined as the inverse of the *Fisher Matrix*:

$$\mathbf{J} = -E \left(\frac{\partial}{\partial \theta} \left[\frac{\partial}{\partial \theta} \ln f_{\boldsymbol{\theta}}(\mathbf{Z}) \right] \right)$$

For the problem with log-likelihood function described as equation (10), *Fisher matrix* is:

$$\mathbf{J} = \frac{\partial \left(\mathbf{DS} \right)^T}{\partial \theta} \mathbf{G}^T \mathbf{G} \frac{\partial \left(\mathbf{DS} \right)}{\partial \theta^T} \tag{19}$$

$$\frac{\partial \mathbf{DS}}{\partial \theta^T} = \left[\begin{array}{cccc} \frac{\partial \mathbf{DS}}{\partial \rho_1^T} & \frac{\partial \mathbf{DS}}{\partial \rho_2^T} & \cdots & \frac{\partial \mathbf{DS}}{\partial \rho_K^T} & \frac{\partial \mathbf{DS}}{\partial \mathbf{S}^T} \end{array} \right] \tag{20}$$

$$\frac{\partial \mathbf{DS}}{\partial \mathbf{S}^T} = \mathbf{D} \tag{21}$$

$$\mathbf{B}_j = \frac{\partial \mathbf{DS}^T}{\partial \rho_j} = \left[\begin{array}{cccc} \frac{-2S_j}{d_{1j}^3} \mathbf{b}_{1j} & \frac{-2S_j}{d_{2j}^3} \mathbf{b}_{2j} & \cdots & \frac{-2S_j}{d_{Nj}^3} \mathbf{b}_{Nj} \end{array} \right]^T \tag{22}$$

In above equation, $\mathbf{b}_{ij}$ is the unit vector from source j to sensor i, which can be expressed as:

$$\mathbf{b}_{ij} = \frac{\partial d_{ij}}{\partial \rho_j} = \frac{\rho_j - \mathbf{r}_i}{d_{ij}}$$

Define:

$$\mathbf{B} = \left[\begin{array}{cccc} \mathbf{B}_1 & \mathbf{B}_2 & \cdots & \mathbf{B}_K \end{array} \right] \tag{23}$$

We get the *Fisher Matrix* **J** as follows:

$$\mathbf{J} = \begin{bmatrix} \mathbf{B^T} \\ \mathbf{D^T} \end{bmatrix} \mathbf{G^T G} \begin{bmatrix} \mathbf{B} & \mathbf{D} \end{bmatrix} \tag{24}$$

Note that in the above equations, **J** is $(p+1)K \times (p+1)K$ matrix, $\mathbf{B}_j$ is $N \times p$ matrix, **B** is $n \times Kp$, **D** is $N \times K$ matrix, **G** is $N \times N$ matrix and $\mathbf{b}_{ij}$ is $p \times 1$ vector

The CRB is:

$$\mathbf{J^{-1}} = \left(\begin{bmatrix} \mathbf{B^T} \\ \mathbf{D^T} \end{bmatrix} \mathbf{G^T G} \begin{bmatrix} \mathbf{B} & \mathbf{D} \end{bmatrix} \right)^{-1} \tag{25}$$

For single target, the formula is reduced to:

$$\mathbf{J} = \begin{bmatrix} \mathbf{J}_{11} & \mathbf{J}_{12} \\ \mathbf{J}_{21} & \mathbf{J}_{22} \end{bmatrix} \tag{26}$$

Where:

$$\mathbf{J}_{11} = \sum_{i=1}^{n} \frac{4s^2 g_i^2}{\sigma_i^2 d_i^6} \mathbf{b}_i \mathbf{b}_i^T \tag{27}$$

$$\mathbf{J}_{21}^T = \mathbf{J}_{12} = -2s \sum_{i=1}^{n} \frac{g_i^2}{\sigma_i^2 d_i^5} \mathbf{b}_i \tag{28}$$

$$J_{22} = \sum_{i=1}^{n} \frac{g_i^2}{\sigma_i^2 d_i^4} \tag{29}$$

The variance of the unknown parameter estimation is bounded by the CRB, i.e.

$$var\left(\widehat{\rho_{ij}}\right) \geq \left(J^{-1}\right)_{(i-1)p+j,(i-1)p+j} \quad \{i = 1 \cdots K, \ j = 1 \cdots p\}$$

Where $var\left(\widehat{\rho_{ij}}\right)$ is the variance of the estimation location for i^{th} source $(\boldsymbol{\rho}_i)$, at j^{th} coordinate direction.

From above *CRB* equation, we know that *CRB* is sensitive to the overall weighted $\left(\frac{g_i}{\sigma_i}\right)$ distance from the targets to the sensors. The longer the distance, the bigger *CRB* could be. When the sensors are deployed close to the road, the weighted overall distance from the targets to the sensors is reduced. Therefore, we can get smaller *CRB*. When the sensors are dense, there are more sensors close to the targets, therefore, smaller *CRB* we can approach. By *Chebyshev's* inequality, we know that the probability of estimation error is less than the ratio of the variance of that random variable and the square of that estimation error, i.e.

$$P\left(\mid X - E\left(X\right)\mid \geq a\right) \leq \frac{Var(X)}{a^2}$$

Since the variance is lower bounded by the *CRB* and for *ML* estimation, variance asymptotically approaches its *CRB*, the bigger the *CRB*, the higher probability of the estimation error we might get. Using dense sensors that are close to the road gives smaller *CRB*, and therefore, improves the performance in the sense that, $\{\forall a > 0, P(|\widehat{X} - X| > a)\}$ is smaller.

Simulations of different sensor deployment with two targets producing similar acoustic energy moving in opposite direction are conducted to check the relation between *CRB* and the sensor deployment. The results are shown in Fig.1 and Fig.2. These results are consistent to our theoretical analysis. Note that when two targets are close to each other, we have more ambiguity, and therefore, the *CRB* increases abruptly at the middle part in Fig. 2.

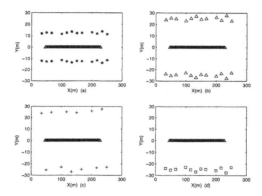

Fig. 1. Sensor Deployment, (a) dense sensor, (b) dense sensor close to road, (c) loose sensor located at one side, (d) loose sensor located at two side.

4   Experiments and Simulations

4.1   Experiments

Sensor Network System. The raw signals were recorded by 29 sensor nodes deployed along the road in the sensor field, CA in November 2001, sponsored by the DARPA ITO SensIT project. The data we used to evaluate *EBL* algorithms were taken from 15 acoustic sensors recording the signatures of AAV vehicle going from east to west during a time period of ∼ 2 minutes. Figure 3 shows the road coordinates and sensor node positions, both supplied by the global positioning system (GPS). The sensor field is divided into two regions as shown in the above figure. Region 1 is composed of node $1, 41, 42, 46, 48, 49, 50, 51$. Region 2 is composed of node $52, 53, 54, 55, 56, 58, 59$. In region 1, node 1 is chosen as manager node, others are detection node. In region 2, node 58 is chosen as manager node, others are detection node.

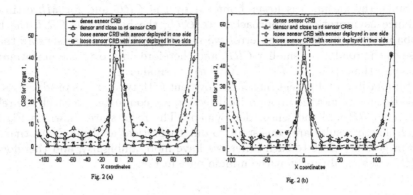

Fig. 2. CRB for different sensor deployment shown as Fig. 1, (a) *CRB* for target 1, (b) *CRB* for target 2.

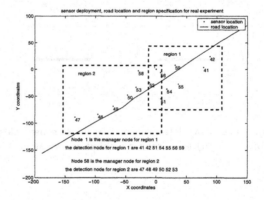

Fig. 3. Sensor deployment, road coordinate and region specification for experiments

The region is activated by our tracking algorithm implemented by Kalman filter. When the region is activated, multi-modality node detection and region detection are performed. Once region detection announces the detection of the target, *EBL* localization algorithm is activated and performed to locate the targets using the most recent reported acoustic energy, noise mean and variance from its detection nodes. The sampling frequency is fs = 4960Hz. The energy is computed by averaging the T=0.75sec non-overlapping data segment (3720 data points).

Fig. 4(a) shows the AAV ground truth and the localization results based on the *ML* algorithm with projection solution and *NLS* algorithm. *MR* search is used to estimate the location. The grid size we chose is: 4*4, 2*2, 1*1. Note that the missing ground-truth points in this figure are the miss-detection points by our multi-modality detector and therefore, there is no localization operation at these points.

To evaluate *ML* algorithm and compare it with *NLS* we proposed in [13] for *EBL* problem, we first compute the localization errors defined as the Euclidian distance between the location estimates and the true target locations for the time when region detection is announced. The true target location can be determined since they must be positioned on the target trajectory which can be extracted from GPS log. These localization errors are then grouped into different error range, i.e., $0 \sim 10, 10 \sim 20, ...40 \sim 50, \geq 50$. We call it as error histogram of our localization algorithm. Fig. 4(b) shows this localization error histogram for AAV localization.

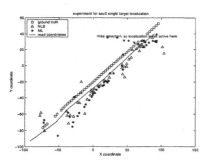 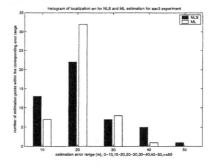

(a) AAV ground truth and localization estimation results

(b) Estimation error histogram for AAV experiment data

Fig. 4. AAV ground truth, localization estimation results and estimation error histogram based on ML algorithm with projection solution and NLS algorithm (MR search is used, grid size is 4*4, 2*2 and 1*1. Estimation results look bias from the ground-truth, see discussion for reasoning)

From experiment, we can see that, overall, both *ML* and *NLS* algorithms perform well estimations of target location. It verifies that inverse distance square acoustic energy decay model is suitable in the free space in normal situation. *ML* algorithm with projection solution outperforms to *NLS* algorithm in the sense that it has less estimation error. Besides, there are some points having estimation error bigger than 30 meters using *NLS* estimation. This says that *NLS* is not as stable as *ML* estimation with projection solution. However, *NLS* algorithm needs less bandwidth. This is because *NLS* doesn't use noise variance for its estimation while *ML* algorithm does need it. So, for *NLS* algorithm, we save about 1/4 bandwidth. (For *ML* estimation, detection nodes need to report acoustic energy, noise mean, noise variance and multi-modality binary node detection results in every 0.75 second).

Fig. 4 shows that the localization estimation results look bias from the real ground-truth. This can be caused by inaccurate GPS measurement. It can be seen that ground truth also looks bias from the road while in the experiment, vehicle moved along the road. We can also see that estimation results are closer and less biased to the road than to the ground-truth. In our works on parameter sensitivity analysis, we found that *EBL* algorithms are sensitive to the sensor gain, sharp background noise or sensor faults. Inaccurate measurement or estimation of these parameters can cause the estimation bias.

4.2 Simulations

Simulations for *ML* Estimation with *EM* Solution and *Projection* Solution for Multi-Target Localization. The simulation parameters were designed according to the experiment data described previously. From the experiment, we know that, for AAV vehicle, the maximum average energy (y_{max}) received by the acoustic sensor is around $y_{max} = 1.324e^{11}/2^{30}$ when the sensors are deployed as Fig. 3. Note that with this sensor deployment, the closest distance from the sensor to the road is about 15 meters. Using energy decay model, we know that AAV acoustic source energy is about $S = 2.78e^4$. Noise mean μ detected by our *CFAR* detector is from $0.01y_{max}$ to $0.04y_{max}$. Noise variance is in the range of $(1 \sim 2)\mu$. So, the maximum SNR received by the acoustic sensor for AAV is around $14db$ to $20db$.

Follow the experiment data, we designed a sensor field with twenty-one sensors scattering along the two sides of the road. The size of sensor field is 200×80 $meter^2$. Simulations were conducted by moving two-targets in opposite direction in the above sensor field. Fig. 5 shows the sensor deployment for this sensor field and the ground truth of the two targets.

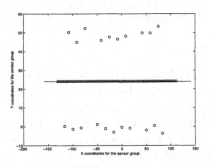

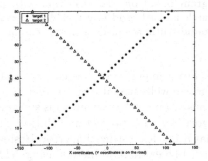

(a) sensor deployment and road coordinate for simulations

(b) Ground truth for two targets moving in the opposite direction

Fig. 5. Sensor deployment, road coordinate and ground truth of the two targets for the simulation

Two cases were run in the simulation. For case 1, the source energy of the two targets are similar, i.e., $S_1 = S = 2.78e^4$, $S_2 = 1.2S_1$. For case 2, the source energy of the two targets have significant difference, i.e., $S_1 = S$, $S_2 = 3S_1$. For each simulation case, we assume the acoustic source energy, S_1 and S_2, keep constant in the simulation time.

Background noise ε_i was generated by *matlab* noise generator. It is gaussian distributed with mean uniformly distributed on $(0.01 \sim 0.04)y_{max}$ and variance uniformly distributed on $(1 \sim 2)\mu$.

Using *ML* estimation algorithm with *projection* solution and *EM* solution, we can solve the location of the two targets at every time period. For *projection* solution, grid size we used for the *exhaustive* search is $8 * 8$. The grid size of *MR* search is $16 * 16$, $8 * 8$. Direct Monte Carlo simulations were performed with 100 trials for each simulation case.

To evaluate the *ML* algorithm with *projection* solution and *EM* solution for energy based multi-target source localization problem, we calculate the localization error which is defined as the distance error between the target ground-truth and the mean of estimation of 100 trials of the Direct Monte Carlo simulation at each target ground-truth. We also calculate the estimation standard deviation (*std*), and compare the *std* with the root of CRB. Fig.6 and Fig.7 show the estimation error and *std* of case 1.

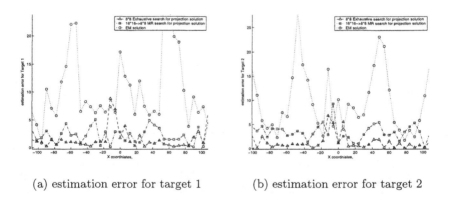

(a) estimation error for target 1   (b) estimation error for target 2

Fig. 6. Estimation errors for *projection* solution using *MR* search, *projection* solution using *exhaustive* search and *EM* solution.(a) target 1, (b) target 2 (sensor deployment and ground truth for the two targets are shown in Fig. 5; Noise is uniformly distributed from $0.01y_{max}$ to $0.04y_{max}$, $S_1 = y_{max}$, $S_2 = 1.2S_1$).

To evaluate the effects of different target energy ratio (S_2/S_1) on our algorithm, we calculate the estimation error difference for the two cases at every estimation point. The result was shown in Fig. 8.

From Fig.6 and Fig.7, we know that, for *projection* solution, *exhaustive* search has better performance than *MR* search since *MR* search is just approximate

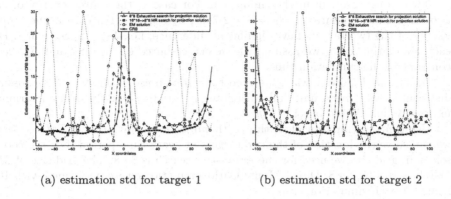

(a) estimation std for target 1   (b) estimation std for target 2

Fig. 7. Estimation standard deviation for *projection* solution using *MR* search, *projection* solution using *MR* search using *exhaustive* search and *EM* solution.(a) target 1, (b) target 2 (simulation condition is the same as Fig.6)

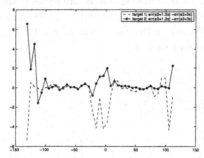

Fig. 8. Estimation error difference when two targets have different S_2/S_1

ML estimation. Yet, the degradation using *MR* search is small for most of time. Performance of *EM* solution is much worse than that of the projection solution. This is because *EM* solution is easy to track into the local minimum. Besides, *EM* solution is sensitive to the initial condition. The advantage of *EM* solution is that it has much less computation complexity. For most of time, it can get results within 6 or 7 iteration and so, it has less computation complexity while exhaustive search and *MR* search for the *projection* solution need to search in the entire effective sensor region. Fig.7 shows that the estimation variance of *ML* estimation with projection solution approaches its CRB. It concludes that *ML* estimation with projection solution is the optimum solution for the *EBL* problem when the prior probability of target location is unknown.

From Fig.8, we know that estimation error decreases for the target with higher acoustic energy. For the target with lower acoustic energy, estimation error increases, especially at the area where the two targets are close to each other or at the boundary of the sensor field. This is because the target with low energy is more ambiguous when the source of other target is much stronger.

The above multi-target localization is based on the assumption that we already detect the active region where the target is inside by our region detect algorithm and we know the number of targets in that active region. The region detection has been developed by the combination of CFAR detector, classification, data fusion and decision fusion. The number of multi-targets can be determined by multi-modality detection we have developed and space-time analysis of the energy sequences that we are developing recently.

5   Conclusion and Future Work

Collaborative energy-based acoustic source localization method has been presented. This method is based on the inverse distance square acoustic energy decay model under certain conditions. *ML* algorithm with different solutions is proposed to estimate multi-target source location. *CRB* is derived and be used for sensor deployment analysis. Experiments and simulations were conducted to evaluate the *ML* algorithm with different solutions and to compare the *ML* algorithm with *NLS* algorithm. Results show that energy based *ML* estimation using *projection* solution and *MR* search is robust, accurate, efficient.

Overall, *EBL* algorithms need low communication bandwidth since each sensor only reports energy reading, noise mean and variance (*NLS* doesn't need variance), and detection binary results to the manager node at every time period rather than at every time instant. Besides, it is power efficient. For detection node, it only calculates the average energy in the time period and performs energy-based CFAR detector (simple algorithm). For manager node, it performs simple voting algorithm and decision fusion algorithm. Manager node performs localization algorithm only if the region detection announces the targets. *ML* estimation with projection solution and MR search under the reduced search region saves the computation burden and so, saves the manager node battery further more. Detection node energy computation requires averaging of instantaneous power over a pre-defined time interval. Hence it is less susceptible to parameter perturbations, and so, the algorithm is robust.

From *CRB* analysis, we know that the performance of our localizer is related to the sensor deployment. The performance of the region detection is also related to the sensor deployment. Besides, our initial research on target number prediction based on the space-time analysis also shows the importance of the sensor deployment. In addition, sensor deployment also affects the sensitivity of the parameter perturbation. Therefore, the sensor deployment is very important in our sensor network communication. The optimum sensor deployment based on all these consideration will be conducted as our future work.

References

1. Li,D. Wong, K.D., Hu, Y. H., Sayeed, A. M.: Detection, classification, and tracking of targets. IEEE Signal Processing Magazine, **19**, (2002), 17–29
2. Haykin, S.: Array Signal Processing, Englewood-Cliffs, NJ: Prentice-Hall, (1985)

3. Taff, L. G.: Target localization from bearings-only observations, IEEE Trans. Aerosp. Electron., **3**, issue 1, (1997) 2–10
4. Oshman, Y., and Davidson, P.: Optimization of observer trajectories for bearings-only target localization, IEEE Trans. Aerosp. Electron., **35**, issue 3, (1999), 892–902
5. Kaplan, K. M., Le, Q., and Molnar, P.: Maximum likelihood methods for bearings-only target localization, Proc IEEE ICASSP, **5**, (2001), 3001–3004
6. Carter G. C.: Coherence and Time Delay Estimation, IEEE Press, 1993.
7. Brandstein, M., and Silverman, H.: A localization-error-based method for microphone-array design, Proc. ICASSP'96, Atlanta, GA, (1996), 901–904
8. Brandstein, M. S., Adcock, J. E., and Silverman,H. F.: A closed form location estimator for use with room environment microphone arrays, IEEE Trans. Speech and Audio Processing, vol. 5 (1997), 45–50
9. Yao, K., Hudson, R. E., Reed, C. W., Chen, D., and Lorenzelli, F.: Blind beamforming on a randomly distributed sensor array system, IEEE J. Selected areas in communications, **16** (1998) 1555–1567
10. Reed, C.W., Hudson, R., and Yao, K.: Direct joint source localization and propagation speed estimation. In Proc. ICASSP'99, Phoenix, AZ, (1999) 1169–1172
11. Special issue on time-delay estimation, IEEE Trans. ASSP **29**, (1981)
12. Smith, J.O., and Abel, J.S.: Closed form least square source location estimation from range difference measurements. IEEE Trans. ASSP **35** (1987) 1661–1669
13. Hu, Y.H., and Li, D.: Energy based source localization, IEEE Trans. ASSP, submitted, 2002
14. Kinsler, L.E., et al.: Fundamentals of Acoustics. NY, NY: John Wiley and Sons, Inc., 1982
15. Rabiner, L. R.: A Tutorial on Hidden Markov models and selected applications in speech recognition, Proceedings of the IEEE, vol. 77 **2**, (1989) 257–287
16. Bishop, L.M.: Neural Network for Pattern Recognition, Oxford University press, 1995, Chapter 2.

A Collaborative Approach to In-Place Sensor Calibration

Vladimir Bychkovskiy, Seapahn Megerian, Deborah Estrin, and
Miodrag Potkonjak

Department of Computer Science,
University of California, Los Angeles
{vladimir, destrin, seapahn, miodrag}@cs.ucla.edu

Abstract. Numerous factors contribute to errors in sensor measurements. In order to be useful, any sensor device must be calibrated to adjust its accuracy against the expected measurement scale. In large-scale sensor networks, calibration will be an exceptionally difficult task since sensor nodes are often not easily accessible and manual device-by-device calibration is intractable. In this paper, we present a two-phase post-deployment calibration technique for large-scale, dense sensor deployments. In its first phase, the algorithm derives relative calibration relationships between pairs of co-located sensors, while in the second phase, it maximizes the consistency of the pair-wise calibration functions among groups of sensor nodes. The key idea in the first phase is to use temporal correlation of signals received at neighboring sensors when the signals are highly correlated (i.e. sensors are observing the same phenomenon) to derive the function relating their bias in amplitude. We formulate the second phase as an optimization problem and present an algorithm suitable for localized implementation. We evaluate the performance of the first phase of the algorithm using empirical and simulated data.

Keywords: Sensor calibration, distributed calibration, consistency maximization, sensor networks, distributed algorithms, in-network processing, calibration routing

1 Introduction

The recent advent of sensor networks as enablers for completely new classes of applications, has not only captured the imagination of many a scientist and engineer in many a domain, but has also sparked the recognition of new classes of problems for the developers of sensor network systems and technology. Data inaccuracy and imprecision are two examples of inevitable challenges when dealing with the measurement of physical phenomena. These errors must be dealt with properly if sensor data are to be useful. Furthermore, these errors must ultimately be dealt with in the network to enable collaborative signal processing. Calibration traditionally refers to the process of correcting systematic errors

F. Zhao and L. Guibas (Eds.): IPSN 2003, LNCS 2634, pp. 301–316, 2003.

(biases) in sensor readings. The term has also often been used in reference to the procedure by which the raw outputs of sensors are mapped to standardized units. Traditional single-sensor calibration often relies on providing a specific stimulus with a known result, thus creating a direct mapping between sensor outputs and expected values. Consequently, such calibration for a sensor is often subject to specific ranges and operating condition restrictions, which are reported in the manufacturer specifications of the sensor. This type of calibration can be performed at the factory, during the production stage, and/or manually in the field. In addition to component level calibrations, sensors usually must be calibrated at the device level when used as part of a measurement system. Moreover, re-calibration is usually required in order to ensure proper operation of a measurement device, as ageing and other factors impact sensors and measurement hardware over time.

However, with large scale sensor networks, manual, single-sensor calibration schemes will not work well. In addition to the obvious scaling issues, the following are examples of factors that will also hinder such methods:

− Limited access to the sensors in the field
− Complex dynamic environmental effects on the sensors
− Sensor drift (age, decay, damage, etc)

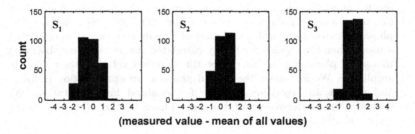

Fig. 1. Distribution of the noise in measured values reported by three light sensors measuring the same source

Consider the three histograms shown in figure 1 which correspond to the raw outputs of three photovoltaic elements connected to an analog to digital conversion circuit. Photovoltaic elements are small electronic devices that produce a voltage at their output pins based on the amount of incident light on their surface. This specific component is readily available in electronic supply stores and is quite inexpensive. It produces roughly 500mV in an average well-lit office space. The histograms correspond to the outputs of three individual sensors of this same type, each measuring the same light source under controlled conditions. The mean of the time-series data has been subtracted so that only the noise component in the measurement remains. The horizontal axis represents raw, uncalibrated values and thus, does not have a standard unit associated with it.

In the light-sensor example above, the errors in the measurements can be classified into 2 major categories as abstracted in figure 2. The vertical axis in the figure represents the probability and the horizontal axis represents the amplitude of a sensor output (i.e. the reported value). Note that figure 2 is only meant as an illustrative diagram and does not necessarily represent the exact characteristics of any specific sensor device. The two major classification of sensor errors are:

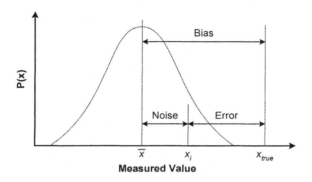

Fig. 2. Sensor measurement error terminology

- **Systematic Errors (*Bias*):** The bias is an offset in the mean amplitude of sensor readings $\bar{x}$ from the true value x_{true}. The bias may depend on time, the sensed phenomena, the environment, or other factors.
- **Random Errors (*Noise*):** This random component in the error may be due to external events that influence sensor readings, hardware noise, or other difficult-to-predict transient events. In some cases, the noise in measurements may be modeled using a specific distribution (such as Gaussian).

Throughout our discussions, we assume that the output characteristics of sensors are of this general type. For a given measurement (at a given time), the error is the difference from the reported value of the sensor and the true value, which we refer to as ground truth. The goal of calibration in general, and our collaborative calibration in particular, is to determine and correct *systematic* biases in sensor readings. In case of a light sensor, the bias can be due to the sensor or supporting hardware, or external factors such as dust particles on the protective lens of the sensor. In our subsequent discussions, when we refer to sensor "readings" we assume that the measurement noise has been filtered out, for example by using averaging over time, but that the systematic bias remains.

The main challenge in detecting the systematic errors autonomously is the lack of known stimuli against which sensor measurements can be calibrated. In this paper, we present a collaborative calibration scheme that addresses this problem. The scheme exploits the redundancies in sensor measurements under dense deployment scenarios and dynamically and autonomously derives calibration functions relating the biases of pairs of sensors. This scheme is in essence different than traditional calibration since it calibrates sensor outputs against the outputs of other sensors, utilizing redundancy. To achieve true calibrated results, one must have a reference point to the ground truth. In typical systems, this can be achieved by manually calibrating a subset of the sensors in the system, and allowing the calibration to adjust the remaining sensors based on the calibrated subset. Clearly the final calibration accuracy with respect to the real ground truth will also depend on the number and distribution of such reference points. However, in this paper, we focus our attention on the relative calibration errors between sensors.

1.1   Paper Organization

In the next section, we present the related work followed by the technical preliminaries section including several assumptions and definitions used in subsequent discussions. Section 4 contains the details of our two-phase calibration algorithm. Phase 1 is the main highlight of this paper which proposes an algorithm for deriving calibration relationships between pairs of co-located sensors. In phase 2, the goal is to improve the results of the first phase at a local level (including several nodes) since errors in measurements and inaccuracies in results will often yield inconsistent pair-wise relationships between different sensors. Results using both measured and simulated data are presented and discussed in section 5.2.

2   Related Work

The topic of sensor calibration is as old as sensors themselves. It is impractical to list all of the work that has been done in this area over centuries of human science. Thus, we focus on calibration techniques proposed for sensor networks
    In [1] authors address calibration of transmission power in the context of a signal strength based localization system. Even though a radio transceiver is not usually considered a sensor per se, the technique described in that paper can, potentially, be applied to more traditional sensors. The approach described in [1] formulates signal strength calibration as a global optimization problem and as written was not intended for distributed on-line deployment. Sensor fault-tolerance is an issue that is closely related to sensor calibration. In [2] the author suggests a methodology for the design of a fault-tolerant sensor. The author advocates increasing the reliability of a virtual sensor through the use of appropriate models of the phenomenon and replication of physical sensors. Our approach is similar to [2] in that it assumes particular models for sensor failures and phenomena. However, we focus on calibration of a network of physically distributed sensors as opposed to the fault-tolerance of a single sensor.
    A significant amount of calibration research work has been done in the context of array signal processing[3]. This research focuses on acoustic and radio

signals. Receiver *equalization* is defined as the calibration of the frequency response of a device. Issues such as time synchronization also come up in practice. Our approach is similar to *blind equalization*; it does not rely on known calibration sources. However, unlike blind equalization, our method does not assume any large-scale propagation models. Our method only requires understanding of the sensed phenomenon at a small scale, because sensors are assumed to be densely deployed.

The field of robotics has also contributed to in-place sensor calibration. Some of these calibration techniques take advantage of intrinsic sensor mobility. In [4], the authors suggest an approach to calibrating the perceived map of the world based on the data received from an inaccurate odometric sensor. Even though their work is drastically different for ours in its applications, the overall philosophy of the approaches is similar. The authors of [4] propose to derive the initial map of the world (a set of calibration functions in our case) based on the current information from a sensor. The inconsistencies of this map are later "relaxed" through a global optimization procedure.

3   Technical Preliminaries

We make the following assumptions about our target sensor systems

- Phenomenon
  - Known and limited spatial frequency (Nyquist)
  - High temporal frequency
- Sensors
  - Dense deployment: This indicates that we have multiple neighboring sensors sensing the same phenomenon and that calibration partitions do not occur.
  - Sensing is slow and has no drift within a calibration epoch with respect to the calibration process.
  - No angle-dependent gains in sensor measurements.
  - Due to time-synchronized nature of our calibration process, we assume there is no hysteresis or delay in sensor response.

Throughout this paper, we use the set S to denote the set of sensor nodes being considered. We denote the measurement reported by sensor $s_i \in S$ at time instance t as $s_i(t)$. We assume all reported measurements are real valued scalars.

Definition: A calibration function (CF), denoted as $F_{i,j}(x)$ is a real-valued function mapping the output x of sensor s_i to sensor s_j. For the sake of simplicity, we often omit the parameter x. Each function $F_{i,j}$ can also have an associated confidence weight $0 \le w_{i,j} \le 1$.

Definition: A calibration matrix (CM), denoted as $\mathbf{F}$, is a 2 dimensional $|S| \times |S|$ matrix such that each element $F_{i,j} \in \mathbf{F}$ is the calibration function mapping the output of sensors $s_i \in S$ to $s_j \in S$.

4   Calibration Algorithm

4.1   Overview

Our calibration algorithm consists of two phases. In its first phase, the algorithm derives relative calibration relationships between pairs of co-located sensors, while in the second phase, it maximizes the consistency of the pair-wise functions among groups of sensor nodes. The key idea in the first phase is to use temporal correlation of signals received at neighboring sensors when the signals are highly correlated (i.e. sensors are observing the same phenomenon) to derive the function relating their bias in amplitude. We formulate the second phase as an optimization problem.

4.2   Phase 1: Pair-Wise Calibration Functions

In the first phase of our algorithm we rely on a pairwise approach because of its scaling properties. This phase of the algorithm will perform well for any number and densities of sensors under the assumptions stated in section (sect. 3). Since all the computation here is based on only local data, scalability is unbounded.

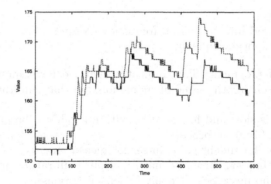

Fig. 3. Time-series data produced by a pair of uncalibrated sensors. Y-axis represents sensor values, X-axis depicts time at which a sample was taken.

Our algorithm consists of the following steps:

1. Collect time-series data in a synchronized manner.
2. Weight each potential data point.
3. Filter out irrelevant data points.
4. Fit a calibration function to the filtered data set.

Time synchronization of sampling is critical because we use temporal correlation to detect periods of time when sensors are observing the same event. A pair of values collected at exactly the same time by two sensors, i and j,

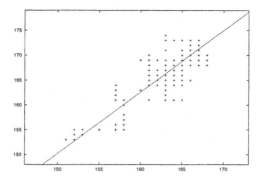

Fig. 4. Scatter plot of time synchronized signals. A data point on this plot is pair of data values taken by the two sensors at exactly the same instant in time. Y-axis corresponds to a value reported by the first sensor; X-axis corresponds to the value reported the second sensor.

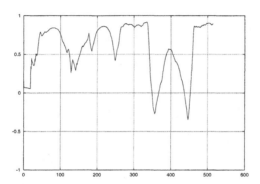

Fig. 5. Sliding window correlation of raw data as a function window time. Y-axis corresponds to the correlation value; X-axis corresponds to the window offset(time).

represents a *potential data point* of a calibration function $F_{i,j}$ between these sensors. It is *potential* because it may correspond to the same external stimulus. Fig. 3 shows two raw data streams aligned in time. If this pair of sensors had been observing the same phenomenon over the course of the whole experiment, we would be able to establish a relationship between them by fitting a line[1] through points on a scatter plot, Fig. 4. Uncorrelated events make it impossible to establish a relation from this data directly. For this reason, our algorithm filters out data points corresponding to periods of time when sensors observed uncorrelated phenomena.

---

[1] In general, a relationship between sensors can be represented by an arbitrary function. However, a line seems to be a good approximation for the class of sensor that we have used.

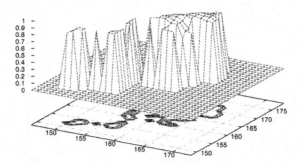

Fig. 6. 3D scatter plot. (x, y) value of each point of a surface corresponds to two sensor values taken at the same time. z-value of each point corresponds to the weight of the point derived through sliding window correlation.

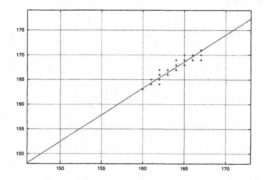

Fig. 7. Filtered scatter plot. It contains only the points believed to be relevant to the calibration relationship.

We use linear correlation to identify periods of time when co-located sensors observe the same phenomena. Our sensor devices exhibited linear behavior in the range of data values collected in the experiments[2]. High sensor density allows us to assume that neighboring sensors are likely to observe the same amplitude of the phenomenon. Fig. 5 shows a sliding window correlation of the same two sensors as a function of window offset. The size of the correlation window depends on the temporal frequency of the phenomenon. If correlated events come and go very quickly, large window size will fail to identify short periods of correlation. Small windows, on the other hand, may render the results of correlation insignificant from the statistical point of view. In our experiments we had the luxury of controlling the rate of change of the phenomenon; therefore, the window size was based on the known duration of correlation periods. A systematic method

---

[2] The ratio of the variances of the linear fit to a quadratic fit was around 2, whereas the ratios of quadratic to cubic and cubic to the forth power fit were close to 1

for deriving the correlation window size for different sensing applications is an open problem and is a subject of future work.

Based on the result of the sliding window correlation we establish weights of all potential data points. Initially weights of all potential data points are set to zero. Then, for all positions of a sliding window that produce a positive correlation coefficient we evaluate all potential data points included. If a point had positively contributed to the correlation of the current window, we increment its weight by the correlation coefficient of the window. The result of this procedure can be visualized as a 3D version of the scatter plot (see Fig. 6), where the height of each point determines its final weight.

The above heuristic provides means to rank potential data points according to their relevance to the relationship between the sensors. This allows us to filter out irrelevant points by picking potential data points with top ranks[3], *the top set*. The level of confidence in $F_{i,j}$ derived from this set can be related to the distribution of ranks in the top set. Choosing an appropriate size of the top set is not straight forward. Small set size may result in large error in the final relationship, due to filtering out of relevant data points. Large sets, on the other hand, are bound to contain more irrelevant data points, and thus may be noisy. In this study we have picked an arbitrary set size of 20 points. A systematic method for deriving a set size that maximizes "correctness" of the relationship is a subject of the future work.

After we have computed the top set, we proceed to fitting the calibration function, $F_{i,j}$. This procedure is similar to in-factory sensor calibration, but the stimuli are unknown. The nature of the calibration function depends on the type of sensors used[4]. For example, if the linear error in substrate doping in a semiconductor sensor are known to result in second order changes to sensor sensitivity, the calibration function for sensors of this type is very likely to be quadratic. For the purposes of this study we have assumed a linear calibration function. The result of fitting a line to the top set is shown in Fig. 7.[5]

4.3   Phase 2: Localized Consistency Maximization

Due to errors, the pair-wise calibration functions $F_{i,j}$ between pair of different nodes s_i and s_j, derived in the first phase of the algorithm, will not be globally consistent. More specifically, traversing the CFs along different paths will yield different calibrated results for a given node. In order to illustrate this problem,

---

[3] Direct thresholding may also be used. However, in some cases, the procedure may fail to establish the relationship due to the lack of potential data points above the threshold.

[4] If the difference in coupling of sensor to the environment needs to be accounted for, the relationship function should include corresponding terms.

[5] The pair-wise calibration algorithm described here does not limit the choice of calibration relationship. However, the use of linear correlation assumes that the inter-sensor relationship can be approximated by a linear transformation within the correlation window. In cases where this is not acceptable, it may be possible to use Spearman (rank) correlation instead of linear correlation.

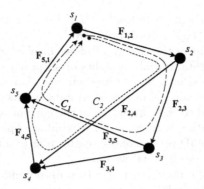

Fig. 8. An example of a calibration graph (CG)

consider the calibration graph (CG) depicted in figure 8. A CG in essence is the graphical representation of a calibration matrix. Each vertex in the CG represents a sensor node and each edge represents the corresponding CF $F_{i,j}$. The figure shows two possible calibration cycles C_1 and C_2 for the node s_1. For the sake of simplicity, we only show the CFs in one direction and omit the reverse mappings in the figure.

For a measured sensor value s_1:

$$\mathbf{C_1} : s_1' = F_{5,1}(F_{3,5}(F_{2,3}(F_{1,2}(s_1)))) \tag{1}$$
$$\mathbf{C_2} : s_1'' = F_{5,1}(F_{4,5}(F_{2,4}(F_{1,2}(s_1)))) \tag{2}$$

and in general, due to errors, $s_1 \neq s_1' \neq s_1''$.

Our goal here is, given a calibration matrix $\mathbf{F}$, to compute a new calibration matrix $\mathbf{F'}$ such that consistency is maximized. In order to formally discuss this problem, we must first establish our definition of consistency followed by an objective function which quantifies the consistency for $\mathbf{F}$.

As mentioned above, traversing different paths in the CG can result in inconsistent calibrated values for a node. Furthermore, the number of such paths in a CG will often grow exponentially with the size of the CG. We should also note here that for linear calibration functions, traversing two consecutive edges of the CG results in a quadratic relationship, while for quadratic calibration functions, traversing two consecutive edges will result in a 4th-degree polynomial. It is easy to see that even for relatively simple calibration functions in low order polynomial form, even short CG path traversals results in very high-degree polynomials quickly. For example, consider the following CF:

$$F_{i,j}(x) = a_{i,j} \cdot x + b_{i,j} \tag{3}$$

Traversing a path from nodes s_1 to s_2 to s_3 we have:

$$F_{2,3}(F_{1,2}(x)) = a_{2,3} \cdot (a_{1,2} \cdot x + b_{1,2}) + b_{2,3} \tag{4}$$

$$= a_{2,3} \cdot a_{1,2} \cdot x + a_{2,3} \cdot b_{1,2} + b_{2,3} \tag{5}$$

which is quadratic in terms of the coefficients $a_{i,j}$ and $b_{i,j}$. However, we make two observations:

1) Since calibration relationships are inherently derived using local information, we should focus more on achieving consistency at a local level, i.e. consider paths in the CG of relatively short lengths.

2) Since each path in the CG is comprised of traversing CFs with different confidence levels, we should expect higher consistency levels from higher confidence traversals.

Definition: The calibration-matrix consistency objective function CMCOF for a calibration matrix $\mathbf{F}$, denoted as $\Gamma(\mathbf{F})$, is a real-valued function such that if $\alpha_1 = \Gamma(F_1)$ and $\alpha_2 = \Gamma(F_2)$, then F_1 is more consistent than F_2 if and only if $\alpha_1 > \alpha_2$.

The exact choice of the appropriate CMCOF depends in large part on the nature and types of errors of the sensors, the environment, and also on how the sensor results will be used. We have relied on the standard L_1, L_2, and L_∞ norms of the discrepancies resulting from different paths in the CG as candidates for experimentation. However, the exact choice of a CMCOF function will depend on the application at hand, as well as analysis of experimental data from sensors under real-life conditions. The data from our experiments which have been of relatively small size with a small number of nodes, have not provided convincing indications for us regarding which function performs better. In general, in a laboratory setting, creating experiments which can truly capture the full effects of the real errors on sensors is in itself a difficult undertaking.

4.4   Consistency Optimization Algorithm

Solving the non-linear programming problem which results by trying to maximize a general CMCOF, directly, under the constraints of given pairwise relation functions is computationally intractable. In the next subsection we present our heuristic-based algorithm that attempts to improve the consistency of the calibration functions on a local scale, subject to the computational and storage limitations of typical sensor nodes. In addition, in order to be practical, our goal has been to create an algorithm which lends itself well to localized and distributed implementation in sensor networks.

The algorithm generates a set of data-point values for each sensor based on the derived calibration functions in phase 1. Each value is obtained by picking a starting value, and calculating the weighted averages of the result produced by traversing different paths in the CG. The weights correspond to combined confidence levels of each traversal and is obtained by multiplying the confidence values along each segment of a path. Thus, higher confidence traversals have a higher weight in the averaging process. The resulting data-points are used to derive a new pair-wise calibration matrix.

```
Enumerate calibration paths P given the CM F
Step 1: Pick a random starting value x
    For every node s_i ∈ S, s'_i = 0 and count_{s_i} = 0
    For every path p_i ∈ P {
        s_prev = first node in p_i
        CurrentValue = x, α = 1
        While cycle not done {
            s_curr = next node in p_i
            CurrentValue = F_{s_prev,s_curr}(CurrentValue)
            α = α x the confidence of F_{s_prev,s_curr}
            s'_curr = s'_curr + α · CurrentValue
            count_{s_curr} ++
            s_prev = s_curr
        }
    }
    For every node s_i ∈ S, s'_i = s'_i/count_{s_i}

Repeat step 1 n times to get n "data points" for each sensor
Step 2: Compute new CM F' using the data-points
```

Fig. 9. Pseudo-code for localized calibration matrix consistency optimiztion

The algorithm is presented as pseudo-code in figure 9. The initial part of the algorithm enumerates the calibration paths which will be used in the rest of the algorithm. A user specified parameter is used to indicate the maximum length of paths which we consider. We enumerate the paths by exhaustively searching the CG graph using breadth-first-search, starting from each node. We discard paths whose confidence levels are below a user-specified threshold. Note that due to the sparsity of the F matrix, and these threshold values, the number of paths that are enumerated can be kept to manageable levels (dictated by available memory, speed of processing, and allotted runtime), given the strict resource constraints of the sensor nodes.

After the data points (n) have been generated by the averaging process, the calibration matrix F is recalculated by fitting pairwise relationship functions based on the new data points, similar to the corresponding step in phase 1.

5   Experiments

We ran our algorithms on temperature data collected using a set of uncalibrated sensors. Because an important contributor to sensor error may be the differences in electronics supporting the sensing components, we used a COTS wireless sensor node system as our experimental uncalibrated sensor node. Co-located calibrated sensor components directly wired to a data aquisition system were used to collect ground truth data. The experimental setup and results are described below.

5.1   Experimental Setup

We chose to use real wireless sensor nodes (MICA motes [5]) to collect the raw data from uncalibrated sensors. This decision is motivated by our plans to run distributed versions of our algorithms on these nodes in future deployments. The heart of the mote is an Atmel [6] ATMEGA103L micro-controller. This chip has a builtin analog to digital converter and can be connected to a resistive sensor through a voltage divider. We have used a YSI44006 [7] precision thermistor to perform our measurements. This is a very stable sensor, but it is not factory calibrated. The observed calibration error was as high as 10%. The ATMEGA 103L is also equipped with 4KB of EEPROM, which we used to store data collected during the experiments.

In order to verify the quality of the calibration algorithms, we collected the ground truth measurements using an industrial quality data acquisition system(DAQ) from National Instruments [8]. We used the SCXI-1001 chassis with SCXI-1102 module for analog input. Type J thermocouples were used as temperature sensors.

Since the pair-wise algorithm (sect. 4.2) uses temporal correlation of the sensed data, we had to synchronize all sampling. In order to synchronize motes among themselves, we implemented the Reference Broadcast Synchronization algorithm [9]. We also implemented *time routing* to make sampling requests more robust to packet loss and enable synchronized sampling across multiple broadcast domains. We synchronized mote sampling with the DAQ by using one of the DAQ's input channels to trigger the sampling. This channel was controlled by flipping a GPIO pin on the mote.

The experiment was conducted on a flat surface of a table indoors. Separation between the mote's thermistor and the DAQ's ground truth sensor was less then 5mm for all sensor nodes. 9 sensor nodes were placed on the flat surface in a 3×3 square grid. Each square of this grid had dimensions of 5cm×5cm. The ambient temperature in the lab during the experiment was approximately 26° Celsius. The sampling rate was set to 2 samples/sec.

We used a commercial hand-held hair dryer as a heat source. This heat source was positioned 10-20cm above the surface of the table. During the experiment the nozzle of the hair dryer was directed towards the sensors. In order to create temperature variations we moved the heat source over the sensor grid in a ran-

dom fashion at a velocity no greater than 1cm/sec. We limited the velocity of
heat source to avoid undersampling.

5.2   Experimental Results

After collecting the data as described above, we analyzed it in the following way.
We derived the relationships between all uncalibrated sensor using the pairwise
algorithm described in Sect. 4.2. We also mapped each uncalibrated sensor onto
its corresponding ground truth sensor[6]. In order to verify the quality of the
calibration relationships we calculated the difference between a value derived
though direct translation and a value derived through the ground truth.

The result of the above procedure is shown in Fig. 10. The vertical axis corresponds to percentage of the conversions. The horizontal axis corresponds to the
difference between a value derived directly through the calibration relationship
and a value derived through the ground truth sensor. In our experiment 0 80%
of the translations were off by less than 5°C.

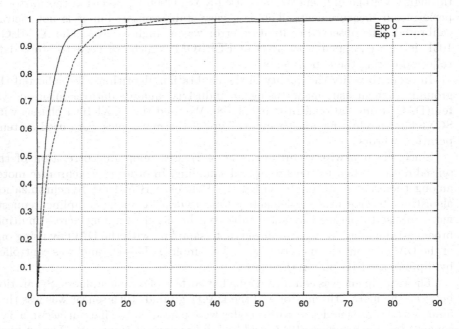

Fig. 10. Calibration error CDFs for two experiments. Y-axis is a fraction(percentage)
of inter-sensor translations. X-axis is a error in the translation in degrees C.

---

[6] For the purposes for this study we neglected the difference among the calibrated
sensors since we measured it previously to be less than 1.0°C.

5.3   Discussion and Future Work

While this scheme requires significant development and study before it will become deployable in the field, the results are promising. The distribution of calibration error is such that in 70% of the cases we were able to derive calibration relationships for the sensors with less 5°C. It is important to note that our algorithm does not make *any* assumptions about initial sensor calibration.

However, more than 10% of all translations were greater than 10°C. We have identified several potential sources of error, each of which will be investigated in future work:

- A possible reason for these errors is undersampling of the phenomenon. The velocity of the heat source may have been too high at times resulting in undersampling of the signal and associated aliasing. This, in turn, would have resulted in additional, possibly correlated, noise in the scatter diagram.
- Another source of error may come from our inability to determine the correct ground truth value. In particular, type J thermocouples have much higher mass than precision thermistors; therefore, thermocouples have slower response to changes in temperature. This may have invalidated ground truth data collected during the periods of high variability of the phenomenon.

As mentioned above, a systematic method for deriving the correlation window as well as choosing an appropriate size of the "top" set in the correlation process are subjects of future research. In addition, our future work also aims to address the applicability of these techniques to higher frequency phenomena such as light, acoustic, and seismic, where our assumption about neighboring sensors sensing the same phenomena and no angle-dependent gains may not hold. In such cases, we believe insights about the nature of the phenomena, the environment, and sensor response characteristics will help in building the appropriate calibration models.

Development of evaluation metrics for calibration quality is another important issue. Different applications may have different requirements. For example, an isotherm finding application may not be concerned with the RMS calibration error. For this application one can define a utility function in terms of the overlap between the isotherm based on the ground truth data and a measured isotherm. We are currently developing this and other methods for calibration quality evaluation.

6   Conclusions

We presented a method that can be used to address the difficult problem of sensor calibration in large-scale autonomous sensor networks. The scheme relies on redundancy in senor measurements due to overdeployment, and assumptions about the nature of the phenomena being sensed, to derive functions relating the output discrepancies (biases) of neighboring sensors. Due to inaccuracies and processing based on purely local information, the pairwise relationship functions will be inconsistent in the network. In the second phase, new pairwise relationships are derived by a heuristic method that is designed to increase the consistency in the system. Early experimental results indicate that the pairwise relative calibration scheme is promising. However, significant experimentation with relatively larger scale sensor networks are required to determine the true performance, especially for the second phase of the algorithm.

References

1. Whitehouse, K., Culler, D.: Calibration as parameter estimation in sensor networks. In: 2002 ACM International Workshop on Wireless Sensor Networks and Applications (WSNA'02), Atlanta, Georgia (2002) 67
2. Marzullo, K.: Tolerating failures of continuous-valued sensors. ACM Transactions on Computer Systems (TOCS) 8 (1990) 284–304
3. Cevher, V., McClellan, J.: Sensor array calibration via tracking with the extended kalman filter. In: 2001 IEEE International Conference on Acoustics, Speech, and Signal Processing. Volume 5. (2001) 2817–2820
4. Andrew Howard, M.M., Sukhatme, G.: Relaxation on a mesh: a formalism for generalized localization. In: IROS 2001. (2001)
5. URL: Crossbow corporation, http://www.xbow.com (2002)
6. URL: Atmel corporation, http://www.atmel.com (2002)
7. URL: Ysi corporation, http://www.ysi.com (2002)
8. URL: National instruments, http://www.ni.com (2002)
9. Jeremy Elson, L.G., Estrin, D.: Fine-grained network time synchronization using reference broadcasts. In: Proc. OSDI 2002 (to appear), Boston, MA (2002)

On the Error Characteristics of Multihop Node Localization in Ad-Hoc Sensor Networks

Andreas Savvides[1], Wendy Garber[2], Sachin Adlakha[1], Randolph Moses[2], and Mani B. Srivastava[1]

[1] Networked and Embedded Systems Lab
Electrical Engineering Department
University of California, Los Angeles
{asavvide, sachin, mbs}@ee.ucla.edu
[2] Department of Electrical Engineering,
Ohio State University
{garberw, randy}@ee.eng.ohio-state.edu

Abstract. Ad-hoc localization in multihop setups is a vital component of numerous sensor network applications. Although considerable effort has been invested in the development of multihop localization protocols, to the best of our knowledge the sensitivity of localization to its different setup parameters (network density, ranging system measurement error and beacon density) that are usually known prior to deployment has not been systematically studied. In an effort to reveal the trends and to gain better understanding of the error behavior in various deployment patterns, in this paper we study the Cramer Rao Bound behavior in carefully controlled scenarios. This analysis has a dual purpose. First, to provide valuable design time suggestions by revealing the error trends associated with deployment and second to provide a benchmark for the performance evaluation of existing localization algorithms.

1 Introduction

Ad-hoc node localization is widely recognized to be an integral component for a diverse set of applications in wireless sensor networks and ubiquitous computing. Although several ad-hoc localization approaches have been recently proposed in the literature [2,4,5,6,7], the trends in localization error behavior in multihop setups have not been studied in a systematic manner. The majority of previously proposed localization approaches evaluate the 'goodness' of their solution with randomly generated scenarios and comparison of the computed results to ground truth. While this is a good starting point, it does not provide an intimate understanding of the different error components that come into play in multi-hop localization systems.

Ideally, node localization would result in error-free position estimates if sensor measurements were to be perfect, and the algorithms were not to make any approximations such as operating on partial information and ignoring finite-precision arithmetic effects. In reality however, sensor measurements are noisy

F. Zhao and L. Guibas (Eds.): IPSN 2003, LNCS 2634, pp. 317–332, 2003.

and produce noisy location estimates. Zooming into the origins of these errors we observe that measurement errors consist two main components, *intrinsic* and *extrinsic*. The intrinsic component is caused by imperfections in the sensor hardware or software. The extrinsic component is more complex and it is attributed to the physical effects on the measurement channel such as obstructions or fading that vary significantly according to the deployment environment. Although, the first type of error can be easily characterized in a lab setup, it is important to note that it also induces additional error that affect both the network setup aspects as well the choice of localization algorithms used.

This paper investigates the different aspects of the error induced by the intrinsic measurement error component in multihop localization setups. To explore the different aspects of error trends we study the Cramér-Rao Lower Bound (CRLB) behavior of carefully controlled deployment scenarios under different configuration parameters. In particular, we study the effect of network density, pre-characterized measurement accuracy, beacon (or other landmark density) and network size. The analysis presented here serves a dual purpose. First, to provide algorithm-independent design time insight in to the error trends associated with the different network setup parameters. This can help optimize the multihop localization performance prior to deployment. Second, the CRLB results can be used as an evaluation benchmark for multihop localization algorithms.

The remainder of this paper is organized as follows. The next section motivates our work by providing an overview of the sources of error in multihop localization systems. Section 3 provides the formulation of CRLB for multihop localization and explains the scenario structures used in this evaluation. Section 4 presents our simulation results. Section 5 discusses the evaluation of existing localization algorithms and section 6 concludes the paper.

2   Sources of Error in Multihop Localization Systems

2.1   Multihop Localization Problem Statement

Assume we have a set of A sensors in a plane, each with unknown location $\{r_i = (x_i, y_i)\}_{i=1}^{A}$. In addition, a set of B beacon with known locations $r_i = (x_i, y_i)_{i=-B+1}^{0}$ are placed in the plane. Each beacon node advertises its location and this information is forwarded to the other nodes in the network. Furthermore, each sensor node and beacon node emits some known signals that allow neighboring nodes to estimate their distance from the emitting node.

The distance measurements contain measurement error. We denote the error as e_{ij}, where

$$\hat{d}_{ij} = d_{ij} + e_{ij} \tag{1}$$

$$d_{ij} = \|r_i - r_j\| = \sqrt{(x_i - x_j)^2 + (y_i - y_j)^2} \tag{2}$$

and where d_{ij} is the true distance between nodes i and j.

In this paper we assume the measurement errors are independent Gaussian random variables with zero mean and known variance σ^2. Although this White-Gaussian measurement error does not capture all practical cases, it is a good starting point for exposing some of the error trends in multihop networks. More general cases are considered in [9]. We denote the availability of a measurement using the indicator function I_{ij} where $I_{ij} = 1$ if node j receives a calibration signal from node i, and $I_{ij} = 0$ otherwise.

The general localization problem statement is as follows: Given noisy measurements of $\hat{d}_{ij}$ and known locations r_i for $i = -B + 1, \ldots, 0$, estimate the locations $\hat{r}_i$ for $i = 1, \ldots, A$.

2.2   A Classification of Error Components

As a first step in understanding the different sources of errors in multihop localization systems we categorize them in three broad classes *setup error, channel error* and *algorithmic error*.

Setup error is induced by intrinsic measurement error and it is reflected in the network configuration parameters such as network density, concentration of beacons (or other landmarks), network size and measurement error characteristics known prior to deployment. For the purposes of our discussion, we assume that intrinsic measurement error can be characterized in a lab setup to provide an indication of the measurement accuracy of a particular ranging technology. Table 1 lists the measurement accuracies of four different ranging systems, an ultrasonic ranging system used in the AHLoS project [6], an ultra wide band (UWB) system [3], and RF Time-of-Flight system from Bluesoft [1] and a SICK laser range finder [10].

Table 1. Accuracy of different measurement technologies

Technology	System	Measurement Accuracy	Range
Ultrasound	AHLoS	2cm	3m
Ultra Wide Band	PAL UWB	1.5m	N/A
RF Time of Flight	Bluesoft	0.5 m	100m
Laser Time of Flight	Laser range finder	1cm	75m

Channel error is a result of the extrinsic measurement error and represents the physical channel effects on sensor measurements. Multipath and shadowing, multiple access interference, the presence of obstructions that results in unpredictable non-line of sight components, and fluctuations in the signal propagation speeds are just a few of these effects that can introduce error into the computation of locations. The magnitude of these effects on the distance measurement process is typically specific to the particular measurement technology and the environment in which they operate; hence different considerations should be applied for each technology.

Finally, the multihop nature of the problem and the different operational requirements introduce another level of complexity and subsequently more error. Many settings that require the random deployment of low cost resource constrained sensor nodes, call for fully distributed operation that has limited power consumption overhead. Such requirements may lead in approximate localization algorithms that have some additional error associated with them. The distributed computation model of *collaborative multilateration* described in [7] is an example of such an algorithm. In this case, the proposed fully distributed algorithm is an approximation of a centralized algorithm that conserves computation and communication energy. This design choice however introduces a small, yet tolerable error. We refer to this error as algorithmic error.

Although the goal of our research is to explore all aspects of error by building an operational ad-hoc localization system[1], in this paper we focus on setup error. The analysis presented here examines the setup error behavior inside specific segments within a sensor network. These segments are comprised of a small number of beacon nodes surrounding a large number of sensor nodes with unknown locations as shown in figure 1. These sensor nodes are expected to estimate their locations by combining their inter-node distance measurements and beacon locations. We evaluate the error trends in such setups using the Cramér-Rao Bound (CRB).

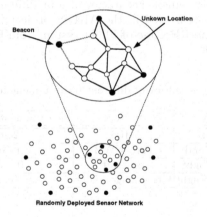

Fig. 1. Typical in network localization region

---

[1] We refer the reader to our project website http://nesl.ee.ucla.edu/projects/ahlos for the details specific to our implementation including all released hardware and software

3 Localization Bounds in a Multihop Setup

3.1 The Cramér-Rao Bound

The accuracy for mean square location estimate can be evaluated using Cramér Rao bound (CRB) [9]. The CRB is a classical result from statistics that gives a lower bound on the error covariance matrix for an unbiased estimate of parameter θ (see, eg, [11]). The lower bound is given in terms of Fisher Information Matrix $J(\theta)$. Let $\hat{\theta}$ be any unbiased estimate of parameter θ based on observation vector X having a pdf of $f_X(x)$. The error covariance matrix is defined as

$$C = E\{(\hat{\theta} - \theta)(\hat{\theta} - \theta)^T\} \tag{3}$$

This error covariance matrix is bounded below by the CR bound, which is given by

$$CRB = [J(\theta)]^{-1} \tag{4}$$

where the matrix $J(\theta)$ has elements given by

$$[J(\theta)]_{mn} = E\left\{\left[\frac{\partial \ln(f_X(X))}{\partial \theta_m}\right]\left[\frac{\partial \ln(f_X(X))}{\partial \theta_n}\right]\right\} \tag{5}$$

The matrix $J(\theta)$ is called the Fisher Information Matrix (FIM).

3.2 Obtaining the CRB for Multihop Topologies

In the multihop problem, the parameter vector θ of interest is the $2A \times 1$ vector

$$\theta = [x_1, y_1, x_2, y_2, \ldots, x_A, y_A]^T \tag{6}$$

The measurement vector X is a vector formed by stacking the distance measurements $\hat{d}_{ij}$. Since it is assumed that the measurement is white Gaussian, the measurement pdf is the vector Gaussian pdf

$$f_X(x; \theta) = \mathcal{N}(\mu(\theta), \Sigma) = \frac{1}{(2\pi)^{2A}|\Sigma|^{\frac{1}{2}}} \exp\left\{-\frac{1}{2}[X - \mu(\theta)]^T \Sigma^{-1}[X - \mu(\theta)]\right\} \tag{7}$$

where the mean vector $\mu(\theta)$ is a vector of true distances whose elements are given by equation 2. The covariance matrix in equation 7 is given by

$$\Sigma = \sigma^2 I \tag{8}$$

where I is the $2A \times 2A$ identity matrix and where σ^2 is the variance of each measurement error e_{ij} in 1. Note that for this application the pdf depends on θ only through its mean value.

The vector X contains measurements of distances $\hat{d}_{ij}$ stacked in some order, and $\mu(\theta)$ is a vector of d_{ij} distances stacked in the same order. Let M denote the total number of $\hat{d}_{ij}$ measurements.

The CRB can be computed from the Fisher Information Matrix (FIM) of θ from equation 5. The Fisher Information Matrix is given by

$$J_\theta = E\left\{ [\nabla_\theta \ln f_X(X; \theta)][\nabla_\theta \ln f_X(X; \theta)]^T \right\}$$

The partial derivatives are readily computed from equations (2), (6), and (7); we find that

$$J_\theta = \frac{1}{\sigma^2}[G'(\theta)]^T[G'(\theta)] \tag{9}$$

where $G'(\theta)$ is the $M \times 2A$ matrix whose mnth element is $\partial\mu_m(\theta)/\partial\theta_n$. Each element of $G'(\theta)$ is readily computed from equation 2. Let the mth element of $\mu(\theta)$ be d_{ij} for some corresponding values of i and j, and note that θ_n is either $x_{i'}$ or $y_{i'}$ for some corresponding i'. Then from equation 2,

$$G'(\theta)_{mn} = \begin{cases} 0 & \text{if } i' \neq i \text{ and } i' \neq j \\ \frac{x_i - x_j}{d_{ij}} & \text{if } \theta_n = x_i \\ \frac{x_j - x_i}{d_{ij}} & \text{if } \theta_n = x_j \\ \frac{y_i - y_j}{d_{ij}} & \text{if } \theta_n = y_i \\ \frac{y_j - y_i}{d_{ij}} & \text{if } \theta_n = y_j \end{cases} \tag{10}$$

The CRB is then given by the inverse of the FIM as in 4.

3.3   Scenario Setup

To evaluate the effects of density variation and measurement error on the overall localization result, we generated a set of scenarios for which density and therefore node connectivity can be controlled. For the purposes of our experiments we define node density D to be the number of nodes per unit area. For N nodes deployed on a circular area A, $D = \frac{N}{A}$. Given this we can control the radius L of a circular field to be

$$L = \sqrt{\frac{A}{\pi}} = \sqrt{\frac{N}{D\pi}} \tag{11}$$

In a circular field, the probability of a node having d neighbors can be expressed as

$$P(d) = \binom{N-1}{d} P_R^d (1 - P_R)^{N-d-1} \tag{12}$$

where P_R is the probability that a node is within transmission range R from another node

$$P_R = \frac{\pi R^2}{A} = \frac{D\pi R^2}{N} \tag{13}$$

As N goes to infinity, the binomial distribution in equation 12 converges to a Poisson distribution (equation 14) with $\lambda = NP_R$

$$P(d) = \frac{\lambda^d}{d!} e^{-\lambda} \tag{14}$$

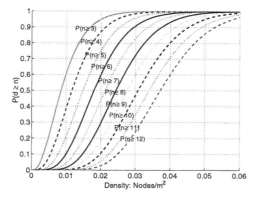

Fig. 2. Probability of n or more neighbors at different densities

Also from this the probability of a node having n or more neighbors is

$$P(d \geq n) = 1 - \sum_{i=0}^{n-1} P(i)$$

In our simulation experiments sensor nodes have a 10-meter range. For this range the corresponding probabilities of having n or more neighbors and for different network densities are shown in figure 2. The scenarios used in this study are generated on a circular plane following the above analysis. To ensure even distribution of nodes per unit area, we divide the circle into rings of width $\frac{1}{\pi\sqrt{D}}$. In each ring we generate node positions in polar coordinates by generating a radius r and an angle θ for each node. The number of nodes in each ring is proportional to the area of the circle covered by the ring.

As it will be shown in section 4.1, this scenario pattern generation method was chosen to isolate error incurred from bad geometry setups. These effects arise when angles between beacons (or other anchor nodes) as seen by the node trying to determine their location are very small. This effect can be prevented when nodes are deployed using the circular pattern described above.

4   Simulation Results

Using the CRLB bounds derived in the previous section, we try to answer some fundamental questions related to setup error. This evaluation is performed by computing the Cramer-Rao bound on a comprehensive set of approximately 2,000 scenarios generated using the algorithm described in the previous section.

4.1   How Does Deployment Geometry Affect the Solution?

Geometry setup alone can affect localization accuracy. This is a known effect frequently referred to as *geometric dilution of precision* (GDOP). The same effects come into play in a multihop setup where neighboring nodes with unknown positions help other nodes to estimate their locations by acting as *anchor points*. In both cases, the best estimates can be obtained when the nodes are placed within the convex hull of the beacons. These effects are demonstrated on a small set of simple scenarios. Figures 3 to 7 show the CLRB bound on a 10×10 grid. In figure 3, four beacons are deployed on the vertices of a 8×8 square. The error is maximum outside the square, and behind the beacons where the angles between diagonally adjacent beacons is very small or zero. Figure 5 shows how the error behaves if the beacon square is shrunk to 2×2. By scaling the beacon square from 2×2 to 8×8 we note that the variance in the bounds at different points on the grid changes significantly. This effect can be seen by comparing figures 3 and 5. This also explains or choice of scenario generation algorithms. By keeping the beacons on the perimeter of the network we ensure that for the rest of our experiments, we operate in the places where the variance of the bounds is more uniform (i.e. similar to the flat region within the beacon square in figure 3.

Figures 6 and 7 show the error bounds when three beacons are used in a triangular configuration. In the first case the beacons are found at locations $B1 = 3, 3$, $B2 = 3, 8$, $B3 = 5.5, 5.5$. In the second case the beacons are placed at locations $B1 = 3, 3$, $B2 = 3, 4$, $B3 = 3.2, 5.5$. These two cases show the effect of geometry then the angles between each of the beacons as seen by a sensor node change. The largest error occurs when the angles to each beacon are very small. Furthermore, we note that the ratio between the incidence angles to each of the beacons is also important. This is illustrated in figure 4, which follows the $8 \times 8m$ beacon pattern as the one in figure 3 with the beacon node at position $(8, 8)$ removed.

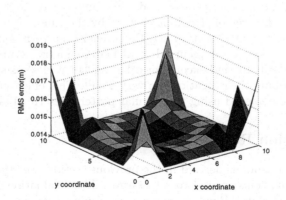

Fig. 3. Effects of geometry on $8 \times 8m$ square beacon pattern

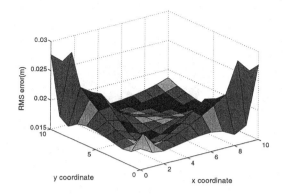

Fig. 4. Effect of removing 1 beacon from the $8 \times 8m$ square beacon pattern

4.2   How Does Network Density Affect Localization Accuracy?

Intuitively, one would expect that localization accuracy would improve as the network density increases. This is because increasing network density, and subsequently the number of neighbors for each node with unknown location adds more constraints to the optimization problem. After some critical density, the effect of density on location accuracy becomes less apparent. Our simulation results in figure 8 verify this expectation. The critical point occurs in the case where the majority of the nodes have at least 6 neighbors. For the particular range used in our experiments, this takes place at a density of 0.35 nodes/m^2. This result is consistent for a test suite of more than 1,000 scenarios at different ranging accuracies as shown in the figure.

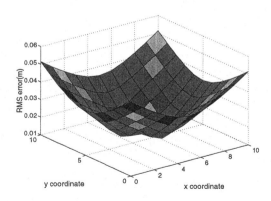

Fig. 5. Effects of geometry on $2 \times 2m$ square beacon pattern

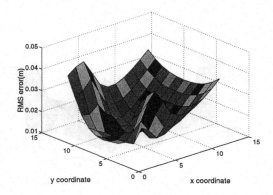

Fig. 6. Effects of geometry on an isosceles beacon triangle

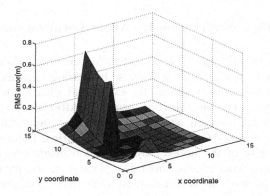

Fig. 7. Effects of geometry on a flat triangle

Furthermore, we note that the different CRLB plots for different values of ranging error σ^2 are scaled versions of one another. In figure 8 and in figures from subsequent sections, our plots show the bounds at different ranging errors to allow the user to associate these results to specific ranging technologies such as the ones listed in table 1.

4.3 What Is the Best Solution One Can Achieve with a Given Measurement Technology?

This question can be answered by observing the bounds on the same set of scenarios as the previous subsection. In general based on our simulations we not that if the network density is sufficient (6 or more neighbors per node), the bound predicts that the localization error will be close to (slightly lower) than the ranging error. The trend lines for different levels of ranging error are shown in figure 9.

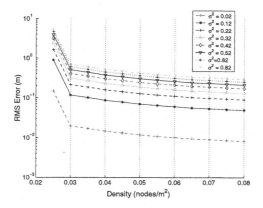

Fig. 8. Density trends at different values of measurement error variance σ^2

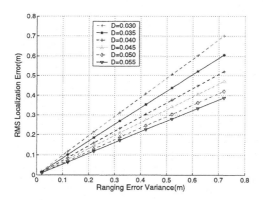

Fig. 9. Density and range error scaling

4.4 How Does Error Behave as the Network Scales?

If the density is kept fixed, the error bound degrades very showly as the network scales. A representative result from our experiments for different measurement accuracies is shown in figure 10. In this experiment, the network size is varied from 40 nodes to 200 nodes while the network density is kept constant at 6 neighbors per node, and 10% beacons.

4.5 What Is the Effect of Beacon Density on the Computed Solution?

To test the effect of beacon density on the localization bounds we used a set of scenarios with fixed density (0.45) and fixed number of nodes (100 nodes). The percentage of beacons was varied from 4% to 20%. The results are (shown in

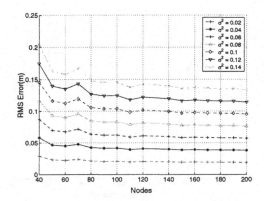

Fig. 10. Error propagation as network scales at 10% beacons, 6 neighbors per node

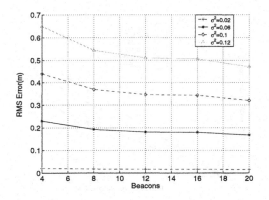

Fig. 11. The effect of beacon density on localization, 100 nodes, 4-20% beacons

figure 11) indicate that increasing the number of beacon nodes does not dramatically reduce the localization bound. This is more profound when the ranging error is very small. As shown in the figure, at a range error variance of $0.02m$, using 4 beacon nodes on a 100 node network performs just as well as 20 beacons. Also for higher levels of ranging error, adding more beacons yields a modest improvement.

5   A Case Study on Algorithmic Error: Collaborative Multilateration

In this section we present a comparison of a specific multihop localization algorithm, *collaborative multilateration*, and corresponding the Cramér-Rao bound. The measurement error characteristics used for this evaluation are drawn from the lab characterization of the ultrasonic distance measurement system described in [6].

5.1 Collaborative Multilateration Overview

Collaborative multilateration is a method for performing node localization in multihop setups. The algorithm, which is described in detail in [7] relies on a small set of beacon nodes and inter-node distance measurements to estimate node locations in multihop setups while trying to prevent error accumulation inside the network. Collaborative multilateration supports two computation models, *centralized* and *distributed*. The centralized model estimates node locations at a central point in the network that has a global vantage point. All the inter-node distance measurements and beacons locations are used to set up a global non-linear optimization problem, which is solved using least squares.

Even though the centralized computation model can yield high quality estimates, it is not always suitable for sensor networks. First, it requires significant computation, which would require more processing and memory resources than what low cost sensor nodes can accommodate. Second, a centralized approach exposes a single point of failure in the network. Third, a centralized approach also requires some routing protocol support to propagate measurements and locations to the central computation point (and sometimes to also propagate the position estimates back to the nodes).

To address the issues of the centralized computation model, the distributed collaborative multilateration computation model was designed to operate in a fully distributed fashion. In this model, each node in the network is responsible for estimating its own location using distance measurements and location information from its one-hop neighbors. To compute an estimate of its location each node uses its neighbors as anchors. If these neighbors do not have a final estimate of their location, then an intermediate rough estimate of the node locations is used. All nodes compute an updated estimate of their locations and they pass it to their neighbors, which in turn use this information to update their own location estimate. The process continues until a certain tolerance is met. In this computation model, the estimate updates at each node happen in a consistent sequence that is repeated until the convergence criteria are met. This forms a gradient with respect to the global topology constraints that allows the nodes in the network to estimate their location with respect to the global constraint while computing their estimate locally.

The distributed computation mode of collaborative multilateration is an approximation of the centralized model that is designed to meet some of the operational requirements of a practical setup. This design decision however introduces some algorithmic error in the location estimates. In the next subsection we compare the error from the two approaches to the bounds.

5.2 Comparison to the Bounds

To evaluate the quality of location estimates of the two computation models of collaborative multilateration, we compare the two computation models to the CRLB bounds, using the same scenarios as the ones used in section 4.1. For these scenarios the ranging error variance was set to $0.02m$ to match the characteristics of the ultrasonic ranging system described in [6]. The results from this comparison are shown in figure 12. The results shown here are averages from 10 different scenarios for each density.

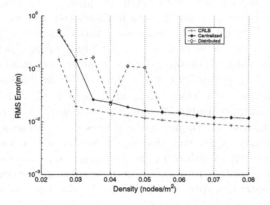

Fig. 12. Algorithmic error in centralized and distributed collaborative multilateration computation models

From this comparison both computation models follow a similar trend to the CRLB bound but we also note some differences, which we classify as part of the *algorithmic error*. The critical density point has moved from 0.03 nodes/m^2 to 0.035 nodes/m^2. This corresponds to the point where the majority of nodes have 8 neighbors instead of 6 as predicted by the bound. We also note the discrepancy in the results of the distributed computation model. Although in most cases, the location estimates provided by distributed collaborative multilateration are almost identical to its centralized counterpart, for some cases the averages shown in figure 12 suggest that the position estimates are sometimes significantly different. A closer examination of the simulation data has shown that this discrepancy arises from very few isolated scenarios where the distributed process does not converge. Repeating the experiments has shown that this discrepancy can be prevented if some consistency checks are added to detect divergence. The distributed computation can converge it a different starting node is selected. This choice however would also incur increased algorithm complexity. At densities of 12 or more neighbors, the results of the two computation models are consistent. We attribute this to the fact that increased densities offer significantly more constraints that keep the process from diverging.

6   Conclusions

In this paper we explored some of the trends in localization error for multihop localization scenarios. Our simulation experiments have shown how intrinsic error from the sensor measurements incurs additional error with respect to different network parameters. This contributes some insight on what the deployment parameters should be for a multihop localization process to be successful. The beacon nodes should be deployed on the perimeter of the network to ensure that localization algorithms operate in the region where variance on the bounds is minimal. We also noted that there is a critical density after which localization improvement is much more gradual. By comparing this to collaborative multilateration we concluded that algorithmic error should also considered prior to deployment and deployment decisions should be more conservative than the ones predicted by the bounds. Furthermore, the study of the bounds has shown that multiple localization approaches are scalable and the position of a large number of nodes can be determined with a very small number of beacons that are found multiple hops away. As part of our future work, we plan to investigate the effects of the extrinsic measurement error on location estimates and how can this be handled at the network level by utilizing network redundancy and the trends exposed in this paper.

Acknowledgments. This paper is based in part on research funded through NSF under grant number ANI-008577, and through DARPA SensIT and Rome Laboratory, Air Force Material Command, USAF, under agreement number F30602-99-1-0529. The U.S. Government is authorized to reproduce and distribute reprints for Governmental purposes notwithstanding any copyright annotation thereon. Any opinions, findings, and conclusions or recommendations expressed in this paper are those of the authors and do not necessarily reflect the views of the NSF, DARPA, or Rome Laboratory, USAF.

References

1. Bluesoft Inc *http://www.bluesoft-inc.com*
2. L. Doherty, L. El Ghaoui, K. S. J. Pister, *Convex Position Estimation in Wireless Sensor Networks*, Proceedings of Infocom 2001, Anchorage, AK, April 2001.
3. R. Fontana, S. Gunderson *Ultra Wideband Precision Asset Location System* Proceedings of IEEE Conference on Ultra Wideband Systems and Technologies, May 2002
4. D. Nicolescu and B. Nath *Ad-Hoc Positioning System* In proceedings of IEEE GlobeCom, November 2001
5. C. Savarese, J. Rabay and K. Langendoen *Robust Positioning Algorithms for Distributed Ad-Hoc Wireless Sensor Networks* USENIX Technical Annual Conference, Monterey, CA, June 2002
6. A. Savvides, C. C Han and M.B Srivastava *Dynamic Fine-Grained Localization in Ad-Hoc Networks of Sensors* Proceedings of fifth Annual International Conference on Mobile Computing and Networking, Mobicom pp. 166–179, Rome, Italy, July 2001

7. A. Savvides, H. Park and M. B. Srivastava, "The Bits and Flops of the n-Hop Multilateration Primitive for Node localization Problems", Proceedings of the first International Conference on Wireless Sensor Networks and Applications held with Mobicom, September 2002
8. R. L. Moses and R. M. Patterson, "Self-calibration of sensor networks," in *Unattended Ground Sensor Technologies and Applications IV (Proc. SPIE Vol. 4743)* (E. M. Carapezza, ed.), pp. 108–119, April 1–4 2002.
9. R. L. Moses, D. Krishnamurthy, and R. Patterson, "A self-localization method for wireless sensor networks," *Eurasip Journal on Applied Signal Processing, Special Issue on Sensor Networks.* (submitted November 2001).
10. SICK http://www.sick.de
11. H. L. Van Trees, *Detection, Estimation, and Modulation Theory: Part I.* New York: Wiley, 1968.

Organizing a Global Coordinate System from Local Information on an Ad Hoc Sensor Network

Radhika Nagpal, Howard Shrobe, and Jonathan Bachrach

Artificial Intelligence Laboratory
Massachusetts Institute of Technology
Cambridge, MA 02139
{radhi, hes, jrb}@ai.mit.edu

Abstract. We demonstrate that it is possible to achieve accurate localization and tracking of a target in a randomly placed wireless sensor network composed of inexpensive components of limited accuracy. The crucial enabler for this is a reasonably accurate local coordinate system aligned with the global coordinates. We present an algorithm for creating such a coordinate system without the use of global control, globally accessible beacon signals, or accurate estimates of inter-sensor distances. The coordinate system is robust and automatically adapts to the failure or addition of sensors. Extensive theoretical analysis and simulation results are presented. Two key theoretical results are: there is a critical minimum average neighborhood size of 15 for good accuracy and there is a fundamental limit on the resolution of any coordinate system determined strictly from local communication. Our simulation results show that we can achieve position accuracy to within 20% of the radio range even when there is variation of up to 10% in the signal strength of the radios. The algorithm improves with finer quantizations of inter-sensor distance estimates: with 6 levels of quantization position errors better than 10% are achieved. Finally we show how the algorithm gracefully generalizes to target tracking tasks.

1 Introduction

Advances in technology have made it possible to build ad hoc sensor networks using inexpensive nodes consisting of a low power processor, a modest amount of memory, a wireless network transceiver and a sensor board; a typical node is comparable in size to 2 AA batteries [5]. Many novel applications are emerging: habitat monitoring, smart building reporting failures, target tracking, etc. In these applications it is necessary to accurately orient the nodes with respect to the global coordinate system. Ad hoc sensor networks present novel tradeoffs in system design. On the one hand, the low cost of the nodes facilitates massive scale and highly parallel computation. On the other hand, each node is likely to have limited power, limited reliability, and only local communication with a modest number of neighbors. The application context and massive scale make it unrealistic to rely on careful placement or uniform arrangement of sensors.

F. Zhao and L. Guibas (Eds.): IPSN 2003, LNCS 2634, pp. 333–348, 2003.

Rather than use globally accessible beacons or expensive GPS to localize each sensor, we would like the sensors to be able to self-organize a coordinate system.

In this paper, we present an algorithm that exploits the characteristics of ad hoc wireless sensor networks to discover position information even when the elements have literally been sprinkled over the terrain. The algorithm exploits two principles: (1) the communication hops between two sensors can give us an easily obtainable and reasonably accurate distance estimate and (2) by using imperfect distance estimates from many sources we can minimize position error. Both of these steps can easily be computed locally by a sensor, without assuming sophisticated radio capabilities. We can theoretically bound the error in the distance estimates, allowing us to predict the localization accuracy. The resulting coordinate system automatically adapts to failures and the addition of sensors.

There are many different localization systems that depend on having direct distance estimates to globally accessible beacons such as the Global Positioning System [6], indoor localization [1] [14], and cell phone location determination [3]. Recently there has been some research in localization in the context of wireless sensor networks where globally accessible beacons are not available. Doherty et al [4] present a technique based on constraint satisfaction using inter-sensor distance estimates (and a percentage of known sensor positions). This method critically depends on the availability of inter-sensor distance measurements and requires expensive centralized computation. Savvides et al [15] describe a distributed localization algorithm that recursively infers the positions of sensors with unknown position from the current set of sensors with known positions, using inter-sensor distance estimates. However, there is no analysis of how the error accumulates with each inference and what parameters affect the error. By contrast, our algorithm does not rely on inter-sensor distance estimates, is fully distributed, and we can theoretically characterize how the density of the sensors affects the error. Our algorithm is based on a simpler method introduced by one of the authors in [11] but also independently suggested in [9].

Section 2 presents the algorithm for organizing the global coordinate system from local information. We present a theoretical analysis of the accuracy of the coordinate system along with simulation results is presented in section 3. Section 4 reports simulation results that generalize the basic algorithm to include more accurate distance information based on signal strength. Section 5 investigates the robustness of the algorithm to variations in communication radius as well as sensor failures. Section 6 introduces a variation of the coordinate estimation algorithm that tracks moving targets.

2   Coordinate System Formation Algorithm

In this section we describe our algorithm for organizing a global coordinate system from local information. Our model of an ad hoc sensor network is randomly distributed sensors on a two dimensional plane. Sensors do not have global knowledge of the topology or their physical location. Each sensor communicates with physically nearby sensors within a fixed distance r, where r is much smaller than the dimensions of the plane. All sensors within the distance r of a sensor are called its communication neighborhood. In the first pass we assume that all sensors have the same communication radius and that signal strength is not used to determine relative position of neighbors within a neighborhood. Later in sections 4 and 5 we relax both of these constraints. We also assume that some set of sensors are "seed" sensors - they are identical to other sensors in capabilities, except that they are preprogrammed with their global position. This may be either through GPS or manual programming of position. The main point is for the seeds to be similar in cost to the sensors, and for it to be easy to add and discard seeds.

The algorithm is based on the fact that the position of a point on a two dimensional plane can be uniquely described by its distance from at least three non-collinear reference points. The basic algorithm consists of two parts: (1) each seed produces a locally propagating *gradient* that allows other sensors to estimate their distance from the seed and (2) each sensor uses a *multilateration* procedure to combine the distance estimates from all the seeds to produce its own position. The following subsections describe both parts of the algorithm in more detail.

2.1   Gradient Algorithm

A seed sensor initiates a gradient by sending its neighbors a message with its location and a count set to one. Each recipient remembers the value of the count and forwards the message to its neighbors with the count incremented by one. Hence a wave of messages propagates outwards from the seed. Each sensor maintains the minimum counter value received and ignores messages containing larger values, which prevents the wave from traveling backwards. If two sensors can communicate with each other directly (i.e. without forwarding the message through other sensors) then they are considered to be within one communication hop of each other. The minimum hop count value, h_i, that a sensor i maintains will eventually be the length of the shortest path to the seed in communication hops. Hence a gradient is essentially a breadth-first-search tree [8].

In our ad hoc sensor network, a communication hop has a maximum physical distance of r associated with it. This implies that a sensor i is at most distance $h_i r$ from the seed. However as the average density of sensors increases, sensors with the same hop count tend to form concentric circular rings, of width approximately r, around the seed sensor. Figure 1 shows a gradient originating from a seed with sensors colored based on their hop count. At these densities the hop count gives an estimate of the straight line distance which is then improved by sensors computing a local average of their neighbors' hop counts.

2.2   Multilateration Algorithm

After receiving at least three gradient values, sensors combine the distances from the seeds to estimate their position relative to the positions of the seed sensors. In particular, each sensor estimates its coordinates by finding coordinates that

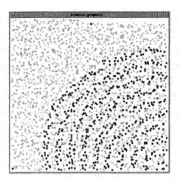

Fig. 1. Gradients propagating from a seed. Each dot represents a sensor. Sensors are colored based on their gradient value.

minimize the total squared error between calculated distances and estimated distances. Sensor j's calculated distance to seed i is:

$$d_{ji} = \sqrt{(x_i - x_j)^2 + (y_i - y_j)^2} \tag{1}$$

and sensor j's total error is:

$$E_j = \sum_{i=1}^{n} (d_{ji} - \hat{d}_{ji})^2 \tag{2}$$

where n is the number of seed sensors and $\hat{d}_{ji}$ is the estimated distance computed through gradient propagation. The coordinates that minimize least squared error can be found iteratively using gradient descent. More precisely, the coordinate estimate starts with the last estimate if it is available and otherwise with the location of the seed with the minimum estimated distance. The coordinates are then incrementally updated in proportion to the gradient of the total error with respect to that coordinate. The partial derivatives are:

$$\frac{\partial E_j}{\partial x_j} = \sum_{i=1}^{n} (x_j - x_i)(1 - \frac{d_{ji}}{\hat{d}_{ji}}) \text{ and } \frac{\partial E_j}{\partial y_j} = \sum_{i=1}^{n} (y_j - y_i)(1 - \frac{d_{ji}}{\hat{d}_{ji}}) \tag{3}$$

and incremental coordinate updates are:

$$\Delta x_j = -\alpha \frac{\partial E_j}{\partial x_j} \text{ and } \Delta y_j = -\alpha \frac{\partial E_j}{\partial y_j} \tag{4}$$

where $0 < \alpha << 1$.

3   Analysis

In this section we analyze the accuracy of the coordinate system produced by this algorithm. In particular we are interested in the effect of the random distribution of sensors and the average local neighborhood size on the accuracy of the position estimates. Accuracy is measured by computing the average absolute error (distance) between the actual physical location and the logical position. The error comes from two sources: (1) errors in the distance estimates produced by gradients and (2) errors produced by combining the distance estimates using multilateration.

For the purpose of analysis, the sensors are assumed to be distributed independently and randomly on a unit square plane. This means that for each sensor we choose a random x coordinate and random y coordinate on the unit square, independently of all other sensors. The probability that there are k sensors in a given area a can be described by a Poisson distribution [10].

$$Pr(\text{k sensors in area a}) = \frac{(\rho a)^k}{k!} e^{-\rho a}$$

From this formula, we can derive the expected number of sensors in area a to be ρa. ρ is equal to $\frac{N}{S}$ where N is the total number of sensors and S is the total surface area. The value that we are interested in is the expected number of sensors in a local neighborhood, which we will call n_{local}. A sensor communicates with all other sensors within the communication radius r. Thus the expected local neighborhood n_{local} is $\rho \pi r^2$. In reality the sensors are randomly distributed but would probably not arbitrarily overlap, which reduces the variance in local neighborhood sizes. This random distribution represents a worst case analysis where sensors may overlap arbitrarily.

3.1   Error in Distance Estimate

The first source of error in distance estimate arises from the discrete distribution of sensors. A gradient computes the shortest communication path from the source to any sensor. Let the gradient value of sensor i be h_i, then the distance between sensor i and the source is at least $h_i \times r$. In the ideal case the gradient value is equal to the straight-line distance, which would imply that with each communication hop one moved a distance r closer to the source. However given any two sensors, there may not be enough intermediate nodes for the shortest communication path to lie along the straight-line path between the source and destination. In that case, the gradient value overestimates the actual distance between the sensor and the source. Intuitively this is related to the density of sensors within a local neighborhood.

We can characterize the effect of density on the error using results derived in the context of random plane graphs and packet radio networks. In these models, receivers are spatially distributed (usually randomly) and each receiver communicates via broadcast with all neighbors within a fixed radius. The goal is usually to guarantee connectivity and optimize network throughput. Shivendra *et al* showed that the theoretical expected local neighborhood n_{local} to ensure connectedness is between 2.195 and 10.526 and simulation experiments suggest at least 5 [13]. Silvester and Kleinrock proved that $n_{local} = 6$ produces optimal network throughput for randomly distributed receivers [7]. In the process they

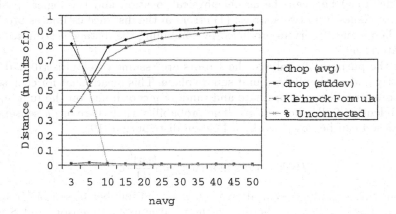

Fig. 2. Theoretical and experimental values for the average distance covered in one communication hop d_{hop}, for different expected local neighborhoods n_{local}. There is significant improvement below $n_{local} = 15$, after which increasing the neighborhood size has diminishing returns.

derived a formula for how the expected distance covered in one communication hop is affected by the parameters of the random distribution. The expected distance covered per communication hop, d_{hop}, is the physical distance between a pair of sensors divided by the expected number of hops in the shortest communication path. Kleinrock and Silvester [7] showed that d_{hop} depends only on the expected local neighborhood n_{local}, not the total number of sensors.[1]

$$d_{hop} = r(1 + e^{-n_{local}} - \int_{-1}^{1} e^{-\frac{n_{local}}{\pi}(\arccos t - t\sqrt{1-t^2})} dt) \qquad (5)$$

In Figure 2, we numerically compute and plot d_{hop} for different n_{local} using this formula. From this graph we can see that when the expected number of local neighbors is small, the distance covered per communication hop is small and the percentage of disconnected sensors is large. But as the expected local neighborhood increases, the probability of nodes along the straight-line path increases rapidly until $n_{local} = 15$, when further increases in local sensor density has diminishing returns. Hence the analysis suggests n_{local} of 15 to be a critical threshold for achieving low errors in the distance estimates.

---

[1] Since n_{local} is proportional to N/S where N is the total number of sensors, it would seem odd to say that the formula does not depend on the total number of sensors. However if n_{local} is kept constant and N is increased (which implies the total area S must increase), then N has no effect. Hence it is appropriate to say that d_{hop} depends on only n_{local}.

In Figure 2, we also show the measured value of the average distance covered per hop for different n_{local}, averaged over several simulations of a gradient from a random source. We also show the percentage of unconnected sensors. The result confirms that the average distance covered per hop does vary as predicted by Kleinrock and Silvester. The formula slightly under-predicts d_{hop} due to an approximation made in the proof when the source and destination are close. Also, the simulation results suggest n_{local} of at least 10 is necessary to significantly reduce the probability of isolated sensors.

Improving the Distance Estimate through Smoothing. Even in the ideal case of infinite density, the distance estimates produced are still integral multiples of the communication radius r. This low resolution adds an average error of approximately $0.5\ r$ to the distance estimates. Therefore we expect the error to asymptote around $0.5\ r$.

The gradient distance estimate is improved by using local averaging. Each sensor collects its neighboring gradient values and computes an average of itself and neighbor values.

$$s_i = \frac{\sum_{j \in nbrs(i)} h_j + h_i}{|nbrs(i)| + 1} - 0.5 \tag{6}$$

where h_i is the gradient value at sensor i (in other words, the integral distance estimate in units of r). $nbrs(i)$ are all the sensors within the communication radius r of sensor i.

Intuitively, sensors can determine if they are on the edge of the band by noticing that a large fraction of their neighbors have an integral distance estimate one lower or one higher than their own. The larger the fraction, the closer they are to the edge. The formula is derived from the effect of smoothing a gradient on a linear array of evenly spaced sensors where it produces the perfect distance (formal derivation in [11]). However in our model the sensors are not evenly spaced and there are variations in density even within a neighborhood. The variations in density are the main source of error in the smoothing process.

Simulation Results on Distance Error. Figure 3 shows results from simulation experiments that calculate the average absolute error in the integral distance estimates for different values of n_{local}. To vary n_{local}, the total number of sensors N is changed while keeping S and r constant. This keeps the physical diameter of the network (in units of r) constant across all simulations, so that all experiments are equally affected by any errors correlated with distance. In each simulation a gradient is produced by a randomly chosen sensor in the lower left corner. The data point for each value of n_{local} is averaged over 10 simulations. The absolute error for a sensor i is computed as $error_i = h_i d_{hop} - d_i$, where h_i is the gradient value, d_i is the Euclidean distance between sensor i and the source, and d_{hop} is the expected distance covered per hop calculated using

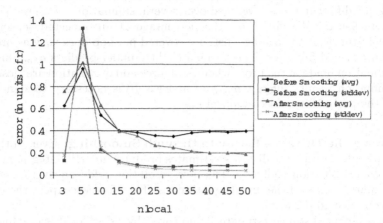

Fig. 3. Average error in gradient distance estimates for different n_{local}. Significant improvements are seen in the integral distance estimates for $n_{local} < 15$. Beyond 15 there is improvement when the distance estimates are smoothed.

formula 5. This takes into account the fact that d_{hop} represents the expected distance traveled in one hop for a given sensor density.

The results confirm our earlier analysis. As the value of n_{local} increases the accuracy of the distance estimate improves, with both the average and standard deviations in error decreasing dramatically. However past $n_{local} = 15$ the error before smoothing asymptotes at 0.4r due to the limited resolution. Further analysis of these simulations shows that the error does not increase significantly with distance from the source because the majority of the per hop error is removed by using Kleinrock and Silvester's formula (5). The error is also not correlated with orientation about the source which is an interesting side-effect of choosing a random distribution versus a rectangular or hexagonal grid where there is anisotropy.

For each of the experiments done for integral gradient values, we also calculated the error in the smoothed gradient value for each sensor. The average error results are also plotted in the same figure. The simulation experiments show that for $n_{local} > 15$ smoothing significantly reduces the average error in the gradient value. Before that the error is dominated by the integral distance error. At $n_{local} = 40$ the average error is as low as 0.2 r. However the error is never reduced to zero due to the uneven distribution of sensors.

3.2   Accuracy of Multilateration

The distance estimates from each of the seeds has a small expected error. We combine these distance estimates by minimizing the squared error from each

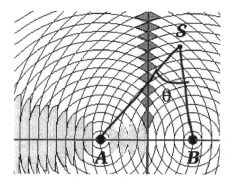

Fig. 4. Error in position relative to two seeds can be approximated as a parallelogram. The area of this parallelogram depends on the angle θ. When θ is 90 degrees the error is minimized, however in certain regions θ is very small resulting in very large error.

of the seeds using a multilateration formula. Multilateration is a well-studied technique that computes the maximum likelihood position estimation. We use gradient descent to compute the multilateration incrementally.

The seed placement has a significant effect on the amount of error in the position of a sensor. The error in the distance estimate from a single seed is radially symmetric. However, when the distances from multiple seeds are combined, the error varies depending on the position of the sensor relative to the seeds. In Figure 4 the concentric bands around each seed represents the uncertainty of the distance estimate from that seed; the width of the band is the expected error in the distance estimate. The intersection region of the two bands represents the region within which a sensor "may" exist — the larger the region, the larger the uncertainty in the position of the sensor. Hence the error in position of a sensor depends not only on the error in the distance estimates, but also in the position of the sensor relative to the two sources. Let ϵ be the expected error in the distance estimates from a seed, and θ be the angle $\angle$ ASB. The overlap region between two bands can be approximated as a parallelogram.

Theorem 1: *The expected error in the position of a sensor S relative to two point sources A and B is determined by the area of the parallelogram with perpendiculars of length 2ϵ and internal angle θ. The area is $\frac{(2\epsilon)^2}{\sin\theta}$.*

The area of the parallelogram is minimized when θ is 90 degrees (square) and when θ is very large or very small the bands appear to be parallel to each other resulting in very large overlaps and hence large uncertainty.

As we add more seeds, the areas of uncertainty will decrease because there will be more bands intersecting. If placed correctly the intersecting regions can be kept small in all regions. This analysis suggests first placing seeds along the perimeter to avoid the large overlaps regions behind seeds. However if seeds are inexpensive then another possibility is simply to place them randomly.

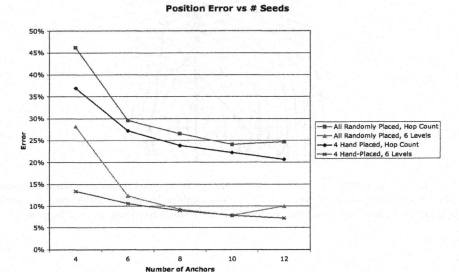

Fig. 5. Graph of position error versus number of seeds for two different seed placement strategies. Position error for smoothed hop count and 6 level radio strength distance estimates are shown.

Simulation results on Position Error. The simulations presented here are motivated by an actual scenario of 200 sensors distributed randomly over a square region $6r \times 6r$. This gives a local neighborhood size of roughly 20, which we know from our previous analysis to give good distance estimates. We investigate two seed placement methods: (1) all seeds are randomly placed and (2) four are hand placed at the corners and the rest are randomly placed. Figure 5 shows the location estimation accuracy averaged over 100 runs with increasing numbers of seeds.

We can see that location accuracy is reasonably high even in the worst case scenario with all randomly placed seeds. Accuracy improves with the hand placement of a few. However, the accuracy of both strategies converge as the number of seeds increases and the improvement levels off at about ten seeds. These results suggest that reasonable accuracy can be achieved by carefully placing a small number of seeds when possible or using a large number of seeds when you are unable to control seed placement.

3.3   Theoretical Limit on Resolution

There is, in fact, a fundamental limit to the accuracy of any coordinate system developed strictly from the topology of the sensor graph. We can think of each sensor as a node in a graph, such that two nodes are connected by an edge if

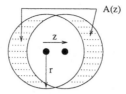

Fig. 6. A sensor can move a distance z without changing the connectivity if there are no sensors in the shaded area.

and only if the sensors can communicate in one hop, i.e. they are less than r distance apart. It is possible to physically move a sensor a non-zero distance without changing the set of sensors it communicates with, and thus without changing any position estimate that is based strictly on communication. The old and new locations of the sensor are indistinguishable from the point of view of the gradient. The average distance a sensor can move without changing the connectivity of the sensor graph gives a lower bound on the expected resolution achievable.

Theorem 2: *The expected distance a sensor can move without changing the connectivity of the sensor graph on an amorphous computer is* $(\frac{\pi}{4n_{local}})r$.

Proof: Let Z be a continuous random variable representing the maximum distance a sensor p can be moved without changing the neighborhood. The probability that Z is less than some real value z is:

$$F(z) = Pr(Z \le z) = 1 - e^{-\rho A(z)}$$

which is the probability that there is at least one sensor in the shaded area $A(z)$ (Figure 6). The area $A(z)$ can be approximated as $4rz$ when z is small compared to r and we expect z to be small for reasonable densities of sensors. The expected value of Z is:

$$E(Z) = \int_0^\infty z\dot{F}(z)dz \tag{7}$$

$$= \int_0^\infty \rho 4rz e^{-\rho 4rz}dz \tag{8}$$

$$= -ze^{-\rho 4rz}\Big|_0^\infty + (-\frac{1}{\rho 4r})e^{-\rho 4rz}\Big|_0^\infty \tag{9}$$

$$= -(z + \frac{1}{\rho 4r})e^{-\rho 4rz}\Big|_0^\infty \tag{10}$$

$$= r(\frac{\pi}{4n_{local}}) \quad \text{q.e.d} \tag{11}$$

where Equation 9 is by the product rule.

Hence, we do not expect to achieve resolutions smaller than $\frac{\pi}{4n_{local}}$ of the local communication radius, r, on an amorphous computer. Whether such a resolution

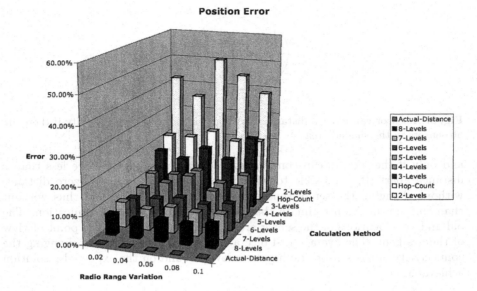

Fig. 7. Graph of the effect of 0-10% communication radius variation and different levels of signal strength quantization on location estimation accuracy.

is achievable is a different question. For n_{local}=15. this implies a resolution limit of .05r, which is far below that achieved by the gradients.

4   Improving Estimates Using Inter-sensor Distance Measurements

One virtue of our algorithm is that it can function in the absence of direct distance measurements. At the same time, our algorithm can be easily generalized to incorporate direct distance measurements if available. For example, suppose that sensors are able to estimate the distance of neighboring sensors through radio strength, then these estimates can easily be used in place of r, or one hop.

In the signal strength simulation experiments, we show the error in position estimates as we allow multiple levels of quantization. What that means is, for a sensor i with 2 levels of quantization, it can tell whether its neighbor is within 1 mini hop or two mini hops. Figure 5 shows the position error for the case of six radio levels in the randomly placed and 4 seeds hand placed seed placement regimes for increasing numbers of seeds. First, we can see that six levels of quantization information gives much improved accuracy over smoothed hop count information. Second, like for hop count, the accuracy improves with increased numbers of seeds tapering off at 10 seeds.

Figure 7 shows the effect of different amounts of signal strength information on location estimation accuracy for eight seeds. We see that position accuracy increases with increased levels of quantization. Beyond 7 levels there are diminishing returns. Our original position estimates based on hop count with no quantization yield a position accuracy between 2 and 3 levels of quantizations. This is because we us local averaging to improve the distance estimates. It unclear how smoothing could be used in conjunction with quantization which we plan to investigate in the future.

We get very high position accuracy with six levels of quantization: error less than 10%. At this level of accuracy with a radius of 20 feet, we could discern locations within 2 feet, which is comparable to commercial GPS. Furthermore, we have found experimentally that this is an achievable level of quantization on the Berkeley mica mote [5] hardware.

5   Robustness

Up to this point we have assumed that each of our sensors had the same communication radius r. In a real-world application we would expect to see variations in radio range from sensor to sensor. Our algorithm can also tolerate variations in communication radius. In Figure 7 we show the error in distance estimate and position estimates when we allow up to 10% random variation in the communication radius. As we can see, the position estimates are reasonably robust to variation in sensor communication radius, tolerating up to 10% variation in range with little degradation.

The algorithm can also adapt automatically to the death and addition of sensors and seeds. If sensors are added, they can locally query neighbors for gradient values and broadcast their value. If this causes any of their neighbors distances estimates to change then those changes will ripple through the network. As a sensor receives new gradient values it can just factor that into the multilateration process. New seeds simply initiate gradients and any sensor that hears a new seed can then incorporate that seed value into the multilateration process. Prior location estimates will serve as good initial locations for multilateration ensuring fast convergence.

If we assume that sensors randomly fail, then the accuracy is not affected unless the average density falls below 15. If sensors in a region die then this affects the distance estimates because the information will travel around the hole and not represent the true distance. However regional failures can be easily corrected by randomly sprinkling new sensors in that area.

The effect of seed failure depends on their placement strategy. Random placement would be more statistically robust in the face of seed failure. Other placement strategies would be more fragile. In these regimes, sensors have to recognize that seeds have failed to then exclude them from multilateration [2].

Our algorithm can tolerate a certain amount of random radio failure, because there are multiple redundant paths from seeds to sensors and therefore distance estimates are repeated many times. In general, the error caused by occasional

---

[2] perhaps using active monitoring of neighbors' aliveness to produce active gradients.

message loss is unlikely to be anywhere close to the error caused by the random distribution of sensors.

6   Application to Tracking

Once a coordinate system is established it is then possible to provide a variety of location based services, two of which we briefly describe here. The first is the *position service*, in which a new (and possibly mobile) member of the ensemble is informed of its own location. The second is *tracking* in which the ensemble members collectively track the position of a mobile (and possibly uncooperative) object based on sensor data.

The position service is a simple application of the multilateration framework. When a sensor broadcasts a position service request, every element of the ensemble within the radio range of the sender responds by sending back its own computed location. The requester then captures the location of each replying element and also estimates the distance to that element using radio strength. Since the requester now knows the estimated position and distance to several other elements in the ensemble, it can use multilateration to compute its own position.

The tracking algorithm employs the multilateration framework in conjunction with ad hoc group formation. We describe an algorithm capable of tracking a single target. We assume that each element of the ensemble is equipped with a sensor that can detect and estimate the distance to the target. Each sensor only attends to targets that are no further away than half a radio range; as a result all sensors that sense a target are within one radio range of one another and may therefore communicate with each other using only *local broadcast* which we use to mean that an element transmits a message over its radio, expecting it to be heard by all elements within its radio range and no others.

The elements that can sense the target form an *ad hoc tracking group*; each member of the group sends to the leader its own position and its estimate of the distance between itself and the target. The group leader then employs multilateration to calculate the estimated position of the target. As the target moves, each group member sends updated estimates of distance to the group leader which then re-estimates the position of the target (using the previous estimate as a seed). The target will initially be roughly at the center of the tracking group, surrounded by the group members. Group members drop out of the group when they cease to be able to sense the target.

Forming the group: Group formation is based on the leader election algorithm presented in [12]. This is a randomized greedy election algorithm that establishes which sensors are *follower* members of the tracking group and which unique sensor is the group *leader*. Initially, all sensors are neither members nor leaders. When a sensor first senses the target it picks a random number (bounded above by the neighborhood size) and begins counting down to 0. If the sensor counts down to 0 without receiving a *recruit* message from another, it then becomes the group leader and immediately locally broadcasts a recruit message containing its own identity. If, however, a sensor receives a *recruit* message before it has counted down to zero, it becomes a follower group member.

Estimating Target Position: When recruited, a follower locally broadcasts a *joining group* message containing its position and its estimate of the distance to the target. Whenever a follower sensor senses a change in the distance to the target it locally broadcasts a *position update* message. The leader captures these distance estimates and periodically uses multilateration to estimate the position of the target.

When a follower sensor notices that it can no longer sense the target it locally broadcasts a *member bailout* message. The group leader then removes this element from the vector of estimated positions and distances. When the group leader notices that it can no longer sense the target, it locally broadcasts a *leader bailout* message. This message contains the identify of that member of the group that the leader estimates is closest to the target. Group members respond to receipt of a leader bailout message in two ways: If the group member is the element named in the bailout message, it immediately becomes the new group leader by locally broadcasts a recruit message. Every other group member, acts as if it had just sensed the target for the first time and begins the countdown of the leader election algorithm. Normally, the follower sensors are recruited by the new leader and the group is reconstituted. However, even if the designated new leader for some reason fails to assume group leadership (for example, the bailout message was garbled in transmission), one of the other sensors will claim leadership and recruit the rest.

We have studied the tracking algorithm by simulating a moving target traversing a path between a series of way points at constant speed. Preliminary results show that the algorithm has positional accuracy comparable to that of the multilateration method used to induce the coordinate system. It also maintains contact with the target quite well, losing the target for about 1% of the cycles.

7 Conclusions and Future Work

In this paper, we present an algorithm to self-organize a global coordinate system on an ad hoc wireless sensor network. Our algorithm relies on distributed simple computation and local communication only, features that an ad hoc sensor network can provide in abundance. At the same time it is able to achieve very reasonable accuracy and the error is theoretically analyzable. The algorithm gracefully adapts to take advantage of any improved sensor capabilities or availability of additional seeds. Given that so much can be achieved from so little, an interesting question is whether more complicated computation is worth it. We are in the process of realizing this algorithm on the Berkeley mote platform [5] towards a implementation of tracking a rover in a field populated by sensors.

Acknowledgements. This research is supported by DARPA under contract number F33615-01-C-1896, and by the National Science Foundation under a grant on Quantum and Biologically Inspired Computing (QuBIC) from the Division of Experimental and Integrative Activities, contract EIA-0130391.

References

1. Paramvir Bahl and Venkata N. Padmanabhan. Radar: An in-building rf-based user location and tracking system. In *Proceedings of Infocom 2000*, 2000.
2. Nirupama Bulusu, John Heidemann, Deborah Estrin, and Tommy Tran. Self-configuring localization systems: Design and experimental evaluation. Submmited to ACM TECS Special Issue on Netowork Embedded Computing, August 2002.
3. US Wireless Corporation. http://www.uswcorp.com/USWCMainPages/our.htm.
4. L. Doherty, L. El Ghaoui, and K. S. J. Pister. Convex position estimation in wireless sensor networks. In *Proceedings of Infocom 2001*, April 2001.
5. J. Hill, R. Szewczyk, A. Woo, S. Hollar, D. Culler, and K. Pister. System architecture directions for networked sensors. In *Proceedings of ASPLOS-IX*, 2000.
6. B. Hofmann-Wellenhoff, H. Lichtennegger, and J. Collins. *Global Positioning System: Theory and Practice, Fourth Edition*. Springer Verlag, 1997.
7. L. Kleinrock and J. Silvester. Optimum tranmission radii for packet radio networks or why six is a magic number. *Proc. Natnl. Telecomm. Conf.*, pages 4.3.1–4.3.5, 1978.
8. N. Lynch. *Distributed Algorithms*. Morgan Kaufmann Publishers, Wonderland, 1996.
9. James D. McLurkin. Algorithms for distributed sensor networks. Master's thesis, UCB, December 1999.
10. W. Mendenhall, D. Wackerly, and R. Scheaffer. *Mathematical Statistics with Applications*. PWS-Kent Publishing Company, Boston, 1989.
11. R. Nagpal. Organizing a global coordinate system from local information on an amorphous computer. AI Memo 1666, MIT, 1999.
12. R. Nagpal and D. Coore. An algorithm for group formation in an amorphous computer. In *Proceedings of the 10th IASTED International Conference on Parallel and Distributed Computing and Systems (PDCS'98)*, October 1998.
13. Philips, Shivendra, Panwar, and Tatami. Connectivity properties of a packet radio network model. *IEEE Transactions on Information Theory*, 35(5), September 1998.
14. Nissanka B. Priyantha, Anit Chakraborty, and Hari Balakrishnan. The cricket location-support system. In *Proceedings of MobiCom 2000*, August 2000.
15. A. Savvides, C. Han, and M. Strivastava. Dynamic fine-grained localization in ad-hoc networks of sensors. In *Proceedings of ACM SIGMOBILE*, July 2001.

A Performance Evaluation of Intrusion-Tolerant Routing in Wireless Sensor Networks

Jing Deng, Richard Han, and Shivakant Mishra

University of Colorado at Boulder, Computer Science Department
{jing,rhan,mishras}@cs.colorado.edu

Abstract. This paper evaluates the performance of INSENS, an INtrusion-tolerant routing protocol for wireless SEnsor Networks. Security in sensor networks is important in battlefield monitoring and home security applications to prevent intruders from eavesdropping, from tampering with sensor data, and from launching denial-of-service (DOS) attacks against the entire network. The resilience of INSENS's multipath performance against various forms of communication-based attacks by intruders is evaluated in simulation. Within the context of INSENS, the paper evaluates implementations on the motes of the RC5 and AES encryption standards, an RC5-based scheme to generate message authentication codes (MACs), and an RC5-based generation of one-way sequence numbers.

1 Introduction

Wireless sensor networks (WSNs) are rapidly emerging as an important new area in the research community. Applications of WSNs are numerous and growing, and range from indoor deployment scenarios in the home and office to outdoor deployment scenarios in natural, military and embedded settings. For military settings, dispersal of WSNs into an adversary's territory enables the detection and tracking of enemy soldiers and vehicles. For home/office environments, indoor sensor networks offer the ability to monitor the health of the elderly and to detect intruders via a wireless home security system. In each of these scenarios, lives and livelihoods may depend on the timeliness and correctness of the sensor data obtained from dispersed sensor nodes. As a result, such WSNs must be secured to prevent an intruder from obstructing the delivery of correct sensor data and from forging sensor data [1] [2] [3]. To address these issues, this paper develops a secure routing system that is resilient to attempts to obstruct data delivery, and in so doing also develops end-to-end data integrity checksums and authentication schemes that can be used to detect tampering with sensor data.

The design and implementation of secure routing in WSNs must simultaneously address three difficult research challenges. First, wireless communication among the sensor nodes increases the vulnerability of the network to eavesdropping, unauthorized access, spoofing, replay and denial-of-service(DOS) attacks. Second, the sensor nodes themselves are highly resource-constrained in terms of limited memory, CPU, communication bandwidth, and especially battery life.

F. Zhao and L. Guibas (Eds.): IPSN 2003, LNCS 2634, pp. 349–364, 2003.

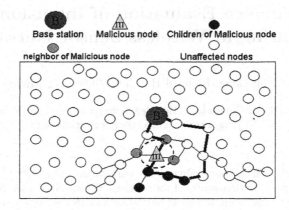

Fig. 1. Sample asymmetric WSN topology rooted at the base station. Triangle node is a malicious node. Black nodes are its downstream nodes. Intrusion-tolerant routing is assisted by multiple paths; downstream nodes can still communicate with the base station.

These resource constraints limit the degree of encryption, decryption, and authentication that can be implemented on individual sensor nodes, and call into question the suitability of traditional security mechanisms such as compute-intensive public-key cryptography. Third, WSNs face the added physical security risk of being deployed in the field, so that individual sensor nodes can be obtained and subject to attacks from a potentially well-equipped intruder in order to compromise a single resource-poor node. Following a successful attack, a compromised sensor node could then be used to instigate such malicious activities as advertising false routing information, possibly unbeknownst to the sensor network, and launching DOS attacks from within the sensor network.

Given these threats and resource constraints, our approach for securing WSNs concedes that a well-equipped intruder can compromise individual sensor nodes, but that the overall design of our secure routing system should tolerate these intrusions such that the network as a whole remains functioning. We assume that the base station has considerably more resources to defend itself against attacks, and therefore concentrate on securing the system against attacks on the weakest links, namely the resource-poor sensor nodes. We have designed and implemented an INtrusion-tolerant routing protocol for wireless SEnsor NetworkS(INSENS) [14] that has the property that a single compromised node can only disrupt a localized portion of the network, and cannot bring down the entire sensor network.

The INSENS secure routing system adheres to the following design principles. First, to prevent DOS-style flooding attacks, individual nodes are not allowed to broadcast to the entire network. Only the base station shown in Figure 1 is allowed to broadcast. The base station acts as a gateway to the wired world, e.g. a satellite uplink connecting to terrestrial networks. The base station is loosely authenticated via a one-way sequence number, so that individual nodes cannot arbitrarily spoof the base station and thereby flood the network. Sensor nodes are restricted to only unicasting a packet, and then only to the base station, thereby preventing DOS/DDOS broadcast attacks. Peer-to-peer sensor communication is not directly supported, though tunneling through the base station permits indirect sensor-to-sensor communication. Second, to prevent advertisement of false routing data, control routing information must be authenticated. A key consequence of this approach is that the base station always receives knowledge of the topology that is correct, though it may only represent a partial picture due to malicious packet dropping. Third, to address resource constraints, 1) symmetric key cryptography is chosen for confidentiality and authentication between the base station and each resource-constrained sensor node, since it is considerably less compute-intensive than public key cryptography, and 2) the resource-rich base station is chosen as the central point for computation and dissemination of the routing tables. Fourth, to address the notion of compromised nodes, redundant multipath routing is built into INSENS to achieve secure routing, as shown in Figure 1. The goal is to have disjoint paths so that even if an intruder takes down a single node or path, secondary paths will exist to forward the packet to the correct destination.

In the remainder of the paper, we provide an overview of the INSENS system in Section 2, present simulation results in Section 3, an implementation of INSENS in Section 4, and address related work in Section 5.

2   Protocol Description

In this section, we provide a brief overview of INSENS. For a more detailed description, see [14]. INSENS is comprised of a route discovery phase and a data forwarding phase. The route discovery phase ascertains the topology of the sensor network and builds appropriate forwarding tables at various nodes. Route discovery is subdivided into three rounds. In the first round, the base station floods (limited flooding) a *request message* to all the reachable sensor nodes in the network. In the second round, each sensor node send its neighborhood topology information back to the base station using a *feedback message*. In the third round, the base station authenticates the neighborhood information, constructs a topological picture of the network, computes the forwarding tables for each sensor node, and sends the tables to the respective nodes using a *routing update message*. The data forwarding phase enables forwarding of data from each sensor node to the base station, and vice versa. A symmetric communication channel is assumed, i.e. if node a can hear a message from node b, then a can send a message to b.

Each node has a shared symmetric key with base station. Every node also possesses a globally known one-way function F and initial sequence number K_0. F and K_0 are used together to loosely authenticate messages from the base station, as explained next. All three pieces of information, namely F, K_0, and the shared symmetric key, are distributed in advance, i.e. they are preprogrammed into each sensor node before deployment. We envision that military applications will for example permit secret keys to be preprogrammed into sensor nodes before deployment.

2.1   Route Discovery: Route Request

The base station initiates the first round whenever it needs to construct the forwarding tables of all sensor nodes. The base station broadcasts a *request message* that is received by all of its neighbors. A request message broadcast by a node x includes a path from the base station to x. When a node receives a request message for the first time, it forwards (broadcasts) this message after appending its identity in the path. It also records the identity of the sender of this message in its neighbor set. When a node receives a duplicate request message, the identity of the sender is added to its neighbor set, but the request is not rebroadcast.

A malicious node in the network can attempt to launch several attacks in this round. First, it can attempt to spoof the base station by sending a spurious request message. Second, it can include a fake path in the request message it forwards. Third, it may not forward a request message, or launch a DOS attack by repeatedly sending several request messages. We use two mechanisms to counter these attacks. Both of these mechanisms require sensor nodes to be pre-configured with appropriate values.

First, the base station uses a one-way cryptographic hash function F to generate a sequence of numbers $K_0, K_1, \ldots, K_n$, such that $K_i = F(K_{i+1})$, where $0 \leq i < n$. Initially, every node knows F and K_0. In the first route discovery phase, the base station includes K_1 in the request message that it broadcasts. In general, the base station uses K_i in the ith route discovery phase. Each node can verify that the sequence number did indeed originate from the base station by computing $K_i = F(K_{i+1})$. An attacker who compromised a sensor node would be unable to guess the next one-way sequence number given the most recent sequence number, i.e. given F, K_0, and the most recent sequence K_i, the attacker cannot invert F to generate the next sequence number K_{i+1}. As a result, a compromised node cannot spoof the base station by generating new sequence numbers. However, a compromised node could repeat the current sequence number in a request message to its downstream nodes, who would then believe that the compromised node is the base station. The damage in this case is localized to the compromised node, which was our design objective. The rest of the network will receive the authentic base station's route request first, and will therefore ignore the compromised node's route request. Our usage of one-way functions leverages the approach taken by the μTESLA protocol [10], but differs in the sense that the numbers in the one-way chain are sequence numbers rather than symmetric keys.

The second mechanism that we use is a keyed MAC algorithm. Each sensor node is configured with a separate secret key that is shared only with the base station. When a node x receives a request message for the first time, it appends its identity to the path list, and then generates a MAC of the complete new path with its key. This MAC is also appended to the request message, before the modified request message is forwarded downstream. This MAC will eventually be used by the base station to verify the integrity of the path contained in the packet. Also, when a node is compromised, only one secret key is revealed, so an attacker cannot compromised the entire network.

The overall effect of these security mechanisms is that a malicious node can attack in the first round only by localized flooding, by not forwarding a request message, and by sending fake path in the request which is later on detected in the second round. The latter two attacks will result in some of the nodes downstream from the malicious node not getting a request message or not being able to forward their feedback message to the base station in the second round.

2.2   Route Discovery: Route Feedback

In the second round, each sensor node sends its local connectivity information (a set of identities of its neighbor nodes as well as the path to itself from the base station) back to the base station using a *feedback message*. After a node x has forwarded its request message in round one, it waits for a certain timeout interval before generating a feedback message. During this time interval, it listens to the local broadcasts from neighboring nodes forwarding the same request message, and stores the neighbor's identity and the neighbor's MAC embedded within the request message. After the timeout, the sensor node will send its list of neighbors (upstream, peer, and downstream) back to the base station, where each neighbor is identified by the neighbor's identity and the neighbor's MAC. The sensor node applies its keyed MAC to the topology data, i.e. the list of neighbors, to further protect the integrity of the feedback message. The messages that reach the base station are guaranteed after verification to be correct and secure from tampering.

Routing of the *feedback message* from a node x to the base station follows the reverse path taken by the request message that initiated the feedback response. To ensure that malicious nodes do not generate false paths while forwarding a feedback message, a node places its parent identification information along with its parent's MAC, that it received in the first request message. Each node will choose one legitimate upstream parent, forming a parental chain of nodes back to the base station. A compromised node will at most be able to flood each of its parents' chains back to the base stations, but no other nodes. This localizes the effect of an attack. To further restrict attacks, rate control is applied at each node; regardless of the incoming traffic rate, the outgoing traffic rate of each node is restricted to some maximum rate, thereby preventing flooding. Also, each node encrypts appropriate information in the feedback message it sends to provide confidentiality against eavesdropping by a malicious node.

The overall effect of these security mechanisms is that a malicious node is limited in the damage it can inflict, whether attacking by DOS attack, by not forwarding a *feedback message* or by modifying the neighborhood information of nodes, which can be detected at the base station. These attacks will result in some of the nodes down-stream from the malicious node not being able to provide their correct connectivity information to the base station. Though a malicious node could launch a battery-drain attack by persistently sending spurious feedback messages at the rate-controlled limit, such an attack would still affect only a limited number of upstream nodes.

2.3 Route Discovery: Computing and Propagating Multipath Routing Tables

After sending its request message in the first round, the base station waits for a certain period of time to collect all the connectivity information received via *feedback messages*. Each node returns an authenticated list of its neighboring nodes. As a result, the base station is able to verify the neighbor information and detect tampering with feedback messages. The base station constructs a topology of the network from these authenticated feedback messages, though this picture of the network may be incomplete due to dropped feedback messages. From this connectivity information, the base station computes the forwarding tables of each node in the network.

INSENS incorporates redundancy in routing by building multiple redundant paths to bypass intruders while routing messages, as shown in Figure 1. These paths are independent of one another in the sense that they share as few common nodes/links as possible; ideally, only the source and the destination nodes are shared among paths. The presence of one or more intruders along some of these paths can jeopardize the delivery of some of the copies of a message. However, as long as there is at least one path that is not affected by an intruder, the destination will receive at least one copy of the message that has not been tampered with.

While INSENS is largely agnostic to the particular criteria for choosing multiple paths, we chose the following multipath heuristic in order to proceed with our implementation of INSENS. For a sensor node A, the first path from A to the base station is chosen using Dijkstra's shortest path algorithm. To determine the second path, three sets of nodes, S_1, S_2, and S_3 are first constructed. S_1 is the set of nodes belonging to the first path, S_2 is the set of nodes belonging to S_1 and any neighbor nodes of the nodes in S_1, and S_3 is the set of nodes belonging S_2 and any neighbor nodes of the nodes in S_2. All three sets exclude A or the base station. The second path is then computed as follows:

1. Remove all nodes in S_3 from the network, and find the shortest path from A to the base station. If such a path is found, terminate the computation. The path found is the second path.
2. Otherwise, remove all nodes in S_2 from the original network. Find the shortest path from A to the base station. If such a path is found, terminate the computation. The path found is the second path.
3. Remove all nodes in S_1 from the original network. Find the shortest path from A to the base station. If such a path is found, it is the second path. Otherwise, there is no second path from A to the base station.

Notice that depending on the network topology, it is possible that no second path is found. In that case, the current implementation of INSENS maintains only a single path. Finding a better algorithm to compute multiple paths in INSENS is part of our future work.

After computing the redundant paths for each node, the base station computes the forwarding tables of each node. These forwarding tables are propagated to the respective nodes in a breadth-first manner. The base station first sends the forwarding tables of all nodes that are its immediate neighbors. It then sends the forwarding tables of nodes that are at a distance of two hops from it, and so on. This mechanism cleverly uses the redundant routing mechanism just built to distribute the forwarding tables. Standard security techniques such as those proposed in [10] can be used to preserve the authentication, integrity, and confidentiality of the forwarding tables.

2.4   Data Forwarding

A node maintains a forwarding table that has several entries, one for each route to which the node belongs. Each entry is a 3-tuple: $<$*destination, source, immediate sender*$>$. *Destination* is the node id of the destination node to which a data packet is sent, *source* is the node id of the node that created this data packet, and *immediate sender* is the node id of the node that just forwarded this packet. For example, given a route from node S to D: $S \rightarrow a \rightarrow b \rightarrow c \rightarrow D$, the forwarding table of node a will contain an entry $< D, S, S >$, forwarding table of b will contain an entry $< D, S, a >$, and the forwarding table of c will contain an entry $< D, S, b >$. With forwarding tables constructed in this way, forwarding data packets is quite simple. On receiving a data packet, a node searches for a matching entry $<$*destination, source, immediate sender*$>$ in its forwarding table. If it finds a match, it forwards (broadcasts) the data packet.

3   Simulation

We have simulated INSENS on nsclick [16], a network simulation tool that combines the ns-2 network simulator with the Click Modular Router. We implemented our own Click element to simulate the behavior of INSENS on sensor nodes and the base station. Ns-2 was used to simulate the wireless network environment, including the MAC (Medium Access Control) protocol and the lower layers of the wireless network, as well as the geographic distribution of nodes.

3.1   Malicious Attack during Data Forwarding

INSENS builds two paths to bypass malicious nodes. With two independent routes available between every node and the base station, our protocol's goal is to route messages correctly in the presence of a single malicious node. Interestingly, our protocol deals quite well with multiple malicious nodes as well. We have performed a set of experiments to measure the number of nodes that can be blocked when a set of multiple nodes turn malicious and drop data packets. Figure 2 shows the average number of nodes that can be blocked as a function of the number of malicious nodes. For comparison, we have also calculated this number when a single-path routing algorithm is used instead.

These results are based on a network of 100 nodes and 200 nodes randomly distributed over a $1500 \times 1500m^2$ space. The numbers reported in this figure are averaged over 50 different combinations of nodes randomly selected to be malicious. For example, for 10 malicious nodes, we measured the number of blocked nodes for 50 different combinations selected randomly of 10 nodes turning malicious. For each test, 20 random topologies were chosen.

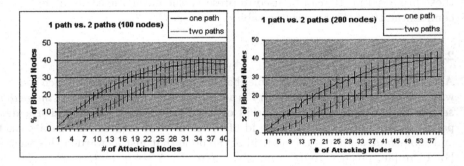

Fig. 2. Multi-node attack on a sensor network that has secure single path and multipath routing. Left graph shows 100 nodes, and right graph shows 200 nodes. X axis: #of attacking nodes. Y axis: #of blocked nodes unable to send packets.

3.2   DOS Attacks

We have performed a set of experiments to analyze the effect of DOS attacks that a malicious node may launch. The DOS attack we have simulated in these experiments is comprised of repeatedly sending data packets to the base station to block the wireless medium and not allow other nodes to send their data packets. DOS attacks are difficult to address completely at the network level. In our opinion, these attacks must be addressed at multiple levels. In our analysis, we have assumed the following: (1) Sensor nodes use an appropriate rate-based control mechanism while forwarding data packets. This implies that a malicious node that repeatedly sends data packets will be able to block its neighbors, but not other (upstream) nodes. (2) The base station has sufficiently large bandwidth available so that a malicious sensor node in its vicinity cannot block the base station by using a DOS attack.

Figure 3 shows the damage a malicious node may cause by launching a DOS attack. The damage caused by a DOS attack depends on the effectiveness of multi-path routing, the density of interconnection of the sensor network, and the topology of the graph. In this experiment, two network densities (sparse and dense) and two topologies (random and grid) are tested. In random generated topologies, the position of each node is randomly selected, and the base station is positioned in the center. The total number of nodes for each random topology is 200. In the grid topology, each node is placed on a square grid. To accommodate the simulator, it was necessary to perturb each position to a small region around each vertex in a square grid graph. In this way, random topologies could be generated even for a nearly uniform square grid. The grid is a 14 × 14 square.

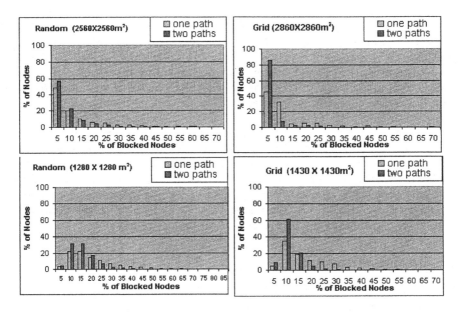

Fig. 3. Histograms of simulated DOS attacks for sparse and dense random and grid topologies.

Figure 3 reveals the performance of INSENS against a single node launching a DOS attack. For either uniform grids or random positioning, we first generate a given topology of scattered nodes. For this topology, we let each node at a time become a DOS intruder and measure the number of blocked nodes downstream affected by the DOS intruder. This generates a histogram per topology. The x-axis records the percentage of nodes that may be blocked by a single-node DOS attack, and the y-axis records the percentage of such nodes in the topology who, if they turned malicious, would have the power to block the number of nodes listed in the x-axis. For clarity, we have grouped the x-axis into bins of 0-5 %, 6-10 %, etc. For both random and grid topologies, we generate 50 such topologies and plot the averaged histogram shown above.

From this figure, we can see that the protection against DOS attacks varies significantly across different network densities and different topologies. As expected, in all cases, the multi-path algorithm provides better protection against DOS attacks than the single path approach. The multi-path approach performs far better for the grid topology, because the grid nearly always offers a valid redundant second path. The best performance of the multi-path approach is obtained for sparse grids (upper right graph), where 85% of intruder nodes are limited to blocking five or fewer nodes. The sparseness limits an intruder to blocking only a few nodes, while the grid almost always offers the sender a valid secondary path. The worst performance of the multi-path approach is obtained for sparse random topologies (upper left graph), in which nodes have few neighbors and few alternate paths (usually only one path) to the base station. In this case, the multi-path approach performs only slightly better than single path routing.

As the network becomes denser, moving from the top row of graphs to the bottom row in Figure 3, attackers are able to block increasing numbers of nodes, and the histograms shift to the right. This is true for both random and grid topologies.

While the figures measure the average response of INSENS, an attacker would benefit by exploiting the topology's structure and identifying the weakest nodes that would partition the graph. Such a partitioning attack would be largely ineffective in grids and/or dense topologies, because such topologies do not easily partition because of alternate paths. Partitioning is a more effective attack for topologies that are both random and sparse. We have not specifically measured INSENS's performance against such a partitioning attack.

4   Implementation

In our implementation, we use UC Berkeley MICA sensor motes [13] as the sensor nodes. The program runs on Atmel Atmega128 microcontroller. The motes support a 4MHZ processor with 128K Bytes code memory and 4K Bytes internal data memory, and an RFM Monolithics TR 1000 radio at 19.2Kbps. INSENS is running on TinyOS 1.0, which is a small, open source, event-driven, energy efficient operating system developed for sensor networks at UC Berkeley.

4.1   Cryptographic Algorithm

To implement INSENS on motes, we need to choose a secure, efficient cryptographic algorithm that can operate correctly, given the resource constraints of motes. To save memory, we should reuse a single cryptographic algorithm for data encryption, MAC generation, and one-way sequence number, as long as their implementations are secure. We chose RC4, RC5, and Rijndael (AES) as candidates. RC5's implementation varies according to the number of rounds. More rounds result in higher security, but require more resources. We implemented RC5 with 5 rounds and 12 rounds. The output of 5 rounds is statistically no different from a random number, and 12 rounds is recommended by

Rivest [17]. We tested the performance of a stream cipher RC4 to compare its performance with block cipher algorithms. RC4 is a very fast stream cipher, but has some weaknesses when used in wireless networks. [18] We also implemented Rijndael on the motes and compared its performance with RC5. We used a standard version of Rijndael [19]. It uses about 1KB memory. There is a fast version that uses about 4KB lookup tables, but that exceeds the memory capabilities of the mote.

To measure performance, we implemented RC4, RC5, and Rijndael on motes to encrypt 200×128 bits of data with CBC mode. To measure the speed of these algorithms on motes, we let the base station send a *"begin"* signal to a mote. On receiving this signal, a mote begins its computation, and after completing the computation, it sends back the result to the base station. The base station records the time interval between when it sent the signal and when it got the data back, verifies the result, subtracts the round-trip time (which is measured in the same way without the mote doing any encryption), and gets the computing time. For each algorithm, we tested it for 20 times. Table 1 shows the calculated average time for computing 128 bits of data for each algorithm.

From Table 1 we see that: 1) RC5 is a good candidate for motes. It uses less memory (both in code size and data size), and it is very efficient. 2) Compared with RC5, Rijndael is very slow. Based on our result, to encrypt a 30Bytes packet, it would spend about 0.2 seconds. However, we believe that in the near future, as sensor nodes become faster and acquire more memory, Rijndael will become a good candidate for cryptographic algorithm on sensor networks. In our implementation, we used RC5 with 5 rounds. We think it is good enough for sensor networks. We can also use RC5 with 12 rounds.

Table 1. Cryptographic Algorithm Overhead

	RC4	RC5		AES
		5 Rounds	12 Rounds	
Speed (128bits/ms)	1.299	5.471	12.475	102.483
Data Size (B)	258	68	124	1165
Code Size (B)	580	1436	1436	9492

We have also implemented RSA public key cryptography on the mote platform and report the following preliminary results. We decrypted 64 bytes of data on the mote with a 1024-bit RSA public key. We found that the measured delay for decryption was approximately 15 seconds. This suggests that public key cryptography could be used in a limited way, e.g. for symmetric key exchange, for certain sensor networks. We also attempted to implement encryption with an RSA private key on the mote, but found that the encryption code died during execution. We hypothesize that encryption exceeded the mote's memory capacity, since RSA encryption consumes more memory than decryption, though more tests are needed to confirm this hypothesis.

Message Authentication Code generation. MAC plays a critical role in INSENS. It is used to authenticate each node, its path, and its neighbor information. We use standard CBC mode to generate MAC with block cipher RC5 [20].

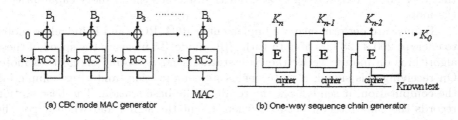

(a) CBC mode MAC generator   (b) One-way sequence chain generator

Fig. 4. CBC-based MAC generation

One-way sequence number generation. The one-way sequence number is used to loosely authenticate the base station. To generate the one-way sequence number, we need a secure one-way function. Our approach is based on the following criteria: By knowing a plaintext and the corresponding ciphertext computed using a block cipher algorithm, such as RC5, we cannot know the key that was used to generate the ciphertext. Our one-way sequence number generator is shown in Figure 4(b). The base station chooses a random key K_n and uses it to encrypt a well-known plaintext and gets a cipher. This cipher is K_{n-1} and the base station uses it as a key to encrypt the same known plaintext. This process continues until we get K_0.

4.2   Implementation Issues

Base Station and Node. We implemented base station in Java. The base station gets information from the mote on the programming board and processes the information, and sends routing tables back to each mote. In our implementation, we used the same strategy described in [14] to find two paths for each node. But we choose BFS (Breadth First Search) algorithm instead of Dijkstra because we assume the cost of each link is same. We implemented INSENS on TinyOS 1.0 with NesC. All of our computing intensive functions are written as tasks, to prevent them from blocking packets or timer interrupts.

Feedback Message Segmentation. On the current TinyOS, the default packet size is 30 bytes, though this can be modified. However the feedback message of INSENS can be far longer, because it contains an authenticated list of neighbors. In our implementation, we segment one feedback message into multiples of 30 byte feedback packets. We add two constraints for feedback packet segmentation to make it work with INSENS and prevent possible attacks. 1) Every segment packet has a sequence number. Any node must forward lower sequence packet before forwarding a higher sequence packet. When a node gets a higher sequence packet while it hasn't got a lower sequence packet, it must drop that packet. 2) The whole path information must be put in the first packet. Upstream nodes need it to forward packets. That limits the longest path at 9. This is suitable for a moderately sized network. Because every feedback message contains a MAC number, which is generated by CBC mode, the malicious node cannot change the sequence of segment packet, or replace a segment packet. The base station can verify the integrity of feedback message sequence packets with the MAC.

Packet Loss. During our experiments, we found that there were many packet losses. The reasons for this may be: 1) The MAC (media access control) layer of TinyOS cannot deal with loss of packets, and INSENS needs to send lots of packets. 2) The packet sending/receiving components of TinyOS cannot receive packets in time.

We employed the following methods to alleviate packet loss. First, random delay is introduced in each mote before forwarding to reduce collisions. Second, when a mote gets a packet, it copies the packet to its frame variable immediately. With these mechanisms, the packet loss was significantly reduced. We note improved MAC protocols [15] could be adopted in the future.

4.3   Performance Evaluation

We have implemented INSENS on motes to build 3-node, 6-node and 10-node networks. Figure 5(a) shows the network topology setup by INSENS for a network of 6 nodes. Every node has its own routing table to route packets. We see that the node 5 has two paths to base station, the first goes through node 6, the second traverses nodes 4 and 1. Because of packet losses, the base station cannot obtain complete network topology information, yet it can still build part of the network based on the request and feed-back messages that do arrive. This is an important feature of INSENS. We measured the memory usage of INSENS and total time to setup the whole network with INSENS, to assess the practicality of INSENS.

Memory Usage of INSENS on Motes. Table 2 shows the memory usage of INSENS. "*Feedback*" is for saving the whole feedback message before segmenting it. "*Packet*" is for saving the incoming packets. In our implementation, we didn't focus on saving memory space, but the result shows that the memory requirements of INSENS can be easily satisfied by the constraints of current mote-based sensor networks. Additional memory savings could be achieved. For example, with a good packet processing mechanism, we don't need "*packet*" space, and with a better packet segmentation implementation, we don't need "*feedback*".

Table 2. Memory Consumption of INSENS (Unit:byte)

code	total data	Crypto	neighbor info	msg & MAC	feedback	packet	OS and others
19000	1200	68	105	105	200	360	360

Network Setup Time. In our implementation, the base station broadcasts a request message, receives all feedback messages, and computes the routing tables. It sends each node's routing table, and waits for a *"routing table received"* message from every node. We measure the time interval between the time the base station broadcasts its request message and the time it gets all *"routing table received"* messages. We set the network as a dense network, so every node has several neighbors. As the number of nodes increased, we experienced more packet losses. But because of the redundancy in neighbor information, the base station was usually able to setup the network based on the limited number of feedback messages that did arrive.

There are several factors affecting the setup time: 1) execution time of cryptographic algorithm, 2) execution time of packet processing, such as sending, receiving, copying, and routing, and 3) waiting time in INSENS, that includes random delay, feedback message waiting time, and the base station waiting time. The base station waits at most 500 ms after receiving a feedback packet. This wait time is reset with each new feedback message. Eventually, no more feedback messages will arrive and the base station will timeout and move on to computing the routing tables. Each sensor node also waits at most 500 ms for neighbor information to be collected. We also tested 700 ms timeouts for the sensor nodes only (not base station). The base station unicast a custom routing table to each mote, and waits 100 ms between sending each routing table. We found that the total network setup time is dominated by the waiting time of the sensor nodes. In comparison, the computation time of RC5-based cryptographic algorithms is relatively short. Figure 5(b) shows our aggregate test results.

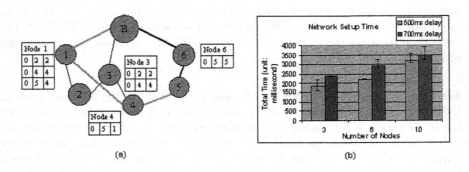

Fig. 5. (a) Routing tables built by INSENS (b) Network setup time

5   Related Work

Sensor network security is a critical issue in sensor network research [4]. Ganesan et al propose a redundant "multipath" routing approach for a sensor network [5] in order to provide fault tolerance and reliable data dissemination. INSENS is largely agnostic to the particular multipath approach employed.

In the field of ad hoc wireless networking, previous work on secure routing employs public key cryptography to perform authentication [6] [4] [7] [8] [9]. Unfortunately, resource constraints in sensor network limit the applicability of these current public/asymmetric key standards.

SPINS [10] addresses secure communication in resource-constrained sensor networks, introducing two low-level secure building blocks, SNEP and μTESLA. Our work uses ideas from SNEP and μTESLA to build INSENS. Like μTESLA, we employ one-way functions, but differ in the sense that the numbers in the one-way chain are sequence numbers rather than symmetric keys. In addition, we are not constrained by time synchronization or a delayed release schedule.

SEADS [11] and Ariadne [12] use symmetric cryptography, a one-way hash function, TESLA, and MACs to build secure wireless network routing. INSENS differs in that it focuses on an asymmetric or hierarchical architecture with a base station and sensors, rather than on peer-to-peer routing.

Staddon et al [21] proposes an efficient algorithm to trace failed nodes in sensor network. Their work also puts intensive computing on the base station, and employs route discovery in a manner similar to our first two rounds. The paper does not address the issue of compromised nodes.

6   Conclusions

In this paper, we have provided an experimental evaluation of INSENS, which is an intrusion-tolerant routing protocol for wireless sensor networks. The resilience of INSENS's multipath performance against various forms of communication-based attacks by intruders is evaluated in simulation. The paper describes practical experiences with implementations of RC5 and AES encryption standards on motes, an RC5-based scheme to generate message authentication codes (MACs), and an RC5-based generation of one-way sequence numbers.

References

1. Wood, A., Stankovic, J.: Denial of Service in Sensor Networks, IEEE Computer, Oct 2002, pp. 54–62.
2. Slijepcevic, S., Potkonjak, M., Tsiatsis, V., Zimbeck, S., Srivastava, M.: On Communication Security in Wireless Ad -Hoc Sensor Networks, Eleventh IEEE International Workshop on Enabling Technologies: Infrastructure for Collaborative Enterprises (WETICE'02), pp. 139–144.
3. Karlof, C., Wagner, D.: Secure Routing in Wireless Sensor Networks: Attacks and Countermeasures, First IEEE International Workshop on Sensor Network Protocols and Applications, May 2003.

4. NAI Lab: http://www.nai.com/nai_labs/asp_set/crypto/crypt_senseit.asp.
5. Ganesan, D., Govindan, R., Shenker, S., Estrin, D.: Highly Resilient, Energy Efficient Multipath Routing in Wireless Sensor Networks. Mobile Computing and Communica-tion Review (MC2R) Vol 1., No.2. 2002.
6. Kong, J.J., Zerfos, P., Luo, H., Lu, S., Zhang, L.X.: Providing Robust and Ubiquitous Security Support for Mobile Ad-Hoc Networks. International Conference on Network Protocols (ICNP 2001).
7. Papadimitratos, P., Haas, Z.: Secure Routing for Mobile Ad hoc Networks. Proceedings of the SCS Communication Networks and Distributed Systems Modeling and Simula-tion Conference (CNDS 2002).
8. Zhou, L., Haas, Z.: Securing Ad Hoc Networks. IEEE Network Magazine, vol. 13, no.6, November/December 1999.
9. Zhang, K.: Efficient protocols for signing routing messages. In Proceedings of the Symposium on Network and Distributed Systems Security (NDSS '98), San Diego, California, March 1998.
10. Perrig, A., Szewczyk, R., Wen, V., Culler, D., Tygar, J.D.: SPINS: Security Protocols for Sensor Networks. Proceedings of Seventh Annual International Conference on Mobile Computing and Networks MOBICOM 2001, July 2001.
11. Hu, Y., Johnson, D., Perrig, A.: SEAD: Secure Efficient Distance Vector Routing for Mobile Wireless Ad Hoc Networks. Fourth IEEE Workshop on Mobile Computing Systems and Applications (WMCSA '02).
12. Hu, Y., Perrig, A., Johnson, D.: Ariadne: A Secure On-Demand Routing Protocol for Ad Hoc Networks. Proceedings of the Eighth Annual International Conference on Mobile Computing and Networking (MobiCom 2002).
13. Hill, J., Szewczyk, R., Woo, A., Hollar, S., Culler, D., Pister, K.: System architecture directions for network sensors. ASPLOS 2000
14. Deng, J., Han, R., Mishra, S.: INSENS: Intrusion-tolerant routing in wireless Sensor NetworkS. Technical Report CU_CS-939-02, Department of Computer Science, University of Colorado, November 2002.
15. Ye, W., Heidemann, J., Estrin, D.: An Energy-Efficient MAC Protocol for Wireless Sensor Networks. Proceedings of the 21st International Annual Joint Conference of the IEEE Computer and Communications Societies (INFOCOM 2002), New York, NY, USA.
16. Neufeld, M., Jain, A., Grunwald, D.: Nsclick: Bridging Network Simulation and Deployment. MSWiM'02, September 28, 2002. Atlanta, Georgia, USA.
17. Schneier, B.: Applied Cryptography, second edition. John Wiley & Sons, Inc. 1996
18. Borisov, N., Goldberg, I., Wagner, D.: Intercepting mobile communications: The insecurity of 802.11. In Proceedings of MOBICOM 2001.
19. Daemen, J., Rijmen, V.: The Design of Rijndael. Springer, (2001) 221–227
20. Menezes, A., etc: Handbook of Applied Cryptography. CRC Press, (1996) 353–354.
21. Staddon, J., Balfanz, D., Durfee, G.: Efficient Tracing of Failed Nodes in Sensor Networks. First Workshop on Sensor Networks and Applications, WSNA'02, Atlanta, Georgia, USA.

Scalable Decentralized Control for Sensor Networks via Distributed Lattices

Baruch Awerbuch[1] and Jonathan Stanton[2]

[1]Department of Computer Science
Johns Hopkins University
Baltimore, MD 21218
baruch@cs.jhu.edu
[2]Department of Computer Science
George Washington University
Washington, DC 20052
jstanton@gwu.edu

Abstract. A network of embedded devices needs to be able to execute queries for dynamically changing content. Even in a completely reliable network, this is a formidable task because of the enormous scale of the networks, severely limited resources of individual devices (bandwidth and battery power) and the heterogeneity of resources being managed. In this work we introduce a novel information query methodology for designing online solutions for heterogeneous sensor networks with various resources (e.g., battery, bandwidth, CPU). This provides a route selection and query management mechanism that will enable a sensor network to find sensor level information without a routing algorithm specialized for the particular form of information. In order to execute such a methodology in a scalable, limited resource environment such as sensor networks we employ a novel lattice data structure, which is basically a combination of trees with small overlap that provably enables extension of any routing or directory infrastructure to an arbitrary scale, with only small overhead. We show how to use such data structures (lattices) that will enable scaling to millions of devices with an overhead that only grows logarithmically in the number of network nodes and with provably small distortion of paths. Moreover, we show a completely distributed implementation of such structures, that creates minimal overload on the client sensors.

1 Introduction

Content addressable routing, namely routing towards the location storing certain data is quite appropriate for embedded networks of many small devices. Instead of addressing a specific device, one needs to route a query to a device that has specific information, e.g. a sensor on (some) bridge. Notice, that content addressable routing greatly increases the scale of the problem (the number of queries is much larger than the number of nodes). In some way, since contents is variable, content addressable routing is equivalent to routing in a network where nodal names are changing arbitrarily (based on the contents).

F. Zhao and L. Guibas (Eds.): IPSN 2003, LNCS 2634, pp. 365–375, 2003.
© Springer-Verlag Berlin Heidelberg 2003

The sheer scale of embedded and sensor networks appears to force a decision based on local information, since the overhead of obtaining the global information may overwhelm the benefit of using it. There is an analogy between routing, content retrieval, and maintenance of local databases of topology and resource depletion information. This analogy is expressed in trade-offs between different generic approaches.

Flooding each piece of information through the network is one extreme. This guarantees the highest quality of information and in a sense simulates global decision making, which results in efficient queries of content or routing of a message. However, the overhead of maintenance is prohibitive and overwhelms the benefits of obtaining the information.

Another extreme is on-demand DSR routing [5] which proceeds by flooding a routing (or information) query upon each request. While this is very expensive operation, it may be meaningful for content-addressable routing, e.g. "connect to the sensor near a human", where there is simply too much content to keep track of.

The above arguments indicate an inherent trade-off between overhead in lookup and overhead in maintenance of data structures. This trade-off has been considered in a number of different papers. Sophisticated methods to examine various trade-offs in matching the sources of queries with sources of content such as directed diffusion [12] illustrate this approach. There is also work on aggregating data from different sources via distributed approximate set cover algorithms [11].

One attempt to avoid this trade-off is geographic "Location aided routing" [18] where the routing request is indicative of the position of the destination; e.g. its GPS coordinates; routing proceeds by making incremental steps toward the destination. This certainly does not work for dynamic content-addressable routing.

Note the assumption that addresses of routing destinations are bound to their geographic location, which inherently assumes that both naming and geography are static. The major (and not so obvious) fallacy of such an approach is the assumption that greedy progress in terms of geographic proximity to the destination is the right strategy. Such a strategy may work well assuming uniform distribution of devices in each geographic region, as well as completely uniform traffic distribution. However, it is easy to see that in fact traffic distribution is highly non-uniform (e.g. few producers and consumers of information). In this case, this strategy may deplete batteries of nodes along the geographically shortest paths, and shut these nodes off. This invalidates the "uniform geographic distribution" assumption, as well as the binding between names and geography leading to potentially catastrophic consequences, since geography is assumed to be static.

Attempts have been made to combine geography with battery utilization, such as GEAR [17] (geographical and energy aware routing); yet there is no rigorous mathematical argument for this strategy being close to optimal. Obviously, the geographic approach is not applicable in this case since the name has nothing to do with the underlying geography.

We address this tradeoff between content dissemination costs and query costs with a general routing algorithm and distributed data-structure that balances the costs while requiring very small storage at each node and small communication over each link.

In the rest of this paper we present this routing algorithm and it's properties in several stages. First, in Section 2 we discuss the core idea in the context of a basic distributed tree. We then present the lattice based algorithm, that resolves the limitations of the tree-based one in Section 3. Section 4 discusses the related work and Section 5 presents our conclusions.

2 Tree-Based Routing

Imagine that our communication network was a tree, and that the costs of communication over edges of the tree would increase exponentially with the distance from the leaves; we will call such a network a "fat tree''. Imagine that all the content is stored at the leaves of the tree, also called clients, and all the control information is stored at the internal nodes. The internal nodes may be separate embedded "server" devices which have additional memory and energy, or they may be a subset of the sensor devices. Since the internal nodes do work, by storing aggregated content and handling routing messages for other nodes they will use up resources faster then the leaf nodes (pure sensors). Thus, the actual devices acting as internal nodes will either need additional resources, or will have to be rotated in and out of providing those services to maximize the lifetime of the nodes. We will discuss later, when the distributed algorithm is presented how these trees can be dynamically modified and maintained in the context of these type of heterogeneous nodes.

2.1 Our Approach – Tree Version

We can aggregate information and accomplish content addressable routing, as well as dissemination of resource utilization information on such fat tree as follows.

Content, originating at a leaf sensor, is registered at all levels of its tree ancestors. This is easily accomplished by climbing up the hierarchy. A query climbs up the hierarchy to locate the lowest common ancestor storing the content, and then descends down the hierarchy to the location of the contents.

Once this hierarchical structure has been created, it can also be used to aggregate the resource costs in a scalable way. The cost information is fairly simple data to aggregate because different costs can simply be added together to reach a combined cost. As long as all the costs have been calculated as opportunity costs, the sum of them, say from one cluster of nodes in the network, represents the aggregate opportunity cost of traversing that cluster of nodes.

Servers on level n can aggregate the resource costs reported by the level $n-1$ nodes (servers or sensors), and forward them further as a single value, usually the summation of the costs received. By doing this the cost updates only need to be sent locally among the sensors local level 1 cluster, then the controller (or server) of that cluster will incorporate that cost into the aggregate cluster cost and only send that cluster cost to other level 1 neighboring clusters and to the parent level 2 cluster leader. By using this aggregated cost information a controller at the n-th level of hierarchy can avoid a congested $n-1$ area as a whole, without knowing resource costs of each individual sensor.

2.2 Simple Distributed Implementation

We could try in principle to implement such a data structure in an embedded network. In order to do this we need to accomplish three tasks: decide which nodes should play a role at each level of the tree; build the tree; and specify the algorithm for routing within the tree.

For the first task of determining which nodes should participate at each level of the tree, we want to create the tree such that a nodes who are have a "small" communication cost between them are close together in the tree. We do not want to only consider physical or network distance because other factors such as bandwidth and battery life can substantially change the *effective* cost of traversing nodes – even if the nodes are physically close. The distance metric used for this purpose is derived from the opportunity cost framework [2] which allows one to incorporate and aggregate a multitude of incomparable parameters such as battery life, reliability and security level, bandwidth, etc.

For example, to construct the lowest level of the hierarchy, let us pick the closest node acting as a server for each client. To construct the next levels, we can select next level servers probabilistically by say flipping coins with probability 1/2, and repeating the process. If a server's coin comes up heads, then it will act as server also for the next level of the hierarchy, if it is tails then it is finished and will not acquire any more roles. Thus each round of coin flipping involves fewer and fewer of the potential servers. This defines a hierarchy of partitions which are very refined close the leaves and quite coarse close to the tree. Each server node acts as a server for at least level 1, and may act as a server for levels 2-k where k is the highest level the server reached in the coin flipping rounds. (We comment that [8] considers a similar setting where servers get chosen probabilistically on a rotating basis.)

To build the tree, each server selected at each level simply floods the message to determine which nodes will enter its tree. Flooding will establish an uplink pointer at each intermediate node eventually leading to the root of each tree. Each server node will rerun the flooding algorithm periodically for the clusters that they are responsible for. This is required to deal with moving sensors and servers, to adapt to changing resource costs (a node may have its battery drained and so the trees should change), and to detect new sensors. The frequency of these floods is a tradeoff between the overhead of flooding and the quality of routes. Although a fixed frequency is simple, since each server conducts their own flood, the frequency can be adjusted separately and dynamically by each server.

Third, the routing algorithm consists of two operations – routing upstream towards the root of the tree, and routing downstream towards a leaf node. The messages being routed can either be content generated by the leaf sensors, or queries that originate at any node (leaf or internal) in the system.

Upstream routing: In order for a node to reach its parent on the hierarchy, it simply sends the message on its uplink, and each intermediate node relays the message on its own uplink.

Downstream routing: It is more difficult for nodes to relay messages downstream, since intermediate tree nodes cannot keep downlinks for each possible child (this is too expensive for sensors). We consider now the problem of routing from root of a cluster to any other node in that cluster, and solve this problem recursively. Namely, we assume we can use similar procedure at one level below as a sub-routine.

The data structure needed for the purpose of downstream routing consists of

1. A collection of lateral "bridges" connecting clusters to sibling clusters, as well as
2. A "sibling routing" table indicating which cluster is the next sibling cluster to be traversed on the way to destination sibling cluster.

This data structure is constructed in a preprocessing stage as follows. Bridges are detected upon termination of flooding process as edges whose end-points were "conquered" by different flood-ID's. Sibling routing tables are built by having each cluster flood a message with its ID thru the whole parent cluster. Upon receipt of such flooded message over a bridge from another cluster, that bridge is designated locally as a preferred gateway en route to the destination cluster, and notification to that effect is sent to the root. The root may receive messages from a number of potential gateway nodes for a particular sibling cluster. In that case it randomly picks one of them. Flooding needs to be performed upon introducing new sibling to the cluster. The total cost of all flooding procedures, in terms of message traffic per edge, is upper-bounded by a term proportional to the product of the number of levels of the recursion, and the degree of tree, i.e., maximal number of sub-cluster in a given cluster.

Finally, we describe how the downstream routing actually works.

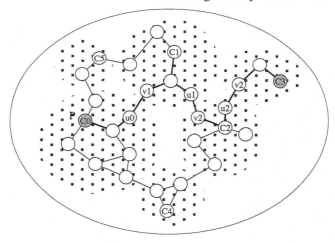

Fig. 1. Downstream and Lateral Routing

In order for a node to reach its child on the hierarchy, it proceeds recursively. Suppose a low-level server C0, selected as high-level server P, wishes to reach, say, C3 who is a child of P. Let C1, C2...Cn also be children of P. The path from C0 to C3 starts at the territory of cluster of C0 and proceeds through the territory of clusters for C1, C2, etc. until reaching cluster of C3. Let bridge (u0-v1) be the edge emanating from cluster of C0 into cluster of C1 on that shortest path. Then, it is enough to send message from C0 to u0 inside lower level cluster of C0, and instruct it to cross the bridge (u0,v1). This can be handled recursively since this is taking place on the territory of the lower-level cluster. After crossing the bridge, the message will go to the root of C1 and find out about next bridge (u1,v2) into territory of C2, etc. The process will continue till we reach lowest level of the hierarchy (see Figure 1).

With these two routing primitives ready, we can describe the whole process.

1. *Registration of content by climbing the hierarchy*: content generated by a client "climbs the hierarchy" by registering at the parent of that client, and then proceeding to grandparent, etc. This process simply involves forwarding all the informa-

tion received from children and aggregating information at the servers of given level before continuing to the next level.

2. *Query for contents by climbing the hierarchy*: Query generated at a client climbs the hierarchy exactly like the content registration process. This process simply involves forwarding all the queries received from children. Upon reaching a server on a given level, the query is successful at that level if the content is locally available; otherwise the query is a failure at this level. In the former case the query is stored at a buffer together with the name of the lower-level server who originated it, and is forwarded on an uplink to the next level up, until is eventually succeeds or fails at the top level.

3. *Query for contents by descending the hierarchy*: Once a query succeeds at some level j, it means that that server keeps the desired content, as well as location of lower level child who reported it. The query proceeds downstream recursively, using downstream routing above.

2.3 Extensions to Battery-Sensitive Routing

The above algorithm classifies nodes into just two levels of computing power: servers and clients. In the case of heterogeneous devices with highly different capabilities, it is obvious that higher level servers need to chosen among stronger devices (ones with higher battery life, higher bandwidth, higher CPU. It is quite possible, however, that servers themselves are not much more powerful than the sensors. In the extreme case, we may consider a completely symmetric peer-to-peer situation where the collectors are the sensors themselves, i.e. clients are no different than servers.

What this means is that clients need to emulate servers. Because of limited battery, and the concentration of traffic at different levels of the hierarchy, the nodes selected to be servers at a given level will quickly run out of battery. This means that their weight will dramatically increase, and the radius of their flooding will be decreased dramatically.

Effectively, this means that the clients they used to be parents of will be reconquered by others floods emanating from higher-battery nodes. This will automatically lead to rotation between different nodes for the role of servers of a given level. If this rotation is accompanied by occasional energy refueling, then the system can keep working indefinitely.

This method applies to a more general setting (with multi-hop connectivity) than the method in [8]. We can prove that our method provides a very precise mathematic guarantees on its performance. As we will see below, this is a serious issue.

2.4 Performance Analysis

The efficiency of the above query publishing and processing can be evaluated by considering the cost of retrieving the content through the hierarchy versus the optimum cost of the retrieval.

Consider for example a segment of length n with a hierarchy in the form of a perfect binary tree. Namely, this segment is broken into two segments of length n/2, each corresponding to lower level clusters. Consider now a bridge edge from one cluster to another. Note that a query emanating from one endpoint of that edge may traverse the whole tree to find a common ancestor with the other endpoint. Thus, the distance distortion exhibited by such a hierarchy grows linearly with the number of nodes.

It is highly unsettling that by managing to reduce the space overhead through aggregation, from linear to constant, we actually damage our routing efficiency by a linear factor. In a sense, this indicates that we have not dealt with the issue of scalability in a satisfactory manner.

3 Lattices versus Trees

This paper suggests a universal mathematical framework for handling the issue of scalability, that we refer to as Hierarchical Redundant Aggregation. The essence of the framework is that it enables one to represent complex structures such as networks with heterogeneous and arbitrarily connected components in a relatively simple format, which is called a "distance preserving lattice".

In a hierarchical distance preserving lattice, we have levels of hierarchy imposed on the network, where all nodes belong to the lower level of the hierarchy, and just a handful of nodes belong to the top level. Each node has a handful of parents on the next level of the lattice; for simplicity imagine each node has just two parents. One can easily imagine that if each node has two parents, it may have four grand-parents, 16 grand grand-parents, etc. However, a lattice is constructed in such a way that each node has handful ancestors at each level of the lattice hierarchy. Figure 2 shows an example of a zone of sensors of which some have two parents in order to provide relay service for messages from sensors who do not have their server.

Since the tree contains less edges than the cycle, we can say that the tree is an "aggregation" of the cycle. The "distortion" of the aggregate structure is the worst case distance deterioration of the original graph. The above discussion indicate that aggregating a cycle into a tree exhibits distortion whose quality degrades linearly with the size of the network, and thus such aggregation will be considered of "poor quality" for large size networks. One can easily see that any tree will be a poor quality aggregation for very simple graphs, such as, for example a grid graph.

The difference between a tree and a lattice is manifested exactly in that in a tree, each node has a single parent in the next layer, and each node has a single ancestor at each level. This difference is crucial in that a lattice is immensely superior to a tree in terms of the ability to capture distances, without the need to introduce exorbitant overhead. In some sense, a lattice can be viewed as a number of trees super-imposed on each other. Observe that two trees can faithfully capture distance on a circle, while it is impossible to achieve this effect with a single tree. Indeed, each tree will fail to contain some edge; and the path on the tree connecting endpoints of that edge is linearly longer than the direct connection. In the next section we provide specific lattice constructions based on the work by Awerbuch and Peleg [1] (we comment that this is the theoretically best data structure for distributed routing).

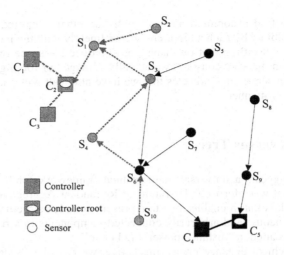

Fig. 2. Sensors with two Controllers and Lattice

3.1 Our Approach – Lattice Version

As we have indicated earlier, it is easy to implement a hierarchy where each node enters the next level with small probability, and partition the graph with spanning trees where each node has a single uplink. This is a very scalable data structure, but as we pointed out it cannot possibly be accurate in representing the metric space.

If we are talking about representation of a regular graph, such a heuristic can work. However, even in a regular deployment of sensors, the distance/cost graph will not remain regular for long because due to factors such as battery depletion, any effective embedded sensor system will have to distort a regular graph into an irregular arbitrary structure.

The idea is that adding a couple more uplinks to nodes (which does not really hurt scalability) will have a crucial impact on the distance distortion, reducing the maximal possible distortion from linear to logarithmic. We rigorously support the claim in a form of a concrete algorithm, a theorem, and a mathematical proof of performance guarantees.

The algorithm to construct one level of the hierarchy is very simple. Select a desired range, say r. Our goal is to construct a collection of clusters each one around a single client (who will now be called a server), and a spanning tree for each cluster such that the following properties hold.

Lattice Properties
1. Any two clients at distance r from each other will be spanned by a common tree (and thus will be able to locate each other).
2. The tree overlap is at most logarithmic.
3. The radius of each tree is at most logarithmically larger than r.
The lattice algorithm: The algorithm consists of logarithmic number of iterations.

In each iteration, each node selects a random integer, from 1 to log n, with exponentially decreasing probability (next integer half as likely as the current), and floods its ID to radius limited by "distance to live" which is the product of the random value and r. Each node propagates the flood if "distance to live" is positive and the ID of this flood is higher than the highest previously seen ID. In this case, it remembers the node from which it receives this flood as an uplink on the link to the corresponding ID, subtracts its (opportunity) cost from "distance-to-live" and broadcasts the new ID to the neighbors. The set of recorded uplinks forms the desired lattice, which is simply the collection of trees rooted at winning ID's.

Distributed Lattice Construction Theorem: For every network of size n nodes, an arbitrary set of clients, and every value of radius r, with overwhelming probability, the following properties hold:

1. Lattice properties above are met
2. Each edge is traversed by logarithmic number of messages

Proof: The radius of each tree is at most logarithmically larger than r by construction; thus 3) holds.

Tree overlap is the expected number of maxima in random sequence; the probability of j's member to be maximum is $1/j$ and summation of $1/j$ is approximately the logarithm of the number of nodes, proving 2). To prove 1), consider two such nodes x and y at distance r at most. The highest ID that have been seen by x was not seen by y or vice versa. Notice that exponential probability is memoryless, thus with probability 0.5 the highest ID flood that reaches x will also reach y, in which case x and y cannot have different parents, **QED.**

4 Related Work

Some ideas related to imposing hierarchy on top of uniform network of sensors were presented in [8] where the LEACH protocol chooses cluster heads probabilistically on a rotating basis. LEACH assumes that all nodes have the ability to communicate with the final destination, but must pay a higher energy cost to do so. Our cost-benefit method can provide the same advantages as LEACH at the lowest levels of the hierarchy where all the nodes are within maximum range of each other, and can also provide the more general multi-hop capabilities by using minimum cost forwarding at higher levels of the hierarchy.

Heterogeneous resource routing has also being described in GEAR project by Estrin et al [GEAR]. We now describe the Geographical and Energy Aware Routing(GEAR) algorithm. GEAR uses a geographical and energy aware neighbor selection heuristic to route the packet towards the target region. At least from the algorithmic point of view, we believe that we should be able to greatly improve on the performance of such solution by using a cost-benefit framework which will unify bandwidth-based and energy-based optimization in a provable manner.

Also utilizing geographic information, but for a different purpose, GAF described in [17] is built using a different methodology of evaluating power usage. The paper offers evidence that the power consumed while idle/listening is significant in comparison to that consumed while transmitting or receiving, and in the low traffic case dominates the power consumption of the network. This results in an accounting methodology that does not ignore idle/listening power consumption and a strategy of utilizing the sleep capabilities of wireless transceivers in order to save some of the power used while nodes are idle. GAF uses location information and a virtual grid in order to approximate a maximal independent set of nodes that must stay awake. Because this approach relies on finding sets of nodes that are all interchangeable, it only provides savings for the most trivial cases, and isn't robust in the case of complex radio propagation phenomenon. The opportunity-cost framework provides an alternative strategy where the cost of keeping a node awake can be compared with the benefit it provides to the network. This analysis can be used to select a randomized duty cycle appropriate for each node.

5 Conclusion

We have presented a general-purpose highly, scalable distributed algorithm for content and query routing on heterogeneous sensor networks. This algorithm has provably strong bounds on the distance distortion it produces, and provides logarithmic message costs for both content distribution and query routing. We believe the lattice routing architecture offers substantial potential for providing a general-purpose routing architecture that can incorporate much of the research on sensor network routing (by choosing different cost metrics, the lattices formed will adapt to many different researchers specific algorithms).

References

1. B. Awerbuch and D. Peleg. Routing with polynomial communication-space trade-off. *SIAM Journal on Discrete Mathematics*, 5(2):151–162, May 1992.
2. B. Awerbuch and Y. Azar and S. Plotkin: Throughput-Competitive On-Line Routing. Proceedings IEEE FOCS 1993, 32–40
3. D. Braginsky and D. Estrin. Rumor routing algorithm for sensor networks.
4. N. Bulusu, D. Estrin, L. Girod, and J. Heidemann. Scalable coordination for wireless sensor networks: Self-configuring localization systems. In *The 6th International Symposium on Communication Theory and Applications*, July 2001.
5. Demand Source routing by Johnson and Maltz , 1996.
6. D. Estrin, R. Govindan, J. Heidemann, and S. Kumar. Next century challenges: Scalable coordination in sensor networks. In *The 5th Annual International Conference on Mobile Computing and Networks*, August 1999.
7. D. Ganesan, R. Govindan, S. Shenker, and D. Estrin. Highly resilient, energy efficient multipath routing in wireless sensor networks. Mobile Computing and Communications Review, 1(2), 2002.
8. W. Heinzelman, A. Chandrakasan, and H. Balakrishnan. Energy-Efficient Communication Protocols for Wireless Microsensor Networks. Proc. Hawaian Int'l Conf. on Systems Science, January 2000
9. W. Heinzelman, J. Kulik, and H. Balakrishnan. Adaptive protocols for information dissemination in wireless sensor networks. In *The 5th ACM/IEEE Mobicom Conference*, August 1999.

10. J. Heidemann, F. Silva, C. Intanagonwiwat, R. Govindan, D. Estrin, and D. Ganesan. Building efficient wireless sensor networks with low-level naming. In *Symposium on Operating Systems Principles*, October 2001.

11. C. Intanagonwiwat, D. Estrin, R. Govindan, and J. Heidemann. Impact of network density on data aggregation in wireless sensor networks.

12. C. Intanagonwiwat, R. Govindan, and D. Estrin. Directed diffusion: A scalable and robust communication paradigm for sensor networks. In *The 6th Annual International Conference on Mobile Computing and Networks*, August 2000.

13. D. B. Johnson, D. A. Maltz, and J. Broch. *DSR: The Dynamic Source Routing Protocol for Multi-Hop Wireless Ad Hoc Networks. in Ad Hoc Networking*, chapter 5, pages 139–172. Addison-Wesley, 2001.

14. S. Kumar, C. Alaettinoglu, and D. Estrin. Scalable object-tracking through unattended techniques. In *The 8th International Conference on Network Protocols*, November 2000.

15. B. Krishanamachari, D. Estrin, and S. Wicker. Modeling data-centric routing in wireless sensor networks.

16. Y. Xu, J. Heidemann, and D. Estrin. Adaptive energy-conserving routing for multihop ad hoc networks. Technical Report Research report 527, USC/Information Sciences Institute, October 2000.

17. Y. Xu, J. Heidemann, and D. Estrin. Geography-informed energy conservation for ad-hoc routing. In *The 7th ACM/IEEE International Conference on Mobile Computing and Networking*, July 2001.

18. Y. Yu, R. Govindan, and D. Estrin. Geographical and energy aware routing: A recursive data dissemination protocol for wireless sensor networks. Technical Report UCLA/CSD-TR-01-0023, UCLA Computer Science Department, May 2001.

19. W. Ye, J. Heidemann, and D. Estrin. An energy-efficient MAC protocol for wireless sensor networks. In *The 21st International Annual Joint Conference of the IEEE Computer and Communications Societies*, June 2002.

Coverage, Exploration, and Deployment by a Mobile Robot and Communication Network

Maxim A. Batalin and Gaurav S. Sukhatme

Robotic Embedded Systems Lab
Computer Science Department
Center for Robotics and Embedded Systems
University of Southern California
Los Angeles, CA 90089

Abstract. We consider the problem of coverage and exploration of an unknown dynamic environment using a mobile robot(s). The environment is assumed to be large enough such that constant motion by the robot(s) is needed to cover the environment. We present an efficient minimalist algorithm which assumes that global information is not available (neither a map, nor GPS). Our algorithm deploys a network of radio beacons which assists the robot(s) in coverage. This network is also used for navigation. The deployed network can also be used for applications other than coverage. Simulation experiments are presented which show the collaboration between the deployed network and mobile robot(s) for the tasks of coverage/exploration, network deployment and maintenance (repair), and mobile robot(s) recovery (homing behavior). We present a theoretical basis for our algorithm on graphs and show the results of the simulated scenario experiments.

1 Introduction

We consider two problems from traditionally different backgrounds. The first is the **exploration and coverage of a space by a mobile robot**. The coverage problem has been defined [1] as the maximization of the total area covered by robot's sensors. There are many applications of coverage such as tracking unfriendly targets (e.g military operations), demining or monitoring (e.g. security), and urban search and rescue (USAR) in the aftermath of a natural or man-made disaster (e.g. building rubble due to an earthquake or other causes). We require the robot to cover all areas of the space, and to occasionally navigate to a designated target location in the -space. The second problem is the **deployment of a sensor and communication network** into an environment. Such a network may be used for monitoring, or as an ad-hoc communication infrastructure. Our claim is that these two problems are best solved together i.e. a *combined* solution exists which satisfies both objectives. The basic idea is simple - the robot deploys the network into the environment as it explores, and the network guides future robot exploration.

Coverage can be considered as a *static* or more generally as a *dynamic* problem. The *static* coverage problem is addressed by algorithms [2,3,4]. The goal of

F. Zhao and L. Guibas (Eds.): IPSN 2003, LNCS 2634, pp. 376–391, 2003.

these algorithms is to converge to a static configuration (an equilibrium state), such that every point in the environment is under the robots' sensor shadow (i.e. covered) at every instant of time. For complete static coverage of an environment the robot team should have a certain critical number of robots (depending on environment size, complexity, and robot sensor ranges). Determining the critical number is difficult or impossible [2] if the environment is unknown *a priori*. *Dynamic* coverage, on the other hand, is addressed by algorithms which explore and hence 'cover' the environment with constant motion and neither settle to a particular configuration [5], nor necessarily to a particular pattern of traversal. Coverage of the environment can be accomplished over time with any number of robots.

In this paper we consider the case of a single robot in an environment that is large enough that complete *static* coverage of the environment is not possible. The robot must thus continually move in order to observe all points in the environment frequently. In other words, we study the *dynamic* coverage problem with a single robot. We briefly discuss various multi-robot extensions at the end of the paper.

Single robot exploration of unknown environments has been studied before [6, 7,8]. The frontier-based approach [6,7] incrementally constructs a global occupancy map of the environment. The map is analyzed to locate the 'frontiers' between the free and unknown space. Exploration proceeds in the direction of the closest 'frontier'. The multi-robot version of the same problem was addressed in [9]. The problem of coverage was considered from the graph theoretic viewpoint in [10,11]. In both cases the authors study the problem of *dynamic* single robot coverage on an environment consisting of nodes and edges (a graph). The key result was that the ability to tag a limited number of nodes (in some cases only one node) with unique *markers* dramatically improved the cover time. It may be noted that both papers consider the coverage problem, but in the process also created topological maps of the environment graph being explored.

The algorithm we propose (a variation of more general *Node Counting* and *Edge Counting* algorithms discussed in detail in [12,13]) differs from the above mentioned approaches in a number of ways. We use neither a map, nor localization in a shared frame of reference. Our algorithm is based on the deployment of a set of static nodes into the environment by the robot. The nodes form a communication network. We term every node in the network a *marker*. The markers we use act as a support infrastructure, which the mobile robot uses to solve the coverage problem efficiently. The robot explores the environment, and based on certain *local criteria*, drops a marker into the environment, from time to time. Each marker is equipped with a small processor and a radio of limited range. Our algorithm performs the coverage task successfully using only local sensing and local interactions between the robot and markers. The approach builds on our prior work [5], and strives to maintain connectivity in the network.

We thus propose an algorithm for robot exploration and coverage that relies on the deployment of a communication network. Once deployed the network is used by the robot for efficient exploration and navigation. We note that our

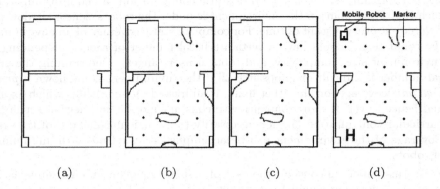

(a)   (b)   (c)   (d)

Fig. 1. A schematic of a) Initial Environment (before the experiment); b) Environment after changes with deployed network(beginning of experiment); c) Some of the nodes require replacement (malfunctioned, damaged, etc.); d) Another alteration to environment and a robot that has to return to marker H;

approach for navigation is similar to [14], which needs potential fields whereas we use value iteration.

Analysis of the deployed network as a graph shows that our algorithm is *complete* i.e. it covers every vertex of the graph and *efficient* (cover time linear in the size of the network graph).

We discuss data from one long term continuous experiment which includes a dynamic environment and exhibits the major functionalities of our approach: the ability to provide full coverage/exploration of the environment, robustness to changes in the environment, ability to replace damaged markers, navigation and extensions to multi-robot applications utilizing the deployed network.

2   Experimental Scenario

Imagine a scenario where the environment changes dramatically in a short time-span; for example a collapsing building. In such a situation a mobile robot, or a group of robots, could be sent into the building to search for people. Our system allows a mobile robot to explore (and completely cover) the environment without access to a prior map, by deploying markers into the environment. Subsequently, the robot is able to 'home' to a given location using the same set of markers.

Figure 1a shows the floor plan of the environment prior to changes. Conventional approaches to covering this environment and exploring it, could use a map-based technique (such as the ones in [6,7]). Suppose however that due to a catastrophic event (e.g. earthquake, fire) debris is introduced into the environment, thereby altering it (Figure 1b). Even though the map of the environment might be available initially, an altered environment would be difficult or impos-

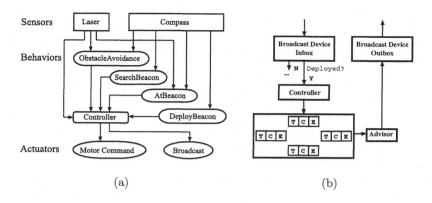

Fig. 2. a) System Architecture showing Robot Behaviors; b) Beacon Architecture

sible to cover and explore, with approaches relying on metric/topological map usage. The experimental work reported in this paper starts at this point. A robot is introduced into the environment of Figure 1b. The robot explores the environment by populating it with markers that form a network. Figure 1c shows the network with some of the nodes removed (malfunctioned, destroyed, etc.). Using our algorithm, the robot repairs the gap in the network by deploying new nodes. The last step of the scenario is depicted in Figure 1d. The environment was altered again so that extra space in the environment is uncovered. The robot is now required to explore and cover the extra space by deploying markers. In addition, the robot is required to use deployed network for homing - returning to a special marker (H on Figure 1d).

3   Architecture

Our algorithm uses two entities: the markers and the mobile robot. The task of each marker is to recommend a locally preferred direction of movement for the robot within its communication range. Thus each marker acts as a local signpost telling the robot which direction to explore next. The robot treats this information as a recommendation, and combines it with local range sensing (to avoid obstacles) to make a decision about which direction to actually pursue.

As shown in Figure 2(b), each marker has a state associated with four cardinal directions (South, East, North, West). The choice of four directions is arbitrary. It implies that each marker is equipped with a 2 bit compass. For each direction, the marker maintains a binary state (T), a counter (C) and block E which might be used for additional information. The state T can be either OPEN or EXPLORED, signifying whether the particular direction was explored by the robot previously. The counter C associated with each direction stores the time since that particular direction was last explored.

When deployed, a marker emits two data packets with different signal strengths. The packet with the lower signal strength is called the *MIN*-packet and the one with the higher signal strength is called the *MAX*-packet. The *MAX*-packet is used for data propagation within the deployed network. We discuss it in section 5.2. The *MIN*-packet contains two pieces of information: a) the suggested direction the robot should take for coverage/exploration and b) the suggested direction the robot should take for homing. This implies that the robot's compass and the marker's compass agree locally on their measurement of direction. Given the coarse coding of direction we have chosen, this is not a problem in realistic settings. The algorithm used by the markers to compute the suggested direction for exploration/coverage is a 'least recently visited direction' policy. All OPEN directions are recommended first (in order from South to West), followed by the EXPLORED directions with largest last update value (largest value of C). Note that this algorithm does not use inter-marker communication. The computation of the suggested direction for homing is discussed in a later section (section 5.1).

The robot uses a behavior-based approach [15] with arbitration [16] for behavior coordination. Priorities are assigned to every behavior *a priori*. As shown in Figure 2(a), the robot executes four behaviors: *ObstacleAvoidance*, *AtBeacon*, *DeployBeacon* and *SearchBeacon*. In addition to priority, every behavior has an activation level, which decides, given the sensory input, whether the behavior should be in an active or passive state (1 or 0 respectively). Each behavior computes the product of its activation level and corresponding priority and sends the result to the Controller, which picks the maximum value, and assigns the corresponding behavior to command the Motor Controller for the next command cycle.

During motion, the robot maintains the notion of a current marker (Figure 3a). This is the node whose *MIN*-packets are received by the robot most frequently. When the robot moves to the vicinity of a new marker, the *AtBeacon* behavior is triggered and the robot's current marker is updated (Figure 3b). *AtBeacon* analyzes the *MIN*-packets received from the current marker and orients the robot along the suggested direction contained in those packets. In addition, the robot sends an update message to the marker telling it to mark the direction from which the robot approached it as EXPLORED. This ensures that the direction of recent approach will not be recommended soon. We term this the *last-neighbor-update*. After the robot has been oriented in a new direction, it checks its range sensor for obstacles. If the scan does not return any obstacles, the robot proceeds in the suggested direction (Figure 3c), while sending a message to its current marker updating the state of the suggested direction to EXPLORED (the marker also resets the corresponding C value). If, however, the suggested direction is obstructed, the *AtBeacon* behavior updates the marker with this information and requests a new suggested direction (Figure 3d). The *Obstacle Avoidance* behavior is triggered if an obstacle is detected in front of the robot, in which case an avoidance maneuver takes place.

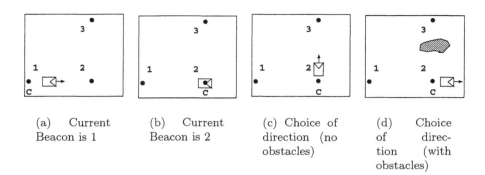

(a)   Current Beacon is 1

(b)   Current Beacon is 2

(c) Choice of direction (no obstacles)

(d)   Choice of direction (with obstacles)

Fig. 3. Behavior Switching. a) The robot is executing *SearchBeacon* behavior traversing suggested direction; b) The robot is executing *AtBeacon* behavior, analyzing sensor readings; c) The robot is executing *SearchBeacon* behavior, supposing the beacon suggests direction *UP* and there are no obstacles detected in the sensor data; d) The robot is executing *SearchBeacon* behavior traversing in direction, not originally suggested by the marker.

Once the robot is oriented in a new direction (whether as a result of taking the advice of the marker, or as a result of avoiding an obstacle), the *SearchBeacon* behavior is triggered. *SearchBeacon* causes the robot to travel a predetermined distance without a change in heading (assuming there are no obstacles in the way). The *DeployBeacon* behavior is triggered if the robot does not receive a *MIN*-packet from any marker after a certain timeout value. In this case the robot deploys a new marker into the environment.

During its exploration of the environment, the robot builds a transition graph. We call this **deployed network graph**. The vertices of the graph represent the deployed markers. A directed edge from vertex A to B is labeled with the probability of arriving at node B from node A by proceeding in a particular direction. In section 5 we discuss the use of this graph for computing probabilistic paths through the environment between any two nodes, and thus, using the marker network for probabilistic navigation.

4   Graph Model

For purposes of analysis, consider an open environment (no obstacles). Given our marker deployment strategy described in the previous section, we can model the steady state spatial configuration of the markers as a regular square lattice. In fact, the analysis applies to any graph of degree 4 isomorphic to a regular lattice. Without loss of generality we ignore the boundary of the graph in the analysis. In the general case the deployed network graph would be a regular graph of degree 4. The *cover time* [17], is the time it takes a robot to cover (visit) every

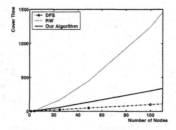

Fig. 4. A comparison between DFS, RW and our algorithm.

node in the graph and can be computed as the number of actions taken by the robot to visit every node of the graph. The problem of coverage on the graph is to minimize the average *cover time*, considering every vertex of the graph as a starting point.

We assert that our algorithm covers the environment completely i.e. the robot visits every node of the graph. In the most simple case where the environment is unknown, and localization cannot be used, and there are no *markers* available, the problem of coverage can be solved by a random walk (RW). It has been shown [17] that the *cover time* of a random walk on a regular graph of n nodes is bounded below by $n \ln n$ and above by $2n^2$. If we assume that passive markers can be used, and the graph $G = (V, E)$ is known (a topological map is available) and the robot has *markers* of three independent colors, then the problem of coverage can be solved optimally by applying depth first search (DFS) which is linear in n. DFS assumes that all resources are available - markers, map, localization and perfect navigation.

We conducted experiments running RW, DFS and our algorithm on graphs with $n = 25, 49$ and 100 nodes. For every experiment each grid point was tried as the starting point. We conducted 50 experiments per starting point, such that as soon as robot covers all nodes, the nodes become uncovered and the coverage task starts from the node where the robot finished its last coverage. Then the next starting point is considered and so on. The average cover time over all experiments was computed. The results of this experiment are shown in Figure 4; our algorithm and DFS both perform asymptotically better than the RW.

Note that in order to determine the color of neighboring vertices and navigate from one vertex to another, DFS assumes that the map of the environment is available and the robot is localized. Our algorithm, on the other hand, does not have access to global information and the robot does not localize itself. The *markers* used in our algorithm are more complicated than those used in DFS, and the cover times are asymptotically somewhat larger than the cover times of DFS.

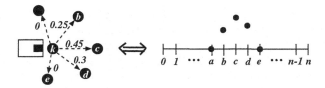

Fig. 5. An example of a discrete probability distribution of vertex (marker) k for direction (action) "East"(i.e. right).

5   Connectivity Map and Probabilistic Navigation

In order for the robot to be able to navigate through the environment from point A to point B, assuming neither map nor GPS are available, the robot should be able to recognize that it has arrived at the goal (B), be able to measure progress and be able to choose an action that maximizes its chances of getting to its goal.

5.1   Value Iteration

We assume finite set of vertices S in the deployed network graph and a finite set of actions A the robot can take at each node (marker). Given a subset of actions $A(s) \subseteq A$, for every two vertices in the deployed network graph $s, s' \in S$ and $a \in A(s)$ the robot should determine the transitional probability $P(s'|s, a)$ (probability of arriving at vertex s' given that the robot started at vertex s and commanded an action a). In our algorithm four actions are possible at every vertex (marker) - East, West, South and North. Thus, for every action a_i at a given vertex $s \in S$ and all other vertices $s' \in S - s$ the robot computes the probability $P(s'|s, a_i)$ as the ratio of the number of transitions from s to s' with action a_i to the number of times a_i was commanded at vertex s. This ratio is normalized to ensure that $\sum_{a_i} P(s'|s, a_i) = 1$. Figure 5 shows a typical discrete probability distribution for a vertex (marker) per action (direction). Note that in practice the probability mass is distributed around neighboring nodes and zero otherwise.

Our model for the proposed system is Markovian - the state the robot transitions to depends only on the current state and action. We simply model the navigation problem as a Markov Decision Process [18]. To compute the best action at a given vertex we use the Value Iteration [19] algorithm on the set of vertices $S - s_g$, where s_g is the goal state. The general idea behind Value Iteration is to compute the utilities for every state and then pick the actions that yield a path towards the goal with maximum expected utility. The utility is incrementally computed:

$$U_{t+1}(s) = C(s, a) + \max_{a \in A(s)} \sum_{s' \in S - s} P(s'|s, a) \times U_t(s') \tag{1}$$

where $C(s, a)$ is the cost associated with moving to the next vertex. Usually the cost is chosen to be a negative number which is smaller than $-1/k$ where k is the number of vertices. The rationale is that the robot should 'pay' for taking an action (otherwise any path that the robot might take would have the same utility), however, the cost should not be to big (otherwise the robot might prefer to stay at the same state).

Initially the utility of the goal state is set to 1 and of the other states to 0. Given the utilities, an *action policy* is computed for every state s as follows:

$$P(s) = \arg \max_{a \in A(s)} \sum_{s' \in S - s} P(s'|s, a) \times U(s'); \qquad (2)$$

The robot maintains a probabilistic transition model for the deployed network graph, and can compute the action policy at each node for any destination point. In practice however, this is limiting, since it requires the robot to traverse the network many times over to learn the transition model. Further, another robot deployed into the same environment would need to first traverse the deployed network before it can navigate between any two points optimally.

One solution is for the robot to compute the action policy as above, and while traversing the network record the optimal action for the current marker as it passes by. Each marker can store this action and can emit it as part of the direction suggestion packet (see Section 3). This would help other robots (which may not yet have explored the entire space) use the information for navigation. However, this solution is inefficient, since it is slow to adapt if the navigation goal is changed.

5.2 Distributed Computation and In-Network Processing

A much more attractive solution is to compute the action policy distributively in the deployed network. The idea is that every node in the network updates its utility and computes the optimal navigation action (for a robot in its vicinity) on its own. While traversing the deployed network the robot stores the transition probabilities $P(s'|s, a)$ on the corresponding markers. Then, if a robot wants to navigate to a point in the environment it injects a *Start Computation* packet into the network containing the target marker's id. Every marker redirects this packet to its neighbors using flooding. Markers that receive the *Start Computation* packet initialize utilities and the cost values depending on whether this particular marker specified as a target or not. Every marker updates the utilities according to equation 5.1. Note that the utilities of neighboring markers are needed as well, hence, the marker queries its neighbors for corresponding utilities. Since computation of some markers can proceed faster than of the others, every marker stores computed utilities in a list, so that even if it's being queried by its neighbors for a utility several steps prior to the current one, the list is accessed and the corresponding utility is sent.

After the utilities are computed, every marker computes an optimal policy for itself according to equation 5.1. Neighboring markers are queried once again for the final utility values. The computed optimal action is stored at each marker and is emitted as part of the MIN-packet (refer to section 3) for homing to the goal.

This technique allows the robot to navigate through the environment between any two nodes of the deployed network. Note that the action policy computation is done only once, and does not need to be recomputed, unless the goal changes. Also, note that utility update equations have to be executed until the desired accuracy is achieved. For practical reasons the accuracy in our algorithm is set to 10^{-3}, which requires a reasonable number of executions of the utility update equation per state and thus, the list of utilities that every marker needs to store is small. Since the computation and memory requirements are small it is possible to implement this approach on the real marker device that we are using (the Mote [20]).

6   Simulation Experiment

We conducted a continuous experiment that would test the algorithm for reliability and robustness to environmental changes, problems in the network and would show the ability to deploy and maintain a network and use it for coverage/exploration and navigation. Thus, the scenario consists of four phases. In Phase 1 the robot's task is to deploy a network and cover/explore the environment completely. In Phase 2 we assume that certain nodes in the network failed and require replacement, thus, the goal of the algorithm is to find the gap in the network and replace the damaged nodes, while covering the environment. Phase 3 distorts the environment further, by introducing an extra space - a "hidden room" which also has to be covered. Then, the robot computes the transition probabilities and stores the appropriate constants at every marker. In Phase 4, we assume that another robot appears on the scene, which does not have any prior knowledge about environment and the deployed sensor network. It executes the same algorithm as the robot-deployer, but in this case the part of data packet containing action policy for homing is preferred and used as a suggested direction of the marker. Note that even though the algorithm is robust against loss of some data packets or imprecise compass readings, in simulations we assume that the compass and radio properties are ideal.

6.1   First Phase

As shown in Figure 1b, the environment has been altered so that an initial map of the environment would not be useful in coverage. Assuming that a mobile robot with a set of markers have been introduced into the environment (thrown in, dropped by an air vehicle, etc.). The robot starts deployment and coverage/exploration process at the same time. While deploying markers, the robot updates its connectivity map. The deployment of the sensor network for this stage of the scenario is presented on Figure 6 in sequence.

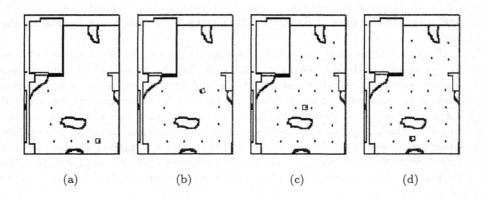

(a)   (b)   (c)   (d)

Fig. 6. Sequential deployment of network.

As shown on the above figure, the robot deployed the network over the whole environment, while at the same time accomplishing coverage. Figure 9 represents coverage values over the first three phases of the experiment.

6.2   Second Phase

As shown in Figure 7a, several nodes of the sensor network were removed (nodes in the upper part of the figure are assumed to be malfunctioned or damaged). As seen in the Figure 7, the gap in the network has been detected by the robot and repaired. Note that the robot continued coverage of the environment(Figure 9) and was not affected by the problems in the network.

6.3   Third Phase

In this phase of the experiment, we assume that certain perturbations occurred in the environment so that the robot starts with the environment shown in Figure 8a. Figure 8bc show expansion of the network by deployment of additional markers into new open space by the robot. Note, that the problem of coverage was not abandoned by the robot under the circumstances depicted in last three phases. A unified view of cover time for three phases is shown in Figure 9. In addition, the robot injects a *Start Computation* packet and the *navigation field* is computed.

6.4   Fourth Phase

In the fourth, last phase, the trapped robot discovered a deployed sensor network. The task is to use the navigational constant and to drive to the home area marked with H (Figure 10a). Figure 10b shows the navigational field that was produced by distributive computation of the optimal policy by the deployed network. The path that the robot traverses is shown on Figure 10c.

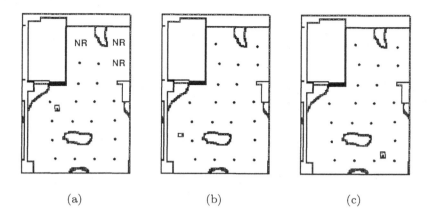

(a)   (b)   (c)

Fig. 7. Network repair. NR - area requiring repair

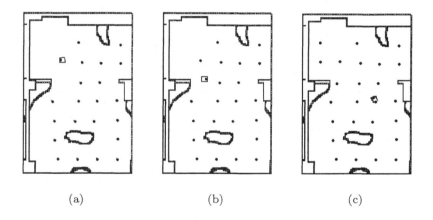

(a)   (b)   (c)

Fig. 8. Deployment of additional markers into the discovered open space.

7 Multi-robot Extensions

In this paper we presented an approach with several different capabilities and applications. The system has potential for the multi-robot domain (robot-deployer and robot-navigator is one example). The ability of the deployed network to respond to queries of different robots (with distinguishing tasks) in a different manner and thus, serving as a multi purpose infrastructure, enables, for example, solutions to problems requiring heterogeneous groups of robots. Imagine a scenario of a construction site which requires cooperation of two distinguishing

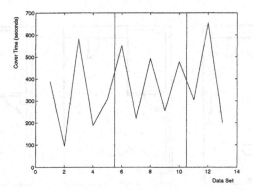

Fig. 9. Coverage over the three stages of the experiment.

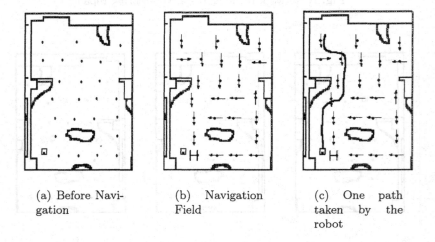

(a) Before Navigation

(b) Navigation Field

(c) One path taken by the robot

Fig. 10. Robot navigation through the environment

groups of robots - transporters and builders. Transporters concentrate on delivering the materials to several piles while builders choose the type of material they need at the moment from a corresponding pile and continue construction. Thus, the query of a transporter robot leads to a shortest path towards the material storage or towards the pile that requires certain material the most. While the builder robot would be directed towards a pile with required material or towards another builder needing assistance. In other words, the network can be used as a *distributed* multi functional manager, which can also be used for task coordination.

Another path for multi-robot extensions of the proposed approach is that the network can be used as an intermediate storage of local data. For example,

Fig. 11. Screen shots of a preliminary physical experiment.

a group of robots might be working on coverage or mapping in local sub areas. Robots then can exchange information about their local discoveries through the deployed network.

8   Conclusions and Future Work

We presented an algorithm for coverage and exploration through the utilization of a deployed network. Several capabilities of the algorithm were demonstrated - network deployment and repair, probabilistic navigation, coverage and exploration, and robustness to environmental and network changes. An experimental scenario was executed which tested the above mentioned capabilities. Throughout the execution of the scenario cover time was measured. The cover time shows that despite perturbations to the environment and network, the robot was able to maintain coverage. As mentioned in the previous section, the presented approach is extendable to multi-robot applications, in which the network can be thought of as a multi-purpose task manager.

A scheme for probabilistic navigation is also presented, however, not extensively tested. In this instance, the network assists the robot in the navigation by the fact that the robot is always localized within the sensor network, and therefore there is no need for feature detection or prior knowledge of a map. Note, however, that the probabilistic navigation was not incorporated to assist the coverage task itself. A clear extension is to navigate from an explored subset of nodes to an unexplored subset, which would essentially reduce the problem of coverage to that of search.

The proposed probabilistic navigation scheme is distributed, which improves performance and allows robots that do not have prior information about the deployed network to navigate between any two markers in the environment.

One of the major ideas behind our approach is that the deployed network can be used in collaboration with mobile robots. This allows us to design a minimalist algorithm which does not require a map of the environment or GPS. In addition, metric localization does not take place. The tradeoff is the assumption that the number of available markers is infinite and that markers are not a scarce resource, which is a reasonable assumption nowadays [20].

The results presented in this work were conducted in simulation. Figure 11 shows some of the screen shots of a preliminary experiment using hardware. Experiments are in progress using a Pioneer 2DX mobile robot equipped with 180° laser range finder, compass and wireless ethernet and a set of Motes (as markers) equipped with CPU, RAM and radio of adjustable signal strength. The experiments suggest that the proposed approach is valid.

Acknowledgment. This work is supported in part by NSF grants ANI-0082498, IIS-0133947, and EIA-0121141.

References

1. Gage, D.W.: Command control for many-robot systems. In: the Nineteenth Annual AUVS Technical Symposium, Huntsville, Alabama, USA (1992) 22–24
2. O'Rourke, J.: Art Gallery Theorems and Algorithms. Oxford University Press, New York (1987)
3. Howard, A., Mataric, M.J., Sukhatme, G.S.: Mobile sensor network deployment using potential fields: A distributed, scalable solution to the area coverage problem. In: Proc. of 6th International Symposium on Distributed Autonomous Robotic Systems, Fukuoka, Japan (2002) 299–308
4. Batalin, M.A., Sukhatme, G.S.: Spreading out: A local approach to multi-robot coverage. In: Proc. of 6th International Symposium on Distributed Autonomous Robotic Systems, Fukuoka, Japan (2002) 373–382
5. Batalin, M.A., Sukhatme, G.S.: Sensor coverage using mobile robots and stationary nodes. In: SPIE2002. Volume 4868. (2002) 269–276
6. Yamauchi, B.: Frontier-based approach for autonomous exploration. In: In Proceedings of the IEEE International Symposium on Computational Intelligence, Robotics and Automation. (1997) 146–151
7. Yamauchi, B., Schultz, A., Adams, W.: Mobile robot exploration and map-building with continuous localization. In: In Proceedings of the 1998 IEEE/RSJ International Conference on Robotics and Automation. Volume 4. (1998) 3175–3720
8. Zelinsky, A.: A mobile robot exploration algorithm. In: IEEE Transactions on Robotics and Automation. Volume 8. (1992) 707–717
9. Burgard, W., Fox, D., Moors, M., Simmons, R., Thrun, S.: Collaborative multirobot exploration. In: Proc. of IEEE International Conferenceon Robotics and Automation (ICRA). Volume 1. (2000) 476–481
10. Dudek, G., Jenkin, M., Milios, E., Wilkes, D.: Robotic exploration as graph construction. In: IEEE Transactions on Robotics and Automation, 7–6. (1991)
11. Bender, M.A., Fernandez, A., Ron, D., Sahai, A., Vadhan, S.: The power of a pebble: Exploring and mapping directed graphs. In: Annual ACM Symposium on Theory of Computing (STOC '98). (1998)
12. Koenig, S., Simmons, R.: Easy and hard testbeds for real-time search algorithms. In: Proccedings of National Conference on Artificial Intelligence. (1996) 279–285
13. Szymanski, B., Koenig, S.: The complexity of node counting on undirected graphs. Technical report, Computer Science Department, Rensselaer Technical Institute, Troy(New York) (1998)
14. Li, Q., DeRosa, M., Rus, D.: Distributed algorithms for guiding navigation across a sensor network. In: The 2nd International Workshop on Information Processing in Sensor Networks (IPSN '03), Palo Alto (2003)

15. Mataric, M.J.: Behavior-based control: Examples from navigation, learning, and group behavior. Journal of Experimental and Theoretical Artificial Intelligence, special issue on Software Architectures for Physical Agents **9** (1997) 323–336

16. Pirjanian, P.: Behavior coordination mechanisms – state-of-the-art. Technical Report IRIS-99-375, Institute for Robotics and Intelligent Systems, University of Southern California (1999)

17. Lovasz, L. In: Random Walks on Graphs: A Survey. Volume 2 of Combinatorics, Paul Erdos is Eighty, Keszthely, Hungary (1993) 1–46

18. White, D.J.: Markov Decision Process. John Wiley & Sons, West Sussex, England (1993)

19. Koenig, S., Simmons, R.G.: Complexity analysis of real-time reinforcement learning applied to finding shortest paths in deterministic domains. Technical Report CMU-CS-93-106, Carnegie Mellon University, School of Computer Science, Carnegie Mellon University, Pittsburg, PA 15213 (1992)

20. Pister, K.S.J., Kahn, J.M., Boser, B.E.: Smart dust: Wireless networks of millimeter-scale sensor nodes. Electronics Research Laboratory Research Summary (1999)

Distance Based Decision Fusion in a Distributed Wireless Sensor Network

Marco Duarte and Yu-Hen Hu

University of Wisconsin – Madison
Department of Electrical and Computer Engineering
Madison WI 53706, USA
mfduarte@wisc.edu, hu@engr.wisc.edu
http://www.ece.wisc.edu/~sensit

Abstract. Target classification fusion problem in a distributed, wireless sensor network is investigated. We propose a distance-based decision fusion scheme exploiting the relationship between sensor to target distance, signal to noise ratio and classification rate, which requires less communication while achieving higher region classification rate when compared to conventional majority-vote based fusion schemes. Several different methods are tested, and very encouraging simulation results using real world experimental data samples are also observed.

1 Introduction

It will soon become feasible to deploy massive amount of low-cost miniature sensors to monitor large regions over ground surface, underwater, or atmosphere. These sensor nodes will be integrated with miniature power supply, sensors, on-board processors, and wireless radio communication modules, capable of forming a large-scale ad hoc wireless network [3]. Common signal processing tasks performed in a sensor system include event detection, and parameter estimation. While these detection, classification, and tracking algorithms have been well developed for conventional centralized signal processing systems, much less is known for a distributed wireless sensor network system. A distinct feature of such a system is that it contains multiple, physically scattered sensing and processing modules that must collaborate with each other to achieve high performance. Conventional centralized information and data fusion techniques are unsuited for such an application because too much data must be communicated from individual sensors to a centralized fusion center. Instead, a family of novel distributed, localized, and location centric signal processing and information fusion algorithms must be developed to meet this demand.

In this paper, we propose a distance-based decision fusion method for the collaborative target classification of moving vehicles using acoustic spectral features. A key innovation of this approach is to use the distance between the target and the sensor as a parameter to select sensors that give reliable classification result to participate decision fusion. Intuitively, sensors that are far from the

F. Zhao and L. Guibas (Eds.): IPSN 2003, LNCS 2634, pp. 392–404, 2003.

target will have lower probability of making correct classification decisions. This intuitive concept is verified using real world experimental data recorded at a military training ground using a prototype wireless sensor network. In the rest of this paper, the background of wireless sensor network architecture will be introduced in section 2.1. The sensor network signal processing algorithms will be surveyed in section 2.2 with special attention to the task of target classification and its performance with respect to sensor-target distance. The distance-based classification fusion method will be discussed in section 3, completed with simulation results using real world experimental data.

2 Distributed Wireless Sensor Network Signal Processing

2.1 Wireless Sensor Nodes and Network

We assume that a number of sensor nodes are deployed in an outdoor sensor field. Each sensor node consists of an on-board computer, power source (battery), one or more sensors with different modalities, and wireless transceivers. Depicted in Figure 1(a) is a prototype sensor node used in the DARPA SensIT project, manufactured by Sensoria, Inc. With this sensor node, there are three sensing modalities: acoustic (microphone), seismic (geophone), and infrared (polarized IR sensor). The acoustic signal is sampled at 5 kHz at 12 bit resolution. The on-board computer is a 32-bit RISC processor running the Linux operating system.

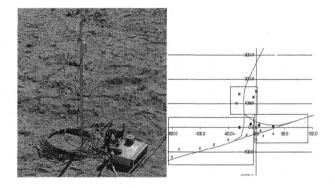

Fig. 1. (a) A Sensoria sensor node, (b) sensor field layout

The sensor field (c.f. Figure 1(b)) is an area of approximately 900 × 300 meters in a California Marine training ground. The sensors, denoted by dots of different colors in Figure 1(b) are layout along side the road. The separation of adjacent sensors ranges from 20-40 meters. We partition the sensors into three geographically local *regions*. Sensors within each region will be able to communicate freely. One sensor within each region is designated as a *manager node*.

The manager node will be given the authority to communicate with manager nodes of surrounding regions. This hierarchy of communication ensures that only local wireless traffic will be engaged, and hence contributes to the goal of energy conservation.

Military vehicles, including the *Assault Amphibian Vehicle* (AAV), the *Dragon Wagon* (DW), the *High Mobility Multipurpose Wheeled Vehicle* (HMMWV), and others are driving passing through the roads. The objective is to detect the vehicles when they pass through each region. The type of the passing vehicle then will be identified, and the accurate location of that vehicle will be estimated using an *energy-based localization algorithm*. In the following discussion, we will assume there is at most one vehicle in each region. During the experimentation in November 2001, multi-gigabyte data samples have been recorded and are used in this paper. We will call these data Sitex02 data set.

2.2   Sensor Network Signal Processing Tasks

In a distributed wireless sensor network, the bulk of signal processing tasks are distributed over individual nodes. In particular, at each sensor node, the on-board computer will process the sensed acoustic, seismic and PIR data to detect the presence of a potential target, and to classify the type of vehicle that is detected. In this paper, we will focus on the processing of acoustic sensing channel only.

CFAR Target Detection. For each of the 0.75 second duration, the energy of the acoustic signal will be computed. This single energy reading then will be fed into a *constant false alarm rate* (CFAR) energy detector [6] to determine whether the current energy reading has a magnitude that exceeds a computed threshold. If so, a *node-detection* event will be declared for this duration. Otherwise, the energy reading is considered as contributions from the background noise.

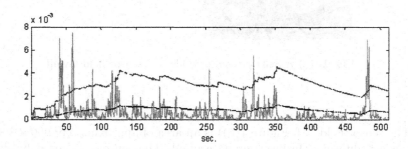

Fig. 2. Illustration of CFAR detection. The upper line is the threshold. Vertical axis is energy. When the energy exceeds the threshold, detection is made

In Figure 2, a sample energy time series is plotted for a period of 500 seconds. The two horizontal lines represent the threshold with two different false alarm rates. These thresholds vary with time as they are updated by the energy readings that do not exceed the thresholds.

From Figure 2, it is clear that when the background noise energy increases, the threshold increases as well. If the signal energy distribution, which is assumed to be unknown in the CFAR detection, remains unchanged, the probability of miss will increase. Furthermore, in this out-door, unrestricted environment, we observe that when the wind-gusts blow directly into the microphone, it often create a surge of false detection events. These anomalies are likely to cause performance degradation.

Target Classification. Once a positive target-detection decision has been made, a pattern classifier using Maximum likelihood pattern classifier [6] is invoked. The acoustic signal is recording usinga sampling frequency of 4960 Hz. We use a 50 dimensional feature vector based on the Fourier power spectrum of the corresponding acoustic time series within the 0.75-second duration. This feature is created by averaging by pairs the first 100 points of the 512-point FFT, which are then normalized; the resolution of the frequency spectrum sampling is 19.375 Hz due to the averaging. Some typical features can be seen in Figure 3.

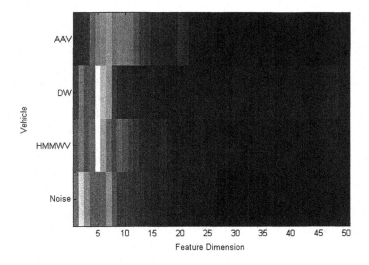

Fig. 3. Figure of typical normalized acoustic features for different vehicle classes.

Since the original acoustic time series contains both the acoustic signal sensed from the moving vehicle as well as background noise, the probability of correct classification may vary as the signal to noise ratio changes. It is intuitive to predict that if a sensor node is far away from the target vehicle, its SNR is lower, and hence the probability of correct classification will be lower. This is particularly easy to explain based on the maximum likelihood classifier architecture. In the ML classifier, we assume that the feature vector x is drawn from a conditional probability (*likelihood function*):

$$P(x|k) \sim \exp\left\{ \frac{-1}{2}(x - x_k)^T \Sigma_k^{-1}(x - x_k) \right\} . \tag{1}$$

where $x|k$ is the mean feature vector of k_{th} type of vehicle and Σ_k is the co-variance matrix estimated from the training data samples. The ML classifier determines that x belongs to the $k*$ class of vehicle if $P(x|k*) > P(x|k)$ for any $k \neq k*$. As x is perturbed with higher background noise, it is more likely that the margin

$$P(x|k*) - \max_{k \neq k*}(P(x|k)) . \tag{2}$$

will shrink. As such, the probability of misclassification will increase. The level of noise can be determined calculating the signal to noise ratio SNRdB, and should be inversely proportional to the distance between the node and the vehicle. To validate this conclusion, we conducted an experiment using a portion of the Sitex02 data set that was recorded when a vehicle is cruising across the east-west segment of the road in the sensor field. With the ground-truth data, we calculate the relative average distance between each sensor to the vehicle as well as the SNRdB for each node during each 0.75-second interval. We also perform target classification using the FFT spectrum of the acoustic signal during that interval, and record the classification result based on Distance and SNRdB.

Then, we collect such results for all the nodes in both regions that cover the road segment and compiled them into a histogram as shown in Figure 4. It is quite clear that as the target-sensor distance increases and the signal to noise ratio decreases, the probability of correct target classification decreases. In fact, this probability dropped below 0.5 when the target-sensor distance is greater than 100 meters. This empirically derived probability of correct classification will offer great information to facilitate the development of a distance-based, region-wide classification fusion method to be discussed in a moment.

Region-Based Information Fusion. Within a short message submitted by individual sensor nodes to the manager node of the region, information is sent on the corresponding energy reading (a non-negative number), CFAR detection result (yes/no), classification result (one integer k), and detection results of PIR and seismic channels. Hence, its length is less than 30 bytes and would take little energy and bandwidth to transmit via the wireless channel.

At the region manager node, information fusion tasks will be performed. First, a region-wide detection decision will be made by majority votes from all sensor nodes that reported detection at any of the three sensing modality channels. If the sum of all these votes exceeds a preset threshold, it is deemed that there is indeed a vehicle present within the region. This will then trigger

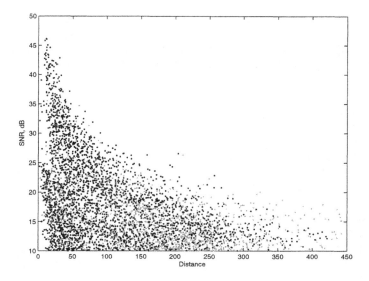

Fig. 4. Distribution of correct (*dark marks*) and incorrect (*light marks*) classifications based on distance and SNR_{dB}

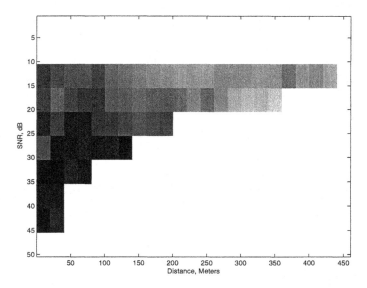

Fig. 5. Probability of correct target classification versus distance betweens sensor node and the target and the signal to noise ratio. Darker marks represent higher correct classification probability

an energy-based target localization algorithm [5] to yield an estimate of the vehicle location. The location information then will be sent to a Kalman filter based tracking algorithm to facilitate data association, track filtering and track prediction. Details of these tasks will be reported in the near future.

3   Distance Based Classification Fusion

Apart from the localization and tracking of the target, it is also necessary to classify the type of vehicle within the region based on target classification results reported from member sensor nodes. Note that in our current system architecture, the target localization may be performed prior to region-wide target classification. Hence, if the target position is relatively accurate, it is possible to use the estimated target location and known sensor coordinates to calculate the target-sensor distance. Then, one may estimate the empirically derived probability of correct classification at a particular sensor node based on the distance information as described in section 3.

3.1   Data Fusion

Statistically speaking, data fusion [2] is the process of estimating the joint posterior probability (likelihood function in the uninformed prior case) based on estimates of the marginal posterior probability. Let $x(i)$ denote the feature vector observed at the ith sensor node within the region, C_k denotes the kth type of vehicle, the goal is to identify a function $f(\cdot)$ such that

$$P(x \in C_k | x(1), \ldots, x(N)) \triangleq P(x \in C_k | \underline{x}).$$
$$\approx f(g(P(x \in C_k | x(i))), 1 \leq i \leq N) . \qquad (3)$$

In our current work, we let the maximum function $g(z_k) = 1$ if $z_k > z_j$, $k \neq j$, and $g(z_k) = 0$ otherwise. Hence, our approach is known as *decision fusion*. Conventionally, there are two basic forms of the fusion function f.

Multiplicative Form. If we assume that $x(i)$ and $x(j)$ are statistically independent feature vectors, then

$$P(x \in C_k | \underline{x}) = \prod_{i=1}^{N} P(x \in C_k | x(i)) . \qquad (4)$$

This approach is not realistic in the sensor network application and cannot be easily adapted to a decision fusion framework.

Additive Form. The fusion function is represented as a weighted sum of the marginal posterior probability or local decisions:

$$\hat{P}(x \in C_k) = \sum_{i=1}^{N} w_i g_i (P(x \in C_k | x(i))) \ . \tag{5}$$

A baseline approach of region-based decision fusion would be simply choose $w_i = 1$ for $1 \leq i \leq N$. This would be called the *simple voting* fusion method.

3.2 Maximum A Posterior Decision Fusion

With distance-based decision fusion, we make each of the weighting factors w_i in equation 4 a function of distance and signal to noise ratio, that is $w_i = h(d_i, s_i)$ where d_i is the distance between the ith sensor and the target and s_i is the signal to noise ratio defined as

$$\mathrm{SNR_{dB}} = 10 \cdot \log_{10} \left(\frac{E_s - E_n}{E_n} \right) \ . \tag{6}$$

where E_s is the signal energy and E_n is the noise mean energy, both determined by the CFAR detection algorithm. We can use then the characterization gathered from the experiment referred in section 2 to formulate a Maximum A Posterior (MAP) Probability Gating network, using the Bayesian estimation

$$\hat{P}(x \in C_k) = P(x \in C_k | \underline{x}, d_i, s_i) \cdot P(\underline{x} | d_i, s_i) \cdot P(d_i, s_i) \ . \tag{7}$$

The prior probability $P(d_i, s_i)$ is the probability that the target is at the distance range d_i, and the acoustic signal $\mathrm{SNR_{dB}}$ is at the s_i range, and can be estimated empirically from the experiments. The conditional probability $P(\underline{x} | d_i, s_i)$ is also available from the empirically gathered data. With these, we may simply assign the following weights in eq. 5:

$$w_i = P(\underline{x} | d_i, s_i) \cdot P(d_i, s_i) \ . \tag{8}$$

In other words, if a particular sensor's classification result is deemed as less likely to be correct, it will be excluded from the classification fusion.

We now have another possible choice of w_i. That is,

$$w_i = \begin{cases} 1 & d_i < d_j, j \neq i \\ 0 & \text{otherwise} \end{cases} \ . \tag{9}$$

This choice of weights represents a nearest neighbor approach, where the result of the closest node to the target is assumed to be the region result.

We can use other choices that are functions only of distance. In this work, we use a simple threshold function:

$$w_i = \begin{cases} 1 & d_i \leq d_{max} \\ 0 & \text{otherwise} \end{cases} \ . \tag{10}$$

We compare these three different methods of choosing w_i to the baseline method of setting $w_i = 1$ for all i, and test them using seven different experiments in the Sitex02 data set, using one out of n training and testing. Our metrics are the classification rate and the rejection rate.

The classification rate is the ratio between the number of correctly classified samples and the total numbered of samples classified as vehicles. The rejection rate is the rate between the number of samples rejected by the classifier and the total number of samples ran through the classification algorithm. Consequentially, the acceptance rate is the complement of the rejection rate.

There are two rejection scenarios with our current classifier scheme; one is at the node level, where one of the classes characterized during training collects typical samples of events with high energy that do not correspond to vehicles. These events are incorrectly detected and include such noises as wind, radio chatter and speech. The other is at the region level, where the region fusion algorithm does not specify satisfactorily a region classification result, i.e. no nodes were closer than d_{max} to the vehicle for the distance-based region fusion algorithm.

It is desired to obtain high classification rates while preserving low rejection rates. The results are listed in Tables 1 and 2. To analyze the impact of localization errors in the different methods, errors were injected to the ground truth coordinates following a zero-mean Gaussian distribution with several standard deviations. The results are shown in Tables 3 to 8.

Table 1. Classification rate fusion results using 4 methods

Fusion Method	MAP Bayesian	$d_{max} = 50$ m	Nearest Neighbor	Majority Voting
	77.19%	80.82%	**83.55%**	75.58%
AAV3	33.87%	50.79%	**73.33%**	27.12%
AAV6	**100.00%**	**100.00%**	**100.00%**	**100.00%**
AAV9	89.80%	90.63%	84.31%	**91.84%**
DW3	80.00%	83.78%	**85.71%**	82.50%
DW6	**100.00%**	**100.00%**	**100.00%**	**100.00%**
DW9	66.67%	75.00%	**75.86%**	63.33%
DW12	**70.00%**	65.52%	65.63%	64.29%

3.3   Results and Analysis

For Tables 1 to 8, the cells that give the highest classification rate are highlighted, including tied cases. It is seen that Nearest Neighbor method yields out the best results consistently when the error is low or nonexistent - in 9 out of 14 cases. The distance-based and MAP-based methods give comparable results in cases where the error is larger (each method has the highest rate in 4 to 6 cases out of 14). However, the rejection rates are unacceptable for the distance-based method, even with nonexistent error, with an average of 35%.

Table 2. Rejection rate fusion results using 4 methods

Fusion Method	MAP Bayesian	$d_{max} = 50$ m	Nearest Neighbor	Majority Voting
	9.53%	21.56%	**7.40%**	10.40%
AAV3	3.13%	**1.56%**	6.25%	7.81%
AAV6	4.29%	27.14%	**2.86%**	7.14%
AAV9	3.92%	37.25%	**0.00%**	3.92%
DW3	4.76%	11.90%	**0.00%**	4.76%
DW6	6.06%	9.09%	**0.00%**	**0.00%**
DW9	**14.29%**	31.43%	17.14%	**14.29%**
DW12	30.23%	32.56%	**25.58%**	34.86%

Table 3. Classification rate fusion results using 4 methods, and error injection with $\sigma = 12.5$ m

Fusion Method	MAP Bayesian	$d_{max} = 50$ m	Nearest Neighbor	Majority Voting
	77.14%	80.51%	**81.89%**	75.58%
AAV3	32.79%	56.45%	**67.21%**	27.12%
AAV6	**100.00%**	**100.00%**	**100.00%**	**100.00%**
AAV9	**93.88%**	90.63%	84.31%	91.84%
DW3	80.00%	81.08%	**83.33%**	82.50%
DW6	**100.00%**	**100.00%**	**100.00%**	**100.00%**
DW9	66.67%	**78.26%**	75.86%	63.33%
DW12	**66.67%**	57.14%	62.50%	64.29%

Table 4. Rejection rate fusion results using 4 methods, and error injection with $\sigma = 12.5$ m

Fusion Method	MAP Bayesian	$d_{max} = 50$ m	Nearest Neighbor	Majority Voting
	9.75%	22.32%	**7.40%**	10.40%
AAV3	4.69%	**3.13%**	6.25%	7.81%
AAV6	4.29%	25.71%	**2.86%**	7.14%
AAV9	3.92%	37.25%	**0.00%**	3.92%
DW3	4.76%	11.90%	**0.00%**	4.76%
DW6	6.06%	9.09%	**0.00%**	**0.00%**
DW9	**14.29%**	34.29%	17.14%	**14.29%**
DW12	30.23%	34.88%	**25.58%**	34.86%

Figure 6 shows the average performance of the different methods for all the error injection scenarios. The results of the error impact experiments show that the MAP-based classification fusion is not heavily affected by the error injection; the change for the classification rate is less than 0.1% in average for an error injection up to $\sigma = 50$ m and the rejection rate increases 0.1% in average. The effects on the other methods are more pronounced, with a change of 3% in average in classification rate for the Nearest Neighbor method and an increase of 24% in the rejection rate of the distance-based method.

Table 5. Classification rate fusion results using 4 methods, and error injection with $\sigma = 25$ m

Fusion Method	MAP Bayesian 77.74%	$d_{max} = 50$ m 79.42%	Nearest Neighbor 79.29%	Majority Voting **75.56%**
AAV3	37.70%	54.39%	**55.36%**	27.12%
AAV6	**100.00%**	**100.00%**	**100.00%**	**100.00%**
AAV9	89.80%	**100.00%**	88.24%	91.84%
DW3	80.00%	**82.86%**	80.95%	82.50%
DW6	**100.00%**	**100.00%**	**100.00%**	**100.00%**
DW9	66.67%	72.00%	**72.41%**	63.33%
DW12	**70.00%**	46.67%	58.06%	64.29%

Table 6. Rejection rate fusion results using 4 methods, and error injection with $\sigma = 25$ m

Fusion Method	MAP Bayesian 9.75%	$d_{max} = 50$ m 24.78%	Nearest Neighbor **8.63%**	Majority Voting 10.40%
AAV3	**4.69%**	10.94%	12.50%	7.81%
AAV6	4.29%	30.00%	**2.86%**	7.14%
AAV9	3.92%	50.98%	**0.00%**	3.92%
DW3	4.76%	16.67%	**0.00%**	4.76%
DW6	6.06%	6.06%	**0.00%**	**0.00%**
DW9	**14.29%**	28.57%	17.14%	**14.29%**
DW12	30.23%	30.23%	**27.91%**	34.88%

Table 7. Classification rate fusion results using 4 methods, and error injection with $\sigma = 50$ m

Fusion Method	MAP Bayesian 77.74%	$d_{max} = 50$ m **80.48%**	Nearest Neighbor 76.72%	Majority Voting 75.58%
AAV3	37.70%	**51.28%**	39.29%	27.12%
AAV6	**100.00%**	**100.00%**	**100.00%**	**100.00%**
AAV9	89.80%	**95.00%**	86.27%	91.84%
DW3	80.00%	**84.62%**	78.57%	82.50%
DW6	**100.00%**	95.24%	96.97%	**100.00%**
DW9	66.67%	**72.22%**	71.43%	63.33%
DW12	**70.00%**	65.00%	64.52%	64.29%

These experiments show higher classification rates for the MAP and Nearest Neighbor approaches compared to the baseline majority voting approach, while maintaining comparable acceptance rates. Further research is needed on additional considerations to avoid transmission of node classifications that have low probability of being correct; it is expected that both the Nearest Neighbor method and an adapted minimum-threshold MAP-based method will easily allow for these additions.

Table 8. Rejection rate fusion results using 4 methods, and error injection with $\sigma = 50$ m

Fusion Method	MAP Bayesian	$d_{max} = 50$ m	Nearest Neighbor	Majority Voting
	9.95%	46.01%	**9.24%**	10.40%
AAV3	**4.69%**	39.06%	12.50%	7.81%
AAV6	5.71%	45.71%	**4.29%**	7.14%
AAV9	3.92%	60.78%	**0.00%**	3.92%
DW3	4.76%	38.10%	**0.00%**	4.76%
DW6	6.06%	36.36%	**0.00%**	**0.00%**
DW9	**14.29%**	48.57%	20.00%	**14.29%**
DW12	30.23%	53.49%	**27.91%**	34.88%

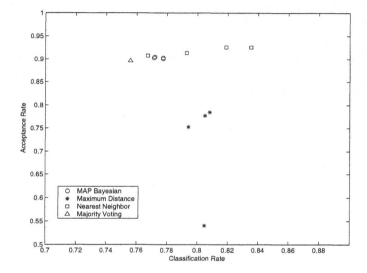

Fig. 6. Average classification and acceptance rate results for different classification region fusion methods

Acknowledgment. This work was supported in part by DARPA under grant no. F 30602-00-2-0555.

References

1. Averbuch, A., Hulata, E., Zheludev, V., Kozlov, I.: A wavelet packet algorithm for classification and detection of moving vehicles. Multidimensional Systems and Signal Processing **12**, (2001) 9–31
2. Brooks, R. R., Iyengar, S. S.: Multi-sensor fusion: fundamentals and applications with software. Upper Saddle River, NJ: Prentice Hall PTR (1998)

3. Estrin, D., Girod, L. Pottie, G., Srivastava, M.: Instrumenting the world with wireless sensor network. Proc. ICASSP'2001. Salt Lake City, UT, (2001) 2675–2678.
4. Lennartsson, R. K., Pentek, A., Kadtke, J.B.: Classification of acoustic and seismic data using nonlinear dynamical signal models. Proc. IEEE Workshop Statistical Signal and Array Processing (2000) 722–726
5. Li, D., Hu, Y.H.: Energy Based Collaborative Source Localization Using Acoustic Micro-Sensor Array. J. Applied Signal Processing, pp. (to appear)
6. Li, D., Wong, K.D., Hu, Y. H., Sayeed, A. M.: Detection, classification and tracking of targets. IEEE Signal Processing Magazine 19 (2002) 17–29
7. Nooralahiyan, A. Y., Dougherty, M., McKeown, D., Kirkby, H.R.: A field trial of acoustic signature analysis for vehicle classification. Transportation Research Part C 5C (1997) 165–177
8. Nooralahiyan, A.Y., Lopez, L., McKewon, D., Ahmadi, M.: Time-delay neural network for audio monitoring of road traffic and vehicle classification. Proceedings of the SPIE. (1997) 193–200
9. Nooralahiyan, A.Y., Kirby, H.R., McKeown, D.: Vehicle classification by acoustic signature. Mathematical and Computer Modelling 27 (1998) 205–214
10. Tung, T.L., Kung, Y.: Classification of vehicles using nonlinear dynamics and array processing. Proceedings of the SPIE (1999) 234–246

Maximum Mutual Information Principle for Dynamic Sensor Query Problems

Emre Ertin[1], John W. Fisher[2], and Lee C. Potter[1]

[1] The Ohio State University, Columbus, OH
{ertin.1,potter}@osu.edu,
[2] MIT Artificial Intelligence Laboratory, Cambridge, MA
fisher@ai.mit.edu

Abstract. In this paper we study a dynamic sensor selection method for Bayesian filtering problems. In particular we consider the distributed Bayesian Filtering strategy given in [1] and show that the principle of mutual information maximization follows naturally from the expected uncertainty minimization criterion in a Bayesian filtering framework. This equivalence results in a computationally feasible approach to state estimation in sensor networks. We illustrate the application of the proposed dynamic sensor selection method to both discrete and linear Gaussian models for distributed tracking as well as to stationary target localization using acoustic arrays.

1   Introduction

There has been renewed interest in the notion of deploying large numbers of networked sensors for applications ranging from environmental monitoring to surveillance to "intelligent" rooms(c.f. [2]). Envisioned are smart sensor nodes with on-board sensing, computation, storage and communication capability. Such sensor networks simultaneously present unprecedented opportunities and unique challenges in collaborative signal processing. A particular challenge in the wireless sensor network setting is the need for distributed estimation algorithms which balance the limited energy resources at a node with costs of communication and sensing.

If one considers the distributed tracking problem, for example, it is not hard to imagine that one need not incorporate *every* sensor measurement in order to compute a reliable, if not optimal, estimate of the state of an object (or more properly the posterior distribution thereof). This is particularly true in the case where sensors have a limited field of regard with limited overlap between sensors. Distributed processing strategies that use a subset of sensor measurements directly mitigate the volume of inter-node communication thereby conserving power. The challenge is to decide in an intelligent manner which sensor measurements to use.

In the context of just such a scenario, Zhao *et al.* [1] recently suggested a novel approach, the Information-Driven Sensor Querying (IDSQ) algorithm, as a means of selecting the "best" sensor measurement for updating the posterior

F. Zhao and L. Guibas (Eds.): IPSN 2003, LNCS 2634, pp. 405–416, 2003.

belief of an object's state. In that work, a utility measure of a node measurement was proposed based on an estimate of the *expected* posterior state distribution conditioned on the, as yet unobserved, measurement at that node. This led to a direct method of selecting which node to query.

In this paper we further investigate aspects of one of the information utility functions suggested in [1,3], specifically state uncertainty as quantified by conditional entropy. We begin by formulating the problem in a Bayesian estimation framework (as is commonly done) and decomposing state estimation into prediction (prior belief) and update (posterior belief) steps. We first show that, not surprisingly, functions which attempt to select the next sensor measurement based on *expected* posterior belief do nothing more than exploit information already contained in the prior belief as both are the same prior to taking a measurement. Consequently, utility functions based on *expected* posterior beliefs are more properly cast as utility functions on the prior belief (i.e. the belief over the current set of measurements). Next we consider the expected posterior uncertainty as quantified by conditional entropy (conditioned on previous measurements and a single new measurement) indexed by sensors. We show that this utility function simplifies to selecting the sensor measurement which has maximum mutual information with the object state at the next time step. The primary consequence of this analysis is that the utility function can be computed in a lower-dimensional space and, importantly, in a computationally feasible manner.

We present three experimental examples. The first example uses a simple discrete model to illustrate the maximum mutual information principle. The second example discusses the application of the maximum mutual information based sensor selection method to linear Gaussian Models. The third example is a simulation study of a stationary target localization problem using an acoustic array.

2   Bayesian Filtering with Dynamic Sensor Selection

We adopt a probabilistic state space model for the tracking problem. The state of the target at time step (t) is denoted by $x^{(t)}$. In this paper we will assume that the state space for the tracking problem can be approximated with a finite state space $\{x_i\}_{i=1}^N$. The sensor network consists of M sensors. Each sensor can be queried to provide a noisy measurements $z_j^{(t)}$ of the state of the target. The state transition and observation model is given as:

$$x^{(t+1)} = F(x^{(t)}, v^{(t)})$$
$$\Rightarrow q(x^{(t+1)}|x^{(t)}) \tag{1}$$
$$z_j^{(t)} = H_j(x^{(t)}, w^{(t)})$$
$$\Rightarrow f_j(z_j^{(t)}|x_j) \tag{2}$$

where F and H_j are arbitrary functions of the state and unknown disturbance variables $v^{(t)}$ and $w^{(t)}$. The state space model suggests a conditional probability distribution $q(x^{(t+1)}|x^{(t)})$ for the target state at time $(t+1)$ and a conditional probability density $f_j(z_j^{(t)}|x_j)$ for the j'th sensors measurement.

The Bayesian filtering solution recursively calculates degree of belief in a state $x^{(t+1)}$, given the sensor measurements. The prediction step computes the prior belief in state $x^{(t+1)}$ before a measurement is taken at $(t+1)$:

$$p(x^{(t+1)}|z^{\overline{(t)}}) = \sum_i q(x^{(t+1)}|x_i^{(t)})p(x_i^{(t)}|z^{(t)}) . \tag{3}$$

The update step computes the posterior belief in state $x^{(t+1)}$ after the measurement at $(t+1)$:

$$p(x^{(t+1)}|z^{\overline{(t+1)}}) = \frac{f_j(z^{(t+1)}|x^{(t+1)})p(x^{(t+1)}|z^{\overline{(t)}})}{g_j(z^{(t+1)}|z^{\overline{(t)}})} , \tag{4}$$

where $z^{\overline{(t)}}$ denotes the measurements $\{z^{(1)}, z^{(2)}, \ldots, z^{(t)}\}$ up to time (t). The normalization constant $g_j(z^{(t+1)}|z^{\overline{(t)}})$ can be computed using:

$$g_j(z^{(t+1)}|z^{\overline{(t)}}) = \sum_i f_j(z^{(t+1)}|x_i)p(x_i|z^{\overline{(t+1)}}) . \tag{5}$$

Zhao *et al.* [1] describes a strategy for tracking problems to implement Bayesian Filtering in a distributed setting. At each time step one sensor node labeled as the leader makes a measurement and computes the belief $p(x^{(t+1)}|z^{\overline{(t)}})$. Then it select a sensor node to lead the tracking effort and passes the current belief to the chosen leader node. The next sensor to lead the tracking algorithm can be chosen to maximize a utility function of the form:

$$U(z^{\overline{(t)}} \cup z_j^{(t+1)}) = -H[p(x^{(t+1)}|z^{\overline{(t)}} \cup z_j^{(t+1)})]$$
$$= \sum_i p(x_i^{(t+1)}|z^{\overline{(t)}} \cup z_j^{(t+1)}) \log p(x_i^{(t+1)}|z^{\overline{(t)}} \cup z_j^{(t+1)}) ,$$

where $U(z^{\overline{(t)}} \cup z_j^t)$ is the utility received from decreased uncertainty in the state of the target, which is measured as the entropy of the conditional probability density of $x^{(t+1)}$ given the sensor measurements up to time $(t+1)$. This utility function can be augmented with the communication cost of relaying the current belief from the current leader to the next. For example, the communication cost component of the utility can encompass the bandwidth utilization, transmission and reception power costs.

In this paper we focus on estimable measures of information utility, but a suitable communication cost can easily be integrated with our approach. Typically the measurement for the next sensor is unknown at $(t+1)$. Further, the expectation of the posterior belief $p(x^{(t+1)}|z^{\overline{(t)}} \cup z_j^t)$ is equal to the predicted belief $p(x^{(t+1)}|z^{\overline{(t)}}))$.

$$E[p(x^{(t+1)}|z^{\overline{(t)}} \cup z_j^{(t+1)})|z^{\overline{(t)}}]$$

$$= E\left[\frac{f_j(z_j^{(t+1)}|x^{(t+1)})p(x^{(t+1)}|z^{\overline{(t)}})}{g_j(z_j^{(t+1)}|z^{\overline{(t)}})}\Bigg|z^{\overline{(t)}}\right]$$

$$= p(x^{(t+1)}|z^{\overline{(t)}})E\left[\frac{f_j(z_j^{(t+1)}|x^{(t+1)})}{g_j(z_j^{(t+1)}|z^{\overline{(t)}})}\Bigg|z^{\overline{(t)}}\right]$$

$$= p(x^{(t+1)}|z^{\overline{(t)}})\int_{z\in Z_j}\frac{f_j(z|x^{(t+1)})}{g_j(z|z^{\overline{(t)}})}g_j(z|z^{\overline{(t)}})dz$$

$$= p(x^{(t+1)}|z^{\overline{(t)}})\int_{z\in Z_j}f_j(z|x^{(t+1)})dz$$

$$= p(x^{(t+1)}|z^{\overline{(t)}})\ .$$

Zhao *et al.* [1] compute a proxy $\hat{p}((x^{(t+1)}|z^{\overline{(t)}}\cup z_j^{(t+1)})$ to the expected posterior belief by averaging $f_j(z_j^{(t+1)}|x^{(t+1)})$ over estimated measurement values using predicted belief. Although, this approximation to the expected posterior belief will not be equal to the predicted belief, the above result indicates that any utility measure based on expected posterior belief will be of limited use for sensor selection. Instead we employ an expected posterior uncertainty measure for sensor selection. In particular, we consider the expected posterior entropy, one of the information measures suggested in [3]:

$$\hat{j} = \arg\max_{j\in V} E\left[-H(p(x^{(t+1)}|z^{\overline{(t)}}\cup z_j^t))|z^{\overline{(t)}}\right]\ .$$

In other words the sensor which will result in the smallest *expected* posterior uncertainty of the target state will be chosen to be the leader node of the tracking algorithm. In general, a direct computation of the expected posterior entropy is computationally infeasible. It requires computing the posterior belief for each possible measurement value and then averaging the entropy of the computed posterior belief over all possible measurement values. Even if the measurement space is discretized it requires computationally expensive calculations in the high dimensional state space. In the following, we show that maximizing the mutual information between the sensor output and target state is equivalent to minimizing expected posterior uncertainty. This observation yields a computationally feasible sensor selection method based on a maximum mutual information principle. The expected entropy of the posterior density can be evaluated using 3 and 4.

$$E\left[-H(p(x^{(t+1)}|z^{\overline{(t)}}\cup z_j^t))|z^{\overline{(t)}}\right]$$

$$= \int_{z\in Z_j}\left(\sum_i p(x_i^{(t+1)}|z^{\overline{(t)}}\cup\{z\})\log p(x_i^{(t+1)}|z^{\overline{(t)}}\cup\{z\})\right)q_j(z|z^{\overline{(t)}})dz$$

$$= \int_{z\in Z_j}\sum_i f_j(z|x_i^{(t+1)})p(x_i^{(t+1)}|z^{\overline{(t)}})\log\frac{f_j(z|x_i^{(t+1)})p(x_i^{(t+1)}|z^{\overline{(t)}})}{g_j(z|z^{\overline{(t)}})}dz$$

$$= \sum_i \left(\int_{z \in Z_j} f_j(z|x_i^{(t+1)}) \log f_j(z|x_i^{(t+1)}) dz \right) p(x_i^{(t+1)}|z^{\overline{(t)}})$$

$$- \int_{z \in Z_j} g_j(z|z^{\overline{(t)}}) \log g_j(z|z^{\overline{(t)}}) dz$$

$$+ \sum_i p(x_i^{(t+1)}|z^{\overline{(t)}}) \log p(x_i^{(t+1)}|z^{\overline{(t)}})$$

$$= -H(Z_j^{(t+1)}|X^{(t+1)}) + H(Z_j^{(t+1)}) - H(X^{(t+1)})$$

$$= I(Z_j^{(t+1)}; X^{(t+1)}) - H(X^{(t+1)})$$

We note that the second term does not depend on the sensor measurement at $(t+1)$. Hence, in a Bayesian Filtering framework minimizing the expected uncertainty in the posterior belief is equivalent to maximizing the mutual information between the state $X^{(t+1)}$ and measurement vector $Z_j^{(t+1)}$.

3   Applications

3.1   Example 1: Discrete Observations

We consider a simple two state, two sensor problem to illustrate the concepts presented in Section 2. There are two possible states for the target $x^{(t)} \in \{-1, 1\}$. The state transition model is given by:

$$x^{(t+1)} = F(x^{(t)}, v^{(t)}) = x^{(t)} v^{(t)} . \tag{6}$$

where $v^{(t)}$ is a binary random variable which takes values $\{-1, 1\}$ with probability q and $1 - q$ respectively. The observation model for the two sensors is given by.

$$z_1^{(t)} = H_1(x^{(t)}, w^{(t)}) = \text{sgn}(x^{(t)} + w_1^{(t)}) \tag{7}$$

$$z_2^{(t)} = H_2(x^{(t)}, w^{(t)}) = \text{sgn}(x^{(t)} - w_2^{(t)}) \tag{8}$$

The state space model suggests the following conditional probability distributions for state $x^{(t+1)}$ and sensor measurement $z_j(t)$.

$$p(x^{(t+1)} = 1|x^{(t)}) = 1 - p(x^{(t+1)} = -1|x^{(t)}) = \begin{cases} 1 - q & \text{if } x^{(t)} = 1 \\ q & \text{if } x^{(t)} = -1 \end{cases}$$

$$f_1(z_1^{(t)} = 1|x^{(t)}) = 1 - f_1(z_1^{(t)} = -1|x^{(t)}) = \begin{cases} 1 & \text{if } x^{(t)} = 1 \\ r & \text{if } x^{(t)} = -1 \end{cases}$$

$$f_2(z_2^{(t)} = -1|x^{(t)}) = 1 - f_2(z_2^{(t)} = 1|x^{(t)}) = \begin{cases} r & \text{if } x^{(t)} = 1 \\ 1 & \text{if } x^{(t)} = -1 \end{cases}$$

i.e., sensor 1 makes an erroneous measurement with probability r if the state is -1, and sensor 2 makes an erroneous measurement with probability r if the state is 1. For this simple model we can parametrize the prior and posterior belief using a scalar variable:

$$p^{(t+1)|\overline{(t)}} \stackrel{\text{def}}{=} p(x^{(t+1)} = 1|z^{\overline{(t)}}) \tag{9}$$

$$p^{(t+1)|\overline{(t+1)}} \stackrel{\text{def}}{=} p(x^{(t+1)} = 1|z^{\overline{(t+1)}}) \tag{10}$$

We can verify that the expected posterior belief $E[p^{(t+1)|\overline{(t+1)}}|z^{\overline{(t)}}]$ is equal to the prior belief $p^{(t+1)|\overline{(t)}}$ irrespective of the sensor choice at time $(t+1)$. If sensor 1 is queried at time $(t+1)$,

$$E[p^{(t+1)|\overline{(t+1)}}|z^{\overline{(t)}}]$$
$$= p(x^{(t+1)} = 1|z^{\overline{(t)}} \cup \{z_1^{(t+1)} = 1\})p(z_1^{(t+1)} = 1|z^{\overline{(t)}})$$
$$+ p(x^{(t+1)} = 1|z^{\overline{(t)}} \cup \{z_1^{(t+1)} = -1\})p(z_1^{(t+1)} = -1|z^{\overline{(t)}})$$
$$= \frac{p^{(t+1)|\overline{(t)}} \cdot 1}{p^{(t+1)|\overline{(t)}} \cdot 1 + (1 - p^{(t+1)|\overline{(t)}}) \cdot r}(p^{(t+1)|\overline{(t)}} \cdot 1 + (1 - p^{(t+1)|\overline{(t)}}) \cdot r)$$
$$+ \frac{p^{(t+1)|\overline{(t)}} \cdot 0}{p^{(t+1)|\overline{(t)}} \cdot 0 + (1 - p^{(t+1)|\overline{(t)}}) \cdot (1 - r)}(p^{(t+1)|\overline{(t)}} \cdot 0 + (1 - p^{(t+1)|\overline{(t)}}) \cdot (1 - r))$$
$$= p^{(t+1)|\overline{(t)}} .$$

Similarly if sensor 2 is queried at time $(t+1)$,

$$E[p^{(t+1)|\overline{(t+1)}}|z^{\overline{(t)}}]$$
$$= p(x^{(t+1)} = 1|z^{\overline{(t)}} \cup \{z_2^{(t+1)} = 1\})p(z_2^{(t+1)} = 1|z^{\overline{(t)}})$$
$$+ p(x^{(t+1)} = 1|z^{\overline{(t)}} \cup \{z_2^{(t+1)} = -1\})p(z_2^{(t+1)} = -1|z^{\overline{(t)}})$$
$$= \frac{p^{(t+1)|\overline{(t)}} \cdot (1-r)}{p^{(t+1)|\overline{(t)}} \cdot (1-r) + (1 - p^{(t+1)|\overline{(t)}}) \cdot 0}(p^{(t+1)|\overline{(t)}} \cdot (1-r) + (1 - p^{(t+1)|\overline{(t)}}) \cdot 0)$$
$$+ \frac{p^{(t+1)|\overline{(t)}} \cdot r}{p^{(t+1)|\overline{(t)}} \cdot r + (1 - p^{(t+1)|\overline{(t)}}) \cdot 1}(p^{(t+1)|\overline{(t)}} \cdot r + (1 - p^{(t+1)|\overline{(t)}}) \cdot 1)$$
$$= p^{(t+1)|\overline{(t)}} .$$

The mutual information between state at time $(t+1)$ and sensor j's output is given by:

$$I(Z_1^{(t+1)}; X^{(t+1)}) = H(Z_1^{(t+1)}) - H(Z_1^{(t+1)}|X^{(t+1)})$$
$$= \mathcal{H}((1 - p^{(t+1)|\overline{(t)}})(1-r)) - (1 - p^{(t+1)|\overline{(t)}})\mathcal{H}((1-r))$$
$$I(Z_2^{(t+1)}; X^{(t+1)}) = H(Z_2^{(t+1)}) - H(Z_2^{(t+1)}|X^{(t+1)})$$
$$= \mathcal{H}(p^{(t+1)|\overline{(t)}}(1-r)) - p^{(t+1)|\overline{(t)}}\mathcal{H}((1-r)) ,$$

where the function $\mathcal{H}$ is defined as $\mathcal{H}(x) = -x\log(x) - (1-x)\log(1-x)$. It is easy to verify that $I(Z_1^{(t+1)}; X^{(t+1)}) > I(Z_2^{(t+1)}; X^{(t+1)})$ for $p^{(t+1)|\overline{(t)}} > 0.5$. For this example minimizing the expected entropy of posterior belief is equivalent to choosing the sensor that is ideal for the most likely state.

3.2   Example 2: Linear Gaussian Model

In this section we consider the sensor selection for the Bayesian filtering problem with linear Gaussian models. We assume the following linear state space model:

$$x^{(t+1)} = Fx^{(t)} + v^{(t)} \tag{11}$$

$$z_j^{(t)} = H_j x^{(t)} + w^{(t)} \tag{12}$$

We assume the disturbances $v^{(t)}, w^{(t)}$ are zero mean Gaussian processes with covariances Σ_v and Σ_w respectively. For a linear Gaussian model and Gaussian prior belief $p(x^{(t)}|z^{\overline{(t)}})$, it can be proved that both $p(x^{(t+1)}|z^{\overline{(t)}})$ and $p(x^{(t+1)}|z^{\overline{(t+1)}})$ are also Gaussian [4]. The mean and covariance for $p(x^{(t+1)}|z^{\overline{(t)}})$ and $p(x^{(t+1)}|z^{\overline{(t+1)}})$ can be computed using the mean and covariance of $p(x^{(t)}|z^{\overline{(t)}})$ and the measurement $z^{(t+1)}$ through Kalman filter recursions.

The observation model in 12 suggests a normal conditional distribution for $z_j^{(t+1)}$:

$$f_j(z_j^{(t+1)}|x^{(t+1)}) = \mathcal{N}(z_j^{(t+1)}; H_j x^{(t+1)}, \Sigma_w) \ , \tag{13}$$

where $\mathcal{N}(y; \mu, \Sigma)$ denotes the Gaussian distribution with mean μ and Σ:

$$\mathcal{N}(y; \mu, \Sigma) \stackrel{\text{def}}{=} ((2\pi)^n |\Sigma|)^{-0.5} \exp\left(-(y - \mu)^T \Sigma^{-1}(y - \mu)\right).$$

Given the predicted belief $p(x^{(t+1)}|z^{\overline{(t)}}) = \mathcal{N}(x^{(t+1)}; \mu^{(t+1)|\overline{(t+1)}}, \Sigma^{(t+1)|\overline{(t+1)}})$ we can derive the distribution for j'th sensors measurement at time $(t+1)$ as:

$$g_j(z_j^{(t+1)}|z^{\overline{(t)}}) = \int f_j(z_j^{(t+1)}|x^{(t+1)})p(x^{(t+1)}|z^{\overline{(t)}})dx^{(t+1)}$$

$$= \int \mathcal{N}(z_j^{(t+1)}; H_j x^{(t+1)}, \Sigma_w)\mathcal{N}(x^{(t+1)}; \mu^{(t+1)|\overline{(t+1)}}, \Sigma^{(t+1)|\overline{(t+1)}})dx^{(t+1)}$$

$$= \mathcal{N}(z_j^{(t+1)}; H_j \mu^{(t+1)|\overline{(t+1)}}, \Sigma_w + H_j \Sigma^{(t+1)|\overline{(t+1)}} H_j^T) \ . \tag{14}$$

The mutual information between the sensor measurement and target state at time $(t+1)$ can be calculated using 13,14

$$I(Z_j^{(t+1)}; X^{(t+1)})$$

$$= H(Z_1^{(t+1)}) - H(Z_1^{(t+1)}|X^{(t+1)})$$

$$= H[\mathcal{N}(z_j^{(t+1)}; H_j \mu^{(t+1)|\overline{(t+1)}}, \Sigma_w + H_j \Sigma^{(t+1)|\overline{(t+1)}} H_j^T)]$$

$$\quad - \int H[\mathcal{N}(z_j^{(t+1)}; H_j x^{(t+1)}, \Sigma_w)]p(x^{(t+1)}|z^{\overline{(t)}})dx^{(t+1)}$$

$$= c \log |\Sigma_w + H_j \Sigma^{(t+1)|\overline{(t+1)}} H_j^T| - \int c \log |\Sigma_w| p(x^{(t+1)}|z^{\overline{(t)}})dx^{(t+1)}$$

$$= c \log \frac{|\Sigma_w + H_j \Sigma^{(t+1)|\overline{(t+1)}} H_j^T|}{|\Sigma_w|}$$

To summarize the sensor selection rule for minimizing the expected posterior entropy is given as:

$$\hat{j} = \arg\max_{j \in V} \frac{|\Sigma_w + H_j \Sigma^{(t+1)|\overline{(t+1)}} H_j^T|}{|\Sigma_w|} .$$

Since the posterior density is Gaussian, this sensor selection rule minimizes the covariance determinant for the posterior belief. We should note that since the covariance (or equivalently the entropy) of the updated belief $p(x^{(t+1)}|z^{\overline{(t+1)}})$ does not depend on the measurement value $z_j^{(t+1)}$, sensor selection for the linear Gaussian model is straightforward.

3.3   Example 3: Acoustic Array

In this section we consider the distributed localization of a single target using an acoustic sensor network. We assume a single target is present in a square 1 km × 1km region, which is divided into 50m × 50m cells. We assume the target is stationary:

$$x^{(t+1)} = F(x^{(t)}, v^{(t)}) = x^{(t)}$$

There are five microphones (range sensors) randomly placed in the region. Each sensor makes a time of arrival measurement (TOA) from an acoustic emission of the target. The sensor measurement model is given as:

$$z_j = \frac{\|x - y_j\|}{c} + n_j .$$

where x denotes the target location and y_j denotes the location of the j'th sensor. The speed of sound is given by c and the disturbances n_j's are Gaussian random variables with variance σ_j. The error variance of the maximum likelihood TOA detector is inversely proportional to the signal to noise ratio, which in general depends on the distance of the target to the sensor location [5,6]. In part A below, we assume constant noise variance for all the sensors and in part B, we consider the general case where the noise variance increases with increasing distance to the target. We assume each sensor can be interrogated only once. We also assume that the sensor locations and target emission time are known. A self localization method for microphone arrays is given in [7].

Part A:
In this case we assume the noise variance $\sigma_j = \sigma_0 = 50$msec is constant for all five sensors. For this case the mutual information between the state $X^{(t+1)}$ and measurement vector Z_j is given by

$$I(Z_j^{(t+1)}; X^{(t+1)}) = H(Z_j^{(t+1)}) - H((Z_j^{(t+1)}|X^{(t+1)}) ,$$

where:

$$H(Z_j^{(t+1)}) = -\int \sum_{x_i} \mathcal{N}(z, \frac{\|x_i - y_j\|}{c}, \sigma_0^2) p(x_i|z^{\overline{(t)}})$$

$$\times \log \left(\sum_{x_i} \mathcal{N}(z, \frac{\|x_i - y_j\|}{c}, \sigma_0^2) p(x_i | z^{\overline{(t)}}) \right) dz$$

$$H(Z_j^{(t+1)} | X) = \frac{1}{2} \log \left(2\pi e \sigma_0^2 \right) .$$

We note that for constant noise variance, maximizing mutual information $I(Z_j^{(t+1)}; X^{(t+1)})$ is equivalent to maximizing the entropy of the Gaussian mixture $H(Z_j^{(t+1)})$. The entropy of the Gaussian mixture can be calculated using numerical integration. Alternatively, we can obtain an approximation to $H(Z_j^{(t+1)})$ by fitting a single Gaussian to the mixture distribution.

$$H(Z_j^{(t+1)}) \approx \frac{1}{2} \log \left(2\pi e \sigma_{Z_j}^2 \right) ,$$

where

$$\sigma_{Z_j}^2 = \sum_{x_i} p(x_i | z^{\overline{(t)}}) \left((\frac{\|x_i - y_j\|}{c})^2 + \sigma_0^2 \right) - \left(\sum_{x_i} p(x_i | z^{\overline{(t)}}) \frac{\|x_i - y_j\|}{c} \right)^2 .$$

In our simulations we observed virtually no difference in sensor selection performance between actual $H(Z_j^{(t+1)})$ and its approximation.

We used 500 monte carlo simulations, for three methods of sensor selection: Random sensor selection, Maximum Mutual Information based sensor selection and Mahalanobis distance based sensor selection discussed in [3]. The results are given in Figure 1. We consider root mean square error as a measure of target localization performance. For this experiment Maximum Mutual Information based sensor selection results in the best localization performance, followed by Mahalanobis distance based method.

Part B:

In this case we assume the noise variance is dependent on the target distance

$$\sigma_j = \sigma(r) = (\frac{r}{r_0})^{\alpha/2} \sigma_0$$

In general the value of alpha depends on temperature and wind conditions and can be anisotropic. For this experiment we used $\alpha = 2$, $r_0 = 0.5$km, and $\sigma_0 = 30$msec. For the distance dependent noise model, the mutual information between the state $X^{(t+1)}$ and measurement vector Z_j is given by

$$I(Z_j^{(t+1)}; X^{(t+1)}) = H(Z_j^{(t+1)}) - H((Z_j^{(t+1)} | X^{(t+1)}) ,$$

where:

$$H(Z_j^{(t+1)}) = - \int \sum_{x_i} \mathcal{N}(z, \frac{\|x_i - y_j\|}{c}, \sigma(\|x_i - y_j\|)^2) p(x_i | z^{\overline{(t)}})$$

$$\times \log \left(\sum_{x_i} \mathcal{N}(z, \frac{\|x_i - y_j\|}{c}, \sigma(\|x_i - y_j\|)^2) p(x_i | z^{\overline{(t)}}) \right) dz$$

$$H(Z_j | X) = \sum_{x_i} \frac{1}{2} \log \left(2\pi e \sigma(\|x_i - y_j\|)^2 \right) p(x_i | z^{\overline{(t)}}) .$$

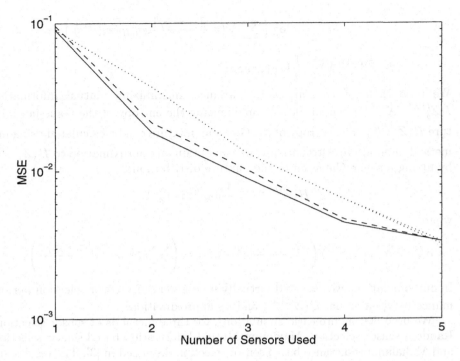

Fig. 1. Performance of the Sensor Selection Methods for constant noise variance. (Solid: Mutual Information, Dashed: Mahalanobis Distance Based Method, Dotted:Random)

Again if the distribution of Z_j can be approximated with a Gaussian we can approximate $H(Z_j^{(t+1)}) \approx \frac{1}{2} \log \left(2\pi e \sigma_{Z_j}^2 \right)$, where

$$\sigma_{Z_j}^2 = \sum_{x_i} p(x_i|z^{\overline{(t)}})((\frac{\|x_i - y_j\|}{c})^2 + \sigma(\|x_i - y_j\|)^2) - \left(\sum_{x_i} p(x_i|z^{\overline{(t)}}) \frac{\|x_i - y_j\|}{c} \right)^2 .$$

We used 500 monte carlo simulations for the range dependent noise case. The results are given in Figure 2. We consider root mean square error as a measure of target localization performance. For this experiment Maximum Mutual Information and Mahalanobis distance based methods are very close in performance. The advantage of dynamic sensor selection over random sensor selection is again evident from the simulation results.

4   Conclusions

Motivated by the work of Zhao *et al.* [1] we have presented an extension to the problem of distributed tracking in sensor networks. Specifically, we considered

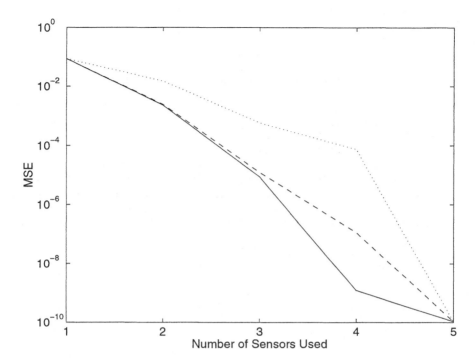

Fig. 2. Performance of the Sensor Selection Methods for range dependent noise variance. (Solid: Mutual Information, Dashed: Mahalanobis Distance Based Method, Dotted:Random)

the expected posterior uncertainty, quantified by conditional entropy as the utility function for choosing the next measurement node in a distributed Bayesian sequential estimation framework. The demonstrated equivalence of expected conditional entropy (over measurements) to the mutual information between future state and the node measurements led to a computationally feasible method for employing the suggested utility function.

Additionally we presented three example problems for which the method could be used along with empirical results. The results indicate that maximum mutual information principle presents a computationally attractive method for dynamic sensor selection problems.

Some interesting questions arise in the context of sensor networks which motivate future research. For example, how does additional attribution of object state (e.g., class) complicate the analysis? How might one incorporate these ideas into heterogeneous networks where measurement models are less well understood? It is unlikely that such modifications will lead to such tractable measurement models; however, it is also the case that estimation of statistical dependence (i.e., mutual information) remains tractable in lower dimensional spaces.

References

1. F. Zhao, J. Shin, and J. Reich, "Information-driven dynamic sensor collaboration," *IEEE Signal Processing Magazine*, vol. 19, no. 1, pp. 61–72, 2002.
2. S. Kumar, D. Shepherd, and F. Zhao, "Collaborative signal and information processing in micro-sensor networks," *IEEE Signal Processing Magazine*, vol. 19, no. 1, 2002.
3. M.Chu, H. Haussecker, and F. Zhao, "Scalable information-driven sensor querying and routing for ad hoc heteregeneneous sensor networks," *Int. J. High-Performance Compu. Applicat.*, 2002. to appear.
4. Y. C. Ho and R. C. K. Lee, "A bayesian approach to problems in stochastic estimation and control," *IEEE Trans. Automat. Contr.*, vol. 9, pp. 333–339, 1964.
5. C. Knapp and G. C. Carter, "The generalized correlation method for estimation of time delay," *IEEE Trans. on ASSP*, vol. 4, pp. 320–326, 1976.
6. D. Krishnamurty, "Self calibration techniques for acoustic sensor arrays," Master's thesis, The Ohio State University, 2002.
7. R. L. Moses, D. Krishnamurthy, and R. M. Patterson, "An auto-calibration method for unattended ground sensors," in *icassp*, vol. 3, (Orlando, FL), 2002.

A Formalism for the Analysis and Design of Time and Path Diversity Schemes in Wireless Sensor Networks

Martin Haenggi

University of Notre Dame, Notre Dame IN 46556, USA
mhaenggi@nd.edu

Abstract. For Rayleigh fading channels, there exists an interesting similarity between resistive circuits and time and path diversity mechanisms in multihop wireless sensor networks. A resistor-like circuit element, the *erristor*, representing the normalized noise-to-signal ratio, is introduced. Given an end-to-end packet delivery probability (as a QoS requirement), the nonlinear mapping from link reception probabilities to erristor values greatly simplifies the problems of power allocation and the selection of time and path diversity schemes. Thanks to its simplicity, the formalism that is developed also provides valuable insight into the benefits of diversity mechanisms, which is illustrated by a number of examples.

1 Introduction

The lifetime of wireless sensor network is crucial, since autonomous operation must be guaranteed over an extended period [1, 2]. Energy and interference considerations often necessitate *multihop routing*, where sensor nodes also act as routers, forwarding other nodes' packets [3]. Routing schemes that were developed for wired networks will perform suboptimally since they are based on virtually error-free point-to-point links, thereby ignoring two fundamental properties of the wireless link: 1) the fragility of the channel due to fading and interference [4, 5] and 2) the inherent broadcast property of wireless transmissions[1]. Whereas the first property is adverse, the second one can be exploited by transmission schemes that are based on the principle of *cooperative diversity* [6], where nodes coordinate both direct and relayed transmissions. Cooperative diversity is a form of spatial diversity, which, in the case of static single-antenna nodes, reduces to path diversity. The other promising strategy (in the case of narrowband channels) against fading is time diversity, which, for slow fading channels and relatively short packets, is mainly exploited in the form of retransmissions.

In this paper, we present a simple but powerful formalism that allows an efficient analysis and design of time and path diversity strategies for Rayleigh fading channels. In the analysis, the transmit power levels are given and the end-to-end reliability p_{EE} is to be determined, whereas in the (more interesting) design

---

[1] We assume that omnidirectional antennas are employed.

F. Zhao and L. Guibas (Eds.): IPSN 2003, LNCS 2634, pp. 417–431, 2003.

problem, we assume that the application dictates a certain end-to-end reliability p_D, and the question is how to choose the transmit powers, the relays (paths), and the number of transmissions over each link in order to minimize energy consumption and/or maximize network lifetime under the constraint $p_{EE} \geqslant p_D$.

Example 1. Consider the simple example in Fig. 1. A packet is transmitted with reception probability p_{01} over the first hop and transmitted twice over the second hop, with probabilities $p_{12,1}$ and $p_{12,2}$, respectively. The end-to-end reliability of the connection is $p_{EE} = p_{01} \cdot \left(1 - (1 - p_{12,1})(1 - p_{12,2})\right)$. Let $p_D = 90\%$. What combination(s) of transmit powers satisfy $p_{EE} \geqslant p_D$, and which one is energy-optimal? $\square$

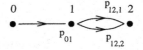

Fig. 1. A two-hop connection with two transmissions over the second hop.

2   The Link Model

We assume a narrowband multipath wireless channel, modeled as a slow Rayleigh fading channel [7] with an additive noise process z. The received signal at time k is $y_k = a_k x_k + z_k$, where a_k is the large-scale path loss multiplied by the fading coefficient. The variance of the noise process is denoted by σ_Z^2.

The transmission from node i to node j is successful if the signal-to-noise-and-interference ratio (SINR) γ is above a certain threshold Θ that is determined by the communication hardware and the modulation and coding scheme [5]. With the assumptions above, γ is a discrete random process with exponential distribution $p_\gamma(x) = 1/\bar{\gamma}\, e^{-x/\bar{\gamma}}$ with mean

$$\bar{\gamma} = \frac{\bar{P}}{\sigma_Z^2 + \sigma_I^2} \,. \tag{1}$$

$\bar{P}$ denotes the average received signal power over a distance $d = \|x_i - x_j\|_2$: $\bar{P} = P_0 d^{-\alpha}$, where P_0 is proportional to the transmit power[2], and the path loss exponent is $2 \leqslant \alpha \leqslant 5$. σ_I^2 is the interference power affecting the transmission. It is the sum of the received power of all the undesired transmitters.

The following theorem shows that for Rayleigh fading networks, it is possible to analyze noise and interference separately.

Theorem 1. *In a Rayleigh fading network, the reception probability $\mathbb{P}[\gamma \geqslant \Theta]$ can be factorized into the reception probability of a zero-noise network and the reception probability of a zero-interference network.*

---

[2] This equation does not hold for very small distances. So, a more accurate model would be $\bar{P} = P_0' \cdot (d/d_0)^{-\alpha}$, valid for $d \geqslant d_0$, with P_0' as the average value at the reference point d_0, which should be in the far field of the transmit antenna. At 916MHz, for example, the near field may extend up to 3-4ft (several wavelengths).

Proof: The probability that the SINR is bigger than a given threshold Θ follows from the cumulative distribution $f_\gamma(x) = 1 - e^{-x/\bar{\gamma}}$:

$$\mathbb{P}[\gamma \geqslant \Theta] = e^{-\Theta/\bar{\gamma}} = e^{-\frac{\Theta}{P}(\sigma_Z^2 + \sigma_I^2)}$$

$$= e^{-\frac{\Theta \sigma_Z^2}{P}} \cdot e^{-\frac{\Theta \sigma_I^2}{P}} = \mathbb{P}[\gamma_Z \geqslant \Theta] \cdot \mathbb{P}[\gamma_I \geqslant \Theta] , \tag{2}$$

where $\gamma_Z := P/\sigma_Z^2$ denotes the signal-to-noise ratio (SNR) and $\gamma_I := P/\sigma_I^2$ denotes the signal-to-interference ratio (SIR). The first factor is the reception probability in a zero-interference network as it depends only on the noise, and the second factor is the reception probability in a zero-noise network, as it depends only on the interference. It follows from (2) that $\bar{\gamma} = (\bar{\gamma}_Z \bar{\gamma}_I)/(\bar{\gamma}_Z + \bar{\gamma}_I)$.   ∎

This allows an independent analysis of the effect caused by noise and the effect caused by interference. The focus of this paper is put on the noise, *i.e.*, on the first factor in (2). If the load is light (low interference probability), then SIR≫SNR, and the noise analysis alone provides accurate results. For high load, a separate interference analysis[3] has to be carried out, as in [9]. Most energy-constrained sensor networks aim at minimizing the communication, which justifies the focus on noise.

In a zero-interference network, the reception probability over a link of distance d at a transmit power P_0, is given by

$$p_r := \mathbb{P}[\gamma_Z \geqslant \Theta] = e^{-\frac{\Theta \sigma_Z^2}{P_0 \, d^{-\alpha}}} . \tag{3}$$

Solving for P_0, we get for the necessary transmit power to achieve p_r:

$$P_0 = \frac{d^\alpha \Theta \sigma_Z^2}{-\ln p_r} . \tag{4}$$

3   The Erristor Representation

3.1   Connections without Retransmission

Assume a n-hop connection from node 0 to node n in a wireless sensor network. The desired end-to-end reliability is p_D. The reception probability over a chain of n nodes is

$$p_{EE} = e^{-\Theta \sum_{i=1}^{n} \frac{1}{\bar{\gamma}_i}} \tag{5}$$

where $\bar{\gamma}_i$ denotes the mean SNR at receiver i. Let R denote the normalized average noise-to-signal ratio (NSR) at the receiver, i.e., $R := \Theta/\bar{\gamma}$. We get

$$-\ln p_{EE} = \sum_{i=1}^{n} R_i = R_{\text{tot}} . \tag{6}$$

---

[3] Note that *power scaling, i.e.,* scaling the transmit powers of all the nodes by the same factor, does not change the SIR, but (slightly) increases the SINR. This has been pointed out also in [8]

Hence the condition $p_{\text{EE}} \geqslant p_{\text{D}}$ translates into the condition that the sum or the *series connection*[4] of the NSR values R_i is at most $R_{\text{D}} := -\ln p_{\text{D}}$. So, the individual R_i's can be replaced by an equivalent R_{tot}. For a single link, we have

$$R = -\ln p_r \quad \Longleftrightarrow \quad p_r = e^{-R}. \tag{7}$$

For probabilities close to 1 (or $R \ll 1$), the following first-order approximations are accurate:

$$\hat{R} := 1 - p_r \lesssim R \quad \Longleftrightarrow \quad \hat{p}_r := 1 - R \gtrsim p_r \tag{8}$$

This approximation shows that for small values, the NSR can be considered equivalent to the packet error probability. To emphasize this fact and the resistor-like series connection property of the NSR, we denote R as an "erristor" and its value as its "erristance".

Eq. (8) shows that, when determining the erristance from a given probability, the approximated value will be on the safe side, and from (6), we see that over a multihop connection, the noise accumulates and the error probabilities simply add up.

The relationship between the transmit power and R is

$$P_0 = d^\alpha \bar{\gamma} \sigma_Z^2 = \frac{d^\alpha \Theta \sigma_Z^2}{R}. \tag{9}$$

Henceforth, $P := d^\alpha / R$ denotes the normalized (by $\Theta \sigma_Z^2$) transmit power.

Example 2. Fig. 2 (left) shows an example with three links and their reception probabilities. From (6) we know that a series of hops translates into a series connection of erristors, hence we find the corresponding erristor network in Fig. 2 (right). For $p_{\text{D}} = 90\%$, for example, the value of $R_1 + R_2 + R_3$ must be at most $-\ln p_{\text{D}} \approx 0.105$. If all the power levels are equal, this can be achieved by setting $R_1 = R_2 = R_3 = 0.105/3 = 0.035$. A possible solution with unequal power is $R_1 = R_2 = 0.05$ and $R_3 = 0.005$. Here, the probability after two links is $e^{-0.05} e^{-0.05} \approx 90.5\%$, which is already close to 90%. Consequently, a lot of of energy is consumed at the third link to ensure packet reception with the required probability $e^{-0.005} = 99.5\%$.

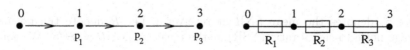

Fig. 2. A three-hop connection with link reception probabilities p_1, p_2, and p_3 (left) and the erristor circuit (right). The erristor values are the normalized noise-to-signal ratios R_1, R_2, and R_3. $R_i = -\ln p_i$.

---

[4] In terms of the SNR values, this corresponds to a parallel connection, which was pointed out in [10].

If the internode distances d_i (between node $i-1$ and node i) are given, a solution can be determined that ensures that all the *transmit* power levels have the same value P. From $(d_1^\alpha + d_2^\alpha + d_3^\alpha)/P \leqslant -\ln p_D$, we get

$$P \geqslant \frac{d_1^\alpha + d_2^\alpha + d_3^\alpha}{-\ln p_D}. \qquad (10)$$

For $d_i = i$, $\alpha = 2$, and $p_D = 90\%$, for example, we get $P \approx 14 \cdot 9.5 \approx 133$ and $R_1 \approx 0.0075$, $R_2 \approx 0.03$, and $R_3 \approx 0.0677$. $\qquad\square$

3.2   Connections with Time Diversity (Retransmissions)

Coming back to example 1 (Fig. 1), the question is how to incorporate retransmissions into the erristor formalism. Considering the second link, we found that $p_{12} = 1 - (1 - p_{12,1})(1 - p_{12,2})$, which is equivalent to

$$p_{12} = 1 - \left(1 - e^{-R_{12,1}}\right)\left(1 - e^{-R_{12,2}}\right). \qquad (11)$$

In general, for n transmissions over one link at NSR levels R_i, we have

$$p_n = 1 - \prod_{i=1}^{n}(1 - e^{-R_i}). \qquad (12)$$

To derive a general rule for the simplification of these expressions, we apply the following theorem.

Theorem 2.
For $(x_1, x_2, \dots, x_n) \in (\mathbb{R}_0^+)^n$,

$$1 - \prod_{i=1}^{n}(1 - e^{-x_i}) \geqslant e^{-\prod_{i=1}^{n} x_i}. \qquad (13)$$

The identity holds if and only if $\prod_{i=1}^{n} x_i = 0$.

The proof is presented in the Appendix.

Example 1 (cont.). So, in example 1, $e^{-R_{12,1}R_{12,2}}$ is a lower bound for p_{12}, and for $R_1 \ll 1$ and $R_2 \ll 1$, the bound is tight. Thus we may replace the erristors R_{21} and R_{22} by an erristor $R_2 = R_{21}R_{22}$. In the erristor diagram, the two transmissions are illustrated by a parallel connection (see Fig. 3). So, erristors connected in series behave like regular resistors, whereas the values of erristors connected in parallel have to be multiplied. Due to the bound

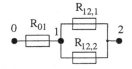

Fig. 3. The erristor circuit of Fig. 1.

derived above, the resultant end-to-end reliability will be slightly higher than the one required. $\qquad\square$

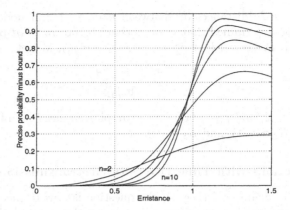

Fig. 4. The difference between the exact probability and the lower bound for $n = 2, 4, 6, 8, 10$ transmissions with equal erristance R.

For n transmissions with the same power level R, the difference between the precise probability value $1 - (1 - e^{-R})^n$ and the lower bound e^{-R^n} is plotted in Fig. 4. The erristance threshold where the bound is within 1% is $R = 0.236$ for $n = 2$ and $R = 0.375$ for $n = 4$. Thus for $R < 1/4$ ($p > 78\%$), the bound is sufficiently tight for all practical purposes.

For values $R \gtrsim 1$, the bound is loose, and the multiplication does not make sense, since the overall erristance increases, although, of course, even a retransmission with low power still leads to an improvement in the total link reception probability. However, for $R \gtrsim 1/2$, a single transmission outperforms splitting the power into two transmissions: For two transmissions at NSR $2R$, the reception probability is $p_r = 1 - (1 - e^{-2R})^2$, whereas for a single transmission at NSR R, we get $p'_r = e^{-R}$. The two probabilities are equal for

$$R = \ln 2 - \ln(\sqrt{5} - 1) \approx 0.48. \tag{14}$$

So, for $R \gtrsim 1/2$, the reception probability is higher for a single transmission at NSR R.

Note that a peak transmit power constraint $P < P_{\max}$ translates into the minimum resistor value that can be used. Over a link of distance d, the minimum erristor value is $R_{\min} = d^\alpha / P_{\max}$.

4   Path Diversity

4.1   Transmissions over Independent Paths

The analysis in the previous Section is valid if retransmissions have independent reception probabilities. This is not guaranteed if the channel's coherence time is substantially larger than a packet transmission time or if shadowing is the cause for packet loss, in which case a form of *path diversity* is required.

Example 3. Fig. 5 displays an example of a network where path independence is guaranteed even when the channels have a long coherence time. By conventional analysis, the end-to-end reception probability is

$$
p_{\text{EE}} = \left(1 - (1 - e^{-R_{01}}e^{-R_{12}})(1 - e^{-R_{02}})\right) \times
$$
$$
\left(1 - (1 - e^{-R_{23}}e^{-R_{34}})(1 - e^{-R_{24}})\right). \tag{15}
$$

How to choose the R_{ij}'s to guarantee $p_{\text{EE}} \geq p_{\text{D}} = 95\%$? This is a non-trivial question that can easily be answered using the erristor formalism. The equivalent erristor (see Fig. 5 (right)) is

$$
R_{\text{tot}} = (R_{01} + R_{12})R_{02} + (R_{23} + R_{34})R_{24}, \tag{16}
$$

and $p_{\text{EE}} = e^{-R_{\text{tot}}}$. For a desired $p_{\text{D}} = 95\%$, we have $R_{\text{tot}} \approx 0.05$. Thanks to the

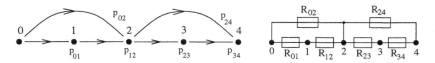

Fig. 5. A network that exploits path diversity (left) and its erristor circuit (right).

symmetry, $(R_{01}+R_{12})R_{02} = (R_{23}+R_{34})R_{24} = 0.025$ is a solution; hence we may set nearest-neighbor hops to $R_{i-1,i} = 0.05$ and $R_{02} = R_{24} = 0.25$. Note that the value for the two longer hops is 5 times bigger, which means that the necessary *transmit* powers are comparable if the nodes have equal distances and the path loss exponent is between 2 and 3. So, using the erristor formalism, the diversity scheme and power allocation should guarantee $p_{\text{EE}} = e^{-0.05} \approx 95.1\% > p_{\text{D}}$. The conventional analysis (15) yields $p_{\text{EE}} \approx 95.8\%$ which is, as expected, slightly bigger than the one from the erristor analysis. The formalism also permits a rapid reallocation of resources, if necessary. Assume node 3 runs out of energy. With $R_{34} \to \infty$, we see immediately that R_{23} becomes useless, and the only path in the lower half of the diagram will be the one with R_{24}. What value does R_{24} need to have to ensure p_{D}? Without changing the other erristances, we immediately find $R_{24} = 0.025$.   □

The total energy consumption (per packet) at each node can easily be determined:

$$
E_i = \sum_{j=1}^{m} \frac{d_{ij}^{\alpha}}{R_{ij}}, \tag{17}
$$

where m is the number of outgoing paths from node i.

4.2 Implicit Transmissions

In the first example (Fig. 1), if node 2 listens to the transmission from node 0 to node 1, then this *implicit transmission* has to be modeled by an additional erristor for an accurate analysis. This implicit erristor is free in terms of transmit power (but still requires power to receive the packet)[5].

Assume $p_D = 99\%$, so $R_{\text{tot}} \approx 0.01$. This is achieved by setting $R_{01} = 0.005$ and $R_{12,1} = R_{12,2} = 0.07$. However, since there is an implicit transmission from 0 to 2, there is a erristor in parallel with a value of $R_{02}^i = R_{01}(d_{02}/d_{01})^\alpha$ (the superscript i indicates an implicit transmission). Assuming $d_{02} = 2d_{01}$ and $\alpha = 3$, we get $R_{02}^i = 0.04$, $R_{\text{tot}} = 0.01 \cdot 0.04$ and $p_{EE} \approx 99.96\%$, which is much better than the target of 99%. So we can reduce R_{01} to a value that guarantees $(R_{01} + 0.005)R_{01} \cdot 88 = 0.01$. Solving the resulting quadratic equation yields $R_{01} \approx 1/30$, which corresponds to less than 1/6 of the original power.

For large path loss exponents and smaller transmit powers, the benefit to listeners that are farther away than the intended receiver becomes small, since the implicit erristances will be close to one or even above However, if the implicit receiver is closer than the intended one or if the transmit power is relatively high, it is worthwhile having the nodes awake and listening.

Example 3 (cont.). In example 3 (Fig. 5), there is an implicit transmission from node 2 to node 3 when node 2 is transmitting to node 4. If node 3 ignores this transmission, then the analysis in the previous Subsection was correct. If it takes advantage of that information, we have to add another erristor, as shown in Fig. 6.

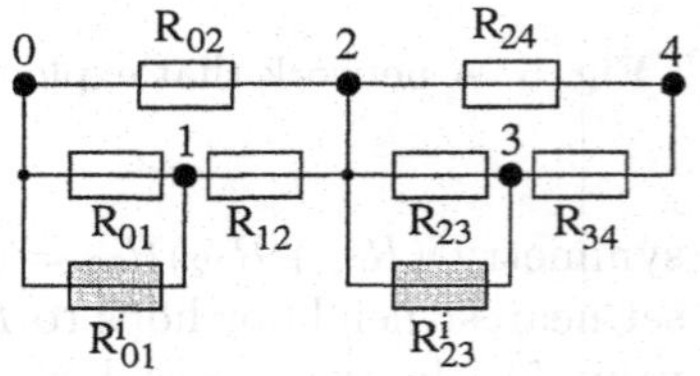

Fig. 6. The erristor circuit for Fig. 5 including implicit transmissions. Implicit erristors are gray-shaded.

Assuming equal distances between neighboring nodes, $R_{01}^i = 2^{-\alpha}R_{02}$ and $R_{23}^i = 2^{-\alpha}R_{24}$. For $\alpha = 2$ and using the same values as before, $R_{i,i-1} = 0.05$ and $R_{02} = R_{24} = 0.25$, we find $R_{01}^i = R_{23}^i = 0.0625$ and

$$R_{\text{tot}} = 2\Big(\frac{1}{20} \cdot \frac{1}{16} + \frac{1}{20}\Big) \cdot \frac{1}{4} \approx 0.027\,, \tag{18}$$

resulting in $p_{EE} \approx 97.3\%$, which is larger than the target of 95%. Considering that $1/16 \ll 1$, we may try to omit the explicit transmission completely, which results in $R_{\text{tot}} = (1/16 + 1/20)/2 \approx 0.056$ and $p_{EE} = 94.4\%$. A slight decrease of R_{02} and R_{24} by 10% each brings p_{EE} to 95.2%.

In general, we can say that whenever there are two erristors in series with one significantly smaller than the other one, the power is better distributed differently.   □

---

[5] This advantage of omnidirectional transmission is often denoted as the *wireless multicast advantage* [11, 5].

Example 4. A simple cooperative scheme. In Fig. 7, a situation is shown where node 0 wants to transmit to node 1, and the cooperative node C may help as a relay. From the erristor circuit it can be seen that there is no explicit transmission from 0 to C. The goal is to determine which transmission strategy minimizes the total transmit energy E_{tot} given a certain total erristance R_{tot}.

Let $D := \left(\frac{d}{2}\right)^\alpha$. With $R_{tot} = R_{01}(R_{0C}^i + R_{C1})$ and $R_{0C}^i = DR_{01}$, we get $R_{tot} = R_{01}(R_{01}D + R_{C1})$ and $E_{tot} = 2^\alpha R_{01} + d^\alpha R_{C1} = 2^\alpha(R_{01} + DR_{C1})$.

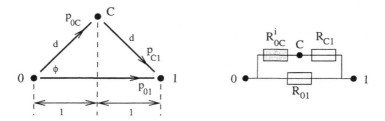

Fig. 7. A simple cooperative scheme (left) and the corresponding erristor circuit (right). Node C is relaying a packet from node 0 to assist node 0. The distancees $\overline{0C}$ and $\overline{C1}$ are $d = 1/\cos\phi$.

Strategy A: Equal received power. A possible strategy is to have C transmit at a power level that makes the received power at node 1 equal to that from the direct transmission 01, i.e., $R_{C1} = R_{01} =: R$. R_{tot} simplifies to $R_{tot} = R^2(1+D)$, and thus $R = \sqrt{\frac{R_{tot}}{1+D}}$. Inserting this expression into the transmit energy $E_{tot} = \frac{2^\alpha}{R}(1+D)$ yields

$$E_{tot}^A = \frac{2^\alpha(1+D)^{3/2}}{\sqrt{R_{tot}}}. \tag{19}$$

Strategy B: Equal transmit power. Here, we assume that both node 0 and C use the same transmit power. With $R := R_{01}$ and $R_{C1} = R_{0C}^i = RD$ we have $R_{tot} = 2DR^2$ and $R = \sqrt{\frac{R_{tot}}{2D}}$. The total energy consumption is simply $E_{tot} = 2 \cdot 2^\alpha/R$, or, as a function of R_{tot},

$$E_{tot}^B = 2^{\alpha+1}\sqrt{\frac{2D}{R_{tot}}}. \tag{20}$$

The energy consumption ratio of strategies A and B is

$$\rho := \frac{E_{tot}^B}{E_{tot}^A} = \frac{2\sqrt{2D}}{(1+D)^{3/2}}. \tag{21}$$

$\rho = 1$ for $D = 1$ and $D = \sqrt{5} - 2 \approx 0.236$. For $\sqrt{5} - 2 < D < 1$, strategy A is preferable ($\rho > 1$). The maximum ρ, however, is only $\frac{4}{9}\sqrt{6} \approx 1.089$, occurring at $D = \frac{1}{2}$. So, strategy A is at most 8.9% better.

To get a complete view, we also discuss the case of a direct one-hop transmission and an explicit two-hop scheme without a direct path from 0 to 1. For the one-hop case, we have $E_{\text{tot}}^{\text{one}} = 2^\alpha/R_{\text{tot}}$, and for the two hop case (assuming equal transmit powers), there are two erristors in series with value $R_{\text{tot}}/2$ and thus $E_{\text{tot}}^{\text{two}} = 4d^\alpha/R_{\text{tot}} = 4DE_{\text{tot}}^{\text{one}}$.

The one-hop strategy is better if $4D \geqslant 1$, or, in terms of the actual distance d, $d > 2^{1-2/\alpha}$. So, for $\alpha = 2$ and for $d \geqslant 2$, one-hop is always better, even for $\alpha \to \infty$, which is easily explained, since node C is then not closer than node 1. As a function of the angle $\phi = \arccos(1/d)$, the condition for one-hop to be better is expressed as $\phi \geqslant \arccos(2^{2/\alpha-1})$. For $\alpha \to \infty$, the critical angle is $\phi = \pi/3$ (corresponding to an equilateral triangle 0C1), as expected.

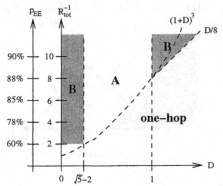

Fig. 8. Visualization of the regions in the (D, R_{tot}^{-1}) plane where the different strategies are optimum. Note that the curves $D/8$ and $(1+D)^3$ intersect at the points $(\sqrt{5}-2, (\sqrt{5}-1)^3)$ and $(1, 8)$. Values $R_{\text{tot}} > 1/2$ are not practical, since the corresponding probability is less than 60%.

The last step is the comparison of these simple schemes with the cooperative strategies A and B. First we note that B always outperforms the two-hop scheme, since it exploits "free" information that is transmitted over the direct path. The tournament between A and one-hop is won by A if $R_{\text{tot}} < (1+D)^{-3}$, and B wins against one-hop if $R_{\text{tot}} < \frac{8}{D}$. The resulting division of the (D, R_{tot}^{-1})-plane in the different strategies is shown in Fig. 8. The erristor formalism transforms complex logarithmic relationships into simple polynomial ones, which permits the analytical derivation of these boundaries.   □

Example 5. Virtual antenna arrays. Several nodes that are close may cooperate and act as a virtual antenna array, exploiting spatial diversity. The performance of such arrays was analyzed in [12] from an information-theoretic perspective. Here, we are using the erristor formalism to compare these schemes with conventional multihop routing. Fig. 9 shows the erristor diagram of a simple scenario with two nodes assisting each other at the source, in the middle, and at the destination. So, instead of individual nodes, we have clusters of two nodes at positions 0, 1, and 2. It is assumed that the intracluster distances are much smaller than the intercluster distances $d/2$. When the source node in cluster 0 is transmitting to cluster 1, his peer will receive that packet with probability (almost) one since $R_{00}^i \ll R_{01}$. In the next time slot, this peer node will transmit the same packet to cluster 0. Hence, the same packet is delivered over four different paths. Similarly, cluster 1 relays the packet to cluster 2 over four paths. In the case that the actual destination node itself in cluster 2 does not correctly receive the packet, an additional short intracluster transmission is required, whose energy is neglected in the following analysis.

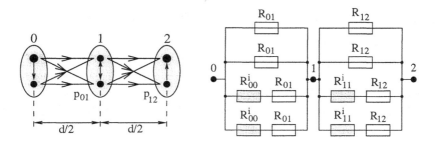

Fig. 9. A virtual antenna scheme and its erristor circuit.

We assume $R_{01} = R_{12} := R$. For the diversity scheme, with $R_{00}^i \ll R$, we get $R_{\text{tot}} = 2R^4$ and

$$E_{\text{tot}} = 4\frac{(d/2)^\alpha}{R} = 4\left(\frac{d}{2}\right)^\alpha \left(\frac{2}{R_{\text{tot}}}\right)^{\frac{1}{4}}. \tag{22}$$

For comparison, for a 4-hop connection with hops of length $d/4$, we have $R_{\text{tot}} = 4R'$ and

$$E'_{\text{tot}} = 4\left(\frac{d}{4}\right)^\alpha \frac{4}{R_{\text{tot}}} = 2^{4-\alpha}\left(\frac{d}{2}\right)^\alpha R_{\text{tot}}^{-1}. \tag{23}$$

The ratio between the two energies is

$$\frac{E_{\text{tot}}}{E'_{\text{tot}}} = R_{\text{tot}}^3 2^{4\alpha-7}. \tag{24}$$

Hence the diversity scheme is more efficient for

$$R_{\text{tot}} < 2^{\frac{4\alpha-7}{3}} \qquad \text{or} \qquad p_{\text{D}} > \exp\left(-2^{\frac{4\alpha-7}{3}}\right). \tag{25}$$

This curve is plotted in Fig. 10 (left). Substantial energy gains are possible for high p_{D} (see Fig. 10 (right)). When the path loss exponent increases by one, the energy gain decreases by a factor of $2^{4/3} \approx 4\text{dB}$.

This diversity scheme can be generalized to clusters of size m that transmit over n hops. In this case, $R_{\text{tot}} = nR^{m^2}$ and

$$E_{\text{tot}} = mn\left(\frac{d}{n}\right)^\alpha \left(\frac{n}{R_{\text{tot}}}\right)^{\frac{1}{m^2}}. \tag{26}$$

For the multihop scheme with mn hops[6], $R_{\text{tot}} = mnR'$ and

$$E'_{\text{tot}} = mn\left(\frac{d}{mn}\right)^\alpha \frac{mn}{R_{\text{tot}}}. \tag{27}$$

---

[6] This comparison is fair both in terms of the number of nodes involved and in the delay, since the total number of transmissions is mn for both schemes.

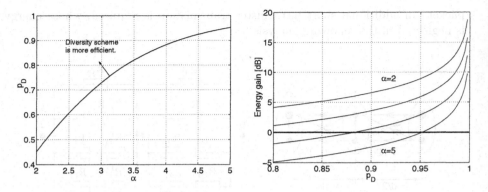

Fig. 10. Left: The region in the (α, p_D) plane where the diversity scheme outperforms conventional multihop routing. Right: The energy gain as a function of the end-to-end probability.

The ratio is

$$\frac{E_{\text{tot}}}{E'_{\text{tot}}} = R_{\text{tot}}^{1-\frac{1}{m^2}} \, n^{\frac{1}{m^2}-1} \, m^{\alpha-1} \, , \tag{28}$$

from which we see that the energy gain is maximized for $m = 2$ (except for $\alpha = 2$, where $m = 3$ performs slightly better) and increases almost linearly in n. We conclude that for high p_D and smaller α, the diversity scheme clearly outperforms conventional multihop routing. $\square$

5   Concluding Remarks

The erristor formalism permits the mapping of unhandy probability expressions into a simple circuit-like framework, which greatly simplifies the analysis and design of transmit schemes that are based on time diversity, path diversity, or a combination thereof. The erristor circuit is topologically equivalent to the network graph and can therefore be drawn in a straightforward manner. Resource allocation and reallocation problems can effortlessly be solved by simple arithmetic, which makes a real-time implementation readily feasible. Further, the formalism may prove useful for educational purposes, since the multiplication property of parallel erristors impressively demonstrates the benefits of diversity schemes, and the series connection shows how the noise and, in turn, the error probability accumulates over multiple hops.

While this work is mainly focused on noise-limited networks, it seems possible to include the interference in the same framework, since SNR and SIR exhibit a parallel combination property similar to the SNR values of subsequent links (see Theorem 1). This will be part of future investigations.

Acknowledgments. The author would like to thank Pascal Vontobel and Joachim Rosenthal for helpful discussions on the proof in the appendix. The partial support of the DARPA/IXO-NEST Program (AF-F30602-01-2-0526), NSF (ECS02-25265), and ORAU is gratefully acknowledged.

References

1. G. J. Pottie and W. J. Kaiser, "Wireless integrated network sensors," *Communications of the ACM*, vol. 43, no. 5, pp. 551–558, 2000.

2. I. F. Akyildiz, W. Su, Y. Sankarasubramaniam, and E. Cayirci, "Wireless sensor networks: a survey," *Computer Networks*, vol. 38, pp. 393–422, Mar. 2002.

3. V. Rodoplu and T. H. Meng, "Minimum Energy Mobile Wireless Networks," *IEEE Journal on Selected Areas in Communications*, vol. 17, no. 8, pp. 1333–1344, 1999.

4. A. J. Goldsmith and S. B. Wicker, "Design Challenges for Energy-Constrained Ad Hoc Wireless Networks," *IEEE Wireless Communications*, vol. 9, pp. 8–27, Aug. 2002.

5. A. Ephremides, "Energy Concerns in Wireless Networks," *IEEE Wireless Communications*, vol. 9, pp. 48–59, Aug. 2002.

6. J. Laneman, D. Tse, and G. Wornell, "Cooperative Diversity in Wireless Networks: Efficient Protocols and Outage Behavior," *IEEE Transactions on Information Theory*. Submitted for publication. Available at:
   http://www.nd.edu/~jnl/pubs/it2002.pdf.

7. T. S. Rappaport, *Wireless Communications – Principles and Practice*. Prentice Hall, 1996. ISBN 0-13-375536-3.

8. T. J. Shepard, "A Channel Access Scheme for Large Dense Packet Radio Networks," in *ACM SIGCOMM*, (Stanford, CA), Aug. 1996. Available at:
   http://www.acm.org/sigcomm/sigcomm96/papers/shepard.ps.

9. M. Haenggi, "Probabilistic Analysis of a Simple MAC Scheme for Ad Hoc Wireless Networks," in *IEEE CAS Workshop on Wireless Communications and Networking*, (Pasadena, CA), Sept. 2002.

10. J. Laneman and G. Wornell, "Energy-Efficient Antenna Sharing and Relaying for Wireless Networks," in *IEEE Wireless Comm. and Netw. Conf. (WCNC)*, (Chicago, IL), pp. 7–12, 2000.

11. J. E. Wieselthier, G. D. Nguyen, and A. Ephremides, "On the Construction of Energy-Efficient Broadcast and Multicast Trees in Wireless Networks," in *IEEE INFOCOM*, (Tel Aviv, Israel), pp. 585–594, Mar. 2000.

12. P. Gupta and P. R. Kumar, "Towards an Information Theory of Large Networks: An Achievable Rate Region," in *IEEE International Symposium on Information Theory*, (Washington DC), p. 159, 2001.

Appendix: Proof of Theorem 2

From the inequality (see (13))

$$1 - \prod_{i=1}^{n}(1 - e^{-x_i}) \geqslant e^{-\prod_{i=1}^{n} x_i} \tag{29}$$

it is easy to see that both expressions are equal (to 1) if one of the x_i is zero. It remains to show that $f(\cdot) : \mathbb{R}^n \to \mathbb{R}$

$$f_n(x_1, x_2, \ldots, x_n) = 1 - \prod_{i=1}^n (1 - e^{-x_i}) - e^{-\prod_{i=1}^n x_i} . \tag{30}$$

is positive if all x_i are positive. We note that f goes to zero if $\forall i, x_i \to \infty$. Hence f is positive for positive x_i if its partial derivatives $\partial f / \partial x_i$ are positive at 0 and have at most one zero for positive x_i. Since the function is symmetric in all x_i, it is sufficient to consider only one partial derivative. An inductive technique is employed, discussing the case $n = 2$ first.

Consider

$$g_2(x) := f_2(x, y) = e^{-x} + e^{-y} - e^{-x-y} - e^{-xy} \tag{31}$$

for a fixed $y \geqslant 0$. For $y = 0$, $g_2(x) \equiv 0$, and for $y > 0$, we note that $g(0) = 0$ and $\lim_{x \to \infty} g(x) = e^{-y} > 0$. Since

$$g'(x) = \frac{dg}{dx} = e^{-x}\left(-1 + e^{-y} + ye^{x(1-y)}\right), \tag{32}$$

there exists a single local extremum $\bar{x}$ for $y > 0$ at

$$\bar{x} = \frac{1}{y-1} \ln\left(\frac{y}{1-e^{-y}}\right). \tag{33}$$

As $y > (1 - e^{-y})$ for $y > 0$, we find $\bar{x} > 0$ for $y > 1$ and $\bar{x} < 0$ for $0 < y < 1$. For $y = 1$, no solution exists, and for $y = 0$, $g'(x) \equiv 0$. Since $g'(0) = -1 + e^{-y} + y > 0$, it is clear that the extremum is a maximum. So, we have $g(0) = 0$, and for $0 < y \leqslant 1$, $g(x)$ is monotonically increasing, whereas for $y > 1$, it is monotonically increasing up to $\bar{x}$ and then monotonically decreasing to $e^{-y} > 0$. Hence $g(x) > 0$ for $x > 0$, and we have proven the theorem for $n = 2$.

Now, assuming it is true for $n - 1$, we show that it holds for n.

For the general function $g_n(x) := f(x, x_2, \ldots, x_n)$ with fixed $x_i \geqslant 0$ for $i > 1$, we note that $g_n(0) = 0$ and

$$\lim_{x \to \infty} = 1 - \prod_{i=2}^n (1 - e^{-x_i}) \geqslant 0. \tag{34}$$

With $Q := \prod_{i=2}^n x_i$, we get

$$g_n'(x) = e^{-x}\left(-\prod_{i=2}^n (1 - e^{-x_i}) + Q e^{x(1-Q)}\right). \tag{35}$$

Evaluation at $x = 0$ yields

$$g'(0) = Q - \prod_{i=2}^{n}(1 - e^{-x_i})$$

$$\geqslant 1 - e^{-Q} - \prod_{i=2}^{n}(1 - e^{-x_i})$$

$$= f_{n-1}(x_2, x_3, \ldots, x_n)$$

$$\geqslant 0 \qquad\qquad (36)$$

where we have made use of the induction. Again, equality holds for $Q = 0$ only. Solving $g'_n(\bar{x}) = 0$ yields the single extremum

$$\bar{x} = \frac{1}{Q - 1}\ln\left(\frac{Q}{\prod_{i=2}^{n}(1 - e^{-x_i})}\right). \qquad\qquad (37)$$

We already established in (36) that the numerator is greater than (or equal to) the denominator in logarithm, so, analogously to (33), we find that $\bar{x} < 0$ for $0 < Q < 1$ and $\bar{x} > 0$ for $Q > 1$. Again, no solution for $Q = 1$ and $g'(x) \equiv 0$ for $Q = 0$. This completes the proof. ∎

Sensor Placement for Isotropic Source Localization

Tamir Hegazy and George Vachtsevanos

Department of Electrical and Computer Engineering
Georgia Institute of Technology
{thegazy, george.vachtsevanos}@ece.gatech.edu

Abstract. This paper proposes a sensor placement method for three-dimensional point source localization using multiple sensors. An observation model of multiple sensors and one source of unknown position is introduced. Given that model, the minimum number of sensors needed to localize the source is determined, and an optimal sensor placement is derived. The placement is optimal in the sense that it minimizes the effect of the measurement error on the localization error bound. The proposed placement is also shown to simplify the computational complexity. The theoretical results are experimentally evaluated through simulation. The simulation results reveal that the proposed placement significantly reduces the relative localization error.

1 Introduction and Related Work

Although source localization is a very active area of research, the literature seems to be rather scarce on sensor placement in the context of point source localization using multiple point sensors. Hence, in this paper we introduce a sensor placement technique for a three-dimensional source localization problem.

Source localization using distributed sensor networks has been an active area of research for many years [1], [2]. The application domain of source localization includes intrusion detection in a surveillance system, contamination source detection in space shuttles, fault detection, and object identification and tracking in military combats. Special attention has been paid to wide-band and acoustic sources, using maximum-likelihood estimators. For example, the authors of [3] derive the maximum-likelihood location estimator based on the Cramér–Rao bound for wideband sources in the near field of the sensor array.

On the other hand, although a lot of work has been done for sensor placement problems, it seems that relatively less work has been done on sensor placement for point source localization using multiple sensors (in comparison with the amount of work done for source localization problem itself). The most relevant published works are presented in [4] and [5]. The author of [4] studied the problem of placing sensors for minimizing the variance of passive position estimates. A simple method was developed for optimally placing the sensors subject to constraints on their positions. The problem of placing sensors constrained to a line segment (originally studied in [6]) was used as an example. In [5], the authors studied three different methods for identifying the location of an impulsive source via point sensor measurements for systems described by partial differential equations (PDE). The authors analyze the minimum

F. Zhao and L. Guibas (Eds.): IPSN 2003, LNCS 2634, pp. 432–441, 2003.
© Springer-Verlag Berlin Heidelberg 2003

number of sensors and "appropriate" sensor locations for each method based on the PDE model.

In this paper, we propose a sensor placement method for the source localization problem driven by the goal of minimizing the localization error bound in a linear-algebraic framework. Further, the minimum number of sensors needed to localize the source is determined. To evaluate the proposed method, a set of simulation experiments is conducted. The experimental results show that the proposed placement greatly reduces the localization error.

The paper is organized as follows: Section 2 introduces the observation model and states the problem addressed in this paper. A solution model and a derivation of the proposed sensor placement are given in Section 3. The proposed placement is evaluated in Section 4. Finally, Section 5 concludes the paper.

2 Observation Model and Problem Statement

The observation model and the problem statement are introduced in Section 2.1 and Section 2.2 respectively.

2.1 Observation Model

The observation model includes one isotropic radiation point source whose intensity is known but its position vector $\mathbf{p}_s$ is unknown. Since the source is isotropic, the energy flows equally in all directions out of the source. Hence, the intensity of the source observed at a distance d from the source is inversely proportional to d^2. This is known as the *inverse square law* [7]. This model applies to a wide variety of sources including light, magnetic, and electric charge sources.

The model includes a set of N sensors $\{s_i | 0 \leq i \leq N-1\}$, where the position $\mathbf{p}_i$ of each sensor s_i is known. Based on the discussion given above, the signal $\hat{u}_i$ picked from the sensor s_i is given by

$$\hat{u}_i = u_i + e_i = \frac{k}{\|\mathbf{p}_i - \mathbf{p}_s\|^2} + e_i \tag{1}$$

where e_i is the measurement error, due to calibration error, noise, etc. The source signal is assumed to propagate at a large enough speed so that we can ignore propagation delays.

2.2 Problem Statement

The end goal of a general source localization problem is to find the position of the source, given the measurements of the sensors. The main objectives to be addressed in this paper are (1) to derive a sensor placement configuration that will minimize the effect of the error component e_i of the sensor measurement on the localization error, and (2) to minimize the number of the sensors required to localize the source.

3 Error-Bound Driven Sensor Placement

This section presents the proposed approach. Section 3.1 derives the solution model for the problem and, as a byproduct, answers the question of "what is the minimum number of sensors needed to find the source location?" Section 3.2 proposes a sensor placement configuration for minimizing the effect of the measurement error on the relative error of the source localization.

3.1 Solution Model

In the case of error-free measurement, Equation (1) can be rewritten as

$$\left\|\mathbf{p}_i - \mathbf{p}_s\right\|^2 = \frac{k}{u_i}; \quad e_i = 0 \tag{2}$$

This means that if the sensor signal is error-free, we can determine that the source is on a spherical locus (or a circle in the case of two-dimensional localization) whose center is the sensor location $\mathbf{p}_i$ and whose radius is k/u_i . Equation (3) can be expanded as follows

$$\left\|\mathbf{p}_i\right\|^2 + \left\|\mathbf{p}_s\right\|^2 - 2\mathbf{p}_i \cdot \mathbf{p}_s = \frac{k}{u_i} \tag{3}$$

where "." indicates scalar product. A similar equation can be obtained for each sensor. As a result, to find the location of the source, we need to solve multiple sphere equations. To make the equations linear, consider the sphere equation obtained for the sensor s_m

$$\left\|\mathbf{p}_m\right\|^2 + \left\|\mathbf{p}_s\right\|^2 - 2\mathbf{p}_m \cdot \mathbf{p}_s = \frac{k}{u_m} \tag{4}$$

Subtracting (5) from (4) and rearranging, we obtain the following linear equation, which represents the common chord of the two spheres described by (4) and (5)

$$-2(\mathbf{p}_i - \mathbf{p}_m) \cdot \mathbf{p}_s = k\left(\frac{1}{u_i} - \frac{1}{u_m}\right) - \left(\left\|\mathbf{p}_i\right\|^2 - \left\|\mathbf{p}_m\right\|^2\right) \tag{5}$$

To localize a source in three dimensions, we need at least three linear equations of the form (6). To obtain three linearly-independent equations of the form (6), we need a set of four sensors $\{s_i | 0 \le i \le 3\}$.

Without loss of generality, s_0 is placed at the origin of the system of coordinates. The three linearly-independent equations can then be obtained by repeating Equation (6) three times. m will be fixed to zero, while i will vary from 1 to 3. Thus, the system of linear equations can be written as $\mathbf{Ap}_s = \mathbf{b}$ where

$$\mathbf{A} = -2 \begin{bmatrix} \mathbf{p}_1^T \\ \mathbf{p}_2^T \\ \mathbf{p}_3^T \end{bmatrix} = -2 \begin{bmatrix} x_1 & y_1 & z_1 \\ x_2 & y_2 & z_2 \\ x_3 & y_3 & z_3 \end{bmatrix}$$

$$, \mathbf{b} = \begin{bmatrix} k\left(\dfrac{1}{u_1} - \dfrac{1}{u_0}\right) - \|\mathbf{p}_1\|^2 \\ k\left(\dfrac{1}{u_2} - \dfrac{1}{u_0}\right) - \|\mathbf{p}_2\|^2 \\ k\left(\dfrac{1}{u_3} - \dfrac{1}{u_0}\right) - \|\mathbf{p}_3\|^2 \end{bmatrix} \qquad (6)$$

The matrix $\mathbf{A}$ is a 3×3 coefficient matrix expressed in terms of the sensor positions. $\mathbf{b}$ is the vector of constants for the system of equations.

3.2 Sensor Placement

The system of linear equations derived in the last section can be solved as $\mathbf{p}_s = \mathbf{A}^{-1}\mathbf{b}$. Note that this is the error-free solution. Now, let us introduce the error into the computation.

The measurement error only affects the vector $\mathbf{b}$, while $\mathbf{A}$ remains unchanged because its elements depend only on the sensor positions, and hence it is always fixed for a given sensor placement. After introducing the error, the system of linear equations becomes

$$\mathbf{A}(\mathbf{p}_s + \Delta\mathbf{p}_s) = \mathbf{b} + \Delta\mathbf{b} \qquad (7)$$

where $\Delta\mathbf{p}_s$ is the localization error and $\Delta\mathbf{b}$ is the error that occurs in the constant vector due to the measurements error. We assume that the error e_i is bounded, otherwise arbitrary, i.e. $|e_i| \le \varepsilon$, where ε is a small positive real number. Furthermore, we assume that $|\varepsilon/u_i| \ll 1$. This can be achieved by imposing the following constraint which is derived by combining $|\varepsilon/u_i| \ll 1$ and Equation (1).

$$\frac{\varepsilon\left\|\mathbf{p}_i - \mathbf{p}_s\right\|^2}{k} << 1 \Rightarrow \left\|\mathbf{p}_i - \mathbf{p}_s\right\| << \sqrt{\frac{k}{\varepsilon}} \tag{8}$$

The physical implication of this constraint is that the less the measurement error bound, the further the source can be from the sensors without introducing a significant localization error. With this in mind, it can be shown (using the binomial expansion with negative powers) that the norm of the error vector $\Delta\mathbf{b}$ is bounded according to the following inequality.

$$\left\|\Delta\mathbf{b}\right\| \leq \varepsilon \left\|\begin{bmatrix} \dfrac{1}{u_1^2} + \dfrac{1}{u_0^2} \\ \dfrac{1}{u_1^2} + \dfrac{1}{u_0^2} \\ \dfrac{1}{u_1^2} + \dfrac{1}{u_0^2} \end{bmatrix}\right\| \tag{9}$$

Now, the localization error bound can be expressed as follows [8]

$$\frac{\left\|\Delta\mathbf{p}_s\right\|}{\left\|\mathbf{p}_s\right\|} \leq \kappa(\mathbf{A})\frac{\left\|\Delta\mathbf{b}\right\|}{\left\|\mathbf{b}\right\|} \tag{10}$$

where $\kappa(\mathbf{A})$ is the condition number of $\mathbf{A}$, which is the ratio between the largest singular value to the smallest singular value of $\mathbf{A}$ in the singular value decomposition (SVD) of $\mathbf{A}$, given by

$$\mathbf{A} = \mathbf{U}\,\mathbf{\Sigma}\,\mathbf{V}^T \tag{11}$$

where $\mathbf{U}$ and $\mathbf{V}$ are orthogonal matrices (note that $\mathbf{A}$ is a real matrix) and $\mathbf{\Sigma}$ is a diagonal matrix whose diagonal elements are the singular values of $\mathbf{A}$ [9].

From the definition of the condition number, it is clear that the "best-conditioned" matrix has a condition number of 1. This is achieved by having equal singular values, i.e. $\mathbf{\Sigma} = \alpha\,\mathbf{I}$, where $\mathbf{I}$ is the identity matrix, and α is a real number that is equal to all the singular values of $\mathbf{A}$. Thus, having $\mathbf{\Sigma} = \alpha\,\mathbf{I}$ corresponds to the optimal placement of the sensors in the sense of minimizing the condition number of $\mathbf{A}$.

If $\mathbf{U}$ and $\mathbf{V}$ are chosen to be any arbitrary orthogonal matrices, the resulting placement is a rotated version of the placement shown in Fig. 1. If we choose $\mathbf{U}$ and $\mathbf{V}$ so that each of them is equal to the identity matrix, as a special case, this will lead to the placement shown in Fig. 1. In this case, we have $\mathbf{A} = \alpha\,\mathbf{I}$. Not only does this placement minimize the localization error bound by minimizing the condition number of $\mathbf{A}$, but it also eliminates the need to invert the matrix $\mathbf{A}$, which in turn simplifies the computations and eliminates the effect of the round off error due to the inversion process. We call this placement "best-conditioned aligned pyramid" (BCAP). The placement is identified as a pyramid since the sensors are on the vertices of a 4-vertex symmetric pyramid whose base is the triangle $s_1\ s_2\ s_3$, and whose top is s_0. The pyramid is described as "aligned" to indicate that its edges are aligned with the coordinate axes.

The solution to the system of equations in this case is given as follows. As mentioned above no matrix inversion is required.

$$\hat{\mathbf{p}}_s = -\frac{1}{2}\begin{bmatrix} \dfrac{k}{\alpha}\left(\dfrac{1}{\hat{u}_1}-\dfrac{1}{\hat{u}_0}\right)-\alpha \\[2ex] \dfrac{k}{\alpha}\left(\dfrac{1}{\hat{u}_2}-\dfrac{1}{\hat{u}_0}\right)-\alpha \\[2ex] \dfrac{k}{\alpha}\left(\dfrac{1}{\hat{u}_3}-\dfrac{1}{\hat{u}_0}\right)-\alpha \end{bmatrix} \tag{12}$$

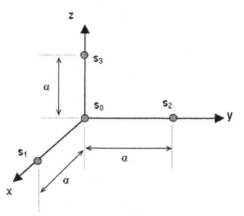

Fig. 1. Sensor placement that minimizes the coefficient matrix condition number

4 Experimental Evaluation

To verify the theoretical results obtained in the previous section, a set of simulation experiments are conducted where the source is moving slowly along a helical path as shown in Fig. 2. The experiments are performed for three different sensor placements. The first placement is the BCAP placement with $\alpha = 100$. The second placement corresponds to a matrix $\mathbf{A}$ that is "badly-conditioned", with a condition number of 10^6. The third placement results in a coefficient matrix with a condition number of 10^3. Note that the condition number only depends on the sensor positions and does not depend on the source position. Fig. 3 depicts the second placement used in the experiments.

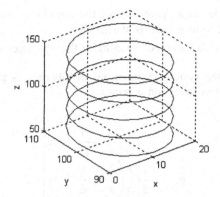

Fig. 2. The source moves along a helical path

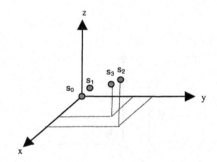

Fig. 3. Sensor configuration that leads to a badly-conditioned matrix: s_0 at $(0, 0, 0)^T$, s_1 at $(1.55, 1.87, 2.61)^T$, s_2 at $(36.31, 43.08, 57.92)^T$, and s_2 at $(26.47, 31.39, 42.11)^T$

To conduct the simulation, the path is sampled into a number sample points. At each sample point, the location of the source is estimated according to the solution model derived in the previous section. The simulation is conducted for different measurement relative error bounds $|\varepsilon/u_i|$. For each bound and for each placement the absolute value of the relative root mean square (RMS) error is computed along the path. Fig. 4 shows a plot of the results for the different placements on a log scale. Thus, each point on the x-axis corresponds to a complete experiment for the source moving along the path with a measurement relative error bound equal to the value on the x-axis at that point. The proposed BCAP placement consistently results in less RMS relative localization errors.

Fig. 5 shows an example of the estimated path using the BCAP placement versus the placement that corresponds to the condition number of 10^3 for the cases where the bound of the relative measurement error is 1% and 0.1%. The case of the "1e3 conditioned" placement with 1% error results in so huge localization error that the actual path and the estimated path cannot be shown on the same scale (hence, will not be

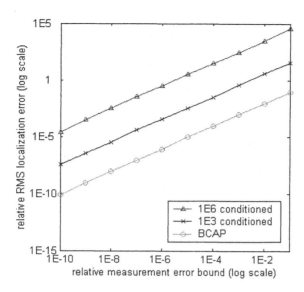

Fig. 4. A plot of the path RMS error vs. the relative measurement error

shown in the figure), whereas the corresponding BCAP case shows that the estimated path is still close to the actual path (Fig. 5a). In the case of 0.1% relative error bound, the estimated path using BCAP follows the actual path to a great precision (Fig. 5c), while the localization error of the "1e3 conditioned" is so high (Fig. 5b) that the estimated path is useless in the sense that it does not provide any good estimation of the actual path.

5   Conclusion

In this paper we present a three-dimensional observation model for a source localization problem. Based on the model, we impose two questions: (1) "What is the minimum number of sensors needed to find the location of the source?" and (2) "What is the optimal sensor placement that minimizes the localization error?" We formulate the problem in a linear-algebraic framework, which directly answers the first question. Then, we use the formulation to derive an error bound for the localization error, based on which, we derive a sensor placement configuration that minimizes the error bound of the localization error and eliminates the round-off error due to inversion. To verify the theoretical results, a set of simulations are conducted. The experimental results reveal that the proposed placement outperforms other placements in terms of the localization error.

Thus, the contribution of this paper is (1) formulating the source localization problem for the given model in a linear-algebraic framework for the goal of obtaining an optimal sensor placement, and (2) the proposed sensor placement (BCAP) that is optimal in the sense that it minimizes the effect of the measurement error on the localization error.

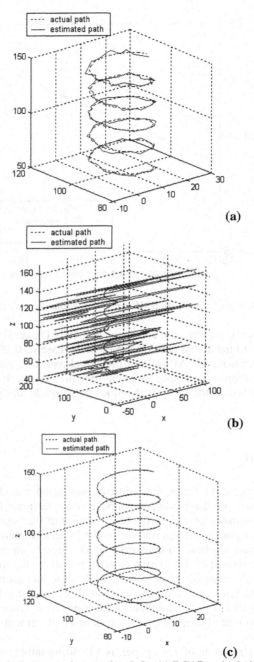

Fig. 5. The estimated path shown vs. the actual path for (a) BCAP and relative measurement error of 1%, (b) a badly-conditioned placement and relative measurement error of 0.1%, and (c) BCAP and relative measurement error of 0.1%

References

1. Chen, J., Yao, K., Hudson, R.: Source Localization and Beamforming. IEEE Signal Processing Magazine. Vol. 19. No. 2 (2002)30–39
2. Chen, J., Hudson, R., Yao, K.: A Maximum-Likelihood Parametric Approach to Source Localizations. Proceedings of IEEE International Acoustics, Speech, and Signal Processing. Vol. 5 (2001) 3013–3016
3. Chen, J., Hudson R., Yao, K.: Maximum-Likelihood Source Localization and Unknown Sensor Location Estimation for Wideband Signals in the Near-Field. IEEE Transactions on Signal Processing. Vol. 50. No. 8 (2002) 1843–1854
4. Abel, J.: Optimal Sensor Placement for Passive Source Localization. International Conference on Acoustics, Speech, and Signal Processing. Vol. 5 (1990) 2927–2930
5. Alpay, M., Shor, M.: Model-Based Solution Techniques for the Source Localization Problem. IEEE Transactions on Control Systems Technology. Vol. 8. No. 6 (2000) 895–904
6. Carter, G.: Variance Bounds for Passively Locating an Acoustic Source with a Symmetric Line Array. J. Acoust. Soc. Am. Vol. 62. No. 4 (1977) 922–926
7. Parker, S. (ed): McGraw-Hill Encyclopedia of Physics. 2nd edn. McGraw-Hill. New York (1993)
8. Heath, T.: Scientific Computing. 2nd edn. McGraw-Hill. New York (2002)
9. Shores, T.: Applied Linear Algebra and Matrix Analysis. 2nd edn. McGraw-Hill. New York (1999)

Mobicast: Just-in-Time Multicast for Sensor Networks under Spatiotemporal Constraints

Qingfeng Huang, Chenyang Lu, and Gruia-Catalin Roman

Department of Computer Science and Engineering
Washington University, Saint Louis, MO 63130.
{qingfeng,lu,roman}@cse.wustl.edu

Abstract. This paper is concerned with coordinated delivery of messages in sensor networks. The notion of multicast is re-examined in light of a new set of requirements that are specific to such networks. The result of this investigation is a new concept called *mobicast*. It entails the delivery of messages to large sets of nodes in a manner that satisfies a potentially dynamic set of spatiotemporal constraints. In order to demonstrate the feasibility of *mobicast*, we present a novel topology-aware protocol for sensor networks. Worst-case analysis shows that the protocol provides strong spatial and temporal delivery guarantees under a set of reasonable assumptions about the network. The design of the protocol relies on new notions of compactness for spatially distributed networks. By explicitly addressing the temporal domain associated with message delivery, *mobicast* is more general than geocast and makes it possible to save precious resources in sensor networks by exploiting its inherent just-in-time delivery semantics.

1 Introduction

Large-scale wireless sensor networks will be deployed in various physical environments to support a broad range of applications such as precision agriculture, smart highway, security, emergency response and disaster recovery systems [1]. These applications need to collect data from sensor networks, aggregate data from multiple sensors inside the network, and communicate aggregated information to end users over multi-hop ad hoc networks. Due to the need for high data fidelity and the severe energy constraint in sensor networks, in-network data aggregation has recently received significant attention [2,3,4]. While some forms of data aggregation can be performed on the end-to-end route from the source to the base station [2,4], explicit group coordination among sensors in the locality of a monitored physical entity (e.g., an intruder) are needed by many applications. In the latter case, a group management protocol maintains a sensor group in the vicinity of a physical entity, and a multicast or unicast protocol provides the communication mechanism for data aggregation inside the group.

Local coordination is often subject to spatiotemporal constraints due to mobility in the physical environment. Environmental mobility, i.e., the movement of monitored physical entities, is common to many sensor network applications

F. Zhao and L. Guibas (Eds.): IPSN 2003, LNCS 2634, pp. 442–457, 2003.
© Springer-Verlag Berlin Heidelberg 2003

(e.g., personnel tracking in emergency sites, mobile robots in factories, and habitat monitoring of wildlife). To illustrate the kind of spatiotemporal constraints likely to be encountered in such applications, let us consider the deployment of acoustic sensors in a security area designed to track intruders. When there are no intruders, most sensors sleep and only periodically wake up to check for interesting events. A small number of sensors remain active to provide continuous vigilance and to activate other sensors when necessary. To track an intruder, sensors in its vicinity form a group to share their data and determine the location of the intruder through triangulation. Only the sensors within the vicinity of an intruder should contribute data for the triangulation operation. It is unnecessary and even incorrect to aggregate the data from sensors that are far away from the intruder because their data may have no correlation with the intruder's actual location. Hence the group is subject to a spatial constraint that requires it to be composed of sensors within a zone surrounding the moving intruder (e.g., a circle centered at the estimated location of the intruder). Meanwhile, the group is also subject to a timing constraint that requires it to move at the same speed as the intruder with sensors dynamically joining and leaving the group. Thus, sensors in the group must actively multicast the location of the intruder to other sensors that are likely to meet the moving zone within a certain deadline. The set of sensors to be notified depends on the moving speed of the intruder and the time it takes for a sensor to wake up and get ready to join the group. In addition, in order to conserve energy and maintain spatial locality as related to data aggregation, nodes should receive the multicast message as late as possible. We call this property "just-in-time" delivery.

We propose a novel class of multicast mechanisms that exhibit "just-in-time" temporal delivery semantics for disseminating data spatially in sensor networks. The distinctive trait of this new form of multicast, called *mobicast*, is the delivery of all nodes that happen to be in a prescribed region of space at a particular point of time. Spatial constraints are combined with temporal constraints by offering the application the ability to request the routing of a message to all points inside a delivery zone while allowing the latter to be defined as a function of time, thus having a continuously changing configuration. The first major challenge derives from the fact that early delivery may not be desirable as it leads to unnecessary energy consumption as the sensors become ready too far in advance relative to the required delivery time. It is the energy minimization constraint that rules out trivial solutions such as full network flooding. The second challenge arises from the fact that any protocol likely to succeed must factor in network topology and geometry. The strong "just-in-time" spatial delivery guarantee can be provided only if the protocol takes into account the spatial distribution of the sensors across the network. Sophisticated analysis will be required to ensure that the demanded guarantees are actually met. The use of spatiotemporal constraints in the specification, the focus on energy minimization, and the reliance on novel geometric analysis are the defining features of this research.

While *mobicast* is conceptually powerful, its implementation on sensor networks is fraught with difficulties. Key among them is the ability to ensure just-in-time delivery guarantees over a wide range of network topologies. The paper introduces two topological compactness metrics for spatially distributed networks designed to facilitate the analysis of information propagation behaviors across networks, and presents a protocol that uses these topological values for the network to meet the strong just-in-time delivery requirement of *mobicast*.

The remainder of the paper is organized as follows. We specify *mobicast* formally in Section 2. A protocol to achieve reliable *mobicast* in sensor networks is described in Section 3. An analysis of the protocol follows in Section 4. Discussion, related work and conclusions appear in sections 5, 6 and 7, respectively.

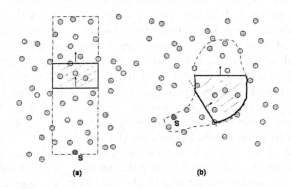

Fig. 1. Sample mobicast delivery zones

2   Problem Definition

The ultimate goal of *mobicast* is to achieve just-in-time information dissemination to all nodes in some prescribed spatial area in the network. We use a "delivery zone," denoted as $Z[t]$, to represent the area where information D should be delivered at time t. As the *mobicast* delivery zone $Z[t]$ evolves over time, the set of recipients for D changes as well. Accordingly, we characterize a *mobicast* by the information D to be delivered and its associated delivery zone $Z[t]$ whose coverage changes over a period of time T:

$$\langle D, Z[t], T \rangle \tag{1}$$

Fig. 1 shows two examples of *mobicast* with different kinds of delivery zones. Fig. 1(a) depicts a rectangle-shaped zone (shaded) that moves from the source located at the bottom of the figure to the top. As the delivery zone moves, some nodes enter the zone and some others leave the zone. *Mobicast* may require that a node be delivered the message D at the time it gets in the zone, or before the time it moves out of the zone. Note that the shape and motion of a delivery zone are defined/specified by *mobicast* users (for their spatiotemporal delivery requirement of information D). A *mobicast* protocol then needs to achieve this spatiotemporal delivery requirements efficiently in various network topologies. Fig. 1(b) shows a more general example where the delivery zone assumes an arbitrary shape, with both its shape and location evolving over time. This may be the case when the delivery requirements change in response to unexpected developments in the delivery zone.

The complexity of a *mobicast* protocol in general depends on the level of the delivery guarantee it wants to achieve. In this paper, we first consider the following strong delivery guarantee: once a node α is in a delivery zone $Z[t]$, it should receive the information D immediately. Let Ω be the set of all nodes in space, let $r(j)$ be the location of node j, and let $D[j,t]$ denote the fact that j has been delivered the information D at time t. Let the time when the *mobicast* is initiated be zero. This *mobicast* delivery property can be formally stated as

$$\langle \forall j, t : j \in \Omega \wedge 0 \leq t \leq T :: r(j) \in Z[t] \implies D[j,t] \rangle^1 \qquad (2)$$

This statement can be interpreted as "During the *mobicast* session, all nodes inside zone Z at time t should have information D."

Unfortunately, delivery property (2) is practically impossible to realize in most wireless ad hoc networks. The reasons include:

- First, communication latency is often not negligible in wireless ad hoc networks. This is especially true in wireless sensor networks where sensor nodes might have a sleeping schedule in order to save energy. Note that (2) implies instantaneous delivery to all nodes at the initial delivery zone $Z[0]$. If $Z[0]$ contains a node other than the sender node, it is impossible for the node to receive information D instantly at time 0 when considering the communication latency.
- Second, a wireless ad hoc network may be partitioned. A delivery zone, specified by some geometric property alone, might cover nodes in multiple network partitions, which in turn renders the delivery impossible.
- Third, we did not put any restrictions on the evolving behavior of the delivery zone. One can imagine cases where a user-specified delivery zone evolves too fast such that its speed of change over space is faster than the maximum delivery speed a network can support.

As such, we are forced to weaken the ideal *mobicast* delivery property in the following practically-minded manner: *mobicast* satisfies property (2) only after some initialization time t_{init} on a connected network. That is

$$\langle \forall j, t : j \in \Omega \wedge t_{init} < t \leq T :: r(j) \in Z[t] \implies D[j,t] \rangle \qquad (3)$$

Thus, each *mobicast* session has two phases. The first, from time 0 to t_{init}, is an initialization phase in which no delivery guarantee is specified. The second phase, from time t_{init} to T, is a stable phase in which the strong spatiotemporal guarantee is required.

2.1   Three Optimization Concerns

Note that, because communication latency is a random variable, it is impossible for one to schedule the delivery of a message to a node at an exact time. In order to achieve the delivery property (3), one has to consider the worst case scenario and schedule the delivery of *mobicast* message ahead of time. Let $t_r(j)$ denote the time a node j first receives the *mobicast* message, $t_{in}(j)$ be the first instant of time j enters the delivery zone. We call the time difference $t_{in}(j) - t_r(j)$ the "slack time" of message delivery. Note that specification (3) implies that t_{in} is the deadline of message delivery, and the slack time measures how early the message is delivered to a node comparing to its deadline to be there.

One optimization concern for any *mobicast* protocol is to reduce the overall time interval between the reception of a message and its required delivery to the application, i.e., the slack time. Minimizing the average slack time t_{slack} for all nodes that were ever in the delivery zone leads to less energy consumption and better locality in spatial data aggregation.

Another optimization dimension for *mobicast* is to reduce the total number of retransmissions needed for each *mobicast* session while delivering the spatial and temporal guarantees. This direction is similar to that of all broadcast and multicast protocols for ad hoc networks.

The third optimization concern is to make the initialization phase as short as possible. In general, the length of the initialization time depends on the size of the delivery zone, the network connectivity pattern within the region, and the protocol execution behavior. While a *mobicast* protocol has no control over the former two factors, it can try to make t_{init} as short as possible by optimizing its execution strategy.

Next we consider the domain of sensor networks and present a *mobicast* protocol that satisfies property (3) in an efficient way.

3   Description of a *Mobicast* Protocol

As a proof of concept, we present a *mobicast* protocol for the case when the delivery zone is a convex polygon P that moves through space at constant velocity v for a duration T. For simplicity, we use an example where the convex polygon is a rectangle and whose shape does not change over time. While conceptually simple, this mobicast protocol is useful for coordination scenarios where the mobile event does not change its velocity and spatial confinement very often, and is very challenging to implement. Our effort in deriving the protocol yields a few insights and new concepts useful for the study of spatiotemporal information dissemination strategies in sensor networks. We will also discuss the potential implications of entertaining more general cases in later sections. Before presenting the protocol, we first describe its key assumptions regarding the network.

3.1   Sensor Network Model

The sensor network model for our protocol is as follows. The network does not have any partition, and all nodes are location-aware, i.e., they know their location r in space with reasonable accuracy. The maximum clock-drift among the sensors in the system is small enough to be negligible. All nodes support wireless communication and are able to act as routers for other nodes. Local wireless broadcast is reliable, i.e., once a local broadcast is executed, it will be heard by all its neighbors within latency τ_1.

3.2   A *Mobicast* Protocol

In order to describe the *mobicast* protocol more concisely, we introduce some terminology. The reader is reminded that the delivery zone is an area where the delivery of messages to the application takes place and is specified by the application itself. Our protocol also uses a "forwarding zone" $F[t]$ that is moving at some distance ahead of the delivery zone, as shown in Fig. 2. We call the distance between the forwarding zone and its associated delivery zone the "headway distance" (of the forwarding zone). The shape of the forwarding zone is related to the shape of the delivery zone, and the topology of the underlying network. The choice of the headway distance and the size of the forwarding zone is such that it guarantees that all nodes entering the delivery zone will have received the *mobicast* message in advance, even if some of them are not directly connected (1-hop) to any nodes already in the delivery zone. In the meantime, the forwarding zone also serves to limit the retransmission to a bounded space while ensuring that all nodes that need to get the message will get it. We will discuss how the forwarding zone is determined in the next section. While nodes in a forwarding zone retransmit the *mobicast* message as soon as they receive it, the nodes in front of the forwarding zone enter a "hold-and-forward" state if they receive the *mobicast* message. They do not retransmit the message until becoming members of the forwarding zone. It is the action of the nodes in the hold-and-forward zone that ensures the "just-in-time" feature of the *mobicast* delivery policy while keeping the average slack time t_{slack} small. This behavior results in a virtual "hold-and-forward zone" in front of the forwarding zone, as also indicated in Fig. 2.

When a request $\langle D, Z[t], T \rangle$ is presented to the *mobicast* service at time t_0, it constructs and broadcasts a *mobicast* message to all the neighbors. A *mobicast* packet $\tilde{m}$ contains the following information: a unique message identifier, a delivery zone descriptor, a forwarding zone descriptor, the session start time t_0, the session lifetime T, and the message data D. The unique message identifier is created from the combination of the location of the source and the time t_0 of the request. The delivery zone descriptor encodes the original location, the shape of the zone, and its velocity. The forwarding zone descriptor encodes the shape and the original location of the forwarding zone, which is computed using some knowledge about the network and the shape of the delivery zone. We will discuss in detail the computation of the forwarding zone in later sections.

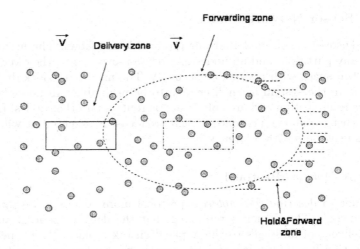

Fig. 2. Mobicast example

The *mobicast* protocol is described in Fig. 3. While not explicitly shown in the code, this *mobicast* protocol exhibits two phases in its spatial and temporal behavior. The first is an initialization phase, in which the nodes are trying to "catch-up" with the spatial and temporal demands of the *mobicast* . When a node in the path of the forwarding zone receives a message for the first time, it rebroadcasts the message as soon as possible. This phase continues until a stable forwarding zone that travels at a certain distance d_s ahead of the delivery zone is created.

The second phase is a cruising phase in which the forwarding zone moves at the same velocity as the delivery zone. The protocol enters this phase after the delivery zone and the forwarding zone reach the stable headway distance d_s. This cruising effect is achieved by having the nodes at the moving front of the forwarding zone retransmit the *mobicast* message in a controlled "hold-and-forward" fashion to make the forwarding zone move at the velocity v. The initialization and the cruising phases together establish *mobicast* property (3) with t_{init} being the time required by the initialization phase.

In the next section we turn our attention to: how the forwarding zone and its stable headway distance are computed; what is the value of t_{init} given a specific *mobicast* request and the spatial properties of the underlying network; and how the protocol delivers on its guarantees.

4   Analysis

A key element in the *mobicast* protocol (Fig. 3) is the forwarding zone. As we mentioned earlier, the purpose of the forwarding zone is to ensure that all the

Upon hearing a mobicast message $\tilde{m}$ at time t.

1.**if** $(\tilde{m}$) is new and $t < t_0 + T$
2.   **if** (I am in F[t]) **then**
3.   broadcast $\tilde{m}$ immediately ;   // fast forward
4.   **if** (I am in Z[t]) **then**
5.   deliver the message data D to the application layer;
6.   **else**
7.   compute the earliest time t_{in} for me to enter the delivery zone;
8.   **if** t_{in} exists and $t_{in} < t_0 + T$
9.   schedule delivery of data D to the application layer at t_{in};
10.   **end if**
11.   **end if**
12.   **else**
13.   compute the earliest time t' for me to enter the forwarding zone;
14.   **if** t' exists
15.   **if** $t_0 \le t' \le t$
16.   broadcast $\tilde{m}$ immediately ;   // catch-up!
17.   **else if** $t < t' < t_0 + T$
18.   schedule a broadcast of $\tilde{m}$ at t';   //hold and forward
19.   **end if**
20.   **end if**
21.   **end if**
22. **end if**

Fig. 3. A mobicast protocol

nodes in a delivery zone receive the *mobicast* message, and that they receive the message before entering the delivery zone. The latter is guaranteed by sustaining a headway distance d_s between the forwarding zone and the delivery zone. The shape of a forwarding zone depends on the following three factors: the shape of the delivery zone, the spatial distribution of the network nodes, and the topology of the network. Fig. 4 shows a rectangle *mobicast* example to illustrate why this is the case. The source node S initiates a mobicast. For node A to be able to deliver the message when it becomes a member of the delivery zone, it should have received the message by that time. In scenario Fig. 4(a), this means the message should have gone through G (in order for it to reach A). This implies that A and G should be in the forwarding zone together at some point in time before A can receive the message. On the other hand, if the network connectivity is "denser", as in Fig. 4(b), it is obvious that the width of the forwarding zone can be relatively smaller. Furthermore, in Fig. 4(a) the height of the forwarding zone has to be bigger than the height of the delivery zone to include D. Without being so, nodes A, B, C would be effectively partitioned from the rest of the nodes in the network, as node D would not participate in forwarding (retransmission) as it was not in the forwarding zone. This is just one special example with an ad

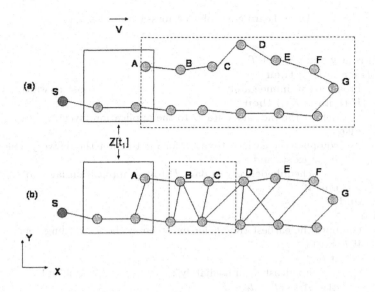

Fig. 4. Effect of network topology on the size of forwarding zone

hoc choice of forwarding zone. The question we would like to answer is, in an arbitrary sensor network, how do we determine the forwarding zone for a specific delivery zone?

In the rest of this section we first discuss how to compute the forwarding zone, then show what headway distance is needed for ensuring the delivery guarantee. Finally, we show that our protocol provides the desired spatiotemporal guarantees given a proper choice for the forwarding zone and the headway distance.

4.1   Computing the Forwarding Zone

In order to compute the size of the forwarding zone for a specific delivery zone on an arbitrary network, we first introduce a compactness measure for the network, called "Δ-compactness."

Δ-Compactness. Given a geometric graph/network $G(V, E)$, Δ-compactness seeks to quantify the relation between the Euclidean distance and the *network spatial distance* among network nodes. The network spatial distance $\tilde{d}(i, j)$ between two nodes i and j is defined in the following manner. Let $d(e)$ denote the Euclidean distance of a network edge e. If a network path l contains an edge e, we say e is in l. We define the "edge-length" of path l to be the sum of the physical distances along its edges:

$$L(l) = \sum_{e \text{ in } l} d(e) \tag{4}$$

Let $M(i, j)$ be the set of shortest network paths between nodes i and j. The network spatial distance $\tilde{d}(i, j)$ is

$$\tilde{d}(i, j) = \min_{l \in M(i,j)} L(l) \tag{5}$$

The Δ-compactness of a geometric graph $G(V, E)$ is defined as the smallest Euclidean distance to network spatial distance ratio among the nodes:

$$\delta = \min_{i,j \in V} \frac{d(i, j)}{\tilde{d}(i, j)} \tag{6}$$

Theorem 1. *Let i, j be any two nodes in a network with Δ-compactness value δ. Let $E(i, j, \delta)$ be an ellipse using i, j as two foci and with eccentricity δ. There is at least one shortest path between i and j inside the ellipse $E(i, j, \delta)$.*

Proof: (We can prove this theorem by contradiction. Proof omitted due to page limit. Reader can find a proof of this theorem and other theorems presented in this paper in [5].)

This theorem is very useful for limiting the flooding region while guaranteeing fastest point to point message delivery in a geometric network. In our case, this metric helps us to decide the size of the forwarding zone.

δ-Cover. We also introduce a notion called the "δ-cover" of a polygon to simplify the mathematical description of the forwarding zone. The δ-cover of a convex polygon P is defined as the locus of all points p in the plane such that there exists two points q and r in the polygon P that satisfy the constraints

$$d(p, q) + d(p, r) \leq \frac{1}{\delta} d(q, r) \tag{7}$$

where $d(x, y)$ is the distance between points x and y.

Theorem 2. *Let i, j be two nodes in a network with Δ-compactness value δ. If i, j are inside a convex polygon P, then the δ-cover of P contains at least one shortest path between i and j.*

Given this theorem, we now have a way to determine the size of the forwarding zone for any convex-shaped delivery zone.

The Forwarding Zone. Given a *mobicast* delivery zone of convex shape P, if the *mobicast* is executed on a network with Δ-compactness value δ, then we choose the shape of the forwarding zone to be the δ-cover of P. We call the area of P in the forwarding zone the "core" of the forwarding zone. One may easily see the following corollary.

Corollary 1. *Let i, j be two nodes in the core of a forwarding zone in a network of Δ-compactness δ. Then the forwarding zone contains at least one shortest path between i and j.*

Note that this corollary provides the following guarantee: inside the δ-cover of a delivery zone, there is a shortest network path between any two nodes in the delivery zone. This also means that if one node in the delivery zone has a message for all other nodes in the delivery zone, it can choose only to flood the δ-cover of a delivery zone, i.e., forwarding zone, to ensure that they all get the message, with an additional property: the message is delivered through shortest paths.

Note also that, so far we are only concerned with guaranteed spatial delivery. In order for all nodes in the delivery zone to receive the multicast message on time, we need to have the forwarding zone moving ahead of the delivery zone.

4.2   Computing the Stable Headway Distance

The headway distance of the forwarding zone is a way to tell the protocol how far ahead to prepare the message delivery in order not to miss the delivery deadline due to some unexpected "twists and turns" on the related network path. One may imagine that networks with more "curved" network paths require longer headway distances than those that are more "direct." In order to capture this notion more precisely, we introduce another compactness metric for the network, called "Γ-compactness."

Γ-compactness. Γ-compactness quantifies the relation between the network distance (in terms of *hops*) and the Euclidean distance among the nodes in a geometric network. Let $h(i, j)$ be the minimum number of network hops between nodes i and j, and $d(i, j)$ be the Euclidean distance between them. We define the Γ-compactness of a geometric graph $G(V, E)$ to be the minimum ratio of the Euclidean distance to the network hop distance between any two nodes, i.e.,

$$\gamma = \min_{i,j \in V} \frac{d(i,j)}{h(i,j)} \tag{8}$$

Intuitively, if a network's Γ-compactness value is γ, then any two nodes in the network separated by a distance d must have a shortest path between them no greater than d/γ hops.

Theorem 3. *Let N be a network with a Γ-compactness value γ, and let τ_1 be its maximum 1-hop communication latency. The lower bound of the maximum message delivery speed over the space of N is $\frac{\gamma}{\tau_1}$.*

This theorem tells us that given a geometric network with Γ-compactness value γ, the delivery zone cannot move at a higher velocity than $\frac{\gamma}{\tau_1}$ if one wants delivery guarantee in all cases.

The Headway Distance. The stable headway distance d_s must be large enough to ensure that when the delivery zone reaches the current location of the core of the forwarding zone, all the nodes in the core have received the message, i.e., $t_{in} > t_r$ is achieved for all nodes.

Theorem 4. *Let S_d be the maximum distance between the boundary points of the delivery zone, let v be the speed of the delivery zone, let τ_1 be the 1-hop maximum network latency of the network and let γ be its Γ-compactness. If we select $d_s = v\tau_1 \lfloor \frac{S_d}{\gamma} \rfloor$, then all nodes in the core of the forwarding zone will have received the mobicast message when the delivery zone reaches them, assuming at least one node in the core has received the message.*

Given the headway distance d and the shape F of the forwarding zone, a node can easily determine the current location of the forwarding zone using velocity v, current time t, sending time t_0 and the source location r_0. Note that t_0 and r_0 can be obtained from the mobicast protocol message ID.

4.3   Length of the Initialization Phase

As we pointed out earlier, it is in the cruising phase that the *mobicast* protocol guarantees on-time delivery. In the initialization phase, the timing constraint of *mobicast* is realized in a best-effort way. It is possible that during the initialization phase, some nodes do not get the messages on-time. In general, the shorter the initialization phase, the more deliveries are on-time. The initialization phase continues until one node inside the core of the forwarding zone that is d_s ahead of the delivery zone receives the *mobicast* message. From discussions in the last section, we know that after this, the timing constraints of *mobicast* are always satisfied.

The time (t_{init}) taken by the *mobicast* protocol to enter the cruising phase is related to the stable headway distance needed, the delivery zone speed, and the maximum admissible spatial information propagation speed of the network. The upper bound of t_{init} that our mobicast protocol achieves is addressed by the following theorem.

Theorem 5. *Let d_s be the required headway stable distance between the forwarding zone and the delivery zone. Let w be the width of the delivery zone. Let v be the speed of the delivery zone and u be lower bound of the maximum message delivery speed achievable on the network. The mobicast protocol initialization time t_{init} is no greater than $\frac{(d_s+w)}{u-v}$*

The Spatiotemporal Guarantees of the Protocol. The spatiotemporal guarantee of the presented *mobicast* protocol is addressed by the following theorem:

Theorem 6. *If at any instant of time in a mobicast session, its (user-defined) delivery zone covers at least one node in the network, our mobicast protocol delivers property (3).*

We provide only a sketch of the proof of this theorem here.
Proof: If a delivery zone covers at least one node in the network at any instant of time, then whenever the last node in a delivery zone is leaving a delivery

zone, there must be another node entering it. The same is true for the core of the forwarding zone, because it is of the same shape as the delivery zone and moves on the same path. So that if at one point in time, a node in the core of the forwarding zone has received the mobicast message, it will always be able to pass on to all others nodes on its path, because of theorem (4). From theorem (5), it is easy to see property (3) is satisfied.   □

Note that if the network has a big "hole" such that the delivery zone may fall into it at some instant of time, i.e., the delivery zone covers no network node, then, our protocol does not provide the guaranteed spatiotemporal delivery. That is why theorem (6) requires the condition "at any instant of time in a *mobicast* session, its user defined delivery zone covers at least one node in the network".

5   Discussion

In the last section we introduced two network compactness metrics to help us choose the right forwarding zone and its headway distance from the delivery zone to achieve the *mobicast* delivery guarantee without unnecessary flooding. The higher the compactness, the smaller the forwarding zone and its headway distance. These compactness values must to be computed for supporting mobicast. Calculating them involves computing the shortest path and Euclidean distances of each pair of nodes in a given network. The all-pair shortest path of a graph $G(V, E)$ can be computed in $O(VE \log V)$ time by using Johnson's algorithm [6]. All-pair distance can be computed in $O(V^2)$ time. So we can compute the the Γ-compactness of the graph in $O(VE \log V)$ time. Δ-compactness can also be computed in $O(VE \log V)$ time. Thus it is not feasible for individual sensor nodes to compute these values in a large network. In practice, one may have a central server collect all the location and connectivity information, do the computation and use one broadcast to inform all the nodes this value. Note that the compactness metrics are defined for the whole network. Different areas in the network could have their regional compactness values. When those values are available to the corresponding nodes, the size of the forwarding zone can change from one area to another in the network. We expect that this adaptive behavior will reduce the overall retransmission overhead. Computing only regional compactness also is computationally less intensive. The tradeoff for doing this is one may not be able to support reliable *mobicast* with delivery zones larger than the size of the region used for the compactness computation. Note also that these compactness metrics are geared for worst-case analysis of a "communication unfriendly" network topology in any area of the network. They are chosen in this manner because the *mobicast* property as specified by (3) is an absolute guarantee. If one prefers a weaker, probabilistic delivery guarantee, weaker (e.g., average) compactness measures would be more appropriate.

For simplicity, our protocol carries out an "as soon as possible" flooding inside the forwarding zone. If nodes have accurate pictures regarding the locations of their one hop or two hop neighbors, one can reduce the number of necessary re-transmissions in a manner similar to techniques proposed for improving broadcast efficiency [7,8]. In a probabilistic guarantee scenario, one may also use probabilistic retransmission-reduction techniques such as the one described in [9]. A review of these and other related methods can be found in [10].

Furthermore, in order to focus on the essential characteristics of *mobicast*, we assume that the local broadcast is reliable, i.e., any message broadcast by a node is to be heard by its neighbors in τ_1 time. Because of the possibility of "hidden nodes" and the high cost of coordination mechanisms to solve the hidden nodes problem, a more realistic choice would be to relax the reliability assumption about local broadcast and, in turn, weaken the delivery guarantee to a probabilistic one.

Finally, while the *mobicast* protocol we presented applies to cases where the delivery zone is a convex polygon P that moves through the space at constant velocity v for a duration T, *mobicast* in general applies to a much wider set of spatiotemporal constraints. The delivery zone can exhibit any evolving characteristics as long as it is sustainable by the underlying system. While they may all require similar ideas of forwarding zone and headway distance to maintain the spatiotemporal properties inherent in *mobicast*, a different type of delivery zone may require different protocol handling details. Classification of a useful set of mobicast delivery zone scenarios and design of the corresponding *mobicast* protocols are part of our plans for future work.

6   Related Work

Mobicast is a multicast mechanism that involves both the spatial and the temporal domains. The idea of disseminating information to nodes in a geographic area is not new. Navas and Imielinski proposed geographic multicast addressing and routing [11,12], dubbed as "geocast," for the Internet. They argued that geocast was a more natural and economic alternative for building geographic service applications than the conventional IP address-based multicast addressing and routing. In a geocast protocol, the multicast group members are determined by their locations. The initiator of a geocast specifies an area for a message to be delivered, and the geocast protocol tries to deliver the message only to the nodes in that area. Ko and Vaidya investigated the problem of geocast in mobile ad hoc networks [13] and proposed to use a "forwarding zone" to decrease delivery overhead of geocast packets. Various other mechanisms [14,15,16] have been proposed to improve geocast efficiency and delivery accuracy in mobile ad hoc networks. Zhou and Singh proposed a content-based multicast [17] in which sensor event information is delivered to nodes in some geographic area that is determined by the velocity and type of the detected events. While different in style and approach, all these techniques assume the delivery zone to be fixed. They also assume the same information delivery semantics along the temporal domain, i.e., information is to be delivered "as soon as possible". However, local coordination often requires just-in-time delivery in sensor networks. Data aggregation is an important information processing step in sensor networks. Several techniques have been proposed to support data aggregation in sensor networks. For example, both directed diffusion [2,18] and TAG [4] allow data to be aggregated on their route from the sources to a base station. No explicit local coordination is supported by these techniques. LEACH [3] organizes sensors into local clusters where each cluster head is responsible for aggregating the data from the whole cluster. However, there is no notion of mobility and the clusters do not move in space following a physical entity. In contrast, supporting local coordination for mobile physical entities is a primary goal of mobicast. Perhaps the EnviroTrack project [19] is closest in spirit to our work. EnviroTrack can dynamically create and maintain a group that tracks mobile entities in the environment. A transport layer protocol maintains connections between mobile groups. However, both Envirotrack and the other aforementioned projects do not provide any guarantees regarding spatiotemporal constraints.

7   Conclusion

In this paper we have presented the basic idea of *mobicast*, a new multicast paradigm for disseminating information to a set of nodes in a sensor network under spatiotemporal constraints. To demonstrate the feasibility of *mobicast*, we designed a protocol and explored its ability to deliver strong spatiotemporal guarantees. The key element in the protocol is a dynamic forwarding zone moving ahead of the delivery zone. Furthermore, we introduced two new notions of network compactness and proved several related theorems useful in the analysis of the information propagation over sensor networks. Using these results we were able to determine the shape of the forwarding zone and the headway distance needed for our protocol to ensure strong multicast delivery guarantees in space and time while keeping retransmission overhead and average slack time small. The powerful just-in-time spatial delivery semantics of *mobicast* serves to optimize resource utilization for multicast tasks in sensor networks and enables application programmers to address both spatial and temporal perspectives of communication and coordination explicitly, in a manner atypical of current multicast models.

References

1. D. Estrin, e.a.: Embedded everywhere: A research agenda for networked systems of embedded computers. National Academy Press (2001) Computer Science and Telecommunications Board (CSTB) Report.
2. Intanagonwiwat, C., Govindan, R., Estrin, D.: Directed diffusion: a scalable and robust communication paradigm for sensor networks. In: Mobile Computing and Networking. (2000) 56–67
3. Heinzelman, W.R., Chandrakasan, A., Balakrishnan, H.: Energy-efficient communication protocol for wireless microsensor networks. In: HICSS. (2000)
4. Madden, S., Franklin, M., Hellerstein, J., Hong, W.: Tag: a tiny aggregation service for ad-hoc sensor networks. (OSDI 2002, Boston MA)

5. Huang, Q., Lu, C., Roman, G.C.: Mobicast: Just-in-time multicast for sensor networks under spatiotemporal constraints. WUCS 42, Washington University in Saint Louis (2002)
6. Cormen, T.H., Leiserson, C.E., Rivest, R.L.: Introduction to Algorithms. The MIT Press (1999)
7. Peng, W., Lu, X.: On the reduction of broadcast redundancy in mobile ad hoc networks. In: Proceedings of the ACM Symposium on Mobile Ad Hoc Networking and Computing (MOBIHOC). (2000)
8. Qayyum, A., Viennot, L., Laouiti, A.: Multipoint relaying: An efficient technique for flooding in mobile wireless networks. Technical Report Research Report RR-3898, INRIA (2000)
9. Ni, S.Y., Tseng, Y.C., Chen, Y.S., Sheu, J.P.: The broadcast storm problem in a mobile ad hoc network. In: Proceedings of the Fifth Annual ACM/IEEE International Conference on Mobile Computing and Networking. (1999) 152–162
10. Williams, B., Camp, T.: Comparison of broadcasting techniques for mobile ad hoc networks. In: Proceedings of the ACM International Symposium on Mobile Ad Hoc Networking and Computing (MOBIHOC). (2002) 194–205
11. Imielinski, T., Navas, J.C.: Gps-based addressing and routing. RFC2009, Computer Sciece, Rutgers University (1996)
12. Navas, J.C., Imielinski, T.: Geocast – geographic addressing and routing. In: Proceedings of the Third Annual International Conference on Mobile Computing and Networking (MobiCom '97). (1997) 66–76
13. Ko, Y., Vaidya, N.: Geocasting in mobile ad hoc networks: Location-based multicast algorithms (1998)
14. Stojmenovic, I.: Voronoi diagram and convex hull based geocasting and routing in wireless networks. TR TR-99-11, University of Ottawa (1999)
15. Liao, W.H., Tseng, Y.C., Lo, K.L., Sheu, J.P.: Geogrid: A geocasting protocol for mobile ad hoc networks based on grid. Journal of Internet Technology 1 (2000) 23–32
16. Boleng, J., Camp, T., Tolety, V.: Mesh-based geocast routing protocols in an ad hoc network. In: Proceedings of the IEEE International Workshop on Parallel and Distributed Computing Issues in Wireless Networks and Mobile Computing (IPDPS). (2001) 184–193
17. Zhou, H., Singh, S.: Content based multicast (cbm) for ad hoc networks. Mobihoc 2000, Boston, MA (2000)
18. Intanagonwiwat, C., Estrin, D., Govindan, R., Heidemann, J.: Impact of network density on data aggregation in wireless sensor networks. International Conference on Distributed Computing Systems (ICDCS-22) (2001)
19. Blum, B., Nagaraddi, P., Wood, A., Abdelzaher, T., Son, S., Stankovic, J.: An entity maintenance and connection service for sensor networks. (The First International Conference on Mobile Systems, Applications, and Services (MobiSys), San Francisco, CA, May 2003)

Sentry-Based Power Management in Wireless Sensor Networks

Jonathan Hui, Zhiyuan Ren, and Bruce H. Krogh

Carnegie Mellon University, Dept. of Electrical and Computer Engineering
5000 Forbes Avenue, Pittsburgh PA 15213-3890, USA
{jhui@andrew|zren@andrew|krogh@ece}.cmu.edu

Abstract. This paper presents a sentry-based approach to power management in wireless sensor networks for applications such as intruder detection and tracking. To minimize average power consumption while maintaining sufficient node density for coarse sensing, nodes are partitioned dynamically into two sets: sentries and non-sentries. Sentry nodes provide sufficient coverage for continuous monitoring and basic communication services. Non-sentry nodes sleep for designated periods of time to conserve power, and switch to full power only when needed to provide more refined sensing for tracking. Non-sentry nodes check for beacons from sentry nodes to determine when they should remain on. Experimental results are presented demonstrating trade-offs between power savings and tracking performance for a network of seventeen nodes using the first implementation of a basic sentry-based power management scheme. The paper concludes with a brief description of a full set of power-management services being implemented as middle-ware for general wireless sensor applications.

Keywords. Power management, wireless sensor networks, tracking

1 Introduction

This paper introduces a sentry-based approach to power management in wireless sensor networks. Nodes are classified dynamically into two categories, sentries and non-sentries. Sentries operate in full power mode, providing a backbone communication network and basic application functionality. Non-sentries operate in a low-power dormant state whenever they are not required to help with the sensing tasks. Sentries wake up the non-sentries when they are needed, as determined by the current operating context for the network.

We present the concepts of sentry-based power management (SBPM) in the context of intruder detection and tracking as a target application. Wireless sensor nodes form a large-scale, ad-hoc network. For object tracking, the network must respond quickly with respect to the object. This implies that the network must be optimized for low latency and high throughput communications. On the other hand, it is common for nodes to exhibit long periods of inactivity whenever there is no activity within the ranges of their sensors. Therefore, power can be saved by turning off nodes when they are not needed for the tracking task.

F. Zhao and L. Guibas (Eds.): IPSN 2003, LNCS 2634, pp. 458–472, 2003.

Power management should achieve a good trade-off between these objectives. It should allow as many nodes to turn off at any time, while leaving enough nodes on to maintain a multi-hop path between any two nodes. This implies that a coarse network of nodes must remain on to form a connected backbone. Also, the nodes that remain on need to be sufficient to perform the task, at least in a coarse mode. In particular, the nodes that are on need to be sufficient to sense the presence of an intruder in areas where most nodes are turned off. The SBPM approach presented in this paper is designed to fulfill the above requirements.

2   Related Work

The recent SPAN [1] scheme of Chen et al. has similar goals to those of SBPM. In SPAN, a sparse network of coordinators is created. This approach is similar to our sentry-based approach where the sentries can be considered coordinators. However, SPAN attempts to create a network of coordinators with minimal loss of network capacity throughout the entire network. When dealing with object tracking, it is often the case that network capacity is not an issue in areas far away from the object.

In AFECA [2], each node maintains a count of the all their neighboring nodes within radio range by listening to broadcast signals. A node transitions between power-down and power-on states by randomly sleeping for a specific amount of time proportional to the number of nearby nodes. The general effect is that the number of nodes remains roughly constant. As the density increases, the amount of power savings increases. However, AFECA's decisions on sleeping time are fairly conservative to ensure that there is a high probability of creating a fully connected graph among nodes to allow an ad hoc network to form. SBPM differs from AFECA in that a node is not left on unless it is absolutely necessary. Also in SBPM, always-on nodes are chosen so that a fully connected graph is virtually ensured.

In GAF [3], the nodes make use of their geographical location information to divide up all nodes into fixed square grids. The size of these squares stays constant regardless of node density. Nodes within a grid power-down and wake-up with the guarantee that at least one node per square is on at all times to maintain a backbone network amongst all nodes. SBPM differs from GAF in that groups are formed dynamically with nearby neighbors rather than specific geographic coordinates.

Other papers on power management focus on taking advantage of multiple levels of power consumption that are available in wireless sensor nodes. Minimum-energy routing [4] minimizes energy consumption by varying the transmission power. Chang and Tassiulas [5] enhanced this method to allow for more uniform power dissipation across all nodes by varying the transmission power across all nodes fairly. In this method, nodes adjust their transmission power by choosing routes that minimize energy consumption. DPM [6] saves power by taking advantage of multiple power states. Individual components are shut down when not needed and are woken up when necessary. The net effect is a set of power states to which a node can transition. The sleep states differ by the amount of power consumed, the time to transition in and out of the states, and what services they provide. DPM does not make use of sentries to coarsely monitor and maintain the network. Another approach is taken by LEACH [7]. This protocol selects multiple coordinators to aggregate data and send the data to a base station. These techniques for exploiting multiple power states, varying transmission power, and data aggregation complement the issues addressed by SBPM. They can be applied to any system where powered on nodes form a fully connected network. Thus, these methods could potentially be combined with SBPM.

3   SBPM Design

There are several characteristics of wireless sensor nodes that limit their functionality. Wireless sensors often have limited energy due to the use of batteries. They also use unsophisticated wireless links that limit the range, reliability, and throughput of communication between nodes. This implies that total network capacity is limited. SBPM attempts to minimize the total power usage over all nodes, maximize the network capacity utilization, and maintain full connectivity among all nodes. For this approach, we must assume that there exists a multi-hop path between any two nodes when all nodes are powered on. We also assume that the nodes have at least three power states. In the power-on state, all of the node's components required for the application are powered on. In the power-off state, the microprocessor is placed in a low-power state while the rest of the components are turned off. In the checking state, a node is only providing power to the microprocessor and radio transceiver.

3.1   Sentries and Non-sentries

To initialize SBPM, a subset of nodes in the network are selected as *sentries*. In our current implementation, the set of sentries forms a spanning tree, that is, each sentry is able to communicate with at least one other sentry. The remaining *non-sentry* nodes are partitioned into groups assigned to each sentry so that every non-sentry is able to communicate with any other node though one or more sentries. Thus, the sentries provide a backbone network that allows communication between any two nodes in the network.

Sentries must also be chosen so that the sensing task can still be performed in at least a preliminary or degraded manner. For object tracking, each sentry provides coarse tracking information by detecting the presence of an intruder in its sensor range. Thus, the second criterion for the selection of sentries is that they provide complete coverage with respect to sensing. With coarse sensing, the intruder can be detected and surrounding non-sentries can be then be turned on to enable higher-resolution tracking.

Sentries are also responsible for waking up nodes that are in the power-off state. The non-sentries notify their sentries when they transition to the power-off state, and declare when they will check for a beacon to see if they need to return to the power-on state.

Since sentries persist in the power-on state, their power consumption is significantly higher than the non-sentry power consumption. While the sensor network is active, the sentry assignments can be rotated to share this power burden. This rotation is achieved by weighting the costs of assigning sentries according the the available remaining energy at each node. We are currently working on efficient procedures to solve the problem of optimal dynamic sentry assignment.

Figure 1 shows the state transition diagram of a node. The main purpose of the non-sentries is to provide more detailed information about the environment when it is needed. In the power-on state, they continuously monitor the area using onboard sensors. Non-sentries differ from sentries in that they are allowed to enter the power-off state when their contribution is not necessary for accurate object tracking. Non-sentries stay in the power-off state for a specific amount of time. When that time expires, the non-sentry enters the checking state to check if it is necessary to completely power on. If the node is not needed, it returns to the power-off state.

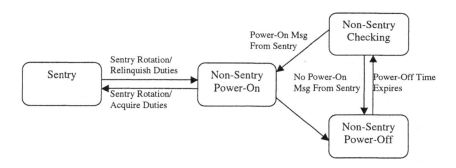

Fig. 1. Node state transition diagram.

The amount of time a non-sentry stays in the power-off state before entering the checking state can be determined right before the non-sentry enters the power-off state. Picking this time correctly is not trivial. A power-off time that is too short does not optimize the amount of energy savings. However, choosing a time that is too long may harm the performance of the sensor network. A node that transitions to a power-off state for a long time may not check to enter the power-on state in time to provide adequate timely information for the task at hand. Section 5 presents results of experiments to study the trade-offs among these considerations for our current implementation.

3.2 Implementation Details

Figure 2 shows where SBPM fits as a service within the overall communication architecture for each node. SBPM communicates directly with both the routing layer and the MAC/physical layer. In our current implementation of SBPM, the routing layer is not notified when nodes transition between the power-on and power-off states. Although optimizations can be made to the routing layer when SBPM provides such notifications, it adds complexity to the integration of the two modules.

Most routing implementations attempt to be fault-tolerant. If a node fails, all paths through that node will be rerouted through other nodes. Due to this feature, we leave the responsibilities of route reconfiguration to the routing layer. Thus, messages can be communicated across any nodes that are powered on. However, when all but a few non-sentries are in the power-down state, the sentries provide a minimal network that can be used to send messages between any two nodes in the power-on state. Although the routing layer plays a passive role, an implementation of SBPM that provides callbacks can be fairly trivial. Since the non-sentry entering the power-off state must send a message to its sentry, this message can be turned into a broadcast, which also notifies neighboring motes of its transition. Our current implementation does not include this callback feature.

SBPM is implemented as two modules as shown in Figure 2. One module provides the services for power management while the other provides the services for sentry management.

SentryGroupManagement. This module provides a generic interface that allows the use of sentries in an application. This module provides the necessary functionality for sentry selection and group management. A group is defined as a sentry and all of the non-sentries that report to it. As shown in Figure 3, the SentryGroupManagement module uses both the routing layer and the power management module. The routing layer is necessary to negotiate with surrounding nodes when selecting sentries and maintaining groups. Also, the PowerManagement module can be helpful during the sentry selection process. Sentries use significantly more power since they generally need to handle more tasks than non-sentries. As a result, selecting a node that has more remaining energy allows for more uniform energy dissipation across all nodes. If such a feature is not requested, the PowerManagement interface should be implemented such that it always returns the same value when sampling a nodes remaining energy. The commands in the SentryGroupMgmnt interface provide the functionality that an application might need when requiring the use of sentries.

PowerManagement. This module provides a generic interface for use of a power management scheme, including the necessary functionality for a node to transition between power states. As shown in Figure 4, the PowerManagement module makes use of both the routing layer and the SentryManagement module. The routing layer is required so that a sentry and its non-sentries can communicate with each other whenever a transition between power states occurs.

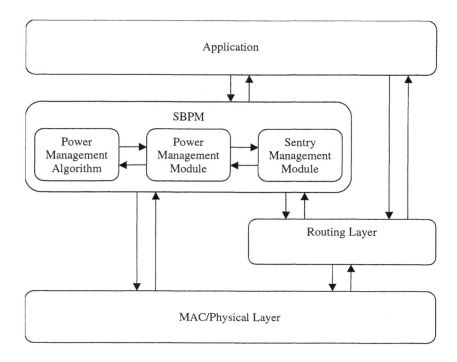

Fig. 2. SBPM is a protocol that uses both the MAC/Physical Layer and the Routing Layer. SBPM is split up into three different modules.

Since SBPM requires the use of sentries, the SentryGroupManagement module is required. This module is needed so that non-sentries can obtain the address of their sentries. The module is also useful when the PowerManagement module requests for a sentry to pass its duties along to another node. The PowerManagement module does not provide the decision making process of when nodes should transition between power states. The PowerMgmtAlgorithm module makes this decision. Having the decision making process as a separate module makes it possible to quickly change between different decision algorithms.

4   Experiment: Intruder Detection and Tracking

Out test bed to implement and study the performance of sentry-based power management is based on a network of *motes*, wireless sensor nodes designed at UC Berkeley and produced at Crossbow Technologies [8]. Each mote has a transceiver, a micro-controller, and a sensor board that includes a photo sensor, temperature sensor, magnetometer, accelerometer, speaker, and microphone. In our experiment, a photo sensor is used to demonstrate intruder detection and tracking. In a real system, sound, sonar, or some other sensor would be used.

```
module SentryGroupManagement {
    provides {
        interface SentryGroupMgmnt;
    }
    uses {
        interface ReceiveMsg as RxMsg;
        interface SendMsg as TxMsg;
        interface PowerMangement;
    }
}

interface SentryGroupMgmnt {
    command result_t startSentryGroupMgmnt(void);
    command result_t stopSentryGroupMgmnt(void);
    command result_t isOn(void);
    command result_t changeSentries(void);
    command addr_t getMySentry(void);
    command result_t getNumNonsentries(void);
    command result_t isSentry(void);
    command result_t isNonsentry(void);
    command result_t isBase(void);
    command result_t declareBase(void);
    command result_t undeclareBase(void);
}
```

Fig. 3. SentryGroupMgmnt module interface and commands.

SBPM is implemented on top of TinyOS [8], a minimal operating system developed for the motes.

Figure 5 shows our experimental setup, which was inspired by the experimental setup described in [9]. Eighteen motes are mounted on a vertical board in a skewed array, as shown in Figure 5. One of the motes is tagged as a base mote and is directly connected to a computer though a serial connection. The base mote does not participate in sensing. In our system, a computer is directly connected to a projector that shines an image on the sensor array. In this experiment, as shown in Figure 5, the "intruder" is a dark circle with a radial gradient. The radial gradient allows a mote to measure its distance from the intruder by measuring the light intensity. The intruder has a radius equal to the distance between any two motes in the system. This forces the intruder to cover at least three motes at any time while inside the sensor array. The motes can then use triangulation to an estimate the position of the intruder.

In our initial implementation we pre-select four motes from the sensor array to act as sentries. The rest of the motes act as non-sentries while the base station serves as a link between the sensor array and the computer. In order to execute the experiment, a simple static routing layer was developed. Due to the static nature of the routes, each non-sentry is assigned a sentry and sends all messages

```
module PowerManagement {
    provides {
        interface PowerMgmnt;
    }
    uses {
        interface ReceiveMsg as RxMsg;
        interface SendMsg as TxMsg;
        interface SentryGroupMgmnt;
        interface PowerMgmntAlgorithm;
    }
}

interface PowerMgmnt {
    command result_t startPowerMgmnt(void);
    command        result_t        stopPowerMgmnt(boolean
    stop_sentry_mgmnt);
    command result_t pausePowerMgmnt(void);
    command result_t isOn(void);
    command result_t updateIdletime(uint16_t idle_time);
    command result_t currentEnergyLevel(void);
}
```

Fig. 4. PowerMgmnt module interface and commands.

Fig. 5. Setup for light-based intruder detection and tracking experiments. The intruder is the dark circle with a radial gradient.

to that sentry. The sentries act as a backbone network forwarding all messages towards the base mote. This allows all non-sentries to power-down and maintain communication throughout the sensor array without changing any of the routing parameters.

Due to variance in ambient light depending on where the experiment is set up and the projector used for the experiment, the sensor array is calibrated whenever the sensor array is first turned on. To calibrate every mote efficiently, we make use of the computer to create an automated calibration process. For simplicity, we have divided the range of light intensity into a fixed number of levels. During calibration, the computer shines a specific light intensity level on every mote and sends a message to the sensor array informing them which light intensity level is currently being projected. Every mote replies upon successful calibration.

Our initial implementation takes a centralized approach to object tracking. Whenever a mote senses a change in light intensity, it sends a message to the computer through the sensor array. The computer takes the data points and triangulates an estimated position of the intruder. A data validation scheme has also been implemented to keep erroneous data from affecting the estimation. In this scheme the computer chooses data points in which the most motes agree. In situations where an equal number of motes agree on different data points, then the motes reporting a stronger presence of the object are chosen for triangulation.

The power management scheme is also centralized in our initial implementation. The computer turns a group of non-sentries off if the intruder is more than one hop away from any of the motes in the sensor array. We consider one hop as a movement from one triangle to another, where lines between neighboring motes define the triangles.

When a non-sentry receives a message commanding it to enter the power-off state, it goes into the power-off state for a set amount of time. This amount of time is constant throughout the operation of the sensor network. Part of the experiment includes the affect of this time on tracking performance and energy consumption. While in the sleep state, power to the transceiver and sensor board is turned off. Also, the micro-controller is placed into a low power mode that preserves the contents of registers and allows a wake-up interrupt. A non-sentry periodically enters the checking state and remains in that state long enough to determine whether or not its sentry is commanding it to enter the power-on state. If there is no beacon from the sentry, it returns to the power-off state.

5   Results

We present results from experiments performed to evaluate the effects of varying several of the design parameters. All experimental results in this section are single-run results. The path of the intruder through the sensor array was fixed to the path shown in Figure 6.

Figure 7 displays the amount of energy consumed with respect to the object movement speed. One curve shows the total energy consumed without power management and another curve shows the total energy consumed with power management. As can be seen in Figure 7, there is a fairly consistent energy savings of about 30% with power management on. This percentage is biased to the low end since the size of the object is large relative to the sensor array.

Expanding the sensor array would decrease the ratio of motes in the power-on state to those in the power-down state.

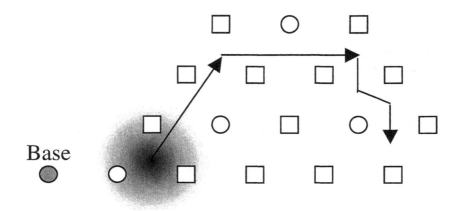

Fig. 6. The path of the intruder through the sensor array used to gather results.

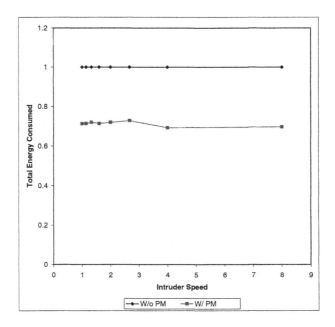

Fig. 7. Energy consumption vs. object movement speed.

For the sentry assignment scheme in our current experimental setup, the ratio of sentries to non-sentries would approach 1/4 as the number of nodes increases. Also, for our current implementation, motes in the power-down state are actually on about 20% of the time (4 seconds sleeping, 1 second checking for power-on message). Thus with a large sensor array, there is a theoretical energy reduction of 60% in our current setup.

We varied the object movement speed while keeping the power-down duration constant. To evaluate the effects of objected movement speed on tracking error, we repeated the experiment for several intruder speeds with power management on and once with power management off. As can be seen in Figure 8, the average tracking error at slow object speeds is roughly equivalent to the quantization error due to the limited light intensity levels. However, as object movement speed increases the amount of tracking error increases in both cases of power management on and off. Due to the limited size of the sensor array, the tracking error is limited to the size of the sensor array. The increase in tracking error can be attributed to the limited network capacity and centralized approach of processing data. As a result of the centralized data processing, this rate increases with the speed of the object for two of reasons. When the object moves more quickly, the motes send messages at a quicker rate because they sense changes in light intensity more often. The increase in number of messages increases the number of collisions, thus increasing the number of retries. The number of retries delays a mote's ability to send a message. As the mote is trying to send a message successfully, the object moves on, which in turn induces even more motes to begin sending messages.

The difference in tracking error when power management is on and power management is off is negligible at slow object movement speeds. When the sensor array can react to the object's motion, all sensors around the object are in the power-on state and provide enough information for accurate estimations. However, at high object movement speeds the tracking error with power management is significantly larger than without power management. Two factors cause this characteristic. When the object is moving quickly, it is more difficult to make correct power management decisions due to the increase in tracking error. Also, if the object moves faster than the sensor array can respond, motes around the object may not be in the power-on state and cannot contribute data that would provide a more accurate estimate.

We also varied the power-down duration while keeping the object movement speed constant. Figure 9 illustrates the relationship between tracking error and power-down duration while keeping the object movement speed constant. The power-down duration directly affects the sensor array's ability to react to object movements. As can be seen by Figure 9, at small values of the predetermined power-down duration, the tracking error remains somewhat constant. When the power-down duration is small enough, the sensor array can react quickly enough to ensure that all nodes around the object are in the power-on state. However, as the predetermined power-down duration increases, there is an increase in

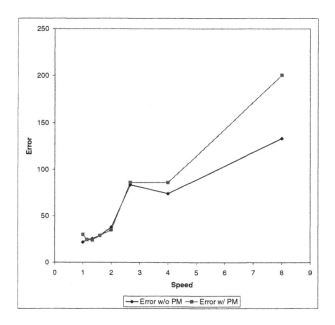

Fig. 8. Tracking error vs. object movement speed with power management on and power management off.

tracking error. This is caused by the sensor array's inability to react quickly enough to ensure that all motes around the object are in the power-on state.

Figure 10 illustrates the relationship between energy consumption and power-down duration while keeping the object movement speed constant. Increasing the power-down duration decreases the frequency at which a mote needs to power on and check whether it needs to switch into the power-on state. As can be seen by Figure 10, there is a small but noticeable decrease in total energy consumption as the power-down duration increases. The small magnitude in difference is due to the fact that the initial power savings is relatively small as explained above.

6   Conclusions

This paper presents SBPM, a sentry-based power management scheme in wireless sensor networks. SBPM makes use of sentries to define a coarse network of nodes that are necessary to perform the task and turn on non-sentry motes when necessary. Our initial implementation demonstrates the feasibility of such a sentry-based approach. Significant issues remain to be explored.

A dynamic sentry selection algorithm would allow for sentry rotation and fault tolerance. In our initial implementation, sentries were pre-selected and fixed. Fixed sentries are not amenable to optimal power savings. Sentries must remain in the power-on state at all times and are burdened with the need to

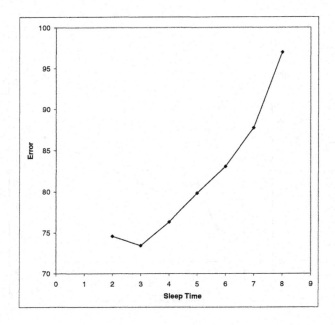

Fig. 9. Tracking error vs. power-down duration.

send messages when non-sentries are in the power-down state. Thus, sentries consume energy much faster. For optimal performance, we would ideally like to have an even rate of energy consumption across all nodes. Fixed sentries also cause problems when dealing with fault tolerance. In our setup, sentries are critical to maintaining both a coarse network and waking up non-sentry motes. Without the ability to dynamically choose sentries, we are assuming that the chosen sentries will never fail.

A distributed object tracking algorithm could minimize messages across the network and ultimately minimizes tracking error. In our current initial implementation, all data is sent to the computer for processing. However, if the processing can be done on the motes themselves, then only one message needs to be sent to the computer. Also, the data can instantly be broadcasted to neighboring motes for other purposes, rather than having the results being sent back out by the computer.

A distributed stochastic-based power management decision algorithm would allow for far less total energy consumption across all nodes. By making power management decisions directly on the motes, the sensor array can react much quicker and require less messages being sent. Our initial implementation also turns whole groups on and off. The nodes in the power-down state also sleep for a fixed amount of time before checking whether to power-on. Varying the amount of time to sleep will allow us to find the optimal point between tracking error and energy savings.

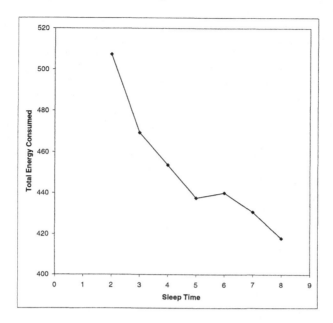

Fig. 10. Energy consumption vs. power-down duration.

As shown by our experiments, the first steps have been taken successfully in implementing a sentry-based object tracking and power management approach for wireless networks. Even in our initial implementation, we have experimentally shown that significant energy can be saved.

Acknowledgment. This research has been supported in part by the DARPA NEST (Network-Enabled Software Technology) program.

References

1. Chen, B., Jamieson, K., Balakrishnan, H., Morris, R.: Span: An energy efficient coordination algorithm for topology maintenance in ad hoc wireless networks. In: Proceedings of Mobicom 2001. (2001) 85–96
2. Xu, Y., Heidemann, J., Estrin, D.: Adaptive energy-conserving routing for multihop ad hoc networks. Technical Report Tech. Rep. 527, USC/ISI (2000)
3. Xu, Y., Heidemann, J., Estrin, D.: Geographically-informed energy conservation for ad hoc routing. In: Proc. Seventh Annual ACM/IEEE International Conference on Mobile Computing and Networking (MobiCom), Rome (2001)
4. Shepard, T.: A channel access scheme for large dense packet radio networks. In: Proc. ACM SIGCOMM. (1996) 219–230
5. Chang, J., Tassiulas, L.: Energy conserving routing in wireless ad hoc networks. In: Proceedings of IEEE INFOCOM, Tel Aviv, Israel (2000)

6. Sinha, A., Chandrakasan, A.: Dynamic power management in wireless sensor networks. IEEE Design and Test of Computers (2001) 62–75
7. Heinzelman, W.R., Chandrakasan, A., Balakrishnan, H.: Energy-efficient communication protocols for wireless microsensor networks. In: Proceedings of the Hawaaian International Confference on Systems Science. (2000)
8. Hill, J., Szewczyk, R., Woo, A., Hollar, S., Culler, D., Pister, K.: System architecture directions for network sensors. In: Proc. Ninth International Conf. on Architectural Support for Programming Languages and Operating Systems, Cambridge, MA (2000)
9. Liu, J., Cheung, P., Guibas, L., Zhao, F.: A dual-space approach to tracking and sensor management in wireless sensor networks. In: First ACM International Workshop On Wireless Sensor Networks and Applications in conjuction with ACM MobiCom 2002. (2002) 131–139

Energy Aware Multi-path Routing for Uniform Resource Utilization in Sensor Networks*

Neha Jain, Dilip K. Madathil, and Dharma P. Agrawal

Center for Distributed and Mobile Computing
ECECS, University of Cincinnati
Cincinnati OH 45221-0030 USA
{njain, kuttymd,dpa}@ececs.uc.edu

Abstract. In a sensor network where every node has a limited energy supply, one of the primary concerns is to maximize the network lifetime through energy-efficient routing. We present an energy efficient, scalable and distributed multipath routing protocol that achieves a substantial improvement in the overall network lifetime. Most of the existing sensor network routing protocols are based on single or shortest path routing. This accelerates the failure of nodes lying along the often used optimal paths, thus adversely affecting the connectivity and hence life of the network. Our scheme is based on a novel deterministic traffic scheduling algorithm that balances the load over multiple paths between source and destination, in proportion to their residual energy. Our protocol focuses on uniformly utilizing the resources of the network, rather than on optimality of routes. With our approach, we are able to minimize the communication and computational overheads involved in dynamically adapting the traffic flow to the energy level of the nodes.

Keywords. Multipath Routing, Energy Awareness, Network Lifetime.

1 Introduction

Wireless sensor networks consist of a large number of tiny, low power devices or nodes equipped with programmable computing, multiple sensing and communication capability. They operate in a dynamic environment to perform distributed sensing tasks. They may be deployed in remote terrains to sense certain attributes of their environment and provide useful information to user queries. The nodes in a sensor network are practically static, forming a large and dense mutihop network, where every node is a router. We refer to the node at which the query is injected in the network as the sink, and the node which responds to this query as the source, as described in the directed diffusion paradigm [1] by Estrin *et. al.* There could be several potential sources for a single sink. The source on receiving the query from the sink, generates query responses for a duration specified in the query and routes them to the sink node. These query responses constitute a majority of the traffic in the network.

---

* This work has been supported by the Ohio Board of Regents, Doctoral Investment Funds and National Science Foundation under Grant No. CCR-0113361

F. Zhao and L. Guibas (Eds.): IPSN 2003, LNCS 2634, pp. 473–487, 2003.

The sensor nodes usually operate on a non-replaceable battery. A large proportion of a node's limited energy resource is consumed in forwarding data [14]. A major design challenge in sensor networks is to increase the operational lifetime of the network as much as possible by employing energy efficient routing. An intuitive approach would be to reduce the number of data transmissions by minimizing the number of hops required for data to reach its destination. Although shortest path routing gives high throughput with minimum response time, nodes lying on this path are drained out of their energy. Therefore, when the offered load on the network increases, packets have to be routed via longer alternate route or they are dropped due to disconnected routes. A wide disparity in the energy levels of the different sensor nodes in the network degrades network performance in the long run. This is because although most of the nodes in the network have plenty of energy, they are no longer connected with each other due to random concentration of dead nodes (with zero battery power) in the network.

The motivation of this work is to improve the network lifetime by avoiding congestion and the consequent partitioning of the network, where we assume the network life to be the time at which the first node in the network is depleted of its energy. Chang and Tassiulas have proved [3] that to improve the overall lifetime of the network, where every node has a limited lifetime, the objective of the protocol should be to maximize the residual energy of every node while routing, rather than minimizing the total energy consumed in routing. In our proposed routing protocol we spread the traffic over the nodes lying on different possible paths connecting the source to the sink, in proportion to their residual energy. The rationale behind traffic spreading is that for a given total energy consumption in the network, at each moment every node should have spent the same amount of energy. To achieve traffic spreading in the sensor network, we make use of multipath routing.

The organization of the paper is as follows: In section 2, we briefly describe the need for multipath routing. This is followed by a discussion on related work in multipath routing for sensor networks in section 3. Section 4 illustrates the details of the proposed protocol, and includes the formulation of the optimal load assignment problem to achieve uniform load distribution. Finally, in section 5 we present the performance evaluation of our scheme under different traffic conditions for regular as well as random deployment of nodes in the field.

2   Multipath Routing

Classical multipath routing has been used extensively in the literature to achieve load balancing and fault tolerance in computer networks, for example in high speed networks [6], and ATM networks [5]. Fault tolerance or robustness is an inherent feature of multipath routing. Robustness is the likelihood that alternate paths can be substituted between the source and the sink when the primary path fails. Load balancing splits the traffic among the multiple paths connecting the source to the sink. The objective is to assign more load to under-utilized paths and less load to over-committed paths to ensure uniform resource utilization of all available paths. In this paper we focus on the load balancing property of multipath routing to improve the lifetime of the network.

There is a need to adapt multipath routing to the design constraints of a sensor network. An important design consideration that drives the design of sensor networks is scalability [1] of the routing protocol. Computation of all possible paths between a source and a sink might be computationally exhaustive. Besides, updating the source about the availability of these paths at any given time might involve considerable communication overhead. The routing algorithm must depend only on the local information [2] or the information piggy-backed with data packets, as global exchange of information is too energy expensive due to large number of nodes. Our algorithm implements multipath routing in a completely distributed manner using localized techniques.

3   Related Work

There has been considerable research in wireless network routing exploiting geographic location information by Karp *et. al.* [17], Ko *et. al.* [16] etc. Motivated by the fact that sensor network queries may often be geographical, Govindan *et. al.* proposed GEAR (Geographic and Energy Aware Routing Algorithm) [15] for single path routing. GEAR complements the data-centric protocol directed diffusion [1] eliminating the overhead of initial and periodic interest and low rate data flooding throughout the network by providing geographic routing support. Instead of using the classical greedy geographic forwarding, GEAR uses an energy aware metric in the estimated cost function to balance energy consumption among neighbors lying in the direction of the sink. Although this delays node failure of nodes lying on the shortest geographic route to the sink, there is limited load balancing as traffic splitting is restricted to immediate neighbors of any node.

More work has been reported on single path routing as compared to multipath routing in wireless ad hoc networks. Some applications of multipath routing for ad hoc networks have been considered by Das and Nasipuri [7], Hass *et. al.* [8], Park *et. al.* [9]. Multipath routing specifically for sensor networks has been explored by Tassiulas and Chang [4], Ganesan *et. al.* [11], Servetto *et. al.* [13], Srivastava *et. al.* [10], etc.

Ganesan *et. al.* [11] have proposed a multipath scheme to achieve high resilience to node failure with low maintenance overhead. In their scheme, the source periodically floods low rate data over all alternate paths in the mutipath in order to keep those paths alive. The frequency of these low rate data events determines how quickly their mechanism recovers from failures on the primary path.

Shah *et. al.* [12] have modified the directed diffusion protocol to improve the overall network lifetime. Instead of reinforcing a single optimal or shortest path for routing, the alternate good paths discovered by the route discovery phase of the directed diffusion are also cached and one of them is chosen for routing in a probabilistic fashion.

Servetto *et. al.* [13] have also implemented multipath routing using random walks between a source and sink, to avoid the overhead of caching paths. They assume the nodes to be powered by a renewable source of energy, hence node failure is temporary. But their assumption of random failure of nodes is not realistic because usually the failure of a node depends on how frequently it is utilized for routing.

4   The Proposed Routing Protocol

The proposed protocol spreads the traffic generated by a query in a geographical area that is symmetric with respect to the location of the source and the sink, which are situated at the opposite ends of the diameter of this symmetric geographical area. The objective is to derive the sequence of path utilization to reduce the disparity in the energy levels of nodes lying in this geographical area bounded by the source and the sink. Our routing protocol can be easily explained by assuming a regular topology of sensor nodes, although in reality the sensor nodes are randomly dispersed in the field. As shown in Fig. 1, the sensor nodes are regularly placed in a two dimensional grid, representing the entire sensor network. Any node in this topology is capable of directly communicating with its eight one-hop neighbors.

We have simulation results in section 5 to prove that our scheme also works for a random deployment of sensor nodes. We now list some of the other basic assumptions that drive the design of our protocol.

4.1   Assumptions

1. All nodes and queries are equally critical.
2. The sink is aware of the geographical location of the source of the query.
3. The query packet contains the rate at which responses are to be generated, and the duration for which the source generates query responses.
4. Every node in the network knows its coordinates in the field and keeps updating its utilization represented by a variable called the *local access count*. We assume utilization or local access count to be the total number of packets a node has transmitted or received at any time since the beginning of the network-cycle.
5. Every node knows the location of all its neighbors and it is periodically updated about the local access count of its neighbors with the aid of beacon signals.

Let us consider a case where a single query q is injected at a sink node P and received by the source node Q in the network, as shown in Fig. 1(a). Let us call the square PQRS bounded by the source R, and the sink P as the *query region* PQRS. The source R on receiving the query q generates the query responses.

In Fig. 1(a), we observe that the shortest straight-line path, i.e., the diagonal joining the source to the sink PR has the minimum number of hops. Let us refer to the diagonal PR as d_1, and the diagonal QS of the *query region* PQRS as d_2. Repeated use of the shortest path d_1 for routing packets will quickly deplete the energy of the nodes on the diagonal d_1 and partition the network along d_1.

Let us construct diagonals parallel to d_2, as shown in Fig. 1(a). Every time a packet travels from the source to the sink or vice versa, the next-hop node lies on one of these diagonals. When the packet begins its journey, it selects a next-hop lying on a diagonal with more number of nodes, till it reaches the next-hop lying on the diagonal d_2 with maximum number of nodes. Thereafter it selects a next-hop lying on diagonals with decreasing number of nodes, till it reaches the destination. Our objective is to split the load uniformly across all these diagonals, unlike minimum energy routing which successively depletes the energy of the node in the center of these diagonals (path d_1

shown in Fig. 1(a)). We establish multiple paths between the source and the sink, such that there is equal load distribution on every diagonal in the query region. These multiple paths resemble the edges of an expanding rhombus, with one pair of its vertices fixed at the source P and the sink R, and diagonal d_2 as the locus of the other pair of vertices as shown in Fig. 1(e).

We observe that most of the available paths are not disjoint. When the traffic originates at the source, it can split in only three directions for the given topology. But as it moves across diagonals of increasing length, the same traffic is split among greater number of nodes. The number of nodes on diagonal d_2 determine the upper bound on the load splitting for a given traffic. Let us refer to these nodes as the *midhops*, and the area in proximity of d_2, where these *midhops* exist as the *midband*. The *midband* neatly divides the network into two sections which we refer to as the upper diagonal region (bounded by the *midhops* and the sink) and the lower diagonal region (bounded by the source and the *midhops*) respectively, as shown in Fig. 1(a).

An optimal traffic-scheduling algorithm should distribute load equally on all *midhops* in a *query region* to ensure an equal load on nodes lying in the *query region*. When the traffic moves towards the *midband*, it diverges with respect to the source along the edges of the rhombus. When the traffic reaches the *midband*, it starts converging towards the sink. Here, we observe that nodes close to the sink obtain traffic from multiple directions. Therefore, although a uniform load distribution is achieved in the entire *query region* which in this case is the entire network, nodes in the immediate proximity of the source and the sink have to relay more packets and consequently have a higher utilization than the rest of the *query region* PQRS.

4.2 Formulation of Traffic Scheduling Algorithm

Let us consider the source sink pair as shown in Fig. 1(b). The query injected at the sink is geographically forwarded (to the neighbor closest to the source) to avoid latency. When the query reaches a *midhop* in the *query region*, while traveling towards the source, it generates an inquiry packet. This inquiry packet is broadcast along the *midband* such that it is received by all the potential *midhops*. On receiving the inquiry packets, the *midhops* generate inquiry responses containing their current utilization information (local access count). These inquiry responses are also geographically forwarded to the source as shown in Fig. 1(c). The source first receives the query and subsequently receives the inquiry responses from the *midhops*. It waits for the responses to pour in from all the *midhops*, for a time that is proportional to the distance between the source and the sink, and stores the local access count corresponding to every *midhop* that responded in a table. When the inquiry response timer at the source expires, it sorts this table in the ascending order of the local access count of each *midhop*. The source then computes the total number of responses or the load P that it has to generate.

Our traffic scheduling algorithm computes the distribution of the total load P, among the possible *midhops*, and the order in which they should be utilized for routing.

We represent the problem of optimal assignment of load to each path as follows:

Let the number of *midhops* or available alternate routes be n. Let $u_1, u_2, u_3, ..., u_n$ represent the local access count of the n *midhops* . Let $p_1, p_2, ..., p_n$ represent the load that will be assigned to the n *midhops*.

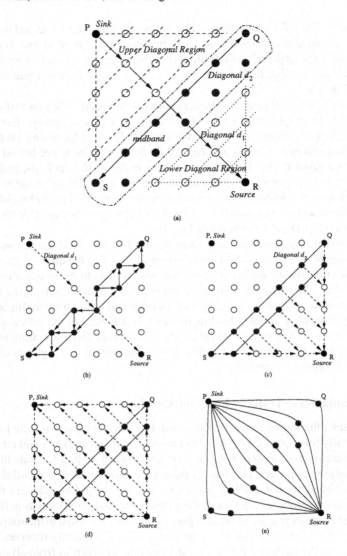

Fig. 1. The different stages of routing. Part (a) shows the general notation used to represent the *query region*. Part (b) shows query injection at the sink P, and subsequent propagation of the query towards the source R, using the shortest available path d_1. Inquiry packets initiated by the query, are broadcast along the diagonal d_2 (QS). Part (c) shows the inquiry responses reaching the source from every *midhop* on d_2. The source transmits the query responses along the multiple paths as shown in part (d) in the order determined by the traffic schedule. These multiple paths resemble the sides of an expanding rhombus as shown in part (e), with one set of vertices fixed at source R, and sink P, and the other pair of vertices expanding along d_2.

To distribute the load P evenly on every *midhop* in the network, the sum of the current utilization and the load to be assigned to each path should be the same.

$$u_1 + p_1 = u_2 + p_2 = \ldots = u_n + p_n = k \tag{1}$$

According to the above equation, *midhops* with lower current utilization are assigned more load than nodes with high current utilization so as to achieve a good load balancing.

Let duration of the query be t. Let r be the rate at which responses have to be generated and P, the total load generated at the source. We know utilization, u_i for all *midhops*, where $1 \leq i \leq n$. Let us try to determine the value of k in Equation (1).

$$P = t \times r \tag{2}$$

From Equation (1)

$$\sum_{i=1}^{i=n} (u_i + p_i) = nk$$

$$\Rightarrow \sum_{i=1}^{i=n} u_i + \sum_{i=1}^{i=n} p_i = nk$$

$$\Rightarrow \quad nk = \sum_{i=1}^{i=n} u_i + P$$

$$or, \Rightarrow \quad k = \frac{\sum_{i=1}^{i=n} u_i + P}{n} \tag{3}$$

We can now determine $p_1, p_2, ..., p_n$ by substituting for k and u_i in Equation (1).

$$p_1 = k - u_1, p_2 = k - u_2, ..., p_n = k - u_n \tag{4}$$

Its possible that there is a wide disparity in the utilization of the *midhops*, and P may not be enough to smooth out the difference in the utilization of all the *midhops*. In this case, the assigned load p_i might be negative for *midhops* with very high utilization with respect to the rest of the nodes. The paths represented by these over-utilized *midhops* must be avoided, and the load P should be redistributed among the rest of the *midhops*. We sort the available paths in the decreasing order of their utilization, such that $u_n < u_{n-1} < ... < u_i < ... < u_1$. We keep eliminating u_{n-i}, where $0 \leq i \leq n-1$, until we obtain $p_{n-i} > 0$ i.e.,

$$u_{n-i} < \frac{\sum_{j=0}^{n-i} u_j + P}{n-i} \tag{5}$$

Let u_m be the first node that satisfies the constraint (4), such that $m \leq n$, we distribute the load P among these m midhops after rejecting the midhops undesirable for routing where p_i for $1 \leq i \leq m$, is the load assigned to the *ith midhop*.

As and when a response packet is routed through a given midhop, the load assigned to that *midhop* is updated in the table at the source. The source transmits the response packet through the *midhop* that has the maximum number of packets remaining to be routed at that time. This ensures that at any time, we use the path that has the minimum local access for its *midhop* to route data.

In order to make sure that the incoming query traffic adapts to the existing query traffic in the network, we introduce acknowledgment packets to reserve the *midhops* for forwarding the number of packets assigned to them. These acknowledgment packets are nothing but the first m response packets of the total load P, routed through each of the m *midhops* once. The *midhops* create a reservation count for the query on receiving the acknowledgment packet to store the value of the load p assigned by the traffic scheduling algorithm. The *midhops* thus update their current utilization to the sum of its local access count and the reservation count. As and when the *midhop* routes the query response to the sink, it decrements the reservation count for that query at the *midhop*. This can be better illustrated from the behavior of the protocol in presence of multiple source sink pairs and is discussed next.

4.3   Routing in Presence of Multiple Source Sink Pairs

Let us consider the example in Fig. 2 with two source sink pairs. Suppose at time t_1, query q_1 was injected in the network at $Sink_1$, for the source at $Source_1$. At time t_2 (later than t_1), query q_2 is injected in the network at $Sink_2$, meant for $Source_2$. We also assume that the nodes in the *query region* 1 and 2 are not serving any other query besides q_1 and q_2. We realize that some *midhops* for q_2 are same as those for q_1. When $source_2$ receives the inquiry responses from the *midhops* of *query region* Q_2, the *midhops* common to q_1 and q_2, will have a higher local access count, and will have a finite reservation count unlike the rest of the *midhops*. Therefore, depending on the sum of the local access count and the reservation count of all *midhops*, the total load P is distributed such that nodes already in use or reserved for future use are successfully avoided. The nodes in the upper and lower diagonal region also keep updating their local access count as and when they are used for routing.

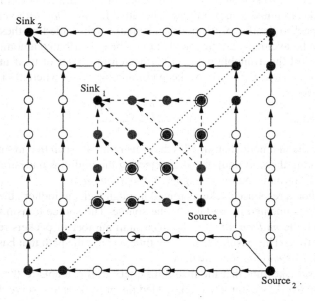

Fig. 2. Queries q_1 and q_2 injected at $Sink_1$ and $Sink_2$ respectively such that the *query region* Q_1 is a subset of the *query region* Q_2. the dashed arrows and the solid arrows show the multiple paths taken by $Source_1$ and $Source_2$ to route the query responses to $Sink_1$ and $Sink_2$ respectively.

The order of injection of the queries affects the ability of our protocol to adapt the incoming traffic to the existing traffic in the network. As long as the query region of any query q_1, already existing in the network is a subset of the query region of any freshly injected query q_2, our protocol reroutes the traffic of the incoming query q_2 along the multiple paths available to q_2, but not common with the multiple paths available to q_1. We are investigating the development of a feedback mechanism in the present scheme to achieve load distribution in the network irrespective of the order in which the queries are injected.

Even though we make sure that different *midhops* are used for routing at different times, there is no guarantee that load is evenly distributed among nodes belonging to the upper and lower diagonal region, primarily because all available paths are not disjoint. We therefore use local energy awareness to route query responses in the upper and lower triangle region. Local energy awareness is same as the energy metric used in protocol GEAR [15] where an intermediate node forwards the packet to the neighbor with least local access count (maximum residual energy) to ensure even load distribution in a neighborhood. Forwarding the packet to the neighboring node that is closer to the destination than itself, ensures that loops are not formed in the network.

4.4   Salient Features of the Protocol

- We successfully eliminate the route discovery phase which involves flooding of the entire network.
- We eliminate the maintenance overhead of exchanging periodic updates to know the availability of the alternate paths, hence the temporal accuracy of the multiple paths is independent of the frequency of the updates exchanged.
- We use limited caching as we do not store the entire sequence of nodes present on each alternate path. Besides the list of *midhops* representing the multiple paths is present only at the source, and not at every intermediate node on the multiple routes.

5   Performance Evaluation

We have simulated a sensor network with utilization as a non-decreasing function of the traffic load. The simulations are carried out using the NS-2 network simulator. We simulate a network of 289 nodes in a square area of 500m x 500m, where the transmission range of a sensor node is 40m. We used the 802.11 medium access layer to conduct our simulations. We use the fact that energy consumption of a node is proportional to the number of packets transmitted or received by it, in choosing node utilization as our primary metric to evaluate the performance of the proposed protocol. For all the experiments we have assumed that a node runs out of its battery after 10000 data transmissions or receptions unless otherwise specified.

We compare the performance of our protocol with the minimum energy or the shortest path protocol under two deployment strategies for the placement of sensor nodes in the sensor field; the regular grid deployment and uniformly distributed random deployment of nodes.

5.1   Regular Grid Deployment

Here the nodes are placed in a two dimensional grid of size 500m x 500m. Any node can wirelessly communicate with its eight one-hop neighbors. We have separately evaluated the performance of the proposed routing protocol in presence of a single query traffic and in presence of traffic generated by multiple queries. In both the cases, the nature of traffic is non uniform.

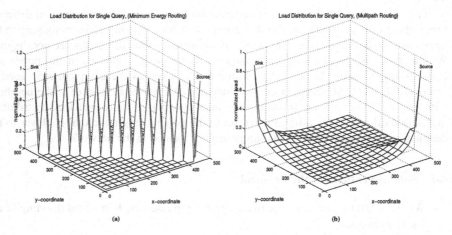

(a)   (b)

Fig. 3. Comparison of load distribution obtained by (a) Minimum Energy Routing with that obtained by (b) Multipath Routing. 5000 query response packets were generated at the Source node [462,14] and routed to the Sink node [14,462] in the network of size 500m X 500m where the total number of nodes are 289. A node's location node [i,j] in the two dimensional sensor network grid is plotted as a point in the x-y plane. The vertical axes represents the number of packets carried by node [i,j].

Single Query Traffic. Fig. 3 shows the comparison of load distribution achieved by the proposed multipath routing protocol with that achieved by minimum energy routing protocol in presence of a single query in the network. A single query is injected at the sink located at one corner of the entire sensor network grid, and the query responses are repeatedly generated by a source situated on the diagonally opposite corner of the grid with respect to the sink as shown in Fig. 3. The effective *query region* for this case is the entire sensor network. The traffic is non uniform in this case because its not originating equally in all parts of the network. Fig. 3 shows that minimum energy routing always selects the nodes lying on the shortest path connecting the source to the sink, hence we observe peaks along the diagonal connecting the source to the sink and the rest of the network remains unutilized. A high utilization of nodes on the shortest path will eventually deplete their energy, partitioning the network along the diagonal. On the other hand, multipath routing shows that most of the nodes in the network share equal routing load. Nodes closer to the source and the sink carry more packets than the rest of the nodes due to reasons explained before in Section 4.1 .

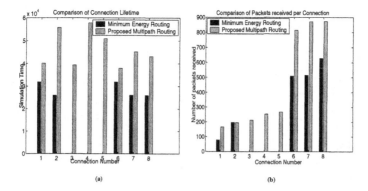

Fig. 4. The above figure shows the improvement in the connection life time and number of packets delivered by eight random connections in the network obtained by the proposed multipath routing over minimum energy routing. The bar graph on connection lifetime (a) shows the time at which the last packet has been received by each of eight connections before the connections expired. The bar graph (b) shows the total number of packets received by a connection before it expires.

Multiple Query Traffic. In this section we discuss the simulation results obtained for random traffic conditions created by multiple queries. We have simulated eight random connections (source sink pairs) in the network which generate traffic for random durations. For this experiment we assumed that a node dies after carrying out 500 data transmissions or receptions. The bar graph on connection lifetime in Fig. 4(a) shows that our scheme improves the lifetime of every individual connection in the network. The total number of packets delivered by any connection before it fails in case of multipath routing are also more or comparable to those delivered by the same connection when minimum energy routing is simulated. This is evident from the bar graph on packets received per connection in Fig. 4(b).

We observe from Fig. 4(b) that some connections in the network are not able to deliver even a single packet in case of minimum energy routing. This is because the shortest path route of those connections was overlapping with the existing connections in the network. Thus, most of the nodes lying on those connections have already been drained out of their energy, causing disconnectivity in the network. On the other hand, we do observe some finite throughput for every connection when multipath routing is used, because we have successfully delayed node failure, improving the overall capacity of the network to route packets.

For the same simulation environment we found out the improvement in overall network life time achieved by multipath routing over minimum energy routing. We varied the location of the source sink pairs in the network, the amount of traffic generated by each source and the time at which a connection became active. We have assumed the lifetime of the network to be the time at which the first node in the network dies due to battery outage. It was found that on an average, a 50% improvement in network lifetime was obtained by the proposed multipath routing over minimum energy routing for the traffic conditions described above.

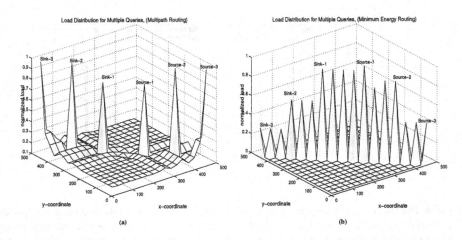

Fig. 5. Comparison of load distribution obtained by (a) Minimum Energy Routing with that obtained by (b) Multipath Routing in presence of three connections. The query responses at $Source_1$ meant for $Sink_1$ are generated first, followed by the query responses generated by $Source_2$ for $Sink_2$, and finally by $Source_3$, for $Sink_3$ respectively. A node's location node[i,j] in the two dimensional sensor network grid is plotted as a point in the x-y plane representing a network of size 500m X 500m. The vertical axes represents the number of packets carried by node[i,j].

Fig. 5 shows simulation results for three connections in the network such that all the three source sink pairs are situated on one of the diagonals of the entire grid. The objective is to show that our traffic scheduling algorithm effectively redistributes the traffic when the *query regions* belonging to different queries overlap, such that some or all of their *midhops* are common with each other, as shown in the diagram in Fig. 2.

When the query q_1 is injected at $Sink_1$, its load is evenly distributed on all nodes in its *query region*. Later when q_2 is injected in the network at $sink_2$, some of its *midhops* are already serving q_1, therefore the rest of the *midhops* are assigned most of the load. Similarly q_3 assigns load to its *midhops* in such a way that it adapts to the existing traffic generated by q_1 and q_2.

In Fig. 5(a) we observe that we are able to split the traffic belonging to the three overlapping queries such that the utilization of all the nodes can be as uniform as possible. Although ulitilization of every node in the network is not exactly the same at any time, we have belts or regions in the network with almost the same utilization, helping the network to collapse gracefully. Fig. 5(b) showing higher peaks or utilization for nodes common to more than one connection when minimum energy routing is simulated. This leads to faster energy depletion of nodes common to the multiple connections. The failure of the nodes in the center of the network limits the life of the network.

5.2   Random Deployment of Nodes

In this section we show simulation results for a random deployment of nodes where the nodes are dispersed with a uniform distribution within the field. There are a total number

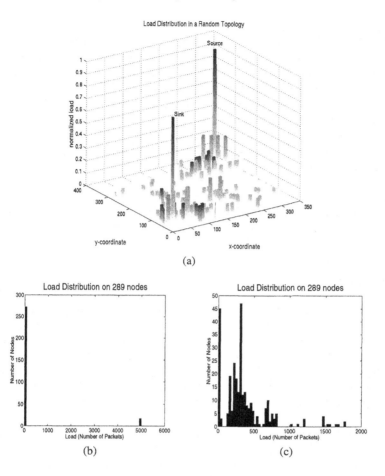

(a)

(b)   (c)

Fig. 6. Load distribution obtained in a network with random distribution of nodes by using the proposed multipath routing is shown in (a). A point in the x-y plane represents the location of a node [i,j] in a sensor field of area 500m X 500m. The total number of nodes is 289. The vertical axis represents the number of packets carried by a node [i,j]. 5000 query response packets were generated at the Source node [342,320] and routed to the Sink node [12,6], where the Source and the Sink are separated by a distance equal to the network diameter. The histogram (b) shows the node utilization obtained by simulating minimum energy routing where most of the nodes are unutilized and the rest of the nodes have very high utilization of the order of 5000 packets. Histogram (c) shows the node utilization obtained by simulating the proposed multipath routing. Here most of the nodes transmit 200 to 600 packets, and there are very few nodes with zero load or very high load.

of 289 nodes in an area of 500m x 500m. We have generated a single query traffic such that the source and the sink are separated by a distance equal to the network diameter as shown in Fig. 6(a).

In such a topology, the number of neighbors of any node is not fixed, therefore the degree of load splitting at every node is different. Unlike a regular topology of nodes, the *midhops* are not equally spaced out in a random topology of nodes. Both these factors make it infeasible to have equal load assignment to every part of the *query region*. Fig. 6(a) shows that we are able to assign load to majority of the nodes in the network, spreading the traffic over approximately the entire sensor network area, with nodes closer to source and the sink being utilized more.

In [10], Srivastava *et. al.* describe the desirable energy histogram as the one, where nodes burn their energy in a more equitable way for the same total energy consumption in the network. The node utilization histogram in Fig. 6(b) shows that our scheme not only distributes the traffic over more number of nodes, the total number of packets carried by these nodes at any time is also similar. Whereas the histogram for minimum energy routing Fig. 6(c) shows wide disparity in the utilization of the various nodes. Most of the nodes are not utilized at all while the rest of the nodes are almost depleted of their energy.

6   Conclusion

We use a localized algorithm with low computational and communication overhead for the construction of alternate paths in our proposed multipath routing protocol. Our protocol ensures that the energy of the nodes is consumed in proportion to their available energy. Besides having a longer lifetime for individual node, we also achieve almost uniform energy depletion by achieving even loading of nodes lying on the possible routes connecting the source to the sink. But, we cannot guarantee the lowest response time by our protocol as we do not control the optimality of the individual path selected for routing.

At present, in our protocol the traffic generated by the queries that are injected later in the network is steered along paths that balance the load on nodes already being used for routing. For future work we would like to enhance our protocol by rerouting the existing traffic to accommodate the freshly generated traffic in the network, in cases where it is not feasible for the incoming traffic to adapt to the current utilization of nodes. Also for this work we assume all queries are equally critical, but in future we plan to extend this work to provide higher priority to queries which may be more time critical than the rest of the queries in the network.

References

1. Intanagonwiwat C., Govindan R., and Estrin D.: Directed Diffusion: A Scalable and Robust Communication Paradigm for Sensor Networks. In *Proceedings of the 6th Annual ACM/IEEE International Conference on Mobile Computing and Networking(MOBICOM)*, pp. 56–67, August 2000.
2. Heinzelman W., Chandrakasan A., and Balakrishnan H.:, Energy-Efficient Communication Protocols for Wireless Microsensor Networks. In *Proceedings Hawaaian International Conference on Systems Science*, January 2000.
3. Chang J. and Tassiulas L.: Energy Conserving Routing in Wireless Ad-hoc Networks. *Proceedings of IEEE Infocom*, pp. 22–31, 2000.

4. Chang J. and Tassiulas L.: Maximum Lifetime Routing in Wireless Sensor Networks. In *Proceedings of Advanced Telecommunications and Information Distribution Research Program*, 2000.
5. Suzuki H. and Tobagi F. A.: Fast Bandwidth Reservation Scheme with Multi link & Multi path routing in ATM networks. In *Proceedings of IEEE Infocom*, 1992.
6. Maxemchuk N.F.: Dispersity Routing in High-speed Networks. *Computer Networks and ISDN System 25*, pp. 645–661, 1993.
7. Nasipuri A. and Das S.: On-Demand Multipath Routing for Mobile Ad Hoc Networks. In *Proceedings of the 8th Annual IEEE International Conference on Computer Communications and Networks (ICCCN)*, pp. 64–70, October 1999.
8. Pearlman M. R., Hass Z. J., Sholander P., and Tabrizi S. S.: On the Impact of Alternate Path Routing for Load Balancing in Mobile Ad Hoc Networks. In *Proceeding of IEEE/ACM MobiHoc*, 2000.
9. Park V. D. and Corson M. S.: A Highly Distributed Routing Algorithm for Mobile Wireless Networks. In *Proceedings IEEE INFOCOM*, pp. 1405–1413, 1997.
10. Schurgers, C. and Srivastava, M. B.: Energy Efficient Routing in Wireless Sensor Networks. *MILCOM'01*, October 2001.
11. Ganesan D., Govindan R., Shenker S. and Estrin D.: Highly Resilient, Energy Efficient Multipath Routing in Wireless Sensor Networks. In *Mobile Computing and Communications Review (MC2R)*, Vol. 1, No. 2, 2002.
12. Shah R.C. and Rabaey, J.: Energy Aware Routing for Low Energy Ad Hoc Sensor Networks. *IEEE Wireless Communications and Networking Conference (WCNC)*, March 2002.
13. Servetto S. D. and Barrenechea G.: Constrained Random Walks on Random Graphs: Routing Algorithms for Large Scale Wireless Sensor Networks. *In Proceedings of the 1st ACM International Workshop on Wireless Sensor Networks and Applications*, pp. 12–21, September 2002.
14. Hill J., Szewczyk R., Woo A., Hollar S., Culler D., and Pister K.: System Architecture Directions for Network Sensors. In *Proceedings of the 9th International Conference on Architectural Support for Programming Languages and Operating Systems*, pp. 93–104, November 2000.
15. Yu Y.,Govindan R., and Estrin D.: Geographical and Energy Aware Routing: A Recursive Data Dissemination Protocol for Wireless Sensor Networks. *UCLA Computer Science Department Technical Report UCLA/CSD-TR-01-0023*, May 2001.
16. Ko Y. and Vaidya N.H.: Location-Aided Routing (LAR) Mobile Ad Hoc Networks. *MOBICOM'98*, October 1998.
17. Karp B. and Kung H.T.: GPSR: Greedy Perimeter Stateless Routing for Wireless Networks. In *Proceedings of ACM MOBICOM'00*, 2000.

Efficient and Fault-Tolerant Feature Extraction in Wireless Sensor Networks

Bhaskar Krishnamachari[1] and S. Sitharama Iyengar[2]

[1] Department of Electrical Engineering, University of Southern California,
Los Angeles, CA 90036, USA
bkrishna@usc.edu, http://ceng.usc.edu/~bkrishna/
[2] Department of Computer Science, Louisiana State University,
Baton Rouge, LA 70802, USA
iyengar@bit.csc.lsu.edu, http://bit.csc.lsu.edu/~iyengar/

Abstract. We consider a canonical task in wireless sensor networks –
the extraction of information about environmental features – and propose
a multi-step solution that is fault-tolerant, self-organizing and energy-
efficient. We explicitly take into account the possibility of sensor measurement faults and study a distributed algorithm for detecting and correcting such faults, showing through theoretical analysis and simulation
results that 85-95% of faults can be corrected using this algorithm even
when as many as 10% of the nodes are faulty. We present a self-organizing
algorithm which combines shortest-path routing mechanisms with leader-
election to permit nodes within each feature region to self-organize into
routing clusters. These clusters are used in data aggregation schemes
that we propose for feature extraction. We show that the best such aggregation scheme can result in an order-of-magnitude improvement in
energy savings.

1 Introduction

In general sensor networks can be tasked to answer any number of queries about
the environment [24]. We focus on one particular class of queries: determining
regions in the environment with a distinguishable, "feature" characteristic. As an
example, consider a network of devices that are capable of sensing concentrations
of some chemical X; an important query in this situation could be "Which regions
in the environment have a chemical concentration greater than λ units?" We will
refer to the process of getting answers to this type of query as *feature extraction*.

Feature extraction can be considered a canonical task in a sensor network.
While feature extraction is useful for static sensor networks, it should be pointed
out that it can also be used as a mechanism for non-uniform sensor deployment.
Information about the location of feature regions can be used to move or deploy
additional sensors to these regions in order to get finer-grained information.

Wireless sensor networks are often unattended, autonomous systems with
severe energy constraints and low-end individual nodes with limited reliability.
In such conditions, self-organizing, energy-efficient, fault-tolerant algorithms are

F. Zhao and L. Guibas (Eds.): IPSN 2003, LNCS 2634, pp. 488–501, 2003.

required for network operation. These design themes will guide the multi-step solution proposed in this paper to the problem of feature extraction.

It is helpful to treat the trivial centralized solution to the feature recognition problem first in order to understand the shortcomings of such an approach. We could have all nodes report their individual sensor measurements, along with their geographical location directly to a central monitoring node. The processing to determine the feature regions can then be performed centrally. While conceptually simple, this scheme does not scale well with the size of the network due to the communication bottlenecks and energy expenses associated with such a centralized scheme. Hence, we would like a solution in which the nodes in a feature region organize themselves and perform localized, in-network processing to determine the extent of the region. This is the approach we will take.

We can decompose the process of extracting features in a sensor network into multiple steps, as follows:

1. Determining feature readings: The sensors need to know what measurement constitutes a feature. Although some work has been done on systems that learn the normal conditions over time so that they can recognize unusual feature readings [33], we consider this issue beyond the scope of this paper. We will instead make the reasonable assumption that a threshold that enables nodes to determine whether their reading corresponds to a feature has been specified with the query, or otherwise made available to the nodes during deployment.

2. Disambiguating "features" from faulty sensor readings: A challenging task is to disambiguate features from faults in the sensor readings, since an unusually high reading could potentially correspond to both. Conversely, a faulty node may report a low measurement even though it is in a feature region. We will present in section 2 a probabilistic decoding mechanism that exploits the fact that sensor faults are likely to be stochastically uncorrelated, while features are likely to be spatially correlated. In analyzing these schemes, we will show that the impact of faults can be reduced by as much as 85-95% even for reasonably high fault rates.

3. Feature clustering: Once the sensors have determined that they do indeed belong to the feature region, we would like to have them self-organize into a cluster. In section 3 we propose a clustering algorithm that develops intra-cluster routing paths and elects a cluster head that would be responsible for collecting the data for the feature region and routing it to the central data sink.

4. Aggregation/Compression of feature information: Finally, a useful additional step would be to aggregate the data by compressing it in some manner. Sending such a compressed version would save energy resources. We discuss this issue in section 4. We will show that the best scheme, stepwise rectangular approximate aggregation (SRA), can result in order-of-magnitude energy savings.

We present the context for our results through a discussion of related work in section 5. Finally, we will present our conclusions in section 6.

2   Fault-Feature Disambiguation

Let the real situation at the sensor node be modelled by a binary variable T_i. This variable $T_i = 0$ if the ground truth is that the node is a normal region, and $T_i = 1$ if the ground truth is that the node is in a "feature" region. We map the real output of the sensor into an abstract binary variable S_i. This variable $S_i = 0$ if the sensor measurement indicates a normal value, and a $S_i = 1$ if it measures an unusual value.

There are thus four possible scenarios: $S_i = 0, T_i = 0$ (sensor correctly reports a normal reading), $S_i = 0, T_i = 1$ (sensor faultily reports a normal reading), $S_i = 1, T_i = 1$ (sensor correctly reports an unusual/feature reading), and $S_i = 1, T_i = 0$ (sensor faultily reports an unusual reading). While each node is aware of the value of S_i, in the presence of a significant probability of a faulty reading, it can happen that $S_i \neq T_i$. We describe below a Bayesian fault-recognition algorithm to determine an estimate R_i of the true reading T_i after obtaining information about the sensor readings of neighboring sensors.

We make one simplifying assumption: the sensor fault probability p is uncorrelated and symmetric. We also wish to model the spatial correlation of feature values. Let each node i have N neighbors (excluding itself). Let's say the evidence $E_i(a, k)$ is that k of the neighboring sensors report the same binary reading a as node i , while $N - k$ of them report the reading $\neg a$, then we can decode according to the following model for using the evidence, giving equal weight to the evidence from each neighbor : $P(R_i = a | E_i(a, k)) = \frac{k}{N}$.

Now, the task for each sensor is to determine a value for R_i given information about its own sensor reading S_i and the evidence $E_i(a, k)$ regarding the readings of its neighbors. The following Bayesian calculations provide the answer:

$$
\begin{aligned}
P_{aak} &= P(R_i = a | S_i = b, E_i(a, k)) \\
&= \frac{P(R_i = a, S_i = b | E_i(a, k))}{P(S_i = b | E_i(a, k))} \\
&= \frac{P(S_i = b | R_i = a)P(R_i = a | E_i(a, k))}{P(S_i = b | R_i = a)P(R_i = a | E_i(a, k)) + P(S_i = b | R_i = \neg a)P(R_i = \neg a | E_i(a, k))} \\
&\approx \frac{P(S_i = b | T_i = a)P(R_i = a | E_i(a, k))}{P(S_i = b | T_i = a)P(R_i = a | E_i(a, k)) + P(S_i = b | T_i = \neg a)P(R_i = \neg a | E_i(a, k))} \\
&= \frac{(1 - p)k}{(1 - p)k + p(N - k)}
\end{aligned}
\tag{1}
$$

Where the approximation follows from the fact that R_i is meant to be an estimate of T_i. Equation (1) shows the statistic with which the sensor node can now make a decision about whether or not to disregard its own sensor reading S_i in the face of the evidence $E_i(a, k)$ from its neighbors. Each node can then use a *threshold decision scheme*, which uses a threshold $0 < \Theta < 1$ as follows: if $P(R_i = a | S_i = a, E_i(a, k)) > \Theta$, then R_i is set to a, and the sensor believes that its sensor reading is correct. If the metric is less than the threshold, then node

i decides that its sensor reading is faulty and sets R_i to $\neg a$. It can be shown that the optimal threshold $\Theta = 1 - p$ corresponds to a median filter (i.e. a node assumes its reading is correct if and only if at least half of its neighbors also have the same value). Equation (1) can be used to obtain analytical expressions for the performance of this fault reduction mechanism.

In order to simplify the analysis of the Bayesian fault-recognition mechanisms, we will make the assumption that for all N neighbors of node i, the ground truth is the same. In other words, if node i is in a feature region, so are all its neighbors; and if i is not in a feature region, neither are any of its neighbors. This assumption is valid everywhere except at nodes which lie on the boundary of a feature region. For sensor networks with high density, this is a reasonable assumption as the number of such boundary nodes will be relatively small. We will first present results for the randomized decision scheme.

Let g_k be the probability that exactly k of node i's N neighbors are not faulty. This probability is the same irrespective of the value of T_i. This can be readily verified:

$$
\begin{aligned}
g_k &= \binom{N}{k} P(S_i = 0 | T_i = 0)^k P(S_i = 1 | T_i = 0)^{(N-k)} \\
&= \binom{N}{k} P(S_i = 1 | T_i = 1)^k P(S_i = 0 | T_i = 0)^{(N-k)} \\
&= \binom{N}{k} (1 - p)^k p^{(N-k)}
\end{aligned}
\tag{2}
$$

For the optimal decision threshold scheme it can be shown (details omitted for brevity) that

$$
P(R_i = a | S_i = a, T_i = a) = \sum_{k=k_{min}}^{N} g_k
\tag{3}
$$

$$
P(R_i = \neg a | S_i = \neg a, T_i = a) = \sum_{k=k_{min}}^{N} g_{N-k}
\tag{4}
$$

The average number of errors after decoding α can then be described by the following expression:

$$
\alpha = \left(1 - \sum_{k=0.5N}^{N} (g_k - g_{N-k})\right) n
\tag{5}
$$

The best policy for each node (in terms of minimizing α, the average number of errors after decoding) is to accept its own sensor reading if and only if at least half of its neighbors have the same reading. This is an intuitive result, following from the equal-weight evidence model that we are using (equation (2)). This means that the sensor nodes can perform an optimal decision without

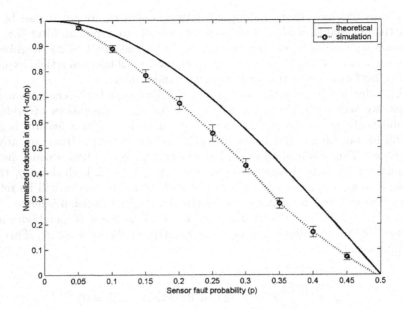

Fig. 1. Normalized reduction in average number of sensor faults for the optimal threshold decision scheme

even having to estimate the value of p. This makes the optimal-threshold decision scheme a very feasible mechanism for minimizing the effect of uncorrelated sensor faults. Figure 1 shows how the optimal threshold scheme results in a significant reduction in the average number of sensor faults. It shows that the impact of faults can be reduced by as much as 85-95% even for fault rates of 10%.

3   Feature Cluster Formation

Once the feature nodes have been identified by the fault-recognition algorithm, we would like to have these nodes self-organize into clusters and elect cluster heads to enable local information processing. We propose to achieve this by combining a distributed election leader algorithm [5] with a distance-vector routing [6] mechanism. The combination is an algorithm in which the immediate neighbors of the leader get the correct information first, then the neighbors of these neighbors, and so on until all nodes within the cluster obtain a path to the same cluster leader. We now give details of this clustering algorithm.

Only nodes which have a feature reading participate in this mechanism. As with most leader election algorithms, it is assumed that each node i within the cluster has a unique ID value ID_i that can be used to determine the cluster head (typically the lowest ID number node is elected, though this can be modified for some other metric easily). One useful way in which unique ID's can be chosen is to base their value on the geographical location of the nodes, particularly on their distance to the central monitoring node. This is likely to result in the cluster head being close to the data sink.

Each node i maintains a 3-tuple (LID_i, K_i, NH_i). The field LID_i is the lowest ID number seen to date by node i; K_i is the number of hops from i to the node with lowest ID; and NH_i is the next hop from i towards the lowest ID node. Initially, for all i, $LID_i = ID_i, K_i = 0$ and the NH_i field is left blank. As the algorithm proceeds, messages are exchanged with nearest neighbors - each node updates its information to reflect the lowest ID number seen to date, the number of hops to that node (which is one plus the value in the received message), and the next hop node (which is the node that delivers the message causing the update. This is similar to the the minimum spanning tree algorithm, and the basic distance vector algorithm used for building routing tables. The algorithm can be performed in a semi-synchronous manner. A node only sends messages when it has updated its own information previously.

If all nodes are at most distance D from the leader node l, all nodes will have their entries frozen in at most D steps, at which point the algorithm terminates. Further, since each node only issues at most one message in each round, no node issues more than D messages.

At the conclusion of this cluster formation mechanism we have a spanning tree incorporating all participating nodes whereby each node can pass information on to the leader/cluster head (the node with the lowest ID). Figure 2 shows a snapshot from the simulator depicting the intra-cluster spanning tree and election of cluster head in the feature region for our sample scenario.

Note the distributed, self-organizing, nature of the entire process - no central commands need to be issued to determine the cluster head for each region and to perform the intra-cluster routing setup. The entire process can be triggered automatically when the feature readings are determined. The algorithm is highly robust to the addition of new nodes to the feature region: any new node i initially advertises its tuple to be $(i, 0, -)$, and the neighbors of this node which are in the feature region would respond by with their current values. If the new node is not going to be the new cluster leader (because its ID number is not low enough), then no additional messages need to be exchanged. If the new node should be the cluster leader, then the clustering algorithm starts afresh in the entire region. It is assumed that complete node failures are rare in the network, but it should be noted that some form of refresh mechanism is required to ensure that the intra-cluster routing information does not become stale. Another approach could be the use of link reversal mechanisms to deal with such failures in the presence of extreme dynamics [34]. Finally, we note that the clustering algorithm can be conducted in parallel throughout the network, resulting in the formation of multiple independent clusters simultaneously in separate feature regions.

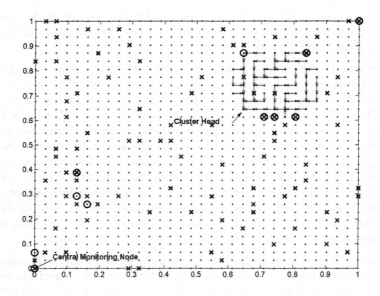

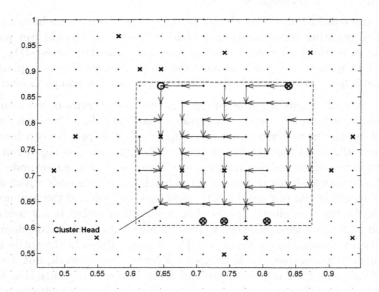

Fig. 2. A simulator snapshot depicting the intra-cluster routing tree within the feature region along with the elected cluster head. The dashed rectangle on the bottom represents the rectangular approximation of the feature region that can be represented compactly. Note that the rectangular approximation is highly robust to faults and decoding errors of nodes on the border of the feature region.

4   Compact Feature Extraction

The central monitoring node may query for the location of the critical event feature region(s), the readings of each individual node in the feature region, or the min/max/average reading in the feature region. Different forms of aggregation may be suitable depending on the query. We focus on the location query. This query says "describe the location of the feature region." The first thing to note is that this is a query that lends itself to both exact and inexact answers. On the one hand we can report the full detailed information of the locations of the nodes in the feature region; on the other hand we can give an approximate parametric description that loosely describes a geometric shape containing all nodes in the feature region.

Let us assume that each node knows the x and y-coordinates for its own location. We also assume that all packets have a fixed header size H, and use B bits to represent each coordinate of a location. Let k refer to the total number of sources, i.e. nodes in the feature region, d the distance in hops from the cluster-head to the sink, and d_i, the shortest distance between the cluster-head and the ith node in the feature region. The following are some aggregation options that can be pursued:

No Aggregation (NA): If no aggregation mechanism is employed, the energy cost of this scheme in terms of the total number of bits transmitted in this case will be $\lambda_{NA} = (2B + H)(kd + \sum d_i)$.

Header Aggregation (HA): In this scheme, all nodes in the feature region send their location information in separate packets through the intra-cluster routing tree to the cluster-head which then combines these without modification into one large packet. The number of bits transmitted, $\lambda_{HA} = 2B(kd + \sum d_i) + H(d + \sum d_i)$.

Header Aggregation with Lossless Compression (HAC): An additional level of savings can be obtained in the header aggregation scheme, if the cluster-head compresses the information it obtains from all nodes in the feature region by a factor of $\rho \leq 1$ before sending it on. The number of bits transmitted, $\lambda_{HAC} = 2B(kd\rho + \sum d_i) + H(d + \sum d_i)$.

Rectangular Approximate Aggregation (RA): If it suffices to know the approximate location and extent of the feature region, significant reduction can be obtained by combining the information into a geometric shape such as the rectangle which contains the nodes in the feature region. The cluster-head collects (x,y) coordinates for all such nodes, and sends the 3-tuple $[XMIN, YMIN, DIAG]$ (which suffices to reconstruct the enclosing rectangle) on to the central monitoring node. The number of bits transmitted, $\lambda_{RA} = 2B \sum d_i + 3Bd + H(d + \sum d_i)$.

Circular Approximate Aggregation (CA): This scheme is similar to the rectangular approximate aggregation, except that the cluster-head instead computes the center and radius of the smallest circle which encloses all nodes in the feature region, represented as the 3-tuple $[XMID, YMID, RADIUS]$. The number of bits transmitted, $\lambda_{CA} = 2B \sum d_i + 3Bd + H(d + \sum d_i)$.

Step-wise Rectangular Aggregation (SRA): If we permit each node within the cluster to aggregate the information coming from all downstream nodes, we can get further gains with the rectangular aggregation scheme. The number of bits transmitted, $\lambda_{SRA} = 3B(k+d-1) + H(d+\sum d_i)$. It is important to note that the final information obtained by the central monitoring node is the same in the case of RA as well as SRA aggregation schemes – the coordinates of the smallest rectangle enclosing the feature nodes.

Step-wise Circular Aggregation (SCA): This scheme is similar to the SRA. Each node sends the 3-tuple $[XMID, YMID, RADIUS]$ upstream. This tuple is used to describe the center and radius of the smallest circular region that includes the intersection of the circular regions of its descendant nodes as well as its own location. The number of bits transmitted, $\lambda_{SCA} = 3B(k + d - 1) + H(d + \sum d_i)$.

Table 1. Comparison of various aggregation schemes for sample simulated scenario

Scheme	Bits Used	Savings	Response Quality
No aggregation (NA)	221544	0%	Exact
Header Aggregation (HA)	117544	46.9 %	Exact
HA with Compression (HAC)	100648	54.6 %	Exact
Rectangular Aggregation (RA)	34984	84.2 %	Tight rect. approximation
Circular Aggregation (CA)	34984	84.2%	Tight circ. approximation
Stepwise Rect. Aggregation (SRA)	9240	95.8%	Tight rect. approximation
Stepwise Circ. Aggregation (SCA)	9240	95.8%	Loose circ. approximation

Table 1 shows a comparison of the above schemes on a sample simulation scenario. In this simulation the values for the size parameters were $H = 40$ and $B = 16$. For HAC, the compression ratio was set to a typical value of $\rho = 0.8$. The number of nodes in the cluster is $k = 66$, the distance between the cluster-head and the central monitoring node is $d = 40$, and the sum of the intra-cluster distances was evaluated to be $\sum d_i = 437$. We can see that since the header size is comparable to the size of the data contents, even header aggregation can reduce the energy costs by nearly half in this case. As noted before, the first three schemes all provide exact information about the location of each individual node, while the remaining schemes provide some form of approximation. Both the RA and CA schemes result in nearly 85% energy savings in this scenario, the additional gains coming chiefly due to the reduction of data being sent from from the cluster-head to the central monitoring node. Both approximations are tight, in the sense that they provide the coordinates of the minimum enclosing rectangle and circle respectively. For applications where the feature is likely to be approximately circular in shape (for example if the chemical concentrations in the environment diffuse uniformly in all directions), the circular approximation may be closer to the real situation. However, when we consider the two step-wise approximate aggregation schemes, the SRA scheme is better since it still provides the minimal enclosing rectangle with significant savings (95% in this scenario), whereas the SCA scheme (which incurs the same costs) can result in a loose overestimate of the region containing all the nodes. Overall, we can conclude the SRA scheme is a robust, reasonably tight approximate aggregation algorithm which provides the most energy gains for this application.

It's also insightful to look at the limiting behavior of the energy gains. An upper-bound on the energy gains is obtained if we let d tend to infinity (when the feature region is really far away from the central monitoring node).

Theorem 1. *If $max(d_i)$ and k are fixed then*

$$\lim_{d \to \infty} 1 - \frac{\lambda_{SRA}}{\lambda_{NA}} = 1 - \frac{(3B + H)}{(2B + H)k} \tag{6}$$

Proof: From the expressions for costs of NA and SRA schemes, we get that

$$\frac{\lambda_{SRA}}{\lambda_{NA}} = \frac{3B(k + d - 1) + H(d + \sum d_i)}{(2B + H)(kd + \sum d_i)} \tag{7}$$

$$\Rightarrow \lim_{d \to \infty} \frac{\lambda_{SRA}}{\lambda_{NA}} = \frac{(3B + H)d + 3B(k - 1) + H\sum d_i}{(2B + H)kd + (2B + H)\sum d_i} \tag{8}$$

$$\Rightarrow \lim_{d \to \infty} \frac{\lambda_{SRA}}{\lambda_{NA}} = \frac{(3B + H)d + o(1)}{(2B + H)kd + o(1)} \tag{9}$$

$$\Rightarrow \lim_{d \to \infty} 1 - \frac{\lambda_{SRA}}{\lambda_{NA}} = 1 - \frac{(3B + H)}{(2B + H)k} \tag{10}$$

$\square$

Theorem 1 represents an upper bound on the gains that can be obtained with SRA. For the sample scenario that we studied, if we let $d \to \infty$, we get a gain of $(1 - 88/(72 \cdot 66))100 = 98.2\%$, which is close to the 95.8% achieved in the simulation for $d = 40$.

The above schemes can be generalized for other queries sent to the feature nodes. For detailed and exact information such as IDs or readings of all nodes in the feature region, approximate schemes are invalid. Thus the HA and HAC schemes are the most appropiate. For queries which require a single number to be sent back, such as query asking for the min/max/average feature reading, a suitable approach is to perform in-cluster aggregation. The information could either be aggregated at the cluster-head after receiving all inputs directly from each node in the cluster, or in a stepwise manner throughout the cluster. The cluster-head then sends this single number on to the central monitoring node. The energy gains through these schemes would be quite comparable to those obtained for the feature-location query with the RA and SRA schemes, respectively.

5   Related Work

Self-configuration and self-organizing mechanisms are needed in sensor networks because of the requirement of unattended operation in uncertain, dynamic environments. Some attention has been given to developing localized, distributed, self-configuration mechanisms in sensor networks [9], [21] and studying conditions under which they are feasible [25].

Sensor networks are characterized by severe energy constraints because the nodes will often operate with finite battery resources and limited recharging. The energy concerns can be addressed by engineering design at all layers. Some of the energy concerns are being addressed at the hardware and architecture level [14], [22], [26]. At the physical layer, there is now a significant body of work on minimizing energy costs by adjusting the transmit powers of nodes while achieving global network properties such as connectivity [27], [28]. At the link layer, some of the work has focused on energy-efficient medium access schemes suitable for sensor networks [10], [16], [31]. At the networking layer, meta-naming of data and data-aggregation during routing has been proposed and analyzed as a significant means for energy savings [1], [7], [8], [12], [13]. At the application layer, it has been recognized that energy savings can be obtained by pushing computation within the network in the form of localized and distributed algorithms [2], [23], [24].

One of the main advantages of the distributed computing paradigm is that it adds a new dimension of robustness and reliability to computing. Computations done by clusters of independent processors need not be sensitive to the failure of a small portion of the network. Wireless sensor networks are an example of large scale distributed computing systems where fault-tolerance is important. For large scale sensor networks to be economically feasible, the individual nodes necessarily have to be low-end inexpensive devices. Such devices are likely to exhibit unreliable behavior. Therefore it's important to guarantee that faulty behavior of individual components does not affect the overall system behavior. Some of the early work in the area of distributed sensor networks focuses on reliable routing with arbitrary network topologies [18], [19], characterizing sensor fault modalities [3], [4], tolerating faults while performing sensor integration [20], and tolerating faults while ensuring sensor coverage [17]. A mechanism for detecting crash faults in wireless sensor networks is described in [29]. There has been little prior work in the literature on detecting and correcting faults in sensor measurements in an application-specific context.

6   Conclusions

With recent advances in technology it has become feasible to consider the deployment of large-scale wireless sensor networks that can provide high-quality environmental monitoring for a range of applications. In this paper we developed a multi-stage solution to a canonical task in such networks – the extraction of information about regions in the environment with identifiable features.

In such networks involving thousands of unattended, low-cost, low-capability devices, reliability, self-organization, and energy-efficiency are paramount concerns. Our solution addresses all these concerns, and illustrates design principles for this emerging space of application-specific networks.

One of the most difficult challenge is that of distinguishing between faulty sensor measurements and unusual environmental conditions. To our knowledge, this is the first paper to propose a solution to the fault-feature disambiguation problem in sensor networks. Our proposed solution, in the form of a Bayesian fault-recognition algorithm, exploits the notion that measurement errors due to faulty equipment are likely to be uncorrelated, while environmental conditions are spatially correlated.

We presented the Bayesian threshold decision scheme and showed an analytical expressions for its performance. Our analysis showed that the threshold decision scheme has good performance in terms of the minimization of errors. The proposed algorithm has the additional advantage of being completely distributed and localized - each node only needs to obtain information from neighboring sensors in order to make its decisions. The theoretical and simulation results show that with the optimal threshold decision scheme, faults can be reduced by as much as 85 to 95% for fault rates as high as 10%.

We then presented a distributed mechanism for nodes in a feature region to self-organize into a cluster. The proposed mechanism combines shortest-path routing techniques with a leader-election mechanism. The final result of the clustering algorithm is the election of a cluster-head and the formation of a minimum spanning tree connecting all the other nodes to the cluster-head.

This cluster is then used as a precursor for in-network processing when information about the feature region is extracted back to the central monitoring node. We presented and analyzed a number of distinct data-aggregation mechanisms that provide energy savings by the elimination of redundant information. We showed that one of these, the stepwise rectangular approximation scheme (SRA) has the advantage of being robust to boundary-errors in the fault recognition algorithm, providing a tight approximation of the feature region, and resulting in order-of-magnitude savings in energy costs. For the simulated scenario, for example, this saving was over 95%.

There are a number of directions in which this work can be extended. The most promising is the extension of our work on fault-recognition and fault-tolerance in sensor networks. We have dealt with a binary fault-feature disambiguation problem here. This could be generalized to the correction of real-valued sensor measurement errors: nodes in a sensor network should be able to exploit the spatial correlation of environmental readings to correct for the noise in their readings. Another related direction is to consider dynamic sensor faults where the same nodes need not always be faulty. Much of the work presented here can also be easily extended to dynamic feature recognition to deal with environmental phenomena that change location or shape over time. We would also like to see the algorithms proposed in this paper implemented and validated on real sensor network hardware in the near future.

References

1. C. Intanagonwiwat, R. Govindan and D. Estrin, "Directed Diffusion: A Scalable and Robust Communication Paradigm for Sensor Networks," *ACM/IEEE International Conference on Mobile Computing and Networks (MobiCom 2000)*, August 2000, Boston, Massachusetts
2. D. Estrin, R. Govindan, J. Heidemann and S. Kumar, "Next Century Challenges: Scalable Coordination in Sensor Networks," *ACM/IEEE International Conference on Mobile Computing and Networks (MobiCom '99)*, Seattle, Washington, August 1999.
3. K. Marzullo, "Implementing fault-tolerant sensors," TR89-997, Dept. of Computer Science, Cornell University, may 1989.
4. L. Prasad, S. S. Iyengar, R. L. Kashyap, and R. N. Madan, "Functional Characterization of Fault Tolerant Interation in Disributed Sensor Networks," *IEEE Transactions on Systems, Man, and Cybernetics*, Vol. 21, No. 5, September/October 1991.
5. N. Lynch, *Distributed Algorithms.*
6. B.A. Forouzan, *Data Communications and Networking*, McGraw Hill, 2001.
7. B. Krishnamachari, D. Estrin, and S. Wicker, "Impact of Data Aggregation in Wireless Sensor Networks," *International Workshop on Distributed Event Based Systems, DEBS'02*, July 2002.
8. S. Madden, R. Szewczyk, M. Franklin, and D. Culler, "Supporting Aggregate Queries over Ad-Hoc Wireless Sensor Networks," *IEEE Workshop on Mobile Computing Systems and Applications*, 2002.
9. A. Cerpa and D. Estrin, "ASCENT: Adaptive Self-Configuring sEnsor Networks Topologies," *INFOCOM*, 2002.
10. Seong-Hwan Cho and A. Chandrakasan, "Energy Efficient Protocols for Low Duty Cycle Wireless Microsensor Networks", *ICASSP 2001*, May 2001.
11. J. Heidemann, F. Silva, C. Intanagonwiwat, R. Govindan, D. Estrin, and D. Ganesan, "Building Efficient Wireless Sensor Networks with Low-Level Naming," *18th ACM Symposium on Operating Systems Principles*, October 21–24, 2001.
12. W.R. Heinzelman, J. Kulik, and H. Balakrishnan "Adaptive Protocols for Information Dissemination in Wireless Sensor Networks," *Proceedings of the Fifth Annual ACM/IEEE International Conference on Mobile Computing and Networking (MobiCom '99)*, Seattle, Washington, August 15–20, 1999, pp. 174–185.
13. W.R. Heinzelman, A. Chandrakasan, and H. Balakrishnan "Energy-Efficient Communication Protocol for Wireless Microsensor Networks," *33rd International Conference on System Sciences (HICSS '00)*, January 2000.
14. J. M. Kahn, R. H. Katz and K. S. J. Pister, "Mobile Networking for Smart Dust", *ACM/IEEE International Conference on Mobile Computing and Networking (MobiCom 99)*, Seattle, WA, August 17–19, 1999
15. Rex Min, Manish Bhardwaj, Seong-Hwan Cho, Amit Sinha, Eugene Shih, Alice Wang, and Anantha Chandrakasan, "Low-Power Wireless Sensor Networks", *VLSI Design 2000*, January 2001.
16. A. Woo and D.E. Culler, "A Transmission Control Scheme for Media Access in Sensor Networks," *ACM/IEEE International Conference on Mobile Computing and Networks (MobiCom '01)*, July 2001, Rome, Italy.
17. K. Chakrabarty, S. S. Iyengar, H. Qi, E.C. Cho, "Grid Coverage of Surveillance and Target location in Distributed Sensor Networks" *To appear in IEEE Transaction on Computers*, May 2002.

18. S.S. Iyengar, M.B. Sharma, and R.L. Kashyap, "Information Routing and Reliability Issues in Distributed Sensor Networks" *IEEE Tran. on Signal Processing,* Vol.40, No.2, pp. 3012–3021, Dec. 1992.

19. S. S. Iyengar, D. N. Jayasimha, D. Nadig, "A Versatile Architecture for the Distributed Sensor Integration Problem," *IEEE Transactions on Computers,* Vol. 43, No. 2, February 1994.

20. L. Prasad, S. S. Iyengar, R. L. Rao, and R. L. Kashyap, "Fault-tolerant sensor integration using multiresolution decomposition," *Physical Review E,* Vol. 49, No. 4, April 1994.

21. K. Sohrabi, J. Gao, V. Ailawadhi, and G.J. Pottie, "Protocols for Self-Organization of a Wireless Sensor Network," *IEEE Personal Communications,* vol. 7, no. 5, pp. 16–27, October 2000.

22. G. Asada *et al.*, "Wireless Integrated Network Sensors: Low Power Systems on a Chip," *Proceedings of the 1998 European Solid State Circuits Conference.*

23. M. Chu, H. Haussecker, F. Zhao, "Scalable information-driven sensor querying and routing for ad hoc heterogeneous sensor networks." *International Journal on High Performance Computing Applications,* to appear, 2002.

24. P. Bonnet, J. E. Gehrke, and P. Seshadri, "Querying the Physical World," *IEEE Personal Communications,* Vol. 7, No. 5, October 2000.

25. B. Krishnamachari, R. Bejar, and S. B. Wicker, "Distributed Problem Solving and the Boundaries of Self-Configuration in Multi-hop Wireless Networks", Hawaii International Conference on System Sciences (HICSS-35), January 2002.

26. R. Min *et al.*, "An Architecture for a Power-Aware Distributed Microsensor Node", *IEEE Workshop on Signal Processing Systems (SiPS '00),* October 2000.

27. P. Gupta and P. R. Kumar, Critical power for asymptotic connectivity in wireless networks. *Stochastic Analysis, Control, Optimization and Applications: A Volume in Honor of W.H. Fleming, W.M. McEneaney, G. Yin, and Q. Zhang (Eds.),* Birkhauser, Boston, 1998.

28. B. Krishnamachari, R. Bejar, and S. B. Wicker, "Phase Transition Phenomena in Wireless Ad-Hoc Networks," *Symposium on Ad-Hoc Wireless Networks, Globecom 2001,* 2001.

29. S.Chessa, P.Santi, "Crash Faults Identification in Wireless Sensor Networks," to appear in *Computer Communications,* Vol. 25, No. 14, pp. 1273–1282, Sept. 2002.

30. D. Estrin *et al. Embedded, Everywhere: A Research Agenda for Networked Systems of Embedded Computers,* National Research Council Report, 2001.

31. W. Ye, J. Heidemann, and D. Estrin, "An Energy-Efficient MAC Protocol for Wireless Sensor Networks," *INFOCOM 2002,* New York, NY, USA, June, 2002.

32. N. Bulusu, J. Heidemann, and D. Estrin, "GPS-less Low Cost Outdoor Localization For Very Small Devices," *IEEE Personal Communications Magazine,* 7 (5), pp. 28–34, October, 2000

33. R. A. Maxion, "Toward diagnosis as an emergent behavior in a network ecosystem," in *Emergent Computation,* Ed. S. Forrest, MIT Press, 1991.

34. V. D. Park and M. S. Corson, "A Highly Adaptive Distributed Routing Algorithm for Mobile Wireless Networks," *INFOCOM 1997.*

35. N. Megiddo, Linear time algorithm for linear programming in R3 and related problems, SIAM J. Comput. 12(4) (1983) 759–776.

36. M.E. Dyer, Linear time algorithms for two and three-variable linear programs, SIAM J. Comput. 13(1) (1984) 31–45.

Event Detection Services Using Data Service Middleware in Distributed Sensor Networks

Shuoqi Li, Sang H. Son, and John A. Stankovic

Department of Computer Science, University of Virginia, USA
{sl7q, son, stankovic}@cs.virginia.edu

Abstract. This paper presents the Real-Time Event Detection Service which is a component of the Data Service Middleware (DSWare). DSWare provides data-centric and group-based services for sensor networks. The real-time event service includes unreliability of individual sensor reports, correlation among different sensor observations, and inherent real-time characteristics of events. The event service supports confidence functions which are designed based on data semantics, including relative importance of sub-events and historical patterns. When the failure rate is high, the event service enables partial detection of critical events to be reported in a timely manner. It can also be applied to differentiate between the occurrences of events and false alarms.

1 Introduction

Sensor networks are large-scale wireless networks that consist of numerous sensor and actuator nodes used to monitor and interact with physical environments [11][14]. From one perspective sensor networks are similar to distributed database systems. They store environmental data on distributed nodes and respond to aperiodic and long-lived periodic queries [7][15][20]. Data interest can be pre-registered to the sensor network so that the corresponding data is collected and transmitted only when needed. These specified interests are similar to views in traditional databases because they filter the data according to the application's data semantics and shield the overwhelming volume of raw data from applications [8][26].

Sensor networks also have inherent real-time properties. The environment that sensor networks interact with is usually dynamic and volatile. The sensor data usually has an absolute validity interval of time after which the data values may not be consistent with the real environment. Transmitting and processing "stale" data wastes communication resources and can result in wrong decisions based on the reported out-of-date data. Besides data freshness, often the data must also be sent to the destination by a deadline. To date, not much research has been performed on real-time data services in sensor networks.

Despite their similarity to conventional distributed real-time databases, sensor networks differ in the following important ways. First, individual sensors are small in size and have limited computing resources. They also must operate for

F. Zhao and L. Guibas (Eds.): IPSN 2003, LNCS 2634, pp. 502–517, 2003.

long periods of time in an unattended fashion. This makes power conservation an important concern in prolonging the lifetime of the system. In current sensor networks, the major source of power consumption is communication. To reduce unnecessary data transmission from each node, data collection and transmission in sensor networks are always initiated by subscriptions or queries. Second, any individual sensor is not reliable. Sensors can be damaged or die after consuming the battery. The wireless communication medium is also unreliable. Packets can collide or be lost. Because of these issues we must build trust on a group of sensor nodes instead of any single node. Previous research emphasizes reliable transmission of important data or control packets at the lower levels, but less emphasis is on the reliability on data semantics at the higher level [23]. Third, the large amount of sensed data produced in sensor networks necessitates in-network processing. If all raw data is sent to base stations for further processing, the volume and burstiness of the traffic may cause many collisions and contribute to significant power loss. To minimize unnecessary data transmission, intermediate nodes or nearby nodes work together to filter and aggregate data before the data arrives at the destination. Fourth, sensor networks can interact with the environment by both sensing and actuating. When certain conditions are met, actuators can initiate an action on the environment. Since such actions are difficult to undo, reducing false alarms is crucial in certain applications.

The remainder of this paper is organized as follows: In section 2, we present related work. In section 3, we present the design of Data Service Middleware (DSWare) and some major components of DSWare. DSWare is a specialized layer that integrates various real-time data services for sensor networks and provides a database-like abstraction to applications. In section 4 we then present a detailed description of the event detection mechanism. Event detection is one of the most important data services in sensor networks because it is a way to "dig" meaningful information out of the huge volume of data produced. It aims to find the "right data" at the "right place" and ensure the data is sent at the "right time". Event Detection Services in DSWare associate a confidence value with each decision it makes based on a pre-specified confidence function. It incorporates the unreliability of sensor behavior, the correlation among different factors, and reduces false alarms by utilizing data semantics. Section 5 presents the preliminary evaluation of the event detection mechanism. We conclude the paper in Section 6.

2 Related Work

There are many ongoing middleware research projects in the area of sensor networks, such as Cougar, Rutgers Dataman, SINA, SCADDS, Smart-msgs, and some virtual-machine-like designs [1][2][3][4][8][12][17][26]. COUGER and SINA are two typical data-centric middleware designs which have goals that are similar to our design goal of providing data services. In COUGER, sensor data is viewed as tables and query execution plans are developed and possibly optimized in this middleware. Our work on DSWare is more tailored to sensor networks, including supporting group-based decision, reliable data-centric storage, and implementing other approaches to improve the performance of real-time execution, reliability of aggregated results and reduction of communication. SINA is a cluster-based middleware design which focuses on the cooperation among sensors to conduct a task. Its extensive SQL-like primitives can be used to issue queries in sensor networks. However, it does not provide schemes to hide the faulty nature of both sensor operations and wireless communication. In SINA it is the application layer that must provide robustness and reliability for data services. In DSWare, the real-time scheduling component and built-in real-time features of other service components make DSWare more suitable than SINA for real-time applications in ad hoc wireless sensor networks.

Multisensor data fusion research focuses on solutions that fuse data from multiple sensors to provide more accurate estimation of the environment [16][22]. In mobile-agent-based data fusion approaches, software that aggregates sensor information are packed and dispatched as *mobile agents* to "hot" areas (e.g., the area where an event occurred) and work independently there. The software migrates among sensors in a cluster, collects observations, then infers the real situation [22]. This approach and our group-based approach both make use of consensus among a number of nearby sensors of the same type to increase the reliability of a single observation. The mobile-agent-based approach, however, leverages on the migration traffic of mobile agents and their appropriate processing at each sensor node in its routes. For instance, if a node in the route inserts wrong data or refuses to forward the mobile agents, the aggregation and subsequent analysis are untrustful. Our approach does not have such limitations: malfunctioning of individual nodes does not infect the entire group.

A fuzzy modelling approach is sometimes used for data fusion in sensor networks. It is used to model the uncertainty in sensor failures and faulty observations [25]. This approach is useful in modelling the sensor error rates due to equipment wear and aggregating local decisions from multiple sensors that measure the same type of data. Some optimal decision schemes focus on the fusion of asynchronously arriving decisions [10][24]. E. Bosse et. al. presented a modelling and simulation approach for a real-time algorithm in multi-source data fusion systems [9]. These data fusion schemes are suitable for increasing the accuracy of decisions, but require extensive computing resources. In our approach to event detection, the computation in fusion nodes is small.

Dempster-Shafer evidential theory is also applied to incorporate uncertainty into decisions in some sensor fusion research [21]. This scheme uses *Belief* and *Plausibility* functions to describe the reliability feature of each source and uses a normalized Dempster's combination rule to integrate decisions from different sources. Our *confidence function* is similar to Dempster-Shafer method except that we place the evidence in both temporal and spatial spectrums to take data real-time validity intervals and possible contexts into consideration.

3 Data Service Middleware (DSWare)

A data services middleware can avoid re-implementing the common data service part of various applications. We develop a Data Service Middleware (DSWare) Layer that exists between the application layer and the network layer. This middleware provides data service abstraction to applications, as depicted in Fig. 1. In this architecture, routing is separated from both DSWare and the network layer since the group management and scheduling components in DSWare can be used to enhance the power-awareness and real-time-awareness of routing protocols. Fig. 2 demonstrates the architecture of DSWare.

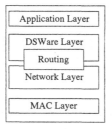

Fig. 1. Software Architecture in Sensor Networks

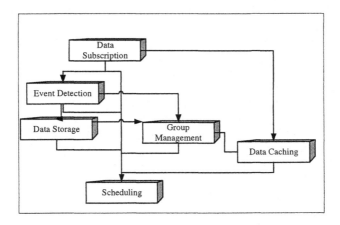

Fig. 2. Framework of DSWare

3.1 Data Storage

Data-centric storage is an implementation of a data storage service [23]. Data that describes different occurrences of some type of activity can be mapped to certain locations so that future queries for this type of data do not require being flooded to the whole network. The Data Storage Component in DSWare provides similar mechanisms to store information according to its semantics with efficient data lookup and supports more robustness during node failures. Correlated data can be stored in geographically adjacent regions to enable possible aggregation and in-network processing.

- Data Lookup
  We use two levels of hashing functions to map data to physical storage nodes. Each type of data has its unique identifier (e.g, the activity name string and the object's privilege profile) and it is used as key for the first level hashing function. The first level hash function maps the key to a logical storage node in the overlay network. At this level, storage nodes establish a hierarchy. In DSWare, we have one more hashing procedure to map a single logical node to multiple physical nodes. When a base station sends queries for this data, the information is fetched from one of these physical locations. Future designs need to consider how to map related data to geographically adjacent locations to promote data aggregation and in-network processing.
- Robustness
  Data stored in an individual node can be lost due to disaster, node damages, energy shortage, and other reasons. If we map a certain type of data to an individual node, when this activity occurs, lots of event data is sent to this node during a short period. The burst of traffic will lead to high collision and power consumption in the storage vicinity and indirectly decrease the reliability and availability of the storage node. In DSWare, data is replicated in multiple physical nodes that can be mapped to a single logical node. Queries are directed to any of these nodes to avoid high traffic collision and heavy load pushed on a single storage node. Load is balanced among the set of physical nodes and the lifetime of an individual node is prolonged. The consistency among these nodes is a key issue for a data storage component. To avoid peak time traffic, we choose "weak consistency" among the nodes. Most of the data on these nodes are identical except a small portion of the newest data. This new data is eventually propagated to the other peer nodes. The size of the portion of data that is inconsistent is bounded and nodes do the replication when their own work load is low.

3.2   Data Caching

The Data Caching Service provides multiple copies of the data most requested. This data is spread out over the routing path to reduce communication, increase availability and accelerate query execution [5]. It uses a simplified feedback control scheme to dynamically decide whether to place copies of the data around the frequently queried nodes.

There is a tradeoff between the query response time and maintenance overhead of data copies. A node can use the total number of queries routed through itself, the proportion of periodic queries, average response time from the data source, the number of copies that already exist in the neighborhood and other observations as inputs to the controller at a node and the controller determines whether to keep a copy. The data caching service in DSWare monitors current usages of the copies and determines whether to increase or reduce the number of copies and whether to move some copies to another location by exchanging information in the neighborhood.

3.3 Group Management

The Group Management component provides localized cooperation among sensor nodes to accomplish a more global objective. There are several reasons why group management is important. First, normally functioning sensors within a geographic area provide similar sensor values. A value that most nodes in a group agree on should have higher confidence, than a value that is in dispute or varies widely. Second, based on the similar observations by nearby sensors in a sufficiently dense area, we can recognize the nodes that keep reporting erroneous results. We may discard the suspicious nodes in later coordination and computations to provide more reliable measurement. Third, some tasks require cooperation of multiple sensors. Movement and speed approximations require more than one sensor to combine their observations to calculate the direction and velocity. Finally, when a region has adequate density of sensors, a portion of them can be put into sleep mode to save energy.

Based on the different reasons discussed above, there are different ways to formulate a group. For most tasks, groups are formed as the query is sent out and dissolved when the query is expired or the task is accomplished. In this case, the group formulation criterion is sent to the queried area first. Nodes decide whether to join this group by checking whether they match the criterion. Some groups are relatively stable after formulation, such as those measuring temperature. Some groups are more dynamic, such as the groups tracking the movement of a vehicle [6]. For a dynamic group, changed criterion is broadcast persistently in a small area whose center is the current group. Hence, nodes can join and leave the group when the target moves. There are other groups designed for geographically stable goals. These groups are not sensitive to tasks, so they can be formulated during system deployment or when explicitly specified by the applications. These groups are not necessary for the accomplishment of a task, but they have significant effects in reliability and reduction of energy consumption and communication.

3.4 Event Detection

In the event detection service, events are pre-registered according to the specific application. Event detection is a common and important service in sensor networks. We present a detailed protocol for event detection in section 4.

3.5   Data Subscription

As a type of data dissemination service, Data Subscription queries are very common in sensor networks. These queries have their own characteristics, including relatively fixed data feeding paths, stable traffic loads for nodes on the paths, and possible merges of multiple data feeding paths. For example, a base station embedded in a policeman's PDA sends a subscription request to the sensor network : "Show me the traffic status at the crossing of Ivy Road and Alderman Road and keep providing the traffic information every 3 minutes for the next two hours (query duration)." In this case, the base station subscribes to the data of node A for duration D (two hours) and rate R (1 per 3 minutes). When several base stations subscribe for the data from the same node at different rates, the Data Subscription Service places copies of the data at some intermediate nodes to minimize the total amount of communication. It changes the data feeding paths when necessary, as shown in Fig. 3.

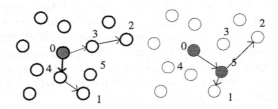

Fig. 3. When there are multiple subscribers (node 1 and node 2) for the data at node 0, the Data Subscription Service detects the proximity of the two paths and merges these two paths by placing a copy of the data at node 5 and lets node 5 send data to the two subscribers during each requesting interval.

3.6   Scheduling

The Scheduling component is a special component because it provides the scheduling service for all components in DSWare. Two most important scheduling options are energy-aware and real-time scheduling. By default, we apply a real-time scheduling mechanism (EDF, EDDF, with or without admission control) as the main scheduling scheme because most queries in sensor networks are inherently real-time tasks. We can also apply the energy-aware mechanism when we have already met the requirements of real-time scheduling. Applications can specify the actual scheduling schema in the sensor networks based on the most important concerns.

4   Event Detection Services

In this section, we present the event detection services of DSWare. We first discuss some of the key concepts of the event detection services, including event hierarchy, confidence, and time semantics, followed by implementation issues.

4.1   Event Hierarchy

An *observation* is the low-level output of a sensing device during a sensing interval. It is a measurement of the environment. An event is an activity that can be monitored or detected in the environment and is of interest to the application.

We group events into two different types: *atomic events* and *compound events*. An *atomic event* refers to an event that can be determined merely based on an observation of a sensor. Suppose we have registered the following events:

High temperature event represents the observation that the temperature is higher than a specified threshold.
Light event represents an occurrence of a sharp change in the light intensity.
Acoustic event represents the occurrence of an unusual sound matching a certain signature.
Explosion event might be defined as the three events above are reported in the same region within a specified time interval.

In this example, whether a high temperature event occurs or not can be determined from an observation of a single temperature sensor. Such event is an atomic event.

A *compound event* can not be detected directly from observations; instead, it must be inferred from detections of other atomic or compound events(i.e. sub-events of this compound event). In the example above, the explosion event is a compound event. High temperature, light and acoustic events are sub-events of the explosion event.

4.2   Confidence, Confidence Function, and Phase

When a compound event occurs, it is possible that not all sub-events are detected. For example, when an explosion actually occurs, only two atomic sub-events – the high temperature and the light sub-events – could be detected, if the sensors that detect the acoustic signals are damaged in the explosion. We use the notion of *confidence* to address this problem.

A *confidence function* takes whether the sub-events have been reported or not as boolean parameters and produces a numeric value of output based on the event's semantics. The *confidence* is the return value of the confidence function specified in event registration. An event with a confidence higher than 1.0 is regarded as "confirmed", i.e., the sensor network is highly confident that the event actually occurred.

A *confidence function* specifies the relationships among sub-events of a compound event with other factors that affect the decision such as relative importance, sensing reliability, historic data, statistical model, fitness of a known pattern and proximity of detections. The information is derived from event semantics in real life. A confidence function can be a simple linear equation or a complex statistical model. For example, if the temperature has been continuously going up for a period of time, combined with light sub-event, then a report of fire event carries a higher confidence compared to the report that is based on the observations only on temperatures going up and down rapidly in a short period of time.

In reality, an event always has its meaningful contexts, which can be modelled using a Finite State Machine (FSM). For example, in a residential monitoring system, morning, afternoon, and evening can be the states of this system. We call these states *phases*. In each *phase*, there is a set of events that are likely to occur with meaningful context, while other events are less likely to occur [27]. Consider a chemical factory. Dissemination of a chemical might not happen except during a specific production phase. If all sub-events of this chemical event are detected during a phase in which the event is very unlikely to happen, the system could either give this event detection a low confidence or report the possible malfunction of the sensors. Using phases in this manner not only saves power in monitoring and event detection, but also increases the reliability of event detection.

4.3   Real-Time Semantics

Each sub-event has an *absolute validity interval (avi)* associated with it. The avi depicts the temporal consistency between the environment and its observed measurement. Continuing the explosion example, the temperature sub-event can have a longer avi because high temperature usually will last for a while, while the light sub-event may not last long because in an explosion, a sharp increase in the intensity of light would happen only for a short period of time. It is the responsibility of the application developer to determine the appropriate avi values.

When an event consists of more than one sub-event, the time an aggregating node should wait for the arrivals of all these sub-events becomes an important issue. The delay of a sub-event's detection varies according to sensors' sampling period and communication delay. We should preserve a time window to allow all possible reports of sub-events to arrive to the aggregating node. Wireless media and unpredictable environment in which a sensor network exists make both the loss of messages and failures of nodes common. For this reason, we can't risk reporting an urgent event late. If before the timer expires the confidence value has reached 1, the event is reported to registrants without waiting any more. If the confidence value exceeds the min_confidence value specified in sub-event list when the timer expires, the event is reported to registrants with this confidence value. If the confidence value hasn't reached the min_confidence value when the timer expires, the event is not reported.

After an event is detected, it should be sent to the registrants before the reporting deadline. For example, we can use the Velocity Monotonic Scheduling or SPEED protocol [13][18].

4.4   Registration and Cancellation

To register an event of interest, an application submits a request in the following SQL-like statement:

```
INSERT INTO EVENT_LIST
    (EVENT_ID, RANGE_TYPE, DETECTING_RANGE,
     SUBEVENT_SET, REGISTRANT_SET, REPORT_DEADLINE,
     DETECTION_DURATION [, SPATIAL_RESOLUTION ]
       [, ACTIONS])
VALUES    ()
```

Range_Type and Detecting_Range together specify a set of sensor nodes that should be responsible for detecting this event. The Range_Type can be GROUP or AREA. The Detecting_Range is the group's description (e.g., Group ID) or the area's coordinates' range. If an application specifies an area in its registration request, one or more groups will be established in this area. Because of the limited space, we cannot describe different options of group formulations and their contexts in this paper. It will be covered in a separate paper. When an event is detected, it will be reported before the Report_Deadline to every node in the Registrant_Set. If an application receives an event detection report with a expired Report_Deadline, it can decide whether to ignore this "stale" report, or take it and reduce its associated confidence. Detection_Duration denotes the ending time for this event detection task. After the duration time, the event's information is void and nodes stop detecting this event. Event information will be deleted from this group or area. Temporary groups built for this event are dissolved. The Spatial_Resolution defines the geographical granularity for the event's detection. The Subevent_Set defines a set of sub-events and their timing constraints. Here we give its definition:

```
Subevent_Set { Time_window,
               Phase_set,
               Confidence_function,
               Min_confidence,
               (sub-event_1, avi1),
               [(sub-event_2, avi2),...]}
```

The Time_window specifies the time interval during which the sub-events reports are collected. The Phase_set identifies the phase to which the event belongs. The Confidence_function and Min_confidence represent the function to be used for computing the confidence and the minimum confidence required to report the occurrence of the sub-event, respectively.

Let P denote the current Phase in the group or area and S denote the set of sub-events for event E, i.e., $S = (sub-event1, sub-event2...)$.

E is detected when the following are true:

1) P belongs to Phase_set of E.

2) For every s in S, calculate B(s): B(s) = 1 when s has been detected and (current_time - detected_time) $\leq$ avi of s; B(s) = 0 otherwise.

3) Calculate confidence = f(B($s1$), B($s2$), ...,), where f is the confidence function.

4) When Time_window expires: if (confidence $\geq$ min_confidence) report the event with confidence value.

Registered events can be cancelled even before the Detection_duration is terminated by submitting a cancellation request. Event cancellation is similar to event detection. The difference is that it only needs to specify the event's id instead of describing an event's criteria.

```
DELETE FROM EVENT_LIST
    WHERE EVENT_ID = event_id
```

After an event is cancelled, the event's information is void and nodes stop detecting the event. Event information is deleted from the group or area. Any groups assembled for this event are dissolved.

4.5   Discussion

In the current version of the prototype, we made some simplifications to demonstrate the main ideas on data semantics, real-time constraints, and reliability of decisions. We understand the complexity and various choices on issues including the formats for registration and cancellation, group formations, confidence function, and spatial/temporal resolutions. In this part, we provide some discussion on important issues in event detection services.

SQL-like Language in Event Detection: As presented in Section 4.4, we use SQL-like statements for the registration and cancellation of an event. This approach provides a simple interface for applications [8][19]. The syntax of the statements is the same as standard SQL statements. So the application can insert events to a traditional database or a sensor network without any changes in the code. This is effective for applications that need event detection services, without paying any special attention to the actual type of the database and data service middleware that is providing the service.

In some cases, this approach is unsuitable because of its parsing overhead. After an SQL-like statement is issued, DSWare parses it, generates an execution plan, and calls the corresponding methods to execute the registration, execution, and cancellation. Parsing consumes memory and processing power. For sensor networks in which sensors are very limited in processing and memory capacities, it might be better to provide method signatures to applications instead of standard SQL. However, we believe that the SQL-like approach is the right one, since it provides the flexibility and expressiveness of SQL to cover a large number of possible event specifications. This is the main reason why we include an optional SQL-parser module in our DSWare.

Spatial and Temporal Resolutions: Spatial resolution indicates the possible detection radius of an event. If the size of a detection group is too small compared to this event, there might be several groups in this event's coverage that report this event. The Event Detection component should be able to tell whether these are different occurrences or just repeated reports of a same event.

Temporal resolution has a similar property to spatial resolution, except that it specifies the detection granularity in the time dimension. Some events last much longer than the sensing interval of a sensor. It is unnecessary for some applications to report a single occurrence repetitively. For example, an application sets the temporal resolution of a fire event as 10 minutes. At the beginning of the fire, the group that detects the fire reports the fire event to the registrants. Assume that there is some mechanism to guarantee that the registrants have received the report, this group can ignore any subsequent occurrence of this event's sub-events within 10 minutes, because that is possibly the same event. The temporal resolution is not required for every application because some applications require the sensors to report an event's existence no matter whether it is a new one or not.

5 Evaluation of Real-Time Event Detection Services

For the preliminary evaluation, we have implemented the real-time event detection services in GloMoSim[29]. Within a terrain of $2000 * 2000 m^2$, which is uniformly divided into 16 groups, we place 100 sensor nodes to sense temperature, light or acoustics. The simulator simulates the detection of an Explosion(E) event that consists of a high temperature atomic event(T), a light atomic event(L) and an acoustic atomic event(A). T and A are modelled as circles whose coverage radius expands over time, denoting the actual energy expansion in a real system [28]. L is modelled as spatially distributed events that occur repetitively during explosions with a very short lifetime.

To simulate the error distribution around a hazard event as an explosion, the failure rate of sensors decreases quadratically with the distance between a sensor and the center of explosion. The Explosion event is registered by node 1 (at upper-left corner of the terrain) to the entire network. In our simulation, we assume high temperature is a more consistent indicator of an explosion among the three sub-events and temperature sensing devices are more robust in the physical environment. Accordingly, we specify a simplistic confidence function as follows:

$$Confidence_E := 0.6 * B(T) + 0.3 * B(L) + 0.3 * B(A). \tag{1}$$

B(x)=1 if x is detected within time window of 3 seconds; 0 otherwise.

The weights of sub-events are consistent with our application and experimental settings. The min_confidence is set as 0.9, which means an explosion event will be reported if the $Confidence\_E$ is not less than 0.9.

5.1   Performance in Reduction of Communication

Previous work [11] uses group coordination or in-network processing to reduce the number of reports generated from a group. In the best case, only one report of a environment property is generated from a group during each sensing interval. However, for correlated events, such an algorithm has to detect the events separately, send all reports (at least one for each atomic event) to an outside node and the entire analysis will be done there. We use this algorithm as our Baseline in the experiments. Fig 4 is the comparison between real-time event services (denoted by the DSWare curve in the figure) and the Baseline on the number of messages transmitted in the network and the explosion reports received by the registrant. In this experiment, explosion events appear randomly with an initial radius of 300m. The figure demonstrates that an event detection scheme which is established upon data and application semantics can further process and aggregate data and thus reducing unnecessary communication without sacrificing real-time constraints.

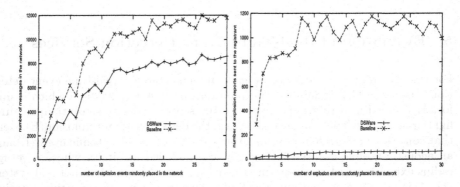

Fig. 4. Comparison between DSWare and Baseline in Communication

5.2   Performance in Differentiating Events and Event-Like Factors

One of the key features of the real-time event services is that it can be used to differentiate between events and pseudo events (event-like factors [28]) happening in physical environment to avoid false alarms.

In this experiment, we place an explosion event with initial radius of 300m at (1000.0, 1000.0) in each run. We place High Temperature events with initial radius of 150m randomly in the network and plot the number of reports sent to the registrant in Fig 5. The figure indicates that with time windows and a carefully designed confidence function, our approach can achieve a performance close to ideal detection (no false alarms). The slight difference between the DSWare reports and the ideal case reports is due to the randomness of sensor types in the explosion event area.

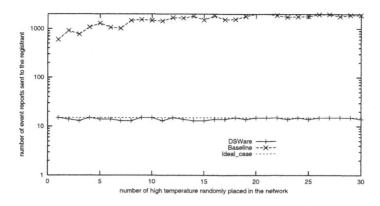

Fig. 5. Performance in Differentiating Events and Event-like Factors

6   Conclusions

A sensor network should be able to provide the abstraction of data services to applications. However, because of the lack of basic data-centric services in sensor networks, current applications need to implement the entire stack of application-specific data services including group management, query optimization, local data processing, and event detection. Such a tight coupling of data services and application logic has several disadvantages and increases the complexity of applying sensor networks as databases in a large software system. We have developed a data-centric service middleware in sensor networks called DSWare. DSWare is a flexible middleware designed to hide unattractive characteristics of sensor networks including the unreliability of individual sensing and communication, complexity and necessity of group coordination, and large volume of dynamic data distributed all over the networks, to present a more general data service interface to applications. Applications are freed from complicated low level operations of sensor networks and are able to retrieve data from sensor networks using similar interfaces as conventional databases.

Event detection is a one of the services that is most widely used in sensor network applications. Instead of providing only simple detection of atomic events, we have developed a middleware architecture that accommodates the data semantics of real-life compound events and tolerates the uncertainty and faultiness in sensor networks.

The current version of DSWare including the event detection services is the first step to deliver a flexible and efficient data service middleware for sensor networks. Our future work includes extending the event detection services to support applications for mobile event tracking and implementing other services in DSWare.

References

1. Cougar Project. www.cs.cornell.edu/database/cougar.
2. Rutgers Dataman Project. www.cs.rutgers.edu/dataman.
3. SCADDS: Scalable Coordination Architectures for Deeply Distributed Systems. www.isi.edu/scadds.
4. Smart Messages Project. discolab.rutgers.edu/sm.
5. S. Bhattacharya, H. Kim, S. Prabh, and T. Abdelzaher. Energy-Conserving Data Placement and Asynchronous Multicast in Wireless Sensor Networks. In *Proceedings of the 1st International Conference on Mobile Systems, Applications, and Services*, San Francisco, CA, 2003.
6. B. Blum, P. Nagaraddi, A. Wood, T. Abdelzaher, S. H. Son, and J. A. Stankovic. An Entity Maintenance and Connection Service for Sensor Networks. In *Proceedings of the 1st International Conference on Mobile Systems, Applications, and Services*, San Francisco, CA, 2003.
7. P. Bonnet, J. Gehrke, and P. Seshadri. Querying the Physical World. *IEEE Personal Communication Magazine*, (7):10–15, Oct 2000.
8. P. Bonnet, J. Gehrke, and P. Seshadri. Towards Sensor Database Systems. In *Proceedings of the 2nd International Conference on Mobile Data Management*, Hong Kong, 2001.
9. E. Bosse, J. Roy, and S. Paradis. Modelling and Simulation in Support of Design of a Data Fusion System. *Information Fusion*, (1):77–87, Dec 2000.
10. W. Chang and M. Kam. Asynchronous Distributed Detection. *IEEE Transactions on Aerospace Electronic Systems*, pages 818–826, 1994.
11. D. Estrin, R. Govindan, J. Heidemann, and S. Kumar. Next Century Challenges: Scalable Coordination in Sensor Networks. In *Proceedings of the 5th Annual International Conference on Mobile Computing and Networks*, Seattle, WA, 1999.
12. J. Feng, F. Koushanfar, and M. Potkonjak. System-Architectures for Sensor Networks: Issues, Alternatives, and Directions. In *Proceedings of the 20th International Conference on Computer Design*, Freiburg, Germany, 2002.
13. T. He, J. A. Stankovic, C. Lu, and T. Abdelzaher. SPEED: A Stateless Protocol for Real-Time Communication in Ad Hoc Sensor Networks. In *Proceedings of the 23rd International Conference on Distributed Computing Systems*, Providence, RI, 2003.
14. J. Hill, R. Szewczyk, A. Woo, S. Hollar, D. E. Culler, and K. S. J. Pister. System Architecture Directions for Networked Sensors. *Architectural Support for Programming Languages and Operating Systems*, pages 93–104, 2000.
15. C. Jaikaeo, C. Srisathapornphat, and C.-C. Shen. Querying and Tasking in Sensor Networks. In *Proceedings of SPIE's 14th Annual International Symposium on Aerospace/Defense Sensing, Simulation, and Control (Digitization of the Battlespace V)*, Orlando, FL, 2000.
16. D. Jayasimha, S. Ivengar, and R. Kashyap Information Integration and Synchronization in Distributed Sensor Networks. *IEEE Transactions on Systems, Man and Cybernetics*, 21(5):1032–1043, Sep/Oct 1991.
17. F. Mattern, K. Römer, O. Kasten. Middleware Challenges for Wireless Sensor Networks. *ACM SIGMOBILE Mobile Computing and Communication Review (MC2R)*, 2002.
18. C. Lu, B. Blum, T. Abdelzaher, J. A. Stankovic, and T. He. RAP: A Real-Time Communication Architecture for Large-Scale Wireless Sensor Networks. In *Proceedings of the 8th IEEE Real-Time Technology and Applications Symposium*, San Jose, CA, 2002.

19. S. Madden, M. Franklin, J. Hellerstein, and W. Hong. TAG: A Tiny Aggregation Service for Ad-Hoc Sensor Networks. In *Proceedings of the 18th International Conference on Data Engeneering*, San Jose, CA, 2002.
20. S. Madden and M. J. Franklin. Fjording The Stream: An Architecture for Queries over Streaming Sensor Data. In *Proceedings of the 18th International Conference on Data Engeneering*, San Jose, CA, 2002.
21. P. R. Murphy. Dempster-Shafer Theory for Sensor Fusion in Autonomous Mobile Robots. *IEEE Transactions on Robotics and Automation*, 14(2):197–206, Apr 1999.
22. H. Qi, X. Wang, S. S. Iyengar, and K. Chakrabarty. Multisensor Data Fusion in Distributed Sensor Networks Using Mobile Agents. In *Proceedings of 5th International Conference on Information Fusion*, Annapolis, MD, 2001.
23. S. Ratnasamy, D. Estrin, R. Govindan, B. Karp, S. Shenker, L. Yin, and F. Yu. Data-Centric Storage in Sensornets. In *Proceedings of the 1st Workshop on Sensor Networks and Applications*, Atlantic, GA, 2002.
24. V. N. S. Samarasooriya and P. K. Varshney. A Sequential Approach to Asynchronous Decision Fusion. *Optical Engineering*, 35(3):625–633, Mar 1996.
25. V. N. S. Samarasooriya and P. K. Varshney. A Fuzzy Modeling Approach to Decision Fusion under Uncertainty. *Fuzzy Sets and Systems*, 114(1):59–69, Aug 2000.
26. C-C Shen, C. Srisathapornphat, and C. Jaikaeo. Sensor Information Networking Architecture and Applications. *IEEE Personel Communication Magazine*, 8(4):52–59, Aug 2001.
27. M. R. Tremblay and M. R. Cutkosky. Using Sensor Fusion and Contextual Information to Perform Event Detection during a Phase-Based Manipulation Task. In *Proceedings of the IEEE/RSJ International Conference on Intelligent Robots and Systems*, Pittsburgh, PA, 1995.
28. S. Yan, S. Wang, and Z. Dou. An Energy Model in Fire Detection and Integrated Analysis on False Alarms. In *Proceedings of the 12th International Conference on Automatic Fire Detection*, Gaithersburg, MD, 2001.
29. X. Zeng, R. Bagrodia, and M. Gerla. GloMoSim: A Library for Parallel Simulation of Large-Scale Wireless Networks. In *Proceedings of the 12th Workshop on Parallel and Distributed Simulation*, Alberta, Canada, 1998.

Meteorology and Hydrology in Yosemite National Park: A Sensor Network Application

Jessica D. Lundquist[1], Daniel R. Cayan[1,2], and Michael D. Dettinger[2,1]

[1] Scripps Institution of Oceanography (SIO), UCSD MC-0213, 9500 Gilman Drive, La Jolla, CA 92039
{jlundquist, dcayan}@ucsd.edu
[2] United States Geological Survey, 9500 Gilman Drive, La Jolla, CA 92039
dettinge@tenaya.ucsd.edu

Abstract. Over half of California's water supply comes from high elevations in the snowmelt-dominated Sierra Nevada. Natural climate fluctuations, global warming, and the growing needs of water consumers demand intelligent management of this water resource. This requires a comprehensive monitoring system across and within the Sierra Nevada. Unfortunately, because of severe terrain and limited access, few measurements exist. Thus, meteorological and hydrologic processes are not well understood at high altitudes. However, new sensor and wireless communication technologies are beginning to provide sensor packages designed for low maintenance operation, low power consumption and unobtrusive footprints. A prototype network of meteorological and hydrological sensors has been deployed in Yosemite National Park, traversing elevation zones from 1,200 to 3,700 m. Communication techniques must be tailored to suit each location, resulting in a hybrid network of radio, cell-phone, land-line, and satellite transmissions. Results are showing how, in some years, snowmelt may occur quite uniformly over the Sierra, while in others it varies with elevation.

1 Introduction

California's water resources depend vitally upon runoff from its high elevations, particularly the snowmelt-dominated Sierra Nevada. In addition to providing over half of the state's water supply, rivers and river basins in the Sierra Nevada carry sediment, nutrients and pollutants and act as vital arteries in the regional airshed. Climate variability in the region is high, and annual precipitation and runoff fluctuate from under 50% to over 200% of climatological averages. In recent decades, streamflow records from watersheds in western North America, collected at relatively low elevation gages, suggest that an alarming change toward earlier snowmelt and snowmelt runoff has been occurring (Cayan et al 2001, Stewart et al 2002, Dettinger and Cayan 1995). Whether this reflects a natural climate variation or an early symptom of anthropogenic climate warming is not known. In the long run, it is estimated that, in response to projected global warming of 3 degrees C, the spring-summer snowmelt would be diminished by one third to one half (Roos 1987). Additionally, virtually all modern climate models suggest there will be higher annual

F. Zhao and L. Guibas (Eds.): IPSN 2003, LNCS 2634, pp. 518–528, 2003.

evaporative demands as climate warming develops, and some models have predicted substantial changes in the State's precipitation. However, the data necessary to detect and understand these changes, and provide ground truth for numerical models is sparse, to the point that many of the variations and processes involved are ill-known and can only be inferred.

Much of the problem arises from our historic monitoring system. Currently, most meteorological observations are collected near highly populated, low elevation regions (Figure 1), while many of the important hydrologic processes occur in unpopulated wilderness areas, often in rugged terrain and high elevations. For example, snowmelt processes are spatially complex and thus difficult to forecast and incorporate in large-scale hydrologic and atmospheric models. Much of the difficulty arises because snow occurs in patches of nonuniform depth and density, particularly in mountainous regions. In situ measurements of the snowpack are both difficult to make and not necessarily representative of region-wide characteristics. Satellite images and geographical information systems have increased spatial coverage, but this data, which is often infrequent in time, is still difficult to relate to the actual river discharge originating from a basin. Apparently simple characteristics, such as the distribution and timing of snow accumulation, snowmelt, and runoff into rivers with elevation, are not routinely quantified.

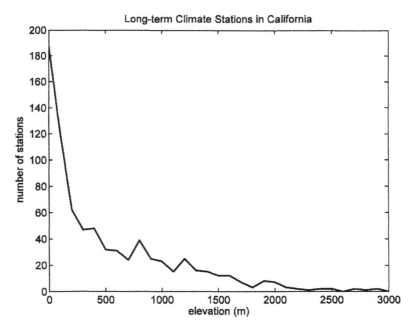

Fig. 1. Number of long-term climate stations in each 100 m elevation band in California. Only two stations, operated by the White Mountain Research Center, exist above 3000 m

Data collection in high elevation wilderness areas historically has been difficult and expensive because of the extra costs and logistics required to visit snowy sites and preserve their undisturbed character. Many such regions are designated as

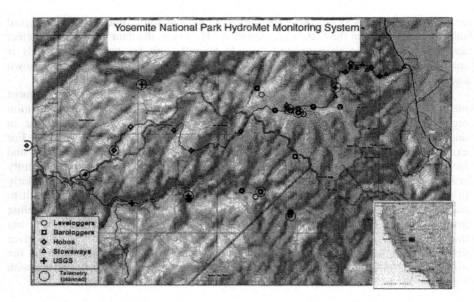

Fig. 2. Map of sensor locations in Yosemite National Park, as of September 2002. Sensors include water level and temperature (*circles*), stream chemistry (*crosses*), air pressure (*squares*), air temperature and humidity (*diamonds*), and air temperature alone (*triangles*). Circled stations have been approved by the National Park Service for telemetry

national parks and wilderness, requiring special permission for instrument installation and access. However, new sensor and wireless communication technologies designed for low maintenance operation, low power consumption and small, unobtrusive footprints are providing new opportunities to monitor mountainous watersheds. Such technologies will allow a significant expansion of data collection vital for understanding, predicting and informing about the variability of climate and water resources in the State and the Nation.

2   Sensor Network: Yosemite National Park

For high altitude monitoring, the most immediate concerns are access – both in terms of transportation to the monitoring sites and in terms of permission to use the given sites – and scientific merit. With these factors in mind, the Merced and Tuolumne Rivers in Yosemite National Park, which drain the western slope of the Southern Sierra from a range of snowmelt-contributing elevations from 1,200 to 3,700 m, have been chosen as test basins. One of the greatest assets of this region is the Tioga Road (Highway 120), which crosses the range at elevations from 1,200 to 3,050 m. This is one of only five highways transecting the Sierra Nevada, and of the five, it has the highest summit. The river basins have been protected by the National Park Service for over 100 years. Not only does this make the region an excellent laboratory for

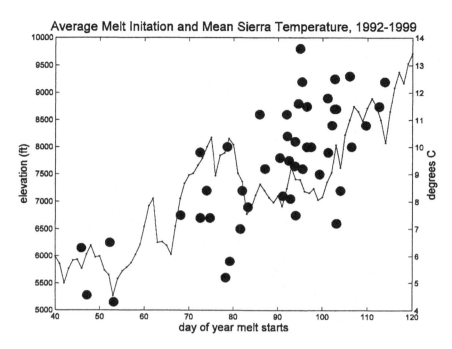

Fig. 3. A weighted average of mean temperatures at Nevada City, Tahoe City, Sacramento, and Hetch Hetchy (*line, right axis*) from 1992 to 1999 shows that, on average, temperature increases smoothly through the spring. Average days of maximum snow accumulation (*circles, left axis*) at 44 CDWR snowpillows over the same period show that higher elevations start melting later in the season, on average

natural, unimpaired processes, but it provides an important opportunity for designing instruments for wilderness areas.

Scientifically, the Merced River gage at Happy Isles has a long daily record (1916-present) of unimpaired flows, and a spatially-distributed USGS watershed model is available for testing hypotheses. Several studies (Cayan et al 2001, Peterson et al 2000) have shown that the Merced's flow characteristics are representative of basins throughout the Western United States. Since 1999, instruments measuring hourly water levels, conductivities, and temperatures have been installed at Pohono Bridge, on Tenaya Creek, and at Happy Isles on the Merced River. Starting in summer 2000, hourly measurements of snow depth and downward shortwave radiation have been added to augment measurements of air temperature, humidity, precipitation, and snow liquid water content measurements at five California Department of Water Resources (CDWR) telemetered snow pillow stations at elevations ranging from 2,000 to 3,000 m.

In summer 2001, in consultation with Park planners and scientists, the USGS, and the CDWR, we obtained necessary research permits and began installing a river monitoring network in the high country of Yosemite National Park. As a result,

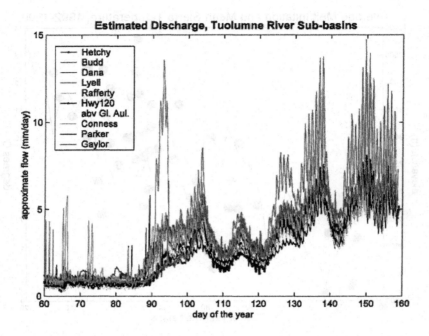

Fig. 4. Spring runoff began simultaneously in ten instrumented sub-basins of the Tuolumne River in Yosemite Natrional Park in spring 2002

twenty instruments recording hourly water level and temperature were installed in the upper reaches of the Merced and Tuolumne Rivers (Figure 2) to provide information about how and when different subbasins contribute to the river's flow. Sensor locations were selected to monitor subbasins with a variety of topographic characteristics. For example, some drain primarily north-facing slopes, and some drain primarily south-facing slopes. These measurements will be combined with remote-sensing and models to understand where and when snowmelt occurs and how it moves through these basins. Four water conductivity sensors were also deployed to make hourly measurements in the Merced and Tuolumne Basins. In summer 2002, stream chemistry measurements were made by NPS personnel at various points along both watersheds to measure water quality and composition throughout the summer. At the same time, discharge measurements were made at each station to establish curves relating discharge rates to water levels.

Along Highway 120, during Summer 2002, we also began to establish a set of meteorological stations (Figure 2) that augment the snow/meteorological stations operated by the CDWR Snow Surveys. Presently, our stations consist of approximately 25 internally-recording temperature/relative humidity sensors, stationed along Highway 120, along the west slope of the Sierra up to the crest of Tioga Pass, and down to the Mono Basin at Lee Vining. This array will monitor weather systems and air masses as they sweep across the Sierra from the Pacific, or occasionally, from the Western Great Basin. We have plans to expand the sensor suite at several of these stations to include other elements such as wind and solar radiation. We also expect to install a webcam at Tioga Pass to view snow in surrounding alpine areas. In addition to our stream and atmospheric temperature/humidity gages, we are collaborating with Frank Gehrke of CDWR to install a full snow/meteorological station at Merced Lake, in the Upper Merced River drainage, complete with GOES satellite telemetry.

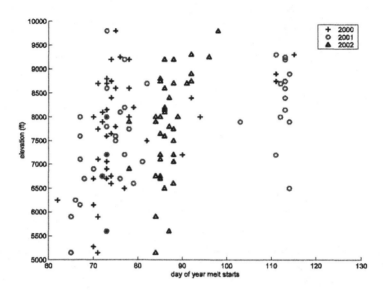

Fig. 5. The dates of maximum snow accumulation (shown here) and snowmelt initiation at 44 snow pillows in the Central Sierra were remarkably similar from elevation to elevation in spring 2002 (*triangles*). Similarly, in 2000 (*crosses*) and 2001 (*circles*), snow at most elevations began melting at the same time (before day 80, March 21st), but several stations at higher altitudes waited until weeks later

3 Preliminary Results

Because of the scarcity of high elevation data, our first year's measurements already provide interesting new insights into how snow melts and spring runoff begins at different altitudes in the Sierra. Common experience and intuition suggest that snow at lower elevations melts first. The standard atmospheric lapse rate describes a decrease in temperature of 6.5°C per 1000 m elevation gain. Reece and Aguado (1992) studied snow pillow stations in the Truckee River Basin and found an approximate 4-day delay in the start of the snowmelt season for each 100 m increase in altitude. Averaged over many years (Figure 3), these results are typical. Sierra Nevada temperature (Figure 3, right axis) increases steadily through the spring.

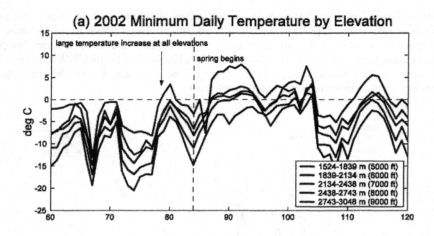

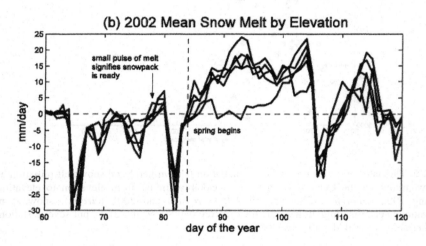

Fig. 6. Average temperatures (*a*) and snowmelt rates (*b*) by elevation for 44 snow pillows in the Central Sierra. In each graph, the top curve is the lowest elevation bin (1524–1839 m, 5000–6000 ft) and the lowest curve is the highest elevation bin (2743–3048 m, 9000–10000 ft)

Because temperatures decrease with increasing elevation, the average day of maximum snow accumulation, which we are using as an index of snowmelt initiation (Figure 3, dots, left axis), is later in the season for higher elevation snow pillow stations. However, what happens in a given year, as exemplified by spring 2002, may vary widely from the average values.

In Spring 2002, ten water-pressure sensors measured the onset of spring runoff in subbasins of the Tuolumne River in Yosemite National Park, California. Subbasin areas ranged from 6 km² to 775 km², and measurement elevations ranged from 1200 m (3,800 ft) at Hetch Hetchy to 2900 m (9,600 ft) at Gaylor Creek. Some were

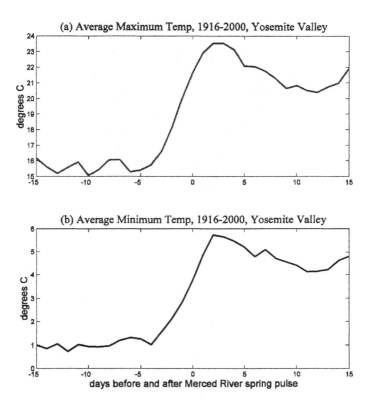

Fig. 7. Average maximum temperatures (*a*) and minimum temperatures (*b*) in Yosemite Valley, 1916-2000, for the 15 days before and after the start of spring runoff in the Merced River at Happy Isles

northfacing and some were south-facing. Estimated mean April radiation varied from 552 W/m² in Budd Creek Basin to 635 W/m² in Gaylor Creek Basin. Despite these differences, streamflow rose simultaneously, just before April 1st, at all gages (Figure 4). The date of maximum snow accumulation and initiation of spring melt also was remarkably uniform from elevation to elevation (Figure 5). Using the same stations, mean temperature and melt rates were calculated in five elevation bands. In 2002, two large increases in temperature preceded spring snowmelt (Figure 6a). After the first, a small amount of melting occurred at all elevations (Figure 6b) so that, during the second temperature increase, melting began in earnest everywhere. Notice that stream runoff only began in earnest after minimum temperatures exceeded 0°C at most elevations.

The rapid and simultaneous initiation of snowmelt and runoff at all elevations in 2002 shows that the onset of spring can differ greatly from the long-term average conditions. How common are sudden springs compared to gradual ones? The 85 years of Yosemite Valley temperature and Merced River discharge data suggest that spring

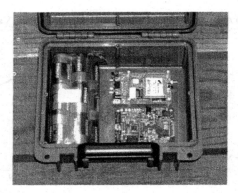

Fig. 8. View of interior of data logger being developed by Douglas Alden. Battery pack (to the left) provides power for data storage and transmission (electronics on right)

most often occurs suddenly. Averaging the temperatures before and after the day the river started rising (spring pulse days, as described in Cayan et al. 2001) reveals that maximum temperatures (Figure 7a) rise about 8°C and minimum temperatures (Figure 7b) rise about 5°C during the weeks surrounding the spring pulse. Out of 85 years, only 8 years had rapid flow increases that were not accompanied by dramatic temperature rises. This suggests that spring runoff is closely tied to large-scale atmospheric circulation patterns, and further study may reveal ways to use this link to improve forecasts of water supply and timing. However, before forecasts can improve, real-time data is essential.

4   Communications Issues

Communications in the Park are difficult because of the high relief. Conditions are especially challenging in river valleys, which are crucial to our study but are typically isolated by surrounding topography. We are exploring potential wireless communications options that include digital cellular, satellite, and land line (phone line) links to the Internet. At several sites (circled sites on map, Figure 2), we have obtained or requested Park approval to install communications equipment. There is tension between the resource-management interests of the Park, which seek more environmental information, and the wilderness-preservation interests, which seek to protect wilderness values from instrument installations. Seeking to balance these interests, our communications will depend on site location and will likely include radio, cell phone and satellite transmissions. The equipment will need to interface with the variety of existing and new sensors and data loggers used by the agencies working in this area. Implementing workable communications solutions in Yosemite will serve as a prototype for other instrumental nodes and networks that will need to be developed to serve California's increasingly multifaceted environmental monitoring needs.

Because access is often difficult in these remote and snowy settings, power consumption and long-term backups of data collected are important design considerations. Thus, SIO Development Engineer Douglas Alden is building a low cost, low power data logger (Figure 8) that will log, record and wirelessly transmit data from several meteorological and hydrological sensors. The logger is designed for wilderness applications and will accommodate several standard meteorological and hydrological sensors. The current version will be powered by a small battery pack, and its 32MB of memory is adequate to store several months of data (while logging measurements at three-minute intervals).

Installing and monitoring a high density of sensors in Yosemite will reveal the spatial variability of meteorological properties at high altitudes. Data intercomparison within the region will also help identify sensors that may not be properly calibrated or indicative of region characteristics, prompting timely repairs and replacements. Connecting the instruments to the internet will eliminate the limitations of data storage and will minimize the travel costs involved in data retrieval. However, battery power will continue to be a limiting factor. Solar panels, in conjunction with 12-volt batteries, are currently used at the CDWR snow pillows, but the large visible panels are not unobtrusive enough for protected wilderness areas. Further technological advances in power generation and consumption are desirable.

5 Future Directions

High altitude observations are necessary to improve understanding of mountain snowpacks, a crucial resource that provides over half of California's water supply. Because the settings are in remote, protected areas, instruments must be designed for low maintenance operation, low power consumption and small, unobtrusive packaging. The technology also must perform despite the lack of traditional cell phone coverage in these regions and the isolated nature of river valleys surrounded by steep terrain. Fortunately, the demand for these measurements is such that any communications advances will be quickly incorporated, and more real-time highaltitude measurements will become available online in the future.

Acknowledgments. Funding for this research was provided by the California Institute for Telecommunications and Information Technology (Cal-(IT)2), NOAA, NSF ROADNet, California Energy Commission, and Cannon National Parks Foundation.

References

1. Cayan, D. R., S. A. Kammerdiener, M. D. Dettinger, J. M. Caprio, and D. H. Peterson, 2001. Changes in the onset of spring in the Western United States. Bull. Am. Met. Soc., 82, 399–415.
2. Dettinger, M. D. and D. R. Cayan, 1995. Large-scale atmospheric forcing of recent trends toward early snowmelt runoff in California. J. Climate, 8, 606–623.
3. Peterson, D. H., R. E. Smith, M. D. Dettinger, D. R. Cayan, and L. Riddle, 2000: An organized signal in snowmelt runoff in the western United States. J. Am. Water Resour. Ass., 36, 421–432.

4.   Reece, B. and E. Aguado, 1992. Accumulation and melt characteristics of Northeastern Sierra Nevada snowpacks. Managing water resources during global change: AWRA 28th annual conference and symposium: Reno, NV, Nov. 1-5, 1992, 631–640.
5.   Roos, M., 1987. Possible changes in California snowmelt runoff patterns. Proceedings of the 4th Annual PACLIM Workshop, Pacific Grove, CA., 22–31.
6.   Stewart, I.T., D.R. Cayan, M.D. Dettinger, 2002. Changes in Snowmelt Runoff Timing in Western North America under a "Business as Usual" Climate Change Scenario. Submitted to Climate Change 10/31/02.

Detection, Classification, and Collaborative Tracking of Multiple Targets Using Video Sensors

P.V. Pahalawatta, D. Depalov, T.N. Pappas, and A.K. Katsaggelos

ECE Dept. Northwestern University, 2145 Sheridan Rd, Evanston, IL 60208
{pesh, depalov, pappas, aggk}@ece.northwestern.edu

Abstract. The study of collaborative, distributed, real-time sensor networks is an emerging research area. Such networks are expected to play an essential role in a number of applications such as, surveillance and tracking of vehicles in the battlefield of the future. This paper proposes an approach to detect and classify multiple targets, and collaboratively track their position and velocity utilizing video cameras. Arbitrarily placed cameras collaboratively perform self-calibration and provide complete battlefield coverage. If some of the cameras are equipped with a GPS system, they are able to metrically reconstruct the scene and determine the absolute coordinates of the tracked targets. A background subtraction scheme combined with a Markov random field based approach is used to detect the target even when it becomes stationary. Targets are continuously tracked using a distributed Kalman filter approach. As the targets move the coverage is handed over to the "best" neighboring cluster of sensors. This paper demonstrates the potential for the development of distributed optical sensor networks and addresses problems and tradeoffs associated with this particular implementation.

1 Introduction

In the past few decades, we have seen many advances in wireless communication techniques and in microsensor technology. These advances combined with growing interest in both the military and the civilian domain in using sensor networks for remote monitoring applications have led to the concept of a wireless sensor network. A wireless sensor network can consist of a densely distributed set of sensors of various modalities (e.g., acoustic, seismic, infrared, imaging) that gather data from the physical environment and then process the data collaboratively to obtain a coherent high level description of the current state of the system.

Due to their low production costs and low energy consumption, acoustic and seismic sensors are among the most commonly studied types of wireless microsensors for battlefield surveillance. However, these sensors have some weaknesses. Since acoustic sensors depend on the acoustic signature of the target, they will not be able to detect a vehicle when it becomes stationary with its engines off. They can also be distracted by acoustic changes caused by gearshifts as well as accelerations and decelerations of a vehicle. Also, these sensors can be affected by acoustic noise caused by wind. Similar problems exist with seismic sensors.

F. Zhao and L. Guibas (Eds.): IPSN 2003, LNCS 2634, pp. 529–544, 2003.
© Springer-Verlag Berlin Heidelberg 2003

We propose the use of multiple video sensors to enhance the capabilities of a wireless sensor network. Video sensors can track accelerating or decelerating targets with relative ease. They continue to "see" targets that become stationary even if the targets are completely silent. Also, video sensors can obtain unique attributes of a target such as its shape, color, and texture that can be used for classification as well as for pose estimation.

Automatic video-based vehicle surveillance has been studied mainly in the context of traffic monitoring applications. We can identify three main approaches that have been used with some success in these applications.

One approach uses three-dimensional models in order to classify a vehicle as well as to identify its position and orientation [1,2,3]. In this method, a sample taken from a database of geometrical wireframe models of possible vehicle shapes is projected on to the image plane and then compared with the object seen in the image. The main advantage of this method is that the vehicle can be classified as a part of the detection process. A disadvantage is that detailed geometrical models of vehicles must be available. Also, this approach can be very computationally intensive.

The second approach uses a contour of the motion-segmented image (i.e., pixels belonging to moving vehicle) to track the dynamics of the vehicle [4][5][8]. The weakness inherent to this method is that if multiple vehicles are in the field of view of the camera, and some vehicles are partially occluded by others as they are initially detected, then the vehicle contours cannot be correctly initialized.

The third approach, which is the one explored in this paper, simply tracks specific features within the vehicle instead of tracking the entire object. An example of a feature-based vehicle tracking system is presented in [6]. An advantage of this method is that some features of an object will still be visible even under partial occlusion.

The first phase or our system requires the detection of the moving target in each camera image. This can be achieved through background subtraction. An early approach to background subtraction was to assume that changes in intensity of a pixel that does not belong to a moving object can only occur due to camera noise and to model each pixel in the background to have a Gaussian intensity distribution. Then, for each pixel in a new frame, a significance test could be used to determine whether it belonged to the background model, or not [7]. However, this method assumes that the background image is completely static, which is not true for outdoor scenes involving foliage, or dust. One approach to deal with this problem has been to model each pixel with a mixture of Gaussians instead of as a single mode distribution [8]. In [9], a non-parametric approach is used to model the statistics of the background. In this case, one does not assume that the shape of the pdf of the pixel intensity is known, but instead, one assumes that the pixel intensities obtained from actual measurements represent samples taken from the pdf of the distribution. In this paper, we have used a simplified version of the approach proposed in [9] with a few modifications.

The next phase of our system is to compute matching feature points from images of the target taken by two cameras and by each camera at different points in time. Due to its key applications in the self-calibration of cameras and in object motion tracking, feature point correspondence is an area that has received much attention in the field of computer vision. The proposed methods can be placed in two broad categories based on the applications for which they are used.

The first category of methods can be used for applications in which the cameras are set up with a short baseline (the baseline is the distance between the centers of projection of each camera) relative to the viewing distance of the object from each camera. In this case, the appearance of the images will be more or less uniform in the two cameras, and matching feature points will be within a searchable local area of the image.

In our application, however, the baseline between the cameras is unlikely to be small compared to the distance from each camera to the target vehicle. The main difference in a wide baseline setup is that different cameras will have significantly different viewpoints of the scene. Therefore, the image of an object will undergo a perspective transformation when it is viewed from a different camera. In this case, a direct correlation of the pixel intensity neighborhood will not provide a correct measure of the similarity between features. Also, feature detection itself becomes a much harder problem in a wide baseline setup because it is not guaranteed that different cameras will detect the same points of the object as feature points.

In [10] and [11], a scale space approach is used to detect scale invariant feature points in images. Typically, the points that can be detected consistently in images from different viewpoints are the points of the object that cause the local pixel intensities in the image to vary two-dimensionally. Such points are generally referred to as corners and a measure based on the horizontal and vertical image gradients can be used as a measure of their "cornerness" [12].

Even if the same feature points are detected from images in both cameras, the matching task is still difficult due to the significant differences in viewpoint between the two images. In [13], the concept of affine Gaussian scale space is introduced whereby image neighborhoods are smoothed using non-symmetric Gaussians in order to make them invariant to affine transformations. It is shown in [14] that affine scale space methods can be used for feature matching in wide baseline applications.

The feature point correspondences are used for camera calibration. There are two main approaches to camera calibration: (i) Calibration using a calibration object, usually a grid with features of known dimensions [15], and (ii) Self-calibration, which exploits the constraints contained in the images themselves (epipolar, image of the absolute conic) [16]. Due to the nature of our problem we must use a self-calibration technique since it does not require the placement of any foreign object in the scene.

2   Problem Formulation

We consider a scenario in which an approaching vehicle must be continuously detected and its position and velocity tracked by a set of video sensors located in the field. We assume the sensors have been placed arbitrarily in the field and that they are not calibrated. We also assume that the sensors are able to communicate with each other and that they are capable of using GPS or some other method to determine their position. We do not assume that the target movement is constrained in anyway other than that it will be moving on the ground plane.

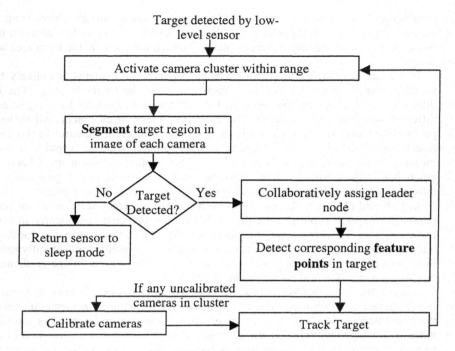

Fig. 1. Block diagram of system.

While the basic goal of the system is to simply detect and track any target vehicle that enters the sensor field, we must also consider the issue of power efficiency in the system. Wireless sensor nodes have access to a limited power supply, and therefore, we must utilize the available power in a way that would maximize the lifetime of the network. Since video sensors require a relatively large amount of processing, our system should be such that a video sensor is used only when a target is approaching the field of view of the sensor. Other less power-consuming sensors such as passive infrared sensors can be used as *tripwires* to turn on the video cameras in the perimeter of the sensor field. Also, due to the large energy cost associated with data transmission, we must avoid transmitting raw video data, and instead, transmit higher-level information generated at each sensor node whenever it is possible to do so.

The system we propose performs two main functions. The first is to automatically calibrate the video cameras in the sensor network based on point correspondences obtained from the moving target. The other is to use feature point correspondences obtained from subsequent frames in the video sequence combined with the camera calibration parameters, to detect the exact position of the target in the field. Then, we use this information to track the target over time and determine its velocity and predict its future state. A general block diagram of the proposed system is given in figure 1.

3 Background Subtraction

In our method, an initial estimate of the moving target region is obtained using a non-parametric model for the background — a method originally proposed in [9]. Then, this estimate is refined using spatial and temporal constraints within a Markov random field framework that has previously been used for image and video segmentation applications [17,18].

We can identify a few main requirements for the background subtraction algorithm. They are:

1. Adaptability to gradual changes in illumination

    As the time of day or weather conditions change, the lighting conditions of the system will also change. Therefore, it is essential that the background model be updated temporally based on the current lighting conditions of the scene.

2. Robustness to vacillations in background

    In outdoor scenes, trees waving in the wind can cause a particular pixel in the image frame to be a projection of a part of a leaf (green), a branch of the tree (brown), or the sky (blue). In all these cases, the particular pixel should be labeled as background although its intensity may differ significantly between successive frames.

3. Small training period

    Due to energy considerations in a wireless sensor network, the camera should not be expected to be on at all times. Therefore, the background subtraction algorithm needs to initialize and generate a background model within a few seconds.

4. Maintaining detection of objects that become stationary

    In our application, it is important to continue to detect a target vehicle for as long as possible even if it comes to a complete stop.

An approach based on the kernel density estimation technique presented in [9] can satisfy most of the requirements specified above. The basic idea behind this technique is that the underlying pdf of any distribution can be approximated by a weighted average of a set of kernel functions defined around sample data points taken from the distribution.

In this technique, we let $x_s(\mathbf{q})$ be an intensity value at location $\mathbf{q}$, and time s, that takes values from the set $\{0,\dots,255\}$. Then, we can estimate the probability that a new pixel at time t, has intensity $x_t(\mathbf{q})$ if it belongs to the background (**B**) by,

$$\Pr(x_t \mid x_t \in \mathbf{B}) \approx \frac{1}{N} \sum_{s \in S_N} \frac{1}{\sqrt{2\pi}\sigma} e^{-\frac{1}{2\sigma^2}(x_t - x_s)} \tag{1}$$

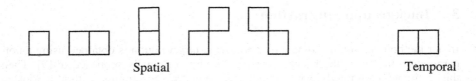

Spatial   Temporal

Fig. 2. Spatial and temporal clique shapes

where S_N is a set of N time instances prior to the current time t. Note that the pixel location $\mathbf{q}$ is omitted for clarity. Here, the kernel function is assumed to be a Gaussian with width σ. A suitable kernel width can be estimated from the sample data in the background pixels [9].

If the estimated probability is greater than a threshold, then the pixel can be labeled as a background pixel. Otherwise, it can be assumed that it belongs to a moving target.

3.1 Spatial and Temporal Constraints

We use a three-dimensional Markov random field (or equivalently, Gibbs random field) approach, previously used in image segmentation [17,18], to further refine the foreground segmentation. In this approach, each pixel in the image is modeled as belonging to two regions- background ($X_t = B$) and foreground ($X_t = B'$). Then, by Bayes theorem, the *a posteriori* probability density that a given pixel, X_t, is in the background can be expressed using the *a priori* density of the background process as:

$$p(X_t \mid x_t) \propto p(x_t \mid X_t) \cdot p(X_t) \tag{2}$$

where x_t is the intensity of the pixel. We have already shown how the density $p(x_t \mid X_t = B)$ can be found using kernel density estimation. The *a priori* density, $p(X_t)$, can be found by modeling the background region using a 3D Gibbs random field. This is done by assuming that the region process satisfies the Markov property. That is, if $\mathbf{N}_t(\mathbf{s})$ is the spatio-temporal neighborhood of a pixel in location $\mathbf{s}$ at time t, then

$$p[X_t(\mathbf{s}) \mid X_r(\mathbf{q}),\ \text{all}\,(\mathbf{q},r) \neq (\mathbf{s},t)] = p[X_t(\mathbf{s}) \mid X_r(\mathbf{q}),\ (\mathbf{q},r) \in \mathbf{N}_t(\mathbf{s})] \tag{3}$$

If this property is satisfied, the Gibbs density for the process can be expressed as

$$p(X_t) = \frac{1}{Z} e^{-\sum_c V_C(X_t)} \tag{4}$$

where Z is a normalizing constant, and $V_c(X_t)$ is the clique potential for a given clique C. We only use two-point cliques (spatial and temporal) and assume that all

Fig. 3. Some results of background subtraction algorithm. Vehicle traveling at 20mph.

one-point cliques have an equal potential of zero. The clique shapes are shown in figure 2. This amounts to an assumption that the probability of classification of the pixel depends only on the immediate (3x3 pixel) spatial neighborhood of the pixel, and temporally only on the previous and next pixel at the same location.

The two-point spatial and temporal clique potentials are defined such that for any two points **s** and **q** in a clique C, and for $\beta > 0$,

$$V_C(X) = \begin{cases} -\beta, & \text{if } X(\mathbf{s}) = X(\mathbf{q}), \quad \mathbf{s}, \mathbf{q} \in C \\ +\beta, & \text{if } X(\mathbf{s}) \neq X(\mathbf{q}), \quad \mathbf{s}, \mathbf{q} \in C \end{cases} \tag{5}$$

3.2 Implementation

An important step in the model generation process is that of updating the background model. In our application, we wished to continue to detect a target even when it becomes stationary. We solve that problem by only updating the background pixels that do not belong to the detected foreground object.

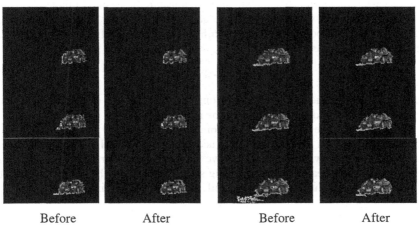

Before   After   Before   After

Fig. 4. Sequence of background frames before and after applying MRF

As input to the algorithm, we use the previously classified frame (background and foreground) and obtain the new classifications for the current and future frame based on the non-parametric model without GRF constraints. Then, a new classification for the current and future frame is found by adding spatial and temporal constraints as specified above. This is iterated until the number of pixels whose classification is changed over a new iteration is below a given threshold. The newly classified frame is now fixed and is used as input for the next iteration of the algorithm.

Figures 3 and 4 show some results of the background subtraction algorithm. In figure 4, we show the improvements made by including spatial and temporal constraints based on Markov random fields.

4   Feature Point Detection and Matching

This method uses a Harris detector [12] for the initial detection of affine invariant feature points. The Harris feature point detector attempts to detect points of interest within the image around which the image intensities change two-dimensionally. The image intensity variation is represented by the second moment matrix, μ, which is calculated using image gradient statistics over a neighborhood of each point.

$$\mu(\mathbf{x}) = \int_{q \in I} g(\mathbf{x} - \mathbf{q}, \sigma_s) \cdot \nabla(\mathbf{q}, \sigma_d) \cdot \nabla(\mathbf{q}, \sigma_d)^T d\mathbf{q} \tag{6}$$

where $g()$ is a Gaussian window with a scale of σ_s, $\mathbf{I}$ is the image intensity function, and

$$\nabla(\mathbf{q}, \sigma_d) = g(\sigma_d) * \mathbf{L}(\mathbf{q}) \tag{7}$$

where $g(\sigma_d)$ is a Gaussian and $\mathbf{L}(\mathbf{q})$ is the image gradient function evaluated at $\mathbf{q}$. The Gaussian function is used to smooth the noise in the original image.

It has been shown in [12] that we can define a corner strength measure, $C(\mathbf{x})$, which represents a point whose neighborhood exhibits significant intensity variations in both dimensions as,

$$C(\mathbf{x}) = \det(\mu(\mathbf{x})) - k \cdot trace^2(\mu(\mathbf{x})) \tag{8}$$

where k is an empirically determined constant. Points with corner strengths above a given threshold could be considered to be interest points.

We can determine the best feature points in the image by choosing the points that give the maximum corner strength according to the Harris measure over all integration and derivation scales. However, since the error in the localization of a feature point is increased with increasing scale, we localize the detected interest point in the smallest scale using a method similar to that proposed in [19].

4.1 Affine Gaussian Scale Space

Affine Gaussian scale space is presented in [14], as a framework within which to solve the wide baseline correspondence problem. An important assumption in using this method is that locally smooth regions of the image of an object will only undergo an affine transformation when viewed from different viewpoints.

The difference between affine Gaussian and linear scale space is that in the former, the Gaussian functions used for convolution of the image prior to finding the second moment matrix will not be rotationally symmetric. Therefore, the scale parameter for an affine Gaussian window will be a covariance matrix instead of a scalar variance.

Then, the second moment matrix of a point in affine Gaussian scale space is,

$$\mu(\mathbf{x}; \Sigma_d; \Sigma_s) = \int_{q \in I} g(\mathbf{x} - \mathbf{q}, \Sigma_s) \cdot \nabla(\mathbf{q}, \Sigma_d) \cdot \nabla(\mathbf{q}, \Sigma_d)^T \, d\mathbf{q} \tag{9}$$

where, Σ_d, and Σ_s are the covariance matrices associated with the scales of derivation and integration.

Assume that the second moment matrix in affine Gaussian scale space of a given image $\mathbf{L}$, is shown to be $\mathbf{M_L}$, and

$$\Sigma_{\mathbf{d,L}} = t\mathbf{M_L^{-1}} \text{ and } \Sigma_{\mathbf{s,L}} = s\mathbf{M_L^{-1}} \tag{10}$$

Then, if $\mathbf{q_R}$ is a point in a transformed image, $\mathbf{R}$, such that $\mathbf{q_R} = \mathbf{A}\mathbf{q_L}$ and, $\mu_\mathbf{R} = \mathbf{M_R}$, it can be shown [13] that,

$$\Sigma_{d,\mathbf{R}} = t\mathbf{M_R^{-1}}, \text{ and } \Sigma_{s,\mathbf{R}} = s\mathbf{M_R^{-1}} \tag{11}$$

Therefore, the fixed point conditions are preserved under linear transformations. Moreover, it is shown in [14] that if we define $\mathbf{L}'$ to be a *square root transformed* image of $\mathbf{L}$, such that $\mathbf{L}'(\mathbf{x}) = \mathbf{L}(\mathbf{M_L^{-\frac{1}{2}}} \cdot \mathbf{x})$, then

$$\mu_\mathbf{L}'(\mathbf{q_L}'; t\mathbf{I}, s\mathbf{I}) = \mathbf{I} \tag{12}$$

Since the same would be true for images $\mathbf{R}$ and $\mathbf{R}'$, and assuming that the affine transformation from $\mathbf{L}'$ to $\mathbf{R}'$ can be written as $\mathbf{A}'$, we get,

$$\mu_\mathbf{L}'(\mathbf{q_L}'; t\mathbf{I}, s\mathbf{I}) = \mathbf{I} = \mathbf{A}'^T \mu_\mathbf{R}'(\mathbf{q_R}'; t\mathbf{I}, s\mathbf{I})\mathbf{A}' = \mathbf{A}'^T \mathbf{A}' = \mathbf{I} \tag{13}$$

Therefore, $\mathbf{A}'$ is a rotation matrix. This implies that, if we are given two images where one is a linear transformation of the other, and we can find the fixed points for each image, then the square root transformed versions of the two images will be related by a simple rotation.

In the wide baseline matching application, we can obtain the local neighborhoods of points detected by the multi-scale Harris feature detector, and find their corresponding square root transformed image neighborhoods. Then, we can use conventional rotation invariant descriptors to represent the transformed images and match them using the minimum distance between such descriptors.

4.2 Implementation

In our implementation, we calculated the corner strength of each point in the image at multiple values of σ_s and σ_d. The values of σ_d were kept proportional to σ_s, and σ_s was chosen to be in the range [2.0, 16.0]. The points with the maximum corner strengths across all possible scales were considered to be feature points of the image.

Then, the goal was to transform the local neighborhood, L, around each feature point, x, to a fixed point and to find its square root form. This transformation, A, is accomplished by iterating through the following basic steps.

1) Set $A^{(0)} = I$.

2) Set $L'(q) = L(A^{(k)} \cdot q)$.

3) Find $\mu'_L(x; t\mathbf{I}, s\mathbf{I})$ where t,s are kept constant and equal to the characteristic scales found by the multi-scale Harris detector.

4) Normalize μ'_L to have a unit determinant.

5) If $\mu'_L \neq I$, then set $A^{(k+1)} = (\mu'_L)^{-\frac{1}{2}} \cdot A^{(k)}$.

6) Normalize $A^{(k)}$ by its largest eigenvalue.

7) If $\mu'_L = I$, then stop. Otherwise, return to step 2.

The normalization of the second moment matrix in step 2 amounts to a rescaling of the local intensity values in the neighborhood of the pixel and the normalization of the transformation matrix in step 6 will ensure that the original image will not be under-sampled.

4.3 Feature Point Correspondence

Before matching the transformed image neighborhoods around the feature points obtained using the above method, they need to be made invariant to changes in intensity since they are viewed by different cameras from different viewpoints. We have used a simple approach, which consists of normalizing each pixel in the feature neighborhood by the maximum intensity value for the neighborhood.

Then, since the images obtained from the two viewpoints will be similar only up to a rotation, the next step is to obtain rotation invariant feature descriptors for each of the images. The descriptors we use are based on a method suggested in [14] and consist of a vector of 15 elements, which correspond to higher order derivatives of the image.

Once the descriptors are obtained we match them using the minimum Mahalanobis distance between each two descriptors taken from different viewpoints. If a point in one image is close to multiple points in another image with a larger spatial variance, then we discard the point since the matching is too ambiguous. Also, if a point does not have any points in the other image which are within a threshold distance, that point is discarded since it may not exist at all in the other image.

4.4 Results

The feature point matching algorithm is successful if the difference in viewpoint between two images is within reasonable limits. For example, the matching algorithm detected 20 corresponding points between figure 5(a) and figure 5(b). Of them, 17 were correct matches. However, of the 17 detected correspondences between 5(a)

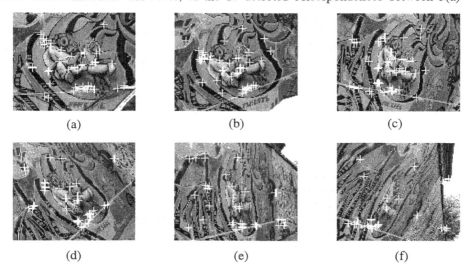

(a)   (b)   (c)

(d)   (e)   (f)

Fig. 5. Results of corner detection. White crosses indicate position of detected corners.

and 5(c), only 9 were correct matches. This shows that, in order to be used for self-calibration, we will need to take images of the target from cameras that have relatively similar viewpoints. On the other hand, if the cameras are already calibrated, then we can use the epipolar constraint to find better correspondences, and a relatively low number of correct correspondences will be sufficient to perform feature point based tracking.

5 Camera Calibration

The sensors need to be calibrated for their intrinsic and extrinsic parameters. Intrinsic camera parameters describe image formation, and they are focal length, aspect ratio, principal point and skew. Extrinsic camera parameters describe position and orientation of the cameras relative to some reference frame and they are described in terms of translation and rotation.

We assume that the relationship between the world coordinates, $[x\ y\ z]$, and the pixel coordinates, $[u\ v]$, is linear projective. This allows for use of projective geometry, which greatly simplifies mathematical representation. In the new generation of cameras distortion is reasonably small, and this model is a good approximation.

$$[u \quad v \quad s]' = P[x \quad y \quad z \quad 1]', \; P = A[R \mid t] \tag{14}$$

Here A is the intrinsic parameter matrix and R, t, describe the rotation and translation parameters.

In addition, we can use several more simplifying assumptions about the camera model that will ease our calibration task and will not seriously degrade the accuracy of reconstruction. Skew can be assumed to be equal to zero, $\theta = \pi/2$, (reasonable for new generations of cameras), and the principal point, $[u_o, v_o]$, can be assumed to be at the center of the image. It is well known that variation in location of the principal point of several pixels does not affect the reconstruction in a great manner [15].

$$A = \begin{bmatrix} fk_u & fk_u \cot\theta & u_0 \\ & \dfrac{fk_v}{\sin\theta} & v_0 \\ & & 1 \end{bmatrix} \rightarrow A = \begin{bmatrix} fk_u & & \\ & fk_v & \\ & & 1 \end{bmatrix} \tag{15}$$

If aspect ratio is known in advance (from manufacturers specifications,) and if we have a good guess for the focal lengths of each camera, we are then able to reconstruct the scene from one snapshot of the stereo pair.

Scene reconstruction involves obtaining pixel correspondences between a pair of images, which are used to estimate the fundamental matrix, F [20]. The fundamental matrix defines an epipolar constraint between images in terms of pixels. Since the estimation of the fundamental matrix is very sensitive to errors in feature point correspondences, and our Harris feature based matcher can produce some false matches, we use the random sample and consensus algorithm (RANSAC) [21] using the epipolar constraint as a criterion to detect false matches and eliminate outliers. For corresponding points m_2 and m_1 in two images, the epipolar constraint is expressed as,

$$m_2^T F m_1 = 0 \tag{16}$$

F is calculated using a normalized eight-point algorithm [22].

Knowing the intrinsic parameters and the fundamental matrix we can calculate the essential matrix, which can further be decomposed into rotational and translational components to obtain initial guesses for the extrinsic parameters [23]. We then optimize the results in terms of the discrepancy from the epipolar constraint by solving a nonlinear least squares problem [15].

$$\min\left[\sum_{i=1}^{m} \left((m_{2i})^T A_2^{-T} T R A_1^{-1} m_{1i} \right)^2 \right] \tag{17}$$

Here T is a skew symmetric matrix made from the translation vector, A_2, and A_1 are the intrinsic matrices of the two cameras, and m_2, m_1 are corresponding points.

If we do not have an accurate guess for the focal lengths, we can obtain them by self-calibrating the cameras. Since we have only one unknown intrinsic parameter for each camera, we need only one synchronized snapshot from each camera to be able to solve for the focal lengths. To self-calibrate cameras, we need to solve the set of Kruppa equations. Kruppa equations require the fundamental matrix to be known and they relate the correspondence of epipolar lines tangent to a dual image of the absolute conic [24].

In the more general case, if we do not know the aspect ratio in advance, then we can still self-calibrate the cameras by using two snapshots of a moving target taken from each camera. Then, if we only obtain correspondence points detected within the target, we can equate the motion of the target to a motion of the stereo rig. It has been shown in [25] that this provides enough additional constraints to solve for the unknown intrinsic parameters.

Since with this approach we can only reconstruct the scene up to an unknown scale factor, we need some external information to perform the metric reconstruction. For example, if the cameras are equipped with GPS device, then we can obtain the scale factor by calculating the baseline distance between the cameras. Figure 6 shows results of the camera calibration algorithm and metric reconstruction procedure.

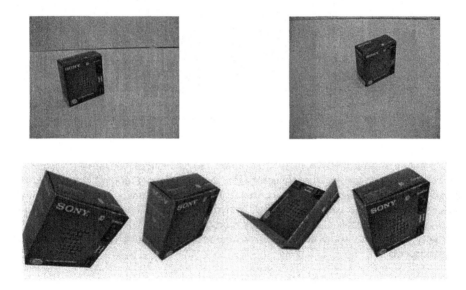

Fig.6. Original images and reconstructed scene using two cameras

6   Tracking Results

For the tracking experiment, we used a sequence of images taken from two cameras in a wide baseline setup. The images were taken with a resolution of 1024x768 pixels and they consisted of two moving objects in an indoor environment. We assumed that the focal lengths of the cameras were known and that aspect ratios were equal to one.

After the cameras were calibrated, the detected feature points on the target were tracked over the entire sequence. The tracking was performed using a Kalman filter. We assume a linear constant velocity dynamic model for the Kalman filter. Figure 7 shows an example of a tracked point as the object moves in the field of view of both cameras.

Fig. 7. Tracked Feature Point. Top: right camera view, bottom: left camera view

The position and velocity plots of the point are shown in figure 8. The position of the point is shown relative to the XZ plane in the camera coordinate system. This corresponds to viewing the trajectory of the point from above. There are some missing points in the position plot that correspond to frames in which the feature points could not be extracted with sufficient certainty. There are also a couple of outliers that are caused by false point correspondences between the images. The velocity plot shows some deviation from the ground truth due to errors in the metric reconstruction.

7   Conclusions

We have concluded that computer vision based target tracking is a viable approach for a wide-baseline configuration involving multiple cameras. Feature point based tracking algorithms enable real time operation, and also reduce communication requirements between sensors. The main difficulty in this approach is establishing wide-baseline feature point correspondences from uncalibrated camera views for the purpose of camera calibration. We plan to further investigate this topic in the future.

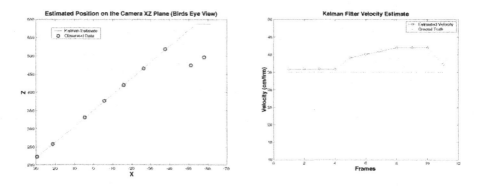

Fig. 8. Position and velocity estimates of tracked point.

Acknowledgements. This project has been funded in part by the Defense Advanced Research Projects Agency (DARPA) through the Sensor Information Technology Program (SensIT).

References

1.   G. D. Sullivan, "Visual Interpretation of Known Objects in Constrained Scenes," *Philosophical Transactions B of the Royal Society*, vol. 337, pp. 361–370, 1992.
2.   D. Koller, K. Daniilidis, and H.-H. Nagel, "Model-based Object Tracking in Monocular Image Sequences of Road Traffic Scenes," *International Journal of Computer Vision*, vol. 10, pp. 257–281, 1993.
3.   J. M. Ferryman, S. J. Maybank, and A. D. Worall, "Visual Surveillance for Moving Vehicles," *International Journal of Computer Vision*, vol. 37, no. 2, pp. 187–197, 2000.
4.   D. Koller, J. Weber, and J. Malik, "Robust Multiple Car Tracking with Occlusion Reasoning," *Proceedings of the European Conference on Computer Vision*, vol. 1, pp. 189–196, 1994.
5.   D. Koller, J. Weber, T. Huang, J. Malik, G. Ogasawara, B. Rao, and S. Russell, "Towards Robust Automatic Traffic Scene Analysis in Real-Time," *Proceedings of the 12th International Conference on Pattern Recognition*, pp. 126–131, 1994.
6.   D. Beymer, P. McLauchlan, B. Coifmann, J. Malik, "A Real-Time Computer Vision System for Measuring Traffic Parameters," *Proceedings of the IEEE Conference on Computer Vision and Pattern Recognition*, pp. 495–501, 1997.
7.   T. Aach and A. Kaup, "Statistical Model-based Change Detection in Moving Video," *Signal Processing*, vol. 31, pp. 165–180, 1993.
8.   C. Stauffer and W. E. L. Grimson, "Adaptive Background Mixture Models for Real-Time Tracking," *Proceedings of the IEEE Conference on Computer Vision and Pattern Recognition*, vol. 1, pp. 22–29, 1999.
9.   A. Elgammal, R. Duraiswamy, D. Harwood, and L. Davis, "Background and Foreground Modeling Using Nonparametric Kernel Density Estimation for Visual Surveillance," *Proceedings of the IEEE*, vol. 90, no. 7, pp. 1151–1163, July 2002.

10. D. G. Lowe, "Object Recognition from Scale Invariant Features," *Proceedings of the International Conference on Computer Vision*, pp. 1150–1157, 1999.
11. K. Mikolajczyk, and C. Schmid, "Indexing Based on Scale Invariant Interest Points," *Proceedings of the 8th International Conference on Computer Vision*, pp. 525–531, 2001.
12. C. Harris, and M. Stephens, "A Combined Corner and Edge Detector," *Proceedings of the Alvey Vision Conference*, pp. 147–151, 1988.
13. T. Lindeberg, and J. Gårding, "Shape-Adapted Smoothing in Estimation of 3-D Shape Cues from Affine Distortions of Local 2-D Brightness Structure," *Image and Vision Computing*, vol. 15, no. 6, pp. 415–434, 1997.
14. A. Baumberg, "Reliable Feature Matching Across Widely Separated Views," *Proceedings of the Conference on Computer Vision and Pattern Recognition*, pp. 774–781, 2000.
15. Z. Zhang, "A Flexible New Technique for Camera Calibration," *IEEE Transactions on Pattern Analysis and Machine Intelligence,* vol. 22, no. 11, November 2000.
16. M. Pollefeys, R. Kock, and L. Van Gool, "Self-Calibration and Metric Reconstruction in spite of Varying and Unknown Intrinsic Camera Parameters," *International Journal of Computer Vision*, vol. 32, no. 1, pp. 7–25, Aug 1999.
17. T. Pappas, "An Adaptive Clustering Algorithm for Image Segmentation," *IEEE Transactions on Signal Processing*, vol. 40, no. 4, April 1992.
18. R. O. Hinds, T. N. Pappas, "An Adaptive Clustering Algorithm for Segmentation of Video Sequences," *Proceedings of the International Conference on Acoustics, Speech and Signal Processing (ICASSP)*, vol. 4, pp. 2427–2430, May 1995.
19. A. P. Witkin, "Scale-Space Filtering," *Proceedings of the 8th International Joint Conference on Artificial Intelligence*, pp. 1019–1022, 1983.
20. Q.T. Luong, O. Faugeras, "The Fundamental Matrix: Theory, Algorithms and Stability Analysis,"*The International Journal of Computer Vision*, vol.17, pp 43–76, 1996.
21. M. A. Fischler, R. C. Bolles. "Random Sample Consensus: A Paradigm for Model Fitting with Applications to Image Analysis and Automated Cartography," *Comm. of the ACM*, Vol 24, pp 381–395, 1981.
22. R. Hartley, "In Defence of the 8-Point Algorithm," *ICCV*, pp. 1064–1070, 1996.
23. O. Faugeras, Q.T. Luong, "The Geometry of Multiple Images," The MIT Press, 2001.
24. R. Hartly, A. Zissereman, "Multiple View geometry", Cambridge University Press, 2000.
25. Z. Zhang, Q.-T.Luong, and O. Faugeras, "Motion of an Uncalibrated Stereo Rig: Self-Calibration and Metric Reconstruction," *IEEE Trans. on Robotics and Automation,* vol. 12, no. 1, pp. 103–113, 1996.

Decentralised Ground Target Tracking with Heterogeneous Sensing Nodes on Multiple UAVs

Matthew Ridley, Eric Nettleton, Ali Göktoğan, Graham Brooker, Salah Sukkarieh, and Hugh F. Durrant-Whyte

School of Aerospace, Mechanical and Mechatronic Engineering
Australian Centre for Field Robotics
The Rose Street Building J04
The University of Sydney 2006 NSW Australia
{m.ridley, ericn, agoktogan, gbrooker, salah, hugh}@acfr.usyd.edu.au
http://www.acfr.usyd.edu.au

Abstract. This paper presents real time results of a decentralised airborne data fusion system tracking multiple ground based targets. These target estimates are then used to construct a map of the environment. A decentralised communication strategy is employed which is robust to communication latencies and dropouts and results in each sensing node having a local estimate using global information.
In addition, this paper describes both hardware and algorithms used to deploy two sensor nodes for such a task. Two sensor types will be discussed, vision and mm wave radar. The problems introduced by locating the sensors on air vehicles are both interesting and challenging. A total of four unmanned air vehicles will be employed to carry node payloads. Weight and power restrictions of the payloads coupled with the vehicle dynamics make the task of processing and fusing vision and radar based data a challenging problem indeed. This paper aims to highlight many of the problems that have been encountered in developing both hardware and software to operate under such constraints.

1 Introduction

The primary objective of this research is the implementation of Decentralised Data Fusion (DDF) algorithms. The algorithms are applied to a tracking problem and are demonstrated in real time on multiple Unmanned Air Vehicles (UAVs). This implementation environment is arguably the most difficult arena in which to demonstrate this research due to the dynamics and complexity of flight vehicles.

The tracking problem formulated in this research involves multiple aircraft flying over some region and estimating the position and velocity of ground based targets. These tracks are then used to form a map of all targets in the area. When using multiple aircraft in the decentralised framework, each aircraft has a local target estimate using global information. The decentralised architecture therefore gives each aircraft more information, which in turn results in a more accurate state estimate. For this reason, there has been a great deal of research in the area over recent years[3,6,13].

F. Zhao and L. Guibas (Eds.): IPSN 2003, LNCS 2634, pp. 545–565, 2003.

The flight vehicle is the Brumby MKIII UAV, capable of carrying a 45kg payload. Each is equipped with GPS and inertial sensors and carries two terrain payloads; a vision system and either a mm-wave radar or laser sensor. Each payload incorporates it's own modular, fully decentralised processing hardware. On-board, the payloads communicate with each other using a CAN bus. Inter-vehicle communication is via radio Ethernet. Each payload processor implements a fully decentralised data fusion algorithm. Payloads communicate with each other directly in terms of terrain information; all data fusion and assimilation occurs at the payload site. There is no separate fusion centre on any flight platform and no fusion centre elsewhere on the ground. The architecture is thus decentralised, fully modular and scalable.

2   Decentralised Data Fusion

A decentralised data fusion system is comprised of a network of independent nodes which include a sensor with some processing and communication hardware attached. Each node then uses this hardware to run its own local estimation algorithm and to communicate its results to other nodes. This communication results in a decentralised network where each node has a local estimate of global information without the need for any central processing or communication facility.

A general decentralised data fusion system can be characterised by three basic constraints [7]:

1. There is no single central fusion centre and no node should be central to the operation of the network.
2. There is no common communications facility - communications must be kept on a strictly node-to-node basis.
3. Each node has knowledge only of its immediate neighbours - there is no global knowledge of the network topology.

These constraints combine to ensure that there is no single element that is critical to the operation of the network. If any node or communication link should fail, the result is a gradual degradation in network performance rather than catastrophic failure. The results presented in this paper were obtained using a DDF network which satisfied these constraints using a peer to peer communication topology.

3   Problem Formulation

Consider a system given by the discrete model

$$\mathbf{x}(k) = \mathbf{F}_k \mathbf{x}(k-1) + \mathbf{B}_k \mathbf{u}(k) + \mathbf{G}_k \mathbf{v}(k), \tag{1}$$

where $\mathbf{x}(k)$ is the state of interest, $\mathbf{u}(k)$ is the control input vector and $\mathbf{v}(k)$ a zero mean, white noise sequence with variance $\mathbf{Q}_k$. The matrices $\mathbf{F}_k$, $\mathbf{B}_k$ and $\mathbf{G}_k$

define the propagation of the state, control and noise inputs respectively over the period t_{k-1} to t_k. To simplify notation, the time index $k-1$ is used to represent t_{k-1} and k to represent t_k. The system is observed by a sensor according to the linear equation

$$\mathbf{z}(k) = \mathbf{H}_k\mathbf{x}(k) + \mathbf{v}(k) \tag{2}$$

where $\mathbf{z}(k)$ is the vector of observations made at time k, $\mathbf{H}_k$ the observation model, and $\mathbf{v}(k)$ is the associated observation noise modeled as an uncorrelated white sequence with $\mathrm{E}\{\mathbf{v}(i)\mathbf{v}^T(j)\} = \delta_{ij}\mathbf{R}(i)$. The Kalman filter algorithm generates estimates for the state $\hat{\mathbf{x}}(k \mid k)$ at a time k given all observations up to time k, together with a corresponding estimate covariance $\mathbf{P}(k \mid k)$.

The information form of the Kalman filter is obtained by re-writing the state estimate and covariance in terms of two new variables

$$\hat{\mathbf{y}}(i \mid j) \overset{\triangle}{=} \mathbf{P}^{-1}(i \mid j)\hat{\mathbf{x}}(i \mid j), \qquad \mathbf{Y}(i \mid j) \overset{\triangle}{=} \mathbf{P}^{-1}(i \mid j), \tag{3}$$

These are known as the information vector and information matrix respectively. The prediction of these quantities is done using

$$\mathbf{Y}(k \mid k-1) = \mathbf{M}_k - \mathbf{M}_k\mathbf{G}_k\boldsymbol{\Sigma}_k^{-1}\mathbf{G}_k^T\mathbf{M}_k$$
$$\hat{\mathbf{y}}(k \mid k-1) = \left[1 - \mathbf{M}_k\mathbf{G}_k\boldsymbol{\Sigma}_k^{-1}\mathbf{G}_k^T\right]\mathbf{F}_k^{-T}\hat{\mathbf{y}}(k-1 \mid k-1) + \mathbf{Y}(k \mid k-1)\mathbf{B}_{k-1}\mathbf{u}(k),$$

where

$$\boldsymbol{\Sigma}_k = \mathbf{G}_k^T\mathbf{M}_k\mathbf{G}_k + \mathbf{Q}_k^{-1} \tag{4}$$
$$\mathbf{M}_k = \mathbf{F}_k^{-T}\mathbf{Y}(k-1 \mid k-1)\mathbf{F}_k^{-1}, \tag{5}$$

When an observation is made, the information it contains is calculated using

$$\mathbf{i}(k) \overset{\triangle}{=} \mathbf{H}^T(k)\mathbf{R}^{-1}(k)\mathbf{z}(k), \qquad \mathbf{I}(k) \overset{\triangle}{=} \mathbf{H}^T(k)\mathbf{R}^{-1}(k)\mathbf{H}(k) \tag{6}$$

With these definitions, the information filter update equations are written

$$\hat{\mathbf{y}}(k \mid k) = \hat{\mathbf{y}}(k \mid k-1) + \mathbf{i}(k) \tag{7}$$
$$\mathbf{Y}(k \mid k) = \mathbf{Y}(k \mid k-1) + \mathbf{I}(k) \tag{8}$$

For a complete derivation of the information filter, the reader is referred to Maybeck [11] and Manyika [10]. The former of these derives the filter equations from the well known Kalman filter, while the latter derives the information filter directly from Bayes Theorem.

The information form of the Kalman filter, while widely known, is not commonly used because the update terms are of dimension of the state, whereas in the distributed Kalman filter updates are of dimension of the observation. For single sensor estimation problems, this argues for the use of the Kalman filter over the information filter. However, in multiple sensor problems, the opposite is true. The reason is that with multiple sensor observations

$$\mathbf{z}_i(k) = \mathbf{H}_i(k)\mathbf{x}(k) + \mathbf{v}_i(k), \qquad i = 1, \cdots, N$$

the estimate can not be constructed from a simple linear combination of contributions from individual sensors

$$\hat{\mathbf{x}}(k \mid k) \neq \hat{\mathbf{x}}(k \mid k - 1) + \sum_{i=1}^{N} \mathbf{W}_i(k) \left[\mathbf{z}_i(k) - \mathbf{H}_i(k)\hat{\mathbf{x}}(k \mid k - 1) \right],$$

as the innovation $\mathbf{z}_i(k) - \mathbf{H}_i(k)\hat{\mathbf{x}}(k \mid k - 1)$ generated from each sensor is correlated because they share common information through the prediction $\hat{\mathbf{x}}(k \mid k - 1)$. However, in information form, estimates can be constructed from linear combinations of observation information

$$\hat{\mathbf{y}}(k \mid k) = \hat{\mathbf{y}}(k \mid k - 1) + \sum_{i=1}^{N} \mathbf{i}_i(k),$$

as the information terms $\mathbf{i}_i(k)$ from each sensor i are uncorrelated. Once the update equations have been written in this simple additive form, it is straightforward to distribute the data fusion problem (unlike for a Kalman filter); each sensor node simply generates the information terms $\mathbf{i}_i(k)$, and these are summed at the fusion centre to produce a global information estimate.

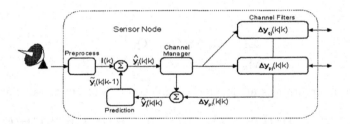

Fig. 1. Structure of a decentralised node.

To decentralise the information filter all that is necessary is to replicate the central fusion algorithm (summation) at each sensor node and simplify the result. This yields a surprisingly simple nodal fusion algorithm. The algorithm is described graphically in Figure 1. Essentially, local estimates are first generated at each node by fusing (adding) locally available observation information $\mathbf{i}_i(k)$ with locally available prior information $\hat{\mathbf{y}}_i(k \mid k - 1)$. This yields a local information estimate $\tilde{\mathbf{y}}_i(k \mid k)$. This complete information state estimate is then transmitted to other nodes, where the difference between it and previously communicated information is calculated. This difference is the increment of new information that can then be fused with the local information state estimate using the additive update equations. The algorithm that calculates the difference is known as the channel filter as it resides on a communication channel and keeps track of what any connected nodes have in common. An important point to note is that, after this, the locally available estimates are *exactly* the same as if the data fusion problem had been solved on a single central processor using a monolithic formulation of the conventional Kalman filter.

One of the most important properties of this decentralised architecture is that it is completely robust to communication failure. If any transmissions are lost or corrupted, the information they contained is implicitly contained in all future messages as each node always sends its complete information state estimate. Thus, when communication is re-established, the first message which is received automatically updates the receiving node with any information that may have been lost in earlier messages.

3.1   Target Model

The state vector is is defined as:

$$\mathbf{x}(k) = [x(k), \dot{x}(k), y(k), \dot{y}(k), z(k)]^T \tag{9}$$

It does not include a vertical velocity as the assumption is that ground based targets will never have significant vertical motion.

The target x and y position and velocity are modeled as an Integrated Ornstein-Uhlenbeck (IOU) process [14]. This process has a Brownian velocity which can be bounded by appropriate choice of the model parameter γ. The z position is modeled as a simple Brownian process. The IOU process model was selected because of the velocity bounding property, which can be used to prevent a Brownian velocity uncertainty from increasing beyond reasonable values. For example, if tracking a wheeled land vehicle then the upper bound on the velocity uncertainty is the maximum speed of the vehicle.

The state transition matrix for this process model is given by Equation 10 below.

$$\mathbf{F}_k = \begin{bmatrix} 1 & \Delta T & 0 & 0 & 0 \\ 0 & F_v & 0 & 0 & 0 \\ 0 & 0 & 1 & \Delta T & 0 \\ 0 & 0 & 0 & F_v & 0 \\ 0 & 0 & 0 & 0 & 1 \end{bmatrix} \tag{10}$$

where

$$F_v = e^{-\Delta T \gamma} \tag{11}$$

The process noise is written as $\mathbf{G}_k \mathbf{Q}_k \mathbf{G}_k^T$ where

$$\mathbf{Q}_k = \begin{bmatrix} q_x & 0 & 0 \\ 0 & q_y & 0 \\ 0 & 0 & q_z \end{bmatrix} \tag{12}$$

and

$$\mathbf{G}_k = \begin{bmatrix} 0 & 0 & 0 \\ \sqrt{\Delta T}(1 - F_v) & 0 & 0 \\ 0 & 0 & 0 \\ 0 & \sqrt{\Delta T}(1 - F_v) & 0 \\ 0 & 0 & 1 \end{bmatrix} \tag{13}$$

As the targets in this implementation where known to be stationary, the IOU process was tuned to decay velocity to zero.

4   Sensors

The task of each sensor node is to assimilate both the navigation solution and raw sensor data into the information matrix and vector **I** and **i** respectively. Sensor control is also required in some implementations (radar) as sensor repositioning may be required to compensate for platform orientation.

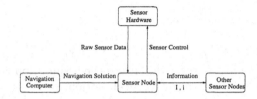

Fig. 2. Flow of data in and out of a sensor node.

Observations are made from a moving platform. These observations must take into account the relative position and orientation (pose) of the vehicle, location of sensor payload relative to the vehicle and sensor model characteristics. The observation is transform to Cartesian space in the sensor frame of reference with the use of Equation 14. [1]

$$\mathbf{z}_t^s = \begin{bmatrix} r_t^s \cos \theta_t^s \cos \psi_t^s \\ r_t^s \cos \theta_t^s \sin \psi_t^s \\ r_t^s \sin \theta_t^s \end{bmatrix} \tag{14}$$

Figure 3 depicts the result of this operation for a vision sensor. Translation and rotation operations bring this observation into earth coordinates. Accounting for body pose and sensor pose (relative to body) results in:

$$\mathbf{z}_t^e = \mathbf{x}_b^e + \mathbf{C}_b^e \mathbf{x}_s^b + \mathbf{C}_b^e \mathbf{C}_s^b \mathbf{z}_t^s \tag{15}$$

The associated uncertainty of the observation is required in the form of the covariance matrix **R**. An approximation converted to Cartesian space relative to the axis defined by the observation itself is:

$$\mathbf{R}_t^t = \begin{bmatrix} \sigma_r^2 & 0 & 0 \\ 0 & r^2 \sigma_\psi^2 & 0 \\ 0 & 0 & r^2 \sigma_\theta^2 \end{bmatrix} \tag{16}$$

---

[1] The scripting of the rotation matrices and vectors defines what particular frame (body,earth,sensor,target) they refer to. For example $\mathbf{C}_b^e$ defines the rotation matrix between earth and vehicle body coordinate frames.

Figure 3 shows more explicitly how this approximation relates geometrically in 2D to the world and sensor axes. The total error in the observation due to the properties of the sensor are:

$$\mathbf{R}_t^e(sensor) = [\mathbf{C}_b^e \mathbf{C}_s^b \mathbf{C}_t^s] \mathbf{R}_t^t [\mathbf{C}_b^e \mathbf{C}_s^b \mathbf{C}_t^s]^T \tag{17}$$

Addition errors induced by the uncertainty in the vehicle body location, roll, pitch and yaw must also be accounted for. Following flight tests it became apparent that these errors are the major contributors to the uncertainty of the observation. The total observation error in earth coordinates is therefore:

$$\mathbf{R}_t^e = \mathbf{R}_t^e(sensor) + \mathbf{R}_b^e(body) + \mathbf{R}_t^e(roll) + \mathbf{R}_t^e(pitch) + \mathbf{R}_t^e(yaw) \tag{18}$$

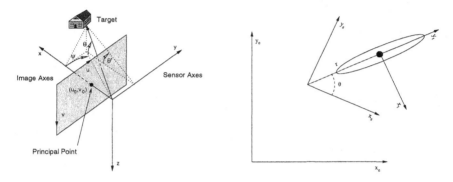

Fig. 3. Principal point, Image and Sensor axes (left). Observation axis relative to sensor and world axis (right).

4.1   Radar Payload

It is important for decentralised data fusion and control amongst multiple platforms that at least one carries a sensor which returns Range, Bearing and Elevation (RBE) of the ground targets [4][12].

The MMW radar described has been built in house and mounted on a specially designed attitude stabilising gimbal with a scanning mirror. The whole radar unit is compact and light enough to be mounted into the nose of the Brumby Mark-III UAV as shown in Figure 4.

Overview. The MMW radar presented in this paper uses frequency modulated continuous-wave (FMCW) principles for range measurement [1][2]. The FMCW radar front end transmits a linear frequency chirp Δf of duration T_d. The radiated electromagnetic waves propagate along the beam axis and reflect back from the

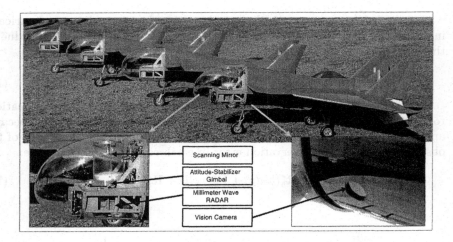

Fig. 4. 77GHz MMW radar on attitude-stabiliser gimbal mechanism with scanning mirror is mounted in the nose cone of Brumby Mark-III UAV. The vision camera is located under the fuselage.

target in a round trip time of T_p. The received signal, which is shifted in frequency proportional to the round-trip time, is mixed with transmitted signal. The result of this mixing is the frequency difference which is known as the intermediate frequency (IF) or beat frequency f_b. This is a measure of the range.

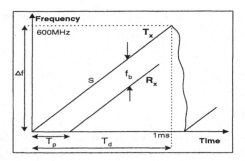

Fig. 5. In FMCW radar, range is calculated from the difference between transmitted and received signal frequencies.

The range resolution depends on the sweep bandwidth Δf and the linearity of the sweep. For a sweep bandwidth of Δf=600MHz and sweep duration of T_d=1ms the theoretical range resolution from Equation 19 is obtained as $\delta R_{chrip} = 0.25m$. Where c is the velocity of propagation.

$$\delta R_{chrip} = \frac{c}{2\Delta f} \tag{19}$$

Linearity of the sweep, Lin is defined in Equation 20 where $S=\delta f/\delta t$ is the chirp slope in Hz/s as shown in Figure 5.

$$Lin = \frac{S_{max} - S_{min}}{S_{min}} \qquad (20)$$

Nominal linearity of the radar chirp is about 0.1%. From Equation 21, the resolution for a target at R=500m is obtained as δR_{lin}=0.5m.

$$\delta R_{lin} = R\ Lin \qquad (21)$$

The final system range resolution δR, can be determined from Equation 22 which resolves as δR=0.56m.

$$\delta R = \sqrt{\delta R_{chrip}^2 + \delta R_{lin}^2} \qquad (22)$$

Hardware. The transmitter and receiver in the MMW radar front end are configured to operate at 77GHz with a transmit power of 10mW.

The MMW radar front end is connected to a high speed 12 bit Analogue to Digital Converter (ADC) unit. Digitised data is stored on a 4096 word buffer and then transferred to the DSP memory.

The Digital Signal Processing (DSP) unit applies a hamming window to the digitised signal to limit the effect of probable discontinuities at the start and end of the sampling period, which contribute to range side-lobes. This improves signal integrity at the expense of slightly poorer range resolution. After the window operation, digitised data is subjected to the Fast Fourier Transform (FFT) operation.

As the UAV manoeuvres during the flight, it's attitude angles (ie. roll and pitch) change continuously. The MMW radar sensor is mounted on a 2 degree of freedom attitude-stabilising gimbal which is controlled to keep the grazing angle of the MMW radar fixed. The shaped scanning mirror rotating at a frequency of 2.5Hz above the gimbal reflects the signal radiated from the horn-lens antenna. A simplified scan pattern is shown in Figure 6.

The DSP unit passes the result of the FFT analysis (ie. measured target ranges), to the control computer. The control computer combines the range data with the gimbal and scanning mirror positions acquired from the servo controllers to form RBE observations The control computer receives aircraft attitude data from the navigation computer. This data is then used to command the servo controllers.

4.2   Vision Payload

During the flight trials, over 150 visual beacons were laid on the ground in surveyed locations. The flight area consisted of relatively featureless farmland. The beacons were 0.9m x 0.9m square plastic sheets and appeared quite clearly in the captured images as can be seen in Figure 7. An algorithm had to be developed to reliably extract these features with minimal use of processing resources.

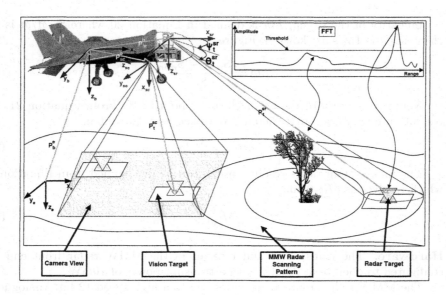

Fig. 6. Scanning mirror rotates around z_{sr} axis. The look-down angle θ_t^{sr}, of the radar beam is fixed. Analysis of the FFT power spectrum reveals the target range.

Hardware. A PC104 embedded computer operating at 266MHz, equipped with a framegrabber provides low cost vision capability. Initial flights of the UAVs enabled several minutes of flight video to be recorded from a low cost monochrome camera. As the PAL imaging system is interlaced each captured images is effectively two separate images taken 20ms apart. An image stream of size 384x288 @ 50Hz was obtained by extracting the odd and even fields of an interlaced stream of size 384x576 @ 25Hz.

Sensor Model. The camera was calibrated with methods similar to that described in [8] with a readily available tool-box. The calibration procedure provides the principal point (u_0, v_0) and focal lengths f_u, f_v (in pixels) for each axis and the expected error in the pinhole model. From this model a mapping from sensor coordinates (x, y, z) to image coordinates (u, v) can be defined as:

$$
\begin{bmatrix} u \\ v \end{bmatrix} = \begin{bmatrix} \frac{yf_u}{x} \\ \frac{zf_v}{x} \end{bmatrix} + \begin{bmatrix} u_0 \\ v_0 \end{bmatrix}
\tag{23}
$$

Parameters for image distortion compensation are also supplied. However, the computational expense of a fifth order polynomial, and the fact that the particular lens used had minimal distortion allowed the step to be omitted.

The inverse mapping is unable to recover the loss of range information. However, a direction to the feature can be recovered. It is convenient to define this information in a similar form to the Euler angles defining the current vehicle state.

$$\psi = \arctan((u - u_0)f_u) \tag{24}$$
$$\theta' = \arctan((v - v_0)f_v) \tag{25}$$
$$\theta = -\arctan(\tan(\theta')\cos(\psi)) \tag{26}$$

Feature Extraction. Due to the modest processing resources being available, a simple but fast method of point based feature extraction is employed. The algorithm operates as follows:

- Statistics of the image intensities are gathered to determine a suitable intensity threshold.
- All pixels above this threshold are converted into line segments.
- A range gate performs data association on these segments to establish clusters of pixels.
- The mass and centre of mass of each pixel cluster is obtained.
- Aspect ratio and density of the cluster of pixels is also obtained.

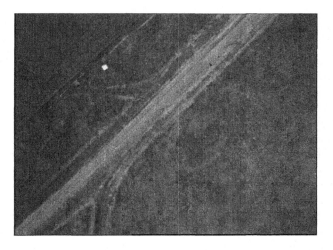

Fig. 7. Image showing artificial feature. Road and fencelines are clearly visible

Although the inverse mapping equations do not provide any range information it is possible to recover some range information due to the fact that the beacons are of a known size. Utilising Equation 23 and assuming the beacon is parallel to the image plane, the height h_v , width w_u and corresponding area (in pixels) A_{uv} of an object can be defined. Where A_{yz} is the beacon area, h_z height and w_y width in the sensor axes.

$$w_u = \frac{w_y f_u}{x} \tag{27}$$

$$h_v = \frac{h_z f_v}{x} \tag{28}$$

$$A_{uv} \approx \frac{f_u f_v A_{yz}}{x^2} \tag{29}$$

Re-arranging Equation 29 provides an expression for an estimate of the perpendicular height (x) above the beacon. The area being expressed in terms of effective side length in pixels(p). Differentiating with respect to p provides an expression for the error in the height estimate. Where $\sigma_p{}^2$ is the variance in the pixels. The range estimate is then obtained by correcting the height estimate with the direction to the target.

$$x = \sqrt{\frac{f_u f_v A_{yz}}{p^2}} \tag{30}$$

$$\sigma_x = \frac{f_u f_v A_{yz}}{xp^3}\sigma_p \tag{31}$$

$$r = \frac{x}{\cos(\theta)\cos(\psi)} \tag{32}$$

5   Postprocessed Flight Data

The DDF algorithm was initially run offline using real logged flight data. A single 15 minute flight was spliced into four separate 3 minute segments such that no segments were overlapping. These were then used to simulate four separate aircraft. The aircraft pose was obtained by fusing the logged GPS/IMU information[9], and tracking information was obtained using vision sensor which logged frames at 50Hz. Artificial vision targets ($0.9m$x$0.9m$ white plastic sheets) were deployed at surveyed locations in order to allow the camera to track known objects.

The data sets were used initially with all four aircraft acting independently and not sharing any information. The entire process was then repeated with the aircraft configured in a DDF network in the topology illustrated in Figure 8. All data association was done using the information gate [5], which is the information form of the state space innovation gate. Results of running in these two configurations are presented in Section 5.1.

5.1   Postprocessed Results

When the platforms operated independently, they each generated target tracks using only the information from their locally attached sensor. The maps of 50 targets generated by each aircraft under these conditions are plotted in Figure 9. Each of these maps is completely independent as they were generated without any sharing of information. An inspection of the plots confirms that each aircraft tracked their own group of 50 targets and that the maps are quite different.

The result of processing the same data sets for the scenario where the four aircraft operated in a DDF network is shown in Figure 10. This illustrates the

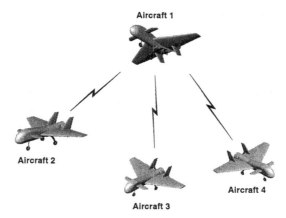

Fig. 8. The topology of the 4 aircraft DDF network when post processing the flight data.

target map generated on aircraft 1, and includes a zoomed in section of one part of the map. As a result of the communication of information in the DDF network, the maps on all aircraft are identical to that presented here and are therefore omitted for brevity.

6   Real Time Implementation

Results are now presented of a real time demonstration of the algorithm. The system consisted of two aircraft equipped with vision payloads and two ground nodes with no sensor attached. The topology of this DDF network is illustrated in Figure 11. As the ground nodes have no sensor attached, they do not contribute any information to the network. They simply receive DDF information from the aircraft they are connected to and use it to construct their own estimates. Thus, the ground nodes will replicate the estimates on the aircraft even though they do not have any sensors attached. The system was implemented in this way for two reasons:

1. To make the network more complex than just the two aircraft nodes.
2. As the ground nodes replicate the estimates on each aircraft, they are able to provide target information for a GUI without the need for the aircraft to communicate anything other than DDF information.

When running the DDF tracking system in real time, the vision system was operating at 25Hz or half its maximum rate. This was necessary as the decentralised tracker and the image processing software shared the same processor. In order to limit the maximum processing requirements of the tracking software, it was limited to a maximum of 17 targets. This number could be increased on future flights, but was initially set to a conservative figure to ensure system

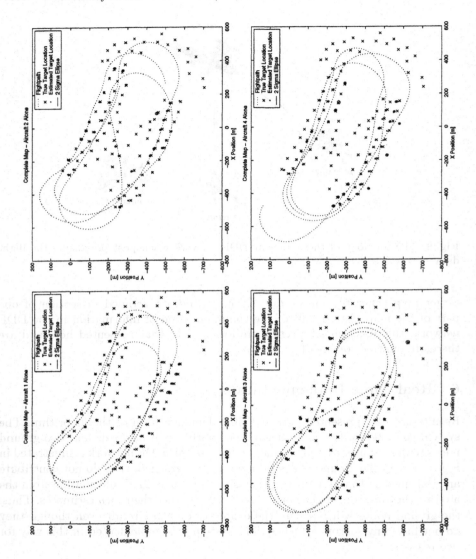

Fig. 9. A map of the 50 targets that aircraft 1,2,3 and 4 generated when operating independently. Note that the maps are different as there was no sharing of information.

stability. Artificial vision targets were again deployed at surveyed locations to allow the system to track known objects. All data association was done in real time using the information gate. If there was any ambiguity in the association, the observation was discarded.

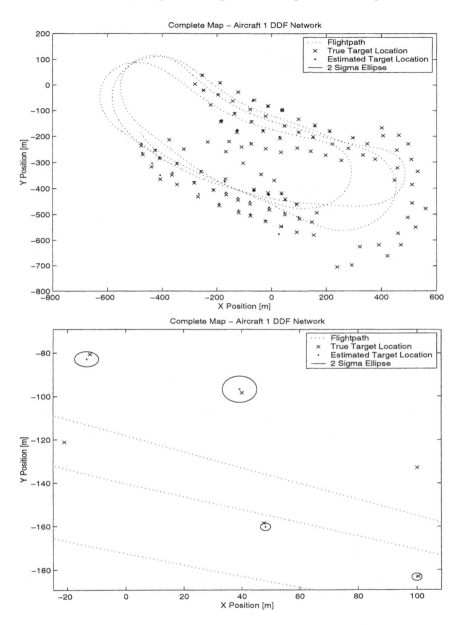

Fig. 10. When operating in a DDF network, all aircraft communicated target information between themselves in order to build a single common map. As the map is the same on all nodes, only that from aircraft 1 is illustrated.

6.1   Real Time Vision Sensor Results

The most recent flight saw the vision algorithms operating in real-time. The results from this flight for a single target are shown in Figure 12. Observations

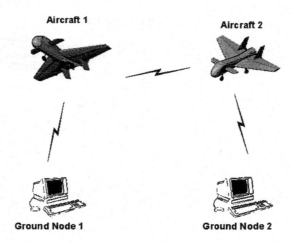

Fig. 11. The topology of the 4 node DDF network when demonstrating the DDF algorithm in real time. While the aircraft nodes are each connected to a camera, the ground nodes have no local sensor at all.

from two distinct aircraft are present. The raw observations (in two axes) and errors in three axes are shown. Range was typically underestimated. This is most likely due to saturation induced leakage of the image sensors elements.

A side effect of this underestimation is that additional errors may be induced in both Northing and Easting when transformation to Cartesian space is performed. This is clearly visible in the Northing error plot (Figure 12) as consecutive measurements drift linearly as the air vehicle passes over the target. The overall effect of this is minimal however as the full covariance of the observation (expressed as the information matrix) combined with the information filtering stage serves to eliminate the majority of this error as results in Section 6.2 show.

6.2   Real Time DDF Results

The results of running the DDF tracking algorithm in real time are presented in Figures 13 and 14. Figure 13 presents the complete map of targets from aircraft 1, along with the true target locations and the flight path of the aircraft. The area containing the 17 targets has been enlarged in the lower plot. Similarly, Figure 14 contains the same information from the second aircraft. The results generated by the ground nodes are identical to those of their corresponding aircraft as expected and are omitted for brevity.

An inspection of the results illustrates that the maps on aircraft 1 and ground node 1 are both identical, as are the maps on aircraft 2 and ground node 2. This is the expected result as the DDF information from the respective aircraft was the only source on information for each of the ground nodes. However, there is a slight difference between the maps on the two aircraft. While the majority

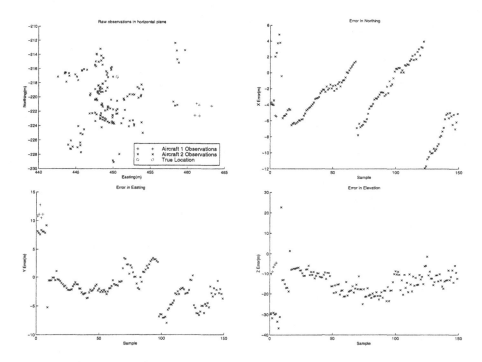

Fig. 12. Clockwise from top left: Raw observations of sample target, errors in Northing, Elevation and Easting.

of targets in the maps are common, there are a small number of targets that aircraft 1 tracks that 2 does not, and vise versa. This result is also expected in a real system, and occurs due to the delay in transmitting target information between nodes. Each node will track the first 17 targets it encounters, whether they be targets the node observes directly or tracks received from other nodes via DDF information.

What tends to occur in practice is that each of the nodes observes targets directly and initiates tracks, then communicates these tracks to neighbouring nodes at the next communication step. If the neighbouring nodes have unused tracking filters they then allocate one of these and maintain a track estimate. This process works up until the point where each of the nodes has only a small number of filters free. When this happens, it is not unusual for each node to allocate its last remaining filters to targets it directly observes. If all nodes do this, there are no spare filters to use to allocate to new tracks communicated from another node. This gives the result illustrated in this implementation where although the majority of targets are common between nodes, there are a small number that are different.

As the target estimates are generated relative to the aircraft pose, an error in the location of the vehicle will result in a corresponding error in the target

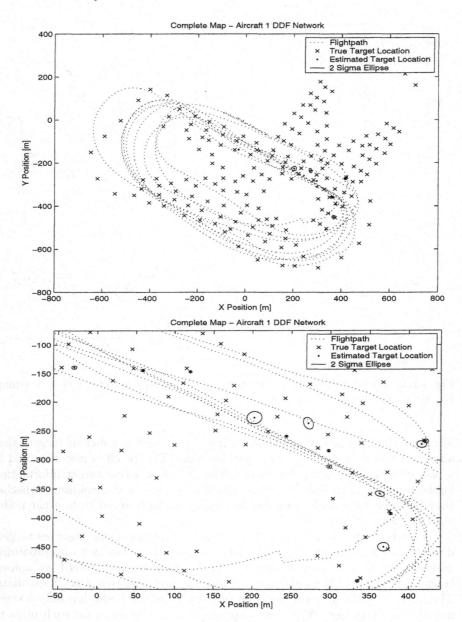

Fig. 13. The map generated by aircraft 1 is shown with the true target locations and the vehicle flightpath. Note the jumps in the flightpath which are a result of poor GPS coverage during the flight.

location. Over multiple passes of a target this error is assumed to be zero mean. However, as the real time flight was only of a relatively short duration and

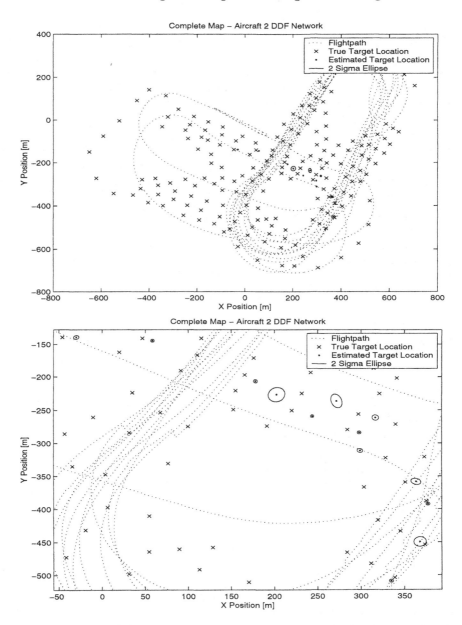

Fig. 14. The map generated by aircraft 2 differs from that on aircraft 1 for only a few targets. This is an expected result which occurs due to limiting the number of tracks that a node can maintain.

not all targets were observed on each circuit, the errors in the vehicle location did result in an offset from the true target location. This can be seen in the results as the 2σ ellipses do not always encapsulate the true target locations. This effect was amplified during the flight as there was poor GPS coverage at the time, which degraded the estimate of vehicle pose significantly. This can be seen by viewing the flightpath of aircraft 1, and noting the jumps of up to $10m$ which occur periodically. The errors in the height of the vehicle were significantly worse than this, and were often in the region of $10 - 20m$. As a result, there are some estimates which sit midway between two real targets as the vehicle uncertainty was sufficiently large to allow two different targets to be associated with a single track. This issue has been addressed for future flights by improving the GPS/IMU navigation loop, decreasing the target density and by making the data association more stringent. Notwithstanding these problems, the majority of estimates were still within $10m$ of the true location.

As the focus of this demonstration was on the DDF architecture, there was no track to track fusion implemented. This can be seen in the results from aircraft 1 as there are two tracks for one of the targets. While this does result in a poor allocation of resources, it does not hinder the demonstration of the DDF technology. As the ANSER project evolves, the inclusion of a track to track fusion algorithm will occur.

7   Conclusion

This paper has presented results of tracking multiple ground targets from aircraft using a decentralised algorithm. Initial results of post processed flight data were included to illustrate the advantages of the DDF architecture under controlled conditions. Results of a real time demonstration using two aircraft are also shown.

The DDF algorithms allowed multiple aircraft to share information. This results in each node in the DDF system having global information which in turn ensures that the estimates are the same on every vehicle. In the tracking and map building problem presented in this research it results each aircraft having the same target map.

The extra information available to node in a DDF network improves the estimate of the all nodes. Furthermore, the fact that the information is shared makes the system extremely robust. For example, if one of the aircraft in this research had of been destroyed for some reason, the information it gathered was already contained in the estimates on every other node. If the aircraft had been operating independently and a vehicle was destroyed, the information it had gathered would be lost.

In implementing the DDF algorithms on aircraft operating in six degrees of freedom at speeds of approximately $180km/h$, they have been operating in arguably the most difficult of environments. While some issues such as track to track fusion and an improved vehicle localisation filter still need to be addressed, the results do indicate the DDF architecture performs very well.

Acknowledgements. This work is funded by BAE SYSTEMS UK and BAE SYSTEMS Australia as part of the Autonomous Navigation and Sensing Experimental Research (ANSER) project.

References

1. G. Brooker, M. Bishop, and Steve Scheding. Millimetre waves for robotics. In *Australasian Conference on Robotics and Automation*, Sydney, 2001.
2. Stephen Clark. *Autonomous Land Vehicle Navigation Using Millimeter Wave Radar*. Phd thesis, University of Sydney, 1999.
3. R. Deaves. *The Management of Communications in Decentralised Bayesian Data Fusion Systems*. Ph.D Thesis, Bristol University, Dept of Electrical and Electronic Engineering, 1999.
4. Salah Sukkarieh, Ali Göktoğan, Jong-Hyuk Kim, Eric Nettleton, Jeremy Randle, Matthew Ridley, Stuart Wishart,and Hugh Durrant-Whyte. Cooperative data fusion and control amongst multiple uninhabited air vehicles. In *ISER 2002 Seventh International Symposium on Experimental Robotics*, 2002.
5. M. Fernandez. *Failure Detection and Isolation in Decentralised Multisensor Systems*. Ph.D Thesis, The University of Oxford, 1993.
6. S. Grime and H. Durrant-Whyte. Data fusion in decentralized sensor networks. *Control Engineering Practice*, 2, No 5:849–863, 1994.
7. Stewart Harper Grime. *Communication in Decentralised Sensing Architectures*. PhD thesis, Department of Engineering Science, University of Oxford, 1992.
8. O. Heikkilä, J. & Silvén. A four-step camera calibration procedure with implicit image correction. In *IEEE Computer Society Conference on Computer Vision and Pattern Recognition (CVPR'97)*, San Juan, Puerto Rico, pages 1106–1112, 1997.
9. J. Kim and S. Sukkarieh. Flight test results of gps/ins navigation loop for an autonomous unmanned aerial vehicle (uav). In *Proceedings of ION GPS*, pages 510–517, 2002.
10. J. Manyika. *An Information Theoretic Approach to Data Fusion and Sensor Management*. PhD Thesis, The University of Oxford, 1993.
11. P. Maybeck. *Stochastic Models, Estimation and Control, Volume 1*. Academic Press Inc, New York, 1979.
12. E. Nettleton, H. Durrant-Whyte, P. Gibbens, and A.Göktoğan. Multiple platform localisation and map building. In G.T. McKee and P.S. Schenker, editors, *Sensor Fusion and Decentralised Control in Robotic Stystems III*, volume 4196, pages 337–347, Bellingham, 2000.
13. D. Nicholson, C. Lloyd, S. Julier, and J. Uhlmann. Scalable distributed data fusion. In *Proceedings of the Fifth International Conference on Information Fusion*, volume 1, pages 630–635, Sunnyvale, 2002.
14. Lawrence D. Stone, Carl A. Barlow, and Thomas L. Corwin. *Bayesian Multiple Target Tracking*. Artech House, 1999.

Power-Aware Acoustic Processing[1]

Ronald Riley[1], Brian Schott [1], Joseph Czarnaski[1], and Sohil Thakkar[2]

[1] USC Information Sciences Institute, 3811 N. Fairfax Dr., Suite 200
Arlington VA 22203-1707
{RRiley, BSchott, JCzarn}@isi.edu
http://www.east.isi.edu
[2] University of Maryland
College Park, MD 20742
sohil@Glue.umd.edu

Abstract. We investigated tradeoffs between accuracy and battery-energy longevity of acoustic beamforming on disposable sensor nodes subject to varying
key parameters: number of microphones, duration of sampling, number of
search angles, and CPU clock. Beyond finding the most energy efficient implementation of the beamforming algorithm at a specified accuracy, we enable application-level selection of accuracy based on the energy required to achieve this
accuracy. We measured the energy consumed by the HiDRA node, provided by
Rockwell Science Center, employing a 133-MHz StrongARM processor. We
compared the accuracy and energy of our time-domain beamformer to a Fourier-
domain algorithm provided by the Army Research Laboratory (ARL). With statistically identical accuracy, we measured a 300x improvement in energy efficiency of the CPU relative to this baseline. We present other algorithms under
development that combine results from multiple nodes to provide more accurate
line-of-bearing estimates despite wind and target elevation.

1 Introduction

Our objective is to develop software and hardware that support dynamic control of the
use of energy and computational resources at various levels according to the need for
precision and the readiness to expend the required resources. We envision sensor
nodes lying almost dormant for months before a sound emitting target comes within
range. During this long quiescent period, the nodes must remain active enough to

[1] This work was sponsored by the Defense Advanced Research Projects Agency and Air Force
Research Laboratory, Air Force Materiel Command, USAF, under agreement number
F30602-99-1-0529. The U.S. Government is authorized to reproduce and distribute reprints
for Governmental purposes notwithstanding any copyright annotation thereon. The views and
conclusions contained herein are those of the authors and should not be interpreted as neces-
sarily representing the official policies or endorsements, either expressed or implied, of the
Defense Advanced Research Projects Agency, the Air Force Research Laboratory, or the U.S.
Government.

F. Zhao and L. Guibas (Eds.): IPSN 2003, LNCS 2634, pp. 566–581, 2003.
© Springer-Verlag Berlin Heidelberg 2003

detect the incursion of an emitter and remain in contact with neighboring nodes to alert them of the detection. At this stage there is no need to determine the direction to an emitter with any accuracy, it is sufficient to detect it as a "tripwire."

Once detected, application level algorithms will determine how often the line of bearing (LOB) is needed and the accuracy required to identify and to track the emitter. These decisions will depend on the perceived importance of the emitter and the available energy resources. This paper summarizes our efforts to find the key parameters in acoustic beamforming and determine their relative contributions to the accuracy and energy consumption.

2   Beamforming Algorithms

Acoustic beamforming algorithms estimate the LOB to distant acoustic emitters by time-shifting signals from microphones at known relative locations to form beams from selected directions. The two beamforming algorithms compared in this paper differ primarily in how they implement time-shifting the sig-

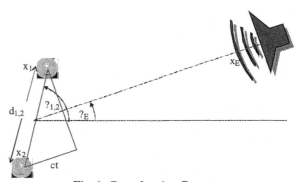

Fig. 1. Beamforming Geometry.

nals. The LOB can be thought of as a by-product of the optimal reconstruction of the signal from an emitter by shifting and adding the signals from a number of microphones [1].

As illustrated in Fig. 1, sound from a distant emitter arrives at two microphones at $\vec{x}_1$ and $\vec{x}_2$ with a relative delay

$$\tau_{1,2} = \lfloor d_{1,2} \cos\left(\theta_{1,2}\right)\rfloor\alpha - \lfloor d_{1,2} \sin\left(\theta_{1,2}\right)\rfloor\beta, \tag{1}$$

where $d_{1,2} \equiv |\vec{x}_2 - \vec{x}_1|$ is the distance between the microphones, $\theta_{1,2}$ is the direction of the separation vector between the microphones, $\alpha = cos(\theta_E)/c$, $\beta = sin(\theta_E)/c$, θ_E is the LOB of the emitter, and $c \sim 332$ *m/s* is the speed of sound in air.

If the microphones rigidly placed or calibrated after deployment, and the speed of sound is adjusted to the local climate, the LOB to the emitter, relative to the microphone separation vector, can be calculated from an estimate of this delay as

$$\theta_E - \theta_{1,2} = \pm\cos^{-1}\left(c\tau_{1,2} / d_{1,2}\right), \tag{2}$$

where the sign ambiguity is due to taking the inverse of the cosine, an even function.

The delays can be estimated by minimizing the differences between signals S^1 and S^2 recorded at microphones 1 and 2,

$$S^1(t) = gS^2(t - \tau_{1,2}),\qquad(3)$$

where g is the relative gain between the two signals. The search for the best delay is limited by (1) to $|\tau_{1,2}| < d_{1,2}/c$. Once the shift has been determined, the signals from the microphones can be shifted and added to provide an enhanced estimate of the signal from the emitter. The background noise and sounds from other emitters will be reduced in proportion to the number of microphones.

Methods for determining the LOB based on reconstructing the emitted signal, as in (3), from an acoustic array with M microphones can distinguish at most $M-1$ emitters. The additional uncertainty of the position of the emitters results in an underdetermined system of linear equations if we try to resolve M emitters. Resolving more emitters requires additional constraints such as knowing the power-spectrum of the emitters. Algorithms, such as MUSIC[2] and ESPRIT[3], which do not attempt to reconstruct the emitted signals can resolve, at most, M emitters from an array of M microphones. They perform eigenvector decomposition of the MxM covariance matrix of the signals from the M microphones and so do not lend themselves to efficient implementation in integer-math oriented processors in sensor nodes.

Beamforming is accomplished by time-shifting the signals from an array of microphones to a common position with time delays prescribed by (1), for an assumed LOB. Beams are formed for a number of LOB search angles. As the search angle approaches the correct LOB of the emitter, the signals constructively interfere as in (3). As shown in Fig.2, the search angle with the maximum power in the delay-summed signal is selected as the estimated LOB.

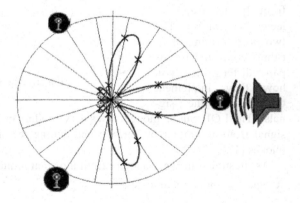

Fig. 2. Beam power at 18 search angles.

This LOB estimate is refined by parabolic interpolation of the power over the adjacent search angles.

The two algorithms compared in this paper differ primarily in how they shift the signals. The baseline algorithm from the Army Research Laboratory (ARL) performs a floating-point Fourier transform on each signal then shifts, sums, and computes the beam power in the Fourier domain. Our beamformer performs all of these operations in the time domain in integer math.

We implemented shifting signals by a fraction of the time between samples by linear interpolation of samples. Interpolative shifting introduces a small error in higher frequency components of signals. These artifacts are mitigated by oversampling the signal and filtering out the highest frequency components.

Our beamformer assumes a single target and employs common integer code to re-port the LOB as the direction with the delay-summed combined signal of loudest total acoustic energy. These results do not include code for false alarm rejection such as Harmonic Line Analysis. We will add these capabilities into future implementations.

Our algorithm is **300x** more efficient in CPU time and energy than the baseline al-gorithms provided by ARL. The largest contribution (**~20x**) is due to developing our algorithm in integer math and avoiding *floating-point* emulation on the StrongARM processor. Operating in the time domain enables the next most significant contribution (**~10x**) by providing a more continuous range of time and energy requirements based on varying the *number of samples*. Fast Fourier transforms operate on signals con-taining integer powers of 2 samples ($S=2^n$). Collecting fewer samples and padding with zeros before taking the transform would reduce the accuracy and provide little or no benefit to the execution time and energy of Fourier-domain algorithms. For this reason, we did not modify the baseline algorithm to vary the number of samples from its hard-coded value of $S=1024$. *Avoiding Fourier transforms* by using interpolative shifts in the time-domain provided the final contribution of (**~3/2x**).

3   Line of Bearing (LOB) Beyond Beamforming

The algorithms discussed in this section are under development and optimization for sensor nodes. We anticipate that these will lead to significant improvements over beamforming in accuracy/noise insensitivity, false-alarm rejection, and an extended range in tradeoffs between accuracy and energy.

Beamforming makes a number of limiting assumptions 1) that the microphones are fixed on a rigid plane, 2) that the emitter lies on the same plane, and 3) that there is little or no wind. While beamforming uses (1) to construct a set of delays correspond-ing to various search angles and selects the "best", the LOB can also be estimated directly from (1) based on the time shifts between pairs of microphones. Given a set of $M>2$ microphones with synchronized sampling, we can select up to $M! / [2 (M-2)!]$ pairs. For example, three microphones provide three pairs. Assuming that the ge-ometry of the M microphones has been calibrated, (1) provides a system of $M! / [2 (M-2)!]$ equations in two unknowns (α and β,) the sine and cosine of the LOB divided by the speed of sound. For more than two pairs, the over-determined system of equations can be solved by standard weighted least-squares methods. Increasing the number of microphones and pairs should improve the accuracy.

The LOB and speed of sound are extracted with the integer math CORDIC[4] as

$$\theta_E = \tan^{-1}[\alpha, \beta], \tag{4}$$

and

$$c = [\alpha^2 + \beta^2]^{-1/2}. \tag{5}$$

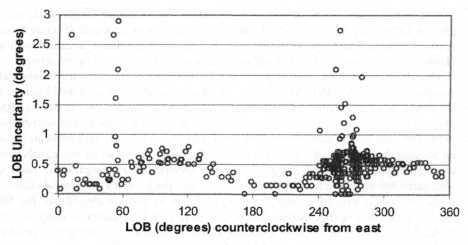

Fig. 3. Uncertainty in LOB of tracked vehicle.

When noise results in nonphysical estimates of the apparent speed of sound, the LOB estimated in (4) can be iteratively refined based on small angle corrections with the speed of sound held to the predicted constant in (1) as

$$\{d_{1,2} \sin(\theta_E - \theta_{1,2})\}\delta\theta_E = c\tau_{1,2} - \{d_{1,2} \cos(\theta_E - \theta_{1,2})\}. \qquad (6)$$

The RMS error of the system of equations defined by (6), or (1), provides a measure of the angular uncertainty of the LOB estimate. If some pairs of microphones produce multiple delays due to multiple targets, this error and the apparent speed of sound provided by (5) could be used to select delays into sets for each target.

Fig. 3 shows a plot of this uncertainty for a tracked vehicle driving around an oval track. The vehicle is farthest from the sensor node (~600 m) when it is 280° counterclockwise from east (~south). These results are based on data we collected at the Aberdeen Proving Grounds with Highly Deployable Remote Access Network Sensors & Systems (HiDRA) sensor nodes, described in section 6, using three microphones deployed on an equilateral triangle with a 7-foot separation.

3.1 Emitter Elevation

If the emitter is elevated above the plane on which the microphones are distributed, as shown in Fig. 4, this decreases the delays between signals and increases the apparent speed of sound estimated by (5) as

$$c = c_0 / \cos(\phi_E), \qquad (7)$$

where φ_E is the elevation angle of the emitter. As the emitter moves directly above the microphones, the apparent speed would tend toward infinity as all of the time shifts approach zero. The elevation angle of the emitter could be estimated by generalizing

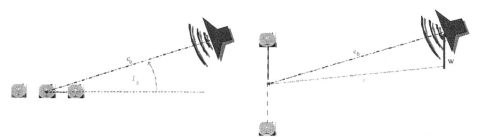

Fig. 4. Elevation angle of emitter.   **Fig. 5.** Wind speed geometry.

our analysis to 3D and elevating one or more microphones above a plane containing three or more microphones[5]. If we can segregate the contribution due to elevation from other effects, such as wind, by collaboration between sensor nodes, each with three or more microphones, we could estimate the elevation angle from (7).

3.2 Wind-Speed Vector Effects

As illustrated in Fig. 5, the average wind speed W between the emitter and the microphones will add as a vector to the sound radiating from the emitter at speed c_0 resulting in an apparent speed of sound of

$$c = \sqrt{[c_0 + W \cos(\theta_E - \theta_W)]^2 + W^2 \sin^2(\theta_E - \theta_W)}, \tag{8}$$

where θ_W is the direction that the wind is from. The LOB would also be shifted by

$$\delta\theta_E = \tan^{-1}[c_0 + W \cos(\theta_E - \theta_W), W \sin(\theta_E - \theta_W)]. \tag{9}$$

Assuming that the wind speed is small compared to that of sound we can approximate

$$(c - c_0) \sim W \cos(\theta_E - \theta_W) = \cos(\theta_E)\{W \cos(\theta_W)\} + \sin(\theta_E)\{W \sin(\theta_W)\}, \tag{10}$$

and

$$\delta\theta_E \sim \frac{(c - c_0)}{c} \tan(\theta_E - \theta_W). \tag{11}$$

A wind speed of 14 mph orthogonal to the LOB would result in a 1° LOB error.

   The deviation from the expected sound speed is plotted in Fig. 6 for a tracked vehicle driven several orbits around an oval track. These preliminary estimates of the apparent sound speed are based on delays of maximum correlation (13), described in the next section. These points are compared to the continuous curve of expected deviation based on (10) for a wind speed of W=30 mph, from the north-east (θ_W~50°.) This is somewhat larger than the 10-mph average wind speed measured near the ground during data collection. The wind direction, taken from the ground truth, agrees well with the estimated deviations in sound speed.

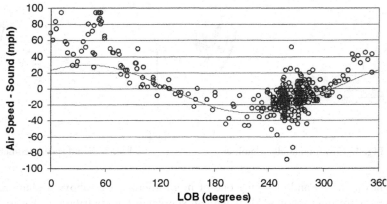

Fig. 6. Deviation of sound speed vs. angle.

Given an estimate of the wind direction, we can estimate and correct the offset in the LOB from (11) based on the apparent speed of sound, if we can assume that there are no other contributions such as elevation of the emitter above the sensor plane.

If we combine the apparent sound speed and estimated LOB from two or more sensor nodes with enough separation transverse to the LOB of the emitter such that they provide significantly different estimated LOBs, and assume that the wind is roughly the same for all sensor nodes, we can solve the resulting system of linear equations given by (10) for the wind vector components. The wind direction can be computed using the CORDIC algorithm as

$$\theta_W = \tan^{-1}[W \cos(\theta_W), W \sin(\theta_W)], \tag{12}$$

and the result can be used in (11) to infer the offset of the LOB's due to the wind.

The LOB and apparent speed of sound from three or more nodes can be combined to solve for the wind and elevation simultaneously by combining (7) and (10) as

$$c \sim \left\{ \frac{c_0}{\cos(\varphi_E)} \right\} + \cos(\theta_E)\{W \cos(\theta_W)\} + \sin(\theta_E)\{W \sin(\theta_W)\}. \tag{13}$$

This assumes that all of the nodes have the same emitter elevation, which could be satisfied if all of the nodes are at the same elevation and roughly the same distance from the emitter. We would have to constrain the added unknown such that the inferred cosine is in the assumed range (0, 1) and would interpret the elevation angle to be positive, forcing the object to lie above the sensor plane.

3.3 Signal-Pair Delay Estimation

All of this analysis is based on the ability to estimate the delay between signals collected by a pair of microphones. One estimate of the delays can be obtained by finding the shift between the signals that produces a peak in correlation between the signals from microphone 1 (S^1) and 2 (S^2)

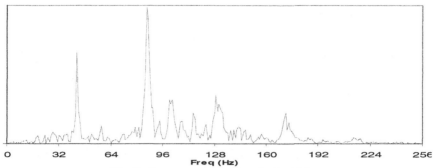

Fig. 7. Power spectrum of tracked vehicle.

$$C^{1,2}(\tau_{1,2}) = \sum_t S^1(t)S^2(t - \tau_{1,2}).$$ (14)

This estimate is best suited to emissions of short duration, such as gunfire or explosions, and is sufficient for cases with high signal to noise and broad band signals.

Much of the recent work in noise-tolerant LOB estimates are based on the fact that many targets of interest, such as vehicles, emit sound in a number of narrow acoustic bands[6], as shown by the acoustic power spectrum of a tracked vehicle shown in Fig. 7. Power spectrums are plotted in relative units since the absolute magnitude is of less interest than the relative magnitudes of the spectral peaks and background. If multiple targets emit primarily in different narrow frequency ranges, their LOBs could be determined by a single sensor node with as few as three microphones.

The LOB of frequencies from 32 to 128 Hz are plotted as points in Fig. 8 for a sensor node with three microphones and two tracked vehicles. The average power spectrum of the three microphones is also plotted as a continuous curve in relative units. The LOBs cluster around 240° and 77° corresponding to the two vehicles. The LOB is plotted as zero for frequencies where it is undefined. Once the LOBs of the two vehicles are estimated, it is straight forward to separate their line-spectra as a basis for target classification.

For each spectral component, the LOB of is based on time shifts of microphone pairs estimated as

$$\tau_{1,2}(\omega) = \frac{\left\{\varphi[S^1(\omega)] - \varphi[S^2(\omega)]\right\} + 2n\pi}{\omega},$$ (15)

where the phase of the Fourier component of the signal $\varphi[S^1(\omega)]$ can be computed with the CORDIC algorithm and the time shift is limited to the range $[-d_{1,2}/c, \ d_{1,2}/c]$. For higher frequencies $(f>c/(2d_{1,2}))$, there can be more than one solution to (15). This degeneracy can be resolved by selecting the solution that is most consistent with lower frequency components or is most consistent with the expected speed of sound and error of fit based on the solution to (1). This ambiguity can be avoided by restricting microphone separations to $d<c/(2f)$, where f is the highest frequency of interest in the emitters spectrum.

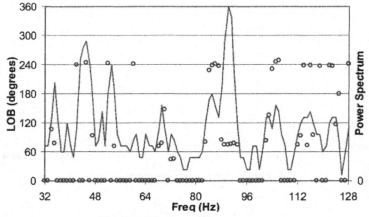

Fig. 8. LOB of spectral components

Our current implementation of the acoustic beamformer operates in the time rather than the frequency domain to reduce CPU time and energy requirements. We will also implement algorithms in the frequency domain, such as described in this section, for those rare occasions when we are required to discriminate a greater number of targets than available microphones.

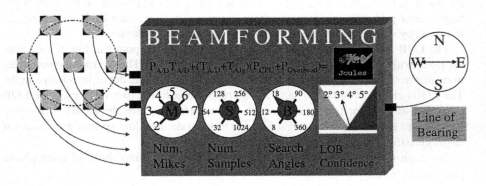

Fig. 9. Beamforming Algorithmic Knobs.

4   Algorithmic "Knobs"

The accuracy and energy requirements of acoustic beamforming depend on a number of parameters, as suggested by Fig. 9. Some are largely dictated by the application. We have chosen as our set of independent variables: **1)** number of microphones M, **2)** number of acoustic samples S, **3)** number of beams B, and **4)** CPU clock speed f_{CPU}.

4.1 Number of Microphones (M)

The number and placement of microphones is principally a hardware design parameter but can also be used as an algorithmic parameter by selecting a subset of the signals collected. We will show that the system energy required for beamforming is *proportional* to the number of microphones, but there are negligible improvements in accuracy due to adding more microphones beyond the number of emitters.

We limit our analysis to nodes supporting at least two microphones. Although single-microphone nodes could collaborate to determine the direction to an emitter, we exclude this case due to the requirements of a large amount of energy to move raw data between nodes, of 10-us synchronization between nodes, and of 5-mm accuracy in relative positioning of microphones. Although the ambiguities resulting from two-microphone beamforming would require collaboration, only a trivial amount of data need be exchanged. Synchronization to a fraction of a second is sufficient, and the required accuracy of relative positioning is similarly relaxed.

4.2 Number of Acoustic Samples (S)

For a fixed sampling rate, in our case 1024 Hz, the system energy required for beamforming is *proportional* to the number of samples simultaneously collected from each microphone. The number of samples collected per second for each microphone is typically selected to be 1 kHz for acoustic tracking of vehicles to facilitate beamforming with the spectrum above 250 Hz attenuated to filter out wind noise. We implemented this as analog anti-aliasing filtering.

4.3 Number of Beams (B)

The beam power is computed at a number of evenly spaced search angles, and interpolated by a parabolic fit to estimate the angle with maximum power. The number of beams only affects the execution speed of the algorithm, *not data acquisition*. The system energy for beamforming depends linearly with the number of beams searched.

4.4 CPU Clock Speed (fCPU)

The sensor node used supports software-control of the clock speed of the CPU over the range 59-133 MHz. Although running at a lower speed should enable reducing the voltage, voltage scaling is not supported. Clock scaling alone changes how long the algorithms run without changing the energy requirements. However, the power consumed by other components in the system during execution of the algorithm and the power consumed by the CPU during data collection give this parameter utility in reducing system energy required for beamforming.

5   System Power Equation for HiDRA Sensor Node

The energy consumed by the Highly Deployable Remote Access Network Sensors & Systems (HiDRA) provided by Rockwell Science Center (RSC)[7][8][9], see Fig. 10, to capture data and compute the LOB is modeled by

$$E = \frac{S}{f_S} P_{AD} + \left[\frac{S}{f_S} + \frac{f_{133}}{f_{CPU}} T_{A\lg} \right]\left[P_{Ovr} + \frac{f_{CPU}}{f_{133}} P_{CPU} \right], \qquad (16)$$

where f_{CPU} is the clock rate of the StrongARM CPU and $f_{133} = 133$ MHz is the maximum clock rate.

This equation reflects that the power required by the A/D board, P_{AD}, is only consumed during the data acquisition time which is the number of samples acquired, S, divided by the sampling rate $f_s = 1024$ Hz. Also implicit in this equation is that, for the HiDRA node, the CPU and memory consume power, P_{CPU}, while the samples are acquired, but the algorithm does not begin to run, for a period T_{Alg}, until after data collection is complete. There is also a significant overhead power, P_{Ovr}, consumed by other supporting components such as the radio.

Fig. 10. RSC HiDRA sensor node stack.

The CPU power and execution time of the algorithm are proportional and inversely proportional, respectively, to the CPU clock rate, f_{CPU}. The clock rate resulting in the minimal energy consumption can be found by setting the derivative of (16) with respect to f_{CPU} to zero, resulting in

$$f_{CPU} = f_{133} \sqrt{P_{Ovr} T_{A\lg} / T_{AD} P_{CPU}} , \qquad (17)$$

where T_{Alg} is the execution time of the algorithm and P_{CPU} is the CPU power at the CPU clock rate of 133 MHz.

When the CPU and overhead power components are roughly equal and the execution time at 133 MHz is a small fraction of the sampling window, as with our algorithm, the minimum available CPU clock rate of 59 MHz provides the best efficiency. When the algorithm runs longer than the sampling window, as with the ARL algorithm, the maximum available CPU clock rate of 133 MHz gives the best results.

6 Power Measurements on the HiDRA Node

The power measurement test setup consisted of the HiDRA sensor node and a current sensing resistor placed inline with the input voltage connector. The voltage drop across this resistor was measured using a National Instruments data acquisition card and triggered from the node's CPU module. The HiDRA node, as shown in Fig. 10, contains the following modules:

1) Processor/Memory: StrongARM 1100 CPU board running at 59-133 MHz., with 4 MB of ROM (flash memory), 1 MB of RAM, input voltage 3.3V I/O, and 1.5V core.

2) DC/DC: Our test measurements were taken with a 12-V DC input. This module supplies voltages 3.3V and 1.5V for the I/O lines and processor core respectively and separate analog voltage lines for the A/D and Radio modules.

3) Radio: A 900 MHz Rockwell proprietary radio.

4) A/D: 5 channels, 3 Multiplexed with variable gains of 1x, 2x, 5.02x, 10.09x, 20.12x and 2 individual inputs with variable gains of 10x, 43.32x, 30x, 36.68x, 49.98x. The selectable gains are tuned to specific sensors that RSC uses for this platform. The acoustic data was captured using only the multiplexed sensor input to keep the gains equivalent across all channels. Low-pass anti-aliasing filters with a cutoff frequency of 3 kHz were also added to the inputs of each of these channels to reduce cross-talk between the channels.

The current measurements were taken at the full clock rate of 133 MHz, which is the optimal operating frequency for the HiDRA node, and at various increments down to 59 MHz. Other power measurements were taken for the different operating modes required to form a single LOB. These modes include acquiring the data from the input microphones, executing the algorithms, and putting the processor in sleep mode. The individual power consumption of each module was measured by removing boards from the stack and calculating the difference in current through the sensing resistor.

7 Results

We evaluated the two algorithms on a test set of acoustic data collected by ARL collected at their Aberdeen Proving Grounds. The data was synchronously collected from six microphones uniformly distributed on a 4-foot radius circle, and a seventh microphone in the center. A single military vehicle was driven by this acoustic array with GPS to provide ground-truth position at 1-second intervals. The signals were collected continuously on a seven-channel digitizer at 12-bits per channel at 1024 samples per second.

For our tests, we broke the acoustic data up into 1-second records associated with the available position ground truth. For each 1-second record, we computed the LOB with both algorithms and measured their errors relative to the ground truth. The results presented are of the Root-Mean-Square of these errors over all of the records in the set.

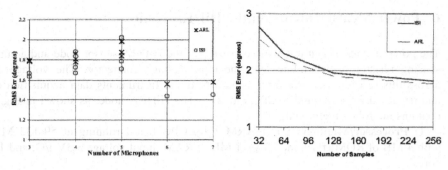

Fig. 11. Error vs. Mikes.   **Fig. 12.** Error vs. Samples.

In addition to validating that our algorithm provided results statistically identical to those of the baseline, we investigated the effect of the various knobs on the accuracy of both algorithms.

As illustrated in Fig. 11, increasing the number of microphones on a circle above the minimum of three provides little, if any, improvement in the accuracy of the LOB estimate.   Doubling the number of microphones from 3 to 6 reduces the RMS error only by 12% for this single emitter. From the errors plotted in Fig. 12, we can see that 32 is the minimum number of samples for which the algorithms can provide a useful result. However, using more than 128 samples provides only modest improvements in accuracy.

As shown in Fig. 13, the error grows rapidly for fewer than eight beams, but improves only slightly for more than sixteen beams. These results depend on the dominant frequency of the acoustic spectra emitted by the target and the "knee" of the curve is likely to shift for other vehicles.

We optimized the execution time of our code using the web-based JouleTrack[10] emulator before porting it to the HiDRA. Although Joule-Track did not provide identical results to what we measured directly from the hardware, it was useful guide in modifying the code to reduce execution time and energy use.

We electronically measured the power consumed by each component of the node during various modes of operation and we measured the execution time of the two algo-

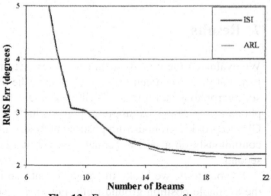

Fig. 13. Error vs. number of beams.

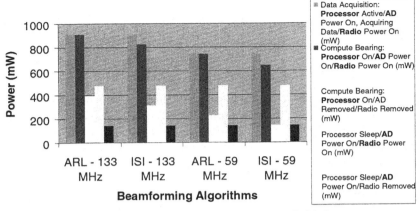

Fig. 14. Power Consumption of Various Node Modes.

rithms at the maximum and minimum clock rates, as shown in Fig. 14. The results of these measurements are summarized in Table 1.

Assuming three microphones (M=3), twelve beams (B=12), and a full second of data (S=1024), applying the values in this table to (16) results in a total system energy of 1614 mJ for the baseline algorithm and 746 mJ for the ISI algorithm, as shown in Fig. 15. Despite a 250x reduction in CPU energy and execution time for the same clock rate, our algorithm results in a modest 2x reduction in overall system energy required to acquire the data and process it to produce a single LOB. By virtually eliminating the energy consumed by the CPU board, the system energy is now dominated by data collection.

Under similar conditions, but with only 0.125 sec sampling window (S=128), the system energy for the baseline would be 816 mJ and the system energy for the ISI algorithm would be 93 mJ. *Our algorithm would provide a 9x reduction in system energy over the baseline algorithm under these conditions.*

8 Conclusions

We have demonstrated the ability to perform acoustic beamforming over a range of accuracy requiring a corresponding range of energy by introducing a number of "knobs" into the basic algorithm. This analysis led us to develop an algorithm that is roughly *300x* more efficient than the baseline algorithms in CPU energy. More importantly, our algorithm provides *9x overall system energy savings* when LOB estimates of slightly lower accuracy are sufficient. We have reduced CPU energy consumption to the point where the system energy is dominated by data collection.

We found that adjusting the number of microphones M offered the largest improvements to energy efficiency with the least impact on accuracy of the LOB for a

Table 1. Power Measurements for the HiDRA node with M, B, and S Knobs.

	P_{Ovr} mW	P_{AD} mW	f_{CPU} MHz	P_{CPU} f_{CPU}/f_{133} mW	T_{Alg} f_{133}/f_{CPU} μs
ISI	274	252	59	132	M B S 0.0555
ARL	358	252	133	302	M B 14300

small number of targets. However, this parameter can only be effectively adjusted during the design of the sensor node. It is difficult to construct a board capable of collecting a large number of synchronized signals but only capture a selected subset without paying much of the power penalty of sampling all of the signals. We determined that three microphones are the minimum required to perform beamforming without collaboration with other nodes.

The number of samples collected, S, for each microphone offers comparable improvements to system energy efficiency with slightly larger impact on accuracy. However, this parameter can be adjusted over a wide range, 32-1024, resulting in a *16x range of system energy requirements*. The memory requirements of future nodes could be reduced by reducing the sampling window and by using our integer algorithm rather than the floating-point baseline.

The number of beams formed in the software, B, only modulates the algorithm execution time which is only a fraction of the sampling window. So this parameter has only a minor effect on the energy efficiency of the whole system.

The clock speed of a CPU, f_{CPU}, typically has a limited range of values, in the case of the HiDRA node 59-133 MHz. We have shown that a faster than real-time algorithm will be most efficient at the lowest available clock speed. This will be even more the case for more power-aware sensor nodes being designed that will be capable of voltage scaling and of computing the algorithm during data collection.

Increased algorithm efficiency will provide a greater impact on total system energy in future generations of sensor nodes by adding the capability to 1) turn off more components when not in use to reduce the overhead power, 2) processing of data during

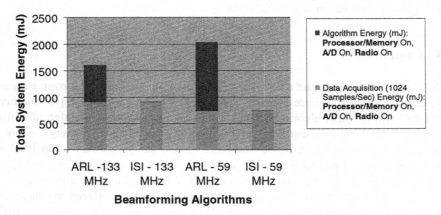

Fig. 15. Acquisition/Proc. Energy to Compute a LOB.

data collection to determine when enough data has been collected, and 3) voltage scaling of the CPU. We are developing a next generation of sensor nodes incorporating these and other power saving features.

References

1. D. K. Campbell, Adaptive Beamforming Using a Microphone Array for Hands-Free Telephony. Masters Thesis, Virginia Polytechnic Institute and State University, 1999. Available: http://scholar.lib.vt.edu/theses/available/etd-022099-122645/
2. R. Schmidt, "Multiple emitter location and signal parameter estimation," IEEE Trans. Antennas Propagat., vol. AP-34, pp. 276–280, 1986.
3. R. Roy and T. Kailath: "ESPRIT—Estimation of Signal Parameters via Rotational Invariance Techniques," IEEE Trans. Accoust. Speech and Signal Proc., vol. 37, no. 7, pp.984–995, July 1989.
4. Ray Andraka, "A survey of CORDIC algorithms for FPGAs (121K),"FPGA '98. Proceedings of the 1998 ACM/SIGDA sixth international symposium on Field programmable gate arrays, Feb. 22-24, 1998, Monterey, CA. pp191-200. Available:
   http://www.fpga-guru.com/cordic.htm
5. M. Walworth and A. Mahajan, "3D Position Sensing Using The Difference In The Time-Of-Flights From A Wave Source To Various Receivers," ICAR '97, Monterey, Ca, July 1997.
6. Tien Pham; Sadler, B.M., "Adaptive wideband aeroacoustic array processing," Statistical Signal and Array Processing, 1996. Proceedings., 8th IEEE Signal Processing Workshop on (Cat. No.96TB10004 , 1996 Page(s): 295 -298. Available:
   http://eewww.eng.ohio-state.edu/~randy/Microphone_Reading_List/index.html
7. J. Agre, L. Clare, G. Pottie and N. Romanov, "Development Platform for Self-Organizing Wireless Sensor Networks," Proceedings of the SPIE Conference on Unattended Ground Sensor Technologies and Applications, Orlando, FL, April, 1999, SPIE Vol. 3713, pp. 257-268.
8. "Highly Deployable Remote Access Network Sensors & Systems", Rockwell Science Center. Available: http://www.rsc.rockwell.com/hidra
9. J. Montague and Control Engineering staff, "Progressive Innovations", Control Engineering, March 1, 2002. Available: http://www.controleng.com/
10. A. Sinha and A. Chandrakasan. "JouleTrack - A Web Based Tool For Software Energy Profiling." Proc. 38th Design Automation Conference, June 2001. Available:
    http://dry-martini.mit.edu/JouleTrack/

Distributed Environmental Monitoring Using Random Sensor Networks*

Slobodan N. Simić and Shankar Sastry

Department of Electrical Engineering and Computer Sciences, University of
California, Berkeley, CA 94720
{simic,sastry}@eecs.berkeley.edu

Abstract. We present a distributed algorithm for environmental monitoring of a scalar field (such as temperature, intensity of light, atmospheric pressure, etc.) using a random sensor network. We derive an error
estimate, discuss the average complexity of the algorithm, and present
some simulation results.

Introduction

We present a distributed algorithm for estimating the gradient of a scalar field
(such as temperature, intensity of light, atmospheric pressure, etc.) using a random wireless sensor network. Environmental monitoring is one of the main applications of the emerging technology of wireless sensor networks. Our algorithm has
potential applications in preventing forest fires, energy conservation, oceanography, building science, etc. We envision using a large number of sensor nodes
to automatically detect the emergence of critical points (such as heat sources in
the context of forest fires) and notifying the base station which can then take
further action.

This work is mainly motivated by the Sensorwebs and Smart Dust [KKP]
projects at UC Berkeley, whose aim is to develop a unified framework for distributed sensor networks. Some previous theoretical work on environmental monitoring using random sensor networks was done in [Doh00]. For a study of wireless sensor networks in real-world habitat monitoring, see [MPS+02]. We also
mention [MEM01], which deals with gradient estimation from scattered data in
geology.

Due to high long range communication costs, low battery power, and need
for robustness to node failures, it is natural to seek decentralized, distributed
algorithms for sensor networks. This means that instead of relaying data to a
central location which does all the computing, the nodes process information in
a collaborative, distributed way. For instance, they can form computational clusters, based on their distance from each other. The outcome of these distributed,
local computations is stored in local memory and can, when necessary, be relayed
to a base station.

---

* Partially supported by the NSF grant ITR/SI: Societal Scale Information Systems:
Technologies, Design and Applications, number EIA-0122599.

F. Zhao and L. Guibas (Eds.): IPSN 2003, LNCS 2634, pp. 582–592, 2003.

The basic idea of our algorithm is the following. Each node communicates with its neighbors and computes the maximal difference quotient of the sensed scalar field. The estimate of the gradient at each node is taken to be the vector in the corresponding direction with norm equal to the maximal difference quotient. The algorithm is not new or sophisticated; however it has two redeeming features: (1) it is sufficiently simple and computationally non-intensive to be implementable on the current sensor network platform [Cul]; (2) it allows us to compute error estimates. We are able to *prove* that, in a probabilistic sense, the algorithm converges (i.e., as the number of nodes goes to infinity, the probability that the error is as small as we want converges to one), and to answer questions like "What should the number of nodes be so that the probability that the error is less than some ϵ, is greater than $1 - \eta$?"

We believe that in the sensor network literature, there is a need for a more precise theoretical analysis of known problems and proposed solutions. We therefore emphasize that the main purpose of this paper is to rigorously analyze the accuracy and complexity of the proposed algorithm from a probabilistic point of view, *not* to discuss any implementation issues, which will be dealt with in future work.

The paper is organized as follows. In Section 1, we introduce the terminology, notation, and the environmental monitoring problem. Section 2 describes the algorithm. In Section 3, we derive error estimates; Section 4 discusses average complexity, followed by simulation results in Section 5. The paper concludes with a summary of results and discussion of future work.

1   Preliminaries

In this section we introduce the basic mathematical framework and formulate the problem.

Assume that a random sensor network consisting of N nodes $S_1, \ldots, S_N$ is deployed in some region $D \subset \mathbb{R}^2$. The number i will be called the ID of the node S_i. We make the following simplifying assumptions:

- Every node is aware of its own position p_i in some fixed coordinate system in D. That is, the network is assumed to have performed node localization (see, e.g., our earlier work [SS02]).
- Each node S_i measures some environmental scalar field V such as temperature, pressure, or the amount of light at its own location. We assume that its measurement v_i is exact, i.e., $v_i = V(p_i)$.
- Each node has a maximal isotropic RF communication range R, i.e., two nodes can communicate if they are less then R meters apart. For every $0 < r \leq R$, each node can adjust it signal strength to achieve communication range r. In this case, two nodes whose distance is $\leq r$ are called *r-neighbors*.

Our *goal* is:

Using only local information, design a distributed algorithm for estimating the gradient of V at $p_1, \ldots, p_N$, and find its error.

We make the following assumptions on D, V, and the network.

- D has unit area and is homeomorphic to the closed unit disk in $\mathbb{R}^2$;
- $V : W \to \mathbb{R}$ is a function of class C^2, i.e., twice continuously differentiable, where W is some neighborhood of D in $\mathbb{R}^2$.
- Random variables $p_1, \ldots, p_N$ are independent and uniformly distributed in D.

This problem formulation has clear limitations. For instance, it does not consider node failures and noise, and the scalar field is deterministic. The simple setting we chose, however, admits hands-on error and complexity analysis and should be taken as the first step towards more exact understanding of the problem of environmental monitoring.

Notation. Throughout this paper, $\cdot$ will denote the standard dot product on $\mathbb{R}^2$. The corresponding 2-norm of a vector $v \in \mathbb{R}^2$ is $|v| = \sqrt{v \cdot v}$. For a matrix $A \in \mathbb{R}^{2 \times 2}$, $\|A\|$ will denote its operator norm relative to $|\ |$,

$$\|A\| = \sup\{|Av| : v \in \mathbb{R}^2, |v| = 1\}.$$

We write ∇V for the gradient of V and denote the second derivative of V (the usual matrix of second partials of V) by D^2V.

For $a, b \in D$, $a \neq b$, denote the difference quotient of V at a relative to b by

$$Q(a, b) = \frac{V(b) - V(a)}{|b - a|}.$$

Finally, let

$$G(a, b) = Q(a, b) \frac{b - a}{|b - a|}.$$

2   The Algorithm

Let $S = S_i$, for some $1 \leq i \leq N$, be a node with position $p = p_i$. Assume the signal strength of all the nodes has been adjusted to achieve maximum communication range of r meters.

We now state our algorithm for estimating $\nabla V(p)$, called $GRAD_S(r)$.

Step 1: *INITIALIZE variables:* $q(S) = 0, n(S) = i$.
Step 2: *COLLECT IDs, positions, and measurements from all r-neighbors.*
Each r-neighbor S_ν contributes (ν, p_ν, v_ν), where ν is its ID, p_ν its position, and v_ν its measurement of V at p_ν.
Step 3: *For each r-neighbor S_ν, COMPUTE $Q(p, p_\nu)$.*
If $Q(p, p_\nu) > q(S)$ then
$n(S) = \nu, q(S) = Q(p, p_\nu)$.
Step 4: *STOP when all data have been processed. The **estimate** of $\nabla V(p)$ is*

$$\text{Grad}(p) = G(p, p_{n(S)}).$$

Note that $v_\nu = V(p_\nu)$; $q(S)$ is the current value of the maximal difference quotient, and $n(S)$ is the ID of the corresponding node.

Remark. The algorithm maximizes the difference quotient $Q(p, p_\nu)$ over all neighbors S_ν of S. Grad(p) is the vector parallel to $p_{n(S)} - p$ of length $Q(p, p_{n(S)})$. Observe that the algorithm is distributed over the nodes of the network. The number of operations it executes is a constant multiple of the number of r-neighbors of S. The only operations a node needs to be able to perform are the four elementary arithmetic operations, squaring, square root, and comparisons.

Presently, we assume that in Step 2 we use one of the existing *data fusion* algorithms. We refer the reader to some of the relevant data fusion literature such as [KM94,QWIC01,IJ01,GDW94]. We are currently investigating this problem in the context of environmental monitoring, but for reasons of space, we postpone its discussion to future work.

3   Error Estimates for $GRAD_S(r)$

In this section we estimate the error of the proposed algorithm. The proofs of all statements are elementary and are therefore included, but can be skipped in first reading.

We will need the following estimate. Here $\angle(u, v)$ will denote the angle between vectors $u, v \in \mathbb{R}^2$, and

$$H = \sup_{p \in D} \|D^2 V(p)\|.$$

Proposition 1 *For all $p, q \in D$, $p \neq q$,*

$$|G(p, q) - \nabla V(p)| \leq |\nabla V(p)| \sin |\angle(\nabla V(p), q - p)| + \frac{1}{2} H |q - p|.$$

Proof. By the Fundamental Theorem of Calculus,

$$V(q) - V(p) = \nabla V(p) \cdot (q - p) + \frac{1}{2} D^2 V(\xi)(q - p) \cdot (q - p),$$

for some ξ lying on the segment connecting p and q. Therefore,

$$
\begin{aligned}
|G(p, q) - \nabla V(p)| &= \left| \frac{V(q) - V(p)}{|q - p|^2}(q - p) - \nabla V(p) \right| \\
&\leq \left| \frac{\nabla V(p) \cdot (q - p)}{|q - p|^2}(q - p) - \nabla V(p) \right| \qquad (1) \\
&\quad + \frac{1}{2} \left| \frac{D^2 V(\xi)(q - p) \cdot (q - p)}{|q - p|^2}(q - p) \right| \\
&= \mathrm{I} + \mathrm{II}.
\end{aligned}
$$

Consider first

$$I = \frac{|[\nabla V(p) \cdot (q-p)](q-p) - |q-p|^2 \nabla V(p)|}{|q-p|^2}. \tag{2}$$

Letting $v = \nabla V(p)$ and $x = q - p$, by elementary linear algebra we obtain that the numerator of (2) is

$$|(v \cdot x)x - |x|^2 v| = \{[(v \cdot x)x - |x|^2 v] \cdot [(v \cdot x)x - |x|^2 v]\}^{1/2}$$
$$= |x|^2 |v| \sin |\angle(v, x)|.$$

Thus,

$$I = |\nabla V(p)| \sin |\angle(\nabla V(p), q - p)|.$$

It is not hard to see that

$$II \le \frac{1}{2} H |q - p|.$$

This completes the proof of the Proposition. ∎

For every $1 \le i \le N$, denote by θ_i the angle between $\nabla V(p_i)$ and the vector $p_{n(S_i)} - p_i$ (Fig. 1).

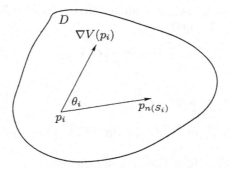

Fig. 1. The angle θ_i.

Corollary 1 *For every* $1 \le i \le N$,

$$|\text{Grad}(p_i) - \nabla V(p_i)| \le |\nabla V(p_i)| \sin |\theta_i| + \frac{1}{2} H |p_{n(S_i)} - p_i|.$$

The following lemma says that if we are sufficiently close to a node, it is the direction that matters in estimating the gradient.

Lemma 1 *Let* $q, q_1, \dots, q_K \in D$ *be distinct points and let*

$$\alpha_i = |\angle(\nabla V(q), q_i - q)|.$$

There exist $\rho > 0$ such that for all q_i, q_j with $|q_i - q|, |q_j - q| < \rho$ and $\alpha_i, \alpha_j < \pi/2$, the following holds:

$$\alpha_i < \alpha_j \Rightarrow Q(q, q_i) > Q(q, q_j).$$

In other words, in a sufficiently small polar coordinate neighborhood of q, $q_i \mapsto Q(q, q_i)$ is a decreasing function of α_i.

Therefore, if q_i's are sufficiently close to q and the angles $\angle(\nabla V(q), q_i - q)$ are not too big, then the difference quotient $Q(q, q_i)$ increases as the vector $q_i - q$ becomes more parallel to $\nabla V(q)$. Note that the lemma is still correct though vacuous if there are no points q_i ρ-close to q. However, in our situation, the probability of that happening is close to zero for large enough K.

Proof. Let $A = |\nabla V(q)|$ and

$$c = \min\{|\cos \alpha_m - \cos \alpha_n| : \alpha_m \neq \alpha_n, \ \alpha_m, \alpha_n < \pi/2, \ 1 \leq m, n \leq K\}.$$

If $H = 0$, then V is an affine (linear + a constant) function, and the statement of the lemma follows easily. So assume $H > 0$. Since $c > 0$, we can choose $\rho > 0$ so that

$$\rho < \frac{Ac}{H}.$$

Assume $|q_i - q|, |q_j - q| < \rho$, $\alpha_i, \alpha_j < \pi/2$, and $\alpha_i < \alpha_j$. Then

$$Q(q, q_i) - Q(q, q_j) = \left\{ \nabla V(q) \frac{q_i - q}{|q_i - q|} + \frac{1}{2} D^2 V(\xi_i)(q_i - q) \cdot \frac{q_i - q}{|q_i - q|} \right\}$$
$$- \left\{ \nabla V(q) \frac{q_j - q}{|q_j - q|} + \frac{1}{2} D^2 V(\xi_j)(q_j - q) \cdot \frac{q_j - q}{|q_j - q|} \right\}$$
$$= |\nabla V(q)|(\cos \alpha_i - \cos \alpha_j)$$
$$+ \frac{1}{2} \left\{ D^2 V(\xi_i)(q_i - q) \cdot \frac{q_i - q}{|q_i - q|} - D^2 V(\xi_j)(q_j - q) \cdot \frac{q_j - q}{|q_j - q|} \right\},$$
$$= \mathrm{I} + \mathrm{II},$$

where ξ_i is a point on the segment connecting q and q_i, and similarly for ξ_j. Further, since $\cos \alpha_i - \cos \alpha_j > 0$, we get $\mathrm{I} \geq Ac$. Also, $|\mathrm{II}| \leq \rho H$. Therefore,

$$\mathrm{I} + \mathrm{II} \geq \mathrm{I} - |\mathrm{II}| \geq Ac - \rho H > 0,$$

implying $Q(q, q_i) > Q(q, q_j)$. ∎

Denote by $\mathbb{P}(\mathcal{A}|\mathcal{B})$ and $\mathbb{E}(\mathcal{A}|\mathcal{B})$ the conditional probability and expectation of $\mathcal{A}$ given $\mathcal{B}$ [GS97]. Let ∂D be the boundary of D, and $d(x, \partial D)$ the distance from x to ∂D. Also, set

$$A_i = |\nabla V(p_i)|.$$

Proposition 2 *For all $1 \leq i \leq N$ and $\epsilon > 0$ small enough,*

$$\mathbb{P}(|\text{Grad}(p_i) - \nabla V(p_i)| < \epsilon \mid d(p_i, \partial D) \geq r) \geq 1 - [1 - \mu_i(\epsilon)]^{N-1},$$

where

$$\mu_i(\epsilon) = \max\{u_2^2 \sin^{-1} u_1 : A_i u_1 + \frac{1}{2} H u_2 = \epsilon, \ u_1, u_2 > 0\}.$$

In particular, if p_i is an equilibrium of ∇V, then

$$\mathbb{P}(|\text{Grad}(p_i)| < \epsilon \mid d(p_i, \partial D) \geq r) \geq 1 - \left(1 - \frac{4\pi\epsilon^2}{H^2}\right)^{N-1}.$$

Proof. Let $C_i(u_1, u_2)$ (Fig. 2) be the circular sector at p_i of radius $u_2 > 0$, angular width $\sin^{-1} u_1$ ($u_1 > 0$), and axis of symmetry $\nabla V(p_i)$. Assume $A_i u_1 + \frac{1}{2} H u_2 < \epsilon$ and $d(p_i, \partial D) \geq r$. If $p_{n(S_i)}$, the node which realizes the maximal difference quotient among the neighbors of S_i, belongs to $C_i(u_1, u_2)$, then by Corollary 1, $|\text{Grad}(p_i) - \nabla V(p_i)| \leq A_i u_1 + \frac{1}{2} H u_2 < \epsilon$. Therefore,

$$\mathbb{P}(|\text{Grad}(p_i) - \nabla V(p_i)| < \epsilon \mid d(p_i, \partial D) \geq r) \geq \mathbb{P}(p_{n(S_i)} \in C_i(u_1, u_2) \mid d(p_i, \partial D) \geq r).$$

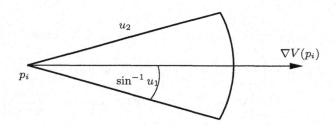

Fig. 2. The circular sector $C_i(u_1, u_2)$.

For ϵ small enough, $C_i(u_1, u_2) \cap D = C_i(u_1, u_2)$; its area is

$$\alpha(u_1, u_2) = u_2^2 \sin^{-1} u_1.$$

If ϵ is sufficiently small, then by Lemma 1, $p_j \mapsto Q(p_i, p_j)$ is a decreasing function of $|\angle(\nabla V(p_i), p_j - p_i)|$ on $C_i(u_1, u_2)$. Therefore, if at least one node is in $C_i(u_1, u_2)$, then $p_{n(S_i)} \in C_i(u_1, u_2)$; the converse is clear enough. Hence the probability that $p_{n(S_i)} \in C_i(u_1, u_2)$ (given $d(p_i, \partial D) \geq r$) equals the probability that at least one node different from S_i lands in $C_i(u_1, u_2)$. Furthermore, note that the conditional probability that exactly k nodes different from S_i lie in $C_i(u_1, u_2)$, given that $d(p_i, \partial D) \geq r$, is

$$\binom{N-1}{k} \alpha(u_1, u_2)^k [1 - \alpha(u_1, u_2)]^{N-1-k}.$$

Therefore,

$$\mathbb{P}(p_{n(S_i)} \in C_i(u_1, u_2) \mid d(p_i, \partial D) \geq r) \tag{3}$$

$$= \sum_{k=1}^{N-1} \binom{N-1}{k} \alpha(u_1, u_2)^k [1 - \alpha(u_1, u_2)]^{N-1-k}$$

$$= 1 - [1 - \alpha(u_1, u_2)]^{N-1}.$$

Since this is true for any pair (u_1, u_2) with the above properties, it follows that

$$\mathbb{P}(|\mathrm{Grad}(p_i) - \nabla V(p_i)| < \epsilon \mid d(p_i, \partial D) \geq r) \geq 1 - [1 - \max_{u_1, u_2} \alpha(u_1, u_2)]^{N-1}$$

$$= 1 - [1 - \mu_i(\epsilon)]^{N-1}.$$

If p_i is an equilibrium of ∇V, then $A_i = 0$. By Corollary 1, $|\mathrm{Grad}(p_i)| < \epsilon$ if $|p_{n(S_i)} - p_i| < 2\epsilon/H$, so $\mathbb{P}(|\mathrm{Grad}(p_i)| < \epsilon \mid d(p_i, \partial D) \geq r)$ is not less than the area of the disk centered at p_i of radius $2\epsilon/H$, proving the second part of the Proposition. ∎

Corollary 2 *For every* $1 \leq i \leq N$ *and* $\epsilon > 0$,

$$\lim_{N \to \infty} \mathbb{P}(|\mathrm{Grad}(p_i) - \nabla V(p_i)| < \epsilon \mid d(p_i, \partial D) \geq r) = 1.$$

Therefore, the algorithm, in the sense specified by the Corollary, "converges in probability".

Proposition 3 *Suppose* p_i *is an equilibrium of* ∇V *and* $0 < \eta < 1$. *If*

$$N \geq N(\epsilon, \eta) = 2 + \frac{\log \eta}{\log \left(1 - \frac{4\pi\epsilon^2}{H^2}\right)}, \tag{4}$$

then

$$\mathbb{P}(|\mathrm{Grad}(p_i)| < \epsilon \mid d(p_i, \partial D) \geq r) > 1 - \eta.$$

Proof. Follows directly from Proposition 2. Observe that as $\epsilon, \eta \to 0$, $N(\epsilon, \eta)$ is of the order $O\left(\frac{1}{\epsilon} \log \frac{1}{\eta}\right)$.

4   Average Complexity

One way to measure the average complexity of $GRAD_S(r)$ is to require that the probability that $|\mathrm{Grad}| < \epsilon$ be greater than $1 - \eta$, and then count the average number of computations and communication steps the algorithm has to perform. The random variable crucial in this count is the number X_r of r-neighbors of a randomly picked but fixed node S_i. If the position of S_i is p_i, it is not difficult to show that

$$\mathbb{E}(X_r \mid d(p_i, \partial D) \geq r) = (N-1)\pi r^2. \tag{5}$$

Proposition 4 *If $\nabla V(p_i) = 0$ and $N \geq N(\epsilon, \eta)$, guaranteeing that*

$$\mathbb{P}(|\mathrm{Grad}(p_i)| < \epsilon \mid d(p_i, \partial D) \geq r) > 1 - \eta,$$

than on average, the number of computations $GRAD_S(r)$ performs is of the order $O\left(\frac{1}{\epsilon} \log \frac{1}{\eta}\right)$, *as $\epsilon, \eta \to 0$.*

Proof. The number of computational steps S performs in $GRAD_S(r)$ is proportional to the number of its r-neighbors, that is, on average, of the order $O(E(X_r \mid d(p_i, \partial D) \geq r)) = O(N)$. The statement then follows from (5) and Proposition 3, since N has to be chosen of the order $O\left(\frac{1}{\epsilon} \log \frac{1}{\eta}\right)$.

Remark. The average communication complexity of the algorithm depends on the data fusion algorithm chosen in Step 2.

5   Simulation Results

Let $F = \nabla V$. If p is not an equilibrium of F, then in a neighborhood of p, F looks essentially like a constant vector field, up to a smooth change of coordinates. This is known as the Flow Box Theorem in dynamical systems. If $F(p) = 0$, then the picture can be much more complicated. However, if $A = DF(p)$ has no eigenvalues on the imaginary axis, then in a neighborhood of p, F looks essentially like A, or, more precisely, up to a continuous coordinate change near p, the flow of F is the same as the flow of A. This is known as the Hartman-Grobman theorem. Observe that the condition "$DF(p)$ has no eigenvalues on the imaginary axis" is generic, i.e., it is satisfied by almost all F. Furthermore, it is well known that, generically (when D^2V is nonsingular), the equilibria of ∇V can only be saddles and stable or unstable nodes.

Therefore, it is sufficient to test our algorithm in three cases: near a nonequilibrium point for ∇V, near a saddle for ∇V, and near an unstable node for ∇V. Consequently, we present three examples: in the first one, V is a linear function (Fig. 3); in the second one, V is quadratic and ∇V has a saddle at $(10, 10)$ (Fig. 4); in the last one, V is quadratic, but ∇V has an unstable node at $(10, 10)$ (Fig. 5). In all cases, the algorithm gives good results away from the boundary of $D = [0, 20] \times [0, 20]$. Observe that if we excluded the edge effects from the calculation of the average relative error (i.e., average absolute error divided by the norm of the gradient at the corresponding point), the accuracy would improve.

6   Conclusion

We presented a distributed algorithm which estimates the gradient of a smooth function using a random sensor network. The method amounts to approximate differentiation of the function given its value on a set of random points. We estimated the probability that the error is small and showed that it converges to one, as the number of nodes goes to infinity.

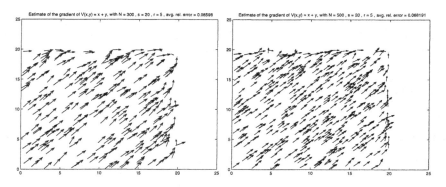

Fig. 3. $V(x, y) = x + y$, $D = [0, 20] \times [0, 20]$.

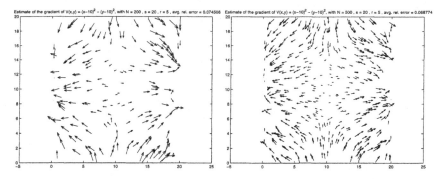

Fig. 4. $V(x, y) = (x - 10)^2 - (y - 10)^2$, $D = [0, 20] \times [0, 20]$.

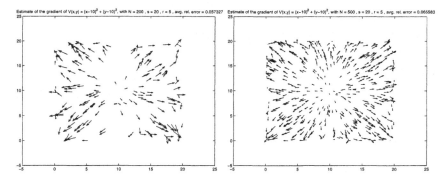

Fig. 5. $V(x, y) = (x - 10)^2 + (y - 10)^2$, $D = [0, 20] \times [0, 20]$.

It would be useful to estimate the expected value of the error and investigate robustness of the algorithm to noise and node failures. Further, it would be interesting to compare this with other algorithms, e.g., the one in [MEM01], which is also sufficiently simple to be implementable on the current platform for sensor network. As the the computers on-board sensor motes get progressively more powerful, it will become possible to use more sophisticated algorithms such as least squares. We plan to do this in future work.

References

[Cul]   D. Culler, http://webs.cs.berkeley.edu.

[Doh00]   L. Doherty, *Algorithms for position and data recovery in wireless sensor networks*, Master's thesis, UC Berkeley, 2000.

[GDW94]   S. Grime and H. F. Durrant-Whyte, *Data fusion in decentralized sensor networks*, Control Enineering Practice **2** (1994), no. 5, 849–863.

[GS97]   G.R. Grimmett and D.R. Strizaker, *Probability and random processes*, 2nd ed., Oxford University Press, 1997.

[IJ01]   S. S. Iyengar and B. Jones, *Information fusion techniques for pattern analysis in large sensor data networks*, Journal of the Franklin Institute **338** (2001), no. 5, 571–582.

[KKP]   J.M. Kahn, R.H. Katz, and K.S.J. Pister, *Mobile networking for Smart Dust*, ACM/IEEE Intl. Conf. on Mobile Computing and Networking (Seattle, WA), August 1999.

[KM94]   A. Knoll and J. Meinkoehn, *Data fusion using large multi-agent networks: an analysis of network structure and performance*, Proceedings of the International Conference on Multisensor Fusion and Integration for Intelligent Systems (MFI) (Las Vegas, NV), Oct. 2–5 1994, pp. 113–120.

[MEM01]   T. H. Meyer, M. Eriksson, and R. C. Maggio, *Gradient estimation from irregularly spaced data sets*, Mathematical Geology **33** (2001), no. 6, 693–717.

[MPS+02]   A. Mainwaring, J. Polastre, R. Szewczyk, D. Culler, and J. Anderson, *Wireless sensor networks for habitat monitoring.*, ACM International Workshop on Wireless Sensor Networks and Applications, WSNA '02 (Atlanta, GA), September 2002.

[QWIC01]   H. Qi, X. Wang, S. S. Iyengar, and K. Chakrabarty, *Multisensor data fusion in distributed sensor networks using mobile agents*, Proc. Intl. Conf. Information Fusion, August 2001, pp. 11–16,.

[SS02]   S. N. Simić and S. Sastry, *Distributed localization in wireless ad hoc networks*, Tech. report, UC Berkeley, 2002, Memorandum No. UCB/ERL M02/26.

Characterization of Location Error in Wireless Sensor Networks: Analysis and Applications*

Sasha Slijepcevic, Seapahn Megerian, and Miodrag Potkonjak

University of California, Los Angeles, CA 90095, USA
{sascha,seapahn,miodrag}@cs.ucla.edu, http://www.cs.ucla.edu/~sascha/

Abstract. One task in which inaccurate measurements are often used is location discovery, a process where the nodes in a network determine their locations. We have focused on location discovery as the primary target of our study since many sensor network tasks are dependent on location information. We demonstrate the benefits of location error analysis for system software and applications in wireless sensor networks. The technical highlight of our work is a statistically validated parameterized model of location errors that can be used to evaluate the impact of a location discovery algorithm on subsequent tasks. We prove that the distribution of location error can be approximated with a family of Weibull distributions. Then, we show that while performing the location discovery task, the nodes in a network can estimate the parameters of the distribution. Finally, we describe how applications can use the estimated statistical parameters to: (i) estimate the confidence intervals for their results, (ii) organize resource consumption to achieve optimal results in presence of estimated magnitude of error.

1 Introduction

Wireless embedded ad-hoc sensor networks (WEASNs) are distributed systems that consist of sensor nodes each equipped with a number of sensors (such as temperature, light, acoustic, seismic, and acceleration), wireless communication systems, storage, processing resources, and in some cases, actuators. One can envision numerous consumer, business, environmental, and scientific applications of WEASNs, ranging from early forest fire detection, indoor energy consumption monitoring, environmental monitoring, target tracking (such as on the battlefields), and earthquake monitoring [6]. Wireless sensor networks monitor the physical world measuring physical phenomena. These measurements and the results computed from them are often inaccurate. In environments where inaccurate measurements are the rule rather than the exception, the ability to detect inaccurate data and to estimate the accuracy of the results must be an intrinsic part of applications and system tasks. Some examples where information about

---

* This work was supported by the NSF under Grant No. ANI-0085773. Any opinions, findings and conclusions expressed in this material are those of the authors and do not necessarily reflect the views of the NSF.

F. Zhao and L. Guibas (Eds.): IPSN 2003, LNCS 2634, pp. 593–608, 2003.

errors could be used in WEASNs are the development of objective functions, optimization algorithms, and measures of confidence for application results.

Information about the locations of sensor nodes is of particular importance for many potential applications of WEASNs. Location information is, however, prone to inaccuracies, since the accuracy of distance measurements, which are essential for all location discovery algorithms, varies widely with the hardware technology and environmental conditions. In this paper, we demonstrate the importance of the estimation of the location errors. The goals and the main contributions of our work presented in this paper are:

1. Examination of impact of the location discovery process parameters on the properties of the distribution of location error.
2. Determination of statistical parameters of the location error at different stages of the location discovery process.
3. Estimation of application performance based on the statistical properties of location error.

We examine the distribution of the location error on different stages of the location discovery process, and we show how we can improve the accuracy of location discovery using the estimates of location errors in different stages of the process. Furthermore, the applications can also benefit from information about the location error distribution. For example, correct predictions of application performance with the presence of error in locations can improve resource management in WEASNs. In some instances, if the estimate of location error is above a certain threshold, applications can determine that the processing based on given locations can create practically useless results. One additional benefit of location error analysis is that accurate modeling of location error can speed up sensor network simulations by generating the locations with appropriate error distributions without running a location discovery algorithm.

The rest of this section contains an example that demonstrates importance of information about the distribution of location error. The notation and statistical methodologies used in this work are presented in Section 2. Section 3 describes distance error models, while Section 4 contains related work. Location errors in the atomic multilateration procedure are examined in Section 5. In Section 6, we determine the properties of location error for the location discovery algorithm, and describe how to determine these parameters. The impact of error on applications is the topic of Section 7. Section 8 concludes the paper.

1.1   Motivation

To better demonstrate the practical importance of estimation of the parameters of the location error distribution, let us consider an application where the goal is to acquire photos of birds, similar to [4]. A camera on a sensor node should be triggered at the moment when a bird is at a particular location. Depending on the accuracy of the locations of sensor nodes and birds, available resources including memory, processing, and power can be dedicated to covering larger or smaller areas in order to have a bird in a picture with a certain probability. Without any information about location error, one can make an educated guess and assume that the average error with which a bird is located is μ, and that the error distribution can be approximated with the Rayleigh distribution, similar to the location error in GPS. Figure 1 shows the distribution of location error for data acquired through simulations, with the average location error of $\mu = 43\,\text{cm}$, and the Rayleigh distribution with the same average location error. The simulations are performed using error models and the algorithms described in this paper. The Rayleigh distribution tells us that in order to take a picture of at least 99% of the birds coming to the area, it is sufficient to cover a 1 m circle, while to photograph 80% of the birds, the covered area should be a 50 cm circle around the estimate of the bird's location. However, the experimental distribution indicates that for a 99% success rate, it is necessary to cover a 4 m circle, while for an 80% success rate it is sufficient to cover a 15 cm circle. In this case, information about the location error distribution would significantly reduce resource consumption, while ensuring that the required success rate is achieved.

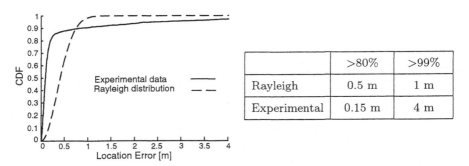

	>80%	>99%
Rayleigh	0.5 m	1 m
Experimental	0.15 m	4 m

Fig. 1. Comparison of the Rayleigh distribution and experimental data, when the average location error is same

2   Preliminaries

In this section, we describe the notation used throughout the paper, the basics of the location discovery process, as well as the statistical methodology for testing the hypotheses and for parameter estimations. We use the following notation for actual locations and distances and their estimates:

(x_i, y_i) Actual location of the sensor node i
(x_i^s, y_i^s) Estimated location of the node i in the solution s
$E_s(x_i, y_i)$ Location error for the node i; distance between (x_i, y_i) and (x_i^s, y_i^s)
d_{ij} Measured distance between the nodes i and j

The basic step of location discovery procedure is atomic multilateration. Node N_0 acquires location estimates (x_i^s, y_i^s) for k of its neighbors, the nodes within its transmission range. The node N_0 also acquires the distance estimates d_{i0}. For each location (x, y), which the node N_0 may choose as an estimate of its location, we can define the values of residuals:

$$R_i(x, y) = \left| \sqrt{(x_i^s - x_i)^2 + (y_i^s - y_i)^2} - d_{i0} \right|.$$

The location that is chosen as the estimate of the location of N_0 is the one for which the extreme value of an objective function is achieved. In this work, we use three objective functions:

$$PDF_{max}(x, y) = \prod_{i=1}^{n} P(R_i), \tag{1}$$

$$L_2(x, y) = \sum_{i=1}^{n} (R_i)^2, \tag{2}$$

$$L_\infty(x, y) = \max_{i=1..N} \frac{R_i}{d_{i0}}. \tag{3}$$

The objective function (1) assumes the complete knowledge of the underlying distance measurement model. For each residual $R_i(x, y)$, the value $P(R_i(x, y))$ corresponds to the probability density function for the distance error R_i, according to a distance error model. The product of these values defines the value of the objective function PDF_{max} at (x, y). The location with the largest value of the objective function (1) is selected. The function (3) uses the knowledge that for all error models in our simulations the error increases with distance. If L_∞ is used, the selected point is the one with the lowest value of L_∞. L_2 is the standard RMS (root mean square) function of the residuals. A global location discovery algorithm starts from a certain number of nodes that initially have their location estimates. These nodes serve as references for initial atomic multilaterations. After the node N_0 acquires its location, it is used as a reference point for other nodes.

The location error distributions for atomic multilateration and for global location discovery algorithms are acquired through simulations of both procedures. After that, we test two different types of hypotheses. The first type determines whether the error distribution can be approximated with some of the theoretical distributions. We selected four theoretical continuous distributions that cover the interval $[0, \infty]$: Rayleigh, Weibull [23], Gamma, and exponential distribution. The parameters of the theoretical distributions are determined using maximum likelihood estimates of the distribution parameters [7] for the given experimental data. In the next step, using the given parameters, random samples are generated for each of the four standard distributions. Finally, we use the Kolmogorov-Smirnov [10] test to compare the random samples for the four distributions and the experimental location error distribution. The Kolomogorov-Smirnov (KS) test tests the hypothesis that the samples are drawn from the same continuous distribution. The hypothesis is accepted or rejected depending on the maximum difference of the cumulative distribution functions (CDF) of the samples. The second type of tests examines whether two different location error distributions are statistically different. Again, the KS test is used to test whether the hypothesis should be rejected. The significance level for all tests is 0.05.

3   Error Models

Distance measurements, and in some cases GPS-generated location estimates, are the input parameters of the location discovery process. They are also main sources of errors in results of location discovery algorithms. Modeling of errors in input parameters, therefore, is of great significance for simulations of algorithms and applications in WEASNs. As wireless sensor networks are intended to be used, among other environments, in remote and inhospitable areas, where the error characteristics of distance measurements cannot be examined in advance, prediction of the performance of the network greatly depends on simulations with carefully chosen error models.

The distance estimates in WEASN are susceptible to different sources of error, including obstacles, interference, and multipath effects. The impact of these sources of error depends on the hardware technology used for measurements. There are three most frequently proposed distance measuring technologies: Received Signal Strength Indicator (RSSI), Time Difference of Arrival (TDoA) combining radio and acoustic signal, and acoustic-based ranging. Each of the given technologies has different error characteristics. However, currently there are not enough published data to precisely characterize the given technologies. We opted for three error models that correspond to each of the hardware technologies. The first error model, mainly intended to capture properties of distance measurement error for RSSI, is based on the path loss models from [17]. The main source of error in RSSI-based distance measurements is the complexity of modeling of environmental effects in the propagation model. Reflection, scattering, and diffraction, as well as the antenna gains, produce significantly different path losses for equal distances. From [17] (pg. 104), the distribution of measured distances $\hat{d}$ is given as

$$10n \log(\frac{\hat{d}}{d_0}) - 10n \log(\frac{d}{d_0}) = X_\sigma [dB], \tag{4}$$

where d is the measured distance, and X_σ is a zero-mean Gaussian random variable with standard deviation σ, both in dB. From (4):

$$\hat{d} = d + d(10^{\frac{X_\sigma}{10n}} - 1). \tag{5}$$

The second term in (5) represents the distance dependent error. The second error model is based on Gaussian distribution. The distance estimate $\hat{d}$ is given as $\hat{d} = d + d * G(0, \sigma)$, where $G(0, \sigma)$ is a white Gaussian noise with the standard deviation σ.

Modeling of the acoustic ranging error is based on the research reported in [8]. There are three important sources of error in acoustic ranging that cannot be eliminated by averaging distance measurements over time [8]:

1. Non-line-of-sight (NLOS) error: This error occurs when there is an obstacle between nodes. We model it as a distance dependent, uniformly distributed, positive error $U_n(0, NLOS\_ERROR_{max}(d))$.
2. Speed of sound error: Atmospheric changes in the environment, as well as different atmospheric conditions in various parts of the network impact the speed of sound. We model this as a distance dependent Gaussian noise $G_1(0, \sigma(d))$.
3. Orientation error: The emitter and the sound sensor may not be aimed towards each other, which creates an error that depends on the angle between them. We model this error as the angle-dependent Gaussian noise $\alpha G_2(0, \sigma)$, where α a is the angle between the emitter and the sound sensor.

Thus, the acoustic distance measurement between the nodes i and j is simulated as:

$$\hat{d} = d + d(U_n + G_1) + \alpha G_2. \tag{6}$$

4   Related Work

Availability of low-cost wireless sensor nodes, and their capability to form distributed network systems is a result of the advances in various scientific disciplines. The research in signal processing [5,21], operating systems [9], low-power design [16], and robotics [20] laid foundation for applications described in [6, 14]. Since the localization is an essential task in WEASNs, and in other wireless systems, there is a large number of research projects related to localization in wireless networks. In [15], a mobile device listens to the available beacons, and can detect its location as well as its orientation within a building with the centimeter-level accuracy. The systems in [15,22] require dedicated infrastructure, while [2] depends only on already existing LAN infrastructure. However, the issue of accuracy of the localization results has not been discussed, except in [19]. A similar problem, the accuracy of the localization of a stationary and a moving target, is examined in [25].

The process of localization in WEASNs is based on two stages. The first stage includes measuring the distance or the angle between two entities in the network. The possibility of using RSSI measurements for distance estimates in WEASNs is discussed in [3]. In [18], the combination of acoustic and radio signal is chosen as a better alternative. The distance is estimated from the difference in time of flight of simultaneously transmitted acoustic and radio signal. The significant difference in speed of these two signals allows the radio signal to be used as a synchronization signal, while the distance is basically derived from the time of travel of the acoustic signal. At the same time, [18] demonstrates unpredictability of RSSI-based distance measurements. Further simulation results in the same paper show that using the given distance measurements, the estimates of locations of the sensor nodes are within 20 cm of the actual locations. The third technology used for distance measurements in WEASNs is acoustic-based [8]. The method is based on measuring the time of travel of the sound between two synchronized nodes.

The examples of the second stage of localization procedure, where the location estimates are distributed through the network to be used for further localization, can be found in several papers [1,13,18]. In the algorithms described in these papers, the location of nodes are determined as soon as the required information is available, without estimating possible errors involved in the given information. In [12], the nodes that receive consistent information from various neighbors determine their locations first. Another localization system where a significant amount of attention is given to error measuring and control is described in [24]. The authors determined certain sources of error in TDoA distance measurements, and they minimized the effect of those error sources by calibrating parameters of the devices.

5   Location Error Distribution for Atomic Multilateration

In this section, we determine characteristics of the location error distribution for the atomic multilateration. The goal of the simulations presented here is to determine the impact of the parameters of the atomic multilateration on the location error distribution. The first parameter that we vary is the atomic multilateration objective function. The second parameter is the percentage of the results of the multilateration that are rejected on the basis of their probability to be inaccurate. That probability is estimated using two tests described in this section. Additionally, in this section we compare the error location distributions for the distance error models from Section 3.

First, we show how the choice of an atomic multilateration objective function, among the ones listed in Section 2, affects the location error distribution. The most frequently used atomic multilateration objective function is L_2 [1,18]. However, the error models used in [1,18], and in most of other simulation-based location discovery projects, is a zero-mean white Gaussian noise. Here, we propose distance dependent error models. The other two objective function that we use, PDF_{max} and L_∞, are tailored to those specific error models. In this experiment, we perform 2000 multilaterations for each error model. The ranging errors are drawn from a distribution corresponding to an error model with the average distance error of 1%. Four nodes are randomly positioned into an area 15x15 m. Three nodes are beacons, while the fourth node determines its location. For each of the 2000 multilaterations, we collect the location errors, and determine cumulative distribution functions (CDF) for each error model. The graphical comparison between the results achieved using different objective functions, for the Gaussian error model, can be seen in Fig. 2. There is no statistically significant difference between the location error distributions for three objective functions according to the KS test with the significance level of 5%. The KS test for the other two error models confirms that there is no difference between the three objective functions for any of the proposed error models. Also, for the average error of 10%, there were no statistically significant difference between the distributions for different error models and objective functions.

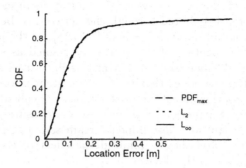

Fig. 2. CDFs of the distribution of the location error for three proposed objective functions

There are two tests that we use to detect the multilateration location estimates that have a high probability of error. The first test is based on the value of the sum of residuals for a particular location. From the correlation between the sum of residuals and location error, displayed in Fig. 3, we can see that a small value of the sum of residuals does not indicate a small value of location error. However, if the residuals sum is above a certain threshold, the distances involved in multilateration are likely to be inaccurate. Thus, a point where the distance measurements can be consistent cannot be found. For the Gaussian error model and an average distance error of 1%, the sums of residuals above 10 cm mostly represent the locations with location error of more than 25 cm.

The second test involves the topology of the referent beacons. If the beacons are almost collinear, or in other words, if the triangle created from the locations of the beacons has an obtuse angle above a certain threshold, a small error in distance measurements can create a small sum of residuals, but a large real location error. In Fig. 3, such locations are the ones along the y-axis, with small sum of residuals, but large location error. If the angle threshold for a largest angle in the triangle increases, the average location error decreases until the point of saturation is reached where the average location error does not change anymore. However, the number of rejected locations also increases. In our simulations, we set the angle limit at $3\pi/4$, where the number of rejected locations due to a large angle in the triangle hits 40%, but the point of saturation is reached close to $\pi/2$. This issue is certainly important and deserves a further research.

In the next experiment, we improve the accuracy of the multilateration procedure by rejecting all locations where the residuals or the beacons topology do not satisfy two tests defined above. The improved accuracy is achieved at the cost of rejecting around 50% of the locations generated during the simulation. The average location error achieved in this experiment is 10 cm, which is an improvement of more than 75% compared to the average value of location error of 43 cm, for experiments when the two tests are not used. Figure 4 shows the distribution for the experimental data and the theoretical distributions with the best-fit parameters.

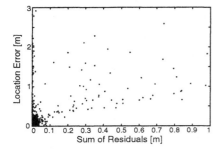
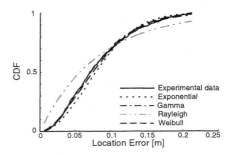

Fig. 3. Correlation between the sum of residuals and the location error

Fig. 4. CDF of the experimental data and theoretical distributions

For this value of the average location error, we can see from Fig. 4 that the experimental data distribution is closest to the Weibull and the Gamma distribution. In order to statistically compare the experimental data distribution and the theoretical distributions, we generated 100 random samples of each of the distributions, and compared them with the experimental data using KS test. The results of the test for the Gaussian error model are given in Table 1. For 94% of the random samples generated using the MLE parameters for the Gamma distribution, the hypothesis H_0 about the same underlying distributions could not be rejected, while the percentage for the Weibull distribution is 54%.

Table 1. Percentage of cases where the hypothesis H_0: "the experimental data and the random sample are from the same distribution" cannot be rejected

Weibull	Rayleigh	Exponential	Gamma
54%	0%	0%	94%

To further confirm that the location error distribution can be approximated with the Gamma distribution, when the average error is below the certain limit, we generated location error distributions with different values of the average location error. We create the distributions with different values of the average location error by changing the parameters of the two tests. For the average location error of less than 17 cm, the acceptance rate, measured in number of random samples statistically not different from the experimental data, does not fall below 90%, while for larger errors the acceptance rate never reaches 90%. Finally, we describe the effects of different error models on the multilateration location error. We give only the corresponding tables to show that the Gamma distribution is still an adequate choice to approximate the experimental data. Table 2 shows that the Gamma distribution represents a good approximation of the location error distribution for the multilateration procedure with the average location error of 10 cm, if the RSSI and the acoustic error model are used.

Table 2. Percentage of cases where the hypothesis H_0: "the experimental data and the random sample are from the same distribution" cannot be rejected, for RSSI and acoustic distance error models

Error model	Weibull	Rayleigh	Exponential	Gamma
RSSI	36%	0%	0%	90%
acoustic	59%	0%	0%	92%

The distributions for the three error models are tested against each other. KS test could not reject the hypothesis that all three location error distributions are samples of the same underlying distribution. The results from the experiments indicate that the distribution based on the atomic multilateration, using the L_2 objective function and the Gaussian model for the distance measurement error, can be accepted as approximation of the distribution if other objective functions from Section 2 and the error models from Section 3 are used. Therefore, we can test the properties of location error in location discovery algorithms with only the Gaussian error model and L_2 objective function without loss of generality.

6   Estimation of Error Distribution Parameters

In this section, we examine the distribution of error amplitudes in nodes' locations determined by the location discovery algorithm. We demonstrate that, for the average location error below a certain threshold, the distribution of location error can be approximated with the Weibull distribution. Then, we describe how the average location error in a network can be estimated using residuals. Finally, we show that there is a correlation between the average location error and the shape parameter of the Weibull distribution, which allows us to estimate parameters of the actual location error distribution.

We perform experiments on networks with 100 nodes positioned in an area 50x50 m. As presented in Section 5, we have found out that the choice of the objective function for the atomic multilateration procedure or the underlying error model does not impact the results, so in this set of experiments we use

L_2 as the objective function and the RSSI model for the distance measurement error. The number of the nodes with initial location information is 15%, while the transmission range is 10 m for all nodes. The details of the location discovery algorithm are described in [12].

First, we examine the possibility to approximate the location error distribution with the Gamma or the Weibull distribution. We compare results for 20 networks with different values of the average location error. For each network, we execute the location discovery algorithm and determine the distribution of error amplitudes from the resulting location estimates. Then, we determine the parameters of the Gamma and the Weibull distribution that are the best fit for the experimental results. Finally, we generate 100 random samples with the best-fit parameters for each of the two standard distributions. Each generated sample is then tested, using the KS test, against the corresponding experimental distribution to determine whether the two distributions are statistically different. The results of the tests are given in Fig. 5. The figure shows the percentage of samples from the Gamma and the Weibull distributions that are not statistically different from the the experimental data at the significance level of 0.05.

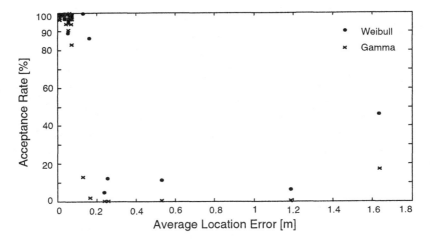

Fig. 5. The percentage of the Gamma and Weibull sample distributions that are statistically not different from the experimental distribution of the location error

We can notice in Fig. 5 that, even with the rejection in the atomic multilateration procedure, there are cases where the average location error reaches 1.8 m, which is large considering the average distance error of 1% of a measured distance. There are still cases where a large error occurs at the beginning of the location discovery process, and then propagates through the network. The second observation is that the acceptance rate for the Weibull and the Gamma distribution sharply increases for the networks with the average location rate lower than 20 cm, where 75% of the networks belong. Finally, for each of the networks, samples from the Weibull distribution achieve better acceptance rate than samples from the Gamma distribution. Consequently, we accepted the former as the better approximation of the location error distribution.

6.1   Average Location Error Estimates

One of the steps in the process of estimating the properties of error in the location discovery procedure is to estimate the average value of location error. While performing a location discovery process, an algorithm deals with a set of initial measurements and intermediate results from which a solution for localization problem is to be found. As we described earlier, initial measurements are often inaccurate, and a solution in which distances between the estimates of nodes' locations are consistent with the initial measurements of the corresponding distances may not be possible. Therefore, solutions always contain a certain level of inconsistencies (residuals) between the initial measurements and the accepted locations: $r_{ij} = d_{ij}^s - d_{ij}$. We use residuals as the base for a simple, but effective solution for the estimation of the average location error. We calculate the sum of all available residuals in the network and we use to estimate the average value of the location error:

$$S = \sum_{i=1}^{N} \sum_{j=1}^{i-1} |r_{ij}| \tag{7}$$

The effectiveness of the given function in estimating the average location error is presented in Fig. 6. We simulated the location discovery algorithm on 70 networks with the average location error below 20 cm, and then we grouped the networks according to their sums of residuals. One group contains all networks with the sum of residuals belonging to one of the noted 5 m intervals, given as the x-axis in Fig. 6.

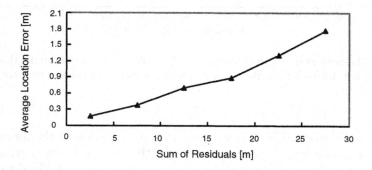

Fig. 6. Correlation between the sums of residuals and the average location errors for 70 networks grouped according to their sums of residuals

For each group we calculated the average location error. Figure 6 shows the relationship between such calculated values. The relationship depends on the size of the networks, connectivity, distance measurement error model, and other parameters. In a practical implementation, these parameters are known or can be modeled in advance, and once the relationship is determined, it can be used to determine the average location error in a real network. After we determined that we can approximate the location error distribution with the Weibull distribution, we need an approach to estimate the parameters of the Weibull distribution. The correlation between the average location error and the shape parameter β, is given in Fig. 7. The results include 70 networks with the average location error below 0.2 m.

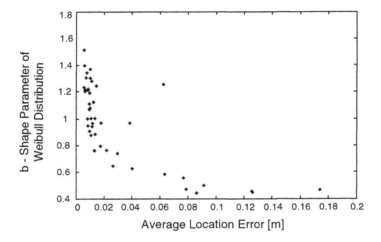

Fig. 7. Correlation between the average location error for the whole network and the shape parameter of the Weibull distribution

It is important to emphasize here is that for one mean value of the Weibull distribution, many different Weibull distributions can be generated, with varying two parameters of the Weibull distribution: the shape parameter β and the scale parameter η. However, in the case of the location error distribution, the range of the shape parameter β is correlated with the average location error, which means that the location error can be described with a limited subset of Weibull distributions, which we consider the most important contribution of this research. At the range of values of the parameter β given in Fig. 7, the parameter η impacts the shape of the distribution significantly less than β.

7   Applications

This section deals with the effect of inaccurate locations on the application in WEASNs. First, we describe two applications with different expected impacts of the error on their performance, and then we present the results. The goal of this experiment is to determine how well we can predict the accuracy of the results of different applications. The first application calculates the shortest paths for each pair of nodes in the network, based on their estimated locations. The most important property of this application is that the locations of all nodes are taken into account in every network where this application is executed. Therefore, if the location error distribution is similar for two networks, which happens when the average errors are close, the impact of location error on the application is similar too. We measure the impact of the location error through the percentage of shortest paths that change, if the estimated locations of the nodes are replaced with the actual locations. For this experiment, we have run the application on 20 different networks, with the locations acquired through the location discovery procedure. We have also run the application on the same networks using the actual locations of the nodes. Then, we compare the results and calculate the percentage of shortest paths that differ. From Fig. 8, we can see that networks with the close values of the average location error experience similar percentage of changed paths, as expected. Networks with the average error below 4 cm have less than 3% different paths, while networks with the average error between 6 cm and 10 cm have between 3% and 8% of different paths.

The second application belongs to a different class of applications, where the impact of the nodes' locations is not uniformly distributed across the network. The application calculates the path on which the exposure from the nodes in the network is minimal. The exposure from one node is inversely proportional to the square of the distance between the node and the point for which the exposure is calculated. The exposure on a path is the integral of the exposures of its points [11]. The nodes that are far from the path has much less impact on the exposure, therefore the impact of error in their locations is also smaller. Since the location error is distributed according to the Weibull distribution, there are always some nodes with larger error. However, in different networks these nodes are closer or further from the minimal exposure path. Fig. 9 displays the difference in the distribution of errors for two set of networks, with networks in one set having similar average location error. The error for this application is defined as the difference between exposure that an object expect to experience along the path calculated using the estimated locations and the real exposure, calculated using the actual locations, along the same path. The networks with the average location error from 1 cm to 3 cm are compared to the networks with the average location error from 8 cm to 12 cm. From Fig. 9, we can predict what is the probability for a network with the average location error, estimated as shown in Section 6.1 to report a result with a certain magnitude of error after running the minimal exposure path application.

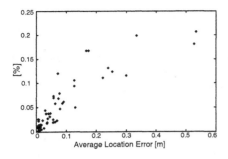

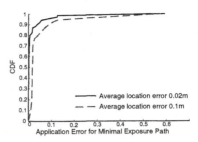

Fig. 8. The percentage of the shortest paths that differ when the paths are calculated using i) estimated and ii) real locations

Fig. 9. Distribution of errors in minimal exposure paths for the networks with different average location error

8   Conclusion

The main goal of this paper has been to analyze location error in WEASNs and to demonstrate the practical use of the results of the analysis. We described here the impact that certain design decisions have on the magnitude and the distribution of location error for atomic multilateration and for location discovery algorithms. We examined the conditions under which location error in atomic multilateration and location discovery algorithms can be approximated with the Gamma and the Weibull distribution, respectively. We determined that the distribution of location error can be approximated well with the Weibull distribution, and that the parameters of the distribution can be unequivocally determined from the inconsistencies in locations and the distance measurements. Knowledge of the error distribution allows us to use the resources for the tasks that can achieve the required results in the presence of error, while the tasks that require higher accuracy can be adapted or canceled. Additional benefit of the results of the location error analysis is that the results of the location discovery process can be simulated accurately without the need for running the location discovery algorithm.

References

1. J. Albowicz, A. Chen, and L. Zhang. Recursive position estimation in sensor networks. In *Proceeding of ICNP*, pages 35–41, Nov 2001.
2. P. Bahl and V. N. Padmanabhan. Radar: an in-building RF-based user location and tracking system. In *Proceedings IEEE INFOCOM 2000*, volume 2, pages 775–84, Apr 2000.
3. N. Bulusu, J. Heidemann, and D. Estrin. GPS-less low cost outdoor localization for very small devices. *IEEE Personal Communications, Special Issue on Smart Spaces and Environments*, 7(5):28–34, Oct 2000.

4. A. Cerpa, J. Elson, D. Estrin, and L. Girrod. Habitat monitoring: Application driver for wireless communication technology. In *2001 ACM SIGCOMM Workshop on Data Communication in Latin America and the Caribbean*, 2001.
5. J.C. Chen, K. Yao, and R.E. Hudson. Source localization and beamforming. *IEEE Signal Processing Magazine*, 19:30–39, Mar 2002.
6. D. Estrin, R. Govindan, and J. Heidemann. Embedding the Internet: Introduction. *Communications of the ACM*, 43(5):43, May 2000.
7. R. A. Fisher. Theory of statistical estimation. *Proceedings of the Cambridge Philosophical Society*, 22:700–725, 1925.
8. L. Girod and D. Estrin. Robust range estimation using acoustic and multimodal sensing. In *IEEE/RSJ International Conference on Intelligent Robots and Systems (IROS 2001)*, Maui, Hawaii, Oct 2001.
9. J. Hill, R. Szewczyk, A. Woo, S. Hollar, D. Culler, and K. Pister. System architecture directions for network sensors. In *ASPLOS 2000*, pages 71–81, Cambridge, MA, Nov 2000.
10. F.J. Massey. The Kolmogorov-Smirnov test of goodness of fit. *Journal of the American Statistical Association*, 46, 1951.
11. S. Meguerdichian, F. Koushanfar, G. Qu, and M. Potkonjak. Exposure in wireless ad hoc sensor networks. In *Procs. of Int. Conf. on Mobile Computing and Networking (MobiCom '01)*, Jul 2001.
12. S. Meguerdichian, S. Slijepcevic, V. Karayan, and M. Potkonjak. Localized algorithms in wireless ad-hoc networks: Location discovery and sensor exposure. In *MobiHOC 2001*, Oct 2001.
13. D. Niculescu and B. Nath. Ad-hoc positioning system. Technical Report DCS-TR-435, Rutgers University, Apr 2001.
14. G. J. Pottie and W. J. Kaiser. Wireless integrated network sensors. *Communications of the ACM*, 43(5):51–58, May 2000.
15. N. B. Priyantha, A. Chakraborty, and H. Balakrishnan. The Cricket location-support system. In *MobiCom 2000*, pages 32–43, 2000.
16. J. M. Rabaey et al. PicoRadio supports ad-hoc ultra-low power wireless networking. *Computer*, 33(7):42–48, Jul 2000.
17. T. S. Rappaport. *Wireless Communications – Principles and Practice*. Prentice-Hall, Inc., New Jersey, 1996.
18. A. Savvides, C. Han, and M. Srivastava. Dynamic fine-grained localization in ad-hoc networks of sensors. In *ACM Sigmobile (Mobicom)*, pages 166–179, 2001.
19. S. Slijepcevic, S. Megerian, and M. Potkonjak. Location errors in wireless embedded sensor networks: Sources, models, and effects on applications. *Mobile Computing and Communications Review*, 6(3):67–78, Jul 2002.
20. G. S. Sukhatme and M. J. Mataric. Embedding robots into the Internet. *Communications of the ACM*, 43:67–73, May 2000.
21. D. L. Tennenhouse and V. G. Bose. The SpectrumWare approach to wireless signal processing. *Wireless Networks*, 2(1):1–12, 1996.
22. A. Ward, A. Jones, and A. Hopper. A new location technique for the active office. *IEEE Personal Communications*, 4(5):42–47, Oct 1997.
23. W. Weibull. A statistical distribution function of wide applicability. *Journal of Applied Mechanics*, Sep 1951.
24. K. Whitehouse and D. Culler. Calibration as parameter estimation in sensor networks. In *ACM Intl. Workshop on Wireless Sensor Networks and Applications*, Atlanta, Sep 2002.
25. F. Zhao, J. Shin, and J. Reich. Information-driven dynamic sensor collaboration for tracking applications. *IEEE Signal Processing Magazine*, Mar 2002.

A Distributed Algorithm for Waking-up in Heterogeneous Sensor Networks[1]

Akis Spyropoulos, Cauligi S. Raghavendra, and Viktor K. Prasanna

Electrical Engineering - Systems
University of Southern California
Los Angeles, California
{spyro, raghu, prasanna}@halcyon.usc.edu

Abstract. In this paper we present a distributed, application-morphable, algorithm for waking up appropriate sensor nodes in a heterogeneous sensor network. We assume a sensor field consisting of a large number of low power, limited functionality, tripwire nodes and a smaller number of powerful, energy-hungry, tracker nodes. Our problem is that when an event is detected by a set of tripwire nodes a specific number of appropriate tracker nodes needs to be woken up. These tracker nodes will subsequently collaborate to perform the sensing task required by the application. Waking up non-suitable tracker nodes or employing more trackers than necessary for a specific task, can lead to significant waste of network resources (e.g. energy). The application indicates the number of nodes that are needed for a sensing task, as well as an optimization function to be used by the algorithm. Therefore, our algorithm is isolated from most application details and is simple and general enough to accommodate a wide range of sensing applications. We prove that our algorithm converges to a uniform optimal global decision for specific classes of optimization functions. Furthermore, we show that it is fast enough (<100ms) to be practical for most sensing applications and exhibits good performance in terms of total messages exchanged. Finally, we demonstrate that our algorithm is very robust, managing to retain its correct and efficient behavior for a wide range of scenarios, even under hostile environmental conditions (e.g. link loss probabilities up to 35%).

1 Introduction

Continuous advances in low power electronics and processor technology have enabled the design of inexpensive sensor nodes capable of performing significant computation and wireless communication. A potentially very large number of such nodes can be deployed either manually or automatically [1] in a field, building or any other area of interest and self-organize into a network to perform a specific application. Various sensor applications have been proposed, ranging from real-time tracking of one or more targets [2] to environmental monitoring [3].

---

[1] This work is supported by the DARPA Power Aware Computing and Communication Program under contract no. F33615-C-00-1633.

F. Zhao and L. Guibas (Eds.): IPSN 2003, LNCS 2634, pp. 609–624, 2003.

A considerable amount of research effort has been devoted during the past couple of years in the area of sensor networks. However, most of the related work adopts a homogeneous sensor network model consisting of a single type of sensor nodes that collaborate to perform a specific sensing task [13] [14] [15]. It has recently been identified [4] [5] [16] that having different classes of sensor nodes may be beneficent to many sensor applications. These classes may be differentiated in terms of processing capabilities, sensing modalities, communication capabilities and size or cost. Specifically, it is envisioned that a large number of inexpensive, low energy, *tripwire* nodes are going to be deployed along with a smaller number of more powerful, specialized, nodes. These specialized nodes will be capable of performing computation-intensive functions (e.g. ranging, tracking, etc.) or communication-specific functions like routing or long-range communication to base station(s).

In this paper, we assume, without loss of generality, that only one such type of specialized nodes is deployed, which we're going to be referring to as *tracker* nodes, hereafter. It is anticipated that tracker nodes are going to be dissipating one to two orders of magnitude more power than tripwire nodes when all their subsystems (i.e. CPU, radio and sensor) are on [16]. Therefore, tracker nodes will have to be "off" most of the time, when no events occur[2], in order to maximize the operational lifetime of the network. On the other hand, tripwire nodes run with low power and may even be self-sufficient by scavenging energy from the environment [6]. However, they only have limited processing and communication capabilities. Their functionality is expected to be that of detecting events, using some simple threshold detection scheme, and waking up appropriate tracker nodes to perform the sensing task.

Our problem is that when an event is detected by a set of tripwire nodes, a specific number of appropriate tracker nodes need to be woken up, that will subsequently collaborate to perform the sensing task required by the application. Waking up more nodes than necessary could result in considerable waste of resources. For example, it has been shown that performing *line of bearing (LOB)* calculation can be achieved with only three tracking nodes with acceptable accuracy. The extra energy consumed by utilizing more tracker nodes for that purpose is not justified by the potential extra accuracy achieved. In addition to that, different sets of chosen tracker nodes may result in considerably different performance, in terms of accuracy, energy-efficiency, etc. Therefore, it is evident that some coordination scheme is needed among the tripwire nodes to wake up an appropriately sized set of tracker nodes that are optimal in respect to the sensor application's specific goal(s).

In this work, we propose a general, efficient and robust distributed algorithm for the tripwires to collaboratively choose a set of specialized nodes for a specific application. In our algorithm, each tripwire node re-evaluates its local decision on the optimal set of tracker nodes to be woken up, whenever it receives a *decision update packet* from a neighboring tripwire. If it learns of or can construct a superior set of tracker nodes, it informs its neighborhood about it. A tripwire terminates its local run of the algorithm if it does not receive any *decision update packet* within a specified time interval. It assumes that a global resolution has been achieved and proceeds with waking up the tracker nodes. The algorithm takes as input from the application the number of nodes that need to be woken up for a sensing task, as well as an optimization function to be used by the algorithm, in order to evaluate the "appropriateness" of a chosen set. This way, the algorithm is isolated from many

---

[2] Typical sensor applications duty cycles may be as low as 5%

application details. Its interface is kept simple and general enough to accommodate a wide range of sensing applications and adapt to each application's specific optimization goals. In this respect, our algorithm is *application-morphable*. Our scheme makes only a minimum number of "helpful" assumptions, in order to be in accordance with typical sensor network operational requirements, which may not hold in other wireless environments (e.g. cellular, ad hoc networks). Specifically, tripwire nodes are not required to have any ids and only single-hop broadcast messages are used for all tripwire communications. Only tracker nodes are assumed to have some kind of local or global id.

We use both analysis and simulations to evaluate the performance of our algorithm. We prove that our algorithm always converges to the optimal set of tracker nodes, for a specific class of optimization functions and show that it does so quickly enough (in less than 100ms) to be of practical value in sensor applications with real-time requirements. We further show that the total number of messages transmitted by all tripwires until the algorithm finished is close to an optimal (but not practical) approach. Finally, we demonstrate that our algorithm is very robust, managing to retain its correct and efficient behavior for a wide range of scenarios, even under hostile environmental conditions (e.g. link loss probabilities up to 35%).

In the next section, we identify the sensor network specific operational requirements and formulate the problem. In section 3, we provide a brief description of the range of approaches that can be taken to solve the basic problem posed in this paper and present our proposed solution. Performance results for our distributed algorithm are given in section 4. Finally, in section 5, we conclude the paper and discuss directions for future work.

2   Problem Formulation and Considerations

We assume that a large number of tripwire nodes are deployed along with a smaller number of tracker nodes in a field of interest. When no event is detected, all tracker nodes are off, performing no sensing, computation or communication. We assume that the tracker node radio either wakes up periodically and listens for incoming messages or has a low-power paging channel that is constantly on, listening for incoming "wake-up" messages. Tripwires are sensing for events at all times, but may keep their processor and radio off, while no event is sensed. When an event occurs, a number of tripwire nodes, say N, detect this event (e.g. receiving signal power exceeded some threshold). Note that N is not fixed, but depends on the strength and type of signal emitted by the event as well as the tripwire node topology and surrounding environment. For example, an acoustic signal can propagate further than a seismic signal and would therefore result in more tripwire nodes (i.e. larger N) detecting the event. In this work, we assume that these N tripwires are close-by and form a connected network. The issues of how to design and deploy the sensor network, in order to guarantee connectivity or full coverage of the field, with a very high probability, have been dealt with elsewhere [17] [18].

Each tripwire is initially *associated* with zero or more tracker nodes, by means of existing paths/gradients [7], established during some initialization phase, or simply by direct communication. Let M be the total number of trackers that are associated with at least one of the N tripwires (M < N). Any tracker j is characterized by a set A_j of attributes, like location, energy level, etc. Tripwire nodes learn about those attributes initially during *association* and subsequently by handshake, when waking up a tracker. Tripwires are not required to have a consistent view of trackers attributes. This may result because of different tripwires inquiring about the same tracker's attributes at different times. However, it is required that at least one tripwire has the correct (most recent) value for the attributes of interest for each of the M trackers.

The problem is to choose a set of K tracker nodes among the M possible ones that is optimal in regards to some optimization function F. Both K and F are application-dependent and are regarded as input parameters to the algorithm. F is an appropriate function of some or all tracker attributes, for the trackers belonging in a specific set of size K. If define as AR the range of all allowable values for an attribute set A_j then: $F:AR^K \rightarrow R$ or $F = f(A_1, A_2, ..., A_K)$. It captures the application-specific optimization goal(s). For example, if the application's goal is to choose the K trackers that have the maximum amount of remaining battery level, the following function F could be used: $F = E_1 + E_2 + ... + E_K$, where E_j is the battery level of tracker j in the chosen set of trackers. As another example, the application may wish to wake-up the *tightest cluster* of K trackers. In this case the application's optimization goal could be captured by

$$F = \sum_{n=1}^{K-1} \sum_{m=n+1}^{K} \left\| \vec{X}_n - \vec{X}_m \right\|,$$ where $\vec{X}_n$ is the position of the n-th tracker. The

optimization function is required to be simple enough to be calculated efficiently by the limited processing resources of the tripwire node.

Any algorithm devised for this problem should have the following goals:

- Correctness: Each tripwire should come up with the same "good" set of trackers.
- Convergence Speed: Sensor applications usually have hard real-time requirements (e.g. tracking of moving target). Therefore, all tripwire nodes should converge quickly enough to allow the tracking nodes time to meet those requirements.
- Message efficiency: The total number of messages exchanged throughout the decision process is a direct indicator of the total energy spent in the network for communication. Consequently, it should be kept low.
- Fault-tolerance and Robustness: Many sensor applications are mission critical. Consequently, it is necessary that the algorithm remains efficient even when a number of failures occur (e.g. node failures, link losses, collisions, etc.)

In addition to these goals, any solution to this problem as well as to many other sensor-related problems must take into account a number of salient features of sensor networks that are not common in other wireless contexts. Many proposed schemes for sensor network problems have been directly transported from the related discipline of wireless ad-hoc networks or other related areas and adapted for the case of sensor networks. However, specific assumptions have been carried along in some cases with these schemes that do not necessarily hold for wireless sensor networks. Failure to take into account the following idiosyncrasies of sensor networks can lead into impractical and inefficient approaches to solving sensor network specific problems.

Sensor applications are most often data-centric [8]. Additionally, sensor nodes are expected to be mass produced and deployed in a dense fashion to achieve high redundancy and fault-tolerance. Hence, it may be impractical or unnecessary to assign each sensor node a unique global id. Furthermore, the environment under which a sensor network is going to operate is expected to be very harsh. Shadowing and fading effects, inadvertent interference or jamming as well as adverse ground reflection effects, due to very low antenna heights, result in frequent and random link losses. Consequently, one should not assume "clean" models (e.g. cells, circles, etc.) for the effective communication range for a sensor node's radio and design protocols that are able to cope with the harsh propagation phenomena in a sensor network. Finally, despite the improvement in hardware and electronics technologies, computational power, memory, communication bandwidth and energy are still expensive and limited resources for wireless sensor nodes, even more than they are for wireless PDAs or laptops.

3   Distributed Wake-up Algorithm

In this section we will present our proposed solution to the problem, which is a fusion-based distributed algorithm. However, we first present the two different edges in the continuum of approaches that can be taken to tackle the basic problem and highlight their advantages and disadvantages, in respect to the 4 goals defined in Sec.2. We do so, in order to provide necessary intuition and justify the decisions we made in our design.

3.1   A Baseline Distributed Approach

A lot of work has been done in the past on a number of different issues related to distributed algorithms and their performance and limitations (see Chandy and Misra [19]). Here we describe a common, simple, approach, which is to have each node acquire global information and individually make a local decision. This way, if all nodes perform the same decision algorithm on the same global set of data, they all will come up with the same set of optimal nodes. In our general application model, this would mean that all N tripwires will need to acquire the necessary data for each of the M trackers, in order to locally choose the optimal set of K trackers, based on F. A general way to reach this state of global knowledge is to have each node flood each local view throughout the network. This exchange of information can be performed either in proactive (e.g. periodical) or reactive (e.g. event-triggered) manner.

An important concern when running any flooding-based algorithm in a wireless, shared media, network is the potential collisions of different update packets transmitted by neighboring nodes at about the same time. One way to deal with this problem would be to use some collision avoidance protocol, like 802.11 [9], which reserves the media before the actual data transmission. The use of the 802.11 protocol has two important drawbacks. First, it is based on the assumption of unique node IDs and can only reserve the media for point-to-point communication. Hence, one should either emulate broadcast by point-to-point transmission to each neighbor or just broadcast and let the back-off algorithm resolve the collisions that will occur. Either case would increase both delay and total number of messages for the algorithm to converge. Therefore, we choose to enforce some randomization to the basic flooding algorithm, in order to prevent synchronization of updates and avoid potential collisions (to a large extent). Specifically, a node periodically broadcasts update messages (if it has any), choosing in every step a different waiting period, uniformly distributed in [0, T], where T is the maximum amount of time that a tripwire node may wait before broadcasting its update.

Assuming that no link or node failures occur during the data exchange, the algorithm will result in each node calculating the same, optimal, set of trackers. This follows from the fact that each node makes its decision by applying the same decision function on the same set of information. Each tripwire node will broadcast an update it receives (or its own initial local info) in at most time T after its reception. Therefore, if D_N is the diameter of the connected network formed by the N tripwires then it will take at most T_{cv} for all local info messages to propagate throughout the whole network and the algorithm to converge, where T_{cv} is given by $T_{CV} = D_N * T$.

Each of the N tripwire nodes has to receive and forward information about all M trackers, at least once. Therefore, in the worst case (e.g. a different update message propagates throughout the network for each of the M trackers) the total number of messages M_{TOT} that needs to be transmitted will be $M_{TOT} = O(N * M)$.

Finally, flooding algorithms can exhibit very good fault-tolerance and robustness properties. This is because they can discover all alternative paths from each node to another in a straightforward manner. Therefore, even if link conditions or a collision results in loss of some update packet to a node from one path, this packet will probably reach the node from some alternative path if there is any

3.2   A Centralized Approach

The opposite end in the continuum of approaches is the centralized one. In the general centralized case, some leader for the whole network needs to be elected [10]. This leader is going to collect data from all other nodes, combine them or make a decision based on the global data, and send back to all the nodes (or some specified sink node, depending on the application) the final result or decision. A path from each node to the leader must be pre-established (during initialization or periodic re-configuration) and be known, before data can be gathered at the leader. Different approaches can be taken to establish those paths, based on the specific application requirements and/or optimization goals. One approach would be to enforce a spanning tree on the network rooted on the elected leader. Then, each node can send its local view (e.g. set of associated trackers along with values for their attributes) up the tree towards the leader. Parent nodes combine data from children nodes with their own and further forward it up the tree. When the root node (leader) has collected all necessary info, it can use this to make a decision and forward that back to all nodes through that tree. Such a tree could be constructed, for example, by implementing diffusion routing [7] to establish gradients towards the leader. Alternatively, one could establish a shortest path (i.e. greedy) chain that spans all nodes in the network. Each node will then send its info to the successor in the chain, which in its turn will combine the received message with its own and forward it to its own successor. When the last node (leader) in the chain is reached, it will make a decision based on the global data and send back this decision through that chain to all nodes. This approach is slower than the spanning tree one, but can be more energy efficient when transmission distances are relatively long or environment is harsh [11].

We claim that adopting any centralized approach for our problem would be conflicting with the fault-tolerance and robustness requirements posed earlier for any algorithm used. Additionally, it is evident that both approaches presented require a number of "helpful" general assumptions to be made, in order to be feasible (e.g. require tripwire nodes to have unique ids, in order to construct the spanning tree or chain). This would ultimately lead in lack of correctness and/or convergence under a broader range of operating conditions. Furthermore, it is well known that centralized approaches do not scale well with large number of nodes, which may be the case in many sensor applications. However, a centralized approach for this problem, albeit impractical in many cases, could be designed to be optimal in theory in terms of specific goals (e.g. energy-efficiency, delay, etc.). Therefore, we will analyze and use the performance of the centralized algorithm as a means to compare our distributed algorithm's performance to the best achievable one.

Since the algorithm is centralized, the leader (i.e. tree root or last node in chain) will eventually receive info by all nodes, assuming no nodes fail and no collisions occur. Therefore, it will be able to make an optimal decision and send it back to all nodes. In the case of the spanning tree, sibling nodes will collide if the try to transmit to their parent at the same time. Therefore, a random waiting interval, uniformly distributed in $[0, T']$, must be enforced, before each sibling will send its message to the parent. Note that the maximum waiting interval T' that is necessary to avoid collisions between neighboring nodes, with a high probability, depends on the average number of children per node compared to the case of the baseline distributed algorithm, where the maximum waiting time interval T depends on the average node degree (i.e. number of neighbors) in the network. In any case T' is at most equal to T. Let us denote the average number of children per node as d. Then the convergence time for the algorithm will be at most $T_{CV} = 2*T'*\log_d N$. The total number of messages in each case will be equal to $M_{TOT} \approx 2*N$, since each node (excluding leader and leaf nodes) has to send one message "upwards" to the leader and forward back the decision message down the tree or chain.

3.3   A Fusion-Based Distributed Algorithm

One drawback of flooding is that it requires each node to maintain a considerable amount of state information, in order to recognize duplicate packets. Additionally, it may propagate non-useful info throughout the network, resulting in a large number of unnecessary transmissions. Specifically, a node will forward a packet containing new info, regardless of whether that info is going to be useful or not in making the final local decision. For example, assume that the tripwires are cooperating in order to choose the 2 trackers with the maximum amount of energy, among the M ones. Assume further that some tripwire j, which has already broadcasted a packet containing two trackers T1 and T2 with their respective energy levels E1 and E2, receives a new packet containing the following info: {T3, E3}, {T4, E4}. If E1,E2>E3,E4, then T3 and T4 do not belong in the optimal solution constitute non-useful information that should not propagate any further. This last argument is the motivation for our distributed fusion-based algorithm.

Our algorithm consists of one basic fusion-and-update step and a back-off mechanism, designed to optimize performance. First, we're going to present the basic algorithm steps and prove the conditions under which the basic algorithm converges to the correct (i.e. optimal) decision. Then, we're going to present the complete algorithm, along with its termination condition, and discuss how the back-off mechanism affects its performance.

3.3.1 Basic Algorithm and Convergence Requirements

We have already formulated the basic problem, but here we'll summarize the assumptions for the sake of clarity:

- There are N tripwires and M trackers. Choose K trackers among M that optimize some function F $(K < M < N)$
- The tripwires form a connected network
- Each tracker j is related with a set of attributes A_j (e.g. energy, location, etc.), that are known by each tripwires associated with tracker j.
- $F = f(A_1, A_2, ..., A_K)$ is a function of the trackers' attributes belonging in a chosen set of size K.
- Each tracker j is associated with at least one tripwire node.

- Function F unambiguously ranks all $\binom{M}{K}$ choices in some total order.

The basic algorithm is the following and is executed by all tripwires:

Initial Step) *Each tripwire is associated with an initial set of (0 to K) tracker nodes. If more than K tracker nodes are within reach of a tripwire, then the tripwire chooses the K "best" ones using function F. It assumes that this initial set is the optimal set of nodes and broadcasts it.*

Fusion-and-Update Step) *Upon receiving a set of nodes from some neighbor, combine(fuse) the received set with the current one using F, to produce a superior, higher-ranked, set if possible.*
- *If a superior set is produced, update the current set and broadcast it.*
- *If not, ignore the received set and do not broadcast an update*

Lemma 1: If any set of nodes S1 = $\{s_{11}, s_{12}, ..., s_{1K}\}$ that contains some number of nodes, say N1, that belong in the optimal set of tracker OS = $\{os_1, os_2, ...,os_K\}$, is ranked higher according to F than any other set containing less than N1 nodes in OS, then: The comparison of two sets S1= $\{s_{11}, s_{12}, ..., s_{1K}\}$ and S2= $\{s_{21}, s_{22},...,s_{2K}\}$ at some tripwire node can only yield a set S3 that is ranked equal or higher than both S1 and S2. Note: $os_i, s_{1i}, s_{2i} \in M$

Proof: There are only to possible cases that cover all scenarios:

<u>Case 1)</u> Assume there is some j for which $s_{1j} \in OS$ and there is no i for which $s_{2i} \in OS$, then S1 wins over S2 at this node. Consequently, S1 continues to be the current set, while S2 gets discarded at this node.

<u>Case 2)</u> If there are "optimal" nodes (i.e. nodes belonging in the optimal set OS) in both S1 and S2, then the combination from S1 and S2 that contains the largest number of "optimal" nodes is ranked the highest among any other combination of choices from S1 and S2. Since all combinations are tried, it is guaranteed that the best one

among those will be discovered and get chosen (i.e. win) over both S1 and S2, which both get discarded at this node.

Lemma 2: Any non-optimal set of trackers S1 will propagate through the network for a finite number of steps, less than N, before it encounters a tripwire node with another set of trackers S2, the combination of which (S1 and S2) results in a set S3 that is higher-ranked than S1.

Proof: According to the basic algorithm, a set S1 that is received by some node L, will be further propagated (as is) by node L, only if it's superior than L's current set (say S2) and L's current set does not contain any optimal nodes (as shown before). Otherwise, S1 will either "lose" to S2, or produce a higher ranked set S3 and trigger a broadcast of the new set S3. If set S1 is non-optimal then it cannot visit all tripwires N and win over the local choices without producing a new better choice. Otherwise, S1 would be optimal.

Theorem 1: The basic distributed fusion-based algorithm converges after a finite number of steps to the optimal set of trackers OS, if and only if: any set of nodes $S1 = \{s_{11}, s_{12}, ..., s_{1K}\}$ that contains some number of nodes, say N1, that belong in OS, is ranked higher according to F than any other set containing less than N1 nodes in OS.

Proof:
Direct) Assume there are I initial sets in the network of tripwires, where $M \leq I \leq \min\left\{N, \binom{M}{K}\right\}$. There are only $\binom{M}{K}$ possible sets of trackers. Each set may be an initial set or get constructed at some step in the algorithm. According to Lemma 1, at any step of the algorithm the comparison of any two sets of trackers will never yield another set that is lower ranked than the initial two. Furthermore, according to Lemma 2, each set will take at most N steps to prevail (if optimal), produce a better one and trigger its broadcast, or lose. Therefore, it will take at most $\binom{M}{K} * N$ steps for all possible sets (including the optimal one) to propagate and the optimal one to prevail.

Converse) We're going to prove the converse, by the use of a counterexample. Assume the problem is to choose 2 among 4 total trackers. Let the 6 possible pairs be ranked by some F from better to worse as follows: (x1,x2), (x3,x4), (x1,x3), (x4,x2), (x1,x4), (x2, x3). It is evident that Lemma 1 cannot be applied for this scenario. Assume there are 3 tripwires, A, B, and C, with the following initial sets: A -> (x3, x4), B -> (x1, x4), C -> (x2, x3). All 4 trackers are associated with some tripwire. However, if A broadcasts his set first, and reaches B and C, then (x3, x4) will win over (x1,x4) and (x2,x3) and prevail. After that, there is no way that the basic algorithm can find the optimal solution (x1,x2), since neither x1 nor x2 are included in any existing set any more.

3.3.2 Complete Algorithm

The complete algorithm is created by introducing some amount of randomization on each step of the basic algorithm and adding a termination condition for it. Here are the modified steps of the distributed fusion-based algorithm:

Initial Step) Each tripwire is associated with an initial set of (0 to K) tracker nodes. If more than K tracker nodes are within reach of a tripwire, then the tripwire chooses the K "best" ones using function F. It assumes that this initial set is the optimal set of nodes. The tripwire waits for an amount of time t1, uniformly distributed in [0, T] and then broadcasts the initial set. T is initially set to maxDelay, where maxDelay is a parameter of the algorithm.

Fusion-and-Update Step) Upon receiving a set of nodes from some neighbor, compare the received set with the current one using F, to produce a superior, higher-ranked, set if possible.
  - *If superior set produced, update the current set. Reduce the maximum backoff time T: $T = max \{T / d, T_{min}\}$, where d is a parameter of the algorithm. Wait for an amount of time t2, uniformly distributed in [0, T] and broadcast the updated set.*
  - *If not, ignore the received set. Continue counting down to the next update broadcast (if one is pending)*

Termination Condition and Actions) If no update message has been received for maxDelay time since the last update has been received, assume that the algorithm has reached a global decision and should terminate. Compare the initial associated set of trackers with the final chosen set. If there are any common trackers in both sets, send a wakeup message to those nodes. A tracker that successfully receives a wakeup message will broadcast an acknowledgement that it has woken up. This acknowledgement prevents other tripwire nodes, from sending redundant wake-up messages to the same trackers. The tripwire terminates its run of the algorithm when acknowledgements by all associated trackers belonging to the final set have been received.

The reason for introducing the random waiting is twofold. First, it helps avoid synchronization effects between nodes' transmissions. If a fixed period was to be used for the updates, then concurrent transmissions by nearby nodes would result in a collision and either retransmission of the packets, if the collision gets detected, or else permanent loss of the transmitted packet. The former would imply an increased number of transmitted messages as well as increased delay. The latter could compromise the correct operation of the algorithm, if the algorithm is not robust enough to overcome a few packet losses of this kind. Second, it tries to dynamically impose some hierarchical structure on the flow of information between tripwires and hence approach the centralized algorithm's performance. However, it does so without requiring any initialization or re-configuration protocol to explicitly enforce this structure beforehand. The price paid for this lack of pre-existing structure is that each link of this structure may potentially be "traversed" more than twice, which is the case for the (optimal) centralized algorithm. Finally, note that only a reasonable amount of computation needs to be performed by each tripwire node during the *fusion-and-*

update step. In the general case, all possible combinations resulting from the merging of two sets of tracker would need to be examined, to make sure that the higher-ranked set will be discovered. This would imply an exponential (on K) amount of work. However, for the classes of converging functions that we're interested in, the higher-ranked set can be produced through only a linear (on K) number of combinations checked. We defer addressing the issue of computational complexity of different fusion algorithms for general optimization functions for future work.

4   Performance

We have simulated our algorithm using a high-level, event-driven, sensor network simulator we're building at USC. The tripwire topology assumed in all scenarios is a NxN *random grid*. A random grid has a grid-like structure, but with the following differences: Each vertex of the grid has a random skew from its position in a perfect grid, in order to model typical deployment processes that provide adequate coverage of the sensor field. Additionally, some links in the grid may not exist. Finally, extra bypass links may exist in the grid. The latter two model random propagation effects (e.g. shadowing, fading, ground reflection, etc.) that result in non-predictable connectivity effects in real sensor network [12]. The tracker nodes are uniformly distributed in the field. In the following paragraphs, we present the performance of our algorithm in terms of message complexity, convergence delay and fault-tolerance/robustness. All results are averaged over a large number of runs for various scenarios.

4.1   Message Complexity

In Fig.1, we depict the number of total messages transmitted by all tripwire nodes involved, until the algorithm converges, as a function of the number of tripwire nodes (N) and the number of trackers (M). It is evident that the number of total messages grows linearly with N, but is not sensitive to M. Specifically, we can see that our algorithm is more efficient and scalable than the distributed baseline (flooding) algorithm, whose message complexity grows linearly with M as well. Furthermore, the total number of messages is in the order of 3N for all M and N, which is quite close to the optimal 2N of the centralized approach.

In Fig.2 we examine another two aspects of the algorithm's behavior, namely the algorithm's dependence on the number K of trackers to be chosen and its load-balancing behavior. We can see that the number of total messages increases with increasing K. However, this dependency is not linear, as in the case of N. This behavior is ratified as follows: While K approaches M the number of extra messages per increase of K decreases, since info about a larger percentage of the tracker nodes is already included in the message. Finally, it is evident that our algorithm is able to balance the load of total messages among all participating tripwire nodes. This is very important in order to avoid depleting any specific tripwire's energy and maximize the network's operational lifetime.

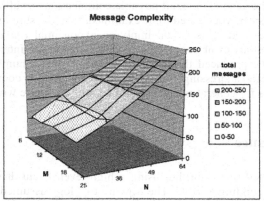

Fig. 1. Number of total messages needed for the algorithm to converge as a function of the number of tripwires (N) and trackers (M). An NxN random grid topology is assumed, with N from 5 to 8. The number of trackers K to be chosen is fixed to 3.

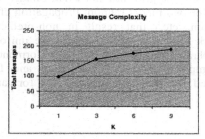 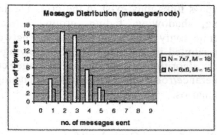

Fig. 2. The graph on the left shows the number of total messages as a function of K. N is fixed to 49 (7x7 random grid) and M is fixed to 18. The graph on the right depicts the distribution of number of messages per tripwire node for two different scenarios.

4.2 Convergence Delay

The basic time unit in our algorithm and implementation is assumed to be the time it takes to transmit a single message. All other waiting interval parameters of our algorithm are calculated as multiples of that time. Therefore, the convergence time of the algorithm is not absolute, but is measured in terms of the basic time unit. However, in order to demonstrate the feasibility and practical value of our algorithm, we present results for its convergence delay, assuming a reasonable message transmission time, derived from current applicable technology specifications. Specifically, we have assumed that the message size is equal to 40 Bytes and transmission rate is 1Mbps for our simulations. The exact message size will depend on K, as well as the attributes that needed by function F. Nonetheless, 40-50 Bytes is a representative value, considering that K will not be too large and F is required to be relatively simple. Faster radios would reduce this time, while large Ks or a function F that depends on a large number of tracker attributes would increase it.

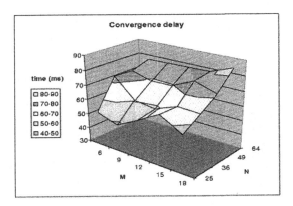

Fig. 3. Convergence delay of distributed wake-up algorithm as a function of the number of tripwire nodes (N) and tracker nodes (M). K is fixed to 3.

In Fig.3 we show the time it takes for the algorithm to converge (i.e. until all tripwires have decided on the final/optimal set of trackers to be woken up) as a function of N (no. tripwires) and M (no. of trackers). It is evident, as in the case of message complexity, that convergence delay is mainly affected by the total number of tripwires N and not as much by the total number of trackers. In all scenarios presented, the convergence time is less than 100ms. Therefore, we conclude that the delay overhead of our waking up algorithm is not very significant and the algorithm is fast enough to allow time to the trackers to do the "useful" work.

4.3   Fault-Tolerance & Robustness

In Fig.4 we examine the behavior of our algorithm under increasing link loss probability (i.e. probability that a message, that should otherwise be received correctly, is lost). It is evident that the algorithm is able to perform very well even in very harsh environments. It manages to overcome almost all losses and perform correctly up to a "threshold point" (~35%), where significantly sized patches of non-optimal decisions start to appear in the field. Such high link loss probabilities may seem unrealistic for the typical sensor network. However, it is interesting to study the behavior of the algorithm under such high losses, since they could realistically model more hostile environments, where adverse ground-propagation effects or jamming may be present.

Intuition for why this threshold point exists is provided in Fig.5. Some link losses result in avoiding some collisions that would otherwise have occurred. Consequently, initially the number of total losses (collisions + link losses) does not grow rapidly and our algorithm can overcome them, by discovering (or re-discovering) alternate paths. However, after a specific point/threshold the number of alternate paths in the topology as well as well as any inherent redundancy in the algorithm is not enough to probabilistically overcome the majority of message losses. At this point, the algorithm starts to allow considerable decision inconsistencies among tripwire nodes.

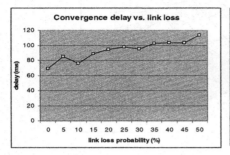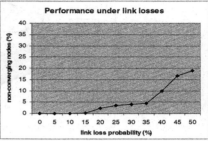

Fig. 4. The left graph depicts the percentage of tripwire nodes that fail to converge to the optimal set of trackers, as a function of the link loss probability, while the graph of the right shows how link loss probability affects the convergence delay of the algorithm.

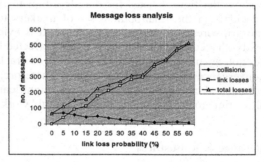

Fig. 5. Message loss analysis. All lost messages (colliding messages or messages lost due to bad link conditions) are counted in terms of messages that should have been received

A final observation that needs to be made is the following. A few (<10%) incorrect tripwire decisions do not necessarily result in incorrect overall behavior. According to the termination step, each tripwire will attempt to wake up a tracker only if that tracker belongs in both its initial and its final set of trackers. In most of the scenarios observed, only a few non-optimal (but high-ranked) tracker nodes, if any, will manage to not lose to the optimal ones after the end of the algorithm. Therefore, the probability of some tripwire having a non-optimal tracker in its final set and having that same tracker in its initial set is low, if the total number of misbehaving tripwires is also low. Consequently, in most cases where more than 90% of the tripwires converge, zero or one extra (non-optimal) trackers are expected be woken up.

4.4   Performance of Fusion-Based Algorithm for General Optimization Functions

We have used simulations to evaluate our algorithm's behavior for general optimization functions, that is, functions that do not provide a partial or total ordering of the different sets. Such functions appear in scenarios like, for example, in the search for the tightest cluster of trackers or functions that are non-trivial combinations of distances between trackers, battery level of trackers and other tracker attributes. Those functions are not covered by Theorem 1, and therefore our algorithm does not provably converge to the optimal set. However, our simulations indicate that our algorithm manages to produce the correct, optimal, set of trackers for the vast majority of trial scenarios and a range of non-conforming optimization functions. Furthermore, it does so with no noticeable extra overhead. We plan to look further into such optimizations functions from a theoretical point of view, in future work.

5   Conclusions and Future Work

In this paper, we have presented a general fusion-based distributed algorithm for waking up in a heterogeneous sensor network, consisting of two types of sensor nodes, namely tripwire and tracker nodes. In our algorithm, tripwire nodes coordinate among each other to decide on an optimal set of a specific number of trackers to perform some sensing task. The number of trackers to be woken up, and an optimization function to be used to evaluate the appropriateness of a set, are provided by the application. We have proven the convergence of our algorithm for specific classes of optimizations functions. Furthermore, we have demonstrated that our algorithm is efficient, in terms of message complexity and convergence delay, for the majority of realistic scenarios. Finally, we have shown that our algorithm exhibits a very robust and fault-tolerant behavior, making it applicable for sensor applications operating in hostile environments, where adverse propagation effects like shadowing, fading and jamming are the rule, rather than the exception.

In the future, we're planning to further explore the behavior of the algorithm for different classes of optimization functions. Specifically, we would like to identify ways to approximate *non-converging* optimization functions with *converging* ones, and devise appropriate variations of the basic algorithm, in order to achieve near-optimal results for a wider range of function classes. Finally, we plan to extend our algorithm and provide a complete framework for event-driven sensor applications where, waking up appropriate tracker nodes when an event is detected, routing the result(s) back to the sink(s) and potentially cueing of a moving event/target, are all handled uniformly and efficiently.

References

1.   J. Kahn, R.H. Katz, and K. Pister, "Emerging Challenges: Mobile Networking for Smart Dust," *in Journal of Communication and Networks*, Sept. 2000, pp. 188–196.
2.   F. Zhao, J. Shin, and J. Reich, "Information-Driven Dynamic Sensor Collaboration for Tracking Applications," *in IEEE Signal Processing Magazine*, March 2002.

3.   A. Mainwaring, J. Polastre, R. Szewczyk, and D. Culler, "Wireless Sensor Networks for Habitat Monitoring," *in Proceedings of ACM 1ˢᵗ International Workshop on Wireless Sensor Networks and Applications (WSNA '02)*, Atlanta, September 2002.
4.   J. Nemeroff, L. Garcia, D. Hampel, and S. DiPierro, "Application of Sensor Network Communication," *in Proceedings of IEEE Milcom 2001, Communication for network-centric operation: Creating the information force*, Vol. 1, 2001, pp. 336–341.
5.   M. Singh, and V. Prasanna, "A Hierarchical Model for Distributed, Collaborative Computation in Wireless Sensor Networks," *submitted to 5ᵗʰ Workshop on Advances in Parallel and Distributed Computation Models 2003*, Nice, France, April 2003.
6.   J. Rabaey, J. Ammer, T. Karalar, S. Li, B. Otis, M. Sheets, and T. Tuan, "PicoRadios for Wireless Sensor Networks: The Next Challenge in Ultra-Low-Power Design", *Proceedings of the International Solid-State Circuits Conference*, San Francisco, CA, February 2002.
7.   C. Intanagonwiway, R. Govindam, and D. Estrin, "Directed Diffusion: a Scalable and Robust Communication Paradigm for Sensor Networks," *in Proceedings of 5th ACM/IEEE Conference on Mobile Computing and Networking (MOBICOM 2000)*, August 2000.
8.   S. Ratnasamy, D. Estrin, R. Govindan, B. Karp, S. Shenker, L. Yin, and F. Yu, "Data-centric Storage in Sensornets," *in Proceedings of First Workshop on Sensor Networks and Applications (WSNA)*, Atlanta, September 2002.
9.   IEEE Local and Metropolitan Area Network Standards Committee, Wireless LAN medium access control (MAC) and physical layer (PHY) specifications, IEEE standard 802.11-1999.
10. K. Nakano, and S. Olariu, "A survey on leader election protocols for radio networks," *in Proceedings of the 6ᵗʰ Internation Symposium on Parallel Architectures, Algorithms and Networks, 2002 (I-SPAN '02)*. May 2002.
11. S. Lindsey, C. S. Raghavendra, and K. Sivalingam, "Data Gathering Algorithms in Sensor Networks Using Energy Metrics," *IEEE Transactions on Parallel and Distributed Systems*, September 2002.
12. D. Ganesan, B. Krishnamachari, A. Woo, D. Culler, D. Estrin, and S. Wicker, "Complex behavior at scale: An experimental study of low-power wireless sensor networks," Technical Report CSD-TR 02-0013, UCLA, 2002.
13. M. Singh, and V. Prasanna, "Optimal Energy-Balanced Algorithm for Selection in a Single Hop Sensor Network," *submitted to 1ˢᵗ IEEE International Workshop on Sensor Network Protocols and Application (SNPA '03)*, May 2003.
14. R. S. Bhuvaneswaran, Jacir L. Bordim, J. Cui, Bordim, and K. Nakano, "Fundamental Protocols for Wireless Sensor Networks," *in International Parallel and Distributed Processing Symposium - IPDPS 2001*, San Francisco, April 2001
15. S. Iyengar, and Q. Wu, "Computational Aspects of Distributed Sensor Networks," *in Proceedings of the Fifth International Conference on Information Fusion*, July 2002.
16. PASTA project. http://neptune.east.isi.edu/pipermail/pasta/
17. Feng Xue and P. R. Kumar, "The number of neighbors needed for connectivity of wireless networks," *Submitted to Wireless Networks*, April 2002.
18. S. Meguerdichian, F. Koushanfar, M. Potkonjak, and M. Srivastava, "Coverage Problems in Wireless Ad-hoc Sensor Networks," *in Proc. of IEEE INFOCOM*, 2001.
19. M. Chandy, and J. Misra, "Parallel Program Design: A Foundation," Addison-Wesley 1988.

Location Tracking in a Wireless Sensor Network by Mobile Agents and Its Data Fusion Strategies*

Yu-Chee Tseng, Sheng-Po Kuo, Hung-Wei Lee, and Chi-Fu Huang

Department of Computer Science and Information Engineering
National Chiao-Tung University
Hsin-Chu, 30050, Taiwan
{yctseng, spkuo, leehw, cfhuang}@csie.nctu.edu.tw

Abstract. The wireless sensor network is an emerging technology that may greatly facilitate human life by providing ubiquitous sensing, computing, and communication capability, through which people can more closely interact with the environment wherever he/she goes. To be context-aware, one of the central issues in sensor networks is *location tracking*, whose goal is to monitor the roaming path of a moving object. While similar to the location-update problem in PCS networks, this problem is more challenging in two senses: (1) there are no central control mechanism and backbone network in such environment, and (2) the wireless communication bandwidth is very limited. In this paper, we propose a novel protocol based on the *mobile agent* paradigm. Once a new object is detected, a mobile agent will be initiated to track the roaming path of the object. The agent is mobile since it will choose the sensor closest to the object to stay. The agent may invite some nearby slave sensors to cooperatively position the object and inhibit other irrelevant (i.e., farther) sensors from tracking the object. As a result, the communication and sensing overheads are greatly reduced. Our prototyping of the location-tracking mobile agent based on IEEE 802.11b NICs and our experimental experiences are also reported.

1   Introduction

The rapid progress of wireless communication and embedded micro-sensing MEMS technologies have made *wireless sensor networks* possible. Such environments may have many inexpensive wireless nodes, each capable of collecting, processing, and storing environmental information, and communicating with neighboring nodes. In the past, sensors are connected by wire lines. Today, this environment is combined with the novel *ad hoc* networking technology to facilitate inter-sensor communication [8]. The flexibility of installation and configuration is greatly improved. A flurry of research activities have recently been commenced in sensor networks.

With sensor networks, the physical world can interact with the internet more closely. Grouping thousands of sensors together may revolutionize information gathering. For example, a disaster detector may be set up so that temperatures of a forest can be

---

* This work is co-sponsored by the Lee and MTI Center for Networking Research at the National Chiao Tung University and the MOE Program for Promoting Academic Excellence of Universities under grant numbers A-91-H-FA07-1-4 and 89-E-FA04-1-4.

F. Zhao and L. Guibas (Eds.): IPSN 2003, LNCS 2634, pp. 625–641, 2003.
© Springer-Verlag Berlin Heidelberg 2003

monitored by sensors to prevent small harmless brush fires from becoming monstrous infernos. Similar techniques can be applied to flood and typhoon detection. Another application is environment control; sensors can monitor factors such as temperature and humidity and feed these information back to a central air conditioning and ventilation system. By attaching sensors on vehicles, roads, and traffic lights, traffic information can be fed back to the traffic control center immediately. Location-based services can be combined with sensor networks. We can dispatch a mobile agent following a person to provide on-site services (such applications might be attractive for disability people who have such as hearing or visual problems). Sensors may also be used in combination with GPS to improve positioning accuracy. However, many issues remain to be resolved for the success of sensor networks.

- *Scalability:* Since a sensor network typically comprises a large number of nodes, how to manage these resources and information is not an easy job. Distributed and localized algorithms are essential in such environments [1,6,7]. Also, scalability is a critical issue in handling the related communication problems. In [17,18,19], the *coverage* and *exposure* of an irregular sensor network are formulated as computational geometry problems. This coverage problem is related to the Art Gallery Problem and can be solved optimally in a 2D plane, but is shown to be NP-hard in the 3D case [10]. Regular placement of sensors and their sensing ability are discussed in [4] and [13].
- *Stability:* Since sensors are likely to be installed in outdoor or even hostile environments, it is reasonable to assume that device failures would be regular and common events. Protocols should be stable and fault-tolerant.
- *Power-saving:* Since no plug-in power is available, sensor devices will be operated by battery powers. Energy conservation should be kept in mind in all cases. Energy consumption of communications might be a major factor. Techniques such as data fusion may be necessary [3], but the timeliness of data should be considered too. Data dissemination is investigated in [5]. Mobile agent-based solutions are sometimes more power-efficient [9].

Since sensor networks are typically used to monitor the environment, one fundamental issue is the *location-tracking problem*, whose goal is to trace the roaming paths of moving objects in the network area [15,21,11,16,14]. This problem is similar to the location-update problem in PCS networks, but is more challenging in two senses: (1) there are no central control mechanism and backbone network in such environment, and (2) the wireless communication bandwidth is very limited. In this paper, we propose a novel protocol based on the *mobile agent* paradigm. Once a new object is detected, a mobile agent will be initiated to track the roaming path of the object. The agent is mobile since it will choose the senor closest to the object to stay. In fact, the agent will follow the object by hopping from sensor to sensor. The agent may invite some nearby slave sensors to cooperatively position the object and inhibit other irrelevant (i.e., farther) sensors from tracking the object. Using mobile agents may have two advantages. First, the sensing, computing, and communication overheads can be greatly reduced. In this work, we will address the delivery and fusion of the tracking results [22]. Second, on-site or follow-me services may be provided by mobile agents. Our prototyping of the location-tracking mobile agent based on IEEE 802.11b NICs and our experimental experiences are also reported. The work reported in this paper is an extended version of our previous work [20]. Irregularity of sensor deployment is considered. The data fusion issue for sensors to process and deliver the collected information is addressed, too. Also, performance of the proposed data fusion strategies are compared through simulations.

The organization of this paper is as follows. Section 2 describes our network model and defines the location-tracking problem. Our protocol based on mobile agents is presented in Section 3. Fusion and delivery of tracking history are discussed in Section 4. Our prototyping experiences and some simulation results are given in Section 5. Section 6 draws our conclusions.

2   Network Model and Problem Statement

We consider a sensor network, which consists of a set of sensor nodes placed in a 2D plane. Sensors may be arranged as a regular or irregular network, as shown in Fig. 1. However, unless otherwise stated, throughout the discussion we will assume a triangular network as illustrated in Fig. 1(a), our framework should be easily extended to other regular, or even irregular, networks (this will be commented in Section 3-3). In order to track objects' routes, each sensor is aware of its physical location as well as the physical locations of its neighboring sensors. Each sensor has sensing capability as well as computing and communication capabilities, so as to execute protocols and exchange messages.

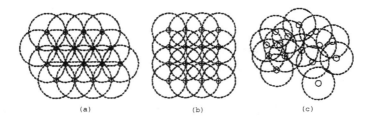

(a)   (b)   (c)

Fig. 1. (a) Triangular, (b) square, and (c) irregular sensor networks.

Each sensor is able to detect the existence of nearby moving objects. We assume that the sensing scope is r, which is equal to the side length of the triangles[1]. Within the detectable distance, a sensor is able to determine its distance to an object. This can be achieved either by the fly time or signal strength that are transmitted by the object, or of the signals that are transmitted by the sensor and reflected by the object.

We assume that three sensors are sufficient to determine the location of an object. Specifically, suppose that an object resides within a triangle formed by three neighboring sensors S_1, S_2, and S_3 and that the distances to the object detected by these sensors are

---

[1] In practice, r should be slightly larger than the side length. We make such an assumption for ease of presentation.

r_1, r_2, and r_3, respectively. As shown in Fig. 2(a), by the intersections of the circles centered at S_1 and S_2, two possible positions of the object can be determined. With the assistance of S_3, the precise position can be determined. (It should be noted that in practice errors may exist, and thus more sensors will be needed to to improve the accuracy.)

The goal of this work is to determine the roaming path of a moving object in the sensor network. The trace of the object should be reported to a location server from time to time, depending on whether this is a real-time application or not. The intersection of the sensing scopes of three neighboring sensors is as shown in Fig. 2(b). We further divide the area into one *working area* A_0 and three *backup areas* A_1, A_2, and A_3. Intuitively, the working area defines the scope where these three sensors work normally, while the backup areas specify when "handover" should be taken.

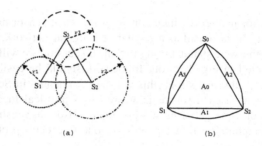

(a)   (b)

Fig. 2. (a) Positioning example and (b) working area and backup areas.

3   The Location Tracking Protocol

3.1   Basic Idea

Our location-tracking protocol is derived by the cooperation of sensors. Whenever an object is detected, an *election process* will be conducted by some nearby sensors to choose a sensor, on which an agent will be initiated, to monitor the roaming behavior of the object. As the object moves, the agent may migrate to a sensor that is closer to the object to keep on monitoring the object. Fig. 3(a) illustrates this concept, where the dash line is the roaming path of the object, and arrows are the migration path of the agent. By so doing, the computation and communication overheads can be reduced significantly.

Recall that positioning an object requires the cooperation of at least three sensors. The mobile agent, called the *master*, will invite two neighboring sensors to participate by dispatching a *slave* agent to each of them. These three agents (master and slaves) will cooperate to perform the trilateration algorithm [1]. From time to time, the slaves will report their sensing results to the master agent, who will then calculate the object's precise locations. As the object moves, these slave agents may be revoked and reassigned. Certain signal strength thresholds will be used to determine when to revoke/reassign a slave agent. The details will be given later. In Fig. 3(a), those sensors that ever host a slave agent are marked by black. We comment that although our development is based on the cooperation of two slave agents, it will be straightforward to extend our work to more slave agents to improve the positioning accuracy. To reduce the amount of data to be carried on, a master may decide to forward some tracking histories to the location server. This issue will be further addressed in Section 4.

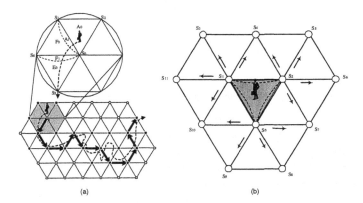

Fig. 3. (a) Roaming path of an object (dash line) and the migration path of the corresponding master agent (arrows). Sensors that ever host a slave agent are marked by black. (b) Inhibiting farther sensors $S_3, S_4, \ldots, S_{11}$ from monitoring the object.

We now discuss how slave agents are revoked and reassigned. Observe the top part of Fig. 3(a). When resident in the working area A_0, the object is tracked by sensors S_0, S_1, and S_2. On entering the backup area A_1, since the signals received by S_2 will reduce to a level below a threshold, the slave agent at S_2 will be revoked and a new slave will be issued to S_6. Similarly, on entering the backup area F_1, the slave at S_1 will be revoked, and a new one will be issued to S_5. As the object passes S_5, the master itself will lose the target, in which case the master will migrate itself to S_5. All old slaves will be revoked and new slaves will be invited.

When an object is in the backup areas of some sensors, it is possible that it can be sensed by more than three sensors. To reduce the sensing overheads, master and slave agents can inhibit other irrelevant sensors from monitoring the object. This concept is illustrated in Fig. 3(b). The object is currently in area A_0. Sensors $S_3, S_4, \ldots, S_{11}$, which may sometimes detect the object, will be inhibited from tracking this object by warning signals that are issued periodically by the agents in S_0, S_1, and S_2.

3.2   Protocol Details

Below, we formally develop our tracking protocol. Since there may exist multiple objects in the network, we have to assume that sensors can distinguish one object from the other. This can be done by having each object periodically send a unique ID code. Otherwise,

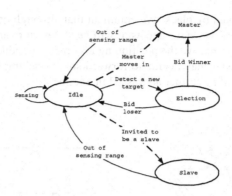

Fig. 4. State transition diagram of a sensor (for one particular object).

some mechanism is needed for sensors to combine proper signals from proper sensors to differentiate objects.

We consider an environment with multiple objects. However, since the processing of each individual object is independent, the following discussion will focus on only one particular object. For each object, three or even more sensors will be able to detect its existence. Fig. 4 shows the state transition diagram of each sensor. (It should be noted that for different objects, a sensor may stay in different states.) Initially, each sensor is in the *idle* state and performs the *Basic Protocol*. Under this state, a sensor will continuously detect any object appearing in its sensing scope. Once detecting a new object, the sensor will enter the *election* state and perform the *Election Protocol* to bid for serving as a master. Most likely, the sensor that is closest to the object will win and become the master agent, which will then dispatch two slave agents to two nearby sensors. The master will go to the *master* state and perform the *Master Protocol*, while the slaves will go to the *slave* state and perform the *Slave Protocol*. To prevent too frequent moves of the agents, as long as the object remains in the working area, the states will not change. However, once the object enters the backup areas, the roles of master and slave may be changed. In this case, an idle sensor may be invited to serve as a master or slave. Another case that a sensor may stay in the idle state is when it detects an object in its backup areas and keeps on receiving inhibiting messages from neighboring sensors. This is reflected by the self-looped transition for the idle state.

Fig. 5 shows six tracks that an object may leave a triangle. Suppose that the master is currently in S_0, and the two slaves are in S_1 and S_2. By symmetry, these can be reduced 3 tracks (numbered by 1 to 3). For track 1, the master discovers two slaves losing the target simultaneously. So the master will revoke all slaves and invite two new slaves. For track 2, only the slave agent in S_1 will be revoked, and a new one will be invited. For track 3, the master discovers one slave as well as itself losing the target. In this case, the master should migrate itself to the sensor that can still detect the object (typically with the strongest receive signals) and revoke all current slaves. After moving to the new sensor, two new slaves should be invited. Finally, we comment that the object may move too fast to be detected. If so, sensors may suddenly lose the target. As a last resort, all agents, when losing the object for a timeout period, will be dissolved. Since no inhibiting

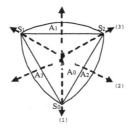

Fig. 5. Possible roaming tracks for an object to leave a triangle.

message will be heard, all sensors must remain in the idle state for this particular object, and new election process will take place to choose a new master to track this object. Our protocol is thus quite fault-tolerant in this sense.

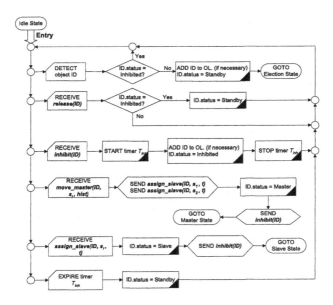

Fig. 6. The Basic Protocol.

Each sensor will keep an *object list (OL)* to record the status of all targets in its sensing scope. Each entry in OL is indexed by the object's unique identity, denoted by ID. For each object, there are two sub-fields: *status* and *time-stamp*. *ID.status* can be one of the four values: *Master*, *Slave*, *Standby*, and *Inhibited*. *ID.time-stamp* is the time when the record is last updated.

Seven types of control messages may be sent by our protocol.

(1) *bid_master(ID, sig):* This is for a sensor to compete as a master for object ID, if no inhibiting record has been created in OL for ID. The parameter *sig* reflects the receive signal strength for this object.

(2) *assign_slave(ID, s_i, t):* This is for a master to invite a nearby sensor s_i to serve as slave agent for object ID for an effective time interval of t.

(3) *revoke_slave(s_i):* This is for a master to revoke its slave at sensor s_i.

(4) *inhibit(ID):* This is a broadcast message for a master/slave to inhibit neighboring irrelevant sensors from tracking object ID. The effective time of the inhibiting message is defined by a system parameter T_{inh}.

(5) *release(ID):* This is to invalidate an earlier inhibiting message.

(6) *move_master(ID, s_i, hist):* A master uses this message to migrate itself from its current sensor to a nearby sensor s_i, where *hist* carries all relevant codes/data/roaming histories related to object ID.

(7) *data(ID, sig, ts):* A slave uses this packet to report to its master the tracking results (*sig* =signal strength and *ts* = timestamp) for ID.

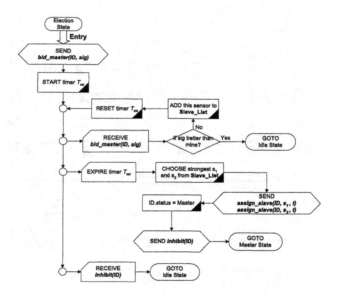

Fig. 7. The Election Protocol.

Below, we formally present our four protocols. The Basic Protocol is shown in Fig. 6. This is an endless loop containing six event-driven actions. The first one describes the reaction when detecting an object. If an inhibiting record exists, it will ignore the object. Otherwise, the sensor will go to the election state. The next four events describe the reactions when receiving a message from a neighboring sensor. In particular, if an *inhibit(ID)* message is received, a timer $T_{inh}(ID)$ will be set. The last event describes the reaction when the above timer expires, in which case the object's status will be changed to Standby and the sensor will be allowed to monitor this object.

The Election Protocol is shown in Fig. 7. In the beginning, a *bid_master* message will be sent and a timer $T_{bid}(ID)$ will be set. Then the sensor will wait for three possible events to occur: receiving *bid_master*, receiving *inhibit*, and finding timer T_{bid} expired. Signal strength will be used in the competition. Depending of different events, the sensor will go to the Master or Idle state.

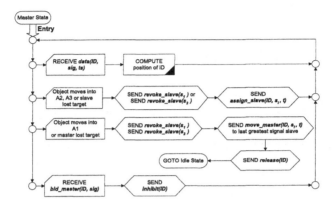

Fig. 8. The Master Protocol.

Fig. 8 shows the Master Protocol. The first event is to collect data from neighboring sensors. The next two events are for slave agents and the master agent when losing the target, respectively. Note that the areas A1, A2, and A3 refer to Fig. 2(b). The last event is to inhibit irrelevant sensors from monitoring the object.

The Slave Protocol is shown in Fig. 9. The first event controls the timing, by timer T_{rep}, to report data to the master. The second event is for the master to revoke the slave. The last event is to inhibit other irrelevant sensors.

3.3 Extension to Irregular Network Topologies

The above discussion has assumed a triangular sensor network topology. In the following, we briefly discuss how to extend our work to handle irregular deployment of sensors.

The election process does not need to be changed because sensors can still bid for serving as a master/slave based on their receive signal strengths. However, the rules to migrate masters/slaves need to be modified slightly as follows. Sensors need to know the locations of at least their two-hop neighbors. The working and backup areas are redefined based on the sensing scope, r, of each sensor. Specifically, there is a predefined value $r' < r$. The working area of a sensor is the circle centered at itself with radius r'. The rest of the area is the backup area. As before, we still use one master and two slaves to track an object (although more slaves may be used). Whenever the master finds the object moves into the backup area of itself or any of the slaves, the corresponding agent will be revoked and new agent will be assigned.

One interesting theoretical problem is how to define the master and two slaves given an object in an irregular network. This can be related to the classical *Voronoi* graph

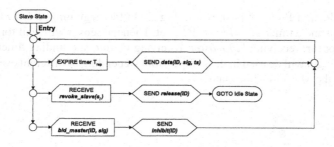

Fig. 9. The Slave Protocol.

problem in geometry [2]. Given a set of points V in a 2D plane, the Voronoi graph partitions the plane into $|V|$ segments such that each segment contains all points that is closest to the (only) vertex in the segment. As a result, if V is the set of all sensors, the sensor of the segment containing the object will serve as its master agent. Fig. 10(a) shows an example. The problem can be solved by a divide-and-conquer solution in time complexity $O(|V| \log |V|)$ [2].

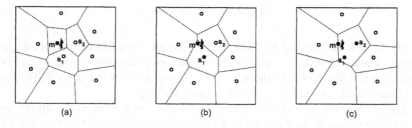

Fig. 10. Using Voronoi graphs to find the master and slaves: (a) the Voronoi graph of all vertics, (b) the Voronoi graph after removing the master, and (c) the Voronoi graph after removing the master and first slave.

The next two sensors that are closest to the object will serve as the slave agents. This can be found recursively as follows. Specifically, let m be the master sensor. We can construct the Voronoi graph again based on the vertex set $V - \{m\}$. Then the sensor, say s_1, of the segment containing the object will serve as the first slave. For example, Fig. 10(b) is the new Voronoi graph after removing the master sensor m. Similarly, to find the second slave, we repeat the process by constructing the Voronoi graph of $V - \{m, s_1\}$. Then the sensor, say s_2, of the segment containing the object will serve as the second slave. An example is in Fig. 10(c).

The advantage of using the Voronoi graph is as follows. For a particular location of the object, we can sort its distance to each sensor and pick the first three sensors closest to it. The complexity is $O(|V| \log |V|)$. However, whenever the object moves, the list needs to be re-sorted. The computational cost increases as time proceeds. If the above approach is used, we only need to pre-compute $1 + \binom{|V|-1}{1} + \binom{|V|-1}{2}$ Voronoi graphs.

So the saving of using Voronoi graphs is clear when we need to track the object for longer time.

4   Fusion and Delivery of Tracking Results

One issue not yet addressed is when a master agent should deliver its tracking result to the outside world. We assume that one of the sensors in the network serves as the gateway connecting to a location server in the wireline network. From time to time, the tracking result should be sent to the location server. We assume that more tracking result will be accumulated as time proceeds. So an optimization problem is that the master agent needs to decide whether it should carry the tracking result from sensor to sensor, or forward the result to the gateway.

We assume that the amount of tracking resulta increases with time at a constant rate. Also, two pieces of tracking results can be combined with a *fusion factor* ρ, where $0 \le \rho < 1$. Specifically, for two consecutive tracking results of sizes N_t and N_{t+1}, they can be merged into one of size $N_t + (1 - \rho)N_{t+1}$. If $\rho = 0$, data fusion has no benefit. Otherwise, the data size reduces after fusion. This is normally the case when data has certain level of dependence. In the following, we propose three data delivery solutions. Note that the first one is in fact not an agent-based solution. It only serves as a referential strategy so as to make comparison to our agent-based solutions.

The first one is called the *Non-Agent-Based (NAB)* strategy. Each sensor works independently and forwards its sensing results back to the gateway from time to time. Note that the sensing result is raw data and needs to be combined with other sensors' sensing results to calculate the object's locations. The shortest paths, which are assumed to be supported by the underlying routing protocol, are always used for data delivery. Also, we assume an ideal situation that only the three sensors nearest to the object will track the object.

The second solution is called the *Threshold-Based (TB)* strategy. A predefined threshold value T is given. The master agent will accumulate the tracking result and "carry" the result with it as long as the amount of result does not exceed T. Whenever the amount reaches T, it will be forwarded to the gateway through a shortest path.

The third solution is called the *Distance-Based (DB)* strategy. The delivery action may be taken only when the master agent moves. Basically, the distances from its current and next sensors' locations to the gateway are considered. Suppose the master agent is currently at sensor S_t and is migrating to sensor S_{t+1}. Let N_t be the current amount of tracking results at S_t, and N_{t+1} the expected amount of tracking results at S_{t+1}. (The value of N_{t+1} may be approximated by the data generation rate times the agent's average sensor residential time from the past experience.) If the master decides to carry the tracking result with it, the expected cost is:

$$C_1 = N_t + (N_t + (1 - \rho)N_{t+1})d(g, S_{t+1}),$$

where the first term is the cost to migrate the current result to the next sensor, and the second term the expected cost to deliver the fused result at the next sensor to the gateway, g. Function $d()$ specifies the minimum number of hops between two sensors.

If the master decides to deliver its current tracking result to the gateway, the expected cost is:

$$C_2 = N_t d(g, S_t) + N_{t+1} d(g, S_{t+1}).$$

So the master agent will carry the results with it if $C_1 \leq C_2$; otherwise, the results will be sent to g. Since sensors S_t and S_{t+1} are neighbors, $|d(g, S_{t+1}) - d(g, S_t)| = 1, 0, or -1$. This simplifies the condition to three cases.

- *Move away:* That is, $d(g, S_{t+1}) - d(g, S_t) = 1$. Then we have

$$C_1 \leq C_2 \equiv d(g, S_t) \geq \frac{2N_t}{\rho N_{t+1}} - 1. \tag{4.1}$$

- *Move parallel:* That is, $d(g, S_{t+1}) = d(g, S_t)$. Then we have

$$C_1 \leq C_2 \equiv d(g, S_t) \geq \frac{N_t}{\rho N_{t+1}}. \tag{4.2}$$

- *Move closer:* That is, $d(g, S_{t+1}) - d(g, S_t) = -1$. Then the agent will always carry the data with it because

$$C_1 \leq C_2 \equiv (\rho N_{t+1} d(g, S_t) \geq 0) \equiv TRUE \tag{4.3}$$

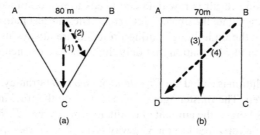

Fig. 11. Experimental environment: (a) triangular sensor network and (b) square sensor network. Dash lines represented tested roaming paths.

5   Prototyping Experiences and Simulation Results

5.1   Prototyping Experiences

In order to verify the feasibility of the proposed protocol, we have prototyped a system based on IEEE 802.11 NICs. Signal strength is used as the criterion to position objects. Specifically, four IBM laptops each equipped with a Lucent ORiNOCO 802.11b Wave-LAN card are used. Three of them are placed as an equilateral triangle each separated by 80 meters to emulate sensor nodes, as shown in Fig. 11(a). One laptop is used to simulate

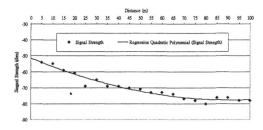

Fig. 12. Experiment of signal strength vs. distance for IEEE 802.11b.

the roaming object by periodically broadcasting beacons. For better sensitivity, an extra WaveLAN Range Extender Antenna is attached to this laptop. The sensor nodes monitor the received beacon strength transmitted by the object using the Client Manager utility.

First, we measure the degradation of signal strength versus distance. Fig. 12 shows one set of data that we collected. For every 5 meters from 0 to 100 meters a measurement is recorded. As can be expected, signal strengths received from IEEE 802.11b are not very stable. We use the "regression quadratic polynomial" to smooth out the curve, as illustrated by the solid line in Fig. 12. The curve is used to convert a received signal strength to an estimated distance.

Since signal strength is not an accurate measurement, the aforementioned trilateration algorithm can not be applied directly. In fact, as one may expect, signal strengths change all the time, even under a motionless situation. Certain gaps inherently exist between estimated distances and actual distances. The real situation is as shown in Fig. 13, where the three estimated circles centered at sensors have no common intersection.

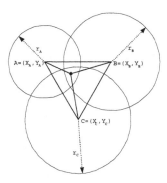

Fig. 13. The position approximation algorithm.

To solve the problem, we propose an approximation algorithm as follows. Let A, B, and C be the sensor nodes, which are located at (x_A, y_A), (x_B, y_B), and (x_C, y_C), respectively. For any point (x, y) on the plane, we then define a difference function

$$\sigma_{x,y} = |\sqrt{(x - x_A)^2 + (y - y_A)^2} - r_A|$$
$$+ |\sqrt{(x - x_B)^2 + (y - y_B)^2} - r_B|$$
$$+ |\sqrt{(x - x_C)^2 + (y - y_C)^2} - r_C|,$$

Where r_A, r_B, and r_C are the estimated distances to A, B, and C respectively. The location of the object is determined to be the point (x, y) among all points such that its difference function $\sigma_{x,y}$ is minimized. In our experiment, we consider only integer grid points on the plane. We measure the location of the object every second. Furthermore, to take sudden fluctuation of signal strength into account, we enforce a condition that the object does not move faster than 5 meters per second. As a result, when searching for the object's location, only those points in $(x \pm 5, y \pm 5)$ are evaluated for their difference functions, where (x, y) represents the location in the previous measurement.

Our experiments were done in an outdoor, plain area with no obstacles. Two roaming paths as illustrated in Fig. 11(a) were tested. For roaming path (1), three sets of results are demonstrated in Fig. 14(a). For roaming path (2), the results are demonstrated in Fig. 14(b). As can be seen, the predicted paths are close to the actual roaming paths, but there are still large gaps yet remaining to be improved further.

We have also tested the arrangement in Fig. 11(b), where four sensors arranged as a square are used. The extension for the tracking protocol and positioning algorithm is straightforward. Our tested results are shown in Fig. 14(c) and Fig. 14(d).

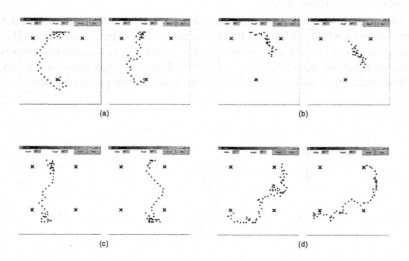

(a)   (b)

(c)   (d)

Fig. 14. Tracking result: (a) path (1) in Fig. 11(a), (b) path (2) in Fig. 11(a), (c) path (3) in Fig. 11(b) and (d) path (4) in Fig. 11(b).

5.2   Simulation Results

To verify the advantage of using our agent-based approach, we have developed a simulator. Sensors are deployed in a 10,000m x 10,000m environment with triangular topology.

The distance between two neighboring sensors is 80m. The gayeway is located at the center of the network.

Each control packet is 2 bytes. Each location is represented by 2 bytes. The IP routing header is assumed, wtih header equal to 2 bytes and MTU as large as 500 bytes.

The Random Way Point Model [12] is used to simulate the mobility of objects. The initial locations of objects are chosen randomly. Each object alternates between moving and pausing states. On entering the moving state, the object's next destination is randomly chosen from $(x \pm 15, y \pm 15)$, where (x, y) is its current location. Note that locations outside the boundary are not considered. Then the object moves at a constant speed of an uniform distribution between 1~3 m/sec. After arriving at its destination, the object will pause a period with an exponential distribution of mean = 5 sec.

We first experiment on different threshold values of T for the TB strategy. The result is in Fig. 15(a). We measure the average traffic load. A T significantly less than the largest MTU is not good due to high packet header overheads. On the contrary, tuning T too large is also inefficient because the master agent will need to carry too much history while traveling. The figure suggests that a T equal to or slightly larger than the largest MTU be a good choice. Fig. 15(b) further demonstrates the effect of the correlation coefficient ρ. We compare different strategies. The DB strategy performs the best. The TB also performs well, if proper T can be selected. In all cases, NAB performs the worst.

In the Fig. 16(a), we change the network size to visualize the effect. It is reasonable that larger networks incur higher traffics due to longer delivery paths. This justifies the importance of using our agent-based strategies. In Fig. 16(b), we further vary the mobility ratio, which is defined to be the ratio of moving time to pausing time. A higher mobility ratio indicates more frequent change of master agents. DB and TB with lower thresholds are less sensitive to mobility. With a too large threshold, TB will degrade significantly because at the time when data delivery is taken place, the distance to the gateway may increase significantly compared to when data was generated.

To summarize, we conclude that DB performs well in all cases. TB is quite simple, but one needs to be cautious in choosing its threshold. These strategies outperform NAB by 60~80% in terms of average traffic load.

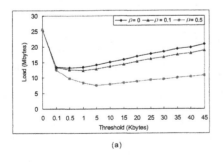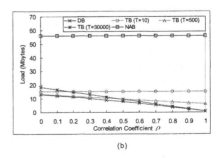

Fig. 15. Simulation results: (a) the threshold T of TB vs traffic load, and (b) the data fusion ratio vs. traffic load.

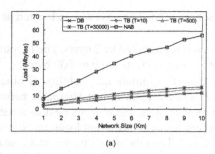
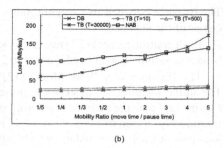

           (a)   (b)

Fig. 16. Simulation results: (a) network size vs. traffic load ($\rho = 0.1$), and (b) mobility ratio vs. traffic load ($\rho = 0.1$).

6   Conclusions

We have proposed a novel location-tracking protocol for regular and irregular sensor networks. A mobile-agent approach is adopted, which enables agents to roam around to follow the moving objects, hence significantly reducing the communication and sensing overheads. A data fusion model is proposed, and several data delivery strategies are proposed and evaluated. We have prototyped a system based on the idea using IEEE 802.11b NICs, where signal strengths are used as the criterion to measure objects' positions. While the prototyping is proved to work correctly, the accuracy still has rooms to be improved further.

References

1. A. Savvides, C.C. Han, M.B. Srivastava. Dynamic fine-grained localization in ad-hoc networks of sensors. In *Procs. of MobiCOM*, 2001.
2. F. Aurenhammer. Voronoi diagrams: a survey of a fundamental geometric data structure. pages 345–405, 1991.
3. B. Horling, R. Vincent, R. Mailler, J. Shen, R. Becker, K. Rawlins, and V. Lesser. Distributed Sensor Network for Real Time Tracking. In *Proc. of the 5th international conference on Autonomous agents*, pages 417–424, 2001.
4. B. Huang, W. Zhang, and Z. Guo. A study of spatial structures of sensor networks and multi-agent negotiation strategies., 2001. http://www.cs.wustl.edu/ zhang/projects/dcmp/.
5. C. Intanagonwiwat, R. Govindan, and D. Estrin. Directed Diffusion: A Scalable and Robust Communication Paradigm for Sensor Networks. In *Proc. of MobiCOM*, pages 56–67, 2000.
6. C. Savarese, J. Rabaey, J. Beutel. Locationing in distributed ad-hoc wireless sensor networks. In *Proc. of the ICASSP*, 2001.
7. D. Estrin, R. Govindan, J. Heidemann, and S. Kumar. Next century challenges: scalable coordination in sensor networks. In *Proc. of MobiCOM*, pages 263–270, 1999.
8. G. J. Pottie and W. J. Kaiser. Wireless integrated network sensors. *Communications of the ACM*, 43(5):51–58, 2000.
9. Hairong Qi, S.S. Iyengar, and K. Chakrabarty. Multiresolution data integration using mobile agents in distributed sensor networks. *IEEE Tran. on Systems, Man, and Cybernetics, Part C: Applications and Reviews*, 31(3):383–391, 2001.

10. J. O'Rourke. Computational geometry column 15. *International Journal of Computational Geometry and Applications*, 2(2):215–217, 1992.
11. J. Rabaey, J. Ammer, J.L. da Silva Jr., D. Patel. Picoradio: Ad-hoc wireless networking of ubiquitous low-energy sensor/monitor nodes. In *VLSI, 2000. Proceedings. IEEE Computer Society Workshop*, pages 9–12, 2000.
12. D. B. Johnson and D. A. Maltz. Dynamic source routing in ad hoc wireless networks. In Imielinski and Korth, editors, *Mobile Computing*, volume 353. Kluwer Academic Publishers, 1996.
13. K. Chakrabarty, S.S. Iyengar, Hairong Qi, and Eungchun Cho. Coding theory framework for target location in distributed sensor networks. In *Proc. Intl. Symposium on Information Technology: Coding and Computing*, pages 130–134, 2001.
14. Nirupama Bulusu, John Heidemann, Deborah Estrin. GPS-less low-cost outdoor localization for very small devices. In *IEEE Personal Communications*, pages 28–34, 2000.
15. P. Enge, and P. Misra. Special issue on GPS: The global positioning system. In *Proc. of the IEEE*, pages 3–15, 1999.
16. Paramvir Bahl, and Venkata N. Padmanabhan. Radar: an in-building rf-based user location and tracking system. In *INFOCOM*, pages 775–784, 2000.
17. S. Meguerdichian, F. Koushanfar, G. Qu, and M. Potkonjak. Exposure in wireless Ad-Hoc sensor networks. In *Proc. of MobiCOM*, pages 139–150, 2001.
18. S. Meguerdichian, F. Koushanfar, M. Potkonjak, and M. Srivastava. Coverage Problems in Wireless Ad-hoc Sensor Networks. In *Proc. of INFOCOM*, pages 1380–1387, 2001.
19. S. Meguerdichian, S. Slijepcevic, V. Karayan and M. Potkonjak. Localized algorithms in wireless ad-hoc networks: location discovery and sensor exposure. In *Proc. of MobiHOC*, pages 106–116, 2001.
20. Y.-C. Tseng, S.-P. Kuo, H.-W. Lee, and C.-F. Huang. A mobile-agent approach for location tracking in a wireless sensor network. In *Int'l Computer Symp.*, 2002.
21. van Diggelen, F. Indoor gps theory & implementation. In *Position Location and Navigation Symposium, 2002 IEEE*, pages 240–247, 2002.
22. K. Whitehouse and D. Culler. Calibration as parameter estimation in sensor networks. In *Proceedings of the first ACM international workshop on Wireless sensor networks and applications*, pages 59–67, 2002.

Acoustic Target Tracking Using Tiny Wireless Sensor Devices*

Qixin Wang, Wei-Peng Chen, Rong Zheng, Kihwal Lee, and Lui Sha

Department of Computer Science
University of Illinois at Urbana-Champaign
Urbana, IL 61801
{qwang4, wchen3, zheng4, klee7, lrs}@cs.uiuc.edu

Abstract. With the advancement of MEMS technologies, wireless networks consist of tiny sensor devices hold the promise of revolutionizing sensing in a wide range of application domains because of their flexibility, low cost and ease of deployment. However, the constrained computation power, battery power, storage capacity and communication bandwidth of the tiny devices pose challenging problems in the design and deployment of such systems. Target localization using acoustic signal with tiny wireless devices is a particularly difficult task due to the amount of signal processing and computation involved. In this paper, we provide an in-depth study of designing such wireless sensor networks for real-world acoustic tracking applications. We layout a cluster-based architecture to address the limitations of the tiny sensing devices. To achieve effective utilization of the scarce wireless bandwidth, a quality-driven paradigm to suppress redundant information and resolve contention is proposed. One instance of the quality-driven approach is implemented in the acoustic tracking system, where the quality of the tracking reports can be quantified numerically. We demonstrate the effectiveness of our proposed architecture and protocols using a sensor network testbed based on UCBerkeley mica motes. Considering the performance limitations of tiny sensor devices, the achieved acoustic target tracking accuracy is extraordinarily good. Our experimental study also shows that the acoustic target tracking quality can be indeed measured and used to assist resource allocation decisions. This application-driven design and implementation exercises also serve to identify important areas of further work in in-network processing and communications.

Keywords. Wireless sensor network, sink tree routing, acoustic target tracking, quality driven, redundancy suppression.

1 Introduction

Fueled by the increasing capabilities and ever-declining cost of computing and communication devices, wireless networks consisting of a large number of tiny

---

* This work is supported by DARPA and ONR MURI project under contract N00014-01-0576, and by DARPA NEST project under contract F33615-5-01-c-1905.

F. Zhao and L. Guibas (Eds.): IPSN 2003, LNCS 2634, pp. 642–657, 2003.

sensors hold the promise of revolutionizing a wide range of application domains such as battlefield surveillance, machine failure diagnosis, biological detection, home security, smart spaces, inventory tracking etc[8]. In surveillance applications, visual and audio data are two key sources of information. Airborne/satellite cameras can easily monitor a wide area while the collection of acoustic information can only be done close to the source due to the limited distance of propagation of sound in the air. As a result, we currently have many eyes in the sky but not enough ears on the ground, so to speak. This makes acoustic tracking of mobile targets using tiny sensing devices very attractive, as massive deployment of wireless sensors in large area can provide more accurate and timely information about the geographical location of the targets. The basic idea of acoustic tracking is to detect the location of a target by analyzing the specific cues such as delay and amplitude received by multiple sensors.

Generally speaking, wireless sensor networks consist of tiny sensory devices deployed in a region of interest. Each device has limited processing and wireless communication capabilities, which enable it to gather information from the environment and deliver this information to actuators for appropriate actions. The major challenges in design and deployment of such wireless sensor networks are the constrained computation power, battery power, storage capacity and communication bandwidth of the tiny devices. Target tracking using acoustic signal is a particular daunting task for the following reasons,

- Acoustic tracking needs collaborative communication/computation among multiple sensors. The information gathered by a single sensor is usually incomplete and inaccurate.
- Acoustic tracking requires a significant amount of signal processing and computation to detect and locate the sources of interest.
- The reports generated by the sensing components need to be delivered to the actuators in a timely fashion. Out-dated reports are of little use.

In this paper, we provide an in-depth study of the *architecture and algorithmic issues* in applying networks of *tiny* wireless sensors to real-world acoustic tracking applications. *The acoustic signal processing techniques used can be quite simplistic, nevertheless, it provides a context for our research.* In addition, in this paper, we only deal with tracking *impulsive* acoustic signals, such as foot steps, sniper shots etc. However, the networking aspect of the system is applicable to any type of target localization.

The overall system architecture consists of two self-contained components, the acoustic target tracking subsystem, which deals with the detection, processing and triangulation of impulsive acoustic signals; and the communication subsystem, which is responsible for reporting high quality tracking results to the data sink in a timely fashion. To address the limited computational and battery power of wireless sensor devices, we organize sensors into clusters. Sensors in each cluster coordinate in sensing and communication to perform the sensing task. To deal with the inaccuracy in measurement and unreliability typical with low-end device in remote or hostile environment, we explore the redundancy in a large number of sensors to obtain more robust results. To achieve effective utilization of the scarce wireless bandwidth, a quality-driven scheme is proposed to suppress redundant data and resolve channel contention. The novelty of quality-driven scheme is that it aims to increase the flow of information as compared to raw bits. One instance of the quality-driven approach is implemented in our testbed, where the quality of the acoustic tracking reports can be quantified.

We demonstrate the effectiveness of our proposed architecture and protocols using a sensor network testbed consisting a number of UCBerkeley mica mote sensor nodes and a few pc/104 single board computers. In our experiments, with an acoustic sensor density of $0.125/ft^2$, we can locate a sound source with an average error of 13.8 inches, among which 35% of the errors are less than 3 inches and 48.3% of the errors are less than 6 inches. Our experimental study shows that the data quality can be indeed measured and used to assist resource allocation decisions. This application-oriented design and implementation exercises also serve to identify and provide insights to important areas in in-network processing and communications.

The organization of this paper is as follows. After the introductory part, we give a brief overview of hardware constraints and the system architecture. Section 3 presents the design and implementation of time synchronization, acoustic signal processing and triangulation for acoustic target tracking. In Section 4, a quality-driven in-network signal processing and communication scheme for redundancy suppression and contention resolution is proposed, together with a novel multi-parent sink-tree routing algorithm. In Section 5, we evaluate the proposed architecture and algorithms using a sensor network testbed and conclude the paper in Section 6 with a list of future work.

2   System Overview

2.1   Networked Wireless Sensor Device

As stated in Section 1, our mission is to implement acoustic target tracking using networked sensors. In designing our system, we face the following challenges:

1. Limited hardware capability (in terms of CPU MIPS, sampling rate, program and data memory, wireless bandwidth etc.);
2. Error- and failure-proneness (e.g., due to the low sampling rate and low sampling accuracy, loss of interrupt events, power constraints, physical damage etc.);
3. Difficulty in programming and debugging embedded systems.

The specific hardware we use is *mica mote*, developed by UC Berkeley [5] [14]. Mica mote uses the ATmega103L micro-controller [3] with a 4MHz CPU cycle frequency and a 4KB data RAM. The wireless networking hardware component on the mica motes is the RFM TR1000 radio transceiver [7], which operates at the unique radio frequency of 916.5MHz. It can achieve a maximal application layer throughput of approximately 520Bytes/sec [13]. The acoustic sensor module on mica mote can at most reach a stable sampling rate of 4kHz. A component-based OS – TinyOS [5] is used as the software system architecture for manipulating motes.

As will become clearer later on, the hardware capability is very limited for data-centric, computational-intensive acoustic tracking applications.

2.2   System Architecture

Due to the aforementioned hardware and software limitation of tiny devices, our system architecture design has to take extra care on the application requirement, availability, robustness and manageability. We adopt the following design philosophies, i) exploring the redundancy in large number of sensing devices, ii) divide-and-conquering acoustic tracking tasks by carrying out role differentiation, and iii) targeting for effective utilization of limited resources rather than nominal utilization. Redundancy is desirable not only for the purpose of better availability (to counteract the impact of high device failure rate), but also for the purpose of robustness. Redundant data can statistically mitigate the negative impact of errors. Role differentiation splits the complex nationalities of the entire system into sub-tasks that are affordable and manageable for each one of the tiny devices. Increasing *effective* resource utilization makes use of limited resources to better serve the application requirements.

Specifically, we divide the overall system into two subsystems: the *acoustic target tracking subsystem* and the *communication subsystem*.

Acoustic target tracking subsystem: The acoustic target tracking subsystem consists of multiple *sensory clusters*. A sensory cluster is the primary unit for tracking the locations of acoustic targets. It has a *cluster head* and several *slavery acoustic sensors* which jointly monitor a specific area. A cluster can be formed using mechanisms such as the one used in Jini [12] to account various application-specific factors (such as geology, algorithm, device capability etc.) Dynamic clustering for moving targets is one of our ongoing research work. Redundancy is achieved by deploying extra sensors within a cluster and allowing the monitoring areas of adjacent clusters to overlap with each other. Traditionally, acoustic tracking needs only three sensors to carry out the *triangulation*. However, in our implementation, we require more than three sensors in each cluster to obtain one tracking report to combat the inaccuracy of individual sensor's data. Role differentiation is done by assigning cluster head and sensors different jobs and coordinating them to jointly carry out acoustic target tracking.

We assume that geographical location of each slavery sensor can be obtained via mechanisms such as described [4,10]. Over the runtime of the system, the cluster head and all its slavery sensors are clock synchronized. When a sound with the specified signature arrives, all sensors record the sound and timing information and report them to the cluster head. By analyzing the differences of the sound arrival times among slavery sensors, the cluster head can estimate the location of the sound source using triangulation and then report the tracking result back to the *data sink* via the *communication subsystem*.

The cluster head needs to handle a significant amount of computation, which is beyond the capability of the current generation of mica motes. Therefore, in our implementation, we use pc/104 single board computers [6] as cluster heads, which are widely used in embedded systems.

Communication Subsystem: The communication subsystem is responsible for relaying the tracking reports from cluster heads to the *data sink.* In order to achieve high *effective* throughput and low latency, we propose a novel scheme called *quality-driven* redundancy suppression and contention resolution to speed up the delivery of higher quality tracking reports and suppress inferior/erroneous reports. Note, the redundancy of acoustic sensory motes reduces the error in a single cluster and thus is desirable. However, due to the overlapping of clusters, multiple reports can be generated for a single acoustic event across multiple adjacent clusters, which may unnecessarily lead to congestion of the network or waste of network resources. Quality-driven redundancy suppression picks the best one from the multiple tracking reports, thus accomplishes the goal of achieving better robustness out of redundant tracking reports. More importantly, quality-driven redundancy suppression and contention resolution is the major mechanism that realized the idea of *effective* utilization of communication subsystem rather than *nominal* utilization. To relay the report to the data sink we introduce multi-parent sink tree routing scheme to provide fast local recovery and higher message delivery ratio.

3   Acoustic Target Tracking Subsystem

In this section, we present the detailed design of the key components for the acoustic tracking system including the time synchronization, onset detection, cross-correlation, triangulation, and determination of the quality of results.

3.1   Time Synchronization

We use delay-based triangulation to locate impulsive sound sources, hence accurate timing information is a necessity. Specifically, all the sensors within the same cluster have to be time-synchronized. The method of time synchronization we adopt in the system is *Reference-Broadcast Synchronization* (RBS)[2], which is a light-weight scheme that can achieve high accuracy. In RBS, a head node broadcasts reference radio beacons to its neighbors. Each receiver records the arrival time based on its local clock and sends this information back to the originator of the head node. Under the assumption that the broadcasted radio beacon arrives at all receivers simultaneously, after a few rounds of the beaconing and replies, the head node can obtain mapping functions of clock readings between any pair of receivers, using statistically methods such as least square linear regression. To this end, the head node can convert any receiver's clock readings into a universal clock reading.

In our implementation, we have a initialization phase when n ($n = 12$ in our practice) rounds of beaconing and replies are performed. After the initialization, timing information can be piggybacked on the packets exchanged between the cluster head and the sensors. Therefore, the clocks can be calibrated without introducing extra control overheads. Experiment results show that the distortion of clock readings can be kept within $30\mu s$, which is sufficient for our delay-based acoustic tracking.

3.2   Onset Detection

Due to the limited computation capability, the current generation of *mica motes* are not capable of sampling and processing acoustic data concurrently. Instead, major functions such as sensing, wireless transceiving and processing have to be serialized. Moreover, because of the limited memory in *motes*, acoustic samples have to be stored in a circular buffer. In order to avoid buffer overflow for useful sample data , an onset detection mechanism is needed to instruct sensors to stop sampling data once the interested acoustic signal is captured. The way a sensor determines whether the incoming acoustic signal is of potential interest is based on the magnitude of the signal. A small sliding window is used to compute the moving average of the magnitude of signals. If the energy within the window exceeds a threshold, the sensor assumes that the current time is close to the onset point of the acoustic signal. The sensor continues recording data into the circular buffer until it winds back and reaches a prelude point prior to the onset point. Once the sound of interest is captured, post-processing is conducted separately at both the cluster head and the sensors. The cluster head extracts the sound signature from the recorded samples and broadcasts it to the sensors in its own cluster. Upon receiving the signature packet from the cluster head, sensors apply cross-correlation to compare the received signature with the buffered data.

3.3   Cross-Correlation

After receiving the sound signature from the cluster head, each sensor cross-correlates the received signature with buffered data to extract the desired pattern and determine the starting portion of signal. There are several advantages in choosing the starting portion as the reference portion. First, the starting portion is less susceptible to echoes. In in-door environments, the effect of echoes is quite significant. Fortunately, the echo is not presented in the starting portion of acoustic signal unless the sensor is very close to a wall. Second, the uniqueness of onset point and the salient change in sound wave shape at the onset point makes the starting portion very easy to be consistently located among distributed independent sensors.

The procedures of cross-correlation are summarized in Fig. 1. Two preprocessing procedures are applied to buffered data before cross-correlation. The first step is to remove the interference of noise. The average magnitude of noise is calculated first, and then the samples whose values are close to the average are replaced with the average so that the results of correlation do not ripple due to the oscillation of noises. In the second step, the signal is passed through a second-order Butterworth low-pass filter to remove the high frequency components. After the pre-processing, cross-correlation is applied to the filtered data with the received sound signature to do pattern matching. The final step is to find the first significant peak in the correlation result using thresholding and thus the arrival time is extracted.

Fig. 1. Procedures of cross-correlation for sensors

3.4 Triangulation (Sound Source Locating) and Evaluation of Quality Rank

Upon receiving the *sound arrival times* from sensors in the cluster, the cluster head translates the time into the universal reference time before executing the triangulation.

Triangulation is done by comparing the differences in sound propagation delays from the source to different acoustic sensors. Suppose the location of sound source is (x, y) and the sound is generated at time t. If a sensor M_1 located at (x_1, y_1) detects the sound reaches it at time t_1 (i.e. sound arrival time). We shall have the following equation:

$$\sqrt{(x - x_1)^2 + (y - y_1)^2} = (t_1 - t) \cdot v \tag{1}$$

where v is the velocity of sound.

Theoretically triangulation can use three such equations generated by three sensors to analytically compute the sound source location. In practice, due to the coarse-grained acoustic sampling data of low-performance sensors, errors generated in cross-correlation are not negligible (for example, the errors can vary from 0.1 to 0.5ms). The above theoretical approach is mostly impractical. How to counteract this problem is a big research topic. Relevant works can be found in [11][1][9] etc. However, this topic is out of the scope of this paper. In this paper we simply consider a maximum likelihood (ML) based heuristic as a context for our research.

Algorithm Description: Consider n sensors, for each hypothetical source location $(\tilde{x}, \tilde{y})$ in the field A, there is a vector $\tilde{p}(\tilde{x}, \tilde{y}) = (\tilde{d}_1, \tilde{d}_2, \ldots, \tilde{d}_n)$ representing the theoretical propagation delay to each one of the n sensors. Let $p = (d_1, d_2, \ldots, d_n)$ be the observed propagation delay vector based on the reports gathered at the cluster head for a single sound events. Then, the estimated location of the sound source $(\hat{x}, \hat{y})$ is given by

$$(\hat{x}, \hat{y}) = \arg_{(\tilde{x}, \tilde{y}) \in A} \min d(\tilde{p}(\tilde{x}, \tilde{y}), p) \tag{2}$$

where d is an algorithm specific difference measurement scheme.

This algorithm only involves multiplicity, additions and comparisons. Compared to equation-based solution, which usually requires division and solving of linear and quadratic equations, our algorithm is more robust to floating point errors or degenerations.

However, since there are infinite points in area A, to make the algorithm work, the monitored area of a cluster is first divided into N-by-N grids (in our implementation, we choose N so that the granularity of the grid is $3 \times 3 \text{inch}^2$). Therefore the time complexity of the algorithm is roughly $O(N^2)$. In addition, it is possible to throw out out-of-bound readings based on the physical laws to avoid unnecessarily degradation of the triangulation result.

The confidence level of estimated location can also be approximated by the percentage of $\tilde{p}$'s elements that falls within the ε boundary of p. This percentage is defined as the *quality rank* of the location report. The higher the percentage, the more confidence in the sensed result and thus the higher the quality rank. Determination of the quality rank of triangulation results is important. In the case of multiple clusters (whose monitored areas may overlap), multiple reports for the same sound event may be generated and delivered to the data sink. Ideally, only the cluster head with the best quality rank (or highest confidence) need to send the report back. Inferior quality reports should be suppressed to better utilize the limited bandwidth and computational power in the wireless networks. This point will be further illustrated in Section 4.1.

The pseudo code for locating the sound source and determining quality rank is given in Fig. 2, where, $\hat{\Delta}$ is the estimation of the fixed time difference between the time reference systems used by $\tilde{p}$ and p. Because $\tilde{p}$ uses the relative time which takes actual sound event happening time as 0; while p can only use universal time which takes the time synchronization initialization time as 0.

---

1. **LocateSoundSource**(observed propagation delay vector $p = (d_1, \ldots, d_n)$):
2.   mark apparently invalid d_i s in p
3. $m \leftarrow$ number of valid elements in p
4.   **for each** point $(\tilde{x}, \tilde{y}) \in Grid$
5.   calculate $\tilde{p} = (\tilde{d_1}, \cdots, \tilde{d_n})$ for $(\tilde{x}, \tilde{y})$ according to Equation (1)
6.   **for each** valid $d_i \in p$
7. $\delta_i \leftarrow \tilde{d_i} - d_i$
8. $\hat{\Delta} \leftarrow$ average of δ_i s
9. $vote \leftarrow 0$
10.   **for each** valid $d_i \in p$
11. $err_i \leftarrow \delta_i - \hat{\Delta}$
12.   **if** $|err_i| \leq \varepsilon$ **then** $vote \leftarrow vote + 1$
13. $QualityRank_{(\tilde{x},\tilde{y})} \leftarrow \frac{vote}{m}$
14. $(\hat{x}, \hat{y}) \leftarrow$ the $(\tilde{x}, \tilde{y})$ with the highest $QualityRank$
15. $\hat{Q} \leftarrow (\hat{x}, \hat{y})$'s corresponding $QualityRank$
16.   **return** $(\hat{x}, \hat{y})$ as the sensed sound source location, with a quality rank of $\hat{Q}$

Fig. 2. Sound Source Locating Algorithm

4   Communication Subsystem

Communication subsystem serves to forward the tracking report from cluster head to the *data sink*. We use the default MAC and routing protocol (i.e., CSMA and sink tree) of TinyOS [5] as a baseline. In order to achieve high robustness in acoustic tracking report, availability, effective throughput and low delay, we propose the idea of *Quality-driven redundancy suppression and contention resolution* (QDR) and *multi-parent routing* .

4.1   Quality-Driven Redundancy Suppression and Contention Resolution

As mentioned before, in the acoustic target tracking subsystem, for the purpose of providing better robustness and availability, we allow the overlapping of clusters' monitoring areas to generate redundant reports for each sound event. Therefore, a mechanism is needed to quantify the quality of reports and select the one with the best quality. Inferior redundant reports can be suppressed from entering the communication subsystem, so as to conserve the scarce wireless bandwidth for effective data. In case of contention resolution, it is desirable to give higher priority to reports with better quality and speed-up their delivery. Inferior reports are assigned lower priority or even dropped in presence of congestion.

To determine the quality of reports during runtime, we use the quality rank defined in acoustic target tracking according to Fig. 2's algorithm. As demonstrated in the experimental result in Section5, quality rank has a strong correlation with the accuracy of the triangulation results.

We implement quality-driven contention resolution and redundancy suppression with the original CSMA MAC protocol in TinyOS. Specifically, we use the quality rank to determine the backoff time for CSMA contention resolution. The better the quality rank, the shorter the backoff. Every time a cluster head/router wants to send out a tracking report packet with a quality rank of Q, its backoff time is computed as,

$$T_{backoff} = Q \cdot interval + random \qquad (3)$$

where *interval* is an implementation-specific constant, Q is the quality rank (with 0 as the highest quality), and *random* is the random backoff generated by the original CSMA protocol. If before the firing of its own back-off timer, a node overhears a report belonging to the same sound event[1] with a higher quality, it drops its pending report.

The pseudo code of the protocol is described in Fig. 3.

---

[1] If the Euclidean distance of the two vectors of the acoustic reports *(sound source location, time)* is smaller than an error bound, the two reports are regarded as "same sound event"

/* Upon generation/reception of an report $R(location, time, QualityRank)$ */
1. enque(R);
2. set_backoff_timer(QualityRank*interval+random);
/* Upon overhearing of an report $R(location, time)$ at node i */
3. if $PacketQueue(i) \neq \emptyset$ {
4.   if $find\_match(R) \equiv true$
5.   drop_inferior_report(QualityRank);
6. }
/* Upon backoff timer expiration */
7. R = dequeue();
8. transmit(R);

Fig. 3. Operation of QDR

4.2   Sink-Tree Construction

We propose a multi-parent sink tree routing algorithm. Compared with the original implementation of sink tree routing [5], the main difference is that instead of maintaining a single upstream node (with respect to the data sink), a node keeps a *candidate parent list* of multiple upstream nodes to reach the data sink. The candidate parent list is ordered by certain preference (e.g., the number of hops to the sink). All the parent candidates are maintained as soft states. The data sink periodically sends out flooding packets to construct the sink tree. New parent candidates are inserted into the router's candidate parent list when a flooding packet from the corresponding node is received.

To forward a data packet, a node always tries to forward it to the first parent candidate. If a link failure is detected (e.g. exceeding the retransmission limit), a node drops the corresponding parent candidate and uses the next one in the list.

The main advantage of multi-parent sink tree protocol is that it improves availability by fast recovery. The link failures can be repaired locally using multi-parent information. Compared with the original sink tree routing algorithm, where the links are not repaired until the next round of sink tree building flooding, local recovery can increase the reliability and throughput for packet delivery in the network.

5   Experiments

In this section, we conduct several experiments in our sensor network testbed. Sensors and routers are made up by a number of mica motes. A few pc/104 single board computers are deployed to serve as the cluster heads. Each pc/104 board is connected via serial port to a mica mote for sensing and wireless communication.

5.1   Sound Source Locating within a Cluster

In this section, we study the performance of the acoustic tracking subsystem. Of primary interests are, i) the accuracy of triangulation result and ii) the correlation between triangulation accuracy and quality rank Q proposed in Section 3.

As mentioned earlier, clusters are the basic units for locating and tracking acoustic target. In this set of experiment, sensors are placed uniformly in a $100 \times 100 inch^2$ 2-D area to form a single cluster (see Fig. 4). Three settings are tested, using 8, 10 and 12 sensors per cluster respectively. A pc/104 is placed at the center of the 2-D area to serve as the cluster head. To understand the sensitivity of triangulation result to the sound source location, we also vary the location of sound source as shown in Fig. 4. In each test setting (8, 10 or 12 sensors/cluster), 10 trials are carried out for each of the 18 sound source locations. Therefore, altogether there are $10 \times 18 \times 3 = 640$ trials.

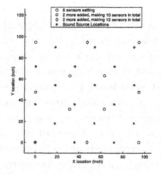

Fig. 4. Locations of sensors and sound sources in a single cluster

Accuracy of triangulation: The accuracy of triangulation result is defined as the Euclidean distance between the actual location (x_a, y_a) and the computed location (x_m, y_m) as,

$$SensingError = \sqrt{(x_a - x_m)^2 + (y_a - y_m)^2} \qquad (4)$$

Fig. 5 gives an example of the tracking results for the 12 sensor case (due to space limit, we only show 6 out of the total 18 locations). Each "*" represents the actual location of the sound source, while each "·" corresponds to the triangulation result in one trial. As shown in Fig. 5, the majorities of the locating reports fall within the vicinity of the sound source. However, the triangulation accuracy degrades as the sound source moves to the corner of the sensing area. This can mitigated by overlapping multiple sensing clusters.

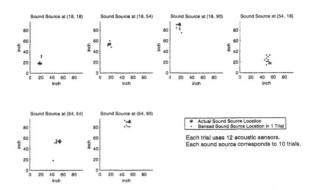

Fig. 5. An example of triangulation results for different sound source location

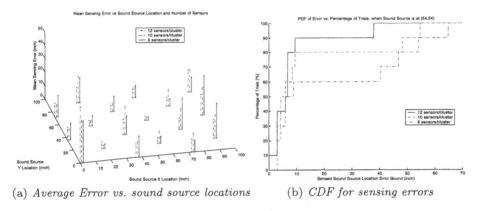

(a) *Average Error vs. sound source locations*   (b) *CDF for sensing errors*

Fig. 6. Distribution of sensing error

Fig. 6(a) shows the average sensing error with respect to different sound location and the number of sensors used. Roughly speaking, with more sensors, the accuracy of triangulation gets higher. The triangulation result is quite satisfying, considering the fact that the sound source itself (a speaker) is approximately a cubic with dimension 4 inches. There are some cases in Fig. 6(a), where using eight sensor gives the best result. This is because "bad" data generated by multiple sensors can potentially "poison" the result. We will further investigate this issue as one of our future work. A closer view of the stochastic property of the triangulation reports is given in Fig. 6(b) for different number of sensors for a fixed sound source location at (54, 54).

Quality of reports: Fig. 7(a) demonstrate the correlation between quality rank and the accuracy of the triangulation result. As expected, the smaller the quality rank (or the higher the quality), the higher the accuracy of the triangulation result. When the quality rank is inferior (with $QualityRank \geq 4$), both the mean and deviation of the sensing errors are very large. On the other hand,

superior quality rank reports are statistically trustworthy. This speaks strongly
for using the quality rank defined in Section 3 as an indication of the quality of
the triangulation results. In addition, as shown in Fig. 7(b), using more sensors
can improve the trustworthiness in superior quality ranks (the percentage of
reports at rank 1 within 3-inch error range is close to 100%).

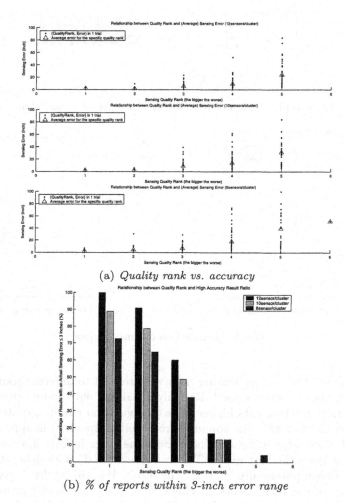

(a) *Quality rank vs. accuracy*

(b) *% of reports within 3-inch error range*

Fig. 7. Relationship between Quality Rank and accuracy of triangulation results

5.2   Study of QDR and Multi-parent Sink Tree Routing

In this section, we study the effectiveness of the quality-driven redundancy suppression and contention resolution (QDR). As mentioned earlier, the benefits of

QDR scheme for communication subsystem are two-folded, i) it alleviates the channel contention thus leads to higher throughout and ii) it increases the information throughput by giving higher priority for high-quality reports to be transmitted. Therefore, the performance metrics of interests are,

- **The average quality rank of received reports ($\overline{Q}$).** As demonstrated in previous section, the quality rank provide a quantitative measurement of the report. The smaller the quality rank, the better the data quality.
- **Deviation from the minimum rank.** Ideally, only the report with the most superior quality rank should be delivered. However, reports may get lost or multiple reports can be delivered since they are generated at different time. Deviation from the minimum rank defined as the difference from the minimum rank, reflects the effectiveness of communication and suppression.
- **Utility.** In attempt to gauge the rate of effective information throughput (rather than nominal throughput of raw bits), we define a utility function $U(k) = \frac{S_k}{Q_k}$ for the kth packet, where Q_k and S_k are the rank and size of the kth packet.

In this set of experiments, there are 3 ajacent clusters, 7 router motes including the ones attached to the sink and the pc/104 board. A sound source can be heard by all of the clusters. However, depending on the location of the sound source and the triangulation result, different clusters can generate reports of different quality. The reports are routed via a 2-hop communication network to the data sink. Transmission of the reports are subject to the quality-driven backoff timer, which is computed as in Equation 3.

Impact of the backoff timer value: In this set of experiment, we vary the interval from 0ms (no backoff) to 400ms. The percentage of suppressed reports are depicted in Fig. 8. Also shown in the graph are the levels of confidence for five runs of experiments. Consistent with our expectation, as the backoff timer value

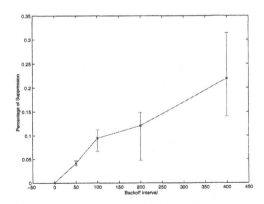

Fig. 8. Effect of backoff timer on the percentage of suppressed reports

gets large, more redundant reports get suppressed. However, this comes at the expense of longer interval to deliver the report. Therefore, in the next set of experiment, we choose the interval to be 100ms.

Study of QDR: In this set of experiment, we fix the interval to be 100ms and compare the scheme with QDR and one without. From Table 1, we can see that

Table 1. Effect of QDR

	rank	dev. rank	utility	% of dropped reports
without QDR	3.4900	1.2517	0.1160	0
with QDR	3.2920	1.1348	0.1312	9.5%

as expected, with the QDR, the average quality of delivered report is better and thus the utility is better. However, the percentage of suppressed reports is not very significant (ideally, it should be around 66.6%). This can be attributed to the fact that the reports are not always generated around the same time. Therefore, a report of inferior quality rank may still get delivered because its backoff period doesn't overlap with the sending of the other reports with superior quality rank.

6   Conclusion and Future Work

In this paper, we investigate the design and implementation of acoustic tracking using tiny wireless devices. To achieve high reliability, availability in a system of networked sensors with only limited computation and communication capability, we propose decomposition of the different roles and divide the system into two components, i) the acoustic target tracking subsystem and ii) the communication subsystem. Our main contributions can be summarized as follows,

- Designed and implemented an acoustic target tracking system using *tiny* wireless devices.
- Proposed a ranking mechanism to decide the quality of tracking result.
- Proposed the idea of quality-driven redundancy suppression and contention resolution, together with an implementation using quality rank.

Experimental results using our sensor network testbed demonstrate the effectiveness of the proposed design and validate the idea of quality rank.

Through our first-hand experience with the system, we identify several agenda for future work, First, protocol design and experimentation with moving targets needs to be investigated. Of particular interest is the real-time issue to deliver high-quality reports in a timely fashion. Secondly, we are interested in applying energy conservation techniques to the acoustic tracking system. Our hierarchical structure can naturally take advantage of the redundancy in highly dense sensor networks for power saving. Lastly, further study of the quality-driven approach and its applicability to other application domain for sensor networks should be studied.

References

1. G. C. Carter, Coherence and Time Delay Estimation, IEEE Press, 1993.
2. Jeremy Elson, Lewis Girod, Deborah Estrin, "Fine-Grained Network Time Synchronization using Reference Broadcasts," in Proc. of the Fifth Symposium on Operating Systems Design and Implementation (OSDI2002), Boston, MA. Dec. 2002.
3. D. V. Gadre, "Programming and Customizing the AVR Microcontroller," McGraw-Hill, 2001.
4. L. Girod, V. Bychkovskiy, J. Elson, D. Estrin, "Locating tiny sensors in time and space: A case study," in Proc. of International Conference on Computer Design (ICCD 2002), Freiburg, Germany. Sep., 2002. (Invited Paper)
5. Jason Hill, Robert Szewczyk, Alec Woo, Seth Hollar, David E. Culler, Kristofer S. J. Pister, "System Architecture Directions for Networked Sensors," in Proc. of ASPLOS-IX, Cambridge, Mass. 2000.
6. http://www.jumptec.de
7. http://www.rfm.com/products/data/tr1000.pdf
8. J. Kahn, R. H. Katz, K. Pister, "Emerging Challenges: Mobile Networking for 'Smart Dust'." Journal of Communications and Networks, vol. 2, no. 3. pp. 188–196, Sep. 2000 (Invited Paper).
9. C. W. Reed, et al., "Direct joint source localization and propagation speed estimation," in Proc. of ICASSP'99, Phoenix, AZ, pp. 1169–1172, 1999.
10. B. Parkinson and S. Gilbert, "NAVSTAR: global positioning information system ten years later," in Proceeding of IEEE, pp. 1177–1186, 1983.
11. X. Sheng, Y. Hu, "Energy Based Acoustic Source Localization," in Proc. of the 2nd International Workshop on Information Processing in Sensor Networks, PARC, Palo Alto, CA, Apr. 2003.
12. Jim Waldo, Ken Arnold, et. al., "The Jini Specifications (2nd edition)," Addison-Wesley Pub Co. Dec., 2000.
13. Qixin Wang, "Mote's throughput test report and source code," in http://www.andrew.cmu.edu/ weizhang/wsn/documents.html
14. B. Warneke, B. Atwood, K. S. J. Pister, "Smart Dust Mote Forerunners," in Proc. of the Fourteenth Annual International Conference on Microelectromechanical Systems (MEMES 2001), Interlaken, Switzerland, Jan. 21–25, 2001, pp. 357–360.

A Robust Data Delivery Protocol for Large Scale Sensor Networks

Fan Ye, Gary Zhong, Songwu Lu, and Lixia Zhang

Computer Science Department, University of California
Los Angeles, CA 90095
{yefan, gzhong, slu, lixia}@cs.ucla.edu

Abstract. Recent technology advances in low-cost, low-power chip designs have made feasible the deployment of large-scale sensor networks. Although data forwarding has been among the first set of issues explored in sensor networking, how to reliably deliver sensing data through a vast field of small, vulnerable sensors remains a research challenge. In this paper we present GRAdient Broadcast (GRAB), a new set of mechanisms and protocols which is designed specifically for robust data delivery in spite of unreliable nodes and fallible wireless links. Similar to previous work [1], GRAB builds and maintains a cost field, providing each sensor in the network the direction to forward sensing data. Different from all the existing approaches, however, GRAB forwards data along an interleaved mesh from each source to the receiver. The width of the forwarding mesh is controlled by the amount of credit carried in each data message, allowing the degree of delivery robustness to be adjusted by the sender. GRAB design harnesses the advantage of large scale and relies on the collective efforts of multiple nodes to deliver data, without dependency on any individual ones. As demonstrated in our extensive simulation experiments, GRAB can successfully deliver above 90% of data with relatively low energy cost even under adverse conditions of up to 30% node failures compounded with 15% link packet losses.

1 Introduction

Recent technology advances in low-cost, low-power chip designs have made it economically feasible to deploy large-scale sensor networks. Thousands or even millions of small, inexpensive, and low-power sensors, such as Berkeley Motes[2], can be quickly deployed to monitor a vast field. The sensors collectively sense the environment and deliver the sensing data via a wireless channel. In near future such sensor networks may play an important role in both civil applications such as agriculture as well as disaster recovery and military surveillance. On the other hand, the above mentioned potential applications also present great challenges to reliable sensing data delivery. Wireless communications among the small, power-limited sensor nodes are prone to errors. Severe operational conditions (e.g. strong wind or high temperature) and disasters (e.g. fire or earthquake) may easily destroy individual sensors, resulting in a constantly changing topology. Furthermore, the short transmission range of small sensors also means that

F. Zhao and L. Guibas (Eds.): IPSN 2003, LNCS 2634, pp. 658–673, 2003.

sensing data may travel through a large number of hops to reach intended destinations, with potential delivery errors and unexpected node failures at each hop.

In this paper we propose GRAdient Broadcast (GRAB) to address the problem of robust data forwarding to a data collecting point (called the *sink*) using unreliable sensor nodes with error-prone wireless links. The objects or events to be monitored are called *stimuli*. All the sensor nodes that detect the same stimulus collectively select the one with strongest sensing signal to generate a sensing report. We call such a node a data *source*. Although several data forwarding protocols have been designed for sensor networks, such as Directed Diffusion [3] and TTDD [4], they typically assume a relatively stable sensor network where nodes do not fail frequently and unexpectedly.

GRAB achieves robust data delivery through building and maintaining a *cost field* for the sink. Each node keeps a cost for forwarding a packet along a certain path to the sink. Nodes "closer" to the sink have smaller costs. A packet can follow the direction of decreasing cost to reach the sink. In stead of a sender appoints which receivers to continue forwarding, GRAB lets each receiver decides whether it should forward by comparing its cost to that of the sender. Multiple such paths exist between a source and the sink.

To further control the redundancy of the multiple paths, a source assigns a *credit* to the packets it sends out. The credit is some extra budget that allows multiple copies of a packet be forwarded over a mesh of *interleaved* paths, each of which has a cost not greater than the total budget. The amount of credit determines the "width" of the mesh, thus the degree of robustness and overhead.

GRAB design harnesses the advantage of large scale. It achieves system robustness by relying on collective efforts from multiple sensors without dependency on any individual ones. A packet is forwarded over multiple paths, which improves reliability. Such paths interleave and recover each other from node failures or link errors, further increasing robustness. Since it is the receivers, not the sender that decide which nodes should forward, a sender merely broadcasts a packet without worrying repairing failed nodes or broken links. The packet is delivered to the sink by those surviving nodes. This receiver-based design eliminates the overhead of repairing paths of failed nodes or broken links. The credit provides a means to trade off between robustness and total cost. A source can assign a credit that achieves required robustness without causing excessive redundancy.

The rest of the paper is organized as follows: We present the design of GRAB in Section 2. Then we evaluate its performance in Section 3. We discuss future work to GRAB in Section 4. In Section 5, we first describe the differences between GRAB and existing work in sensor networking area, then report our performance comparison study of GRAB with an existing protocol [3]. Section 6 concludes the paper.

2   GRAB Data Forwarding Protocol

2.1   Design Overview

In this paper we assume the following sensor network model: Large numbers of small, stationary sensor nodes are densely deployed over a field. A stimulus is detected by multiple nearby sensor nodes for reliable sensing. Nodes are equipped with CSMA MACs. The lack of RTS/CTS/ACK makes packets more easily lost than those sent with 802.11 DCF. External noises and disturbances may further exacerbate the condition. Sensor nodes fail unpredictably due to the harsh environment. Nodes can tune their transmitting powers to control how far the transmission may reach. Such power adjustments save energy and reduce collisions whenever possible[1]. We use an example of one sink and one stimulus to illustrate how GRAB works.

To collect data reports, the sink first builds a *cost field* by propagating advertisement (ADV) packets in the network. The cost at a node is the minimum energy overhead to forward a packet from this node to the sink along a path. We assume each node can estimate the cost of sending data to nearby neighbors. The costs of all nodes in the network form the cost field[2]. If we imagine each node be elevated to a height proportional to its cost, the whole cost field would look like a funnel(see Figure1 for a illustration): nodes "closer" to the sink have smaller costs and are "lower", while those "farther" away have greater costs and are "higher".

The cost field gives the global direction towards the sink implicitly. When a node sends a packet, it does not designate which nodes are the next hop. It just includes its own cost in the packet and broadcasts the packet. Only neighbors with smaller costs may continue forwarding the packet. Neighbors with higher or equal costs silently drop the packet because they are at the "wrong" direction. Thus packets travel in a cost field like water flows down to the bottom of a funnel: they follow the direction of decreasing cost to reach the bottom of the cost field, which is the sink. The paths of decreasing cost interleave and form a mesh.

The selection of the source follows the same mechanism. We want only one node to generate the report since it would be a waste of resources if every node detecting the stimulus sends a report. The stimulus creates a field of sensing signal strength, the "shape" of which is similar to that of the cost field. Each node broadcasts a message indicating its signal strength (with some random delay to avoid collision). A node rebroadcasts its signal strength whenever it hears a neighbor's message with a weaker signal, but stops broadcasting when it hears a stronger one. This way, messages roll towards the center of the signal strength field. Finally the node with the strongest signal generates a report. We call this node the Center of Stimulus (COS).

---

[1] Some existing hardware [2] already have different levels of transmitting power.

[2] The cost may take different forms such as the hop number, the energy overhead or even physical distance. The current energy form is meant to save the scarce energy resources of nodes.

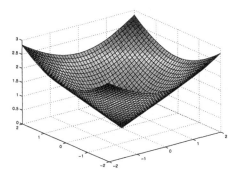

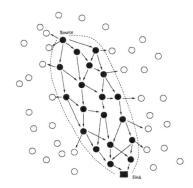

Fig. 1. The "shape" of the cost field is like a funnel, with the sink sitting at the bottom. Packets follow the decreasing cost direction to reach the bottom of the cost field, which is the sink

Fig. 2. The forwarding mesh starts from a source and ends at a sink. All black nodes within the mesh participate data delivery and forward the packet to the sink collectively. Notice that some nodes outside of the mesh also receive the packet but do not forward it.

COS election and data forwarding utilize the same concept of a funnel-shaped field. The differences are: The signal strength field already exists in the physical world, whereas the cost field is an artifact created by the sink; nodes farther to the stimulus have weaker signals, but nodes farther to the sink have greater costs; when a stimulus is detected, data come from all directions to the center, but for forwarding, they come only from the direction of the source.

After the cost field is built, we want to limit the "width" of the forwarding mesh. Otherwise the packet would follow every possible path of decreasing cost, creating excessive redundancy and wasting resources. Ideally, the mesh starts at the source and expands to a certain width quickly, then it keeps the width while going towards the sink until finally it reaches the sink (see Figure 2 for an example). The width of the forwarding mesh determines the robustness of data forwarding.

To control the "width", a source assigns a credit α to the packets it sends out. The credit is some extra budget that can be consumed to forward the packet. The sum of the credit and the source' cost (i.e., $\alpha + C_{source}$) is the total budget that can be used to send a packet to the sink along a path. A packet can take any path that requires a cost less than or equal to, but not beyond, the total budget.

The amount of credit controls the redundancy of the mesh flexibly. If there is no credit, the packet can only be forwarded along the single minimum cost path of the source; when more credit is added to increase the budget, more paths are available to deliver the packet. Such paths surround the minimum cost path and form the forwarding mesh *dynamically* through the combined effect of the cost field and the credit value carried in each packet.

A final point we would like to make before presenting the design is the number of sources and sinks the GRAB design can support. To simplify the presentation we use a simple model of one stationary source (COS) and one stationary sink. However we point out that the GRAB supports data forwarding from multiple, mobile *stimuli* as well. When a stimulus, such as a tank, moves through the field, a different COS sensor is elected to generate the report; the old COS node stops reporting automatically because it finds itself no longer at the center of the stimulus. For multiple stimuli multiple COS's are elected. The exact details of COS election are not presented in this paper, which focuses on data forwarding.

In the rest of this section, we give a brief summary in Section 2.2 about an algorithm proposed in a previous work [5] to build the cost field efficiently. Then we present the GRAB forwarding algorithm in Section 2.3.

2.2 Building and Maintaining the Cost Field

The cost field can be built in the following straightforward way. A sink broadcasts an advertisement packet (ADV) announcing a cost of 0. Each node initially has a cost of ∞. When hearing an ADV packet containing the cost of the sender, a node obtains a cost by adding the link cost to the cost of the sender. It compares this cost to its old one and sets the new cost as the smaller of the two. Whenever it obtains a cost smaller than the old one, it also broadcasts an ADV packet containing the new cost. The "rippling" of ADV packets from the sink outwards builds the cost field for the sink[3].

The problem with the above method is excessive ADV messages, which prevent it from scaling to large numbers of nodes. Before a node settles with the minimum cost, it may hear many ADV packets, each of which results in a smaller cost than the previous one. Thus the node broadcasts many ADV packets. To build the cost field in a scalable manner, we proposed a waiting algorithm in [5] and proved that the waiting algorithm ensures each node broadcasts only once, and with its minimum cost.

The value of a node's cost depends on the topology. The topology changes as nodes fail, exhaust energy, or new nodes are deployed. The initially built cost field thus becomes inaccurate. Although the GRAB forwarding protocol is highly robust against inaccuracies in cost field (we will see that in Section 3), the cost field should be refreshed on time to keep the forwarding efficient.

To avoid the overhead of periodic refreshing, we choose an event-driven design. The sink keeps a profile about the recent history of data reports from the source. It includes the success ratio (packets are numbered so a sink can calculate success ratio), the average consumed budget, the average number of copies received per packet and the average number of hops traveled for recent reports. Once a new packet is received, the sink compares the parameters of the packet to those in the past. If a parameter differs from its past by a certain threshold, the sink broadcasts a new ADV packet to rebuild the cost field. Due to space limit, more details are in a technical report[6].

---

[3] This is originally how GRAB gets its name. "Gradient" stands for the cost, the broadcast of gradients builds the cost field. Notice that although the same word is used, the "gradient" here is completely different from that in [3]

The rationale behind the event-driven refreshing is that topology changes bring variations in data delivery. By monitoring certain parameters which reflect the quality of data delivery, we can tell how much change has happened. Only major changes that make the data delivery deteriorate beyond acceptable levels trigger refreshings. The forwarding algorithm itself is robust enough to withstand significant amount of minor changes, which will be shown in Section 3.

Before we proceed to the forwarding algorithm, we want to point out that [5] solves only the problem of building the cost field. It does not address robust data delivery with unreliable sensor nodes, which is the centerpiece of this paper.

2.3   Realizing a Robust Forwarding Mesh by the Credit

This section describes how to build a forwarding mesh by the credit. To realize the mesh we need to address three issues.

Issues in Realizing the Mesh. First, how to expand the mesh quickly starting from the source. To be robust, the mesh should be wide enough to contain sufficient parallel nodes (paths). When there are node failures or packet losses, a sufficient width ensures some nodes can still deliver packets successfully to the next hop. Since there is only one node (the source) at the first hop, we need to expand the mesh to a sufficient width quickly. Otherwise, the delivery can fail before the mesh is wide enough.

Second, after the mesh has expanded sufficiently, how to maintain the width. Due to node failures and packet losses, the number of parallel nodes that forward a packet tend to decrease from one hop to the next. A failed node or a node that does not receive the packet can reduce the number of parallel forwarding nodes. If no measure is taken to counteract this tendency, the mesh can narrow down later.

Finally, how to prevent packets from traveling along some devious paths or diverting too much from the direction of the sink. For any sender, roughly half of its neighbors have smaller costs. If all such directions of decreasing costs are followed, the forwarding could diffuse into a sector-shape, in which many packets divert significantly from the direction of the sink. We want to stop packets from following such diverting paths.

Solutions to the Issues. To address the first two issues, we divide the total amount of credit among different hops in the right way. Specifically, we want beginning hops to consume larger shares of the credit, while later hops consume some, but smaller shares of the credit. This is because the share of credit a node receives decides whether it can expand the mesh. If a node does not have any "bonus" to use but has only a budget equal to its cost, it should reach only its next hop neighbor on the minimum cost path, without expanding the mesh. When a node has some "bonus" (credit) to use, it can consume more budget, reaching more receivers and expanding the mesh. Beginning hops use more credit to expand the mesh quickly while later hops do not need as much credit because they do not need to expand the mesh. However, they should also receive certain credit to maintain the width. Otherwise node failures and packet losses can "narrow down" the mesh.

Now, how to solve the last issue? If a packet has been traveling on a quite devious path, or divert from the direction of the sink too much, it would consume much credit, without traveling proportionately close towards the sink. An analogy to this is spending most of a month's budget in a few days. Thus by comparing the remaining credit to how far it still ahead we can detect and terminate such packets.

To calculate the remaining credit, we let each packet carry certain information, so a node can first calculate how much credit has been consumed. To tell how "far" a node is to the sink, it uses a threshold function, whose value tells the relative "position" of this node between the source and the sink. By comparing the remaining credit to the threshold value, we can tell if the packet has already consumed too much credit, or there is still enough to use. We choose the format of the threshold function such that it achieves desired division of credit among different hops, solving the first two issues (an analysis will be shown later). We first explain what are carried in a packet, then present the detailed forwarding algorithm.

The Forwarding Algorithm. A packet carries the following fields:

- α: the amount of credit assigned to the packet at the source. A node needs it to calculate how much credit remains. This field does not change as the packet travels towards the sink.
- C_{source}: the cost of the source to send a packet to the sink. It is used to calculate the threshold. This field does not change at different hops, either.
- $P_{consumed}$: the amount of budget that has been consumed from the source to the current hop. It is set to the cost used by the source to broadcast the packet initially and increased by the amount used to forward the packet at each hop.

After a COS assigns an α to a data report, it fills the above three fields and broadcasts the packet. To prevent loops, only receivers with smaller costs may forward the packet. Thus a packet is forwarded by successive nodes of decreasing costs, leading to the sink finally.

If a receiver finds it has a smaller cost, it calculates and compare two ratios R_α and R_{thresh} as follows.

$$R_\alpha = \frac{REP.\alpha - \alpha_{used}}{REP.\alpha} \tag{1}$$

$$R_{thresh} = (\frac{C_{receiver}}{REP.C_{source}})^2 \tag{2}$$

where

$$\alpha_{used} = REP.P_{consumed} + C_{receiver} - REP.C_{source} \tag{3}$$

In the above equations, α_{used} stands for the amount of credit that has been consumed. REP is the report packet received, $C_{receiver}$ is the cost of this node. $REP.P_{consumed} + C_{receiver}$ is the least amount of total budget required should this node forward the packet via any path to the sink. This minimum amount is achieved when the packet took the minimum cost path from this node to the sink. The "extra" amount of this to C_{source}, would be the credit consumed. So Eqn.3 is at least how much credit has been used. Thus R_α represents the fraction of credit that is still available for this node and later hops. R_{thresh} indicates how "far" the node is to the sink. Both R_α and R_{thresh} range between 0 and 1.

The node then compares R_α to R_{thresh}. If R_α is greater than R_{thresh}, we consider the node has sufficient credit to use. It broadcasts at a power to reach multiple neighbors towards the sink (We define neighbors with smaller costs as this node's *nearer neighbors*). How much power depends on the degree of robustness desired. A higher robustness requires more nearer neighbors. In current design, we let the node broadcast the packet at a power to reach three closest nearer neighbors.[4] The node knows this power from the ADV messages it received during cost field building[5]. It increases $P_{consumed}$ by how much budget it is going to consume in broadcasting. Then it broadcasts the packet to reach those nearer neighbors. Different forwarding nodes on the same hop may reach the same nearer neighbor(s) on the next hop. This is how the paths interleave.

If R_α is smaller, however, the node does not have sufficient credit and should forward the packet along its minimum cost path to minimize the total cost. Thus the node sends the packet to the next hop neighbor on its minimum cost path. It increases $P_{consumed}$ in the sent packet similarly.

To reduce collisions, a forwarding node always waits for some random time before sending the packet, so that senders on the same hops do not broadcast simultaneously and result in collisions.

It is possible that a node receives multiple copies of the same packet from different upstream nodes, and each copy has enough credit to use. To suppress such duplicates, each node maintains a cache which stores the signatures of recently forwarded packets. The signature of a packet can be the header of the packet, or a hash of the packet calculated on demand. It serves as an identifier to distinguish packets. If the signature of a received packet is found in the cache, the packet is dropped. Notice that this is an optimization technique, not a fundamental requirement of the design.

Analysis of Credit Allotment. Now we give an analysis of the amount of credit that can be used at any hop. For a node A, its cost is C_A. The maximum share of credit is consumed when the remaining credit ratio R_α is equal to threshold R_{thresh}, i.e.

$$\frac{\alpha - (P_{consumed} + C_A - C_{source})}{\alpha} = \left(\frac{C_A}{C_{source}}\right)^2 \tag{4}$$

---

[4] We call the number of nearer neighbors to reach *the branching factor* . It represents a tradeoff between robustness and energy. Experiments show that three is an appropriate number.

Taking derivatives of C_A for $P_{consumed}$, we have

$$\frac{\partial P_{consumed}}{\partial C_A} = -\left(1 + 2\alpha \frac{C_A}{C_{source}^2}\right).$$

Then, the allowed energy consumption at a hop is:

$$\Delta P_{consumed} \leqq -\Delta C_A - 2\alpha \frac{\Delta C_A}{C_{source}^2} C_A \tag{5}$$

In Eqn.5, $\Delta P_{consumed}$ is the amount of cost that can be consumed at A. ΔC_A denotes the minimum required cost to go to the next hop, which is the link cost to the next hop. $2\alpha \frac{\Delta C_A}{C_{source}^2} C_A$ is roughly the maximum amount of credit that can be used at this hop It is proportional to C_A, the cost from this node to the sink. Thus the higher a node's cost, the more credit it can use. Therefore, as a packet travels from source to sink, it is allowed to consume more credit near the source, and less at later hops. This way, the forwarding mesh can expand aggressively initially, while still having some credit later to maintain the width. We will evaluate other forms of threshold function in Section 3.

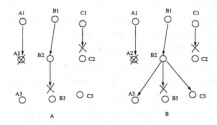

Fig. 3. A: any single node failure or packet loss ruins a single path; B: interleaving paths can recover each other from failures or packet losses

Implicit and Interleaving Paths Add to Robustness. GRAB achieves robustness through the redundancy in the mesh. We carefully make the design choices so that the paths in the mesh are *implicit* and *interleaving*. Implicit means a sender does not appoint which node should continue forwarding. It is up to each receiver to decide whether or not it should forward. When there are node failures or packet losses, each node still perform the same operations. As long as there are some surviving nodes that can continue forwarding the packet, data delivery will not fail. The lack of explicit paths eliminates the need to repair them when they are broken.

Interleaving means these paths are not disjoint, they intersect with each other. This is more robust than multiple disjoint paths. The failure of any single node or loss of packet along a single path destroy the forwarding on the path. When there are many hops between the source and the sink, a single path has a high probability to fail. In contrast, interleaving paths in a forwarding mesh can recover the node failures and packet losses of each other. For example (Figure 3A), there exist three disjoint paths A1-A2-A3, B1-B2-B3 and C1-C2-C3. If A2 fails and both B3 and C2 do not receive the packet, all three paths fail to deliver the packet. In contrast(Figure 3B), given the same failure of A2 and loss of packet at B3 and C2, A3 and C3 can still receive from the broadcast of B2. Thus path A and C can be recovered by B2. Similarly, path B can be recovered by broadcasts from A3 or C3 later.

3   Performance Evaluation

In this section we evaluate the performance of GRAB through simulations. We implemented GRAB forwarding protocol in Parsec [7] due to its ability to scale to large numbers of nodes. We select sensor hardware parameters similar to Berkeley motes [2]. The maximum transmission range of a node is 10 meters, each node can adjusts its transmitting power to reach a given range. We simulated both the two ray ground and the free space signal propagation models. Due to space limit we present the results from the former only[5]. The power consumptions of full power transmitting, receiving and idling are 60mW, 12mW and 12mW. The transmission (receiving) time for a packet is 10 ms. In most scenarios, we use a field size of $150 \times 150 m^2$ where 1200 nodes are uniformly distributed. One sink and one source sit in opposite corners of the field. The source generates a report packet every 10 seconds. In each run 100 reports are generated. The average number of hops of the source' minimum cost path is about 70 hops. To simulate fallible wireless links, packets are dropped at the receiver with a probability, which is called packet loss rate. Node failures are uniformly distributed over time. The fraction of failed nodes is defined as the node failure rate.

To test if GRAB achieves its goal in robust data delivery, we measure the *success ratio*, which is the ratio of the number of report packets successfully received at the sink to the total number generated at the source. It indicates the degree of robustness of GRAB to forward data in the presence of node failures and packet losses. To see if GRAB satisfies robustness at the cost of excessive overhead, we also measure *total energy consumption* and *control packet overhead*. Total energy consumption is the total amount of energy consumed in the simulation. It shows how much energy GRAB incurs for robust data delivery. Control packet overhead is the number of control packets in the simulation. The results are averaged over 10 different runs.

We first evaluate the impact of control parameters, including the amount of credit and the threshold function; then the impact of various environmental settings, including node failure rate, packet loss rate, node density and the size of the field.

---

[5] Results from the free space model are similar

3.1 Impact of Control Parameters

Different amounts of credit α. The amount of credit directly affects the degree of robustness. To find how much credit α is enough for robust delivery, we vary the amount of credit from 1 to 10 times that of the source' cost to reach the sink. A fixed 15% node failure and a fixed 15% packet loss rate are present in all runs.

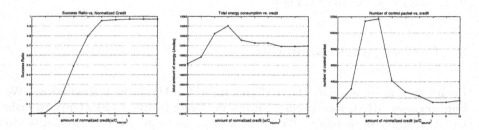

Fig. 4. Success ratio for different α **Fig. 5.** Energy consumption for different α **Fig. 6.** Control packet number for different α

Figure 4 shows the success ratio as a function of α, which is normalized to the source' cost. When the credit is small, the chance of successful delivery is also very small. When $\alpha \leq 2$, almost all reports are lost. This is because there are many hops (around 70) from the source to the sink, along which node failures and packet losses happen frequently. When α increases, the success ratio improves steadily. $\alpha = 5$ gives an 80% success ratio. When the amount of credit is sufficient, the forwarding is very robust. For $\alpha \geq 6$, over 95% report packets are successfully delivered to the sink[6]. This shows that credit decides the degree of robustness. A sufficient credit ensure good robustness.

To find whether GRAB consumes excessive energy to ensure robustness, Figure 5 gives the total energy consumption as a function of α. When α is small($\alpha = 1$), about 16050 Joules are consumed. As α increases, the total energy also increases. At $\alpha = 4$, total energy reaches 16058 Joules, which is 8 Joules more. This is because more energy is used in data delivery and building the cost field. When $\alpha \geq 6$, the total energy decreases to 16054 Joules. The fluctuation is very small compared to the total amount. Thus GRAB is efficient and does not achieve robustness at the cost of excessive energy consumption.

The decrease of total energy when α is high is a little counter-intuitive because more data packets are successfully delivered and more energy should be used. Actually the decrease comes from the reduced control packets. Figure 6 shows the control packet overhead. When α is small(≤ 2) or big(≥ 6), the delivery quality is constantly low or high. The measured parameters about delivery

---

[6] A sufficient $\alpha \geq 6$ because we use transmitting energy as the cost. It does not mean 6 times more total energy is consumed. In two-ray ground model, the transmitting power increases linearly to the 4th power of distance. Six times in power means 1.56 times in distance on average. In free space model, $\alpha \geq 1.2$ is sufficient under the same topologies.

quality at the sink seldom differ from their recent history beyond the thresholds. Thus less refreshings happen, and less total energy consumption. The number of control packet is below 3100, and on average less than 3 cost field (re)buildings happen. When α is medium(from 3 to 5), the delivery quality is not stable, and the measured parameters differ from their recent averages beyond the thresholds more often, triggering more refreshings and thus more energy consumption. The number of control packets reaches 11500, and about 10 cost field (re)buildings happen.

The different control packet overhead also shows that the event-driven cost field refreshing can adapt to the delivery quality. When the delivery quality is stable(either constantly low or constantly high), more refreshings cannot improve the success ratio much(the improvement is less than 1%). So GRAB has less refreshings. When the delivery quality is not stable, the sink refreshes the cost field more often, thus more packets which otherwise could not reach the sink are successfully delivered(the improvement is about 10%).

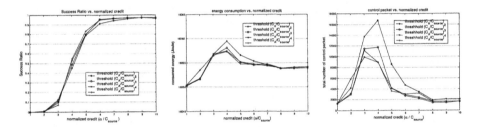

Fig. 7. Success ratio for different threshold functions

Fig. 8. Energy consumption for different threshold functions

Fig. 9. Control packet number for different threshold functions

Different threshold functions. The form of the threshold function decides how credit is alloted among different hops. We evaluate four different threshold functions: (C_A/C_{source}), $(C_A/C_{source})^2$, $(C_A/C_{source})^3$ and $(C_A/C_{source})^4$, where C_A is the cost of the receiving node A and C_{source} is the cost of the source to reach the sink. We repeat the same simulations in Section 3.1. The success ratio, energy consumption and control packet overhead are shown in Figure 7, 8 and 9, respectively. The success ratios for the threshold (C_A/C_{source}) is smaller than the those of the other three. Its energy consumption and control packet overhead are obviously higher, while the other three have similar energy consumption and control packet overhead. The metrics do not change much for the latter three threshold functions($(C_A/C_{source})^2$, $(C_A/C_{source})^3$ and $(C_A/C_{source})^4$). This is because they all give more credit to beginning hops and still allot some amount to later hops[7]. Thus the forwarding mesh can expand quickly and maintain a certain width later.

---

[7] Similar analysis on credit allotment can be made by following the analysis in Section 2.3.

3.2   Impact of Node Failures and Packet Losses

We evaluate the robustness of GRAB by studying how node failures and packet losses affect the success ratio in this section. We first vary the node failure rate from 5% to 50%, while using a fixed 15% packet loss rate. Then we vary the packet loss rate from 5% to 50%, while using a fixed 15% node failure rate. The amount of credit α is set to 6. This is the value that achieves higher than 95% success ratio in the previous section.

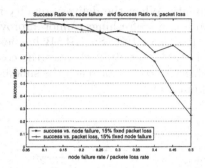

Fig. 10. Success ratio for node failures and success ratio for packet losses

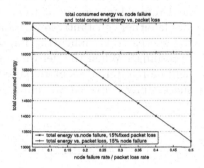

Fig. 11. Energy consumption for node failures and energy consumption for packet losses

Figure 10 shows the success ratio as functions of node failure rate and packet loss rate. We first look at the impact of node failures. The success ratio is above 95% for node failure rates of up to 20%. As the node failure rate continues to increase, although the success ratio tends to decrease, GRAB still maintains very high degrees of robustness. The success ratio remains above 85% when 35% nodes fail, and is around 70% in the extreme case when half of the nodes fail. This shows that GRAB is robust even with severe node failures. For packet loss rates of up to 25%, the success ratio is above 90%. After 25%, the success ratio drops quickly. With a packet loss rate of 65%, the success ratio is about 67%. Compared to node failure cases, GRAB is less robust when the packet loss rate is high. This is because no acknowledgement or retransmission is used to recover a lost packet in CSMA MAC. For node failures, however, as long as there are still enough surviving nodes, a cost field refreshing can resume data delivery. Nevertheless, GRAB delivers over 80% reports successfully for node failure rates or packet loss rates of up to 30%. The high success ratio also demonstrates that GRAB is highly tolerate to inaccurate cost fields because node failures and packet losses both cause inaccuracies during cost field building.

The energy consumptions are shown in Figure 11. When node failure increases, the energy decreases linearly. This is because the idle energy dominates the total energy consumption. A higher node failure rates means more node failures, thus proportionally less energy consumption. For different packet loss rates, the energy remains almost constant around 16054, increasing less than 6 Joules as the packet loss rate grows from 5% to 50%. Again, although less energy is consumed for data delivery, more is spent in rebuilding the cost field. Thus the total energy increases a little.

4 Future Work

We plan to further improve GRAB to make the credit assignment adaptive. The sink may include some information that reflects recent data delivery quality when sending ADV packets. A source can use this feedback to choose an appropriate credit to adapt to network conditions. In addition, the allotment of credit among different hops can also adapt to local failure and noise characteristics. Nodes in a neighborhood with more severe conditions can use greater shares of the credit if they can measure local failures or packet losses. So far we have been focusing on one stationary sink. When there are multiple sinks, each needs to build its own cost field. Every node keeps one cost per sink. This per-sink state may not allow GRAB to scale to large numbers of sinks directly. Sink mobility is not well addressed in the current design, either. Although a sink can simply rebuilds its cost field every time it moves to a new location, such rebuildings may consume much energy and bandwidth when the sink is highly mobile. We plan to apply landmark routing [8] to address the multiple, mobile sink problem in the future.

5 Related Work

There have been a plethora of research efforts in sensor networking area in the last few years. Directed diffusion [3] is a data forwarding protocol designed for sensor networks where a sink floods its interests to build reverse paths from all potential sources to the sink. GRAB also builds a field, but it is a scalar field of cost values, not one of reverse path vectors. Diffusion uses reinforcement and negative reinforcement mechanisms to select a high quality path for the data flow from each source and deactivate low quality ones. Braided diffusion [9] is a variant of directed diffusion. It maintains multiple "braided" paths as backup. When a node on the primary path fails, data can go on an alternate path. Both Directed diffusion and Braided diffusion establish *explicit* paths to forward data; each node forwards data to a specific next hop neighbor. In contract, a sender in GRAB simply transmits data to the radio channel without appointing any neighbor as the next hop; each receiving node decides whether it should further forward the data. There is no explict path in GRAB; data simply follows whichever surviving nodes to reach the destination. Diffusion combats against errors and failures by periodically re-flooding the interests messages to repair the paths. GRAB achieves robustness by exploiting the redundancy from interleaving paths in the forwarding mesh. Diffusion detects forwarding loops by caching previous packets. In GRAB, because packets can only go along the decreasing cost direction (toward the sink), no loop can form.

TTDD [4] solves the problem to delivering data to mobile sinks that are in constant motion. It builds a grid structure for each source. The impact of a mobile sink is confined within a local cell. Data delivery and query forwarding traverse the grid tier and the local cell tier in reverse order. TTDD does not address the robustness issue. Only a single path is used to forward data.

Both Diffusion and TTDD work with 802.11 DCF MAC which has RTS/CTS/ACK. They have yet to demonstrate their robustness using nodes with less reliable CSMA MACs.

Gradient Routing [1] shares similarity in design with GRAB in that it also builds and uses a cost field. However it has no mechanism to control the degree of redundancy in data forwarding. When a sender broadcasts a packet, all neighboring nodes with lower costs forward the packet, leading to much redundancy and higher energy consumption. In GRAB, the credit carried in each packet effectively controls the width of the forwarding mesh, thus the degree of redundancy and energy consumption.

Energy Aware Routing [10] also builds per-sink cost fields to direct data delivery but it uses single path only. A sender probabilistically pick a receiver to forward the packet. GRAB has multiple interleaving paths forming a mesh and senders do not decide who are receivers.

Redundant mesh forwarding is also proposed in [11,12] for robust multicast delivery in wireless ad hoc networks. However these designs exchange control messages to establish explicit path states at each node; the forwarding mesh is made of a set of explicit paths. In contrast, the forwarding mesh in GRAB is *dynamically* formed by the combined effect of the cost field and the credit value carried in each packet, which allows data to flow along any path within the mesh.

Routing has been a very active research area in the context of ad hoc networks, many proposals have appeared in the literature [13,14]. However, they are not designed for sensor networks and do not address the unique issues in sensor networks.

6   Conclusions

As the deployment of large scale sensor networks showing up on the horizon today, we are facing new research challenges of providing reliable sensing and robust data delivery via vast numbers of potentially unreliable sensors. Compared to data networks in general, individual sensors have much lower utilization but potentially much higher failure rate. These special requirements demand new solutions to reliable data delivery. In this paper, we presented the GRAB design which ensures robust data delivery over large numbers of hops of small, unreliable sensor nodes and error-prone wireless channels. GRAB exploits the large scale property of sensor networks and achieves robust data delivery through controlled mesh forwarding. GRAB builds and maintains a cost field for each destination. It controls the "width" of the forwarding mesh, thus the degree of redundancy, by the amount of credit carried in each data packet. Extensive simulations confirmed GRAB's effectiveness in providing reliable delivery under severe operational conditions, demonstrating the principle that a reliable system can be built out of unreliable components.

References

1. Poor, R.: Gradient Routing in Ad Hoc Networks. (http://www.media.mit.edu/pia/Research/ESP/texts/poorieeepaper.pdf)
2. Hill, J., Szewczyk, R., Woo, A., Hollar, S., Culler, D., Pister, K.: System Architecture Directions for Networked Sensors. International Conference on Architectural Support for Programming Languages and Operating Systems (ASPLOS-IX) (2000)
3. Intanagonwiwat, C., Govindan, R., Estrin, D.: Directed Diffusion: A Scalable and Robust Communication Paradigm for Sensor Networks. ACM International Conference on Mobile Computing and Networking (MOBICOM'00) (2000)
4. Ye, F., Luo, H., Cheng, J., Lu, S., Zhang, L.: A two-tier data dissemination model for large-scale wireless sensor networks. In: Mobicom. (2002)
5. Ye, F., Chen, A., Lu, S., Zhang, L.: A Scalable Solution to Minimum Cost Forwarding in Large Scale Sensor Networks. The Tenth International Conference on Computer Communications and Networks (2001)
6. Ye, F., Lu, S., Zhang, L.: GRAdient Broadcast: A Robust, Long-lived Large Sensor Network. http://irl.cs.ucla.edu/papers/grab-tech-report.ps (2001)
7. Parallel Computing Laboratory, Computer Science Department, U.: Parsec. (http://pcl.cs.ucla.edu/projects/parsec/)
8. Tsuchiya, P.F.: The landmark hierarchy: A new hierarchy for routing in very large networks. Computer Communication Review **18** (August 1988)
9. Ganesan, D., Govindan, R., Shenker, S., Estrin, D.: Highly-Resilient, Energy-Efficient Multipath Routing in Wireless Sensor Networks. ACM Mobile Computing and Communications Review, Vol. 5, No. 4 (October 2001.)
10. Shah, R.C., Rabaey, J.: Energy Aware Routing for Low Energy Ad Hoc Sensor Networks. WCNC (2002)
11. Chiang, C.C., Gerla, M., Zhang, L.: Forwarding group multicast protocol (FGMP) for multihop, mobile wireless networks. Cluster Computing **1** (1998) 187–196
12. Garcia-Luna-Aceves, J.J., Madruga, E.L.: A multicast routing protocol for ad-hoc networks. In: INFOCOM (2). (1999) 784–792
13. Johnson, D.B., Maltz, D.A.: Dynamic Source Routing in Ad-hoc Wireless Networks. Mobile Computing, Kluwer Academic Publishers (1996)
14. Perkins, C.: Ad-Hoc On Demand Distance Vector Routing (AODV). Internet-Draft (November 1997)

Author Index

Lecture Notes in Computer Science

For information about Vols. 1–2548

please contact your bookseller or Springer-Verlag

Vol. 2587: P.J. Lee, C.H. Lim (Eds.), Information Security and Cryptology – ICISC 2002. Proceedings, 2002. XI, 536 pages. 2003.

Vol. 2588: A. Gelbukh (Ed.), Computational Linguistics and Intelligent Text Processing. Proceedings, 2003. XV, 648 pages. 2003.

Vol. 2589: E. Börger, A. Gargantini, E. Riccobene (Eds.), Abstract State Machines 2003. Proceedings, 2003. XI, 427 pages. 2003.

Vol. 2590: S. Bressan, A.B. Chaudhri, M.L. Lee, J.X. Yu, Z. Lacroix (Eds.), Efficiency and Effectiveness of XML Tools and Techniques and Data Integration over the Web. Proceedings, 2002. X, 259 pages. 2003.

Vol. 2591: M. Aksit, M. Mezini, R. Unland (Eds.), Objects, Components, Architectures, Services, and Applications for a Networked World. Proceedings, 2002. XI, 431 pages. 2003.

Vol. 2592: R. Kowalczyk, J.P. Müller, H. Tianfield, R. Unland (Eds.), Agent Technologies, Infrastructures, Tools, and Applications for E-Services. Proceedings, 2002. XVII, 371 pages. 2003. (Subseries LNAI).

Vol. 2593: A.B. Chaudhri, M. Jeckle, E. Rahm, R. Unland (Eds.), Web, Web-Services, and Database Systems. Proceedings, 2002. XI, 311 pages. 2003.

Vol. 2594: A. Asperti, B. Buchberger, J.H. Davenport (Eds.), Mathematical Knowledge Management. Proceedings, 2003. X, 225 pages. 2003.

Vol. 2595: K. Nyberg, H. Heys (Eds.), Selected Areas in Cryptography. Proceedings, 2002. XI, 405 pages. 2003.

Vol. 2597: G. Păun, G. Rozenberg, A. Salomaa, C. Zandron (Eds.), Membrane Computing. Proceedings, 2002. VIII, 423 pages. 2003.

Vol. 2598: R. Klein, H.-W. Six, L. Wegner (Eds.), Computer Science in Perspective. X, 357 pages. 2003.

Vol. 2599: E. Sherratt (Ed.), Telecommunications and beyond: The Broader Applicability of SDL and MSC. Proceedings, 2002. X, 253 pages. 2003.

Vol. 2600: S. Mendelson, A.J. Smola, Advanced Lectures on Machine Learning. Proceedings, 2002. IX, 259 pages. 2003. (Subseries LNAI).

Vol. 2601: M. Ajmone Marsan, G. Corazza, M. Listanti, A. Roveri (Eds.) Quality of Service in Multiservice IP Networks. Proceedings, 2003. XV, 759 pages. 2003.

Vol. 2602: C. Priami (Ed.), Computational Methods in Systems Biology. Proceedings, 2003. IX, 214 pages. 2003.

Vol. 2604: N. Guelfi, E. Astesiano, G. Reggio (Eds.), Scientific Engineering for Distributed Java Applications. Proceedings, 2002. X, 205 pages. 2003.

Vol. 2606: A.M. Tyrrell, P.C. Haddow, J. Torresen (Eds.), Evolvable Systems: From Biology to Hardware. Proceedings, 2003. XIV, 468 pages. 2003.

Vol. 2607: H. Alt, M. Habib (Eds.), STACS 2003. Proceedings, 2003. XVII, 700 pages. 2003.

Vol. 2609: M. Okada, B. Pierce, A. Scedrov, H. Tokuda, A. Yonezawa (Eds.), Software Security – Theories and Systems. Proceedings, 2002. XI, 471 pages. 2003.

Vol. 2610: C. Ryan, T. Soule, M. Keijzer, E. Tsang, R. Poli, E. Costa (Eds.), Genetic Programming. Proceedings, 2003. XII, 486 pages. 2003.

Vol. 2611: S. Cagnoni, J.J. Romero Cardalda, D.W. Corne, J. Gottlieb, A. Guillot, E. Hart, C.G. Johnson, E. Marchiori, J.-A. Meyer, M. Middendorf, G.R. Raidl (Eds.), Applications of Evolutionary Computing. Proceedings, 2003. XXI, 708 pages. 2003.

Vol. 2612: M. Joye (Ed.), Topics in Cryptology – CT-RSA 2003. Proceedings, 2003. XI, 417 pages. 2003.

Vol. 2613: F.A.P. Petitcolas, H.J. Kim (Eds.), Digital Watermarking. Proceedings, 2002. XI, 265 pages. 2003.

Vol. 2614: R. Laddaga, P. Robertson, H. Shrobe (Eds.), Self-Adaptive Software: Applications. Proceedings, 2001. VIII, 291 pages. 2003.

Vol. 2615: N. Carbonell, C. Stephanidis (Eds.), Universal Access. Proceedings, 2002. XIV, 534 pages. 2003.

Vol. 2616: T. Asano, R. Klette, C. Ronse (Eds.), Geometry, Morphology, and Computational Imaging. Proceedings, 2002. X, 437 pages. 2003.

Vol. 2617: H.A. Reijers (Eds.), Design and Control of Workflow Processes. Proceedings, 2002. XV, 624 pages. 2003.

Vol. 2618: P. Degano (Ed.), Programming Languages and Systems. Proceedings, 2003. XV, 415 pages. 2003.

Vol. 2619: H. Garavel, J. Hatcliff (Eds.), Tools and Algorithms for the Construction and Analysis of Systems. Proceedings, 2003. XVI, 604 pages. 2003.

Vol. 2620: A.D. Gordon (Ed.), Foundations of Software Science and Computation Structures. Proceedings, 2003. XII, 441 pages. 2003.

Vol. 2621: M. Pezzè (Ed.), Fundamental Approaches to Software Engineering. Proceedings, 2003. XIV, 403 pages. 2003.

Vol. 2622: G. Hedin (Ed.), Compiler Construction. Proceedings, 2003. XII, 335 pages. 2003.

Vol. 2623: O. Maler, A. Pnueli (Eds.), Hybrid Systems: Computation and Control. Proceedings, 2003. XII, 558 pages. 2003.

Vol. 2625: U. Meyer, P. Sanders, J. Sibeyn (Eds.), Algorithms for Memory Hierarchies. Proceedings, 2003. XVIII, 428 pages. 2003.

Vol. 2626: J.L. Crowley, J.H. Piater, M. Vincze, L. Paletta (Eds.), Computer Vision Systems. Proceedings, 2003. XIII, 546 pages. 2003.

Vol. 2627: B. O'Sullivan (Ed.), Recent Advances in Constraints. Proceedings, 2002. X, 201 pages. 2003. (Subseries LNAI).

Vol. 2628: T. Fahringer, B. Scholz, Advanced Symbolic Analysis for Compilers. XII, 129 pages. 2003.

Vol. 2631: R. Falcone, S. Barber, L. Korba, M. Singh (Eds.), Trust, Reputation, and Security: Theories and Practice. Proceedings, 2002. X, 235 pages. 2003. (Subseries LNAI).

Vol. 2632: C.M. Fonseca, P.J. Fleming, E. Zitzler, K. Deb, L. Thiele (Eds.), Evolutionary Multi-Criterion Optimization. Proceedings, 2003. XV, 812 pages. 2003.

Vol. 2633: F. Sebastiani (Ed.), Advances in Information Retrieval. Proceedings, 2003. XIII, 546 pages. 2003.

Vol. 2634: F. Zhao, L. Guibas (Eds.), Information Processing in Sensor Networks. Proceedings, 2003. XII, 692 pages. 2003.